The UK Competition Regime

The UK Competition Regime

A Twenty-Year Retrospective

Edited by

BARRY RODGER, PETER WHELAN, AND
ANGUS MACCULLOCH

OXFORD
UNIVERSITY PRESS

OXFORD
UNIVERSITY PRESS

Great Clarendon Street, Oxford, OX2 6DP,
United Kingdom

Oxford University Press is a department of the University of Oxford.
It furthers the University's objective of excellence in research, scholarship,
and education by publishing worldwide. Oxford is a registered trade mark of
Oxford University Press in the UK and in certain other countries

Published in the United States of America by Oxford University Press
198 Madison Avenue, New York, NY 10016, United States of America

British Library Cataloguing in Publication Data

Data available

Library of Congress Control Number: 2020953002

ISBN 978-0-19-886802-6

DOI: 10.1093/oso/9780198868026.001.0001

Printed and bound in the UK by
TJ Books Limited

Preface

UK competition law has come a long way since I was introduced to the competition law implications of market behaviour on such diverse markets as Breakfast Cereals and Contraceptive Sheaths, by JAK Huntley in a stand-alone competition law class at Strathclyde University Law School, ahead of its time, in the mid-1980s. My second immersion in the subject followed not long after in 1989/1990 on the BCL competition law class at Oxford led by Richard Whish, using the newly published second(!) edition of his leading text, *Competition Law* (now in its ninth edition with David Bailey as co-author), and I was particularly fascinated by the focus on oligopoly in UK competition law, which I later studied in detail at the EUI, Florence. After several years of teaching EU and UK competition law back at Strathclyde in the 1990s, I witnessed UK competition law undergo significant reform in 1998, with the passing of the Competition Act 1998. At that stage, Angus MacCulloch and I co-edited a book (*The UK Competition Act 1998: A New Era for UK Competition Law*, Hart Publishing, 2000) to coincide with the introduction of the key provisions in the Act and to review the fundamental reforms introduced to the UK competition law landscape. Developments in enforcement and case law, new statutory provisions, and modifications to the UK competition law institutions in the following ten years were subsequently discussed and analysed in a follow-on collection edited by myself in 2010 (*Ten Years of UK Competition Law Reform*, Dundee University Press, 2010). UK competition law has since continued its trajectory of transformation over the last ten years with for instance the institutional reforms introduced by the Enterprise and Regulatory Reform Act 2013, notably the creation of the Competition and Markets Authority as the primary competition law agency in the UK.

The UK competition law landscape has changed considerably and has also had to respond to a changing context and new issues such as the increasing significance of the digital economy. Peter Whelan, Angus MacCulloch, and I considered it important to reflect on how UK competition law has been reformed, revised, and developed in relation to a range of contexts and issues over the last twenty years and to revisit some issues considered in the earlier books and additionally consider newer and increasingly significant themes. The book, while not aiming to provide comprehensive coverage of every facet of UK competition law and its enforcement, brings together fourteen contributions from a range of eminently qualified academics and practitioners. It seeks to provide an analytical and critical assessment of core issues relating to the policy-making, institutions, enforcement, substance, and direction of travel of UK competition law over the last twenty years (to 1 May 2020) and to suggest how it may further develop in the coming years. The chapters have generally been updated to reflect recent changes, notably the impact of withdrawal of the UK from the EU following the end of the transition period on 31 December 2020. (For a fuller discussion, see B Rodger and A Stephan, *Brexit and Competition Law* (Taylor &

Francis, 2021)). The Penrose Review Report was published in February 2021 (16 February 2021) and has not been discussed in any of the chapters. Nonetheless, the Report will not have any direct short-term impact on UK competition policy law and institutions, given its key recommendation in this context is basically for a further review of the decision-making and appeal processes involving the CMA and CAT.

Barry Rodger

Table of Contents

Table of Cases   xv
Table of Legislation   xxxi
Overview of Chapters   xxxvii
List of Abbreviations   xliii
Biographies   xlv

1. Towards a World Class Regime—An Overview of Twenty Years of UK
   Competition Enforcement   1
   Peter Freeman QC
   1 Introduction   1
   2 The New Regime, Its Objectives and Its Critics   2
       2.1 The Government's Aims for the New Regime   2
       2.2 The Cycle of Criticism   2
       2.3 Institutional Issues   2
       2.4 The EU Law Aspect   3
       2.5 The Question of Enforcement   4
       2.6 The Appeal System   4
       2.7 Merger Control   4
       2.8 The Financial Crisis   5
       2.9 A Wider Scepticism?   5
       2.10 The Digital Challenge   6
       2.11 The CMA Proposals   6
   3 The Performance of the New Regime in Practice   6
       3.1 Antitrust   6
           3.1.1 The EU Context   6
           3.1.2 Cartels and Restrictive Agreements   7
           3.1.3 The Situation after ERRA 2013   8
           3.1.4 Abuse of Dominant Position   9
           3.1.5 Criminal Enforcement and Directors' Disqualification   9
       3.2 Market Investigations   10
           3.2.1 The EA 2002 Regime   10
           3.2.2 Sclerosis in the System?   11
           3.2.3 The Effect of ERRA 2013   11
           3.2.4 The Retail Banking and Energy Cases   12
       3.3 Mergers   12
           3.3.1 The Period after EA 2002   12
           3.3.2 The Arrival of the CMA   13
           3.3.3 After ERRA 2013   14
           3.3.4 A New Approach?   14
           3.3.5 The System of Voluntary Notification   14
       3.4 The Public Interest   15
           3.4.1 Grounds for Intervention   15
           3.4.2 Merger Cases   15
           3.4.3 A Wider Public Interest?   15

3.5 Private Actions	16
3.5.1 The Original Purpose	16
3.5.2 Early Experience	16
3.5.3 The New Regime	17
3.6 The Role of Ministers	18
3.6.1 Stepping Back	18
3.6.2 A Change of Emphasis?	18
3.7 Concurrent Enforcement by Regulators	19
3.7.1 Initial Problems	19
3.7.2 Improvement	20
4 The Digital Age and New Challenges	20
4.1 The Challenge	20
4.2 The Response	21
5 The EU Legal Framework and the Consequences of Leaving It	22
5.1 The Pursuit of Integration	22
5.2 Effect of Leaving the EU	23
6 Overall Assessment and the Future	25
6.1 A Governmental View	25
6.2 Antitrust and the Appeal System	25
6.3 Other Issues	26
6.4 Populist Pressure	26
6.5 The CMA Proposals	27
6.6 The COVID-19 Pandemic	27
7 Conclusions	28
2. Horizontal Agreements	29
Richard Whish QC	
1 Introduction	29
2 Cartels	30
2.1 2000–2014: Enforcement Action against Cartels by the OFT	30
2.1.1 A Slow Beginning	30
2.1.2 A More Productive Period	32
2.2 Criticism of Under-enforcement and the Establishment of the CMA	35
2.3 2014–2020: Enforcement Action against Cartels by the CMA	36
3 Hub and Spoke Cartels	39
3.1 What Is Meant by a Hub and Spoke Conspiracy?	40
3.2 The UK Cases: *Football Shirts* and *Toys and Games*	41
3.3 *Dairy Products*	42
3.4 Hub and Spoke Agreements in Other Jurisdictions	42
4 Trade Associations	43
5 Paroxetine	43
5.1 The CMA's Finding	44
5.2 The Judgment of the ECJ	44
5.2.1 Actual or Potential Competition	44
5.2.2 Restriction of Competition by Object?	45
5.3 The Outcome	46
6 Notification and Exemption	46
7 Concurrency	49
8 Scotland	50
9 Public Policy and the Coronavirus Crisis	51

10 Brexit and the Future   53
11 Conclusions   54

3. Vertical Agreements   55
    Alison Jones
    1 Introduction   55
    2 Outline and Evolution of the Law   56
       2.1 The Verticals Exclusion Order   56
       2.2 Modernization of EU Law and Removal of the Verticals Exclusion Order   57
            2.2.1 Object Restrictions   58
            2.2.2 De Minimis and the Verticals Block Exemption   60
            2.2.3 Agreements within a Single Economic Unit   61
            2.2.4 Fuller Effects Analysis   61
    3 UK Jurisprudence   62
       3.1 Vertical Agreements and the Competition Act   62
            3.1.1 Overview   62
            3.1.2 Resale Price Maintenance and Online Selling Restraints   63
            3.1.3 Price Relationship Agreements and MFNs   67
            3.1.4 Other Distribution Arrangements   69
       3.2 Vertical Agreements and the Enterprise Act   72
    4 The Future   73
       4.1 Should UK Law Continue to Follow EU Law?   73
       4.2 Presumption of Illegality   75
       4.3 Verticals Block Exemption or Another Safe Harbour   76
       4.4 Provision of Guidance   76
    5 Conclusions   77

4. Exclusionary Abuses   79
    Renato Nazzini
    1 Introduction   79
    2 Dominance   80
       2.1 General Approach   80
       2.2 Dominance in Pharmaceutical Markets   82
            2.2.1 A Gloss on Market Definition in Pharmaceutical Markets   83
       2.3 Dominance and Platforms   85
    3 Legal Test for Abuse: Standard of Foreclosure and Efficiencies   87
       3.1 Clarifying the Law on Retroactive Rebates and Bundled Discounts   87
       3.2 Exclusion in Multi-market Settings   92
       3.3 Exclusivity, MFNs, and Equivalent Clauses   97
       3.4 Discrimination   98
       3.5 Exclusionary Abuses in the Pharmaceutical Sector   105
    4 Conclusions   109

5. Exploitative Abuses   113
    Robert O'Donoghue QC
    1 Introduction   113
    2 The Decisional Practice and Case Law   114
       2.1 CAT Cases/Appeals in CAT Cases   114
            2.1.1 Napp   114
            2.1.2 Albion Water   115
            2.1.3 Phenytoin   117

2.2 High Court Cases/Appeals from High Court Cases   126
3 Distillation of the Core Principles   129
   3.1 The Court of Appeal's Summary in *Phenytoin*   129
   3.2 Comment and Critique   130
4 Conclusions   136

6. 'Jack of All Trades, Master of None': The Ever-increasing Ambit of
the Market Investigation Regime   137
Christian Ahlborn and Will Leslie
1 Introduction   137
2 The Market Investigation Regime   138
   2.1 Background   138
   2.2 Institutions and Procedure   139
      2.2.1 Phase 1: Market Studies and Market Investigation References   139
      2.2.2 Phase 2: Market Investigations   141
      2.2.3 Enforcement Powers and Remedies   141
      2.2.4 Judicial Review   142
   2.3 Substantive Provisions   143
   2.4 Policy Goal   143
3 Overview of the Last Ten years   145
   3.1 Stage 1: Market Studies   145
   3.2 Stage 2: Market Investigations   146
   3.3 Judicial Review: The CAT   148
4 Trends in Market Investigations   150
   4.1 Conventional Competition Cases   151
   4.2 Extended Competition Cases   152
   4.3 Consumer Policy   153
   4.4 State Action   154
5 Market Investigations and the Rise of Behavioural Economics   155
   5.1 The Role of Behavioural Economics in Market Investigations   156
   5.2 The Tension between Competition Policy and Consumer Policy   158
   5.3 Behavioural Economics and the Dangers of Reimagining Markets   159
   5.4 Appropriate Scope of Behavioural Economics   160
6 Market Investigations and the Rule of Law   161
   6.1 Conventional Competition Issues and Regulatory Arbitrage   162
   6.2 Insufficiently Weak Judicial Oversight?   163
7 Other Policy Issues   164
   7.1 Territorial Limitations   164
   7.2 Back to the Future: The Introduction of a Public Interest Test   166
8 Future Developments   167
9 Conclusions   168

7. UK Merger Control: Finely Tailored but Time for a New Suit?   169
David Reader
1 Introduction   169
2 Merger Control under the Enterprise Act 2002: A Primer   170
   2.1 Removing Politicians and Reaffirming Competition   170
   2.2 The Initial 'Bedding Down' Period   171
      2.2.1 Interpreting the OFT's 'Duty to Refer' to Phase 2   171
      2.2.2 The Concept of 'A Relevant Merger Situation'   172
      2.2.3 The Residual Public Interest Regime: A Test of the EA 2002's Integrity   173
      2.2.4 A 'New Era' or 'More of the Same'?   175

3 Fine-tuning and 'Missed Opportunities' under the ERRA 2013   175
    3.1 A Merger Regime for Growth   175
    3.2 Fine-tuning under the ERRA 2013   177
        3.2.1 New Powers for the CMA to Order Interim Measures to
            Halt Integration   177
        3.2.2 Statutory Time Limits for Streamlining the Review Process   179
        3.2.3 Unlocking the Potential for 'Undertakings in Lieu' at Phase 1   180
    3.3 A Missed Opportunity for Radical Change?   181
4 Enforcement Trends under the EA 2002   183
    4.1 A Higher Rate of Enforcement, But Not All Is as It Seems   183
    4.2 A False Dawn for Undertakings in Lieu?   185
    4.3 The Likelihood of Referral Remains Unchanged under the CMA   186
    4.4 No Evidence of Confirmation Bias within the CMA Model   188
    4.5 A Streamlined Regime, But Questions over Pre-Notification Discussions   189
5 Emerging Challenges and the Agenda for Further Reform   190
    5.1 Managing the Post-Brexit Caseload   191
    5.2 Resisting the Rise of Nationalist Sentiment   192
    5.3 Rising to the Challenge Presented by Digital Mergers   195
6 Conclusion   198

8. Unfinished Reform of the Institutions Enforcing UK Competition Law   201
    Bruce Lyons
1 Introduction   201
2 What Matters in Institutional Design and Performance?   202
    2.1 Mandate   203
    2.2 Organizational Design and Decision-making   203
    2.3 Rights of Appeal   204
    2.4 Evaluation of Performance   205
3 Institutional Cultures Inherited from the Twentieth Century   206
    3.1 The 'Monopolies Commission' and Restrictive Practices Court   206
    3.2 The OFT and Sector Regulators   207
    3.3 Inherited Institutional Cultures   208
4 The Competition Test and New Powers of Decision: Institutional
    Implications of CA 1998 and EA 2002   209
    4.1 The Rise of the Economic Approach   209
    4.2 The OFT   209
    4.3 The CC   210
    4.4 The CAT   211
    4.5 Performance of the OFT and the CC   212
5 Compromise(d) Merger: the ERRA 2013 and the CMA   214
    5.1 CMA Design   214
        5.1.1 Mandate   214
        5.1.2 Organizational Design and Decision-making   215
    5.2 CMA Performance   217
6 The Case for Institutional Reform   220
    6.1 Five New Twenty-first Century Challenges   220
        6.1.1 Loss of Public Faith in Markets   220
        6.1.2 Digital Markets and Dominant Platforms   220
        6.1.3 Brexit Including Scrutiny of State Subsidies   221
        6.1.4 Covid-19 Pandemic   222
        6.1.5 Climate Change   223

6.2 CMA's Own Proposals for Reform: The Tyrie Letter 224
  6.2.1 The Consumer Interest as an Overriding Statutory Duty 224
  6.2.2 Anticipated Use of Interim Measures in the Markets Regime 225
  6.2.3 Limited Standard of Review for CA 1998 Enforcement Cases 225
6.3 Coherent Institutional Reform for the CMA 226
7 Conclusion 228

9. Human Rights and the UK Competition Act: Public Enforcement
  and Due Process 231
  Arianna Andreangeli
  1 Introduction 231
  2 Competition Enforcement and Human Rights Observance in the UK—
    'Criminal in Nature' and Its Implications 232
    2.1 From a Registration-based to an Enforcement-based Structure: The
      Competition Act 1998 and Its Implications 232
    2.2 Defining the Benchmark: The Right to a Fair Trial and 'Criminal in
      Nature' Infringements—Article 6 ECHR and the Judicial Scrutiny
      of Competition Cases 234
      2.2.1 Administrative Decisions and the European Convention: What Is
        'Criminal' or 'Civil'? What Is 'Fair'? 234
      2.2.2 Article 6(1) ECHR and Competition Cases in the UK 237
  3 United Kingdom Competition Proceedings Put to the Human Rights Test—
    Article 6 and the Competition Appeals Tribunal 241
    3.1 A 'Fair Trial' in the UK—Between the Common Law and the ECHR:
      Summary Remarks 241
    3.2 UK Competition Proceedings Put to the ECHR Test: The *NAPP* Judgment 243
    3.3 Competition Enforcement, Human Rights, and Judicial Scrutiny—
      A Settled Question? 247
  4 Conclusions 252

10. Concurrency 255
  Niamh Dunne
  1 Introduction 255
  2 The Origins and Evolution of Concurrency 255
  3 'Enhancing' Concurrency: The Enterprise and Regulatory Reform Act 2013 259
  4 Concurrency in Practice: Twenty Years after the Competition Act 1998 262
    4.1 Concurrency in Practice: The Framework of 'Enhanced' Concurrency 263
    4.2 Concurrency in Practice: Case Allocation 265
    4.3 Concurrency in Practice: Enforcement Activity in Regulated Markets 269
  5 Reflections on Concurrency 276
  6 Conclusion 281

11. The Emerging Contribution of Director Disqualification in UK
  Competition Law 283
  Peter Whelan
  1 Introduction 283
  2 The Rationale for Director Disqualification 284
    2.1 Its Normative Role in the Armoury of Non-criminal Antitrust Sanctions 285
    2.2 Its Potential Effectiveness in its Complementary Deterrence Role 287
  3 The Development of the UK Approach to Direction Disqualification 290
    3.1 The Legal Basis for Director Disqualification 290

3.2 Enforcement Practice to Date 293
    3.2.1 The Refinement of the Guidelines on CDOs 294
    3.2.2 The CMA's Reliance Upon Director Disqualification Undertakings 297
4 The UK Regime as an Insightful Example for Other Jurisdictions 300
  4.1 Effectiveness 301
  4.2 Legitimacy 304
    4.2.1 Director Disqualification and Culpability 304
    4.2.2 Transparency of CMA Policy and Practice 306
5 Conclusion 307

12. Private Enforcement in the UK: Effective Redress for Consumers? 311
  Barry J Rodger
  1 Introduction 311
  2 Key Legislative and Institutional Developments 312
    2.1 UK Statutory Developments 312
    2.2 EU Law Developments 313
  3 Overview of the UK Case Law 315
  4 Specific Issues 318
    4.1 Limitation Periods 318
    4.2 Binding Force of Competition Authority Decisions 320
    4.3 The Existence of a Specialist Court/Tribunal 321
    4.4 The Availability of Effective Disclosure Mechanisms 322
    4.5 Damages Awards 324
      4.5.1 The Passing-on Defence and Indirect Purchasers 326
    4.6 Collective Redress Mechanism 327
    4.7 Funding Private Enforcement 331
  5 Learning from the USA 332
  6 Impact of UK Withdrawal from EU 334
  7 Conclusions 335

13. The Quiet Decline of the UK Cartel Offence: A Principled Victory in the Face of Practical Failure 337
  Angus MacCulloch
  1 Introduction 337
  2 The Introduction of the Cartel Offence 338
  3 The Cartel Offence: A Mid-life Crisis 340
    3.1 A Quiet Decline 340
    3.2 The Reshaping of the UK Cartel Offence 346
  4 A Developing Consensus in the Academic Debate 350
    4.1 The Culpability of Cartel Participants 351
    4.2 The Social Harmfulness of Cartel Behaviour 352
    4.3 The Moral Wrongfulness of Cartels 352
    4.4 The Value of Consensus 353
  5 The Future of Criminal Investigations and the Cartel Offence in the UK 354
    5.1 The New Cartel Offence 354
    5.2 Individual Culpability 355
    5.3 The Narrative of Wrongfulness 357
  6 Conclusions 358

14. Competition Law and the Digital Economy in the UK and Beyond   359
    Liza Lovdahl Gormsen
    1 Introduction   359
    2 Antitrust and the Digital Economy   360
        2.1 Digital Platforms, Data, and Anti-competitive Conduct   361
        2.2 Data Sharing and Data Portability   367
        2.3 Killer Acquisitions   370
    3 Enforcement in the Digital Space   376
    4 Regulation   380
        4.1 Regulatory Initiatives around the World   380
    5 Conclusion   386

Index   389

Table of Cases

Competition and Markets Authority is referred to by its initials CMA

2 Travel Group plc v Cardiff City Transport Services Ltd [2019] CAT 19 .... 16–17, 315–16, 324–25, 324n.114, 325nn.128–29

A v Secretary of State for the Home Department [2005] UKHL 71 .... 233n.15
Aberdeen Journals v OFT [2002] CAT 4 9
Aberdeen Journals Limited v Director General of Fair Trading [2003] CAT 11 .... 93n.108
AC-Treuhand, Case C-194/14 P, EU:C:2015:717 .... 272n.143
AC-Treuhand, Case C-194/14 P, Opinion of AG Wahl, EU:C:2015:350 .... 272n.143
Access control and alarm systems, OFT decision of 6 December 2013 35
Access to car parking facilities at East Midlands International Airport. *See* East Midlands International Airport/Prestige Parking Ltd
Achilles Group Ltd v OFT, Case 1067/1/1/06 [2006] CAT 24 32
Achilles Information Ltd v Network Rail Infrastructure Ltd, Case 1298/5/7/18
    [2019] CAT 20 .... 70n.110, 94, 94n.115, 94nn.117–18, 94n.120, 94n.121, 95n.122, 95n.126, 95nn.127–30, 96n.134, 109–10, 317–18, 317n.57
Adidas, Case B3 137/12 (27 June 2014), Bundeskartellamt 59n.25
Aéroports de Paris v Commission, Case T-128/98, EU:T:2000:290 .... 95n.130, 96, 96n.135
Aéroports de Paris v Commission, Case T-128/98, [2000] ECR II-3939 .... 317n.52
Agents' Mutual Ltd v Gascoigne Halman Ltd, Case 1262/5/7/16 (T) [2017] CAT 15, upheld
    [2019] EWCA Civ 24 ....17–18, 70–71, 322
Agents' Mutual Ltd v Gascoigne Halman Ltd [2017] CAT 22 .... 322n.92
Aggregates, OFT 153n.99
Aggregates, Cement and Ready-Mix Concrete Market Investigation—Final Report, CMA (14
    January 2014) 11, 146–48, 146n.66, 148n.79, 149, 152, 152n.95, 153, 163–64, 219, 219n.73
AH Willis & Sons Ltd v OFT, Case 1122/1/1/09, [2011] CAT 13 34
Air cargo, Commission Decision of 9 November 2010 53–54
Airline passenger fuel surcharges for long-haul passenger flights, OFT decision of
    19 April 2012 34–35
AKZO Chemie v Commission, Case C-62/86, [1991] ECR I-3359 .... 82n.20, 93n.107, 103n.188
Akzo Nobel NV/Metlac Holdings Srl (December 2012); on appeal [2013] CAT 13,
    [2014] EWCA Civ 482 13
Albert and Le Compte v Belgium App nos 7299/75 and 7496/76 (1983)
    5 EHRR 533 .... 235, 235n.24, 236, 239n.57, 245
Albion Water v Dwr Cymru Cyfyngedig [2013] CAT 6 .... 16–17, 315–16, 324–25, 324n.115
Albion Water Ltd v Dwr Cymru Cyfyngedig (Water Services Regulation Authority intervening)
    [2008] EWCA Civ 536, [2009] 2 All ER 279 .... 20, 213n.45
Albion Water Limited v Water Services Regulation Authority, Case Nos 1046/2/4/04, 1034/2/4/
    04(IR)[2006] CAT 36, [2007] CompAR 328 (Albion WaterI) 20, 115–16, 115n.18, 116n.19, 117n.23, 133, 134n.96, 136, 213n.45
Albion Water Limited v Water Services Regulation Authority [2008] CAT 31
    (Albion Water II) 20, 115–16, 115n.18, 117n.22, 136
Alrosa v Commission, Case C-441/07 P, Opinion of AG Kokott, [2010] ECR I-05949 8
Aluminium Spacer Bars, OFT decision of 29 June 2006 32
Amazon, AT40153, (28 July 2017) 62n.46
Amazon Retail, Case CE/9692/12, (1 November 2013) 69n.102
AmChem Products Inc v Windsor, 83 F. 3d, 610 .... 334n.213

Anti-competitive conduct in the asset management sector, CMP/01-2016/CA98, Decision of
    21 February 2019 . . . . 275n.170
Apex Asphalt and Paving Co Ltd v OFT, Case 1032/1/1/04, [2005] CAT 4 . . . . 7, 31–32
Applications for leniency and no-action in cartel cases, OFT 1495 (July 2013) 64n.62
Arcadia Group Brands and Others v Visa Inc and Others [2015]
    EWCA Civ 883 . . . . 319n.64, 319, 319n.65
Argos Ltd v OFT and Littlewoods Ltd v OFT, Cases 1014/1/1/03 and 1015/1/1/03 [2004] CAT 24;
    [2006] EWCA Civ 1318 . . . . 39–40, 63n.58, 248nn.119–22, 248–49
Arkin v Borchard Lines Ltd and Others [2003] EWHC 3088 . . . . 324n.116
Arriva Scotland West Ltd v Glasgow Airport Ltd [2011] CSOH 69 . . . . 316–17, 316n.49
Arriva The Shires Ltd v London Luton Airport Operations Ltd [2014]
    EWHC 64 (Ch) 195, 95n.130, 96, 96nn.136, 138, 97, 104,
                                           104n.193, 105n.197, 105n.198, 105n.199, 105n.200,
                                                          105n.201, 109–10, 316–17, 316n.51
Asda Stores Ltd v Mastercard Inc [2017] EWHC 93. . . . . 326n.134
Asset Management, FCA decision of 21 February 2019 50
Association of British Insurers' General Terms of Agreement, OFT decision of 22 April 2004 48
Association of British Insurers v OFT, Case 1036/1/1/04, order of 30 July 2004, Case closure
    notice of 29 January 2007. 48
Association of Convenience Stores and National Federation of Retail Newsagents v OFT, Case
    1191/6/1/12 [2012]. 148n.77
Asus, Case AT/40.46, (26 September 2018) IP/18/4601 . . . . 59n.21, 64n.60
ATG Media: CMA, Decision to accept binding commitments offered by ATG Media in relation
    to live online bidding auction platform services Case No 50408 (29 June 2017) 69, 85–86,
                                                          85–86nn.52–57, 98, 98nn.146–49
Att-Gen v Blake [2001] 1 AC 268 . . . . 325n.127
Attheraces, OFT decision of 10 May 2004 48–49
ATTHERACES Ltd & Anor v The British Horse Racing Board & Anor [2007]
    EWCA Civ 38 . . . . 127–28, 127–28nn.73–74, 133, 133n.94, 134, 134n.99, 136
Ausurus Group/Cu Fe Investments (14 August 2018) 14
Autortiesību un komunicēšanās konsultāciju aģentūra/Latvijas Autoru apvienība,
    Case C-177/16. . . . . 131n.83
AXA PPP Healthcare Limited v CMA, Case 1228/6/12/14, [2015] CAT 5 . . . . 11, 148n.80, 164
AXA PPP Healthcare Limited v CMA Case 1229/6/12/14 . . . . 164n.162

B&M European Value Retail v CMA, Case 1301/6/12/18 [2018] 148n.81
BAA Airports Market Investigation (2009). 11, 148, 148n.76, 149, 213,
                                                          213n.49, 219n.75, 267n.111
BAA Ltd v CC, Case 1110/6/8/09 . . . . 148n.76, 163n.161
BAA Ltd v CC, Case 1185/6/8/11 [2011] 148, 148n.77
BAA Ltd v CC [2009] CAT 35, [2010] EWCA Civ 1097 . . . . 11, 138–39, 139n.12, 267n.111
BAA Ltd v CC (No 2) [2012] CAT 3, [2012] EWCA Civ 1077. 11
Balmoral Tanks v CMA, Case 1277/1/12/17 [2017] CAT 23. 37
Balmoral Tanks Ltd & Anor v CMA [2019] EWCA Civ 162 . . . . 356–57, 357n.114
Bar Council of Northern Ireland, OFT Press Release 02/ 11 (5 January 2011) 43
Barclays Bank v CC [2009] CAT 27. 11
Barrett Estate Services Ltd v OFT, Cases 1125/1/1/09 etc [2011] CAT 9 34
Baustahlgewebe v Commission, Case C-185/95 P [1998] 373, 374n.88
Bayer AG v Commission, Joined Cases C-2 and 3/01 P, EU:C:2004:2 . . . . 64n.65
Bayer AG v Commission, Case T-41/96, EU:T:2000:242. . . . . 64n.65
Beer and Pub Market (CAMRA Super-Complaint) 148, 148n.75, 149
Bertelsmann and Sony Corporation of America v Impala, Case C-413/06 P [2008] . 373, 374nn.90, 91
BetterCare Group v OFT [2002] CAT 6. 7
BHB Enterprises v Victor Chandler (International) Limited [2005] EWHC 1074. . . . . . . 126, 126n.70,
                                                          127n.71, 127n.72, 127–28, 133, 133n.95
Bid Rigging in the Construction Industry in England, Decision of 21 September 2009 7
Blackspur Group plc and Others, In Re [1998] BCC 1. . . . . 288n.55

Bleaching Chemicals 30–31
BMI Healthcare Limited v CMA (I), Case 1218/6/8/13, [2013] CAT 24 . . . . 148n.80
BMI Healthcare v CMA (II), Case 1220/6/8/13, [2013] 148n.80
BMW/Carwow https://www.gov.uk/government/news/bmw-changes-policy-on-car-
    comparison-sites-following-cma-action. 59n.25, 67
Bookmakers' Afternoon Greyhound Services v Amalgamated Racing ('BAGS') [2008] EWHC
    1978 (Ch D), [2009] EWCA Civ 750 (CA) 48–49
Bouyid v Belgium App no 23380/09 (2016) 62 EHRR 32 . . . . 236n.32
Brasserie de Haecht v Wilkin, Case 23/67, EU:C:1967:54 . . . . 61n.44, 70
Bristol Water plc: Decision to accept binding commitments, Decision of
    23 March 2015. . . . . .273–74, 273n.157
BritNed Development Ltd v ABB AB and ABB Ltd [2018] EWHC 2616 and 2913 (Ch); [2019]
    EWCA Civ 1840 . . . . .18, 315–16, 316n.43, 326nn.132, 137
British Airways 9–10
British Airways v Commission, Case C-95/04 P, Opinion of AG Kokott, [2007]
    ECR I-2331 . . . . 101n.170
British Airways v Commission, Case T-219/99, 2003 E.C.R. II-5917 . . . . 80n.4, 101n.170
British Horseracing Board v OFT, Case 1042/2/1/04, [2005] CAT 29 .48–49
British Leyland Plc v Commission, Case 226/84, [1986] ECR 3263 . . . . 113n.4
British Sky Broadcasting Group plc v CC [2008] CAT 36; [2010] EWCA Civ 2 15
British Telecommunications PLC v Ofcom [2016] CAT 3. . . . . .103–4, 103n.187
British Telecommunications plc against British Sky Broadcasting Group plc, Complaint alleging
    abuse of a dominant position regarding the wholesale supply of Sky Sports
    1 and 2,Ofcom. 271n.133
BRT v SABAM, Case 127/73 [1974] ECR 51 . . . . 314n.26
Bryan v United Kingdom App no 19198/91 (1996) 21 EHRR 342 . . . . 236–37, 236n.34, 250n.141
BSkyB/ITV 13

Calor Gas Ltd v Express Fuels (Scotland) Ltd & Anor [2008] CSOH 13 70
Campaign for Real Ale v OFT, Case 1148/6/1/09 [2009] 148n.75
Car Glass, Commission Decision of 12 November 2008 53–54
Car rental in the UK (Market Study 2015). 145n.54
Cardiff Bus, Decision of 18 November 2008 OFT. 9
Casio Electronics, Case 50565-2 (1 August 2019). 64n.66, 64–65
CB v Commission, Case C-67/13, EU:C:2014:25 45
CB v Commission, Case C-67/13 P, judgment of 11 September 2014, EU:C:2014:2204 46
CDK Global, Auto/Mate [2018]—171 0156 . . . . 382n.152
CDS (Credit Default Swaps)—Clearing, closure of proceedings on 4 December 2015 53–54
Celesio AG v OFT [2006] CAT 9. . . . . 172, 172n.27
Centre Belge d'Etudes de Marché-Télémarketing (CBEM) v SA Compagnie Luxembourgeoise
    de Télédiffusion (CLT) and Information Publicité Benelux (IPB), Case 311/84,
    [1985] ECR 3261. . . . . 99n.153
CEPSA, Case C-279/06, EU:C:2008:485 . . . . 61n.39
Certas Energy. See Western Isles Road Fuels
Chloropene Rubber 30–31
Claymore Dairies Ltd and Express Dairies Ltd v OFT [2004] CAT 3 7
Cleanroom laundry services and products, CMA decision of 14 December 2017 38
CMA v Flynn Pharmaceuticals Co Ltd and Pfizer Inc, Decision of 7 December 2016. 9
CMA v Flynn Pharmaceuticals Co Ltd and Pfizer Inc., [2018] CAT 11,
    [2020] EWCA 339 . . . . 9, 113n.8, 117n.25, 122n.59, 122n.60,
                                                    122n.61, 122n.62, 123n.63, 124n.64, 124n.65,
                                                    124n.66, 130n.81, 133n.92, 134n.100, 135n.101,
                                                    135n.102, 248–49, 248–49nn.126–31
CMA v Martin [2020] EWHC 1751 (Ch) 38, 293n.95, 298n.142, 301n.165, 305n.181, 305n.183
CMA v Pfizer UK Limited and Others See CMA v Flynn Pharmaceuticals Co Ltd and Pfizer Inc
Collusive tendering for mastic asphalt flat-roofing contracts in Scotland, OFT decision of
    15 March 2005. 51

Commercial use of consumer data (call for information) (Market Study 2015). 145n.54
Competition and regulation in higher education in England (Market Study 2015). 145n.54
Competition Authority v Beef Industry Development Society Ltd (BIDS), Case C-209/07,
    EU:C:2008:643 . . . . 67n.92
Competition in passenger rail services in GB (Market Study 2016). 145n.54
Concrete Drainage Pipes, CMA decision of 23 October 2019 . . . . 8–9, 38
Condron v Austria App no 35718/97 (ECHR 2 May 2000). 236n.29
Conduct in the modelling sector, CMA decision of 16 December 2016 . . . . 37, 43
Conduct in the opthamology sector, CMA decision of 20 August 2015 . . . . 36–37, 43, 50
Construction bid-rigging, Decision of 21 September 2009. 34
Construction Industry Forum, Decision of 29 September 2009. 7
Construction Recruitment Forum, OFT decision of 29 September 2009 34
Consumer behavioural biases in competition—Final report, OFT (May 2011). 158n.133
Consumers Association v JJB Sports, Case No 1078/7/9/07, Order of the CAT
    (14 January 2008). 16, 31–32, 327n.148, 336
Cooper Tire & Rubber Co v Shell Chemicals UK Ltd [2010] EWCA Civ 864 (CA). 313n.16
Copper Fittings, Commission Decision of 20 September 2006 . . . . 30–31, 53–54
CoreLogic/DataQuick [2014] 131 0199. . . . . 359n.4
Coty, Case C-230/16, EU:C:2017:941. . . . . 59, 76n.133
Courage v Crehan, Case C-453/99 [2001] ECR I-6297 . . . . 313–14, 313n.20, 324
Coventry and Others v Lawrence and Another [2015] UKSC 50. . . . . 331n.198
Crehan v Inntrepreneur Pub Company (CPC), [2004] EWCA Civ 637;
    [2004] ECC 28. . . . . 324n.113, 326n.133
Cross-border access to pay-TV, Case AT. 40023, Commission Decision (7 March 2019). 152n.93

Dairy retail price initiatives (Dairy Products), OFT decision of 10 August 2011,
    [2012] CAT 31. . . . . 7, 8, 39–40, 41, 42
Dairy retail price initiatives (Dairy Products), Appeal Case 1188/1/1/11,
    [2012] CAT 31. . . . . 39–40, 41
Delimitis, Case C-234/89, EU:C:1991:91. . . . . 44, 61, 70
Design, Construction and Fit-Out Services: Director Disqualification... 309
Design, Construction and Fit-Out Services, CMA Statement on
    (10 December 2019). 299–300, 300n.154
Deutsche Bahn AG v Morgan Crucible Company Plc and Others [2012]
    EWCA Civ 1055 . . . . 318, 318n.61
Deutsche Bahn AG v Morgan Crucible co plc and Others, Case 1173/5/7/10 [2013] CAT 18,
    [2013] EWCA Civ 1484 . . . . 335n.222
Deutsche Bahn AG and Others v Mastercard Inc and Others 27 July 2016, Case 1240/5/7/15,
    [2016] CAT 13. . . . . 318n.62
Deutsche Bahn AG and Others v Morgan Advanced Materials Plc [2014]
    UKSC 24 . . . . 318, 318n.61
Deutsche Telekom AG v Commission, Case C-280/08 P, EU:C:2010:603. . . . . 91n.96, 375n.106
Deutsche Telekom AG v European Commission, Case C-80/08 P, [2010] ECR I-9555. . . . . . . 99n.154
Devenish Nutrition Ltd v Sanofi-Aventis SA (France) [2008] EWCA Civ 1086 (CA), [2007]
    EWHC 2394 (Ch). 313n.14, 325, 325n.128
Digital Comparison Tool Services market study, Final Report, CMA,
    (26 September 2017) 145, 145n.55, 162–63, 163n.156
Digital Comparison Tools Services Market Study—Update Paper, CMA. 163n.157
Digital keyboards and guitars, Case 50565-6, (17 July 2020) 64n.63, 64–65n.69
Digital Platforms Inquiry—final report (Australian Competition and Consumer Commission,
    July 2019) (ACCC Final report)) 364nn.31–32, 371n.76,
                              371–72, 372n.80, 374, 375–76nn.95–108,
                              375, 375n.99, 380–81, 383n.157
Dimes v Grand Junction Canal Co [1852] 10 ER 301. . . . . 241–42, 241n.69
Discriminatory pricing in relation to the supply of bulk mail delivery services in the UK,
    CW/ 01122/01/14 Decision of 14 August 2018. . . . . 270n.128

Distribution of Mercedes-Benz commercial vehicles (van), Case CE/ 9161-09,
    (27 March 2013) 63n.59
Dixon Stores Group Ltd/Compaq Computer Ltd/Packard Bell Nec Ltd, Case CA98/3/2001
    (6 April 2001) 56–57
Domestic LPG. 10
Donau Chemie et al, Case C-536/11 [2013] 5 CMLR 19 . . . . 323n.105
DS Smith Paper Limited and Others v MAN SE and Others, Case 1343/5/7/20 (T) 322n.93
DSG Retail Ltd and Others v Mastercard Incorporated and Others CA [2020]
    EWCA Civ 671 . . . . 318n.62, 319–20, 320n.70
Dupont de Nemours v Dupont (2003) EWCA Civ 1368 . . . . 204–5n.12
Durkan Holdings Ltd v OFT, Case 1121/1/1/09, [2011] CAT 6 34
Dutch Beer. 30–31

East Midlands International Airport/Prestige Parking Ltd, Civil Aviation
    Authority decision of 20 December 2016 . . . . 49–50, 64–65n.69
East Midlands International Airport (CAP 1507): Access to car parking facilities CA98-001,
    Decision of 15 December 2016. . . . . 274n.163
e-books, COMP/39.847, [2013] OJ C378/25. . . . . 62n.46
e-books, Case CE/9440-11, (1 December 2011) 62n.46
Economy Energy, E (Gas and Electricity) and Dyball Associates: Infringement of Chapter I of the
    Competition Act 1998 with respect to an anti-competitive agreement, Decision of
    29 May 2019 . . . . 271n.139
Eden Brown Ltd v OFT [2011] CAT 11 7
Eden Brown Ltd v OFT, Cases 1140/1/1/09 etc, [2011] CAT 8 34
Eurotunnel case See Groupe Eurotunnel SA/Sea France SA
Electricity North West Limited: Decision to accept binding commitments over connection
    charges, Case 76/12, Decision of 24 May 2012 . . . . 271n.138
Electronic drum sector, Case 50565-5, (29 June 2020). 64n.62, 64n.63, 64–65n.69
Electrorent/Microlease, CMA decision (17 May 2018); [2019] CAT 4 (appeal on penalty upheld) 14
Elevators and Escalators. 30–31
Elite Greenhouses Limited, Case CP/1709-02 . . . . 64n.65
Emerald Supplies Ltd v British Airways Plc [2015] EWCA Civ 1024. . . . . 323n.99
Emerson III [2008] CAT 8. . . . . 313n.17
Emerson Electric Co v Mersen UK Portslade Limited [2012] EWCA Civ 1557 . . . . 335n.222
Emerson Electric Co v Morgan Crucible [2011] CAT 4; [2012] EWCA Civ 1559 . . . . 79, 16–17,
                                                                                320–21, 320nn.76–78,
Energy Market See Supply and Acquisition of Energy Market Investigation
Engel and Others v Netherlands App no 5100/71 (1979-1980) 1 EHRR 647 . . . . . . 234n.19, 237n.42, 238
English Rugby Ltd, case closure of 6 August 2003 43
English Welsh and Scottish Railway Limited, Decision of 17 November 2006. . . . . 273n.149
Enron Coal Services Ltd (in Liquidation) v English, Welsh and Scottish Railway Ltd [2011]
    EWCA Civ 2 . . . . 76, 320nn.73–75,
Enron Coal Services Ltd (in Liquidation) v English, Welsh and Scottish Railway Ltd [2009]
    CAT 7 and Court of Appeal, [2009] EWCA Civ 647 . . . . 320n.76
Enron Coal Services Limited (in liquidation) v English Welsh & Scottish Railway
    Limited [2009] CAT 36 . . . . 324n.120
Enron Coal Services Ltd (in Liquidation) v English, Welsh and Scottish Railway Ltd
    (EWS Ltd), Case No 1106/5/7/08 . . . . 315, 315n.38, 320–21, 320n.77
Ensign Bus Co v London Southend Airport, Case 1335/5/7/19 . . . . 316n.48
EPEX Spot SE and EEX, Notice of Decision to accept binding commitments in relation to
    electricity wholesale trading activities, Ofgem, (18 June 2019) 272n.146
Epyx Ltd: CMA, Decision to accept commitments offered by epyx Limited and FleetCor
    Technologies, Inc., Supply of service, maintenance and repair platforms
    (9 September 2014) 86, 86nn.58–63, 97, 97nn.140–41,
Établissements Consten Sàrl & Grundig-Verkaufs- GmbH v Commission (Consten and
    Grundig), Cases 56 and 58/64, EU:C:1966:41. . . . . 59n.22, 59n.27

Europemballage Corpn and Continental Can Co Inc Commission, Case 6/72,
    EU:C:1973:22 . . . . 91n.96
EWS Ltd v ENRON Coal Services Ltd [2009] CAT 7; [2009] EWCA Civ 647. 16–17
Exchange of Information on Future Fees by Certain Independent Fee-Paying Schools, OFT
    decision of 20 November 2006 32–33
Expedia Inc v Authorité de la concurrence, Case C-226/11, EU:C:2012:795. . . . . 58n.14
Extended Warranties on Domestic Electrical Goods, OFT Final decision on Market
    Investigation Reference (June 2012) 145, 145n.55, 146, 146n.64,
                                                                             148, 148n.78, 149
Ezeh and Connors v United Kingdom App no 39665/98 (2004)
    39 EHRR 1. . . . . 235n.21, 238n.43, 243, 243n.79

F. Hoffmann-la Roche and Others, Case C-179/16, EU:C:2018:25, judgment of
    23 January 2018 45
Fairfield Competition Act 1998 investigation decision summary, Decision of
    22 December 2015 . . . . 274n.161
Federal Trade Commission v Surescripts, LLC, 1:19-cv-01080-JDB 361n.11
Federation of Independent Practitioner Organisations v CMA, Case 1230/6/12/14,
    [2015] CAT 8. . . . . 148n.80
Felt and Single Ply Roofing Contracts in Western-Central Scotland, OFT decision of
    11 July 2005 . . . . 31–32, 51
Fender Musical Instruments, Case 50565-3 (20 January 2020) 64n.62, 64n.66, 64–65
Financial services 39
FIPO v CMA [2015] CAT 8. 11
Flat Roof and Car Park Surfacing Contracts in England and Scotland, OFT decision of 23
    February 2006. . . . . 31–32, 51, 309
Fludrocortisone, CMA decision of 9 July 2020 . . . . 39, 43–44
Flybe: OFT, No Grounds for Action Decision, Alleged abuse of a dominant position by Flybe
    Limited(OFT1286, 5 November 2010) 81, 81nn.14–15, 92, 92–93nn.102–6,
                                                                 93nn.109–12, 93–94nn.113–14, 109–10
Flynn Pharma Ltd and Flynn Pharma (Holdings) Ltd v CMA; with Pfizer Inc. and Pfizer Limited
    v CMA (Phenytoin) [2018] CAT 117. . . . . 218n.67
Food packaging, Commission Decision of 24 June 2015. 53–54
Football Association Premier League case, Commission Decision of 22 March 2006. 53–54
Football Kit price-fixing (Football Shirts), OFT decision of 1 August 2003 . . . . 39–40, 41
Football Kit price-fixing (Football Shirts) [2006] EWCA Civ 1318 41
Forex (O'Higgins v Barclays and Evans v Barclays) 17, 330–31, 331nn.192–93,
Foster Refrigerator UK (Commercial Refrigeration), Case CE/9856/14,
    (24 May 2016). 64n.64, 64–65n.69, 65
Fourfront Group Ltd, Re [2019] EWHC 3318 (Ch) 286n.34, 299–300n.153
FP McGann v CMA, Case 1337/1/12/19 not yet decided 38
Freight forwarding, Commission Decision of 28 March 2012 53–54
French Competition Authority, Decision 15-D-06 . . . . 152n.91
Funerals—Terms of reference, CMA, (28 March 2019). 12, 146, 146n.63, 147,
                                                                             154, 154n.103, 218–19
Furniture Parts, CMA 8–9

Gallaher Group Ltd v CMA [2016] EWCA Civ 719, rev'd [2018] UKSC 25 . . . . 68n.94
Galvanised steel tanks for water storage information exchange infringement, CMA decision of
    19 December 2016 37
Galvanised steel tanks for water storage main cartel infringement, CMA decision of 19
    December 2016. . . . . 37, 342–43, 354n.108, 355–57
Galvanised Steel Tanks cartel, Southwark Crown Court (24 June 2015) 10
Garden Cottage Foods Ltd v Milk Marketing Board [1984] AC 130 . . . . 312n.5
General Insurance Standard Council, OFT decision of 26 January 2001. 47
General Motors Continental NV v Commission, Case 26/75, [1975] ECR 1367 . . . . 113n.4

Generics (UK) and Others v CMA, Case C-307/18, EU:C:2020:52, CJEU Judgment of
    30 January 2020 in Paroxetine).......................8–9, 44–45, 46, 84nn.46–48, 107n.209,
                                                                107nn.210–13, 107nn.214–16, 107n.216,
                                                                108nn.221–22, 108nn.223–24,
Generics UK Limited v CMA [2018] CAT 4 (CAT judgment in Paroxetine) 45, 83nn.35–37,
                                                                83–84nn.39–42
Genzyme, Decision of 27 March 2003 9
Genzyme v OFT [2004] CAT 4 9
German Competition Authority, Decision B 6–46/12................................. 152n.91
GF Tomlinson Building Ltd v OFT, Cases 1117/1/1/09 etc [2011] CAT 7..................... 34
Gibson (Dorothy) v Pride Mobility Products Ltd, Case 1257/7/16 [2017] CAT 9 ....65n.72, 249,
                                                                249nn.132–39, 321, 321nn.81–82, 322n.88,
                                                                327n.153, 328–29, 328–29nn.167, 169,
                                                                330, 332, 333n.208, 336
Glasgow Solicitors Property Centre, OFT Press Release 154/ 03 (1 December 2003) 43
GlaxoSmithKline plc v CMA [2018] CAT 4 8–9
GlaxoSmithKline Services Unlimited v Commission Cases C-501, 513, 515, & 519/06 P,
    EU:C:2009:610 .... 58n.18, 59n.23
GMI Construction Holdings plc v OFT, Case 1118/1/1/09, [2011] CAT 12 34
Google Android, Case 40099, European Commission 360n.10, 378n.126, 379, 382n.149
Google Search (Ad Sense), Case 40411, European Commission 360n.10, 382n.150
Google Search (Shopping), Case 39470, European Commission.........360n.10, 372n.80, 377–78,
                                                                378n.125, 381nn.137–45, 381n.146, 387n.175
Grande Stevens v ItalyApp no 18640/10 (ECHR 4 March 2014) 236–37, 236–37nn.35–40,
                                                                237n.41, 239, 244
Granville Technology Group Ltd v Infineon Technologies AG 25 Feb 2020 [2020]
    EWHC 415 (Comm) 316n.46, 319–20, 320n.69
Groceries—Final Report, CC (30 April 2008)....................... 11, 148, 149, 159, 159n.137
Groundwork products 39
Groupe Canal+ v Commission, Case T-873/16, EU:T:2018:904 .... 59n.23
Groupe Eurotunnel SA/Sea France SA; on appeal, SCOP v CC [2015] CAT 1; [2015]
    EWCA Civ 487; Supreme Court [2015] UKSC 75 13
Groupement des cartes bancaires v Commission (CB),
    Case C-67/13 P, EU:C:2014:2204 .... 68, 68n.95, 75, 339n.8
Guess, Case AT40428, (17 December 2018) 59n.23, 59n.24
Gutmann (Justin) v First MTR South Western Trains Limited and Another, Case 1305/7/7/19,
    registered 27 February 2019 .... 330, 331n.190, 336

Hand Sanitiser Products: Suspected Excessive and Unfair Pricing, Case reference: 50924.... 223n.88
Hanson Quarry v CC, Case 1223/6/8/13, [2013] 148n.79
Hasbro UK Ltd See Toys and Games
HCA International Ltd v CMA, Case 1228/6/12/14, [2014] CAT 23 ....11, 146n.67, 147, 148n.80,
                                                                149, 163n.161, 219n.72
HCA International Ltd v CMA [2015] EWCA Civ 492 .... 248, 248n.123
Heathrow Airport/Arora Group: Conduct in the transport sector (facilities at airports),
    Case 50523, Decision of 25 October 2018 .... 49–50, 64–65n.69, 266–67, 274
Hoffmann-La Roche v Commission, Case 85/76, EU:C:1979:36 .... 80n.4, 91n.96, 96n.133,
                                                                101n.172, 108n.223
Holcim/Lafarge, Case M.7252, European Commission (15 December 2014) 219n.73
Hope Construction Materials 149
Hotel Online Booking, Case CE/9320-10 (31 January 2014)....................... 68–69, 68n.97
Household Fuels, CMA 8–9
Huawei Technologies, Case C-170/13, EU:C:2015:477 .... 108n.223
Hüls v Commission, Case C199/92 P [1999] ECR I4287............................. 374n.89
Humber Oil Terminals Trustee v Associated British Ports [2011] EWHC 352...... 128–29, 128n.76,
                                                                129n.77, 129nn.78–80

Hutchison 3G UK Ltd v O2 (UK) Ltd [2008] EWHC 50 (Comm) 323n.98
Hutchinson 3G Ltd v OFCOM App no 1083/3/3/07 (ECHR 20 May 2008) [2008] CAT 251n.152
Hydrogen Peroxide Antitrust Litigation, Re 552 F. 3d 305 (3rd Cir. 2008) 334nn.214–15,

IB v The Queen [2009] EWCA Crim 2575. . . . . 339, 339n.9
IBA Health Ltd v OFT [2003] CAT 27 . . . . 171–72, 172n.18, 186
IDEXX: OFT, No Grounds for Action Decision, Alleged abuse of a dominant position by IDEXX
    Laboratories Limited (OFT1387) (1 November 2011) (IDEXX) 81, 81nn.9–13,
                                                                                            89n.87, 90, 90n.89, 109
Iiyama Benelux BV v Schott AG [2016] 5 CMLR 15 (Ch) 334n.219
Iiyama (UK) Ltd v Samsung Electronics Co Ltd [2016] EWHC 1980 (Ch); [2016] 5 CMLR 16;
    [2018] EWCA Civ 220 . . . . 334n.219
Imperial Tobacco v OFT [2011] CAT 41 . . . . 7, 8
Impulse Ice Cream: CMA, No Grounds for Action Decision, Investigation relating to supplies of
    impulse ice cream (9 August 2017) (Impulse Ice Cream) 81, 81n.17, 90–91, 90n.91, 109
IMS Health GmbH & Co OHG v NDC Health GmbH & Co KG, Case C-418/01,
    [2004] ECR I-5039 . . . . 99n.153
Ineos Vinyls Ltd v Huntsman Petrochemicals (UK) Ltd [2006] EWHC 1241 (Ch) 128n.76
Infederation Ltd v Google Inc [2015] EWHC 3705 (Ch). 323n.99
Institute of Independent Insurance Brokers v Director General of Fair Trading,
    Cases 1003/2/1/01 etc. [2001] CAT 4. 47
Intel [2009] OJ C227/13. . . . . 88–89, 88n.79, 92
Intel, Case COMP/C-3/37.990 (13 May 2009) 91n.97
Intel Corporation [2010]—061 0247 . . . . 382n.153
Intel Corp v Commission, Case T-286/09, [2014] ECLI:EU:T:2014:547. . . . . 88n.79, 91–92, 101n.172
Intel Corp v Commission, Case C-413/14, [2017] ECLI:EU:C:2017:632 . . . . . 88–89, 88–89nn.79–83,
                                                                                            90–91, 91n.92, 103–4, 104n.190,
                                                                                            107n.214, 109, 132, 132n.89
Investment Consultancy and Fiduciary Management Services—Final Report, CMA
    (12 December 2018). 147, 154, 154n.103, 155,
                                                                                            155n.110, 160, 160n.140, 161
Investment Consultancy Management Services—Terms of reference, FCA,
    (14 September 2017) 145–46, 145n.58
Investigation of the multilateral interchange fees—MasterCard, OFT decision. 49
ISG Pearce Ltd v OFT, Case 1126/1/1/09, [2011] CAT 10 34
Istituto Chemioterapico Italiano SpA and Commercial Solvents Corp v Commission,
    Case 6/73, [1974] ECR 223 . . . . 99n.153
Italian Competition Authority, Decision dated 21 April 2015 . . . . 152n.91
IVAX-GlaxoSmithKline: CMA Paroxetine investigation, Case closure summary in respect
    of the IVAX-GlaxoSmithKline agreement (CE9531/11, 10 August 2016) 106n.208, 107–9
Ivey v Genting Casinos (UK) Ltd t/a Crockfords [2017] UKSC 67 . . . . 343n.53, 350n.83,
                                                                                            353, 353n.105

Jalloh v Switzerland App no 54810/00 (2007) 44 EHRR 20 . . . . 236n.32
JD Sports Fashion PLC/Footasylum PLC (phase 2 current) 14
Jetivia SA v Bilta (UK) Ltd (in liquidation) [2015] UKSC 23, [2015] 2 WLR 1168. . . . . 324n.113
JJB Sports plc and Allsports Ltd v Office of Fair Trading, Cases 1021/1/1/03 and 1022/1/1/03,
    [2004] CAT 17 and [2004] CAT 22, aff'd [2006] EWCA Civ 1318 . . . . 33, 39–40, 63n.58
John Lewis v OFT, Case 1203/6/1/12, [2012] 148n.78, 149
John Murray v United Kingdom App no 19731/91 (ECHR 8 February 1996) 235n.27
Jussila v Finland App no 73053/01 (2007) 45 EHRR 39 . . . . 235n.26

Kanda v Malaya [1962] AC 322. . . . . 242n.76
Kier Group plc v OFT, Cases 1114/1/1/09 etc [2011] CAT 3. . . . . 34, 248n.122
King Pharmaceuticals, CMA Decision of 4 March 2020 . . . . 8–9, 10
Kingsley v UK App no 35605/97 (2001) 33 EHRR 13 . . . . 236n.34
KME Yorkshire Ltd v Toshiba Carrier UK Ltd [2012] EWCA Civ 1190 40

Kone AG v OBB-Infrastruktur AG, Case C-557/12, [2014] 5 CMLR 5 . . . . 313–14, 314n.29

Konkurrensverket v TeliaSonera AB, Case C-52/09, EU:C:2011:83. . . . . 99n.154, 103n.188,
    107n.214, 370n.71

Kraft/Cadbury. 15–16

Lafarge Tarmac 11, 149

Lafarge Tarmac v CC, Case 1222/6/8/13, [2013]. 148n.79

Latvian Copyright, Case C-177/16, EU:C:2017:286. 132

Lexon (UK) Ltd v CMA, Case 1344/1/12/20 not yet decided 39

LIBOR cases, Commission Decisions of 21 October 2014 and 4 December 2013 53–54

Light fittings, Case 50343, (3 May 2017) 64nn.62–63, 64–65n.69

LINK Interchange Network Ltd, OFT decision of 16 October 2001. 47–48

Lladró Comercial SA: Agreements between Lladró Comercial SA and UK retailers fixing
    the price of porcelain and stoneware figurines (31 March 31 2003),
    DGFT Decision 63n.54, 63n.55

Lloyd v McMahon [1987] AC 625. . . . . 251n.152

Lloyds/HBOS: Anticipated acquisition by Lloyds TSB plc of HBOS plcOFT, (Report to BERR
    Secretary, 24 October 2008) 174n.44, 174–75, 199, 223n.89

Loans to large professional services firms, OFT decision of 20 January 2011 33

Local Bus Services Market investigation—Final report, CC (20 December 2011) 11, 146–48,
    146n.71, 153, 153n.97, 155, 155n.116

Loyalty-inducing discount scheme: CMA, Statement regarding the CMA's decision to close an
    investigation into a suspected breach of competition law in the pharmaceutical sector on the
    grounds of administrative priority (CE/9855-14, June 2015) 89–90, 90n.88, 91–92, 109

Lucazeau v SACEM, Joined Cases 110/88, 241/88, 242/88 [1989] ECR 2811 . . . . 113n.5

Lucite International UK Ltd and BASF plc, Case CP/1288-02, (29 November 2002) 56–57

Lundbeck, Commission decision of 19 June 2013 44

Lundbeck v Commission, Case C-591/16 P, not yet decided 44, 46

Makers UK Ltd v OFT, Case 1061/1/1/06 [2007] CAT 11 31–32

Manchester United plc v OFT, Case 1020/1/1/03 [2004] CAT 22. 39–40

Manfredi v Lloyd Adriatico Assicurazioni SpA, Case C-295/04 [2006] ECR I-6619 313–14,
    313n.20, 324

Marine Hosescase, Commission Decision of 28 January 2009 . . . . . 9–10, 37, 53–54, 297–98, 340, 341

Marine Hose: Criminal Cartel Investigation, CMA (14 November 2008). 340n.17, 340–41

Maritime Car Carriers cases (McLaren v MOL and Others). 17

Mark McLaren Class Representative Limited v MOL (Europe Africa) Ltd and Others
    Case 1339/7/7/20 . . . . 331n.191

Market Investigation References OFT511 (March 2006). 72

Market Sharing by Arriva and FirstGroup, OFT decision of 30 January 2002 30–31

MasterCard UK Members Forum Ltd and Others v Office of Fair Trading Supported by
    The British Retail Consortium (Case Nos 1054/1/1/05, 1055/1/1/05, 1056/1/1/05)
    [2006] CAT 14, [2006] Comp AR 595 . . . . 7, 49, 212–13n.44

Masterfoods, Case C-344/98 [2000] ECR I-11369 . . . . 321n.84

Mastic Asphalt Flat-roofing Contracts in Scotland, OFT decision of 7 April 2005 31–32

Maxima Latvija, Case C-345/14, EU:C:2015:784, judgment of 26 November 2015. 45–46

McKerr, Re [2004] UKHL 12. . . . . 232–33, 233n.5

ME Burgess, JJ Burgess and SJ Burgess (trading as JJ Burgess & Sons) v Office of Fair Trading
    and W Austin & Sons, Harwood Park Crematorium Ltd, Consumers' Association
    Case No 1044/2/1/04 [2005] CAT 25, [2005] CompAR 1151. . . . . 213n.45

Media-Saturn Holding GmbH v Toshiba Information Systems [2019]
    EWHC 1095 (Ch). 334n.219

Melanie Meigh (trading as The Prinknash Bird and Deer Park) v Prinknash Abbey Trustees
    Registered, Case 1303/5/7/19 . . . . 330n.182

Melrose/GKN 194–95

Memorandum of Understanding on the supply of oil fuels in an emergency, OFT
    decision of 25 October 2001 . . . . 48, 52–53, 71

Menarini Diagnostics v Italy App no 43509/08 (ECHR 27 September 2011) 235n.25, 238,
                238n.45, 238nn.47–48, 238nn.49–51, 239, 239n.58,
                240, 240n.64, 244, 244n.85, 250n.142, 251, 252, 253
MEO-Serviços de Comunicações e Multimédia, Case C-525/16, EU:C:2018:270...... 132, 132n.90
Merger Action Group v Secretary of State for Business [2008] CAT 36........................ 15
Merricks (Walter Hugh) v MasterCard Inc [2017] CAT 16; on appeal [2018] EWCA Civ 2527;
    currently before the Supreme Court 17, 311–12, 322, 322n.94, 325, 329–30,
                329nn.171–77, 332, 333nn.208–9, 336
Metro-SB-Grossmärkte GmbH v Commission (Metro I), Case 26/76,
    EU:C:1977:167 .... 59n.20, 61
Michelin I See NV Nederlandsche Banden Industrie Michelin v Commission of the
    European Communities
Microsoft, Case AT.37792 .... 377n.123
Microsoft (Tying), Case AT.39530 .... 378n.124
Microsoft Corp v Commission, Case T-201/04EU:T:2007:289 .... 91n.100, 99n.153, 100n.161,
                101nn.170–71,
Ministère Public v Tournier, Case 395/87, [1989] ECR 2521 .... 113n.5
Mittal Steel South Africa Limited v Harmony Gold Mining, Case 70/CAC/Apr07,
    [2009] ZACAC 1.. 134n.97
Model Agencies, CMA.. 8–9
Monitor Tubes.. 340–41
Montecatini v Commission, Case C235/52 P [1999] ECR I4539 .... 374n.89
Morija plc, Re; Kluk v Secretary of State for Business and Regulatory Reform [2008]
    2 BCLC 313.. 286n.29
Motor Car Insurers, OFT decision of 2 December 2011 34
Movies on Pay-TV—Final Report, CC (2 August 2012) 147, 152, 152n.89, 152n.93
Movies on Pay-TV—Terms of reference, Ofcom (4 August 2010) 145–46, 146n.61

Napp Pharmaceuticals v OFT [2002] CAT 1.. 9
Napp Pharmaceutical Holdings v Director General for Fair Trading [2001] Comp AR 1..... 244n.87
Napp Pharmaceutical Holdings Ltd & Others v DGFT [2002] ECC 3(Napp 3)..... 245n.89, 245n.92,
                245nn.93–96, 245–46nn.97–101,
                246nn.102–3, 246n.110
Napp Pharmaceutical Holdings Ltd & Others v DGFT [2002] ECC 13 (Napp 4)...........244n.88,
                245n.91, 246nn.104–6, 246nn.107–9, 247n.117
Napp Pharmaceuticals Holdings Ltd and Subsidiaries, Case CA98/2/2001, Decision of Director
    General of Fair Trading on 30 March 2001 .... 114, 114n.10, 114–15nn.11–14,
                115n.15, 115n.16, 132n.91
Napp Pharmaceutical Holdings Limited and Subsidiaries v Director General of Fair Trading
    [2002] CAT 1 (Napp)....................... 114, 114n.10, 114–15nn.11–14, 115, 115n.15,
                116, 132, 136, 136n.105, 136n.106, 244n.87, 283n.5
National Grid Electricity Transmission Plc v ABB Ltd [2014] EWHC 1055 (Ch) 323n.99
National Grid Electricity Transmission plc v ABB Ltd and Others [2012]
    EWHC 869 (Ch)...323nn.106–8
National Grid plc v GEMA [2009] CAT 14; [2010] EWCA Civ 114................... 19, 271n.137
National Lighting Co, CMA 8–9
Needles and haberdashery, Commission Decisions of 19 September 2007.................. 53–54
Neste Markkinointi Oy vYotuuli Ky, Case C-214/ 99 EU:C:2000:679 70
Network Rail Infrastructure Limited v Achilles Information Limited [2020]
    EWCA Civ 323 .... 94n.116, 318n.59
New Cars, Cm 4660 (2000) 72
Newspaper and Magazine Distribution...................................... 148, 148n.77, 149
Nokia Corporation v AU Optonics Corporation and Others [2012] EWHC 732 (Ch)....... 313n.16
North Midland Construction plc v OFT, Case 1124/1/1/09, [2011] CAT 14 34
Northern Ireland Livestock and Auctioneers' Association, OFT decision of
    3 February 2003 ....30–31, 43
Northern Irish Banking Services 10

Nortriptylene, CMA decisions of 4 March 2020 . . . . 39, 43–44
Nortriptylene Investigation 309
Notification by the Film Distributors' Association of its Standard Conditions for Licensing the
    Commercial Exhibition of Films, OFT decision of 1 February 2002 43
NV Nederlandsche Banden Industrie Michelin v Commission of the European Communities
    ECLI:EU:C:1983:313 . . . . 378, 382n.147

Office Fit Out cartel 10
Official Receiver v Wadge Rapps & Hunt [2003] UKHL 49 . . . . 290n.76
OFT v IBA Health Ltd [2005] CAT 27, [2004] EWCA Civ 142 . . . . 12–13, 172n.19, 172
O'Halloran and Francis v United Kingdom App no 15809/02 (2008) 46 EHRR 21 . . . . 236n.28
O'Higgins [2020] CAT 8 . . . . 328n.166
O'Higgins FX Class representative Ltd v Barclays Bank and Others: Philip Evans v Barclays Bank
    and Others, Case 1329/7/7/19 [2020] CAT 8 . . . . 330–31, 330n.183, 331nn.192–93,
Oil fuels 52–53
Online platforms and digital advertising market study, CMA Final report
    (1 July 2020) 199n.220, 360–61
Online Platforms and Digital Advertising, CMA Interim report (18 December 2019) 12, 13n.84,
    22, 55–56n.3, 165–66, 165n.168
Online Platforms and Digital Advertising in the UK—Penalty notice under section 174A of the
    Enterprise Act 2002, Case MA/50777/19, CMA, (10 January 2020) 146, 146n.62
Online resale price maintenance in the digital piano and digital keyboard sector,
    Case 50565-2 [2019] 379n.130
Online sales ban in the golf equipment sector, Case 50230 [2017] 379n.128
Online sales of posters and frames, Case 50223 [2016] 379n.127
Online sales of posters and frames, CMA decision of 12 August 2016 37
Online sales of posters and frames: Director Disqualification 309
Ophthalmology sector, conduct in, Case CE/9784-13, Decision of 20 August 2015 . . . . 268n.120
Osborn v Parole Board [2013] 3 WLR 1020 . . . . 233, 233n.13
Oscar Bronner GmbH & Co KG v Mediaprint Zeitungsund Zeitschriftenverlag
    GmbH & Co KG, Case C-7/97, [1998] ECR I-7791 . . . . 99n.153
Oscar Bronner GmbH & Co KG v Mediaprint Zeitungs-und Zeitschriftenverlag GmbH
    & Co. KG, Mediaprint Zeitungsvertriebsgesellschaft mbH & Co. KG and Mediaprint
    Anzeigengesellschaft mbH & Co KG [1998] ECLI:EU:C:1998:569 . . . . 369, 369nn.67–69,
Otis v Land Oberosterreich Case C-435/18 . . . . 314n.29
Öztürk v Germany App no 8544/79 (1984) 6 EHRR 409 237–38

Paroxetine Case No: C3/2018/1847 and 1874 [2020] EWCA Civ 339 . . . . 218n.68
pay TV, Review of the wholesale must-offer obligation, Ofcom (19 November 2015) 271n.134
Paroxetine Investigation, Case CE-9531/11, Decision of 12 February 2016 . . . . 8–9, 29–30, 36–37,
    43–46, 57, 57n.8, 69n.104, 82, 82nn.21–26,
    83, 110, 218, 218n.69
Paroxetine Investigation: Case CE-9531/11, Decision 10 August 2016, Case closure summary in
    respect of the IVAX GlaxoSmithKline agreement 106n.208, 107–9
Paroxetine CJEU Judgment: Generics (UK) and Others v CMA, Case C-307/18, EU:C:2020:52,
    CJEU Judgment of 30 January 2020 in Paroxetine) 8–9, 44, 45, 46, 84nn.46–48,
    107n.209, 107nn.210–13, 107nn.214–16,
    107n.216, 108nn.221–22, 108nn.223–24
Paroxetine CAT Judgment: Generics UK Limited v CMA [2018] CAT 4 (CAT judgment in
    Paroxetine) 45, 83nn.35–37, 83–84nn.39–42
Payday Lending Market Investigation—Final Report, CMA (24 February 2015) 11, 146–48,
    146n.69, 154, 154n.106, 155, 155n.112
PayPal/iZettle (12 June 2019) 14, 197
Payment Protection Insurance (2009) 11
Perindopril (Servier), Case AT.39612, (30/09/2016) Commission Decision 83–84, 84n.44
Pernod Ricard v OFT [2004] CAT 10 8
Peugeot, COMP/36.623, 36.820, and 37.275 (5 October 2005) 64n.60

Peugeot and Others v NSK Ltd [2018] CAT 3 . . . . 322–23, 323n.101
Pfizer Inc v CMA, Cases 1275/1/12/16 and 1276/1/12/17, [2020] EWCA Civ 339 43–44
Pfizer Limited and Others v CMA [2018] CAT 11 . . . . 113, 113n.8, 117n.25, 117n.26,
                    120nn.47–48, 120nn.49–50, 120n.51, 121n.52,
                    121nn.53–55, 121nn.56–58, 125n.67,
                    125n.68, 126n.69, 130n.81
Pfleiderer v AG Bundeskartellamt, Case C-360/09 [2011] ECR I-5161 . . . . 323, 323n.105
Pharmaceuticals 39
Phenytoin, Case CE/ 9742-13, decision (7 December 2016) 25–26, 43–44, 113–14,
                    117–26, 117n.24, 129–30, 132n.86, 132–33,
                    134–35, 136, 216n.60, 218
Pierre Fabre v Président de l'Autorité de la concurrence, Case C-439/09,
    EU:C:2011:277 . . . . 59, 66n.78, 66–67
Pierre Fabre Dermo-Cosmétique SAS v Président de l'Autorité de la concurrence and
    Ministre de l'Économie, de l'Industrie et de l'Emploi ECLI:EU:C:2011:649 . . . . 379n.129
Ping,Case 50230, (24 August 2017) 58n.16, 64n.66, 65–66, 78
Ping Europe Ltd v CMA, Case 1279/1/12/17 [2018] CAT 8 . . . . 66n.76
Ping Europe Ltd v CMA [2020] EWCA Civ 13 . . . . 66n.77, 75
Ping Europe Ltd v CMA [2018] CAT 13 . . . . 218n.70
Polly Peck International plc, Re [1994] 1 BCLC 574 . . . . 292n.94
Pool Reinsurance, OFT decision of 15 April 2004 48
Post Danmark I, Case C-209/10, EU:C:2012:172 . . . . 95, 95n.124, 103n.188, 108nn.221–22,
Post Danmark II, Case C-23/14, EU:C:2015:651 . . . . .91n.100, 96n.133, 101n.172, 103n.188
Power Cables (Cases 1340-41/5/7/20(T)) 17
Premier League Ltd v QC Leisure and Murphy v Media Protection Services Ltd, Cases C- 403
    and 429/08, EU:C:2011:631 . . . . 59n.23
Price Fixing Agreements involving John Bruce (UK) Limited, Fleet Parts Limited and Truck and
    Trailer Components(13 May 2002), DGFT Decision 63n.51
Pride Mobility Products Ltd, Case CE/9578-12 (27 March 2014) 64n.61, 65
Private Motor Insurance market investigation—Final Report, CMA (24 September 2014) 11, 72,
                    146–48, 146n.70, 151n.88, 152,
                    152n.90, 155, 155n.114, 162, 163
Private Motor Insurance market investigation—Provisional findings report, CC
    (17 December 2013) 162n.152
Privately-Funded Health Care Market Investigation—Final Report, CMA
    (02 April 2014) 11, 146–48, 146n.66, 148n.80, 149–50, 152,
                    152n.94, 153, 155, 155n.113, 163–64, 219n.72
Privately funded ophthamology services, CMA decision of 1 July 2020 38–39
Professional Videotapes 30–31
Project Condor Board Review (OFT October 2010) 10
Prokent-Tomra, Case COMP/E-1/38.113 (29 March 2006) 91n.97
Pronuptia de Paris v Schillgallis, Case 161/84, EU:C:1986:41 . . . . 59n.20, 61
Property Sales and Lettings, CMA decision of 8 May 2015 36–37
Public transport (Market Study 2015) 145n.53
Publishers' Association, Case C-360/92 P, EU:C:1995:6 57
Purple Parking Limited and Meteor Parking Limited v Heathrow Airport Limited [2011]
    EWHC 987 (Ch) 97, 99, 99nn.150–52, 99nn.154–55,
                    99n.157, 104, 109–10, 316–17, 316n.50

Quantum Claims Compensation Specialists Ltd v Powell 1998 SC 316 . . . . 332n.201
Quarmby Construction Co Ltd v OFT, Case 1120/1/1/09, [2011] CAT 11 . . . . 7, 34

R v Burns and Others (2010/2141) 9–10
R v Cooper, Unreported, Crown Court at Southwark (15 September 2017) 298n.148
R v George, Burns, Burnett and Crawley [2010] EWCA Crim 1148 . . . . 343n.54
R v Ghosh [1982] EWCA Crim 2 . . . . 343–44, 343n.53, 350n.83
R v Haddock [2006] HRLR 40 . . . . 252n.159
R v Lambert [2001] 2 AC 545 . . . . 233n.9

R v Lyons, Parnes, Ronson, Saunders [2002] UKHL 44 . . . . 241–42, 241n.70, 242nn.71–72,
R v Whittle, Brammar and Allison [2008] EWCA Crim 2560 . . . . .298n.146, 340–41nn.19–30
R v Whittle, Brammar & Allison, Sentencing Remarks, Crown Court at Southwark
     (11 June 2008. . . . . 340n.18
R v Whittle and Others Southwark Crown Court (10 June 2008). 9–10, 298n.145
R (Alconbury Developments and Others) v Secretary of State for the Environment, Transport
     and the Regions [2003] AC 295 . . . . 242, 242n.77, 250n.141
R (Brind) v Secretary of State for the Home Department [1991] 1 AC 696 . . . . 232n.3
R (Guardian News and Media Ltd) v City of Westminster Magistrates' Court[2012]
     EWCA Civ 420 . . . . 233, 233nn.11–12,
R (Hawthorne) v Police Ombudsman for northern Ireland [2018] NIQB 5 . . . . 242n.76
R (Smith) v Parole Board and R (West) v Parole Board [2005] UKHL 1 . . . . 243n.78
R (UNISON) v Lord Chancellor [2017] UKSC 51 . . . . 233–34, 234n.17
R (Witham) v Lord Chancellor [1998] QB 575 . . . . 241, 241n.67
Racecourse Association and Others v Office of Fair Trading; British Horseracing Board v Office
     of Fair Trading, (Case Nos 1035/1/1/04 and 1041/2/1/04) [2005] CAT 29, [2006]
     CompAR 99 . . . . .48–49, 212–13n.44
Radio Telefis Eireann (RTE) and Independent Television Publications Ltd (ITP) v Commission,
     Joined Cases C-241/91 P and C-242/91 P, [1995] ECR I-743 . . . . 99n.153
Reckitt Benckiser: OFT, Abuse of a dominant position by Reckitt Benckiser Healthcare (UK)
     Limited and Reckitt Benckiser Group plc (OFT1368, Decision of 12 April 2011) 9, 83,
          83nn.31–34, 105–6, 106nn.203–5
Regulated Industries: Guidance on concurrent application of competition law to regulated
     industries (CMA10) (March 2014) 263n.71, 264n.78, 264n.84,
          266nn.99–100, 266n.104
Remicade: CMA, No grounds for Action Decision, Remicade (50236, 14 March 2019) 82–83,
          82nn.27–28, 91–92, 91nn.93–95,
          91nn.98–99, 109
Rentokil Initial/Cannon Hygiene, CMA decision (25 January 2019); appeal to the
     CAT withdrawn 14
Replica Football Shirts litigation See Consumers Association v JJB Sports
Residential estate agency services, CMA decision of 31 May 2017. 38
Residential Estate Agency Services in Berkshire, Case 50543, CMA decision of
     17 December 2019 . . . . .38, 357–58, 357n.117
Residential Estate Agency Services in the Berkshire Area: Director Disqualification 309
Residential Estate Agency Services in the Burnham-on-Sea Area: Director Disqualification 309
Retail Banking Market Investigation—Final Report, CMA, (9 August 2016). 12, 146–48,
          146n.69, 154, 154n.104, 155n.112,
          155–56, 159–60, 168
Road Haulage and Others v Daimler AG, Case 1289/7/7/18, [2019] CAT 26 . . . . 316n.47
Roche AG/Spark Therapeutics Inc (phase 1 clearance decision December 2019) 14
Roche Products Limited v Provimi Limited [2003] EWHC 961 (Comm). 335n.222
Rolled lead. 39
Rolling Stock Leasing (2009). 11
Roma Medical Aids Ltd, Case CE/9578-12 (5 August 2013). 64n.61, 65–66
Royal Bournemouth & Christchurch Hospitals NHSFT/Poole Hospital NHSFT report
     (17 October 2013) 13–14
Royal Mail: Discriminatory pricing in relation to the supply of bulk mail delivery services in the
     UK (CW/01122/01/14, OFCOM decision of 14 August 2018) (Royal Mail) 49–50, 81n.16,
          102–3, 102–3nn.180–84, 109–10
Royal Mail Group Ltd v DAF Truck and Others [2020] CAT 321n.84
Royal Mail v Ofcom [2020] CAT 2 . . . . 270n.130
Royal Mail v Ofcom, Case 1299/1/3/18 [2019] CAT 27 . . . . 189, 20, 49–50, 103nn.185–86,
          103n.188, 104n.191, 104, 109–10, 270n.129
Royal Mail/The Sale Group (trading as Despatch Bay), CW/01222/07/18, OFCOM
     decision of 14 November 2019 . . . . 50, 270n.131
Rural Broadband Wayleaves, Short-form Opinion of 23 August 2012. 43
Ryanair Holdings plc v CC [2014] CAT 3; [2015] EWCA Civ 83 . . . . 13, 23

Sabre/Farelogix, (phase 2 prohibition decision April 2020) 14
Safeway Stores Ltd v Twigger [2010] EWCA 1472 . . . . 324n.113
Sainsburys/ASDA (2019),[2019] CAT 1 14
Sainsbury's Supermarkets Ltd v Mastercard Inc and Others, Case 1241/5/7/15 (T)
    [2016] CAT 11. . . . . 315–16, 316n.42, 325nn.121–23, 326, 326nn.140–43
Sainsburys and Others v Mastercard[2020] UKSC 24, [2018] EWCA 1536 (Civ),
    [2016] CAT 26. . . . . .17–18, 316n.42, 322nn.95–96, 325n.124, 326n.144
Salabiaku v France App no 10589/83 (1991) 13 EHRR 79. . . . . 236n.31
Scandlines Sverige AB v Port of Helsingborg, Case COMP/A.36.568/D3, Commission
    Decision of 23 July 2004. . . . . 113n.7, 128
Scottish legal services research (Market Study 2020). 145n.54
SEL-Imperial Ltd v The British Standards Institution [2010] EWHC 854 (Ch) 317n.52
Sepia Logistics Ltd v OFT, Case 1072/1/1/06 [2007] CAT 13 32
Servier, Commission decision of 9 July 2014. 44
Servier v Commission, Case C-201/19, not yet decided 44, 46, 84n.44
Servier SAS and Others v European Commission, Case T-691/14. . . . . 83–84, 84n.44
Sevenoaks, Re [1991] Ch 164 . . . . 301n.165
Showmen's Guild of Great Britain, CMA decision of 26 October 2017 43
Skyscanner, CMA decision of 31 January 2104. 8
Skyscanner v CMA, 2014 [CAT] 16 8
SME Banking (2002) 10
Société de Vente de Ciments et Bétons de l'Est SA v Kerpen & Kerpen GmbH, Case 319/82,
    ECLI:EU:C:1983:374 . . . . 314n.27
Société Stenuit v France App no 11598/85 (ECHR 30 May 1991) (1991) ECC 41 . . . 238n.44, 238–39,
                                                                                       239nn.53–56
Société Technique Minière v Maschinenbau Ulm GmbH (STM), Case 56/65, EU:C:1966:38 61
Socrates Training Ltd v The Law Society of England and Wales, Case 1249/5/7/16
    [2017] CAT 10. . . . . 70, 94n.119, 317–18, 317n.55
Somerfield plc v CC [2006] CAT 4 13
Somerset Estate Agents (2016) 10, 39
Specialist Laundry Services, CMA 8–9
SSE plc: Notice of decision to accept binding commitments, Decision of
    3 November 2016 . . . . 272n.144
Stagecoach v CC [2010] CAT 14. 13
Statutory Audit Services for Large Companies—Final report, CMA (18 April 2019) 11, 12,
                                                                    13n.83, 147, 152n.96, 153, 155, 155n.115,
                                                                                       165–66, 165n.167
Statutory Audit Services for Large Companies—Terms of reference, OFT
    (October 2011) 166n.169
Steel and Morris v United Kingdom App no 24838/94 (ECHR 23 September 1998). 236, 236n.30
Stericycle International LLC v Competition Commission [2006] CAT 21 . . . . 178, 178n.74
Stock Check Pads, OFT decision of 4 April 2006 32
Store Cards 10
Street Furniture (Outside Advertising) (17 May 2012) 69n.105
Streetmap.EU Ltd v Google Inc and Others [2016] EWHC 253 (Ch), [2016]
    All ER (D) 129 (Feb). 94n.120, 95n.125, 95–96,
                                97, 100, 100nn.159–61, 100nn.162–63, 100nn.164–65,
                                101n.166, 101nn.167–68, 101n.169, 101nn.170–72,
                                                        102.173, 102n.174, 102nn.175–77,
                                        102nn.178–79, 104, 109–10, 316–17, 317n.53
Sunday Times v United Kingdom (1979) 2 EHRR 245 . . . . 161n.146
Sundbusserne v Port of Helsingborg, Case COMP/A.36.568/D3, Commission Decision of
    23 July 2004 . . . . 113n.7
Supply and Acquisition of Energy Market Investigation—Final report, CMA
    (24 June 2016). 12, 147, 148nn.73–74, 154, 154n.105,
                                                154n.108, 155n.110, 155–56, 159–60, 159n.139, 168
Supply and Acquisition of Energy—Terms of reference Ofgem, (21 July 2014) 145–46, 145n.59
Supply of care home medicines, OFT decision of 20 March 2014. 35

Supply of medicines (Market Study 2015) 145n.54
Supply of Precast Concrete Drainage Pipes cartel 10, 344–45, 348, 355–58
Supply of Precast Concrete Drainage Products: Criminal Investigation, Case CE/9705/12
    Update CMA (13 June 2017). 345n.57, 355–56, 356n.111
Supply of Precast Concrete Drainage Products: Director Disqualification 309
Supply of Products to the Construction Industry (Pre-cast Concrete Drainage Products) Case
    50299 CMA Decision (23 October 2019) 345nn.58–63
Supply of products to the furniture industry (drawer fronts), CMA decision of
    27 March 2017. 38
Supply of solid fuel and charcoal products, CMA decision of 28 March 2018 38
Swedish Competition Authority, Decision 596/2013 (15 April 2015) 152n.91
Synthesizers and high-tech equipment, Case 50565-4, (29 June 2020) 64n.63, 64–65n.69
Synthetic Rubber 30–31

Tesco v CC [2009] CAT 6. 11
Tesco Stores v OFT, Case 1188/1/1/11 [2012] CAT 31 . . . . 7, 42
Tetra Pak v Commission, Case C-333/94 P, [1996] ECR II-5951 . . . . 92, 92n.101
TGA Mobility Ltd, Case 50469, (19 October 2017) 65
Tiercé Ladbroke SA v Commission of the European Communities, Case T-504/93 [1997]
    ECR II-00923 . . . . 38, 83n.36
T-Mobile Netherlands, Case C-8/08, EU:C:2009:343, [2019] EWCA Civ 162. . . . . 37, 67, 67n.93
Tobacco 25–26, 77
Tobacco, Formal decision of 16 April 2010 7
Tobacco, Case CE/2596–03 (15 April 2010) 67
Tobacco, Cases 1160–5/1/1/10 [2011] CAT 41 . . . . 68n.94
Tobii AB/Smartbox Assistive Technology Ltd, appeal to the CAT dismissed [2020] CAT 1 14
Tomra Systems v Commission, Case C-549/10 P, EU:C:2012:221 . . . . 100n.165, 108n.220
Toshiba Carrier UK Ltd and Others v KME Yorkshire Ltd and Others [2011]
    EWHC 2665 (Ch). 313n.16
Toshiba Corporation and Others v Úřad pro ochranu hospodářské soutěže, Case C-17/10,
    EU:C:2012:72 . . . . 261n.53
Toys and Games 31–32, 41
Toys and Games, [2006] EWCA Civ 1318 41
Toys and Games: Agreements between Hasbro UK Ltd and distributors fixing the price of
    Hasbro toys and games (28 November 2002), DGFT Decision 63n.53
Toys and Games: Agreements between Hasbro UK Ltd/Argos Ltd/Littlewoods Ltd fixing the
    price of Hasbro toys and games (21 November 2003), DGFT Decision 63n.56, 64n.62
Toys and Games: Hasbro UK Ltd/Argos Ltd/Littlewoods Ltd, OFT decision of
    2 December 2003 39–40
Toys 'R' Us, Inc v Federal Trade Commission 42
Trains: Gutmann v First MTR South Western and Another and Gutmann v South Eastern
    Railway). 17
Trucks (cases 1284, 1290-95/5/7/18(T)) 17, 336
Trucks (Road Haulage Association v MAN and Others and UK Trucks
    Claims v Fiat and Others) 17, 336, 340–41

UK Trucks Claim Ltd v Fiat Chrysler, Case 1282/7/7/18. . . . . 316n.47
Ultra Finishing Ltd (Bathroom Fittings), Case CE/9857/14 (10 May 2016) 64n.63, 64n.64,
                                                                                  64–65n.69, 65n.74
Umbro Holdings Ltd v OFT, Case 1019/1/1/03. 30
Unfair pricing in respect of the supply of phenytoin sodium capsules in the UK,
    Case CE/9742-13 [2016] 218n.67
UniChem v OFT [2005] CAT 8. . . . . 171–72, 172n.20, 186
UOP desiccant, Case CE/2464-03, OFT decision of 8 November 2004. . . . . 32, 63n.59
United Brands v Commission, Case 27/76, EU:C:1978:22 . . . . 80n.4, 113n.3, 118n.29,
                                                                      118–19, 119nn.32–36, 119nn.37–39,
                                                                      119nn.40–41, 119n.42, 120nn.43–45,
                                                                      120n.46, 120–21, 124, 127

Unwired Planet International Ltd v Huawei Technologies Co Ltd [2016] EWCA
     Civ 489, [2016] 5 CMLR 11 . . . . 322n.91
US v Apple Inc. 42
US film studios, Case AT40023 . . . . 59n.23

Valico Srl v Italy App no 70074/ 01 (ECHR 21 March 2006) 250n.142
Vanilla Group/Washstation (11 October 2018) 14
Vantaan Kaupunka v Skanska Industrial Solutions Oy 14th March 2019, Case C-274/17 . . . . 314n.31
Verisk/EagleView [2014] 141 0085. . . . . 359n.5
Verwaltungsverfahren, Case B6-22/16 GEM § 32 ABS 1 GWB, Bundeskartellamt 365n.33
Viho Europe BV v Commission, Case C-73/95P, EU:C:1996:405 . . . . 61n.38
Vitamins. 30–31
Vodafone, (5 April 2002), OFTEL decision 62n.48

Walt Wilhelm v Bundeskartellamt, Case 14/68, EU:C:1969:4. 57
West Midland Roofing Contractors, OFT decision of 17 March 2004 . . . . 7, 31–32
Western Isles Road Fuels(24 June 2014) (Certas Energy) 80, 80n.7, 97–98, 97–98nn.142–45
Westmid Packing Services Ltd, Secretary of State for Trade and Industry v Griffiths and others,
     Re [1998] 2 BCLC 646 . . . . 305n.182
WH Newson Holding Ltd v IMI plc [2016] EWCA Civ 773, [2015] EWHC 1676 (Ch) 319n.67
WH Newson Holding Ltd v IMI plc [2013] EWHC 3788 (Ch). 323n.99

Zander v Sweden App no 14282/ 88 (1994) 18 EHRR 175. . . . . 235nn.22–23,
Zinc phosphates, Commission Decision of 11 December 2001 53–54

Table of Legislation

Table of Statutes

Civil Aviation Act 2012
s 68 . . . . 267n.108
Civil Litigation (Expenses and Group
Proceedings) (Scotland) Act 2018 331
s 1 . . . . 332n.203
s 10 . . . . 332n.203
Communications Act 2003 . . . . . 103–4, 174n.39
ss 316–318 20
s 317(2). 260n.39
Companies Act 2006 . . . . 291n.84
Company Directors Disqualification Act
1986 (CDDA 1986). 291n.81,
291nn.84–85, 292n.93, 293,
295–96n.124, 303–4
s 1(a). 292–93
s 1(b). 292–93
ss 2–8 . . . . 290n.78
s 2 . . . . .297–98, 305n.181
s 2(1). 298n.147
s 9 295–96
ss 9A–9E. 290–91
s 9A. 290–91, 291n.83, 292n.90, 297–98
s 9A(1) 290–91
s 9A(2) 290–91
s 9A(3) 290–91
s 9A(5)(a). 290–91
s 9A(5)(b) 292
s 9A(5)(c). 292
s 9A(6) 290–91, 305–6
s 9A(7) 291n.88
s 9A(9) 292
s 9A(10) 292–93
s9A(11) 292n.89
s 9B. 297–98
s 9B(1) 293
s 9B(2) 293
s 9B(3) 293n.98
s 9B(4) 293n.98
s 9B(5) 293n.99
s 9C(1) 292–93
s 9C(2) 292n.92
s 9C(3) 292n.93, 304n.178
s 9C(4) 292n.93, 304n.178
s 9D. 292n.90
s 9E(2) 292n.90
s 9E(3) 292n.91
s9E(4). 292n.89

s 9E(5) 291n.85
s 13 . . . . 293n.100
s 13(a). 293n.96
s 13(b) 293n.96
s 15 . . . . 293n.100
s 15(1)(a) 292–93
s 16(1). 292–93, 292n.93, 304n.178
s 16(3). 292–93
s 17 299–300
s 18(2). 292–93
s 18(2A)(b) 293n.101
s 22(2). 291n.84
ss 22A–22C 291n.84
ss 22E–22H 291n.84
s 24(1). 291n.81
Sch 1 292
Competition Act 1980 . . . . .29, 255–56
ss 2–10 . . . . 257n.12
ss 9–10 . . . . 257n.13
Competition Act 1998 (CA 1998). 1, 2, 3,
4, 6, 7, 9, 12, 16–17, 19, 23, 24, 25, 27–28,
29–31, 32–33, 36, 38, 43, 46–47, 49–50,
52–53, 54, 55, 56–58, 57n.9, 63–64, 65–66,
68n.94, 69, 70–71, 72, 73, 76–78, 109,
113–14, 123, 126, 132, 136, 138–39, 142–43,
145, 145n.57, 151, 152, 162, 163–64, 166–67,
201, 202, 204–5, 207, 209–12, 213, 214,
214n.52, 215–16, 217–18, 219n.76, 221,
225–28, 231, 232, 237, 238–39, 243, 244–47,
249, 250–51, 255, 256–58, 257n.21, 259–60,
261–63, 271–72, 276, 277, 283, 284, 312,
313, 314–15, 335
Chap I prohibition 14, 3, 22–23, 30–31,
32–33, 38–39, 43, 47, 48–50, 55, 56–58,
58n.10, 62n.48, 63, 64–66, 68–69, 70,
73–74, 76–77, 94, 95–96, 106, 106n.206,
144, 152, 153, 162, 204, 210n.34, 213, 218,
221, 237, 238–39, 243–44, 250–51, 252–53,
256–57, 263, 267, 270–71, 274, 275, 283–84,
290–91, 309, 312, 316–18, 320–21, 322,
347–48, 355–57
Chap II prohibition 3, 8–9,
16–17, 22–23, 28, 30, 43–44, 49–50, 56–57,
57n.6, 70, 79, 94, 95–96, 103, 109–10, 129,
162, 163, 204, 210n.34, 213, 218, 221,
222–23, 237, 238–39, 243–44, 250–51,
252–53, 256–57, 263, 270–71, 283–84,
290–91, 312, 316–17, 320–21, 336
s 2 . . . . .31–32, 70, 76, 78

s 2(1).. 71
ss 6 to 8.............................46–47
s 9 ....46–47, 48–49, 52–53,
                            71, 77, 78, 349
s 9(1)..47–48
s 10 ....58n.12
s 11 ....46–47, 349
s 16 17–18
s 18 ....99, 114, 129
s 18(2)(c) 102–3
s25.. 292n.92
ss 26–30 .... 292n.92
s 31A.........................34, 54, 68n.98
s 36 .... 285n.13
s 39 .... 64n.61
s 40(4)..325
s 47A.....16, 312, 312n.12, 320–22, 327n.153
s 47A(3) 322n.89
s 47A(9) 321n.83
s 47A(10) 313n.14
s 47B..................16, 65n.72, 249, 312,
                      315, 321, 327–28, 329–30
s 47B(1) 312n.13, 327n.147
s 47B(4) 33, 312n.13, 327n.147, 328n.157
s 47B(5)(a)...................328nn.157–58,
s 47B(6) 328nn.157–59,
s 47B(7) 328n.160
s 47B(8) 327–28
s 47B(8)(a).......................328n.165
s 47B(8)(b).........................327–28
s 47B(10) 328n.161
s 47B(11) 328n.162
s 47B(11)(b)....................328n.164
s 47C(1) 325
s 47C(6) 332
s 47C(8) 332
s 47E.................................318
s 49A.................................327–28
s 49B.................................327–28
s 50(1)..57n.6
s 54 .... 257n.14
s 58A..........16, 320–21, 321nn.83–84, 334
s 58A(2) 320n.74
s 58A(3) 320n.75
s 59(1B) 328n.163
s 60 ....23, 57, 73, 78,
                      111n.226, 334n.218
s 60A.........................73, 111n.226
Sch 3, para 7.........................52–53
Sch 3, para 7(2) 52–53
Sch 3, para 7(3) 52–53
Sch 8, para 3........................244, 250
Consumer Rights Act 2015
   (CRA 2015)..............17–18, 212, 249,
                      313, 315–16, 318, 321–22,
                      325, 327–28, 327n.153, 332
Pt 2, Chap 3 17
Sch 8, para 31.....................322n.89

Courts and Legal Services Act 1990
   s 58AA 332n.204
Digital Economy Act 2017.................4
Electricity Act 1989
   s 3A.............................257n.10
   s 25(5).........................260n.39
Enterprise Act 2002 (EA 2002) 1, 2, 4–5,
      9–10, 12–13, 15, 16, 37, 55, 56, 57n.6, 69,
      72, 73, 76–78, 137, 138–39, 156, 166–67,
      169, 170–76, 171n.12, 174n.39, 175n.51,
      178, 179–80, 181, 181n.109, 183, 183n.130,
      184, 184n.135, 186, 187–88, 190–91, 193,
      194–95, 196, 198, 199, 201, 202, 209, 210,
      211n.37, 211–12, 222n.84, 227, 228, 231,
      256–57, 258, 259, 261–62, 276, 290–91,
      293, 312, 321–22, 337, 347–48
Chap 1 140
Pt 4 ....137n.3, 257n.17, 263
s 5 142
s 16(6).........................322n.91
s 18 ....312n.10
s 19 ....16, 312
s 20 16
s 22(1)(a) 173n.31
s 22(1)(b) 171n.14
s 23(1).........................173n.32
s 23(1)(b) 173n.33
s 23(2)–(4) 173n.33
s 23A.........................194n.184
s 24(1).........................173n.34
s 25 ....139n.14
s 33(1)(a) 173n.31
s 33(1)(b) 171n.14
s 34ZA 179–80n.95
s 34ZA(3).......................180n.96
s 35(1)(a) 173n.31
s 35(1)(b) 171n.12
s 36(1)(a) 173n.31
s 36(1)(b) 171n.12
s 41A(1) 180n.104
s 41A(2) 180n.106
s 41A(3) 180n.106
s 42(2).........................171n.16
s 42(8)(b) 174n.42
s 58 173–74
s 58(1).........................174n.39
s 58(2).........................195n.194
ss 58(2A)–(2C) 174n.39
s 58(3)...........173–75, 193, 194–95, 199
s 71 ....177n.69
s 71(3).........................178n.73
s 72 ....178n.78
s 72(1)(b) 178n.80
s 72(3)(a) 178n.73
s 72(3B) 178n.81
s 73A(1) 181n.110
s 73A(2) 181n.111
s 73A(3)–(4) 181n.111

s 80(2A) 178n.81
s 81(2). 178n.79
s 81(2A) 178n.81
s 94A. 178n.82
s 96(2A) 180n.97
s 106 . . . . 175n.54
s 107 . . . . 175n.54
s 120(4). 250
s 131(1). 140n.20, 140n.21
s 131(2A) 143n.42
s 132 . . . . 140n.18
s 133 . . . . .141nn.30–31
s 134(1). 143
s 137(2A) 141n.26
s 138 . . . . 141n.35
s 138(2). 143n.41
s 138A. 141n.27
s 140A(7)(a) 143n.45
s 141 . . . . 140n.24
s 142 . . . . 141n.32
s 144 . . . . 140n.24
s 146 . . . . 141n.33
s 146(3). 141n.34
s 146A. 141n.33
s 153 . . . . 143n.43, 144n.48, 144n.51
s 169 140–41
s 172 . . . . 140n.23
s 174 146
s 179 . . . . 137n.3, 142, 148n.74
s 179(4). 250
s 179(6). 143n.39
s 179(7). 143n.39
s 188 . . . . .2, 283n.7, 295–96n.124,
                               305n.181, 338
s 188(1). 347–48, 349
s 188(2). 351
s 188A. 347–48, 349–50
s 188A(1)(a) .347–48
s 188A(1)(b) 347n.72
s 188A(1)(c). 347–48, 349
s 188A(2) 347–48
s 188B. 347–48
s 188B(1) 348
s 188B(2) 348
s 188B(3) 348, 349–50
s 204 290–91
Explanatory Notes, para 292 . . . .138–39nn.9–10
Enterprise and Regulatory Reform Act 2013
     (ERRA 2013). 2–3, 4, 5, 8, 9–10,
          11–13, 14, 18–19, 25, 26, 35, 137, 138,
          139–40, 140n.19, 141, 143–44, 145–46,
          166–67, 168, 170, 175–82, 177n.67, 179–
          80n.95, 183, 183n.131, 185–86, 187–88,
          189–91, 198, 201, 202, 204, 213n.47, 214,
          214n.52, 216, 225, 226–27, 228, 247, 255,
          256, 257–58, 259n.34, 259–61, 262–63,
          264–66, 270, 276–77, 277n.193, 279–80,
          350n.83, 352, 354–55, 358

s 16 . . . . 260n.47
s 16(3)(c) 260n.38
s 25(3). 165n.165, 214n.54
ss 29ff 247n.115
s 33 11–12
s 36 . . . . .10, 11–12
s 38 10
ss 39ff 247n.116
s 47 . . . . .347–48, 347n.71
ss 51 to 53. 259
s 51 260–61
s 51(2). 261
s 51(4). 260n.43
s 51(5). 259–60, 259n.35
s 52 261–62
s 52(1). 262n.57
s 52(6). 261–62
s 53 261–62
Sch 4 . . . . 260–61, 260n.38, 260n.47
Sch 9 11–12
Sch 10 11–12
Sch 12 10
Sch 14. . . . . 259n.35, 260n.40
Explanatory Notes 166, 283n.5
Explanatory Notes, para 264 . . . . 166n.174
Explanatory Notes, para 370 255
Explanatory Notes, para 378 . . . . 260n.40
European Union (Withdrawal)
     Act 2018. . . . . 73n.126
European Union (Withdrawal Agreement)
     Act 2020. . . . . 73n.126, 201n.1
Fair Trading Act 1973. . . . . . 29, 72, 166, 169–70,
                              172–73, 175, 199, 207n.25,
                              210–11, 255–56
Pt 1, s 2 . . . . 208n.26
s 50 . . . . 257n.11
ss 52–55 . . . . 257n.11
s 56 . . . . 257n.13
s 64(1). 173n.30
s 84 . . . . 166n.173, 206n.21
s 84(1)(a)–(e) 170n.7
s 88 . . . . 257n.13
Financial Services and Markets
     Act 2000. 275
s 1E 257n.10
Gas Act
     s 4AA 257n.10
     s 28(5). 260n.39
Health and Social Care Act 2012. . . . .13–14, 258
s 62(3). 257n.10, 276n.183
s 72 . . . . 276n.182
s 73 . . . . 276n.182
Human Rights Act 1998 (HRA) 204–5,
                              204n.11, 226, 231, 232–34,
                              242–43, 246, 247–48
s 3 232–33
Insolvency Act 1986
     Pt 5 . . . . 291n.84

Legal Aid, Sentencing and Punishment of
   Offenders Act 2012 (LASPO) 331
Limitation Act 1980 319–20
   s 2 . . . . 318n.63
   s 32 318–19
   s 32(1)(b) 318–20
Monopolies and Mergers
   Act 1965 . . . . 170, 207n.23
   s 6(2)(ii) 170n.6
Prescription and Limitation (Scotland) Act 1973
   s 6 . . . . 319n.64
   s 11(3) 319n.64
Railways Act 1993
   s 4 . . . . 257n.10
   s 55(5A) 260n.39
Resale Prices Act 1976 29
Restrictive Trade Practices Act 1976 29,
                                      32–33, 207
Scotland Act 1998
   Sch 4 50–51
   Sch 5 50–51
Scotland Act 2016 50–51
Solicitors (Scotland) Act 1980
   s 61A 332n.200
Telecommunications Act 1984 255–56
   s 3(2)(b) 257n.10
Transport Act 2000
   s 2(4) 257n.10
Water Act 1991
   s 2 . . . . 257n.10

TABLE OF STATUTORY
INSTRUMENTS

Claims in respect of Loss or Damage arising
   from Competition Infringements
   (Competition Act 1998 and Other
   Enactments (Amendment))
   Regulations 2017 314–15
Civil Procedure Rules 322–23
   Pt 18 . . . . 322–23, 323n.98
   Pt 31 322–23
   r 31.6(b) 322–23
   Pt 31C 323n.103
Company Directors Disqualification
   (Northern Ireland) Order 2002,
   SI 2002/3150 (NI 4)
   arts 13A–13E 291n.81
Competition Act 1998 and Other
   Enactments (Amendment) Regulations
   2004, SI 2004/1261 . . . . .46–47, 52
Competition Act 1998 (Concurrency)
   Regulations 2004, SI 1077/2004 . . . 257n.18
Competition Act 1998 (Concurrency)
   Regulations 2014 (Concurrency
   Regulations), SI 536/2014 260–61,
                 260n.42, 264–65, 266, 267
   reg 3 . . . . 260n.43

reg 4 . . . . 261n.49, 266n.97
reg 5 . . . . 261n.52
reg 5(4)(b) 261n.51
reg 5(5) 261n.51
reg 6 . . . . 261n.55
reg 8 . . . . 261n.52
reg 8(1)(a) 261n.51
reg 8(1)(b) 261n.51
reg 9 . . . . 260n.44
reg 10 . . . . 260n.46
Explanatory Memorandum 262n.64
Competition Act 1998 (Dairy Produce)
   (Coronavirus) (Public Policy
   Exclusion) Order 2020, SI 2020/481 53,
                              224n.91
Competition Act 1998 (Groceries)
   (Coronavirus)(Public Policy Exclusion)
   Order 2020, SI 2020/369 53
Competition Act 1998 (Health Services for
   Patients in England)(Coronavirus)
   (Public Policy Exclusion) Order 2020,
   SI 2020/368 . . . . .27–28, 53
Competition Act 1998 (Health Services for
   Patients in Wales)(Coronavirus)(Public
   Policy Exclusion) Order 2020,
   SI 2020/435 53
Competition Act 1998 (Land and Vertical
   Agreements Exclusion) Order 2000,
   SI 2000/310 . . . . 56–62, 57n.6, 57n.8,
               63, 69, 77, 106, 106n.207
   arts 2–4 56–57
Competition Act 1998 (Public Policy
   Exclusion) Order 2006,
   SI 2006/605 52–53
Competition Act 1998 (Public Policy
   Exclusion) Order 2007,
   SI 2007/1896 .52–53
Competition Act 1998 (Public Policy
   Exclusion) Order 2008,
   SI 2008/1820 .52–53
Competition Act 1998 (Public Policy
   Exclusion) Order 2012,
   SI 2012/710 . . . . .48, 52–53
Competition Act 1998 (Public Policy
   Exclusion) (Revocation) Order 2011,
   SI 2011/2886 .52–53
Competition Act 1998 (Public Transport
   Ticketing Schemes Block Exemption)
   (Amendment) Order 2005,
   SI 2005/3347 .46–47
Competition Act 1998 (Public Transport
   Ticketing Schemes Block Exemption)
   (Amendment) Order 2011,
   SI 2011/227 46–47
Competition Act 1998 (Public Transport
   Ticketing Schemes Block Exemption)
   (Amendment) Order 2016,
   SI 2016/126 46–47

Competition Act 1998 (Public Transport
  Ticketing Schemes Block Exemption)
  Order 2001, SI 2001/319 46–47
Competition Act 1998 (Solent Maritime
  Crossings)(Coronavirus)(Public Policy
  Exclusion) Order 2020, SI 2020/370. 53
Competition (Amendment etc) (EU Exit)
  Regulations 2019, SI 2019/93 . . . . . 73n.126
Pt 2, reg 22 . . . . 111n.226
Sch 1, para 1(2)(b) 291n.87
Competition Appeal Tribunal Rules 1992 329–30
Competition Appeal Tribunal Rules 1993 329–30
Competition Appeal Tribunal Rules 2015,
  SI 2015/1648 . . . . 327n.153
Pt 4 . . . . 323n.103
Pt 5 . . . . 323n.103, 327–28
rr 60–65 . . . . 323n.97
rr 77–79 327–28
r 78 327–28
r 79 . . . . 327–28, 329–30
r 93(4). 332
r 113 . . . . 332n.204
r 119 . . . . 322n.88, 327n.153
Consumer Rights Act 2015
  (Commencement No 3, Transitional
  Provisions, Savings and Consequential
  Amendments) Order 2015,
  SI 2015/1630 . . . . 313n.15
Damages-Based Agreements Regulations
  2013, SI 2013/609 . . . . 332, 332n.204
Enterprise Act 2002 Regulations 2015,
  SI 2015/1643 . . . . 322, 322n.90
Section 16 . . . . 292n.91, 295n.120,
                                   315n.37, 316n.45, 322
Enterprise Act 2002 (Commencement No 3,
  Transitional and Transitory Provisions
  and Savings) Order 2003
  art 2(1) 291n.82
Enterprise Act 2002 (Specification of
  Additional Section 58 Consideration)
  Order 2008 . . . . 174n.43
Enterprise Act 2002 (Specification of
  Additional Section 58 Consideration)
  Order 2020 . . . . 174n.47
Supply of New Cars Order 2000,
  SI 2000/2088 72

TABLE OF OTHER LEGISLATION

Italy

Law No 287 of 10 October 1990 . . . . 238n.46

United States

Clayton Act
  s 7 379–80

Federal Rules of Civil Procedure
  r 23 332–33
Sherman Act
  s 2 379–80

TABLE OF INTERNATIONAL INSTRUMENTS

Agreement on the Withdrawal of the
  United Kingdom of Great Britain and
  Northern Ireland from the European
  Union and the European Atomic
  Energy Community (the Withdrawal
  Agreement) 79n.1
art 126 . . . . 73n.125
European Convention on Human Rights
  1950 (ECHR) 162, 231, 232–34,
                                235, 237, 239, 240–44,
                                246, 247, 248–49, 251
  Art 6 . . . . 204n.11, 231, 233, 234,
                                236–37, 238–39, 240, 241–52
  Art 6(1) 234–35, 237–40, 241,
                                243–44, 248–49, 250
  Art 8 . . . . 293n.95
  Art 10 233
  Protocol 1, Art 1 249
Hague Convention on the Recognition
  and Enforcement of Foreign
  Judgments in Civil or Commercial
  Matters 2019 . . . . 335n.224
Lugano Convention 335n.224
Treaty establishing the European Economic
  Community (EEC Treaty)
  Art 85 EEC. 29
Treaty on the Functioning of the European
  Union (TFEU)
  Art 101 . . . . 3, 22–24, 29, 40, 46, 49–50,
                       53–54, 55, 56–58, 60–61, 60n.36, 63–66,
                       67, 68–69, 70, 72, 74, 75n.130, 76,
                       105n.201, 106–7, 110, 152, 153,
                       162–63, 201n.1, 207n.22, 209–10, 244,
                       261, 270–71, 275, 280–81, 290–91, 309,
                       312, 322, 325, 326, 338–39, 373, 385
  Art 101(1) 46–47, 56–57, 58,
                       60–62, 62n.46, 63n.55, 70, 76, 320–21
  Art 101(3) 46–47, 52, 58, 58n.17,
                       61, 65–66, 70, 74, 339, 349
  Art 102 . . . . 3, 21, 22–24, 28, 29,
                       43–44, 49–50, 56–57, 62n.46, 79,
                       87–89, 92, 95–96, 99, 103, 106–10,
                       113–14, 129, 132, 152, 162–63, 201n.1,
                       209–10, 221, 244, 261, 270–71, 280–81,
                       290–91, 312, 320–21, 336, 368, 372, 385
  Art 102(c) 102–3
  Art 106 . . . . 150n.84
  Art 267 . . . . 29–30, 44
  Art 346 52–53

TABLE OF EUROPEAN REGULATIONS

17/62Regulation 46–47, 52, 207n.22
4064/89 European Merger
　Regulation 207n.24
2790/1999 Regulation [1999]
　OJ L336/21 . . . . 58n.15, 60–61
1/2003/EC Council Regulation of 16
　December 2002 on the implementation
　of the rules on competition laid down
　in Articles 81 and 82 of the Treaty
　[2002] OJ L1 (Regulation
　1/2003). 3, 4, 6–7, 19, 22–23,
　　　　　　　　　46–47, 52, 57–58, 57n.9, 72,
　　　　　　　　　201n.1, 261, 262n.58,
　　　　　　　　　313–14, 339n.7, 373
　art 2. . . . . 373, 373n.87
　art 3. 338–39
　art 3(1)(2) 72
　art 3(2) 72
　art 5. . . . . 261n.53
　art 9. . . . . 8, 54
　art 11(6) 261n.53
　art 16 . . . . 320n.75
　art 29 . . . . 64n.67
139/2004/EC Council Regulation on the
　control of concentrations between
　undertakings, which replaced Council
　Regulation 4065/89/EC (as amended)
　for transactions after 1 May 2004
　[2004] OJ L24 (EUMR) 4–5, 173,
　　　　　　　　　192–93, 198–99, 373, 376, 377
　art 1. . . . . 173n.36
　art 4(5) 377
　art 21(4) 192–93, 193n.175, 194n.188
　art 22 377
864/2007 Regulation (Rome II Regulation)
　[2007] OJ L299/40 . . . . 334, 335n.223
330/2010Verticals Block Exemption
　Regulation (VBER)[2010]
　OJ L102/1. . . . . 58, 76, 77–78, 162–63
　Recital 15 . . . . 60n.37
　art 3. . . . . 60n.35
　art 4. . . . . 60n.36
　art 5. . . . . 60n.36
　art 6. . . . . 60n.37
1215/2012 Regulation (recast Brussels 1A
　Regulation) [2012] OJ L351/1 334,
　　　　　　　　　335n.221, 335n.224
2016/679/EU Regulation of the European
　Parliament and of the Council of 27
　April 2016 on the protection of natural
　persons with regard to the processing
　of personal data and on the free
　movement such data, and repealing
　Directive 95/46/EC (General Data
　Protection Regulation) 363
　art 1(b) 363n.23
　art 1(c) 363n.23
　art 5. . . . . 363n.23

TABLE OF EUROPEAN DIRECTIVES

2014/104/EU Antitrust DamagesDirective
　OJ 2914 L349/1 (EU Damages
　Directive). 17, 23, 313–15, 321,
　　　　　　　　　323, 324, 325, 326
　Recital 13 . . . . 325n.131
　Chap IV 326
　Art 3 . . . . .313–14, 324, 325
　Art 4 . . . . .313–14, 324n.112
　Art 5 322–23
　Art 6 . . . . 323n.110
　Art 6(6) 323n.110
　Art 7 . . . . 323n.110
　Art 9(1) 321
　Art 9(2) 321n.85
　Art 10 319
　Art 10(4) 319
　Arts 12–14 326
　Art 13 326
　Art 17(2) 324
　Art 21 314–15
　Art 22 319–20
　Art 22(1) 314–15
　Art 22(2) 314–15
2015/2366/EU Payment Services
　Directive 368

Overview of Chapters

Chapter 1, 'Towards a World Class Regime—An Overview of Twenty Years of Competition Enforcement' by Peter Freeman, provides an excellent and informed general backdrop for the remainder of the chapters. It explains the objectives of the competition law regime introduced from 1998 to 2002 and the problems that led to the reforms of 2013. It reviews how the regime has performed in each aspect: antitrust, markets, mergers, the appeal system, and private enforcement, ministers, and the public interest and concurrent application by regulators. It discusses exit from the EU and the 'digital challenge' and it comments on the recent reform proposals from the then chairman of the CMA. It gives an overall assessment and considers the way forward, including the possible effect of the Covid-19 pandemic. It is a must-read for anyone wanting to understand the core aspects and direction of travel of UK competition law in one chapter and sets the scene beautifully for the chapters which follow.

Chapter 2, by Richard Whish, considers the application of the Competition Act 1998 to 'horizontal agreements', and in particular to cartel behaviour, since that piece of legislation entered into force on 1 March 2000. It is a tour de force of the enforcement practice. The chapter notes that early years of the legislation were somewhat disappointing, with a fairly low level of enforcement, although the Office of Fair Trading did score success with pioneering investigations of so-called 'hub-and-spoke' cartels in the *Football Shirts* and *Toys and Games* cases. From about 2006 onwards, there were more decisions from the Office of Fair Trading, and some of the cases, such as *Construction bid-rigging* and *Fuel surcharges*, were high-profile ones. Despite this, criticism of under-performance was voiced, not least by the National Audit Office. It is noted that in due course the Office of Fair Trading was replaced by the Competition and Markets Authority, and there has been a noticeable increase in enforcement in recent years. Whish suggests that in a post-Brexit world it can be anticipated that there will be yet more enforcement, including of larger cartels which historically would have been investigated by the European Commission in Brussels.

Alison Jones looks at 'vertical agreements' in Chapter 3. This chapter charts the development of UK competition law and policy towards vertical agreements over the twenty years since the Competition Act 1998 came into force. It traces how UK policy has evolved, before examining the UK jurisprudence that assesses the compatibility of vertical agreements with competition law. It notes that although many UK cases initially focused on resale price maintenance, more recently a number have analysed vertical restraints affecting online selling, which have proliferated since 2000 with the rapid growth of e-commerce. The chapter also considers how the law could, or should, develop in the future, especially now the transition period following the UK's departure from the EU has ended An important issue considered is whether, post-Brexit, the UK authorities should continue to follow EU competition law in this sphere, which has in significant respects been influenced by internal market considerations, or whether it should take a different course.

Chapter 4, by Renato Nazzini, deals with 'exclusionary abuses' under the Competition Act 1998, covering both public and private enforcement cases. The analysis concerns the approach to dominance as well as tests for abuse, focusing on retroactive rebates and bundled discounts, exclusion in multi-market settings, exclusivity, most favoured nation and equivalent clauses, discrimination, and exclusionary abuses in the pharmaceutical sector. This chapter argues that, in its second decade, modern UK competition law continued a trend that was already clear in the first decade: the prohibition of abuse of dominance is applied in a more economically robust and commercially reasonable way than it is by the EU institutions, the Commission, and the EU Courts, and in certain other Member States. The chapter notes that the third decade of the Competition Act 1998 will see the UK develop its competition policy free from the constraints of EU law and may allow for some divergence in the approach to exclusionary abuses in the future.

Chapter 5, by Robert O'Donoghue, provides a detailed and comprehensive description and analysis of the major 'exploitative abuses' cases considered by the English courts and competition and regulatory authorities since the inception of the Competition Act 1998, including the High Court, the Competition Appeal Tribunal, and the Court of Appeal. This decisional practice and case law have been widely cited and adopted by the EU Courts in Advocate General opinions and in the judgments and opinions of overseas authorities and courts. The chapter also contains a critique of the case law and decisional practice and highlights important practical points and points of principle that have received insufficient (or no) attention, as well as issues on which the case law and decisional practice are arguably wrong. This analysis is timely, since it is clear that the topic of exploitative abuse remains an important one for the UK competition authorities, regulators, and courts, perhaps even more so than authorities and courts in EU Member States.

Chapter 6 allows Christian Ahlborn, together with Will Leslie, to revisit his earlier analytical critique of market investigations in UK competition law (published in *Ten Years of UK Competition Law Reform*, Dundee University Press, 2010), in a chapter entitled, ' "Jack of All Trades, Master of None": The Ever-increasing Ambit of the Market Investigation Regime'! Whereas the beginning of the decade saw the National Audit Office criticizing the market investigation regime's low profile, market investigations had figured amongst the Competition and Markets Authority's most high-profile interventions by the end of it. This chapter considers the extent to which this unique UK competition policy instrument has simultaneously undergone significant legislative reform, as well as a slew of judicial challenges. These events have undoubtedly matured the regime and put its procedures on a firmer statutory footing. However, the same question posed in 2010 has not yet been fully answered: the authors remain unclear at the end of this enlightening chapter just what market investigations are actually for.

In Chapter 7, entitled 'UK Merger Control: Finely Tailored but Time for a New Suit?', David Reader observes that the introduction of the Enterprise Act 2002 formally ended a much-maligned public interest approach to merger control in the UK, oft-criticized for the uncertainty permeated by ministerial decision-making. In its place came a new competition-based test to be applied by independent competition authorities with new powers and resources at their disposal. Despite encountering some teething problems as the authorities sought to interpret their respective roles at Phases 1 and 2, the reforms have proven largely successful in delivering one of the most transparent and predictable merger regimes in the world. This chapter reflects on the evolution of UK merger control under the Enterprise Act, observing that a combination of major—and finer-tuning of the competition authority's Phase 1 enforcement powers has enabled it effectively to deliver upon its mandate. New challenges lie in wait, however, and Reader stresses that the Competition and Markets Authority must be allocated the resources and statutory remit to contend with the increased workload implications presented by Brexit and the novel theories of harm associated with mergers in the digital sector. Of further concern are recent reforms to extend the national security public interest ground, which risk a return to the 'dark ages' of opaque ministerial decision-making if further safeguards are not implemented.

Chapter 8 on institutional reform is entitled 'Unfinished Reform of the Institutions Enforcing UK Competition Law'. Written by Bruce Lyons, it notes that the period since 1998 has seen major changes in competition law, including: public interest was replaced by promotion of competition as the primary duty; anti-competitive agreements and abuse of a dominant position were prohibited, with significant penalties for breach; and the minister withdrew from case decisions making the institutions determinative. There were also major organizational changes, including the merger of the Office of Fair Trading and the Competition Commission to form the Competition and Markets Authority, and establishment of the Competition Appeal Tribunal as a specialist appeals body. In the chapter, Lyons considers the evolution of these institutions from the perspective of how they frame and influence the quality of first instance determinations. Institutions are hostages to their history, and he traces some of the problems faced by the Competition and Markets Authority to its institutional roots. New challenges beyond its control are also identified. Reform is needed. The chapter concludes that some of the Competition and Markets Authority's suggestions for legislation are misguided, particularly in replacing its competition duty with 'the consumer interest', and reducing the standard of review by the Competition Appeal Tribunal. Alternative proposals are appraised, including a potential change to a prosecutorial system. Lyons argues convincingly that genuinely independent decision-making within the Competition and Markets Authority should be preferred and would permit a more limited standard of review.

In Chapter 9, entitled 'Human Rights and the UK Competition Act: Public Enforcement and Due Process', Arianna Andreangeli discusses the approach adopted in the UK towards questions of human rights compliance in UK competition enforcement processes. It examines the nature of competition proceedings in light of Article 6 of the European Convention on Human Rights and the implications that that issue has for the fairness standards applicable to those proceedings. It is argued that, while the recognition that competition cases may have a 'criminal nature' does not justify the wholesale extension of all the safeguards that the Convention reserves to criminal cases, it nonetheless means that investigated parties are entitled to some basic protections that Article 6 ECHR enshrines. The chapter explores the Competition Appeal Tribunal's powers of review of infringement decisions and suggests that at the root of the conferral of a power of scrutiny 'on the merits' is the need to ensure that the public enforcement competition proceedings are 'human rights-proofed'. It concludes that, while demands of effectiveness in the application of the UK competition rules cannot be overlooked, maintaining the CAT's rigorous review role for competition decisions is indispensable for compliance with human rights' standards and for the integrity and reputation of the UK competition framework.

In Chapter 10, Niamh Dunne tackles a key and developing enforcement issue which had not been dealt with in either of the preceding collections: 'concurrency'. The concurrency regime empowers certain sector regulators in the UK to apply the competition rules in tandem with the Competition and Markets Authority. Reflecting a strong ideological preference for the benefits of competition over more prescriptive forms of regulatory super-vision, the regime has, however, struggled to deliver effective enforcement in practice. This chapter discusses the evolution of the concurrency framework with particular emphasis on the enhancements introduced by the Enterprise and Regulatory Reform Act 2013, which sought both to encourage regulators to make greater use of their concurrent powers, and to give the Competition and Markets Authority a more formal leadership role in assisting them to do so. Subsequent enforcement activity is discussed, alongside the future prospects of competition law in the regulated sectors.

Peter Whelan assesses a developing and increasingly significant enforcement tool in the UK competition authority's armoury in Chapter 11, 'The Emerging Contribution of Director Disqualification in UK Competition Law'. in which he notes that the enforce-ment of UK competition law is deterrence-focused and comprises both criminal and non-criminal (i.e. civil/administrative) elements. The chapter concentrates on the non-criminal enforcement apparatus that has been developed over the last twenty years. More specifically, it critically evaluates a particular enforcement mechanism that has been gaining increasing importance throughout the recent development of UK competition enforcement prac-tice: the use of director disqualification. It first establishes the normative role of director disqualification in the UK's armoury of non-criminal antitrust sanctions (i.e. its comple-menting of the deterrent function of corporate antitrust fines), following which it highlights their potential for performing this role effectively. It then outlines the legal basis for the use of director disqualification within the UK and evaluates the policy and enforcement prac-tice to date with respect to such orders, before proceeding to outline some of the insights that the UK director disqualification regime can provide to other jurisdictions. Ultimately it concludes that, on the basis of the promising, albeit nascent, UK experience to date, dir-ector disqualification should be seriously considered by jurisdictions that wish to operate a robust competition law enforcement regime.

In Chapter 12, 'Private Enforcement in the UK: Effective Redress for Consumers?', Barry Rodger retraces his footsteps in relation to his contributions in both earlier collections on the theme of private enforcement in the UK, with a particular slant on the extent to which consumers have benefited, or may benefit, from statutory and case law developments in the area. Accordingly, this chapter assesses how private enforcement of competition law rights has developed in the UK over the last twenty years. Key legislative developments, inter alia the Competition Act 1998, the Enterprise Act 2002, and the Consumer Rights Act 2015, have transformed the private enforcement architecture, notably with the introduction, and increasingly significant and enhanced role of the specialist tribunal, the Competition Appeal Tribunal, and the availability of an opt-out collective redress mechanism. The chapter assesses the key UK statutory and case law developments, in comparison with the US private antitrust enforcement model, to reflect on the disappointing extent to which ef-fective redress for consumers has been provided to date, despite those legal and institutional developments. Nonetheless, the recent Supreme Court ruling in *Merricks*, as discussed here, should be pivotal in this context.

In Chapter 13, entitled 'The Quiet Decline of the UK Cartel Offence: A Principled Victory in the Face of Practical Failure', Angus MacCulloch focuses on criminal enforce-ment. The UK Cartel Offence was introduced in the Enterprise Act 2002 to challenge hard-core cartels and enhance the deterrent effect of the UK competition regime. In its initial phase of operation there was some success. However, a number of significant cases failed to secure convictions. This damaged confidence in the ability of the UK competition authorities to bring successful prosecutions, and ultimately questioned the usefulness of the Cartel Offence. This chapter examines the problems that beset the original Cartel Offence and the lessons learned from the small number of prosecutions brought before the courts. It goes on to examine the reforms in 2013, that removed the controversial 'dishonesty' element from the offence, and replaced it with carve-outs for openness and publication. Alongside the practical issues in relation to the development of the UK Cartel Offence consideration is also given to a parallel process which saw a form of consensus developing in the academic literature as to the nature of the wrong at the heart of individual cartel activity. It is suggested that this greater understanding can be used to direct efforts to rebuild confidence in the reformed UK Cartel Offence going forward. Increased importance should be given to the securing of good evidence of individual culpability in relation to cartel activity during the investigation phase. It argues that, once good evidence is secured, better prosecution cases can be built on the basis of the new narrative of wrongfulness for hard core cartel activity.

In Chapter 14, 'Competition Law and the Digital Economy in the UK and Beyond', Liza Lovdahl Gormsen considers the contemporaneous debate on how best to address aspects of the interaction between competition law and the digital economy. She stressed that data is the pinnacle of the digital economy. It has fuelled amazing innovations in all sectors of the economy, but the accumulation of data in the hands of a few global companies may lead to lock-in, bottleneck issues, and leverage. The chapter notes that, according to the report *Unlocking Digital Competition*, which was prepared for the UK Treasury, competition policy will need to be updated to address the novel challenges posed by the digital economy. Some of these updates can happen within current powers, but legal changes are important to ensure that this job can be done effectively. The Competition and Markets Authority's market study on Online Platforms and Digital Advertising recommends establishing a Digital Markets Unit and ex ante regulation as a possible way forward. Building on the outputs from the Furman Review, the government asked the CMA to lead a Digital Markets Taskforce. In December 2020, the latter published its advice *A New Pro-competition Regime for Digital Markets*, where it sets out the role of the Digital Markets Unit and an overview of its proposed regulatory framework for digital firms. This chapter looks at some of the challenges for UK competition policy in digital markets, in particular in relation to data, enforcement, and regulation. It also touches upon some of the potential issues that the UK faces in the digital economy following Brexit.

List of Abbreviations

AAC	average avoidable costs
ACH	acetone cyanohydrin
AEC test	adverse effect on competition test
AED	anti-epilepsy drug
AGCM	Autorita' Garante per la Concorrenza ed il Mercato
APPAs	across platform parity agreements
BEIS	Department for Business, Energy and Industrial Strategy
CA 1998	Competition Act 1998
CAA	Civil Aviation Authority
CAT	Competition Appeal Tribunal
CC	Competition Commission
CCAT	Competition Commission Appeals Tribunal
CCNS	contract change notices
CDOs	Competition Disqualification Orders
CDUs	Competition Disqualification Undertakings
CEO	chief operating officer
CJEU	Court of Justice of the European Union
CMA	Competition and Markets Authority
CoJ	Court of Justice
CPOs	Collective Proceedings Orders
CRA 2015	Consumer Rights Act 2015
DDOs	Director Disqualification Orders
DECC	Department for Energy and Climate Change
DGFT	Director General for Fair Trading
DTI	Department of Trade and Industry
EA 2002	Enterprise Act 2002
ECHR	European Convention on Human Rights
ECN	European Competition Network
ECtHR	European Court of Human Rights
ERRA 2013	Enterprise and Regulatory Reform Act 2013
EUMR	EU Merger Regulation
FCA	Financial Conduct Authority
FTA	Fair Trading Act 1973
HCN	hydrogen cyanide
HRA 1998	Human Rights Act 1998
ICN	International Competition Network
IUs	initial undertakings
LOB	live online bidding
LRAIC	long-run average incremental costs
MFN	most favoured nation
MIF	multilateral interchange fee
MIR	Market Investigation Regime
MMC	Monopolies and Mergers Commission

MRPC	Monopolies and Restrictive Practices Commission
NAO	National Audit Office
NCAs	national competition authorities
NHSI	NHS Improvement
NIAUR	Northern Ireland Authority for Utility Regulation
OFCOM	Office of Communications
Ofgem	Gas and Electricity Markets Authority
OFT	Office of Fair Trading
Ofwat	Water Services Regulation Authority
ORR	Office of Rail and Road
PPRS	Pharmaceutical Price Regulation Scheme
PSR	Payment Systems Regulator
RISQS	Rail Industry Supplier Qualification Scheme
ROCE	return on capital employed
ROS	return on sales
RPM	minimum resale prices
RTPA	Restrictive Trade Practices Act
SLC	substantial lessening of competition
SMR	supply, maintenance and repair
SO	Statement of Objections
TAR	Tribunale Amminstrativo Regionale
TFEU	Treaty on the Functioning of the European Union
UK	United Kingdom
USO	universal service obligation
VBER	Vertical Block Exemption Regulation

Biographies

Editors

Barry Rodger

Barry has been an academic at Strathclyde University Law School since 1993, having previously studied at Strathclyde, Worcester College, Oxford, and the European University Institute, Florence, and after qualifying as a practising solicitor in Scotland. His primary teaching and research interests are related to EU and UK competition law and international private law, and he also teaches aspects of private law. In recent years, his work has focused on the interface between competition law and private law with various projects related to developments in the private enforcement of competition law in the UK and EU. An AHRC-funded project in this area led to the 2014 publication of *Competition Law Comparative Private Enforcement and Collective Redress Across the EU* (Rodger (ed), Kluwer Law International), and more recently he has coordinated a project which resulted in the co-edited publication (with M Sousa Ferro and F Marcos) by OUP in December 2018 of *The EU Antitrust Damages Directive, Transposition in the Member States*. He is currently working on a range of projects related both to enforcement and substantive issues in EU and UK competition law. He is one of the co-organizers of the Competition Law Scholars' Forum (www.clasf.org), which runs two annual competition law events for competition law academics, is co-editor of the online *Competition Law Review*, and is also the co-author, with Angus MacCulloch, of the student textbook, *Competition Law and Policy in the EU and UK*, now in its 5th edition.

Peter Whelan

Peter is a Professor of Law at the School of Law, University of Leeds, where he is the Director of the Centre for Business Law and Practice. He has a PhD in Law from St John's College, University of Cambridge. A qualified US Attorney-at-Law, Peter is an expert in competition (antitrust) law and criminal law. Peter has published widely in prestigious law journals (including the *Oxford Journal of Legal Studies*, the *Cambridge Law Journal*, and the *Modern Law Review*). He recently completed a monograph analysing the inherent challenges of European cartel criminalization, which was published by Oxford University Press as part of the series entitled Oxford Studies in European Law. He is currently finalizing an academic monograph on parental liability in EU competition law; it will be published in due course by Oxford University Press. To date he has presented his research on six continents and in over thirty countries. Peter has twice provided oral evidence to the New Zealand Parliament on cartel criminalization. He also provided oral evidence to the Competition Law Review Committee, which was set up by the Indian government to propose amendments to its competition law regime. He was appointed as an International Expert by the Finnish Competition and Consumer Authority and wrote a report advising the Finnish Ministry of Justice on the desirability of introducing criminal cartel sanctions in Finland. He has provided training in EU competition law to the Romanian judiciary, the Omani competition authority, and the Eswatini Competition Commission, and he has delivered lectures on his research at the National Economic Prosecutor's Office of Chile, the Competition Tribunal of Chile, and the Peruvian competition authority (INDECOPI). He is a Non-Governmental Advisor to the International Competition Network and recently became a member of the United Nations Working Group on Cross-Border Cartels, which is operated by UNCTAD. He is a member of the editorial boards of five journals and is the Managing Editor of *Oxford Competition Law* (Oxford University Press).

Angus MacCulloch

Angus first graduated with an LLB (Hons) from the University of Dundee (1992), before going on to undertake an LLM (European Law) at the University of Strathclyde (1994) and an MPhil at the University of Manchester (1997). From 1996 he was a Lecturer at the University of Manchester with his research focusing largely on competition law. Angus joined Lancaster University Law School, as Senior Lecturer, in September 2006. His research interests lie primarily in competition law, particularly antitrust and enforcement issues, and EU law, particularly free movement of goods, but he retains a wider interest in regulation, white collar crime, and IP law. The majority of his recent competition law work focuses on the impact of the introduction of the UK's cartel offence and the wider global move towards the criminalization of cartel activity. His recent EU law research has focused on the EU law challenges to the introduction of alcohol minimum unit pricing (MUP) in Scotland, and EU law's attempt to balance the often competition goals of enhancing free trade/competition and protecting public health. He has written extensively on the Scotch Whisky Association's challenge to MUP which has been before the Scottish and EU Courts. Angus' other work includes the interaction between competition law and human rights/due process during contentious competition law investigations, and the provisions in IP law which seek to protect copyright through technological measures, and their impact on the consumer of copyrighted material. Angus also continues to publish a popular Competition Law textbook, *Competition Law and Policy in the EU and UK*, now in its 5th edition, and a cases and materials text. He is also one of the Editors of the *Competition Law Review*, founded in 2004, which is an increasingly important home for competition law scholarship. He is a founding member of the Competition Law Scholars Forum and maintains the 'Who's Competing?' blog.

Contributors

Christian Ahlborn is the Global Practice Head of the Linklaters' Competition & Antitrust Group. Christian is a qualified lawyer in England & Wales, as well as in Germany. Christian is also a trained economist. Christian has a broad range of experience in UK and EU competition law, particularly in relation to complex M&A, behavioural antitrust work, control of dominance, and state aid control. He is well-known for extensive work on high-profile matters which, recently, include advising E.ON on its large-scale asset swap with RWE, including the acquisition of Innogy and Unilever in relation to a Competition and Markets Authority investigation into an alleged abuse of dominance in the impulse ice cream market.

Arianna Andreangeli is a Lecturer in competition law at Edinburgh Law School, University of Edinburgh. Her research interests lie in the area of EU and domestic competition law: she has written widely on questions of due process and human rights' protection in the context of competition enforcement (*EU Competition Enforcement and Human Rights*, Edward Elgar Publishing 2008) and on the role of the EU competition rules in innovative markets; she has also published a monograph examining the issues arising from the collective litigation of competition cases in the EU and the US (*Private Enforcement of Antitrust*, Edward Elgar Publishing 2014). Recent work has focused on the role of devolved administration in UK competition policy, especially in light of Brexit. She was a Scottish Parliament Information Centre (SPICe) Academic Fellow in 2017 and worked on a project in this broad area. She is currently researching the implications of the changing role of platforms in markets where intermediation is important for the effectiveness of competition law enforcement.

Niamh Dunne is an Associate Professor in the Law Department of the London School of Economics, where she researches and teaches in the areas of competition law, market regulation, and EU law. She has worked as a case officer for the Competition Authority of Ireland and as a consultant for the Competition Committee of the OECD, and taught previously at Cambridge University and King's College London. She has published widely on competition law related issues including *Competition Law and Economic Regulation* (Cambridge University Press 2015) and *Jones & Sufrin's EU Competition Law: Texts, Cases, Materials* (7th edition, Oxford University Press 2019) (with Alison Jones and Brenda Sufrin).

Peter Freeman CBE QC (Hon) is one of the Chairmen of the Competition Appeal Tribunal. He is a lawyer who has held senior posts in UK competition enforcement. From 2006 to 2011, he was Chairman of the Competition Commission, having been a Deputy Chairman from 2003. He is a member of the Lloyds Enforcement Appeal Tribunal and a Board Member of the Single Source Regulations Office (SSRO). He was called to the Bar (Middle Temple) in 1972 and admitted as a solicitor in 1977. He was a partner at Simmons & Simmons from 1978 to 2003 and a senior consultant to Cleary Gottlieb Steen & Hamilton from 2011 to 2013. He was a founding member and Chairman of the Regulatory Policy Institute, Oxford, and has written and spoken widely on competition and regulatory law matters.

Liza Lovdahl Gormsen joined the Financial Conduct Authority as a Senior Adviser in May 2020. She is also currently a Senior Research Fellow and the Director of the Competition Law Forum at the British Institute of International and Comparative Law. She chairs the Advisory Board of the Competition Law Forum. Liza obtained a PhD in competition law at King's College London in 2007. Following her PhD, she taught competition law at London School of Economics and University of Manchester. Liza is the author of *A Principled Approach to Abuse of Dominance* (Cambridge University Press 2010) and *State Aid and Tax Rulings* (Edward Elgar Publishing 2019). She has published widely in national and international peer-review journals and regularly addresses audiences at select committees before the House of Commons and House of Lords, the White House, and the European Commission. She sits on the advisory board of the *Journal of Antitrust Enforcement* (Oxford University Press). Besides her academic background, Liza has legal experience from both the private and public sector. She served as a lawyer at the Office of Fair Trading and has worked as a consultant for the World Bank for a number of years. Liza is currently a Board Member of the Open Markets Institute in Washington DC and is a non-governmental Adviser to the International Competition Network, appointed by the Competition and Markets Authority.

Alison Jones is a Professor of Law at King's College London. Prior to joining King's, Alison read law at Girton College, Cambridge, worked at Slaughter & May, and completed a BCL at Christ Church, Oxford. Alison teaches and researches principally in the sphere of competition law (especially EU, UK, and US) and is co-author of *Jones and Sufrin on EU Competition Law: Text, Cases, and Materials* (currently in its seventh edition). Alison has published widely on competition issues, including for instance 'Identifying Anticompetitive Agreements in the United States and the European Union: Developing a Coherent Antitrust Analytical Framework' with W E Kovacic (2017 (62) Antitrust Bulletin 254).

Will Leslie is a Managing Associate in the Linklaters' Competition & Antitrust Group. Will is a qualified lawyer in England & Wales, as well as a registered EU lawyer in Brussels. Will has a broad range of experience advising on EU and UK competition law and economic regulation, including complex M&A, behavioural antitrust work, market investigations, state aid, and UK price control.

Bruce Lyons is Professor of Economics and a founding member of the Centre for Competition Policy at the University of East Anglia. He is also Academic Adviser on competition economics to KPMG. He was formerly Editor of the *Journal of Industrial Economics*, a Member of the European Commission's Economic Advisory Group on Competition Policy (2004–17) and Reporting Member of the UK Competition Commission (2002–11). He has held visiting research positions at the European University Institute Florence and the University of Melbourne. Bruce has published widely on competition economics and market structure. His co-authored books include *Cases in European Competition Policy: The Economic Analysis* (CUP 2009), *Mergers and Merger Remedies in the EU: Assessing the Consequences for Competition* (Edward Elgar Publishing 2007), and *Merger Control in the UK* (OUP 2005). He also co-authored the independent report on *Geographic Market Definition in European Commission Merger Control* (DG Comp 2016). Bruce's current research is on the economics of competition policy, transactional unfairness, and the implications of behavioural consumers. He is co-investigator in the ESRC-funded Network for Integrated Behavioural Science.

Renato Nazzini joined King's College London as Professor of Law in 2012. Previously, he was Professor of Competition Law and Arbitration at the University of Southampton, which he joined from the Office of Fair Trading, then the UK competition authority (now the Competition and Markets Authority), where he was Deputy Director of the Legal and Policy Department and led or advised on major areas of enforcement and policy. His work included the review of the policy on abuse of dominance under Article 102 TFEU, which led to the adoption of the Commission Guidance Paper on Article 102 TFEU, and on the formulation of the policy on actions for damages for competition infringements, which led to major reforms in the UK and in the EU. Professor Nazzini is currently a non-governmental adviser to the International Competition Network (ICN), where he has been particularly active on both the Unilateral Conduct Working Group and the Merger Working Group.

Robert O'Donoghue QC is a barrister practising in London and internationally, specialized in litigation as well as advocacy before regulatory authorities. He has over twenty years' experience of competition law, EU law, utility regulation, and related aspects of commercial and public law. He has appeared in major cases in the High Court, the Competition Appeal Tribunal, the Court of Appeal, the Supreme Court, EU Courts, Irish courts, international arbitral bodies, and in oral hearings before competition authorities and sectoral regulators in these matters. He also advises and acts for public authorities on regulatory and competition law matters in Hong Kong and Ireland. He has written and taught extensively on EU law, competition law, and regulation in publications, conferences, and universities worldwide. He has contributed to a number of published books and is the co-author of a major work on abuse of a dominant position (*The Law and Economics of Article 102 TFEU*, 3rd edition, Hart Publishing, 2020).

David Reader is a Lecturer in Law at Newcastle University and an Honorary Senior Fellow at the Melbourne Law School, having previously worked as a Senior Research Associate at the interdisciplinary Centre for Competition Policy (CCP) at the University of East Anglia. He was awarded a doctorate from the UEA in 2016 for his thesis entitled *Revisiting the Role of the Public Interest in Merger Control*, which uses empirical legal methods to observe patterns and trends among seventy-five merger regimes. His research on cross-border merger control and public interest criteria informed the framework of an OECD roundtable event on public interest clauses, and he continues to work with regulators and government departments in an advisory capacity. He has published in journals such as the IBA's *Competition Law International*, the *Journal of Antitrust Enforcement*, and the *European Competition and Regulatory Law Review (CoRe)*. His empirical work also features in *Comparative and Competition Policy* (Edward Elgar Publishing 2020), a collection of leading articles covering the breadth of comparative competition law between 1994 and 2018. David's recent research extends into issues arising from foreign direct investment (FDI), killer acquisitions, digital markets, and the statutory duties of market regulators.

Richard Whish is Emeritus Professor of Law at King's College London; in 2014 he was appointed QC Honoris Causa. He was a non-executive director of the Office of Fair Trading in the UK from 2003 to 2009, and a non-executive director of the Singaporean Energy Markets Authority from 2005 to 2011. He is the co-author, with David Bailey, of *Competition Law* (9th edn, OUP 2018), and the author of many other books, articles, case notes, and book reviews on various aspects of international competition law and policy. Richard travels the world providing competition law masterclasses and advises lawyers, governments, and competition authorities on a range of competition law and policy issues.

1

Towards a World Class Regime— An Overview of Twenty Years of UK Competition Enforcement

Peter Freeman QC

1 Introduction

It is now more than twenty years since the Competition Act 1998 (CA 1998) introduced radical reform to UK competition law. This followed nearly two decades of discussion and debate. There was more consensus on the need to reform the control of restrictive agreements than on what to do about the abuse of market power. The regime that was introduced, following the election of a Labour government in 1997, opted for the introduction of the EU-style prohibitions on both restrictive agreements and abuse of a dominant position but retained important parts of the existing system for control of monopolies and mergers. Reform of those aspects was delayed for a further four years until the Enterprise Act 2002 (EA 2002).

Writing in 1999, this author, together with Richard Whish, commented that the previously existing system was 'complex, difficult to apply, and in numerous respects defective' and that the new law 'may have to last for a quarter of a century at least'.[1] That last prediction may yet prove optimistic. As we come to the end of the new regime's second decade of operation, its utility and effectiveness are coming under increasing scrutiny.

We therefore begin with a comparison of the regime's original objectives with some of the criticisms that emerged, before examining how the regime has performed over the period. We examine the law on anti-competitive agreements and abuse of dominant position (together referred to as 'antitrust'); the system for investigating markets; and the control of mergers. We consider briefly the role of ministers, the 'concurrent' application of competition law by sectoral regulators, and the system of judicial control. We examine the challenges of the digital economy and leaving the EU. Finally, we offer an overall assessment and some pointers to the future, particularly in the light of the current pandemic.

---

[1] Peter Freeman and Richard Whish, *A Guide to the Competition Act 1998* (Butterworths 1999) Preface, 1.

Peter Freeman, *Towards a World Class Regime—An Overview of Twenty Years of UK Competition Enforcement* In: *The UK Competition Regime*. Edited by: Barry Rodger, Peter Whelan, and Angus MacCulloch, Oxford University Press. © The Contributors 2021.
DOI: 10.1093/oso/9780198868026.003.0001

2 The New Regime, Its Objectives and Its Critics

2.1 The Government's Aims for the New Regime

The policy underpinning the current regime was developed in various official publications over the years preceding the CA 1998 and EA 2002.[2] Recognizing that CA 1998 was only part of what needed to be done, the government moved on to deal with the remaining aspects. The best point of reference for this process is the 2001 *World Class Competition Regime* White Paper,[3] which not only made the economic case for competition as a driver of increased productivity, but also laid out the government's objectives for a competition-based prohibition system, modelled on EU law, an enhanced merger regime, and a revitalized monopolies regime, the last two recast in specifically competition terms.

These were to be administered by strong, proactive, and independent authorities, professionally staffed under expert leadership.[4] The Office of Fair Trading (OFT) was to operate the new antitrust system but also 'shine a light' into the darkest corners of the economy and prosecute individual cartel offenders.[5] The Competition Commission (CC) would, at the invitation of the OFT, sectoral regulators, and ministers, investigate the sectors of the economy where competition was not working and apply remedies. The Competition Appeal Tribunal (CAT)[6] would provide necessary judicial oversight. This new regime settled a long drawn out debate about what the UK competition system should be. That competition settlement has, broadly speaking, lasted for the best part of two decades, although it is now under threat, as we shall see.

2.2 The Cycle of Criticism

A feeling of optimism accompanied the new regime's launch. There was an initial honeymoon period during which the fundamentals of its institutional and operational model were generally accepted. Mounting concerns resulted in a major institutional upheaval in 2012–2013. There followed a second honeymoon period, but, more recently, the regime has once again faced criticism.

2.3 Institutional Issues

The institutional changes in 2013[7] arose mainly from the ambiguity of maintaining two separate authorities which, although in a vertical relationship (in that the OFT referred

---

[2] The Department of Trade and Industry (DTI) had published the reviews by Hans Liesner CB of monopolies and mergers policy in 1978 and of restrictive trade practices policy in 1979. Many other reviews and consultation papers followed over the next two decades.

[3] *Productivity and Enterprise, A World Class Competition Regime* (White Paper Cm 5233, July 2001) (the 2001 White Paper).

[4] The 2001 White Paper (see paras 4.1–4.3) named (Sir) John Vickers, (Sir) Derek Morris, and (Sir) Christopher Bellamy QC as leaders of the OFT, CC, and the (then) CC appeal tribunals, respectively.

[5] The individual cartel offence was in s 188 of the EA 2002.

[6] The appeal system was not discussed in detail in the White Paper as the CAT had not yet been established separately from the CC. This was achieved by the EA 2002.

[7] Enterprise and Regulatory Reform Act 2013 (ERRA 2013).

cases to the CC), sometimes appeared in horizontal competition with each other for the 'high ground' of competition doctrine. The merged authority that was established by the Enterprise and Regulatory Reform Act 2013 (ERRA 2013), the Competition and Markets Authority (CMA), was intended to internalize those potentially competing aspects and embody the best of both former authorities.

2.4 The EU Law Aspect

The OFT and the CC also had different relationships with EU competition law. The OFT, as the operator of the CA 1998 system for antitrust, was embedded in the EU-wide enforcement system. Chapters I and II were closely modelled on Articles 101 and 102 and, from 2003, the OFT was the designated UK competition authority under Regulation 1/2003[8] and a member of the European Competition Network (ECN) through which EU-wide enforcement was coordinated.

The CC, by contrast, had a more indirect link with EU law. It was not a designated authority and its main competition law focus, other than mergers, was the Market Investigation Regime (MIR). This, although using similar terminology ('prevent, restrict or distort competition') to Article 101, was derived from the 'complex monopoly' provisions of the previous legislation and offered a different approach to enforcement, as it did not find infringements or impose penalties.

In the MIR's early years, the overlap between the two approaches caused some concern. Conduct caught by the MIR's 'adverse effect on competition' (AEC) test could also breach Articles 101 and 102. Regulation 1/2003 essentially required Member States to apply EU law in parallel with national competition law and to avoid any inconsistency. The CC could not itself apply EU law and might take inconsistent measures. One solution was to designate the CC to take limited EU law proceedings within the framework of a market investigation, if the relevant conduct also infringed EU law. This idea was pursued for some time but did not attract universal support and was dropped.

Most of the potential difficulties were overcome by a pragmatic approach. The CC made clear that it was not concerned to apply the MIR in a divergent way and played its own part, by invitation, in the work of the ECN. The OFT sought not to refer markets which appeared more suited to enforcement action rather than investigation under the MIR and the CC, when it found infringing conduct, reported this to the OFT. Ironically, other EU regimes which did not have the benefit of a self-standing MIR began to see its value. Nonetheless, the CC was being underused and the MIR was tending to be applied to rather narrow, specific, markets. Moreover, sectoral regulators were not referring markets to the CC to the extent envisaged, as the National Audit Office (NAO) noted in its 2010 Report.[9] The ERRA 2013 was intended to remedy this defect.

---

[8] Council Regulation 1/2003/EC of 16 December 2002 [2003] OJ L1/1 (Regulation 1/2003).
[9] *Review of the UK's Competition Landscape* (22 March 2010) (NAO 2010) para 10.

2.5 The Question of Enforcement

The ERRA 2013 was also intended to overcome a further perceived drawback in the system, namely the dearth of antitrust enforcement. This applied also to criminal cartel cases under the powers provided in EA 2002. There were several possible reasons for this, including the fear of appeal, as we discuss in more detail in section 3 below. The NAO also noted that: 'There is a risk that the length, and uncertainty of outcome, of the enforcement process in its entirety may reduce the appetite of the authorities for using their competition enforcement powers.'[10]

2.6 The Appeal System

The NAO's comment included the appeal system. The CAT had emerged from the CA 1998/ EA 2002 reform process as an independently constituted statutory tribunal, tasked with hearing full merits appeals from OFT antitrust decisions[11] and conducting judicial review of OFT or CC merger and market decisions. In the early years, the CAT heard some significant appeals against enforcement decisions, although it also considered refusals to investigate or findings of non-infringement, where it was trying to encourage the authorities to take action.

Despite the observations of the NAO and the fears of some authorities that an over-intrusive appeal system might be chilling enforcement activity, the government in its response to the pre-ERRA 2013 consultation[12] expressed its commitment to the existing appeal system, whilst at the same time encouraging the new CMA to improve its internal procedures to make appeals less likely.[13] It was therefore perhaps surprising that very soon after this the government included appeals against competition decisions in its Regulatory Appeal Review.[14] The response to its proposals to replace full merits appeals with judicial review (or a specific review system) for competition cases was uniformly hostile and the proposals were quietly dropped.[15]

2.7 Merger Control

The EA 2002 introduced major changes to the merger control regime. The old system of merger investigations by the OFT and MMC/CC in succession, followed by a ministerial decision, normally, but not necessarily, on competition grounds, was replaced by a 'substantial lessening of competition' (SLC) regime where the OFT and CC were empowered

---

[10] ibid.

[11] Many of the communications regulator Ofcom's regulatory decisions were also subject to full merits appeal.

[12] *Growth, Competition and the Competition Regime, Government Response to Consultation,* (March 2012) (ERRA Consultation Response).

[13] The OFT had already introduced some procedural improvements, including separate case decision groups, which were generally well received. See *Review of OFT's Investigative procedures: Summary of Responses* OFT 1455 (2012).

[14] *Streamlining Regulatory and Competition Appeals: Consultation on Options for Reform* (19 June 2013) (Regulatory Appeal Review).

[15] It has re-emerged more recently: see further discussion below. An amendment to the standard of review in Communications Act cases was introduced by the Digital Economy Act 2017.

to decide cases themselves. Ministerial intervention was limited to defined public interest grounds. This was a much more disciplined and accountable system than had operated before. Transparency was enhanced and competition was central to the analysis. It coincided with a similar change to the EU Merger Regulation (EUMR), where a test based on creation of a dominant position was replaced with one focused more on incremental effect.[16]

Although it produced high quality decisions, the UK regime was criticized for being ponderous and lengthy. The preliminary investigation by the OFT, followed by a fresh investigation by the CC, was said to involve unnecessary delays and repetition, whilst some OFT critics believed the CC tended to ignore the work it had done. By placing the two phases of review under a single authority, the ERRA 2013 regime was intended to improve the alignment of the two phases and improve speed and efficiency generally.

2.8 The Financial Crisis

Besides these issues of institutional design and enforcement practice, there were other more fundamental developments that threatened the smooth operation of the new regime. The first of these was the financial crisis that began in 2008. This crisis and the economic downturn that followed threatened the very basis of the liberal economic system, with free competition at its centre. Promotion of competition within the financial system had clearly given rise to problems and the system of regulation had also failed. Some put the blame for the crisis on too much competition at the expense of prudent regulation. Whether or not this was so, the widespread difficulties that followed the collapse of Lehman Brothers, including the very extensive measures needed to support the banking industry, sapped official and public confidence in competition as a policy.

2.9 A Wider Scepticism?

Competition policy also came in for some more general criticism. Its extension into public services such as health, transport, or postal services appeared to some to be clumsy and unfortunate. Scepticism about the reliability of economics-based competition analysis applied by independent authorities appeared to grow.[17] Competition analysis had become highly technical and increasingly difficult to explain to the business or parliamentary worlds, let alone to the consumer.[18] The growth of data and analytical techniques made competition decisions, particularly in relation to market power and mergers, sometimes hard to follow and explain.

---

[16] Council Regulation (EC) No 139/2004 on the control of concentrations between undertakings, which replaced Council Regulation (EC) No 4065/89 (as amended) for transactions after 1 May 2004 [2004] OJ L24 (EUMR).

[17] See eg the *Res Publica* submission to House of Lords (September 2017) (CMP0030) Pt 1 and The Economist Special Report *Trustbusting in the 21st Century* (17 November 2017).

[18] Or to the then President of France, M Sarkozy, who remarked at the time of the Lisbon Treaty negotiations in 2007: 'Competition, as an Ideology, as a Dogma, What Has it Done for Europe'? The Guardian (25 June 2007).

2.10 The Digital Challenge

As the regime entered its second decade, a further challenge came from the growth of digital business activities and the organizations that had created and developed them. These posed a fundamental threat to established ways of making, advertising, selling, and delivering goods and services. The scale and power of the leading players, larger than any national or regional competition authority, combined with the difficulty of challenging their position, presented a major threat to the established competition 'order'. Digital business models, with their multi-sided nature, their emphasis on accumulation of data, and covert pricing models, did not easily fit standard competition analysis.

2.11 The CMA Proposals

The competition regime therefore increasingly faced basic questions as to whether it was making any real difference to economic performance, whether it was relevant to the issues that citizens rated as important and whether it was capable of offering any coherent response to the digital challenge.

In early 2019, the new chairman of the CMA, Lord Tyrie, expressed many of these concerns to the responsible minister.[19] Referring to the procedural and technical complexity of the UK's competition regime, he said: 'Despite relatively recent legislative changes, the UK has an analogue system ... in a digital age.'[20] The solutions he proposed were for the CMA to 'reconnect' with the consumer, become more 'visible and vocal', and accept new duties to 'put the consumer first' and 'conduct its investigations swiftly'. Changes to the markets and mergers regimes were also proposed as well as greater use of interim measures and changes to the standard of appeal review.[21] We will return in more detail to these and other criticisms later in this chapter.

3 The Performance of the New Regime in Practice

3.1 Antitrust

3.1.1 The EU Context
The 'jewel in the crown' of the newly empowered OFT was the CA 1998 prohibition system. This came into force on 1 March 2000 and allowed the OFT, for the first time, to investigate and decide on cases of infringement, to impose financial penalties, and take other enforcement measures. Although some may have emphasized the national basis of the CA 1998, there is little doubt that this was EU competition law applied at the UK level.

The new UK system was introduced just as the EU system was going through its own fundamental change to a more decentralized EU wide partnership. The enactment of

---

[19] Letter from Rt Hon Lord Tyrie to the Secretary of State for Business (Rt Hon Greg Clark MP) of 21 February 2019 (Tyrie Letter) .Lord Tyrie left the CMA in September 2020.
[20] ibid 2.
[21] *Summary of Proposals from the CMA Chair to the Secretary of State* (25 February 2019) (CMA Proposals).

Regulation 1/2003 meant that the UK also abandoned the notification of agreements (which the OFT had never viewed with great enthusiasm) and adopted a similar approach to that of the EU. Major EU-wide cases, and the development of antitrust doctrine, tended to be done by the EU Commission, making it difficult for a national authority such as the OFT to break new ground.

3.1.2 Cartels and Restrictive Agreements

The OFT issued several early cartel decisions but found that bringing cases to a successful conclusion was more difficult than the authors of the CA 1998 had thought. The OFT withdrew its defence before the CAT in the *Mastercard* case[22] but its decisions were upheld in a number of appeals relating to collusion in the construction industry.[23] There was a series of cases about what was an appealable decision, some of which were of considerable economic significance.[24] The OFT sought to prioritize its enforcement activity on major sectors of the economy and to make use of settlement or early resolution procedures as an alternative to formal infringement decisions.

The OFT also developed its leniency policy, under which penalties were reduced for acknowledging liability and agreeing to cooperate. In the *British Airways* case, the company admitted an infringement in relation to air cargo rates and agreed to pay a reduced fine[25]. Some of the undertakings in the *Dairy Products* and *Tobacco* cases (see below) made similar arrangements.

In 2009, the OFT issued a series of major decisions, again involving the construction industry. In *Bid Rigging in the Construction Industry in England*[26] it imposed fines totalling £129 million for numerous infringements associated with the practice of cover pricing and in the *Construction Industry Forum*[27] condemned a collective boycott. Appeals to the CAT clarified important issues about the OFT's investigation process and the use of evidence, but largely endorsed its substantive findings.[28] This success did not, however, lead to a major increase in activity, at least in the short term. There were several possible reasons. First, there were also some setbacks, often stemming from poor case handling. For example, in *Dairy Products*[29] a fine of nearly £50 million was set aside by the CAT and in *Tobacco*[30] the OFT had to discontinue the defence of its decision, as its case was not supported by oral witness evidence.[31]

The OFT also had an important role in advocacy and increasing the awareness of competition amongst businesses and consumers. This 'soft enforcement' policy complemented its work on infringement decisions, which were in any case highly resource intensive. At the same time, the EU Commission was engaged in its own high-profile cartel enforcement activity, which distracted attention from cartel enforcement at national level. As the

---

[22] *Mastercard UK Members Forum Ltd v OFT* [2006] CAT 14.
[23] *West Midland Roofing Contractors*, decision of 17 March 2004, on appeal, *Apex Asphalt and Paving Co Ltd v OFT* [2005] CAT 4.
[24] *BetterCare Group v OFT* [2002] CAT 6 and *Claymore Dairies Ltd and Express Dairies Ltd v OFT* [2004] CAT 3.
[25] OFT press release 113/07 of 1 August 2007.
[26] Decision of 21 September 2009.
[27] Decision of 29 September 2009 upheld on appeal *Eden Brown Ltd v OFT* [2011] CAT 11.
[28] See eg *Quarmby v OFT* [2011] CAT 11.
[29] OFT decision of 10 August 2011. On appeal *Tesco Stores v OFT* [2012] CAT 31.
[30] OFT Early Settlement decision announced 11 July 2007; Formal decision of 16 April 2010. On appeal *Imperial Tobacco v OFT* [2011] CAT 41.
[31] There was no substantive judgment by the CAT.

NAO commented in NAO 2010, the system 'faces challenges in building a richer body of case law'.[32] The situation was summed up in the ERRA Consultation Response: '[T]here is a problem with antitrust enforcement, in relation some or all of the number of cases, the time they take and the quality and robustness of administrative decision-making (including in perceptions of confirmation bias).'[33] This assessment fed directly into the ERRA 2013 reforms.

3.1.3 The Situation after ERRA 2013

The ERRA 2013 did not change the fundamentals of antitrust enforcement but gave it greater emphasis. The government considered, but in the end rejected, moving to a 'prosecutorial system' under which the OFT/CMA would prosecute cases before the CAT. This would have reduced overall case times by eliminating the administrative decision stage but was thought to be too great an upheaval at that time. Instead, as we noted earlier, the CMA was encouraged further to improve its processes.[34]

Since 2013 there have followed seven years of enhanced case work by the CMA, under a new leadership with a new focus. This also involved use of full and partial settlements and formal commitments. In EU law, commitments were provided under Article 9 of Regulation 1/2003. The Court of Justice of the European Union (CJEU) had held that they were a useful means of enforcement.[35] The OFT had used informal commitments as far back as 2002, in proceedings against Bacardi that led to the appeal by Pernod Ricard.[36] In *Skyscanner*, the CMA accepted commitments from two major hotel online booking organizations but a third party complained that this had damaged its competitive position. The CAT upheld this appeal.[37]

Partial settlements also proved problematic, for example where, as in the *Dairy Products* and *Tobacco* cases,[38] a party that declined to settle successfully overturned the decision. Nevertheless, after 2013, there was a growing number of infringement cases and an increase in the level of fines, reflecting the CMA's determination to make progress. A market sharing infringement by Quantum Pharmaceuticals attracted a fine of nearly £400,000; the CMA imposed fines of £775,000 in its decision on property sales and letting agencies; and a fine of £2.2 million on ITW Ltd in relation to online sales.[39]

More recently, there has been a further noticeable increase both in anti-cartel activity and weight of intervention. In 2016, the decision in *Paroxetine*,[40] against several major pharmaceutical companies engaging in 'pay for delay' patent litigation settlements, suggested an increased level of focus (this case was referred to the CJEU by the CAT). The CMA subsequently took several significant decisions with increasingly large fines.[41] The CMA focused

---

[32] NAO 2010 (n 9) para 9. See also para 10.

[33] ibid para 6.8. The OFT had been accused of confirmation bias because it both investigated and decided on its own cases. Internal procedural reforms to separate decision-making from investigation were intended to make this less likely.

[34] See the OFT's procedural changes referred to in n 13.

[35] Case C-441/07 P *Alrosa v Commission* (see in particular the Opinion of AG Kokott) [2010] ECR I-05949.

[36] *Pernod Ricard v OFT* [2004] CAT 10.

[37] CMA decision of 31 January 2104. On appeal, *Skyscanner v CMA* 2014 [CAT] 16.

[38] See nn 28 and 29.

[39] Decisions of 20 March 2014, 19 March, and 24 May 2015, respectively.

[40] Decision of 12 February 2016; on appeal *GlaxoSmithKline plc v CMA* [2018] CAT 4 (CJEU Judgment of 30 January 2020 in Case C-307/18 *Generics (UK) and Others* EU:C:2020:52).

[41] These included *Model Agencies* (£1.53 m), *Furniture Parts* (£2.7 m), *National Lighting Co* (£2.7 m), *Specialist Laundry Services* (£1.71 m), *Household Fuels* (£3.4 m), and *Concrete Drainage Pipes* (£36 m).

on the pharmaceutical sector, where, in addition to *Paroxetine*, it took decisions on market sharing, delaying market entry, information exchange, and other infringements.[42] Some of these cases also involved breach of Chapter II.

3.1.4 Abuse of Dominant Position

The OFT initially concentrated its enforcement activity on Chapter II, with major cases such as *Aberdeen Journals*[43] and *Napp*,[44] which involved appeals to the CAT. On the whole, the OFT emerged with credit from these encounters, although there were some important lessons learnt. In 2004, the CAT partially overturned the OFT's decision in *Genzyme*,[45] which concerned bundling and margin squeeze. In its decision in *Cardiff Bus*, in 2008, the OFT found that the company had abused its dominant position by excluding a low-cost rival.[46] In 2011, the OFT fined Reckitt Benckiser £11.2 million for abusing its dominant position by impeding generic competition to its Gaviscon product.[47]

In the *Phenytoin* case, in 2016, the CMA fined Flynn and Pfizer some £90 million for excessive pricing of a pharmaceutical product.[48] This decision was partially overturned on appeal by the CAT, which ordered remittal to the CMA. The CMA appealed to the Court of Appeal but this appeal was for the most part rejected and the case was once again remitted to the CMA for further consideration.[49]

Nevertheless, the CMA's willingness to take on major cases against companies of significant scale, such as Glaxo SmithKline and Pfizer, suggests that, whatever criticisms may previously have been made, the CMA remains determined to assert its enforcement powers under the CA 1998.

3.1.5 Criminal Enforcement and Directors' Disqualification

Although criminalizing individual cartel conduct was an important aim of the 2001 White Paper, the OFT encountered difficulty in making the system effective. In 2008, it obtained guilty pleas from three individuals following plea bargains agreed with the US Department of Justice in the US marine hose cartel proceedings.[50] In *British Airways*, however, it was obliged to withdraw a case brought against four BA executives because of difficulties in handling electronic evidence.[51] This was later the subject of an internal OFT review by three non-executive directors, which identified errors in case handling and internal oversight.[52] The lack of progress was blamed in part on the restrictive terms of the statutory offence, requiring the establishment of dishonest intent. As part of the ERRA 2013 reforms, this

---

[42] See most recently two CMA Decisions of 4 March 2020 relating to the drug Nortriptyline, one of which was appealed to the CAT: *Lexon (UK) Limited v Competition and Markets Authority*: Case no 1344/1/12/20. See n 40 for reference to the Paroxetine CMA decision.

[43] *Aberdeen Journals v OFT* [2002] CAT 4.

[44] *Napp Pharmaceuticals v OFT* [2002] CAT 1.

[45] Decision of 27 March 2003; on appeal *Genzyme v OFT* [2004] CAT 4.

[46] Decision of 18 November 2008. This case led to a notable follow-on damages action, discussed below.

[47] Decision of 12 April 2011. This case also involved a follow-on damages action.

[48] Decision of 7 December 2016, Case CE/9742-13.

[49] *CMA v Flynn Pharmaceuticals Co Ltd and Pfizer Inc*, CAT decision on appeal 7 June 2018 [2018] CAT 11 and Court of Appeal decision 9 March 2020 [2020] EWCA Civ 339.

[50] *R v Whittle and Others* Southwark Crown Court (10/11 June 2008). The sentences imposed by the Crown Court were reduced on appeal. See [2008] EWCA Crim 2560.

[51] *R v Burns and Others* (2010/2141). See also OFT Press Release 47/0 (10 May 2010).

[52] *Project Condor Board Review* (OFT October 2010).

requirement (which had been much discussed at the time of the EA 2002) was removed and replaced by a defence of disclosure.

Since then there have been further convictions. In 2015, a guilty plea was entered by one participant in the *Galvanised Steel Tanks* cartel but two other executives were acquitted.[53] In 2017, a participant in the *Precast Concrete Drainage Pipes* cartel was given a suspended sentence.[54] It does not appear, however, that changing the legal test made the CMA's task any easier and in 2019 the CMA proposed that it should relinquish its primary role in criminal cartel enforcement.[55]

In contrast, the CMA has recently adopted a vigorous approach to seeking disqualification of company directors implicated in illegal cartels. The convicted director in the *Precast Concrete* case mentioned above was disqualified for seven years, and in a case involving estate agents, two directors were disqualified for three and a half years each.[56] More recently, two further estate agents were disqualified for six and a half years[57] and six directors in the *Office Fit Out* cartel were disqualified for terms from two to five years each.[58] The CMA has said that this aspect of its powers will be made use of whenever possible.[59]

3.2 Market Investigations

3.2.1 The EA 2002 Regime

Until the ERRA 2013 reforms, market investigations were carried out by the CC at the instigation of the OFT or sector regulators. The CC could not itself initiate a market investigation and the parallel power for Ministers to make market references was never exercised.[60] There was considerable use of the MIR during this period but its full potential was not realized. Early cases, such as *Store Cards* (2006), *Domestic LPG* (2006), and *Northern Irish Banking Services* (2006) were important, but the markets involved were narrow and the issues highly focused. There was little sign of the systematic examination of the economy envisaged by the 2001 White Paper. At several points during this period, the OFT found it hard to identify markets suitable for reference to the CC, in other words important enough to justify the time and effort involved, whilst not being more suitable for enforcement action or an OFT market study.[61]

---

[53] Southwark Crown Court (24 June 2015). The cartel itself was the subject of a settlement decision in 2016, with a £2.6 million fine.

[54] CMA announcement (15 September 2017).

[55] CMA Proposals (n 21) 6: 'in practice it has been difficult and costly to bring prosecutions'; see also Tyrie Letter (n 19) 25.

[56] *Somerset Estate Agents.* See https://www.gov.uk/cma-cases/residential-estate-agency-services-in-the-burnham-on-sea-area-director-disqualification.

[57] *Berkshire Estate Agents*: CMA announcement (15 June 2020); see https://www.gov.uk/government/news/estate-agent-directors-disqualified-for-roles-in-illegal-cartel.

[58] CMA announcement 31 July 2019; see https://www.gov.uk/cma-cases/design-construction-and-fit-out-services-director-disqualification.

[59] See also two decisions involving the drug Nortriptyline(n 42), in which disqualification undertakings ranging from two to seven years were obtained by the CMA. See https://www.gov.uk/cma-cases/suppliers-of-antidepressants-director-disqualification. For fuller discussion of the issue of director disqualification see Peter Whelan, 'The Emerging Contribution of Director Disqualification in UK Competition Law', ch 11 in this volume.

[60] A similar power existed before the EA 2002: see eg the CC's investigation into *SME Banking* (2002).

[61] The OFT had established a market study regime under its general duty to keep the economy under observation. ERRA 2013, ss 36 and 38 and Sch 12 introduced time limits and specific investigative powers for market studies.

3.2.2 Sclerosis in the System?

In 2007, the OFT and CC established a working group[62] to examine how things could be improved. The group's recommendations in August 2008 included early identification of suitable cases, tighter timescales, better liaison between the two authorities and a reaffirmation of the value of the MIR. Although these recommendations were endorsed by both the OFT and the CC, they were soon overtaken by discussions about a possible merger between the two authorities.[63]

Although the effectiveness of the MIR system was in doubt, it nevertheless continued to operate during the merger discussions, with a succession of major investigations; *Groceries* (2008), *Payment Protection Insurance* (2009), *Rolling Stock Leasing* (2009), *BAA Airports* (2009), and *Local Bus Services* (2011). These were all significant cases, three of which gave rise to appeals to the CAT. In *Groceries*, where the CC found the industry in general to be competitive, the recommendation to limit supermarket expansion in high concentration areas was challenged by Tesco, remitted by the CAT to the CC[64] and a modified version reissued. A similar process occurred with the PPI report.[65] In *Airports*, the CC found that common ownership of multiple airports by BAA harmed competition. BAA's first appeal against the CC's order to divest two of its London airports and one Scottish airport was successful in the CAT[66] but overturned by the Court of Appeal.[67] After the CC had issued a further divestment order, BAA appealed this also, but the appeal was rejected both by the CAT and the Court of Appeal.[68] This was a significant moment for the MIR as it confirmed that, in the appropriate circumstances, divestment could be used as an effective and powerful remedy.[69]

3.2.3 The Effect of ERRA 2013

Use of the MIR continued as preparations went ahead for the formation of the CMA. In *Statutory Audit Services* (2013) the CC required audit contracts to be retendered every five years; in *Aggregates, Cement and Ready-mix Concrete* (2014) it imposed a divestment requirement for Lafarge Tarmac. *Private Healthcare* (2014) also featured a divestment requirement (for hospitals owned by HCA) but this remedy was overturned on appeal to the CAT.[70] The investigation into *Private Motor Insurance* (2014) produced measures to restrict incumbents' market advantage and *Payday Lending* (2015) led to increased transparency in the cost of borrowing.

The ERRA 2013 strengthened the system of market investigations. Not only was the panel system retained, but it now became possible to investigate issues spanning several markets.[71] There was also more emphasis on public interest aspects, with ministers able to appoint experts from outside the CMA to participate.[72] Important though these reforms

---

[62] Comprising the chief economists and one non-executive director from each authority.

[63] The first specific proposal for this was made by the OFT in October 2008 but was rejected by ministers in November 2008.

[64] *Tesco v CC* [2009] CAT 6; CC Report on remittal (October 2009).

[65] *Barclays Bank v CC* [2009] CAT 27; CC Report on remittal (October 2010).

[66] *BAA Ltd v CC* [2009] CAT 35.

[67] [2010] EWCA Civ 1097.

[68] *BAA Ltd v CC (No 2)* [2012] CAT 3 and [2012] EWCA Civ 1077.

[69] The CMA issued a favourable evaluation report on 16 May 2016.

[70] *HCA International Ltd v CMA* [2014] CAT 23. See also *AXA v CMA* [2015] CAT 5 (anaesthetists' groups) and *FIPO v CMA* [2015] CAT 8 (private medical insurers and consultants); see also [2016] EWCA Civ 777.

[71] 'Cross market references': s 33 and Sch 9.

[72] 'Public interest interventions': s 36 and Sch 10.

were, the post ERRA 2013 period is notable for two major investigations, into retail banking and energy respectively, that involved major markets of direct relevance to consumers, in other words what the 2001 White Paper had envisaged.

3.2.4 The Retail Banking and Energy Cases

Both investigations were, arguably, long overdue. The banking industry had been the subject of many previous studies including a major non-statutory investigation.[73] The UK energy market had been considered extensively both by the energy regulator, Ofgem, and by ministers over several years but neither had been willing to pass the issue to the CC. These were very substantial cases, and not uncontroversial. With the benefit of hindsight, it may not have been altogether wise for a newly formed authority to embark on both of them at the same time.

The *retail banking* case[74] did not impose any divestment remedies, despite calls for these. Instead, the CMA chose to increase switching and to further empower banking consumers. These measures were far-reaching (described as a 'revolution in open banking') but were largely accepted by the industry. Their effect has yet to be fully felt.

The *energy market*[75] investigation gave rise to political controversy. The CMA's overall finding was that suppliers were making excess profits from energy customers. The majority of the CMA panel decided against a price cap, apart from in one niche sector, essentially because this would disadvantage new entrants, who competed mainly on price, and limit customers' ability to switch to cheaper suppliers. The government (following the opposition Labour party) relied on the minority opinion by one panel member and legislated to require Ofgem to impose a general price cap. This is now in place, although it is still too early to assess its effects.[76]

The issue is not whether a price cap would be more effective than what the CMA had proposed but rather the over-ruling of the CMA's majority decision by the government. This may not prove to be a regular occurrence but its significance in relation to the CA 1998/EA 2002 settlement should not be underrated.

The CMA is conducting a market investigation of the funeral services industry[77] as part of its drive to concentrate on markets of direct relevance to consumers. The CMA has recently examined *Statutory Audit Services*[78] and *Online Platforms and Digital Advertising*[79] as market studies without use of the MIR.

3.3 Mergers

3.3.1 The Period after EA 2002

As with the MIR, the ERRA 2013 strengthened the merger control regime by removing any element of rivalry between the institutions. However, several of the largest merger cases

---

[73] In 2011, the Independent Commission on Banking (ICB), chaired by Sir John Vickers, reported on prudential and competition aspects of the banking industry.

[74] Report (9 August 2016).

[75] Report (24 June 2016).

[76] Early indications, however, confirm that the price cap can go up as well as down.

[77] Reference (28 March 2019).

[78] Market study (18 April 2019).

[79] Final report (1 July 2020).

spanned the transition to the new regime. In the period immediately following EA 2002, the newly independent authorities worked to bed down the new system and work out the appropriate lines of demarcation. In the 2003 *IBA Health* case,[80] the OFT's approach to merger references to the CC was criticized by the CAT but was upheld by the Court of Appeal. The OFT increased the quality and depth of its own 'phase 1' scrutiny and, where possible, dealt with cases by obtaining undertakings in lieu of a reference, reserving references to the CC for those cases where either no undertakings were offered, or it had clearly identified the need for an outright prohibition. So successful was this policy that, for extended periods, very few cases went to 'phase 2'.[81]

In terms of substance, the authorities' work in the initial years appears to have been effective. Contentious issues on appeal were largely confined to matters of procedure, specific points of analysis and remedies. In 2006, the CC's store disposal remedies in the *Somerfield* case[82] were upheld by the CAT. In 2008, the CC's assessment of the likelihood of an SLC was upheld in *BSkyB/ITV* (discussed later under public interest) and its decision to prohibit Stagecoach's acquisition of Preston Bus (2010) was also upheld by the CAT, although its choice of counterfactual and other parts of its reasoning were criticized.[83]

3.3.2 The Arrival of the CMA

In *Akzo Nobel/Metlac* the CC prohibited a merger where the UK territorial jurisdiction was based only on the management of subsidiaries within the UK. The decision was nevertheless upheld by the CAT and by the Court of Appeal.[84]

In the protracted *Eurotunnel* case,[85] which concerned cross-channel ferries, the CC/CMA decided that what appeared to be (and had been accepted as such by the French authorities) the purchase of redundant assets was in law an anti-competitive merger of two businesses. The CAT initially criticized but then upheld the CMA's assessment. This decision was overturned by the Court of Appeal but then upheld in the Supreme Court. The CC's assessment of the substance of the case was not criticized in any appeal and the proposed acquisition was eventually abandoned.

In *Ryanair/Aer Lingus*,[86] the EU Commission had required Ryanair to reduce its shareholding in Aer Lingus to not more than 30 per cent. The UK authorities nonetheless intervened under the more flexible merger threshold of 'material influence' to require a further reduction to 5 per cent, provoking a protracted series of disputes, in which the authorities ultimately prevailed.

In 2012, competition control was applied to public hospital mergers.[87] In 2013, the CMA prohibited the proposed merger of two NHS hospital foundation trusts.[88] This aroused

---

[80] *OFT v IBA Health Ltd* [2005] CAT 27, [2004] EWCA Civ 142.

[81] The NAO noted in NAO 2010 (n 9) Pt Five that only seven references were made to the CC in 2008–2009 out of a total of 84 mergers investigated by the OFT; undertakings in lieu were obtained in six cases. This compared to eighteen references to the CC in 2004–2005 out of 257 investigated cases, with undertakings in five cases.

[82] *Somerfield plc v CC* [2006] CAT 4.

[83] *Stagecoach v CC* [2010] CAT 14.

[84] *Akzo Nobel NV/Metlac Holdings Srl* (December 2012); on appeal [2013] CAT 13, [2014] EWCA Civ 482.

[85] *Groupe Eurotunnel SA/Sea France SA*; on appeal, *SCOP v CC* [2015] CAT 1; [2015] EWCA Civ 487; Supreme Court [2015] UKSC 75.

[86] *Ryanair Holdings plc v CC* [2014] CAT 3; [2015] EWCA Civ 83. The litigation effectively began in 2011 and only concluded in 2015.

[87] Health and Social Care Act 2012.

[88] *Royal Bournemouth & Christchurch Hospitals NHSFT/Poole Hospital NHSFT* report (17 October 2013). The parties are currently seeking to revive the merger proposal.

considerable opposition in healthcare circles. The CMA has looked at several hospital mergers since then but has not prohibited any outright.

3.3.3 After ERRA 2013
The flow of merger cases continued in the period after the ERRA 2013. In 2015, the CMA found against the Reckitt Benckiser and Johnson and Johnson merger, requiring a brand to be licensed to a third party, and in 2016 against Ladbrokes and Coral, requiring the divestment of some 350 betting shops. However, in 2017 the CMA allowed the merger of Tesco and Booker, in a sector where such mergers had traditionally been problematic.

During 2018–2019 there was a series of completed mergers where the CMA found not only adverse results but also that unauthorized steps had been taken to implement the merger before clearance had been granted and imposed penalties.[89] The most high-profile merger in this period was in the supermarkets sector. In Sainsburys/ASDA (2019), the CMA condemned the proposed merger of two major supermarket groups. There was no appeal of the decision, the only recourse to the CAT being made during the investigation in relation to the deadlines for commenting on working papers.[90] The proposed merger was abandoned.

3.3.4 A New Approach?
Recently, it has been suggested that the CMA is taking an increasingly aggressive approach to mergers, possibly in anticipation of its future role no longer participating in the EUMR system. The CMA denies that it has changed its policy. The recent Roche/Spark[91] and Sabre/Farelogix[92] cases have been seen by some as indicating a more expansive approach to asserting jurisdiction over mergers where the centre of gravity is outside the UK. It may be significant that the CMA has found an SLC (and required divestiture) in the majority of recent cases, such as Rentokil/Cannon,[93] Electrorent/Microlease,[94] and Tobii/Smartbox[95] also perhaps suggesting a tougher approach.

3.3.5 The System of Voluntary Notification
Many of these cases involved completed mergers. The UK has no compulsory pre-notification requirement, so an adverse finding may involve divestiture and 'unscrambling' of arrangements already made. The JD Sports/Footasylum[96] merger was a completed merger which the CMA prohibited. An appeal to the CAT by JD Sports was successful[97] but the CMA is seeking to reverse this. Whatever the merits of the UK's voluntary notification system, it is unlikely that it will survive either the departure of the UK from the EU, or the rise of the digital economy, as the CMA has stated.[98]

---

[89] See eg Ausurus Group/Cu Fe Investments (14 August 2018), Vanilla Group/Washstation (11 October 2018). See also PayPal/iZettle (12 June 2019), a clearance decision.

[90] [2019] CAT 1.

[91] Roche AG/Spark Therapeutics Inc (phase 1 clearance decision December 2019).

[92] Sabre/Farelogix (phase 2 prohibition decision April 2020); (appealed to the CAT on remedies: case no 1245/4/12/20)

[93] Rentokil Initial/Cannon Hygiene, CMA decision (25 January 2019); appeal to the CAT withdrawn.

[94] Electrorent/Microlease, CMA decision (17 May 2018); see also [2019] CAT 4 (appeal on penalty upheld).

[95] Tobii AB/ Smartbox Assistive Technology Ltd; appeal to the CAT dismissed [2020] CAT 1.

[96] JD Sports Fashion PLC/Footasylum PLC (6 May 2020).

[97] CAT Decision of 13 November 2020 [2020] CAT 24.

[98] CMA Proposals (n 21) 6; Tyrie Letter (n 19) 42.

3.4 The Public Interest

3.4.1 Grounds for Intervention

The EA 2002 retained the right for ministers to intervene in both markets and merger investigations on specific statutory public interest grounds. This power has so far not been exercised for markets, so the interest is in relation to mergers.

3.4.2 Merger Cases

There were several major cases where the government intervened in mergers that would otherwise have been decided on competition grounds alone, and others where it did not. There was also a steady stream of initial interventions, mainly on national security grounds, where no further action was taken. In 2007, News International, part owner of BSkyB, as it then was, purchased a 17.9 per cent stake in ITV. This was below the 20 per cent cross-media threshold set by statute, but still subject to the 'material influence' merger jurisdiction. The government was concerned about reduced plurality of the media from putting Sky News and ITN under common control. The CC decided that the public interest fears were overstated but that the merger should be prohibited on competition grounds. That view was accepted by the government and the decision (in both its aspects) upheld by the Court of Appeal.[99]

In 2008, at the onset of the financial crisis, Lloyds Banking Group offered to buy the ailing Halifax Bank of Scotland (HBoS) bank. The government's concern in this case was that the competition authorities might block all or part of the merger. The government swiftly enacted a new statutory public interest ground and the Secretary of State approved the merger, on the advice of the Bank of England, under this new ground. An appeal by Scottish business interests was dismissed by the CAT.[100]

In 2010, News Corporation proposed to purchase the remaining shares in BSkyB that it did not already own. The merger was cleared by the EU Commission under the EUMR but was subject to national control of media issues. The case was removed from the jurisdiction of the Secretary of State for Business on grounds of possible bias and transferred to the Culture Secretary, who was minded to accept undertakings of editorial independence. These fell away in the aftermath of the *News of the World* scandal and the merger was briefly referred to the CC and then abandoned.

In the different climate of 2018, 21st Century Fox, now the part owner of Sky (as it was now known), sought to purchase the remaining shares. Competition issues were again cleared under the EUMR but public interest aspects were dealt with in the UK. The CMA recommended divestment to a third party. The stake was subsequently acquired by Comcast.[101]

3.4.3 A Wider Public Interest?

Some mergers that aroused the particular interest of the public were not examined by the UK authorities at all. For example, in *Kraft/Cadbury*, also an EUMR case, no attempt was made by the government to claim jurisdiction on public interest grounds. It was asked in

---

[99] *British Sky Broadcasting Group plc v CC* [2008] CAT 36; [2010] EWCA Civ 2.
[100] *Merger Action Group v Secretary of State for Business* [2008] CAT 36.
[101] CMA Report (1 May 2018). Secretary of State's Statement to Parliament of 5 June 2018.

Parliament and in the media why the UK appeared powerless to prevent the takeover by a US corporation of a UK household name.[102]

As a response to the digital challenge and perceived threats to national security, changes have already been made to jurisdictional thresholds to make it easier to control acquisitions of start-up businesses. More radical proposals currently under discussion to establish a completely separate control of mergers that appear to threaten national security would seem more problematic, as they would suggest a radical recasting of the entire public interest merger framework.[103] More generally, the move to decide mergers on public interest, rather than on purely competition, grounds may prove hard to resist. Up to now, the structure set out in the EA 2002, of a competition-based assessment by the CMA supplemented by a parallel assessment on specific public interest grounds, also by the CMA, at the behest of the Secretary of State, has provided a reasonable and predictable basis for resolving issues.

3.5 Private Actions

3.5.1 The Original Purpose

One objective of CA 1998 was to encourage the use of private actions to give redress to the victims of competition law infringements. Initially, this was largely an aspiration, although it was provided that infringement decisions of EU and national authorities were binding on the courts.[104] The EA 2002 conferred on the CAT a special jurisdiction to assess and award damages and provided a procedure for designated representative claimants.[105] The intention was that consumer bodies would routinely seek damages awards by way of 'follow-on' from infringement decisions.

3.5.2 Early Experience

The practice was less encouraging. In the *Replica Football Shirts* litigation, brought by the Consumers Association following an OFT cartel finding, the protracted process, which ended in settlement,[106] resulted in very small monetary compensation for individuals. The association said that it would be hard to justify similar cases in future.

Follow-on claims in the CAT were few in number. This was partly because the CAT was unable to go beyond the limits of the infringement finding[107] and there was often a need to expand this in time or scope properly to assess the damages due. As a consequence, cases tended to be started in the High Court rather than under the special CA 1998 procedure, and normally to be settled. An exception was *Cardiff Bus*,[108] where the liquidator of a failed company sought to recover in the CAT very large sums from the incumbent, which OFT

---

[102] There was no relevant public interest criterion and the government did not enact one, instead obtaining informal commitments from Kraft. The government published its Response to a (very critical) report of the HC Business Select Committee in July 2010 (Cm 7915).

[103] A National Security and Investments Bill, providing for ministers to be able to 'call in' mergers with a 'trigger event' to conduct a national security assessment, was introduced in Parliament in November 2020.

[104] CA 1998, s 58A inserted by EA 2002, s 20.

[105] CA 1998, ss 47A and 47B added by EA 2002, s 19.

[106] *The Consumers Association v JJB Sports*, Order of the CAT (14 January 2008).

[107] *EWS Ltd v ENRON Coal Services Ltd* [2009] CAT 7 and [2009] EWCA Civ 647 and see also *Emerson Electric Co v Morgan Crucible* [2011] CAT 4 and [2012] EWCA Civ 1559.

[108] *2 Travel v Cardiff City Transport Services Ltd* [2019] CAT 19. This was possibly the first and last treble damages award in the UK.

had found to have infringed Chapter II by excluding a competitor.[109] The claimant recovered a small fraction of its claim, mainly because the CAT found that much of the harm was not attributable to the infringement. The intention to exclude was blatant, however, and the CAT awarded exemplary damages, trebling the basic award. Another example was *Albion Water*, where the CAT awarded £1.85 million damages for an abuse of dominant position in relation to water supply. Unusually, this claim 'followed-on' from the CAT's own earlier judgment.[110]

3.5.3 The New Regime

In 2015, the Consumer Rights Act (CRA 2015) gave a substantial boost to private actions.[111] This legislation provided for so called 'opt-in' and 'opt-out' individual and collective (or 'class') actions, with conditions for class representatives, funding, and allocation of costs. It followed, but was largely unaffected by, the EU's Damages Directive[112] that set minimum standards for national law. Control of collective actions was conferred exclusively on the CAT, which had to certify at the initial stage whether the case was suitable for collective proceedings.

The early cases following the CRA 2015 confirmed predictions that the most strongly contested part of any litigation would be the certification stage before the CAT. It was initially thought that the CAT's certification decision was not subject to appeal. However, in the *Walter Merricks* case,[113] which involved a possible class of many tens of millions, the Court of Appeal held that it did have jurisdiction to review the CAT's decision that the case was not suitable for collective treatment and went on to reverse it. The Supreme Court, by a three to two majority decision, upheld the Court of Appeal's judgment, with the result that not only Walter Merricks' own action but other important collective action cases that were dependent on the result could proceed.[114]

There appears to be considerable interest in the new regime. Major cases are under way or contemplated, but given the uncertainty over the requirements for certification, the regime has yet to realize its full potential, and its scope and effectiveness have still to be fully tested.

Individual damages actions also received a boost from the 2015 Act. All aspects of the case could now be considered by the CAT and, with the bringing into force of the so-called 'Lever Amendment',[115] competition aspects of cases taking place in the High Court could be transferred to the CAT for decision. Whilst this was not without its complexities (for example, in the *Agents Mutual* case[116] it was unclear whether the CAT's 'decision' on competition aspects was open to appeal), this transfer power was strongly endorsed by the Court of Appeal in *Sainsburys and Others v Mastercard*.[117] There, the Court of Appeal had

---

[109] See n 45.

[110] *Albion Water v Dwr Cymru Cyfyngedig* [2013] CAT 6.

[111] Consumer Rights Act 2015 Pt 2 Ch 3 (CRA 2015).

[112] Directive 214/14/EU OJ 2914 L349/1 (EU Damages Directive).

[113] *Walter Hugh Merricks CBE v MasterCard Inc and Others* [2017] CAT 16; Court of Appeal decision [2018] EWCA Civ 2527; Supreme Court decision of December 2020 [2020] UKSC 51.

[114] Including *Trucks* (*Road Haulage Association v MAN and Others* and *UK Trucks Claims v Fiat and Others*), *Trains* (*Gutmann v First MTR South Western and Another* and *Gutmann v South Eastern Railway*), *Forex* (*O'Higgins v Barclays* and *Evans v Barclays*), and *Maritime Car Carriers* cases (*McLaren v MOL and Others*).

[115] CA 1998, s 16, promoted by Sir Jeremy Lever KCMG, QC.

[116] [2017] CAT 15.

[117] [2018] EWCA 1536 (Civ).

to examine three conflicting first instance judgments from different courts on damages for infringement arising from Mastercard's multilateral interchange fee (MIF). Perhaps understandably, it ruled that, in future, all such cases should be heard in the CAT and this was subsequently confirmed by the Supreme Court.[118]

As with collective actions, a significant number of major individual damages actions are under way, or contemplated, or in process of transfer from the High Court to the CAT.[119] A notable recent individual damages award was in *BritNed*,[120] where the Court of Appeal largely upheld a judgment of the High Court based on direct evidence of causation rather than economic modelling.

The expectations raised for this new and expanding regime are high. Whether the policy of encouraging damages actions will live up to these expectations remains to be seen.[121] The CAT may have to handle many large and complex cases, possibly simultaneously, in addition to its appeal functions. There is no doubt, however, about the determination of all concerned to make the regime work effectively.

3.6 The Role of Ministers

3.6.1 Stepping Back
The 2001 White Paper emphasized that competition decision-making was to be placed, possibly for the first time in the UK, in the hands of professionally competent bodies, staffed and headed by specialists, if not experts. In line with a worldwide trend, competition law and economics were to be relied on as disciplines that would provide sensible answers to issues that in the past had all too frequently been decided by informed instinct.

The corollary of this was the withdrawal of ministers from the day to day operation of the competition regime. With the important exception of public interest cases, a minister's role was confined to overseeing the operation of the regime, accounting for it to Parliament, and ensuring that the various appointments were filled by individuals of suitable qualifications and calibre. One unintended consequence of this was a reduction in the responsible department's own competition expertise. This 'hollowing out' of capability stemmed directly from the reduced involvement of officials in operations and decision-making. For example, in the OECD's competition deliberations, the places occupied by department officials passed to the OFT and the CC. Other international organizations such as the ECN and, increasingly, the International Competition network (ICN) were the preserve of the competition authorities rather than departmental officials.

3.6.2 A Change of Emphasis?
In the early years this tended to create a gulf between those operating the system and those ultimately responsible for it. When, as the regime became established, the government

---

[118] *Sainsbury's Supermarkets Ltd (Respondents) v Visa Europe Services LLC and Others (Appellants); Sainsbury's Supermarkets Ltd and Others (Respondents) v Mastercard Incorporated and Others (Appellants)* [2020] UKSC 24.

[119] Including *Trucks* (cases 1284, 1290-95/5/7/18(T)) and *Power Cables* (cases 1340-41/5/7/20(T)).

[120] *BritNed Development Ltd v ABB AB and ABB Ltd* [2018] EWHC 2616 and 2913 (Ch); [2019] EWCA Civ 1840.

[121] The 2016 Act also introduced a 'fast track' procedure for smaller cases, in which costs and evidence were capped. The CAT was empowered to grant injunctions but not to make declarations.

wished to make changes, it was placed at a disadvantage. Either it had to rely on the views of the authorities it had created, or it had somehow to replicate the knowledge it had lost. This was apparent in the consultation leading up to the ERRA 2013. The government was sometimes insufficiently informed of the reasons why particular aspects of the regime existed, or what they had achieved in practice. It was also apparent in the Regulatory Appeal Review. This developed rapidly into a radical 'bottom-up' review of the entire appeal framework. Basic issues, such as the reason for having full merits appeals in competition cases, which were well understood within the administrations of 1998 to 2003, had by 2013 apparently been forgotten.

Recent developments are more encouraging. Given the enormous commitment involved in creating the CMA, government now appears to be devoting much more attention than hitherto to understanding its aims and its achievements. It offers the CMA a 'strategic steer' and there are proposals for the CMA to provide the government with an annual 'State of Competition' Report[122]. In the current political climate, pressure for more ministerial involvement in the practical application of competition policy is likely to be strong. It is therefore important that this should happen on a sufficiently informed basis.

3.7 Concurrent Enforcement by Regulators

3.7.1 Initial Problems

Sectoral regulators play an important role in competition enforcement and were empowered by the CA 1998 to apply competition law as well as being designated to apply EU competition law under Regulation 1/2003. The institutional relationship between them and the competition authorities has been a matter of some debate. The 'concurrency working group' was set up to ensure coordination but this was not always achieved. Use of competition powers by regulators was limited, it often proving easier and more flexible to use regulatory powers instead, although there were some important exceptions. One was the £41.6 million fine imposed by Ofgem in 2008 on National Grid for abuse of dominance in relation to household meters.[123] Another was the £4.1 million fine imposed by the rail regulator ORR on EWS in 2006.

The general practice was not satisfactory, however, and various attempts were made to encourage regulators to make greater use of their competition powers. A joint departmental inquiry in 2006 recommended more clarity about which powers regulators were deciding to use, and why, and a greater use of competition powers.[124] The issue was addressed in the ERRA 2013, with the establishment of a more formal coordinating group, the UK Regulators Network (UKRN), greater clarity on when competition powers should be used, and the threat that competition powers would be removed altogether from sectoral regulators if use was not made of them.

---

[122] The CMA issued its first such report on 30 November 2020. See https://www.gov.uk/government/publications/state-of-uk-competition-report-2020.

[123] Upheld on appeal [2009] CAT 14 and [2010] EWCA Civ 114, although the fine was reduced to £15 million.

[124] *Concurrent Competition Powers in Sectoral Regulation*, Department of Trade and Industry and HM Treasury (May 2006) URN 06/1244.

3.7.2 Improvement

These measures seem to have had some effect. For example, in 2012, the communications regulator, Ofcom, brought its *Pay TV* case against BSkyB under its regulatory powers.[125] In 2018 it used competition powers against Royal Mail in relation to bulk mail access.[126] The CMA's annual concurrency report for 2020[127] noted that in the previous two years five infringement cases had been completed in relation to regulated sectors, including two by Ofgem. Nonetheless, as discussed later in section 6, the government in 2019 still regarded the issue as unresolved.

As well as competition cases undertaken by sectoral regulators, there were also significant cases undertaken by competition authorities in regulated sectors. The CC's investigation into BAA followed a reference by the OFT. The extended litigation in the CAT involving *Albion Water*[128] arose because the CAT considered that the facts, on close examination, indicated a serious infringement of Chapter II that the water regulator, Ofwat, had not acknowledged.

4 The Digital Age and New Challenges

4.1 The Challenge

The CMA Proposals in 2019 asserted that, amongst other things, the system for competition enforcement needed to adapt to meet the 'digital challenge'. As we mentioned above in section 2, this derived from the growth of major digital companies that based their business models either on the control of digital platforms, on which others could trade, or on the amassing of data, which could be used to attract advertising or to target other commercial initiatives.

Authorities in many countries besides the UK, for example in Australia, Germany, France, and, significantly, the EU itself, have been aware of this issue for some years. An array of impressive studies and reports, including the Furman Report in the UK, has highlighted not only the scale of the challenge but also the difficulty of fitting these new technologies into established competition orthodoxy.[129] The government considered some of these issues in its 2018 Consumer Green Paper.[130]

Not only were many of the services provided by these new businesses very attractive to consumers, they involved innovation on a grand scale and often were free of charge to the consumer. Whilst their economic power could be observed in general terms, it was hard to

---

[125] Communications Act 2003, ss 316–318. These provisions were carried over from the previous legislation, which preceded the granting of concurrent competition enforcement powers to Ofcom.

[126] On appeal to the CAT, *Royal Mail v Ofcom* [2019] CAT 27. An appeal to the Court of Appeal is pending.

[127] Published on 15 April 2020. The Financial Conduct Authority (FCA) took its first infringement decision in February 2019.

[128] *Albion Water Services Ltd v Water Services Regulation Authority* [2006] CAT 36, [2008] EWCA Civ 536, and [2008] CAT 31.

[129] See eg *Competition Policy for the Digital Era* (Cremer, de Montjoiye, and Schweitzer) DG Comp Brussels 2019; *Unlocking Digital Competition* (Digital Competition Expert Panel) HM Treasury March 2019 (Furman Report); and Diane Coyle *Practical Competition Policy Implications of Digital Platforms* (University of Cambridge, March 2018).

[130] Department for Business, Energy and Industrial Strategy, *Modernising Consumer Markets*, (2018) ch 3.

measure this by normal methods and, particularly when it involved large quantities of data, it was hard to assess whether it was harmful or beneficial to consumer welfare. Moreover, if there was a problem it was sometimes hard to know what to do about it. Controlling the market power (if such it was) that arose from amassing data was complicated by data privacy and ownership considerations, making traditional access remedies difficult. Pricing remedies were, by definition, ineffective if applied to already free services. The size and financial muscle of the larger digital undertakings meant that fines were likely to be insufficient either as punishment or deterrent and the pace of innovation made behavioural remedies unreliable.

The challenge posed therefore had a number of different elements. In relation to dominance and market power, the question was whether traditional market definition techniques and abuse analysis were sufficient. In relation to cartels and restrictive agreements, digital technology and artificial intelligence could make market coordination much easier, without any need for express agreement; or, alternatively, they could increase market transparency and promote competition, which was another difficulty. In relation to merger control, the traditional horizontal/vertical distinction and effects between competitors (which current systems controlled quite well) might be less important than the danger of mergers stifling innovation and growth of future market entrants (which current systems controlled less easily).

4.2 The Response

The response of the competition world to the rapid emergence of this problem has been mixed. Authorities were initially reluctant to accept that digital competition threatened to displace traditional trading methods. The approach to merger control may have been too relaxed and perhaps too much faith was placed in the capacity of markets to self-correct, it being assumed that new entrants would be attracted to profitable, monopolized, sectors.

Given these difficulties, it is hardly surprising that specific interventions have sometimes appeared uncoordinated and not always effective. The EU Commission pursued a series of cases in the digital sector, principally, but not exclusively, against Google, and mainly under Article 102. In Germany, the BKA proceeded against Facebook for unfair trading practices, but encountered difficulties in defending its decision in court. Enforcement action in the UK has focused mainly on aspects of online sales, and there has also been some private litigation. The balance of opinion appears to be that some form of regulation is needed in addition to competition enforcement and, as discussed below, the government has now moved to implement a regulatory regime.

The difficulties in establishing a regulatory system specifically for the digital economy should not be under-rated. Not only is it hard to know where the digital economy starts and finishes (it could soon extend to the bulk of economic activity) but setting new regulatory objectives and duties involves developing a coherent intellectual framework for distinguishing desirable from undesirable features. There are also significant problems of scale and capability. Any regulatory body would need to be strong enough to 'take on' major digital players. This would mean attracting personnel of sufficient expertise and experience to match that of the digital undertakings.

In 2019, as recommended by the Furman Report, the CMA launched a market study of digital advertising.[131] The preliminary conclusions of this were that the numerous issues identified were best addressed, at least in the first instance, by regulation. The CMA was not inclined to go on to conduct a full market investigation, despite calls to do so, on the grounds that any remedial action that resulted would be ineffective if confined to the UK. The same applies, of course, to any regulatory action, which clearly needs to be international and coordinated if it is to be effective.

In relation to merger control, the existing regime is being applied but with increased vigilance. The CMA has said that the UK merger control regime is adequate for the task,[132] whilst acknowledging pressure to introduce some degree of mandatory pre-notification and to adapt the analysis to cover the acquisition by major incumbents of fast-growing, innovative, new companies. An aspect of this is the need to predict what may happen, in both the actual and in the counterfactual situation, in relation to businesses whose products have yet to achieve sales, or even to exist at all. One problem here is that the business model for investment finance often assumes that the start-up will be so acquired within a relatively short time, so there is a danger of unintended consequences. In any event, we may expect a rapid evolution of policy and practice in relation to the digital economy.

In March 2020, as recommended by the Furman Report, the government set up a Digital Markets Taskforce to develop policy in this area. In December 2020, it announced the creation of a Digital Markets Unit (DMU) within the CMA to oversee a binding code of practice that would apply to digital companies with a defined 'strategic market status' (SMS); to intervene where needed to promote competition; and to apply closer scrutiny to mergers involving firms with SMS.[133] How this new regime will operate in practice remains to be worked out.

5 The EU Legal Framework and the Consequences of Leaving It

5.1 The Pursuit of Integration

The 2001 White Paper placed the UK's competition regime squarely in the context of EU law. As it said, '(EU) law has direct effect in the UK—prohibiting the same kinds of behaviour where they have an effect on inter-state trade.'[134] This was before the European Commission had fully developed its modernization plans, embodied in Regulation 1/2003, under which national authorities would be designated to apply EU competition law. The government welcomed these developments and noted that they showed a common commitment to its own principles for competition policy.[135] The OFT, and since 2013 the CMA, has taken duties and obligations under EU law very seriously. Many cases initiated primarily under Chapters I and II relied also on Articles 101 and 102, with the two systems

---

[131] *Online Platforms and Digital Advertising*, Final report published on 1 July 2020. The principal recommendation to set up a digital markets unit was accepted by the government – see below.

[132] Andrea Coscelli (CMA chief executive) Speech at GCR Live: Telecoms, Media, and Technology 2020, published on 2 March 2020.

[133] Press release (8 December 2020) https://www.gov.uk/government/news/cma-advises-government-on-new-regulatory-regime-for-tech-giants.

[134] 2001 White Paper (n 3) 5.

[135] ibid Pt 3.

applied in parallel. The UK authorities participated closely in the ECN and gave assistance and support in investigations conducted on UK territory by DG Comp. It is fair to say that the UK has been a leading player in European-wide competition enforcement.

On the substance of competition law, there were some more subtle aspects. In relation to CA 1998, the UK courts and authorities were required to act so that UK law was interpreted and applied, so far as possible, consistently with EU law.[136] UK competition law was, in respect of antitrust, closely aligned with EU competition law. Similarly, the UK regime for private enforcement had to comply with the EU Damages Directive. As we noted earlier, this was less true for the MIR, which had a purely UK pedigree. The duties of cooperation and consistent rulings embodied in Regulation 1/2003 meant that the UK authorities had to ensure that their actions did not conflict with the application of Articles 101 or 102. The CC, and after it the CMA, had to apply the MIR in a way that did not conflict with EU law.

The position with merger control was different again. Unlike under the CA 1998, the demarcation between national and EU merger control was based on a strict turnover threshold. Mergers falling under the EUMR were examined under EU law; those that fell outside the EU's control or were referred to national authorities under one of the several possible routes, were considered under national law. The two did not have to be the same, although it was undesirable for them to diverge substantially.

We noted above that, in terms of procedure, scope of control, and jurisdiction, the two systems differed in some respects, as shown, for example, by the *Ryanair* case. In terms of substance, however, the approach adopted by both the UK and the EU has been broadly the same. Moreover, throughout the period the UK authorities worked closely with DG Comp and other national authorities to ensure as harmonious a policy of EU-wide merger control as possible.[137]

5.2 Effect of Leaving the EU

At the practical level, and in the short term, the effect of departure is likely to be fairly muted. Not only did many existing arrangements continue to apply during the transition period to the end of 2020, but even afterwards, incentives to diverge, on either side, are not obvious.

In relation to substantive competition law, the obligation to act consistently with EU law remains, but has been relaxed, with the authorities and courts allowed to depart from pre-exit EU law where this can be shown to be appropriate by reference to a list of specific factors.[138]. Articles 101 and 102 and the associated jurisprudence will remain, as will their continuing development by EU courts and authorities. How far the UK authorities and courts will take account of this power to diverge remains to be seen, but they will have to weigh carefully the immediate attraction of doctrinal freedom against the disadvantage of reduced weight and impact of their decisions. As part of a European network, whether at the administrative or the judicial level, the UK's decisions carry considerable authority and

---

[136] CA 1998, s 60.
[137] Including co-chairing the ECN's Mergers Working Party.
[138] CA 1998, s 60A, replacing s 60, enacted by the Competition (Amendment etc)(EU Exit) Regulations 2019 (SI 2019/93).

contribute to the development of the whole system. In isolated divergence, however excellent, they may become interesting only in themselves.

In relation to more practical aspects, we may expect a considerable effort on both sides to maintain contacts and channels of communication, in the interests of coherence and coordination. The UK will probably continue as much collaboration as possible, whilst reserving the right to apply the law differently in particular cases. It is likely that the UK will proceed against undertakings based outside the UK whose activities affect UK territory and that DG Comp will act against UK based companies whose activities have effects within the EU.

The UK will be free to apply the MIR as it wishes, without having to take account of EU law. It will, however, still have to operate it alongside a prohibition system largely based on EU law.

In relation to merger control, without the benefit of the EUMR, many more cases will fall within the UK's jurisdiction. The CMA will have to decide how it will operate in parallel with DG Comp in relation to mergers covered by the EUMR. The CMA will also have to work out how it handles an increased case load, and how to introduce a mandatory pre-notification system. We are likely to see more UK merger decisions involving larger and more complex transactions. The effect of this on the competition regime as a whole in the UK is as yet unclear. One possible effect might be that there will be more appeals to the CAT, with appeals going more to the substance of the ruling rather than remedies or procedure. This may in turn reopen the question of whether the current judicial review standard in merger cases provides a sufficient level of judicial scrutiny on appeal.

Private enforcement is likely to continue its expansion, although there will be fewer 'follow-on' actions based on the decisions of EU authorities. Growth may therefore be slower than would otherwise have been the case.

More generally, outside the EU framework, the need to adhere to the current administrative enforcement structure may also be questioned. Before the CA 1998, the OFT generally did not take substantive decisions. It was more of a prosecutor, whether in relation to monopolies or mergers, where it referred, or advised ministers whether to refer, cases to the Monopolies and Mergers Commission (MMC), or in relation to the Restrictive Trade Practices Act (RTPA) where it referred agreements to the Restrictive Practices Court for adjudication. Giving the OFT the power to take infringement decisions in its own right was a concept borrowed from EU practice, to which the CMA has succeeded.

Departure from the EU framework might permit a sensible debate to take place on whether to adopt the prosecutorial system that was considered in 2013, but seen then as too radical, under which the CMA would present cases before the CAT, as the specialist competition court, for a decisions on substance and penalty.[139]

Apart from this possibly beneficial area of change, however, too much divergence in the substantive law is unlikely to bring many benefits and may do harm to the overall effectiveness of the system. It is to be hoped that wiser counsels will prevail over some of the more enthusiastic plans of those favouring an 'independent' UK competition regime.

---

[139] See earlier discussion of the ERRA 2013. This would also reflect the current position in relation to the individual criminal offence.

6 Overall Assessment and the Future

6.1 A Governmental View

In its 2019 review of the impact of the reforms introduced by the ERRA 2013,[140] the government offered a rather lukewarm assessment. In relation to antitrust enforcement generally,
it said: 'While this review has found some improvement in the speed and number of cases,
questions remain about the effectiveness of the UK's competition enforcement regime' (at
56). In relation to the concurrency arrangements, which, as we noted earlier have been a
source of perennial concern since 2003, it said: 'The improved mechanisms for institutional
co-operation have been well received. Concerns remain over the small number of CA 1998
cases being opened and findings of infringement' (at p 56). On the markets and mergers
regime, it said: 'Overall, while the evidence suggests the changes introduced under ERRA
have had a positive effect on the markets and mergers regimes, there are external factors
which suggest a need for wider reform' (at p 89). These external factors were said to be, first,
the effect on the mergers regime of leaving the EUMR framework; secondly, the overall
length of the MIR process from inception to the imposition of remedies; and, thirdly, the
apparent rigidity of the AEC test applied in phase 2 of the MIR.

The government promised a wider review of the competition and consumer regime later
in 2020,[141] although this has been delayed by the Covid-19 outbreak. In the meantime, the
government commissioned an independent review of UK competition policy from John
Penrose MP, which was due to be published in February 2021.[142] This aimed to address a
wide range of issues, including many of those identified in the ERRA review, such as the
digital challenge, but also others such as the impact of Covid-19, the speed of the competition enforcement process, and, by implication, the amount of judicial scrutiny to which the
authorities' work should be subject.

6.2 Antitrust and the Appeal System

The matter of appeals remains controversial. The idea persists that the CMA, like the OFT
before it, is in some way held back from performing its tasks by the appeal system. But the
record of the authorities on appeal to the CAT and higher courts suggests otherwise. There
are very few cases where an authority decision was not upheld in large measure by the CAT.

The last such case of any significance was *Tobacco* in 2012, but even there the OFT withdrew its case and there was no adverse judgment. The recent *Phenytoin* decision in the CAT
was only a partial annulment.[143] The issue is therefore less one of actual quality of decisions,

---

[140] *Competition Law Review: Post Implementation Review of Statutory Changes in the Enterprise and Regulatory
Reform Act 2013*, Department for Business, Energy and Industrial Strategy 2019 (ERRA Review).

[141] Announcement by Kelly Tolhurst MP: HC 11 February 2020. An earlier BEIS consultation in May 2016 on
'Options to Refine the UK Competition Regime' (including proposals to alter the CMA's panel system) was not
proceeded with.

[142] Report commissioned in September 2020 by the Chancellor of the Exchequer and the Business Secretary
to examine 'how the UK's competition policy can evolve to meet the government's aims of promoting a dynamic,
innovation driven economy which delivers for consumers and businesses across all regions and nations of the UK,
within the context of recovery from COVID-19 and the end of the transition period'.

[143] See n 47.

but more a matter of perception. The issue is now presented more as one of weight of process, the chilling of enforcement activity and in consequence less effective overall enforcement. The Tyrie letter refers to those accused of infringement using 'large teams of private sector lawyers' leading to 'often years of protracted dispute ... far removed from the concerns of ordinary consumers'.[144]

Conducting infringement cases is not easy. Given the potentially penal nature of the process, as well as the large civil liability that may follow from an adverse finding, the stakes for undertakings accused of breaching the law are high. This means the process must be robust, the evidence base for the decision must be sufficient and the analysis sound. A decision made by an authority that meets these requirements will normally not be overturned on appeal. This is not the place to settle the debate on the precise degree of judicial control that should apply to decisions of the authorities. That is likely to continue without easy resolution. What is clear is that, given that the authorities dispose of such a large concentration of enforcement power, the need for supervision by the courts remains paramount. Other aspects of accountability, for example to ministers, to Parliament, to the media, or to the public in general, whilst important, are not sufficient.

6.3 Other Issues

Other issues for consideration, not all of them identified in the ERRA review, include, first, the effect of EU exit, secondly the digital revolution, and, thirdly, for want of a better term, populism. To these must now be added a fourth, the effects of Covid-19.

We have already looked at the effects of leaving the EU and the challenge of the digital economy. In relation to the EU, we concluded that the benefits of cooperation and broad conformity outweigh any possible gains from diverging too far from the EU competition regime. In relation to the digital challenge, we have emphasized the need, alongside greater 'agility' in decision-making, to develop a coherent intellectual framework, in order to avoid the danger of the authorities simply making wrong decisions more speedily. It is crucial to know where to strike the right balance between enforcement and tolerance.

6.4 Populist Pressure

The third issue, which we touched on above, is populism. This has a virtuous aspect and a less virtuous one. On the virtuous side is the generally acknowledged need for competition law to be more readily understandable and less dependent on complex data analysis for its results in every case. On the less virtuous side is the risk of jettisoning any reliable basis for assessment and intervention.

The idea that competition law needs no basis in economics is insidious and dangerous. Taken to its conclusion it involves allowing an authority to intervene whenever it wishes, on the flimsiest of grounds. Such an authority would also be very difficult to control, either judicially or by any other means. It is no answer to say that ministers would remain in overall

---

[144] Tyrie Letter (n 19) 2.

charge. They are as vulnerable to the dangers of populism as are the authorities themselves. What is needed is a sensible balance of powers and responsibilities between different parts of the system, with the limits and controls made explicit in each case. The settlement of 1998–2003 was designed to replace an administrative system which claimed to operate 'in the public interest', under overall ministerial control. It did not work well, which is why it was replaced. It would be a pity if the same lesson had to be learned all over again. We should not discard lightly the model of decisions taken by expert authorities, principally on competition grounds, supervised by specialist courts, under general political oversight.

6.5 The CMA Proposals

Before considering the impact of Covid-19, let us pause to consider the recent CMA proposals, which are directed at many of these issues. There is of course much in the proposals with which to agree. Authorities do need to move more quickly; they must be able to explain what they do in terms that those affected by them can understand. The system has hardly begun to grapple with the emergence of the digital revolution, with new forms of market power, undertakings of unprecedented scale, and fast-moving technology.

Other aspects are more problematic. Placing a duty on authorities and the courts to 'put the consumer first' could be seen as a populist gesture, without real content. Measures to give the authorities greater power, whilst reducing their supervision by the courts, could be seen as contrary to common sense. Tidying up the array of available powers, and simplifying the institutional structure, are valid objectives, albeit requiring careful implementation. It is also easy to understand why the CMA might wish to develop the MIR into a broadly-based regime for intervention in markets; it is already a very powerful instrument. But if it is no longer anchored in competition law, it risks becoming merely a tool for arbitrary enforcement activity.

Finally, as pressure for greater enforcement activity grows, weakening judicial scrutiny of competition decisions looks most unwise. Logically, it should be made stronger rather than weaker. Competition analysis may have become too complex for its own good but that does not mean it should be discarded altogether. Instead, it must be adapted to fit the new era and then applied with vigour and purpose.

6.6 The Covid-19 Pandemic

We must finally consider a new and unexpected source of pressure. At the time of writing, the UK and the rest of the world is being swept by a pandemic which, besides great suffering, has caused large-scale economic disruption, at a level equal to, if not greater than, the 2008 crisis. The disruption of normal physical and economic activity that this has entailed serves as a further, powerful, reminder of the fragility of the current competition settlement and the market economy upon which it rests.

In one rather limited sense, the crisis has shown the inherent flexibility of the CA 1998 regime, with temporary exceptions to competition law being introduced by statutory instrument to facilitate the provision of matters such as medical services, food, and transport.[145]

---

[145] For example, the Competition Act 1998 (Health Services for Patients in England) (Coronavirus) (Public Policy Exclusion) Order 2020.

Similar measures are in place in other countries and systems. In another sense, however, the crisis raises major issues for the future. If a policy of free competition, with only limited state involvement in economic activity, encouragement of free trade, and a general prohibition on cooperation between competitors, has been shown to be incapable of anticipating, let alone dealing with, such a major shock (for example through insufficient innovation or self-sufficiency or immediate capacity to provide treatments or vaccines) it may be asked whether it will be appropriate to rely on this policy once the immediate threat has receded.

Not only may the experience of the current pandemic threaten many accepted assumptions, it may also encourage those who seek a greater role for the state in providing essential infrastructure, promoting innovation and organizing resources. As with the financial crisis of 2008, it might be said that the market economy was not ready for, and could not readily cope with, such a grave situation. If that is indeed the case, it could have profound implications for future policy.

7 Conclusions

The UK competition system has evolved significantly over the past two decades, but it is still recognizable as the system created by the legislation of twenty years ago with the aim of being as good as any in the world. All in all, that aim has been achieved, with the UK recognized as a significant player in the competition world, which was not always so in former times. That achievement ought to survive the UK's departure from the EU, although nothing should be taken for granted in these turbulent times.

Even without departure from the EU and the Covid-19 pandemic, there was already lively debate about the future direction to follow. This can only be intensified by recent events. The current system faces some serious issues, as we have described. Further, significant, change is therefore probable if not inevitable. In normal circumstances, this would follow a rational debate and be a process of evolution rather than something more disruptive, but the combination of current pressures may make this difficult. If the process of change takes a more radical turn, then it will nevertheless be important to remember that the present system has in general performed well and that the one it replaced was less than ideal. It would be foolish indeed to discard the benefits of the past twenty years' experience.

Finally, in this context, it is perhaps ironic that the MIR, comprising a legal framework for market-wide investigations, firmly rooted in competition principles, but with the important power to apply remedies, a regime that was at times seen as the poor relation of the Article 102/Chapter II prohibition, may yet prove, both in the UK and possibly also, after suitable adaptation, in the EU, to be a very effective means of tackling the 'digital challenge'.

2

Horizontal Agreements

Richard Whish QC

1 Introduction

This chapter reviews the application of the Competition Act 1998 CA 1998) to horizontal agreements since it entered into force on 1 March 2000. It is interesting today to reflect on the law that the CA 1998 replaced: between them the Fair Trading Act 1973, the Restrictive Trade Practices Act 1976, the Resale Prices Act 1976, and the Competition Act 1980 provided a somewhat eccentric—or a uniquely British—system of competition law which was at one and the same time highly complex but frustratingly ineffective. Cartels were registrable under the Restrictive Trade Practices Act, an exceedingly technical piece of legislation: in the first edition of my book[1] it required a chapter of sixty two pages to explain it; the chapter on Article 85 EEC (sic!) was fifty four pages in length. The penalty for entering into an unregistered registrable agreement was to be taken to the Restrictive Practices Court, which had the power to tell the recalcitrant firms to abandon the agreement and not to enter into another one like it: there were no other public law sanctions, although theoretically parties harmed by an illegal agreement could sue for damages. As for dominant firms, it was possible for the practices of such a firm to be referred to the Monopolies and Mergers Commission, which would decide whether the firm was doing anything that 'may be expected to operate against the public interest'; if so the Secretary of State could decide whether to ask it to change its behaviour, and sometimes he or she did so. This system could not have been more different from the EU antitrust rules, and the UK agonized for many years over whether to adopt a system based on the EU model. Not normally a country to rush into decisions, the UK decided in 1998, 25 years after joining the European Economic Community, to adopt the CA 1998, in large part replicating what are now Articles 101 and 102 TFEU; the Act invested powers, originally in the Director General of Fair Trading, then the Office of Fair Trading (OFT) and then the Competition and Markets Authority (CMA), to conduct dawn raids, to adopt infringement decisions and—importantly—to impose significant fines for infringements of the law. The UK finally had a modern system of competition law.

This is a good time to reflect on the first twenty years of the CA 1998; but also, for obvious reasons, to think forward to what competition law might look like in a post-Brexit world. This chapter looks specifically at how the CA 1998 has impacted horizontal agreements. Section 2 will specifically consider the application of the Act to cartels; section 3 looks at a particular type of cartel behaviour, namely so-called 'hub and spoke' agreements, with which the OFT was particularly concerned in the early years of the CA 1998. Section 4 will point out that, quite apart from investigating cartels, the UK competition authorities

---

[1] Richard Whish, *Competition Law* (Butterworths 1985).

Richard Whish, *Horizontal Agreements* In: *The UK Competition Regime*. Edited by: Barry Rodger, Peter Whelan, and Angus MacCulloch, Oxford University Press. © The Contributors 2021. DOI: 10.1093/oso/9780198868026.003.0002

have also closely monitored the activities of trade associations, and have often taken action to suppress 'decisions of associations of undertakings' that could be harmful to competition. Section 5 considers so-called 'pay-for-delay' agreements in the pharmaceuticals sector and, in particular, the interesting judgment of the European Court of Justice (CJEU) in the *Paroxetine* case, an Article 267 TFEU reference from the UK Competition Appeal Tribunal (CAT).

In the early years of the CA 1998 it was possible to notify an agreement to the OFT for negative clearance and/or individual exemption: this led to some interesting cases which will be discussed in section 6, together with the provisions on exemption more generally. Sections 7 and 8 will briefly consider how the concurrency arrangements have impacted horizontal agreements and the application of the CA 1998 to such agreements in Scotland. Section 9 discusses the effect of the coronavirus crisis on the application of the legislation to horizontal agreements. The final section of this chapter will make some comments about the effect of Brexit on horizontal cases in the future before some brief conclusions are offered.

2 Cartels

The entry into force of the CA 1998 meant that, for the first time in the UK, there was a system of competition law which categorically prohibited anti-competitive agreements and the abuse of dominance: indeed these two offences were named in the legislation the 'Chapter I prohibition' and the 'Chapter II prohibition', respectively. The Director General of Fair Trading was given powers similar to those of the European Commission to enforce the law, including the ability to impose significant fines. Expectations were high that there would be a significant number of cases; it was said in Parliament when the Competition Bill was being debated, and by OFT officials speaking publicly, that there were expected to be fifteen to thirty cases a year. In practice the early years of the Act were unspectacular in terms of anti-cartel enforcement action, and this led to criticism of the OFT's performance, both of the slowness of the process and the relative paucity of decisions. In due course the OFT (and the Competition Commission) were replaced by a new unitary authority, the CMA, and it was clear that the government intended that there should be more, and quicker, enforcement in the future. In this section of this chapter the OFT's record in investigating cartels will be considered; the background to the formation of the CMA will be discussed; and lastly the CMA's performance in the years since 2014 will be reviewed. There is no doubt that enforcement activity has increased in recent years. The future will be interesting because, in a post-Brexit world, it can be expected that the CMA (and the sectoral regulators, in particular the Financial Conduct Authority (FCA)) will be investigating larger cartels of a type that, until Brexit, would have been investigated by the European Commission in Brussels. We will return to this point at the end of this chapter.

2.1 2000–2014: Enforcement Action against Cartels by the OFT

2.1.1 A Slow Beginning
Anti-cartel enforcement was somewhat limited in the early years of the Competition Act 1998. This was at a time when the European Commission had become very active in

investigating cartels: for example in 2001 the fines imposed by the Commission in cartel cases totalled €1.836 billion, by far the largest amount in any one year up to that point. In 2006 the Commission's cartel fines came to €1.846 billion and in 2007 €3.334 billion fines.[2] The Commission's cases covered numerous sectors, from *Vitamins, Bleaching Chemicals* and various rubber products (for example *Synthetic Rubber* and *Chloropene Rubber*) to *Copper Fittings, Dutch Beer, Professional Videotapes*, and—a particular striking case (giving rise to follow-on actions for damages which are still active today)—*Elevators and Escalators*. Meanwhile in the UK the first decision under the CA 1998 imposing a fine on a cartel came in 2002, *Market Sharing by Arriva and FirstGroup*,[3] where those two companies were found to have shared bus routes in the Leeds area. After discounting for leniency a fine of £203,632 was imposed in this case. There is no evidence that the Boards of the UK's major public limited companies quaked with terror at the adoption of this decision. The next finding of a Chapter I prohibition in a horizontal case was similarly low-key. In *Northern Ireland Livestock and Auctioneers' Association*[4] a recommendation by the Association on the rate of commission that its members should charge for the purchase of livestock in Northern Ireland cattle marts was found to have infringed the Chapter I prohibition; no fine was imposed, not least because the infringement occurred when the beef sector was suffering as a result of so-called 'mad cow' disease that caused havoc in the agricultural sector at that time.[5]

The next cartel decision (leaving aside the very interesting hub and spoke cases, *Replica Football Kits* and *Toys and Games*, which are dealt with later in this chapter[6]) came in 2004, *West Midlands Roofing Contractors*:[7] this was a bid-rigging case in which the fines, after leniency, amounted to £297,625, reduced to £288,625 on appeal, somewhat less than the punishments being handed down in Brussels at that time! The decision in *West Midland Roofing Contractors* led to a useful judgment of the CAT in *Apex Asphalt and Paving Co Ltd v OFT*[8] on the concept of a concerted practice in the Chapter I prohibition and its application to collusive tendering. Various roofing contractors, including Apex, had been found guilty of colluding in relation to the making of tender bids for flat-roofing contracts in the West Midlands. Having set out the principles of relevance when determining whether undertakings are party to a concerted practice,[9] the CAT proceeded to apply them to a tendering process in which some of the participating undertakings had made 'cover bids', that is to say that they had submitted a price for a contract that was not intended actually to win the contract. The reason for doing this was that cover pricing maintained the appearance of competition, and indicated that the firm offering the cover price wished to continue participating in future invitations to tender. In the CAT's view a tendering process is designed to produce competition in a very structured way and bidders are sometimes required to certify that they have not had contact with competitors in the preparation of their bids. The CAT considered that where the tendering is selective rather than open to all potential bidders the

---

[2] These statistics are available on DG COMP's website www.ec.europa.eu.

[3] OFT decision of 30 January 2002.

[4] OFT decision of 3 February 2003.

[5] ibid paras 37–49.

[6] See section 3 below on hub-and-spoke cartels.

[7] OFT decision of 17 March 2004.

[8] Case 1032/1/1/04 [2005] CAT 4.

[9] ibid para 206; on the meaning of a concerted practice in section 2 CA 1998 see Richard Whish and David Bailey, *Competition Law* (9th edn, OUP 2018).

loss of independence through knowledge of the intentions of other selected bidders is particularly likely to distort competition.[10] The CAT was satisfied on the facts of the case that Apex was party to a concerted practice and upheld the finding of an infringement. Several more bid-rigging cases followed in 2005 and 2006: *Mastic Asphalt Flat-roofing Contracts in Scotland*,[11] where the fines were £87,353 after leniency; *Felt and Single Ply Roofing Contracts in Western-Central Scotland*,[12] £138,515 after leniency; and *Flat Roof and Car Park Surfacing Contracts in England and Scotland*,[13] £1.557 million after leniency. The CAT applied the reasoning in the *Apex Asphalt* case in *Makers UK Ltd v OFT*,[14] an unsuccessful appeal against the last of these decisions.

There was a second cartel decision in 2004, *UOP Desiccants*.[15] Four producers had agreed to fix or maintain prices for desiccants. Fines of £1,707,000 were imposed; on appeal one of the fines was reduced from £109,000 to £36,210.

Two further cartel decisions were adopted by the OFT in 2006. In *Stock Check Pads*[16] fines of £168,318 were imposed in the case of price fixing and market sharing of stock check pads, used by staff in cafés and restaurants to record customers' orders. In *Aluminium Spacer Bars*[17] four companies had to pay fines of £898,470 for price fixing, customer allocation, and market sharing for aluminium spacer bars used in double glazing. In a few other cases, allegations of price fixing were settled informally in the early years of the Competition Act.[18]

2.1.2 A More Productive Period

It would be reasonable to say that this early track record of the OFT in relation to cartels failed to meet the expectations that had been aroused when the legislation entered into force. However, from 2006 onwards things began to change as more complex and/or higher profile cases came along.

The decision in *Exchange of Information on Future Fees by Certain Independent Fee-Paying Schools*[19] was certainly a high profile one. Many of the most illustrious private schools[20] in the UK were found to have infringed the Chapter I prohibition. The participant schools submitted details of their current fee levels, proposed fee increases (expressed as a percentage) and the resulting intended fee levels to the bursar of one of the schools, who then circulated the information to all the other participants in a tabular form. The OFT became aware of this arrangement when two pupils at Winchester school discovered e-mails explaining these arrangements, including the phrase 'Confidential please, so that we aren't accused of being a cartel': the pupils sent these emails to the *Times* newspaper. This was not the easiest of cases for the OFT, not least given that the private schools in question were

---

[10] Case 1032/1/1/04 [2005] CAT 4 (n 8) paras 208–12.
[11] OFT decision of 7 April 2005.
[12] OFT decision of 11 July 2005.
[13] OFT decision of 23 February 2006.
[14] Case 1061/1/1/06 [2007] CAT 11, paras 103–110.
[15] OTF decision of 8 November 2004.
[16] OFT decision of 4 April 2006, upheld on appeal in Case 1067/1/1/06 *Achilles Group Ltd v OFT* [2006] CAT 24.
[17] OFT decision of 29 June 2006, upheld on appeal in Case 1072/1/1/06 *Sepia Logistics Ltd v OFT* [2007] CAT 13.
[18] See eg *Royal Institute of British Architects* Weekly Gazette of the OFT, Competition case closure summaries (17–23 May 2003); see similarly the case closures in *The Notaries Society* (30 April 2004) www.nationalarchives.gov.uk.
[19] OFT decision of 20 November 2006.
[20] Those unfamiliar with the British educational system will be forgiven for any confusion caused by the fact that, in the UK, private schools are called public schools.

charities, lacking a profit motive; furthermore they had been exempted from the Restrictive Trade Practices Act 1976, which the CA 1998 replaced. Any fines imposed would presumably have to be paid for by the parents of future pupils of the schools, and yet the theory of harm was precisely that the exchange of information was likely to result in higher fees than would have obtained absent the exchange of information. On the other hand the conduct in question appeared to be an obvious infringement of the Chapter I prohibition: could the OFT turn a 'blind eye' to a clear breach of the law? There were clear policy tensions, not made any easier by the fact that several of the OFT's board members had links with various of the schools implicated in the infringement, who may have been biased in favour of (or, depending on their experience at school, against!) a particular school. In the end a settlement was reached in which the OFT concluded that the information exchange restricted competition by object; it made no finding as to the effect of the agreement: the settling parties were concerned that a finding of effects (higher school fees) would have encouraged the parents concerned to bring follow-on actions for damages.[21] Each school agreed to pay a nominal fine of £10,000, except for Eton and Winchester which earned reductions of 50 per cent for their cooperation with the investigation; the schools also agreed to make *ex gratia* payments of £3 million into a trust fund to benefit pupils who attended the schools during the period of the information exchange.[22] This case was sufficiently interesting to earn its own entry on Wikipedia.[23]

The OFT investigated information-sharing agreements on several occasions after the *Independent Fee-Paying Schools* decision. The hub-and-spoke cases, which all concern the exchange of information, are dealt with in section 3 below. An interesting decision was adopted in *Loans to large professional services firms*.[24] The OFT concluded that Barclays Bank and the Royal Bank of Scotland had participated in an unlawful agreement and/or concerted practice between October 2007 and at least February or March 2008. The unlawful conduct took the form of the provision of confidential, commercially sensitive pricing information by RBS to Barclays during the course of a number of contacts over a period of months: Barclays did not provide information to RBS. Some of the information was generic, some customer-specific. The OFT said in paragraph 3 of its decision that: 'By the contacts between them, the Parties substituted practical cooperation for the risks of competition'.

Barclays Bank had blown the whistle and was therefore granted immunity from paying a fine. RBS was fined £28.59 million; this included a 15 per cent reduction in the fine that it would otherwise have paid, since RBS admitted the infringement and settled the case.

The decision was of interest because it involved the one-way provision of information by RBS to Barclays. In paragraphs 234 to 241 of the decision, the OFT referred to jurisprudence of the Luxembourg Courts and to the judgment of the CAT in *JJB/Allsports v OFT*[25], where it said that: '[e]ven the unilateral disclosure of future pricing intentions can constitute a concerted practice if the effect of disclosure is in fact to reduce uncertainty in the market place'.[26]

---

[21] *Exchange of Information on Future Fees by Certain Independent Fee-Paying Schools*, CA98/05/2006, paras 1348–58.
[22] OFT Press Releases 165/06 (22 November 2006) and 182/06 (21 December 2006).
[23] See 'Independent school fee fixing scandal' on Wikipedia.
[24] OFT decision of 20 January 2011.
[25] *JJB Sports plc and Allsports Ltd v Office of Fair Trading* [2004] CAT 17.
[26] ibid para 658.

The OFT explained why there was an agreement and/or concerted practice on the facts of this particular case in paragraphs 287 to 321 of the decision. There were generic contacts, in which RBS informed Barclays about its general pricing policy: this information high-lighted to Barclays that there was less downward pressure on its prices than might otherwise have been expected. The information was considered to be sufficiently important that it was disseminated within Barclays. Information was also provided about specific loan products for Savills and Knight Frank, two large international property consultancies. Flavour was added to the decision by the OFT's description of the locations at which RBS provided the information in question to Barclays: at a bowling event arranged by an accountancy firm; at a seminar at a law firm; during a lunch at All Bar One in the City; in O'Neill's bar in London Wall; and at a dinner arranged by an accountancy firm.

Another case involving information exchange occurred in the car insurance sector. In *Motor Car Insurers*[27] the OFT accepted commitments under section 31A CA 1998 from private motor insurers, whereby pricing information would be exchanged through an IT product only if it was at least six months old, anonymized, aggregated across at least five in-surers, and already 'live' in the insurance policies sold by brokers.

Construction Recruitment Forum[28] was a different kind of case. Here fines of £39.27 mil-lion were imposed for price fixing in conjunction with a collective boycott: the noticeable feature of this decision was that the fines were much higher than in any previous case. On appeal the CAT held that a collective boycott of a new entrant was among the most serious kind of infringement;[29] but the fines were significantly reduced to £6,900,000 on appeal due to errors in the OFT's calculation of the fines.

In 2009, the *Construction bid-rigging*[30] decision imposed fines of £129.2 million on 103 undertakings involved in unlawful cover pricing and other bid-rigging activities. The de-cision followed the largest investigation ever undertaken under the Competition Act. It also made use of a novel 'fast-track offer', whereby fines for undertakings implicated in bid-rigging (that had not already applied for leniency) were reduced in return for cooperation. On appeal the CAT upheld the decision in four cases,[31] partially annulled the decision in four cases,[32] and reduced the fines in twenty cases.[33] A report in June 2010 found that there had been significant improvements in awareness of competition law and changes in behav-iour since the *Construction bid-rigging* decision.[34]

A very high profile case arose in *Fuel Surcharges*.[35] From the OFT's point of view this was just the kind of case that it needed to run: a consumer-facing product, cartelized by

---

[27] OFT decision of 2 December 2011.

[28] OFT decision of 29 September 2009.

[29] Cases 1140/1/1/09 etc *Eden Brown Ltd v OFT* [2011] CAT 8.

[30] Decision of 21 September 2009.

[31] Case 1121/1/1/09 *Durkan Holdings Ltd v OFT* [2011] CAT 6, paras 13–92; Case 1126/1/1/09 *ISG Pearce Ltd v OFT* [2011] CAT 10, paras 11–36; Case 1120/1/1/09 *Quarmby Construction Co Ltd v OFT* [2011] CAT 11, paras 8–140; Case 1124/1/1/09 *North Midland Construction plc v OFT* [2011] CAT 14, paras 35–63.

[32] Case 1121/1/1/09 *Durkan Holdings Ltd v OFT* [2011] CAT 6, paras 93–125; Case 1118/1/1/09 *GMI Construction Holdings plc v OFT* [2011] CAT 12; Case 1122/1/1/09 *AH Willis & Sons Ltd v OFT* [2011] CAT 13; Case 1124/1/1/09 *North Midland Construction plc v OFT* [2011] CAT 14, paras 14–34.

[33] See Cases 1114/1/1/09 etc *Kier Group plc v OFT* [2011] CAT 3; Cases 1117/1/1/09 etc *GF Tomlinson Building Ltd v OFT* [2011] CAT 7; Cases 1125/1/1/09 etc *Barrett Estate Services Ltd v OFT* [2011] CAT 9; Case 1121/1/1/09 *Durkan Holdings Ltd v OFT* [2011] CAT 6, paras 126–180; Case 1124/1/1/09 *North Midland Construction plc v OFT* [2011] CAT 14, paras 64–111.

[34] *Evaluation of the impact of the OFT's investigation into bid rigging in the construction industry*, OFT 1240, see also OFT Press Release 60/10, 4 June 2010.

[35] *Airline passenger fuel surcharges for long-haul passenger flights*, OFT decision of 19 April 2012.

well-known, household names. British Airways and Virgin Atlantic were found to have co-ordinated their pricing through the exchange of commercially sensitive information about their long-haul passenger fuel surcharges between August 2004 and January 2006: BA agreed to pay a reduced penalty of £58.5 million after admitting the infringement;[36] Virgin blew the whistle and therefore was not fined. The edge was taken off the OFT's investigation in this case when the associated criminal prosecution of four BA employees in Southwark Crown Court collapsed.[37]

The OFT adopted further decisions imposing fines in cartel cases in the period just before its abolition and the creation of the CMA. In March of 2013, it adopted five decisions imposing fines of £2.8 million for arrangements to share markets, coordinate prices, and exchange information in relation to Mercedes-Benz commercial vehicles.[38] Mercedes-Benz was found to have acted as a 'facilitator' to one of its dealers' infringements. In *Access control and alarm systems*[39] fines of £53,410 were imposed for collusive tendering, including a reduction of 20 per cent after settlement with one of the parties. In *Supply of care home medicines* a fine of £370,226 was imposed on Hamsard for agreeing with Lloyds Pharmacy to share the market for prescription medicines supplied to care homes in England.[40]

2.2 Criticism of Under-enforcement and the Establishment of the CMA

Even though there was an increase in enforcement on the part of the OFT, both generally and specifically in relation to horizontal agreements, from about 2006 onwards, there continued to be a perception that the new system was not functioning as well as had been expected. The National Audit Office (NAO) conducted two reviews of the OFT's performance, in 2005[41] and 2009.[42] The NAO's 2009 Report noted that the UK competition regime was well regarded internationally. However, it was not uncritical of the UK competition authorities' performance, and considered that the system needed to be more flexible and to make better use of its resources; that the development of case-law needed to be strengthened; and that the sectoral regulators should consider referring more markets for review. Partly in response to this criticism, the Enterprise and Regulatory Reform Act 2013 (ERRA 2013) made significant changes to UK competition law, which included the replacement of the OFT and the Competition Commission by the CMA. It was clear that the government intended that the regime should be strengthened and that decisions should be adopted more speedily; it was also intended that there should be greater predictability for business.

The CMA became responsible for the enforcement of competition law in the UK on 1 April 2014. Its record of enforcement action against cartels will be considered in section 2.3 below. At this stage it is worth referring to a third report by the NAO published in February

---

[36] BA's fine had originally been agreed at £121.5 million, but was renegotiated following criticism of the OFT's fining methodology in various CAT appeals.

[37] OFT Press Release 93/08 (7 August 2008); on criminal enforcement see Angus MacCulloch, 'The Quiet Decline of the UK Cartel Offence: A Principled Victory in the Face of Practical Failure', ch 13 in this volume.

[38] OFT decisions of 27 March 2013.

[39] OFT decision of 6 December 2013.

[40] OFT decision of 20 March 2014.

[41] *The Office of Fair Trading: Enforcing competition in markets*, HC 593, 2005–2006 (17 November 2005).

[42] *The Office of Fair Trading: Progress report on maintaining competition in markets*, HC 127, 2008–2009 (5 March 2009).

2016, *UK competition authorities: the UK competition regime.*[43] This report set out some key facts about the UK competition regime, including that the estimated annual direct spending on it was £66 million in the preceding year and that the CMA's estimate of the annual direct benefit to consumers of its work was £745 million: assuming that the CMA's estimate was correct, this return on taxpayers' investment was considerable. Three other key facts noted by the NAO were that five non-criminal competition enforcement cases were concluded in 2014; that no criminal ones were; and that 23 per cent of businesses felt that they knew competition law well: this, of course, is a way of saying that 77 per cent of businesses felt that they did not.

The NAO's 2016 Report found that the newly-created CMA had taken significant steps to tackle the failings identified in previous reports, and that action had been taken to improve the detection of anti-competitive behaviour and to build a pipeline of cases. At the time of its Report, the NAO said that there had yet to be a substantial flow of new decisions and also noted that awareness of competition law, especially among small—and medium-sized businesses, was low. Key recommendations of the NAO's 2016 Report included that the CMA should take further action to step up the flow of successful enforcement cases.

In fairness to the OFT and the CMA, it is reasonable to point out that, during the years since the CA 1998 came into force, many UK undertakings have been involved in significant cartels that fell within the jurisdiction of the European Commission;[44] it is not surprising therefore that several of the domestic investigations were of a fairly parochial nature.[45]

2.3 2014–2020: Enforcement Action against Cartels by the CMA

The CMA has adopted numerous infringement decisions in a variety of sectors in relation to horizontal agreements since April 2014, far exceeding the output in any comparable period during the OFT years. Its decision in *Paroxetine* will be discussed in section 4 below. In 2015, in *Property sales and lettings*[46] the CMA imposed fines totalling £735,000 on an association of estate agents in Hampshire, three of its members and a newspaper publisher for agreeing to prevent estate agents from advertising their fees or discounts in the local property newspaper. The CMA found that the trade association had been used by its members 'as a vehicle to facilitate the contractual arrangements on behalf of each of its members'.[47] Another decision in 2015 was *Conduct in the opthamology sector* in which the CMA imposed a fine of £382,500 on the Consultant Eye Surgeons Partnership,[48] which represented thirty-seven partnerships of ophthalmologists who were specialists in medical and surgical procedures. CEPS was guilty of various infringements of the Chapter I prohibition: recommending its members to refuse to accept lower fees offered by an insurer; circulating detailed price lists for ophthalmic procedures such as cataract surgery, which made it harder for insurers and patients to obtain lower prices; and facilitating the sharing of consultants'

---

[43] HC 737, Session 2015–16 (5 February 2016).
[44] For further discussion see section 10 below.
[45] See Barry J Rodger, 'Application of the Domestic and EU Antitrust Prohibitions: an Analysis of the UK Competition Authority's Enforcement Practice', (2020) 8 Journal of Antitrust Enforcement 86.
[46] CMA decision of 8 May 2015.
[47] ibid para 5.57.3.
[48] *Conduct in the ophthalmology sector*, CMA decision of 20 August 2015.

future pricing and business intentions which enabled them to align their behaviour. An interesting feature of this case was that CESP received a discount of 10 per cent on the fine it would have paid specifically because of its commitment to adopt a comprehensive competition law compliance programme. After each of these decisions the CMA communicated with the sectors concerned to raise their awareness of competition law.[49]

There were three cases in 2016. In *Online sales of posters and frames*[50] the CMA imposed a fine of £163,371 on Trod Ltd for agreeing with GB eye Ltd that they would not undercut each other's prices for posters and frames sold on Amazon's UK website. GB eye Ltd was not fined as it had reported the cartel to the CMA. This was the first case in which a company director was disqualified under the powers conferred by the Enterprise Act 2002.[51] The case was also of interest because Trod and GB eye had used automated re-pricing software to implement their agreement on prices; the CMA warned software providers that they themselves risked infringing competition law by supplying this kind of software.[52] In an OFGEM decision of 2019 a software provider, Dyball Associates, was fined for doing so.[53]

In *Galvanised Steel Tanks*[54] the CMA adopted two decisions. The first one condemned a price-fixing and market-sharing cartel and the fines were £2.6 million. The second decision found that three members of the cartel had exchanged their current and future pricing intentions with another company, Balmoral Tanks, at a single meeting in July 2012, which was secretly recorded by the CMA. Balmoral Tanks had been invited to join the cartel, but had declined to do so; nevertheless it was fined £130,000 for participating in an unlawful exchange of information on a single occasion. The CMA applied the EU precedent of *T-Mobile*[55] that a concerted practice can exist where information is exchanged on one occasion; its decision was upheld on appeal to the CAT[56] and to the Court of Appeal.[57] One individual in this case pleaded guilty to committing the criminal cartel offence; two others pleaded not guilty and were acquitted following a jury trial.[58]

In *Conduct in the modelling sector*[59] the CMA imposed fines totalling £1.53 million on five model agencies and a trade association for agreeing to fix minimum prices and a common approach to pricing. The CMA cooperated with the French and Italian competition authorities during this investigation; both authorities also penalized cartels in the modelling services sector.

---

[49] In relation to estate agents see the CMA's open letters to the property industry and to newspaper publishers of 3 June 2015; in relation to medical professionals see *Medical Practitioners: advice on competition law* (3 December 2015).

[50] CMA decision of 12 August 2016.

[51] CMA Press Release (1 December 2016); the disqualifications in the earlier *Marine Hoses* case occurred because the directors in question had committed the criminal cartel offence. See Peter Whelan, 'The Emerging Contribution of Director Disqualification in UK Competition Law', ch 11 in this volume.

[52] CMA Press Release (7 November 2016).

[53] See section 7 below.

[54] *Galvanised steel tanks for water storage main cartel infringement*, CMA decision of 19 December 2016 and *Galvanised steel tanks for water storage information exchange infringement*, CMA decision of 19 December 2016.

[55] Case C-8/08 *T-Mobile Netherlands* EU:C:2009:343, paras 58–59.

[56] Case 1277/1/12/17 *Balmoral Tanks v CMA* [2017] CAT 23.

[57] [2019] EWCA Civ 162.

[58] CMA Press Release of 14 September 2015. See Angus MacCulloch, 'The Quiet Decline of the UK Cartel Offence: A Principled Victory in the Face of Practical Failure', ch 13 in this volume.

[59] CMA decision of 16 December 2016.

In 2017, there were three cartel cases. In *Supply of products to the furniture industry*[60] fines were imposed on members of two distinct bilateral cartels that involved the allocation of customers, bid-rigging, and the exchange of confidential and commercially important information. In *Residential estate agency services*[61] the CMA decided that six Somerset estate agents had participated in a price-fixing cartel in relation to estate agency services. One estate agent was not fined because it had blown the whistle; the CMA imposed fines totalling £370,084 on the other five estate agents, four of whom admitted the infringement, while the fifth denied that it was guilty of an infringement, but did not appeal to the CAT.[62] Two individuals gave director disqualification undertakings in this case. A third, Michael Martin, declined to do so: this led to a four day hearing in the Insolvency and Companies Court in June 2020 (the first case of this kind to be contested) and led to a judgment on 3 July in which he was disqualified for a period of seven years and ordered to pay the CMA's costs.[63] Fines of £1.71 million were imposed for geographical market sharing in *Cleanroom laundry services and products*.[64]

There was one decision in 2018, *Supply of solid fuel and charcoal products*,[65] in which fines of £3.4 million were imposed on two firms that had rigged their responses to competitive tenderers from June 2010 to February 2011 for the supply of those products to Tesco and Sainsbury's supermarkets.

In 2019, the CMA found that six office fit-out firms had engaged in cover bidding; five firms were fined £7 million; a sixth was granted immunity.[66] Six individuals gave director disqualification undertakings in this case.[67] *Concrete drainage products* was a hybrid settlement case in which the CMA imposed fines of £36 million for price fixing and market sharing and sharing competitively sensitive information.[68] In 2019, the CMA penalized another cartel in the real property sector, *Residential estate agency services in Berkshire*.[69] Fines of £605,519 were imposed on three estate agents (a fourth was granted immunity) for agreeing to fix and maintain a minimum level of commission fees for a period from September 2008 to May 2015. This was a hybrid settlement, where one of the four firms contested liability. Two individuals gave director disqualification undertakings;[70] disqualification proceedings have been commenced against two others in Northern Ireland.[71]

In *Privately funded opthamology services*[72] the CMA imposed fines of £1.2 million on Sprie Healthcare Ltd (as a facilitator) and six ophthalmologists for fixing the prices of initial consultation fees for self-pay patients at a hospital in the north of England. Interestingly in this case the natural (as opposed to legal) persons were fined, since each ophthalmologist

---

[60] *Supply of products to the furniture industry (drawer fronts)*, CMA decision of 27 March 2017 and *Supply of products to the furniture industry (drawer wraps)*, CMA decision of 27 March 2017; Thomas Armstrong (Timber) Ltd was a member of both cartels.

[61] CMA decision of 31 May 2017.

[62] *Residential estate agency services*, CMA decision of 31 May 2017; on 10 April 2018, the CMA announced that two individuals had been disqualified from acting as company directors as a result of this infringement of the Competition Act 1998.

[63] *CMA v Martin* [2020] EWHC 1751 (Ch).

[64] CMA decision of 14 December 2017.

[65] CMA decision of 28 March 2018.

[66] CMA decision of 31 May 2019.

[67] CMA Press Releases of 10 May 2019 and 29 July 2019.

[68] CMA decision of 23 October 2019.

[69] CMA decision of 17 December 2019.

[70] CMA Press Release of 31 March 2020.

[71] CMA Press Release of 16 January 2020.

[72] CMA decision of 1 July 2020.

was an undertaking for the purposes of the Chapter I prohibition. One ophthalmologist was not fined as he was the whistleblower.

In the course of 2020, the CMA imposed fines in relation to two pharmaceutical products for cartel behaviour. In the case of *Nortriptyline*[73] the CMA adopted two decisions. The first involved a market-sharing agreement between King Pharmaceuticals and Auden Mckenzie/Accord-UK Ltd for the supply of nortriptyline tables to a large pharmaceutical wholesaler. Kings was fined £75,573 and Auden £1,882,238. Auden also agreed to pay the NHS £1 million. In the second decision fines were imposed for the exchange of commercially sensitive information between King Pharmaceuticals (fined £75,573), Lexon (UK) Ltd (fined £1,220,383), and Alissa Healthcare Research Ltd (fined £174,912). All the parties settled except Lexon, which has appealed to the CAT.[74] The fine on King represented 10 per cent of its turnover, the maximum fine that could be imposed under the CA 1998. Two individuals gave director disqualification undertakings.[75] The other case in the pharmaceutical sector was *Fludrocortisone*,[76] in which fines of £2.3 million were imposed for market sharing by three firms. The CMA has said that Aspen has paid £8 million to the NHS 'to help resolve the CMA's competition concerns' in relation to fludrocortisone. One individual has given a director disqualification undertaking.[77] The CMA announced in June 2020 that two of the UK's largest suppliers of rolled lead have admitted to a market sharing agreement and that they may face fines of £11 million.[78]

The CMA deserves credit for its anti-cartel enforcement since 2014. It was required and expected to increase its enforcement activities, and it has responded accordingly. Not only have there been more cases, but the CMA has been active in proceeding against directors of recalcitrant firms, securing numerous company director disqualifications[79] including, in the *Somerset estate agents* case, the first-ever order imposed by a court. The CMA has also been active in communicating its anti-cartel programme, for example by following up in specific sectors, such as estate agency and the medical profession, after the completion of cases and by running a 'Stop cartels' campaign, which began in October 2018. At the time of writing the CMA is involved in several cartel investigations, for example in relation to *Rolled lead*, *Groundwork products*, *Financial services*, and *Pharmaceuticals*. It is reasonable to expect that, in the years ahead, there will be many more cartel decisions, and that, as a result of Brexit, some of them will relate to larger cartels than was the case during EU membership.

3 Hub and Spoke Cartels

The relatively low level of enforcement action against cartels in the early years of the CA 1998 was noted in section 2.1 above. However, the OFT did achieve success in two cases in 2003, *Football Shirts*[80] and *Toys and Games*[81] in which it established the existence of hub

---

[73] CMA decisions of 4 March 2020.
[74] Case 1344/1/12/20 *Lexon (UK) Ltd v CMA*, not yet decided.
[75] CMA Press Release of 17 July 2020.
[76] CMA decision of 9 July 2020.
[77] CMA Press Release of 4 June 2020.
[78] CMA Press Release of 12 June 2020.
[79] See Peter Whelan, 'The Emerging Contribution of Director Disqualification in UK Competition Law', ch 11 in this volume.
[80] *Football Kit price-fixing*, OFT decision of 1 August 2003.
[81] *Hasbro UK Ltd/Argos Ltd/Littlewoods Ltd*, OFT decision of 2 December 2003.

and spoke cartels. These decisions were for the most part upheld on appeal, although the CAT reduced the fines that the OFT had imposed on Umbro, Manchester United, and JJB Sports; the fine on Allsports Ltd was increased on appeal, as it emerged that that firm had not been as cooperative as it had been given credit for by the OFT.[82] A third hub-and-spoke case followed in 2011 in relation to *Dairy Products*;[83] this decision was partly upheld on appeal.[84] These three cases put the OFT at the forefront of enforcement against hub and spoke conspiracies. Some national competition authorities within the EU have taken an interest in such cases in recent years.[85]

3.1 What Is Meant by a Hub and Spoke Conspiracy?

The idea of a hub and spoke cartel is that laws that prohibit collusion between competitors can be infringed where A, a competitor of C, achieves a collusive outcome as a consequence of contacts with B, the 'hub'.[86] A horizontal agreement or concerted practice is established between A and C as a result of common vertical links that each has with B. The Court of Appeal has pointed out that 'even indirect and isolated instances of contact between competitors may be sufficient to infringe Article 101, if their object is to promote artificial conditions of competition in the market'.[87]

A hub-and-spoke cartel can be presented in diagrammatic form:

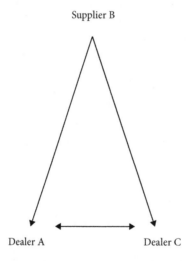

Supplier B

Dealer A   Dealer C

---

[82] In the CAT the *Football Shirts* appeals were Case 1019/1/1/03 *Umbro Holdings Ltd v OFT* and Case 1020/1/1/03 *Manchester United plc v OFT* [2004] CAT 22; and Cases 1021/1/1/03 and 1022/1/1/03 *JJB Sports plc and Allsports Ltd v Office of Fair Trading* [2004] CAT 17 and [2004] CAT 22; the appeals in the case of *Toys* were Cases 1014/1/1/03 and 1015/1/1/03 *Argos Ltd v OFT* and *Littlewoods Ltd v OFT* [2004] CAT 24. In the Court of Appeal there was one single judgment for both cases, [2006] EWCA Civ 1318.

[83] *Dairy retail price initiatives*, OFT decision of 10 August 2011.

[84] Case 1188/1/1/11 [2012] CAT 31.

[85] See section 3.4 below.

[86] See Oke Odudu, 'Indirect Information Exchange: The Constituent Elements of Hub and Spoke Collusion' (2011) 7(2) European Competition Journal 205.

[87] *KME Yorkshire Ltd v Toshiba Carrier UK Ltd* [2012] EWCA Civ 1190, para 19.

3.2 The UK Cases: *Football Shirts* and *Toys and Games*

In *Football Shirts* and *Toys and Games* the OFT found bilateral agreements between B and A and between B and C. The OFT also found that there were concerted practices between A, B, and C which, as between A and C, were horizontal rather than vertical. At no time was there any direct communication between A and C. These horizontal concerted practices had come about as a result of indirect contact between A and C through the medium of B.

Applying the judgment of the Court of Appeal in *Football Shirts* and *Toys and Games*,[88] in *Dairy Products* the CAT held that a concerted practice between A, B, and C exists if five conditions are met:

- retailer A discloses to supplier B its future pricing intentions
- A may be taken to intend that B will make use of that information to influence market conditions by passing that information to other retailers (of whom C is, or may be, one)
- B passes that information to C
- C may be taken to know the circumstances in which the information was disclosed by A to B and
- C uses the information in determining its own future pricing intentions.[89]

The CAT explained that it is necessary to prove each retailer's 'state of mind' to establish that discussions between a supplier and a retailer have gone beyond normal commercial dealings, for example as to the retailer's profit margin or the terms of trade, and have instead given rise to an unlawful, albeit indirect, 'horizontal element'.[90] The absence of any legitimate commercial reason for a disclosure by retailer A of its future pricing intentions to supplier B may indicate the requisite state of mind.[91] The CAT left open whether a lesser state of mind, such as recklessness as to transmission or receipt of A's pricing intentions, would be sufficient.[92]

These cases mean that an undertaking in the position of B must take care to ensure that it does not, consciously or unconsciously, act as the facilitator of horizontal collusion between A and C. Whilst bilateral discussions between a supplier and a dealer of a purely vertical nature about matters such as likely retail prices, profit margins, and wholesale prices are permissible, suppliers must be cautious about how they seek to influence the pricing behaviour of their retailers. Retailers, for their part, must be careful about telling suppliers about their intention to maintain or increase retail prices: an authority may consider that A anticipated that B would disclose that information to C, opening up the possibility of a hub-and-spoke infringement.

---

[88] [2006] EWCA Civ 1318, para 141.
[89] Case 1188/1/1/11 [2012] CAT 31, para 57.
[90] See paras 65–66 of the CAT judgment; see also para 106 of the Court of Appeal's judgment in *Football Shirts* and *Toys and Games*.
[91] [2012] CAT 31, para 72.
[92] ibid paras 73 and 350–54.

3.3 Dairy Products

In 2011, the OFT adopted another decision on hub and spoke conspiracy, *Dairy retail price initiatives*.[93] The OFT concluded that Tesco had participated in two separate concerted practices with other retailers, and imposed a fine of £10.4 million. Tesco appealed to the CAT, which handed down a judgment on liability on 20 December 2012.[94] The OFT had identified nine different concerted practices in relation to the price of cheese: each practice was termed a 'strand'. The CAT dismissed three of Tesco's appeals, in relation to strands 2, 3, and 7, but upheld the appeals in relation to the other strands. The OFT and Tesco subsequently agreed that the fine should be reduced from £10.4 million to £6.5 million.[95]

3.4 Hub and Spoke Agreements in Other Jurisdictions

Within the EU the OFT was a pioneer of hub and spoke cases. It is interesting to note that the Belgian Competition Authority brought a hub and spoke case in relation to perfumes, hygiene products, and drugstores in Belgium. In a settlement decision of 22 June 2015, fines were imposed totalling more than €174 million on a number of producers, such as Colgate-Palmolive, GlaxoSmithKline, and Procter & Gamble, and retailers such as Carrefour, Delhaize, and Makro Cash and Carry.[96]

In passing, it should be pointed out that a hub and spoke conspiracy can occur where the hub, B, is the dealer and A and C are suppliers. Two US cases provide good examples of this. In *Toys 'R' Us, Inc v Federal Trade Commission* the retailer, a case decided in 2000, Toys 'R' Us communicated a policy to its suppliers, the toy manufacturers, that it, Toys 'R' Us, did not wish the manufacturers to supply 'warehouse clubs'—that is to say cut-price dealers. The toy manufacturers had an incentive and a desire to supply the warehouse clubs as this would increase sales and diversify their retail base. However, they did limit such sales, and the evidence showed that this was after Toys 'R' Us had provided assurances that this was a policy that every other toy manufacturer would abide by. Thus, horizontal collusion between the manufacturers was established as a result of the vertical discussions that took place between each manufacturer and the hub, Toys 'R' Us.[97]

In a similar case in 2015, *US v Apple Inc.*, the US Court of Appeals for the Second Circuit dismissed an appeal by Apple and two publishers of e-books against a finding by the US District Court for the Southern District of New York that there was a hub and spoke conspiracy between five major publishing companies orchestrated by Apple, the hub in this case.[98] The Supreme Court refused to allow an appeal in this case.

The Portuguese Competition Authority has more recently announced that it has sent statements of objections to supermarket chains and suppliers in hub and spoke cases in the beverages, bread and cakes, and wine and alcoholic drinks sectors.[99]

---

[93] OFT decision of 26 July 2011.
[94] CAT 1188/1/1/11 *Tesco Stores Ltd v OFT* [2012] CAT 31.
[95] CAT Order of 26 February 2013.
[96] The decision is available at www.belgiancompetition.be.
[97] The case can be found at www.ftc.gov.
[98] The case can be found at www.justice.gov/atr.
[99] See the ADC's Press Releases 2/2019 (22 March 2019); 9/2020 (25 June 2020); and 10/2020 (4 July 2020).

4 Trade Associations

In considering the application of the CA 1998 to cartels, it is worth bearing in mind that the Chapter I prohibition applies to decisions of undertakings as well as to agreements and concerted practices between undertakings. From the earliest days of the CA 1998 the OFT and, subsequently, the CMA have monitored the behaviour of trade associations to ensure their compliance with competition law. The decision in *Northern Ireland Livestock and Auctioneers' Association*[100] was noted in section 2.1.1 above. In 2002, the Standard Conditions of the Film Distributors' Association were found to be a decision of an association of undertakings; the offending clauses that limited the ability of cinemas to determine their own prices and promotional activities were dropped.[101] In *Rural Broadband Wayleaves*[102] a recommendation by the National Farmers' Union as to the rate to be charged by landowners for the grant of wayleaves for the provision of broadband services in rural areas was held to be a decision of an association of undertakings and the OFT issued a 'Short-form opinion' on the circumstances in which the Chapter I prohibition might be infringed. In both *Conduct in the ophthalmology sector*[103] and *Conduct in the modelling sector*[104] trade associations were fined, in the former case the Consultant Eye Surgeons Partnership and in the latter the Association of Model Agents.

In *Showmen's Guild of Great Britain*[105] the CMA accepted legally-binding commitments from the Guild that would open up the market for non-member showmen to participate in fairs and reduce restrictions on rival fairs opening near to the Guild's fares. Files have been closed in several other cases concerning allegedly exclusionary rules of sports and professional associations, often following amendments to ensure open, non-discriminatory access to those associations.[106].

5 Paroxetine

As noted in section 2.3 above, the CMA has recently punished cartels in the pharmaceutical sector, in the cases of *Nortriptylene* and *Fludrocortisone*. It has also fined Pfizer Inc and Flynn Ltd for charging excessive prices, contrary to Article 102 TFEU and the Chapter II prohibition, for a drug known as *Phenytoin*, which is used in the treatment of epilepsy; after appeals to the CAT and the Court of Appeal the CMA is now reconsidering the case.[107] The CMA has also adopted an infringement decision in relation to a so-called 'pay-for-delay' agreement in the pharmaceutical sector. In pay-for-delay cases the owner of a patent, faced

---

[100] OFT decision of 3 February 2003.

[101] *Notification by the Film Distributors' Association of its Standard Conditions for Licensing the Commercial Exhibition of Films*, OFT decision of 1 February 2002, paras 43–45.

[102] Short-form Opinion of 23 August 2012, paras 7.3 and 7.7.

[103] CMA decision of 20 August 2015.

[104] CMA decision of 16 December 2016; in this case the CMA liaised with the French and the Italian NCAs that carried out parallel investigations in the modelling services sector.

[105] CMA decision of 26 October 2017.

[106] See eg *English Rugby Ltd*, case closure of 6 August 2003; *Glasgow Solicitors Property Centre*, OFT Press Release 154/03 (1 December 2003); *Bar Council of Northern Ireland*, OFT Press Release 02/11 (5 January 2011).

[107] CMA decision of 7 December 2016, set aside by the CAT in Cases 1275/1/12/16 and 1276/1/12/17 *Pfizer Inc v CMA*; the Court of Appeal's judgment, [2020] EWCA Civ 339, partly allowed the CMA's appeal and remitted the matter to the CMA.

with a challenge to the validity of its patent by a producer of generic drugs intending to enter the market, settles the dispute or litigation on the basis that the generic company withdraws the challenge, agrees not to enter the market independently of the patent owner, and receives in return a significant transfer of value (in cash or in kind) from the patent owner.

5.1 The CMA's Finding

In *Paroxetine*,[108] a prescription-only anti-depressant medicine, the CMA found that settlement agreements between GlaxoSmithKline and two generic producers unjustifiably delayed the latters' efforts to enter the market independently of Glaxo, and had the effect (as well as the object) of restricting competition. A fine of £84.2 million was imposed on Pfizer; Flynn was fined £5.2 million.[109] On appeal the CAT referred a series of questions to the ECJ: this was a sensible course to take, since the ECJ was also dealing with two appeals against European Commission decisions, *Lundbeck*[110] and *Servier*,[111] in which substantially the same issues were under consideration. Of particular interest to the subject-matter of this chapter was the question whether the pay-for-delay agreements in this case were between actual or potential competitors: that is to say, were they horizontal agreements? If so, a further question was whether such agreements could be restrictive of competition by object.

5.2 The Judgment of the ECJ

5.2.1 Actual or Potential Competition

Assuming that two or more undertakings are already operating on the same relevant product or geographic market, it is clear that they are actual competitors and that therefore there is a horizontal relationship between them. However, the position is less clear where an undertaking not currently active on the market might at some point in the future enter it. What factors are relevant, and how plausible does entry by that undertaking have to be, before it can be regarded as a potential, and therefore a horizontal, competitor? This is a subject on which there is relatively little jurisprudence. In *Generics (UK) Ltd v Competition and Markets Authority*[112] ECJ handed down a very helpful judgment as its response to the CAT's Article 267 reference in the *Paroxetine* case. It will be applied in the future; it is not limited to the issue of pay-for-delay agreements. The ECJ held that, in order to determine whether an undertaking was a potential competitor of one or more other undertakings already present on the market: 'it must be determined whether there are *real and concrete possibilities* of the former joining that market and competing with one or more of the latter'.[113]

---

[108] CMA decision of 12 February 2016.

[109] Each of Pfizer and Flynn was also held to have abused a dominant position contrary to TFEU, art 102 and the Chapter II prohibition.

[110] Commission decision of 19 June 2013, on appeal to the ECJ Cases C-591/16 P *Lundbeck v Commission*, not yet decided.

[111] Commission decision of 9 July 2014, on appeal to the ECJ Cases C-201/19, not yet decided.

[112] Case C-307/18 EU:C:2020:52.

[113] Case C-307/18, EU:C:2020:52, para 36, citing Case C-234/89 *Delimitis* EU:C:1991:91, para 21 (emphasis added).

The Court added that it would be insufficient to establish a potential competitive relationship from the 'purely hypothetical possibility' of entry; but equally that it was not necessary to demonstrate with certainty that a manufacturer would actually enter the market and that, having entered, it would be capable of retaining its place on the market.[114] Rather, the assessment of potential competition must be carried out: 'having regard to the structure of the market and the economic and legal context within which it operates'.[115]

It is also relevant to consider the perception of the undertaking already on the market: if it perceives an undertaking outside the market to be a potential entrant, that may give rise to competitive pressure on the undertaking already established there.[116]

One question in such cases is whether the existence of the patent means, in itself, that the generic company cannot be considered a potential competitor of the patent owner, since it is unlawful to infringe a valid patent. The ECJ held that it is necessary to determine, first, whether the generic company has taken sufficient preparatory steps to enable it to enter the market, and, secondly, whether any barriers to entry are insurmountable.[117] In the context of the pharmaceutical sector, where challenges by generic companies to the validity of patents is commonplace and where generic entry does occur, the patent did not in itself mean that there was an insurmountable barrier to entry by generic companies.[118] Furthermore the facts that there was a genuine dispute between the parties, the outcome of which was uncertain,[119] and that they had entered into settlement agreements, were themselves evidence of a potential competitive relationship between them.[120]

5.2.2 Restriction of Competition by Object?

On the question of whether a pay-for-delay agreement could restrict competition by object, the ECJ cited its three fairly recent judgments in as *Maxima Latvija*,[121] *F. Hoffmann-la Roche and Others*[122] and *CB v Commission*.[123] The general position is set out in paragraphs 67 and 68 of the *Paroxetine* judgment:

67 It is clear from the Court's case-law that the concept of restriction of competition 'by object' must be interpreted strictly and can be applied only to some concerted practices between undertakings which reveal, in themselves and having regard to the content of their provisions, their objectives, and the economic and legal context of which they form part, a sufficient degree of harm to competition for the view to be taken that it is not necessary to assess their effects, since some forms of coordination between undertakings can be regarded, by their very nature, as being harmful to the proper functioning of normal competition (judgments of 26 November 2015, *Maxima Latvija*, C-345/14,

---

[114] Case C-307/18 EU:C:2020:52, para 38.
[115] ibid para 39.
[116] ibid para 42.
[117] Case C-307/18 EU:C:2020:52, paras 43–45.
[118] See generally Case C-307/18 EU:C:2020:52, paras 43–51.
[119] Case C-307/18 EU:C:2020:52, para 52.
[120] ibid para 55.
[121] Case C-345/14 EU:C:2015:784.
[122] Case C-179/16 EU:C:2018:25.
[123] Case C-67/13 EU:C:2014:25.

EU:C:2015:784, paragraph 20, and of 23 January 2018, *F. Hoffmann-La Roche and Others*, C-179/16, EU:C:2018:25, paragraphs 78 and 79).

68   When determining that context, it is necessary to take into consideration the nature of the goods or services affected, as well as the real conditions of the functioning and structure of the market or markets in question (judgment of 11 September 2014, *CB v Commission*, C-67/13 P, EU:C:2014:2204, paragraph 53 and the case-law cited).

The ECJ then made a number of points about the circumstances of the *Paroxetine* case. It discussed the context of the pharmaceutical sector, in which barriers to entry are high, and where there is a pricing mechanism that is strongly influenced by generic entry, which can cause a significant reduction in prices.[124] This meant that the medicines sector is particularly sensitive to a delay in the market entry of the generic version of a drug.[125] The ECJ noted that settlement agreements, in principle, can be subject to Article 101,[126] although they are not necessarily so.[127] The Court considered that a settlement of the kind in *Paroxetine* could be restrictive of competition by object:

> when it is plain from the analysis of the settlement agreement concerned that the transfers of value provided for by it cannot have any explanation other than the commercial interest of both the holder of the patent and the party allegedly infringing the patent not to engage in competition on the merits.[128]

If the transfer of value from the patent owner to the generic manufacturer is sufficiently beneficial to encourage the generic firm to refrain from entering the market and not to compete on the merits the agreement must, in principle, be characterized as a restriction of competition by object.[129]

5.3 The Outcome

When the *Paroxetine* case returned to the CAT it asked the parties to make submissions on what the ECJ had said. At the time of writing that process is now complete and the judgment of the CAT is awaited. The CAT will of course have to apply the *Paroxetine* judgment to the particular facts of the case. However, it is clear from the ECJ's judgment that it is possible, in principle, for a pay-for-delay agreement to be restrictive of competition by object. This is course relevant to the pending appeals in the *Lundbeck* and *Servier* cases.

6 Notification and Exemption

Just as Article 101(3) TFEU provides a defence for agreements that restrict competition under Article 101(1), so too the CA 1998 makes provision for the exemption of agreements.

---

[124] Case C-307/18, para 69.
[125] ibid para 70.
[126] ibid paras 80–82.
[127] ibid para 84.
[128] ibid para 87.
[129] ibid paras 94 and 95.

Block exemption is provided for in sections 6 to 8;[130] individual exemption in section 9; and parallel exemption, for agreements permitted under EU law, in section 11. In the early years of the CA 1998 it was possible (as under Regulation 17 of 1962 in EU law) to notify agreements for negative clearance and/or individual exemption from the OFT. However, just as Regulation 1/2003[131] abolished the system of notification in EU law, so too the Competition Act 1998 and Other Enactments (Amendment) Regulations 2004[132] repealed the notification system in CA 1998.

After the CA 1998 entered into force there were a few notifications to the OFT. The 'nightmare' of a flood of notifications, as happened in the 1960s when Regulation 17 of 1962 established the system of notification under EU competition law and more than 30,000 agreements were notified to (at that time) DG IV, never occurred; no doubt this was partly because of the availability of parallel exemption, that meant that agreements exempt under EU law were also deemed to be exempt under UK law. Nevertheless, some of the early notifications led to lengthy investigations by the OFT and to appeals to the CAT. One is bound to speculate whether the OFT might have been more successful in the early years in its enforcement efforts against cartels had less of its time been spent working on the notified cases.

The first decision to be adopted by the OFT after the CA 1998 entered into force was *General Insurance Standard Council*.[133] GISC had notified its rules to the OFT for negative clearance and/or individual exemption. The OFT concluded that the rules did not infringe the CA 1998. Rule F42 provided that intermediaries could not sell the general insurance products of GISC's members unless they (the intermediaries) were also members of GISC. The rule was challenged by the Institute of Independent Insurance Brokers and by the Association of British Travel Agents. The CAT disagreed with the OFT's position and concluded that Rule F42 amounted to a collective boycott and was therefore a restriction of competition by object contrary to the Chapter I prohibition:[134] such a practice could be upheld, if at all, only by recourse to the criteria in section 9(1) of the Competition Act.[135] The OFT's decision was annulled and the case was remitted to the OFT for reconsideration; in due course a second non-infringement decision was adopted confirming that the GISC rules did not infringe the CA 1998, but only after the offending Rule F42 had been dropped.[136] In the meantime the CAT had handed down a ruling ordering the OFT to pay 85 per cent of the costs of the IIIB's and ABTA's appeals.[137] This was an unfortunate outcome for the first decision to have been adopted by the OFT.

The next decision of the OFT on a notified agreement was *LINK Interchange Network Ltd*,[138] and it was more straightforward. The OFT applied section 9(1) to arrangements that provided for a centrally-set multilateral interchange fee for the operation of the LINK

---

[130] One block exemption has been adopted in the UK, the Competition Act 1998 (Public Transport Ticketing Schemes Block Exemption) Order 2001, SI 2001/319, as amended by three statutory instruments: SI 2005/3347, SI 2011/227, and SI 2016/126; it will expire on 28 February 2026.

[131] OJ [2004] L1/1.

[132] SI 2004/1261.

[133] OFT decision of 26 January 2001.

[134] Cases 1003/2/1/01 etc. *Institute of Independent Insurance Brokers v Director General of Fair Trading* [2001] CAT 4.

[135] ibid para 261.

[136] OFT decision of 22 November 2002.

[137] Order of the CAT of 20 January 2002.

[138] OFT decision of 16 October 2001.

network of automated teller machines, in which the major banks and building societies in the UK participate. The OFT recognized that charging such a fee could lead to an improvement in distribution by preventing one bank from taking a free ride on the investment of others.[139] The OFT considered whether the level of the multilateral interchange fee exceeded the cost of operating the network of cash machines but found that it did not.[140] The OFT granted an individual exemption to the arrangements in question until 16 October 2006.

Individual exemption was granted in the next case as well, *Memorandum of Understanding on the supply of oil fuels in an emergency*.[141] In 2000 the Labour government faced a major emergency when independent lorry drivers protested against the high price of petrol and diesel fuel and demanded a reduction in the duty imposed on fuel. Blockades were imposed on refineries and severe fuel shortages led to panic buying. After the crisis was over the Memorandum was notified to the OFT; it enabled the government to direct supplies of fuel to 'essential users' such as providers of emergency services in the event of a fuel shortage: in the absence of this arrangement the concern was that, in a free and competitive market, fuel would be delivered to the highest bidder. The OFT granted an individual exemption for a period of ten years.[142] The arrangement envisaged in the Memorandum remains in effect today, but is now covered by the Competition Act 1998 (Public Policy Exclusion) Order 2012.[143]

In *Pool Reinsurance*[144] the OFT concluded that rules designed to provide reinsurance against acts of terrorism in the UK restricted competition but satisfied the conditions of section 9. In *Association of British Insurers' General Terms of Agreement*[145] the OFT considered that, if certain provisions of the General Terms of Agreement were amended, it might satisfy section 9(1). This decision was set aside on appeal to the CAT.[146] The OFT subsequently decided to close the file since the case did not constitute an administrative priority.[147]

The OFT spent a great deal of its time in the early 2000s on two other notifications, each of which ended somewhat unfortunately from its point of view. In *Attheraces*[148] the OFT concluded that the collective selling of media rights to horseraces held under the auspices of the British Horseracing Board and the Racecourse Association to Attheraces, a joint venture company which intended to launch a pay-TV channel and an associated website to provide live pictures of British horseracing and an interactive betting services, infringed the Chapter I prohibition and did not qualify for exemption under section 9 CA 1998. Appeals by both the British Horseracing Board and the Racecourse Association against this decision were upheld by the CAT.[149] It fundamentally disagreed with the OFT's market definition in this case; but the CAT also concluded that, in the circumstances of the case, an acquisition of the media rights via a central negotiation was the only realistic way forward from the

---

[139]   ibid paras 42–45.
[140]   ibid paras 47–49.
[141]   OFT decision of 25 October 2001.
[142]   ibid paras 62–63; see now the Competition Act 1998 (Public Policy Exclusion) Order 2012, SI 2012/710.
[143]   SI 2012/710.
[144]   OFT decision of 15 April 2004.
[145]   OFT decision of 22 April 2004.
[146]   Case 1036/1/1/04 *Association of British Insurers v OFT*, order of 30 July 2004.
[147]   Case closure notice of 29 January 2007.
[148]   OFT decision of 10 May 2004.
[149]   Case 1035/1/1/04 *The Racecourse Association v OFT* and Case 1042/2/1/04 *The British Horseracing Board v OFT* [2005] CAT 29.

view point of both bidders and sellers and was therefore necessary for the legitimate commercial objective of launching a new product. The CAT also held that the OFT had failed to prove that the collective selling of the media rights had any appreciable effect on competition, either by increasing prices or by restricting incentives for competition. This was a fairly comprehensive defeat for the OFT: in choosing whether to find an infringement or no infringement, it had certainly backed the wrong horse.[150]

The OFT's decision *Investigation of the multilateral interchange fees—MasterCard* also had an unfortunate outcome. The OFT held that the fixing of the level of the multilateral interchange fee payable by acquiring banks to issuing banks infringed the Chapter I prohibition and was ineligible for exemption. Appeals were launched by MasterCard and the Royal Bank of Scotland before the CAT: it became clear during the hearing that the OFT's decision was likely to be criticized by the CAT on numerous grounds and the OFT indicated that it wished to withdraw the decision before judgment had been given; the investigation was subsequently closed.[151]. As Barry Rodger explains in Chapter 12 of this book,[152] the 'saga' of MasterCard's and Visa's interchanges continues to occupy the time of the UK courts in various stand-alone and follow-on actions.

7 Concurrency

An interesting feature of the Competition Act 1998 is the concurrency regime: many of the UK's sectoral regulators are given concurrent powers with the CMA to enforce the Chapter I and Chapter II prohibitions and, until Brexit, Articles 101 and 102 TFEU. These concurrency arrangements are considered by Niamh Dunne in Chapter 10.[153] For obvious reasons a majority of the cases investigated by the regulators have concerned possible abuses of dominance: in many regulated sectors historical monopolists still have considerable market power, often in markets typified by vertical integration where it may be relatively simple to foreclose market access. An obvious example of this is OFCOM's decision in 2018 in which it fined Royal Mail £50 million for excluding Whistl from the market for bulk business delivery of post.[154] Suffice it to say however that there have also been a few cases in which the sectoral regulators have adopted infringement decisions in relation to horizontal agreements. In *Access to car parking facilities at East Midlands International Airport*[155] the Civil Aviation Authority found that East Midlands International Airport and Prestige had unlawfully agreed that Prestige should not sell its car-parking services at the airport below a minimum price, which was linked to the price of the airport's own car parking services.

---

[150] Note that in a separate private action, *Bookmakers' Afternoon Greyhound Services v Amalgamated Racing* ('*BAGS*'), the Court of Appeal endorsed the High Court's conclusion in that case that the collective negotiation and exclusive licensing of horseracing media rights was to introduce competition into a previously monopsonistic market and that any increase in price was the consequence of that increase in competition. It followed that the arrangements did not have as their object the restriction of competition: [2008] EWHC 1978 (Chancery Division), upheld on appeal, [2009] EWCA Civ 750 (Court of Appeal).

[151] The OFT's decision was formally set aside by the CAT: Cases 1054/1/1/05 etc *MasterCard UK Members Forum Ltd v OFT* [2006] CAT 14.

[152] Barry Rodger, 'Private Enforcement in the UK: Effective Redress for Consumers?', ch 12 in this volume.

[153] Niamh Dunne, 'Concurrency', ch 10 in this volume.

[154] OFCOM decision of 14 August 2018, upheld on appeal Case 1299/1/3/18 *Royal Mail plc v OFCOM* [2019] CAT 27; the case is in appeal to the Court of Appeal, not yet decided.

[155] Civil Aviation Authority decision of 20 December 2016.

Neither party was fined, however, since the airport had blown the whistle and Prestige was no longer trading. Subsequently the CMA fined Heathrow Airport Ltd £1.6 million for entering into a price-fixing agreement with Heathrow T5 Hotel Ltd (part of the Arora Group) in relation to car-parking facilities at the Sofitel Hotel at Terminal 5.[156] The Arora Group was not fined as it had blown the whistle. Warning letters were sent by the CMA to other airports and hotel groups about the risks of infringing competition law.

In February 2019, the FCA adopted its first competition law decision. In *Asset Management*[157] it concluded that three asset management firms had disclosed their confidential bidding intentions in relation to two upcoming IPOs (initial public offerings) on the London Stock Exchange; Newton Investment Management blew the whistle; fines of £306,300 and £108,600 were imposed on Hargreave Hale Ltd and Mercantile Asset Management LLP, respectively.

In May 2019, OFGEM issued a decision in which it found that Economy Energy, EGEL, and Dyball Associates had infringed the Chapter I prohibition by sharing markets and/or allocating customers in relation to the supply of gas and electricity to domestic customers in Great Britain. Dyball was fined as a facilitator of the cartel: it had designed, implemented, and maintained software systems that blocked the acquisition of Economy Energy's and EGEL's customers by each other; it also facilitated the sharing of customer lists. EGEL was fined £650,000, Economy Electricity £200,000 and Dyball, for its role as a facilitator, £20,000.

In November 2019, Ofcomadopted a decision finding an infringement of competition law on the part of Royal Mail and The Sale Group (trading as Despatch Bay): they had entered into an agreement not to supply parcel-delivery services to each other's business customers.[158] A fine of £40,000 was imposed on Sale Group; Royal Mail was the leniency applicant and was not fined.

In some cases, a sectoral regulator may assist with the CMA's investigation; for example NHS Improvement assisted the CMA in *Conduct in the ophthalmology sector*.[159]

8 Scotland

As the UK leaves the EU, it cannot be ruled out that a second referendum in Scotland in the relatively near future might lead to Scotland leaving the UK. The complexity that will be caused by this shift of the tectonic plates cannot be underestimated, not least when contemplating the future of competition law and policy within the UK. Quite apart from the many issues that will have to be settled as to future relations between the UK and the EU, it is also important to contemplate how Brexit will affect the position as between Westminster and the nations. At this stage we know that competition policy is 'reserved' to Westminster under Schedules 4 and 5 of the Scotland Act 1998.[160] The Scottish government had hoped

---

[156] CMA decision of 25 October 2018.
[157] FCA decision of 21 February 2019.
[158] OFCOM decision of 14 November 2019.
[159] CMA decision of 20 August 2015; see *Annual report on concurrency* CMA63 (28 April 2017) n 10.
[160] For a helpful account of the current position see Catriona Munro and Jamie Dunne, 'Serving Two Masters: How Devolution Affects the Enforcement of Competition Law in Scotland' (2017) 16 Competition Law Journal 95; see also R Whish, 'Competition Law in Scotland' (2019) 18 Competition Law Journal 133.

that the Smith Commission[161] would lead to significant devolution of competition and consumer powers to Scotland, but the Scotland Act 2016 did not provide this. This will have been frustrating for the Scottish government, which has expressed the view that insufficient attention has been given by the UK competition authorities to markets in Scotland.[162] The UK position contrasts interestingly with Spain, where several 'autonomous communities' possess their own competition law powers.[163]

The CMA made a submission to the Smith Commission outlining the work that it (and the OFT and the Competition Commission before it) had carried out in relation to Scottish markets, but if anything this seemed to confirm the scarcity of cases: in a period of ten years from 2004 the CMA reported that there had been eleven merger cases involving only Scottish firms or markets, two cartel cases involving only Scottish undertakings, one abuse of dominance case and one market study.[164] Annex A of the *CMA's Response* contains a useful list of the OFT/CC/CMA cases since 2004 with significance for Scotland. The two cartel cases that related specifically to Scottish markets were *Collusive tendering for mastic asphalt flat-roofing contracts in Scotland,*[165] where the fines of £231,445 were reduced to £87,353 after leniency had been taken into consideration, and *Felt and Single Ply Roofing Contracts in Western-Central Scotland,*[166] where the fines of £258,576 were reduced to £138,515. In a third case, not limited to Scotland, *Flat Roof and Car Park Surfacing Contracts in England and Scotland,*[167] fines of £1.852 million were reduced to £1.557 million after leniency.

It will be interesting to see whether this situation of relatively little Scottish enforcement will change in the years ahead. It is important to note that in recent years the CMA has significantly expanded its office in Edinburgh. In its *Annual Report for the year ended 31 March 2019* the CMA reported that it had recently opened an expanded office in Edinburgh with more than 40 staff from a variety of professions including policy, law, and economics: this number has since grown, and it is understood that there is now space to accommodate up to 100 people in Edinburgh, which would represent 10 per cent of the CMA's workforce.

9 Public Policy and the Coronavirus Crisis

The coronavirus crisis of 2020 presented governments worldwide with monumental challenges of a kind never seen before in peacetime. Competition authorities very quickly had to engage with the crisis, for example as complaints flooded in about price-gouging by firms selling essential products such as face masks and hand sanitizers. A specific issue arose in relation to horizontal cooperation agreements where competitors argued that the exigencies of the time required that they should be allowed to enter into agreements in a way that risked infringement of competition law. Competition authorities (and international

---

[161] *Report of the Smith Commission for further devolution of powers to the Scottish Parliament* (27 November 2014).

[162] See the *Scottish Government Response to the Interim Report from the Devolution (Further Powers) Committee on the Smith Commission and the UK Government's Proposals* (7 June 2015) 18 www.parliament/scot.

[163] There are regional competition authorities in Catalunya, Galicia, Valencia, Aragon, Castile and Leon, the Basque Country, Extremadura, and Andalucía; the Spanish competition authority and the regional authorities meet annually in the 'Annual Council for the Defence of Competition'.

[164] *The CMA's Response to the Smith Commission*, CMA36 (31 October 2014)) www.gov.uk.

[165] OFT decision of 15 March 2005.

[166] OFT decision of 11 July 2005.

[167] OFT decision of 23 February 2006.

organizations such as the OECD and ICN) were quick to publish generic guidance as to how they intended to apply competition law during the pandemic.[168] They were clear that the crisis should not be used as a cloak for cartel behaviour; however they would not be unsympathetic to certain types of horizontal agreements which might be needed, for example, to address a problem of excess capacity—perhaps farmers producing too much milk or cheese—or because of under capacity—maybe not enough face masks or hand sanitizers.

In so far as a competition authority might be willing to tolerate cooperation during a time of crisis, an important issue for firms and their legal advisers is risk management: more specifically, can an authority provide a formal exemption from the application of competition law? Or formal guidance? Or informal guidance? Different legal systems provide different answers to these questions. Neither EU nor UK law have provided for formal individual exemption of an agreement that satisfies Article 101(3) TFEU or section 9 of the CA 1998 since Regulation 1/2003 replaced Regulation 17 of 1962 in 2004, and since the UK aligned the CA 1998 with the position in EU law by virtue of the Competition Act 1998 and Other Enactments (Amendment) Regulations 2004.[169] The CMA established a Coronavirus Task Force[170] and provided generic guidance[171] in which it recognized that the Covid-19 crisis might trigger the need for companies to cooperate to ensure the supply and fair distribution of scarce products. At paragraph 2.3 of this guidance the CMA indicated that it would not take enforcement action where temporary measures to coordinate business behaviour are appropriate and necessary in order to avoid a shortage or to ensure security of supply; where this is clearly in the public interest; where this would contribute to the benefit or well-being of customers; where the cooperation deals with critical issues arising as a result of the pandemic; and where the cooperation would last no longer than is necessary to deal with those critical issues.

What was interesting about the position in the UK is that a different possibility existed to address the need of firms for legal certainty, whereby the government (as opposed to the CMA) could *exclude* an agreement or categories of agreement from the legislation altogether, rather than *exempting* them pursuant to section 9 CA 1998, a conceptually different matter. Paragraph 7 of Schedule 3 of the Act gives power to the Secretary of State to make such an order where there are 'exceptional and compelling reasons of public policy' for doing so. The order can provide that the exclusion shall apply only in specified circumstances,[172] and may be retrospective.[173] Between 2000 and 2020 four orders had been made under paragraph 7: three in relation to the defence industry,[174] one of which has been repealed.[175] The fourth concerns arrangements for the supply of oil and petroleum

---

[168] See eg Communication from the Commission: *Temporary Framework for assessing the antitrust issues related to business cooperation in response to situations of urgency stemming from the current COVID-19 outbreak* (8 April 2020) OJ [2020] C116 1/7; *Antitrust: Joint statement by the European Competition Network (ECN) on application of competition law during the Corona crisis* (April 2020); ICN Steering Group Statement: *Competition during and after the COVID-19 Pandemic* (April 2020).

[169] SI 2004/1261.

[170] Details of the work of the Task Force can be followed on www.gov.uk/cma.

[171] *CMA approach to business cooperation in response to COVID-19* (25 March 2020) CMA118.

[172] CA 1998, Sch 3, para 7(2).

[173] ibid Sch 3, para 7(3).

[174] TFEU, art 346 provides an exclusion from the EU competition rules for certain matters related to defence; there are no specific exclusions for this area from the Competition Act 1998.

[175] Competition Act 1998 (Public Policy Exclusion) Order 2006, SI 2006/605 (maintenance and repair of warships); Competition Act 1998 (Public Policy Exclusion) Order 2007, SI 2007/1896 (strategic and tactical weapons and their supporting technology, repealed with effect from 30 December 2011 by Competition Act 1998 (Public Policy Exclusion) (Revocation) Order 2011, SI 2011/2886; Competition Act 1998 (Public Policy Exclusion) Order 2008, SI 2008/1820 (design, construction, maintenance and disposal of nuclear submarines).

products in the event of significant disruption, or threat of significant disruption, to normal supply;[176] as noted in section 6 above, this Order followed the expiry of the individual exemption granted in *Memorandum of Understanding on the supply of oil fuels in an emergency*,[177] granted in the days when the OFT could issue formal exemption decisions. In so far as that *Oil fuels* originated in the 'crisis' of the fuel blockade of 2000, it was something of a 'pilot' for the conditions encountered in the pandemic, when there was genuine anxiety about certain products becoming under-available because of scarcity.

Five orders prompted by the coronavirus crisis had been made under Schedule 3(7) CA 1998 at the time of completion of this chapter: the Competition Act 1998 (Health Services for Patients in England)(Coronavirus)(Public Policy Exclusion) Order 2020;[178] the Competition Act 1998 (Groceries)(Coronavirus)(Public Policy Exclusion) Order 2020;[179] the Competition Act 1998 (Solent Maritime Crossings)(Coronavirus)(Public Policy Exclusion) Order 2020;[180] the Competition Act 1998 (Health Services for Patients in Wales)(Coronavirus)(Public Policy Exclusion) Order 2020;[181] and the Competition Act 1998 (Dairy Produce)(Coronavirus)(Public Policy Exclusion) Order 2020.[182] The first four of these public policy exclusion orders addressed possible problems of scarcity; the last of them with over-production.[183]

10 Brexit and the Future

The UK left the European Union on 31 January 2020. At the time of writing this chapter it is unclear whether the UK will enter into a trade agreement with the EU by the end of 2020; nor is it known what arrangements there may be in relation to cooperation on competition law matters between the EU and the UK. Whatever the answer turns out to be, we can expect to see a significant difference in the enforcement of the Chapter I prohibition against cartels in the future. Criticism of under-enforcement of competition law by the CMA and, before it, the OFT, was referred to in section 2.1 above. Some of this criticism was perhaps misplaced, since many UK firms were in cartels that were investigated by the European Commission. For example, UK firms were fined for their participation in the cartels in *Zinc phosphates*,[184] *Copper fittings*,[185] *Car glass*,[186] *Food packaging*,[187] *Needles and haberdashery*,[188] the *LIBOR* cases,[189] *Air cargo*,[190] *Freight forwarding*,[191] and *Marine hoses*;[192] there are other examples—this is by

---

[176] Competition Act 1998 (Public Policy Exclusion) Order 2012, SI 2012/710.
[177] OFT decision of 25 October 2011.
[178] SI 2020/368.
[179] SI 2020/369.
[180] SI 2020/370.
[181] SI 2020/435.
[182] SI 2020/481.
[183] For discussion see Oke Odudu, 'Feeding the Nation in Times of Crisis: the Relaxation of Competition Law in the United Kingdom' (2020) 19(2) Competition Law Journal 68.
[184] Commission Decision of 11 December 2001.
[185] Commission Decision of 20 September 2006.
[186] Commission Decision of 12 November 2008.
[187] Commission Decision of 24 June 2015.
[188] Commission Decisions of 19 September 2007.
[189] Commission Decisions of 21 October 2014 and 4 December 2013.
[190] Commission Decision of 9 November 2010.
[191] Commission Decision of 28 March 2012.
[192] Commission Decision of 28 January 2009.

no means an exhaustive list. UK undertakings were also investigated, though not fined, in other European Commission cases under Article 101, for example in the *Football Association Premier League* case[193] and in *Credit default swaps*.[194] Absent the jurisdiction of the European Commission—which is another way of saying in a post-Brexit world—these cases might have been investigated by the UK competition authorities. This would have made the pattern and amount of enforcement action look very different, and the fines imposed since 1 March 2004 would have been considerably greater than has been the case.[195] It is not unreasonable to suppose that, in the future, the CMA and the sectoral regulators will investigate larger cartels than in the past, presumably, in some cases, alongside the Commission (or one or more of the national competition authorities). More specifically, given that so many of the Commission's cases in recent years have related to the financial services sector, it may be that the Financial Conduct Authority will be increasingly involved in enforcement action.

In the meantime, one horizontal case being conducted by the CMA is not of a cartel: *Atlantic Joint Business Agreement*. In 2010, the Commission accepted commitments under Article 9 of Regulation 1/2003 from British Airways, American Airlines, and Iberia in relation to the release of certain take-off and landing slots at Heathrow Airport in order to facilitate competition between the oneworld alliance, of which those airlines were members, and other would-be entrants to routes from Heathrow to various US destinations.[196] The CMA adopted an interim measures decision on 17 September 2020 continuing the commitments in effect until 2024. Had the UK not left the EU this case would, presumably, have been taken forward by the European Commission.

11 Conclusions

I distinctly remember the excitement that was generated by the publication of the Competition Bill, and the subsequent royal assent for the Competition Act, that equipped the UK with a modern, fit-for-purpose set of tools. This meant that for the first times cartels could be effectively investigated (for example through the introduction of the power to conduct dawn raids) and severely punished. I equally remember the sense of disappointment after the legislation had entered into force at the relatively low level of enforcement in the early years. As a non-executive director of the OFT from 2003 to 2009 I was able to witness at first hand some of the difficulties involved in building an effective competition authority possessing the numerous different skill sets necessary to enforce competition law fairly, effectively, and in a predictable manner. As I hope this chapter has demonstrated, there has since been a noticeable increase in enforcement action against cartels. The world in August 2020 looks very different than it did in March 2000 when CA 1998 came into effect. However, the CMA today, with the benefit of twenty years of experience behind it (and the OFT), would appear to have the resources, know-how, and determination to take the fight against cartels forward into the new post-Brexit era. Assuming that there is, in due course, a volume to celebrate the thirtieth anniversary of the CA 1998 it will be fascinating to see what happened in the next ten years!

---

[193] Commission Decision of 22 March 2006.
[194] *CDS (Credit Default Swaps)—Clearing*; the Commission closed its proceedings on 4 December 2015.
[195] See Rodger (n 45).
[196] European Commission decision of 14 July 2010.

3

Vertical Agreements

Alison Jones*

1 Introduction

UK competition law and policy towards vertical agreements has developed significantly over the twenty years since the Competition Act 1998 (CA 1998) came into force. First, policy has developed from a more laissez-faire, to a more interventionist, one.[1] At the time of the enactment of the CA 1998, the UK authorities took a permissive approach towards vertical agreements. This led, in rejection of the more heavy-handed EU approach adopted at that time under Article 101 TFEU, to the exclusion of most vertical agreements from the Chapter I prohibition of restrictive agreements. However, the dramatic modernization of the EU attitude towards vertical agreements between 1997-2004, combined with the UK government's decision to withdraw the exclusion for vertical agreements in 2005, resulted both in vertical agreements being more closely scrutinized under the CA 1998 and the UK and EU approach towards them becoming closely aligned. One important distinction between EU and UK law in this sphere nonetheless results from the operation of the market investigation provisions of the Enterprise Act 2002 (EA 2002), which allows for the investigation of markets where it appears that competition is being prevented, restricted, or distorted, but where there is no obvious breach of the CA 1998 provisions (for example, where parallel but non-collusive courses of conduct are being pursued by undertakings operating in an oligopolistic market).[2] These provisions have proved helpful to scrutinize some vertical arrangements, in particular, where similar practices are widespread across a market or access to it is foreclosed to new competitors (perhaps as a result of the cumulative effects).

Secondly, some evolution has been demanded as a result of the exponential growth in the last twenty years of e-commerce which, as in other parts of the world, has had enduring effects on the way that goods and services are distributed in the UK. Numerous products are now sold online or through platforms, and price comparison websites exist to facilitate consumers' buying choices. This creates both opportunities, and challenges, for manufacturers and retailers and has fuelled new distribution practices—for example, more manufactures integrating vertically into online distribution, greater use of selective distribution systems (SDSs, selecting the type or number of outlets in which the supplier's products are sold and precluding dealers from selling to unauthorized distributors outside the network) and restraints on online selling.[3] Like other competition agencies, the CMA has therefore

[*] The author would like to thank Biatriz Hidalgo Silva and Valentina Novoa Hales for their excellent research assistance and Stijn Huijts and Christopher Brown for their extremely helpful comments on an earlier draft of the chapter.

[1] See section 2 below.

[2] Market investigations are discussed more fully in ch 6 (see also section 3.2 below).

[3] See ch 14 below and the CMA's market study into Online Markets and Digital Advertising, Interim Report published 18 December 2019. See also the European Commission's Final Report on the E-commerce Sector

Alison Jones, *Vertical Agreements* In: *The UK Competition Regime*. Edited by: Barry Rodger, Peter Whelan, and Angus MacCulloch, Oxford University Press. © The Contributors 2021. DOI: 10.1093/oso/9780198868026.003.0003

had to consider how traditional competition law rules, designed in a different era, apply to this new context.

This chapter charts these developments, focusing on Chapter I and the EA 2002 and leaving Chapters 4 and 5 to consider how the Chapter II prohibition applies to vertical agreements concluded by dominant undertakings. It commences in section 2 by outlining how Chapter I and the EA 2002 have evolved to deal with vertical agreements and in particular how substantive assessment under the CA 1998 has come to parallel that conducted under EU law. Section 3 appraises some of the core UK jurisprudence and, in the light of this discussion, section 4 considers how the law could, or should, develop in the future, especially now the transition period following the UK's departure from the European Union has ended. An important issue considered is whether, post-Brexit, the UK authorities should continue to follow the EU jurisprudence in this sphere which has, arguably, been more significantly influenced by internal market considerations (and a particular concern about restraints that prohibit and limit the opportunities for parallel or cross-border trade and perpetuate price differences between Member States) than pure competition ones, or whether it should take a different course. Section 5 concludes that despite some important developments in the UK jurisprudence more could be done to develop a coherent approach to vertical agreements, through guidelines and cases focusing on scenarios where established presumptions of illegality do not apply.

2 Outline and Evolution of the Law

2.1 The Verticals Exclusion Order

At the time of the enactment of the CA 1998, the UK authorities were rarely concerned about vertical agreements in the absence of one of the parties having market power or the existence of networks of agreements. Even though the CA 1998 was modelled on Articles 101 and 102 and designed to align domestic law with it,[4] the government was consequently unwilling to follow the then strict EU approach taken to vertical agreements, according to which numerous agreements were, unless de minimis or block exempted, prohibited following a broad, form-based interpretation of Article 101(1).[5] To avoid having to follow EU law, the government excluded all vertical agreements (agreements between undertakings which operated, for the purposes of the agreement, at a different level of the production or distribution chain) from the Chapter I prohibition, other than those that had the effect of

---

Inquiry and accompanying Staff Working Document (Final Report), which summarizes the main findings of the ecommerce sector inquiry and incorporates comments submitted by stakeholders during the public consultation on 10 May [2017] SWD(2017) 154 final. The latter recognize that e-commerce has led: (a) more manufacturers to integrate vertically (b) to wider use of SDSs; (c) to increasing use of vertical restraints that allow for a greater control over the distribution of products, for example, through pricing restrictions, marketplace (platform) bans, restrictions on the use of price comparison tools, and the exclusion of pure online players from distribution networks.

[4] See eg B Rayment, '4 The Consistency Principle: Section 60 of the Competition Act 1998' in B Rodger (ed), *Ten Years of UK Competition Law Reform* (Edinburgh University Press 2010).

[5] For a discussion of this approach and the modernization process see eg A Jones, B Sufrin, and N Dunne, *Jones and Sufrin's EU Competition Law: Text, Cases, and Materials* (7th edn, Oxford University Press 2019) ch 5.

fixing resale or minimum resale prices (RPM).[6] The early cases, between 2000 and 2004, dealing with vertical agreements thus generally concerned RPM, hub and spoke agreements (see further Chapter 2), or the scope of the Verticals Exclusion Order (see further section 3).

One problem with the UK's initial approach was its (albeit deliberate) lack of consistency with EU law. Even though at that time section 60 CA 1998 only provided for consistency with corresponding principles of EU law in so far as is possible and having regard to relevant differences in law and the OFT, like many national competition authorities (NCAs), did not have power to apply Article 101, it was clear that, according to the EU legal order and the principle of supremacy of EU law, national law could not authorize an agreement which was prohibited under EU law.[7] A more permissive approach to vertical agreements under the CA 1998 could not therefore save an agreement which infringed Article 101. The difficulties resulting from this divergence became starker as modernization approached, the EU approach to vertical agreements evolved significantly (following a recognition that appraisal of vertical agreements should be based not on their content and form, but taking account of their competitive effects) and it became evident that NCAs would be obliged to apply EU competition law when applying their own national competition laws to agreements that had an effect on trade between Member States.

Another concern was that the approach might be too permissive leading to a risk that some anti-competitive vertical agreements were going unchecked (a risk of type II errors, arising from an under-inclusive rule); the fact that vertical restraints might provide pro-competitive effects did not mean that they would inevitably result in distributive efficiency. On the contrary vertical agreements can create both collusion risks and, by raising barriers to entry or expansion, exclusionary ones.[8]

2.2 Modernization of EU Law and Removal of the Verticals Exclusion Order

In the light of the concerns identified above the government decided, following consultation and an impact assessment,[9] to remove the exclusion order for vertical agreements

---

[6] See CA 1998, s 50(1) and Competition Act 1998 (Land and Vertical Agreements Exclusion) Order 2000, SI 2000/310, arts 2–4 (the exclusion did not apply to the Chapter II prohibition or the EA02). Although the DGFT was conferred with power to withdraw the exclusion, this was never exercised. Indeed, in Case CP/1288-02 *Lucite International UK Ltd and BASF plc* (29 November 2002), the DGFT declined to exercise his power to withdraw the exclusion from an agreement for the sale of hydrogen cyanide (HCN) concluded between BASF and Lucite (also a producer of HCN) and for the construction of a plant to convert HCN to acetone cyanohydrin (ACH). Although both parties produced HCN, and would jointly be producing ACH in the new plant, the agreement was covered by the order because it related to the conditions for the sale and purchase of HCN and the parties operated, for the purposes of the agreement, at different levels of the production or distribution chain. The DGFT concluded that even if withdrawn the agreement would, given the environmental benefits produced, have been likely to receive an exemption from the Chap I prohibition. He also declined with withdraw the exclusion order in Case CA98/3/2001 *Dixon Stores Group Ltd/ Compaq Computer Ltd/ Packard Bell Nec Ltd* (6 April 2001).

[7] See eg Case 14/68 *Walt Wilhelm v Bundeskartellamt* EU:C:1969:4 and Case C-360/92 P *Publishers' Association* EU:C:1995:6.

[8] A broad consensus supports the view that it is not possible to regard them 'as per se beneficial for competition', European Commission, Green Paper on Vertical Restraints in EC Competition Policy, COM(96) 721, para 54. See also the CMA's no grounds for action decision in Case CE-9531/11 *Paroxetine* (12 February 2016), where the CMA concluded that an agreement between GSK and IVAX, one agreement in a broader investigation into pay-for-delay agreements, had been excluded from the Chapter I prohibition by the Verticals Exclusion Order.

[9] See especially *A World Class Competition Regime* (2001 White Paper Cm 5233) and DTI Modernization—A consultation on the Government's proposals for exclusions and exemption from the Competition Act 1998 in light of Regulation 1/2003 (April 2003).

from 1 May 2005.[10] This change, together with Regulation 1/2003[11] and the CA 1998 parallel exemption procedure,[12] allowed the OFT (and subsequently the CMA) to apply both Articles 101 and the Chapter I prohibition to vertical agreements and for UK competition law to become aligned with 'modernized' EU law. Consequently, since 2005 substantive assessment of vertical agreements under Chapter I has closely mirrored that adopted under Article 101 (see the *Guidance on Vertical agreements*[13] and further section 3), which applies in the following way, relying on certain presumptions and safe harbours.

2.2.1 Object Restrictions

Vertical agreements found to restrict competition by object are presumed to be incompatible with Article 101: they are assumed to restrict competition appreciably under Article 101(1);[14] and the European Commission's view is that they are presumed not to satisfy the conditions of Article 101(3)—hard-core restraints in the Verticals Block Exemption, currently Regulation 330/2010,[15] are aligned closely with likely object restrictions, meaning that the block exemption does not generally provide a safe harbour for such agreements (see 2.2.2 below) and the Commission's view is that provisions so severely restricting rivalry between firms are unlikely individually to satisfy the conditions of Article 101(3).[16] Because in most cases an agreement containing an object restraint is, when uncovered, treated as a serious infringement of the competition rules that attracts fines, firms generally avoid incorporating these restraints in their distribution agreements and having to advance efficiency justifications for them.[17]

Object restraints, which are by their very nature injurious to competition, are identified only through a flexible characterization process involving an analysis of the agreements' content, objective, and context.[18] Consequently, even seemingly severe restraints on competition (such as horizontal price restraints) will not restrict competition by object where the objective and context reveals a plausible efficiency rationale for the conduct.[19] Nonetheless, jurisprudence clarifies that agreements containing certain 'established' clauses

---

[10] Competition Act 1998 (Land Agreements Exclusion and Revocation) Order 2004 SI 2004/1260 (the Land and Vertical Agreements Exclusion Order (n 6) had excluded all vertical agreements, with the exception of those imposing minimum or fixed resale prices, from the Chapter I prohibition from March 2000 until 30 April 2005).

[11] [2003] OJ L1/1.

[12] CA 1998, s10 allows the Verticals Block Exemption, currently Regulation 330/2010 [2010] OJ L102/1, to apply to agreements affecting trade within the UK even if they do not affect trade between Member States.

[13] See OFT 419 (December 2004) https://assets.publishing.service.gov.uk/government/uploads/system/uploads/attachment_data/file/284430/oft419.pdf.

[14] Case C-226/11 *Expedia Inc v Authorité de la concurrence* EU:C:2012:795. For a full discussion of object restraints and the literature discussing the topic see eg Jones, Sufrin, and Dunne (n 5) ch 5.

[15] [2010] OJ L102/1, replacing reg 2790/1999 [1999] OJ L336/21. For a full discussion of this block exemption and the modernization process that led to its adoption see Jones, Sufrin, and Dunne (n 5) ch 11.

[16] They are unlikely to create objective economic benefits for consumers or to be indispensable to the attainment of any efficiencies created by the agreement in question (efficiencies generated can generally be achieved by less restrictive means) see eg Guidelines on the application of art 81(3) [now art 101(3)] [2004] OJ C101/97, paras 46, 79, and 105. But see discussion of Case 50230 *Ping* (24 August 2017) (n 75 and text).

[17] Such restraints are generally perceived by business to be de facto illegal. Although therefore it is frequently argued that the object category in the EU is distinct from the per se rule in the US (which does not allow any justifications for the conduct to be raised), this distinction is in practice more theoretical than real. There is extremely limited clarity as to when agreements incorporating object restraints may exceptionally satisfy the four onerous conditions of art 101(3).

[18] See Jones, Sufrin, and Dunne (n 5) ch 5 and eg Cases C-501, 513, 515, & 519/06 P *GlaxoSmithKline Services Unlimited v Commission* EU:C:2009:610, para 58.

[19] See further section 4.2.

in vertical agreements are highly likely, or liable in principle, to be found to pursue a re-strictive objective, including provisions:

- involving RPM[20] (and online RPM);[21]
- conferring absolute territorial protection (ATP) on a distributor[22] or otherwise aimed 'at prohibiting or limiting parallel trade';[23]
- banning online selling (which reduces the ability of a distributor to sell outside its ter-ritory, see *Pierre Fabre v Président de l'Autorité de la concurrence*)[24] (but not necessarily restraints prohibiting only certain forms of internet selling, such as via a platform, see *Coty*);[25] and, it seems,
- certain selective distribution systems (SDSs—which restrict the number or type of dealers and prohibits sales from authorized to non-authorized distributors).[26]

Indeed, where such restraints have been uncovered EU authorities have, save in the most exceptional circumstances, generally refused to accept that the context of a case supports a finding that the overarching objective is to, for example, enhance efficiency of the supply chain to the benefit of the parties and end customers, rather than to restrict competi-tion.[27] This category of restraints is thus ordinarily found to restrict competition by object irrespective of (i) the rationale for the incorporation of the restraint, (ii) the intensity of interbrand competition and/or (iii) the degree of market power of the parties.

The strict approach towards these vertical restraints—all of which constitute restraints on intra-brand competition (that is competition between distributors of a supplier's product or service)—has attracted considerable controversy over the years. Although rules or presumptions of illegality serve important ends in antitrust systems—particularly the attainment of procedural economy and the clear prohibition, and deterrence, of patently

---

[20] See eg Case 161/84 *Pronuptia de Paris v Schillgallis* EU:C:1986:41, para 25; and Case 26/76 *Metro-SB-Grossmärkte GmbH v Commission (Metro I)* EU:C:1977:167, para 21.

[21] See eg Case AT/40.465 *Asus* (26 September 2018) IP/18/4601.

[22] Where the supplier and no other distributor is entitled to sell within the territory see eg Cases 56 and 58/64 *Établissements Consten Sàrl & Grundig-Verkaufs-GmbH v Commission (Consten and Grundig)* EU:C:1966:41.

[23] '[I]n principle, agreements aimed at prohibiting or limiting parallel trade have as their object the prevention of competition', Case C-501/06 P *GlaxoSmithKline* (n 18) para 59; Cases C-403 and 429/08 *Premier League Ltd v QC Leisure and Murphy v Media Protection Services* EU:C:2011:631; and Case AT40428 *Guess* (17 December 2018) (€40 million fine for geo-blocking, including through a prohibition of selling online without specific author-ization); and Case AT40023 *US film studios* (commitments given to resolve the Commission's concerns about re-straints on cross-border competition in film licensing contracts for Pay-TV, appeal challenging the commitments given by Paramount dismissed; Case T-873/16 *Groupe Canal+ v Commission* EU:T:2018:904).

[24] Case C-439/09 EU:C:2011:277; and *Guess* (n 23).

[25] Case C-230/16 EU:C:2017:941. But see the settlement reached, prior to *Coty*, by the Bundeskartellamt (the German NCA) following its investigation into Adidas, Case B3 137/12 (27 June 2014) (for English summary see http://www.bundeskartellamt.de/SharedDocs/Entscheidung/EN/Fallberichte/Kartellverbot/2014/B3-137-12.pdf?__blob=publicationFile&v=2). See also discussion of *BMW/Carwow* https://www.gov.uk/government/news/bmw-changes-policy-on-car-comparison-sites-following-cma-action (n 87 and text below).

[26] *Pierre Fabre* (n 24).

[27] Rather, as is illustrated by *Consten and Grundig* (n 22), in these cases the Court tends to focus on the restraints imposed and simply assumes that they are disproportionate to any objective pursued. In this case the Court of Justice rejected the parties' argument that the vertical sole distributorship agreement, conferring ATP upon the distributor, was necessary to prevent freeriding and to encourage competition between similar products of dif-ferent makes (inter-brand competition). Instead, focusing on the mechanism the parties adopted to achieve their objective—the isolation of the French market—the Court held that clauses which result in the segregation of a na-tional market, and/or in maintaining separate national markets, were liable to have as their object the restriction of competition. See also section 3.1.2 below.

anti-competitive behaviour[28]—it is argued by some that the EU attitude is overly rigid and requires adjustment.[29] Indeed, it is arguable that because pro-competitive justifications— and an increase in interbrand competition—could be the driving economic motivation for vertical restraints,[30] the application of a virtually irrebuttable[31] presumption of illegality is not justified and creates a risk of type I errors (arising from an over-inclusive rule which sometimes condemns conduct that is competitive, benign or beneficial). Nevertheless, the approach, heavily influenced by market integration concerns, remains entrenched in the EU jurisprudence.[32]

2.2.2 De Minimis and the Verticals Block Exemption

Agreements that do not contain by object restraints may be compatible with Article 101 where the parties' market shares do not exceed certain market share thresholds. Thus, agreements which do not incorporate object restraints fall outside of Article 101(1) altogether where they do not appreciably restrict, or have a de minimis impact on, competition— likely where the parties' market shares do not exceed 15 per cent on the upstream or downstream market.[33] Further, since modernization the Verticals Block Exemption (like its predecessor Regulation 2790/1999)[34] provides a broad, overarching exemption from Article 101(1) for vertical agreements involving parties that: (i) are considered unlikely to have market power—proxied by use of a 30 per cent market share threshold;[35] and (ii) do not contain hard-core restraints, including RPM provisions and, with limited exceptions, restrictions on the territories into which, or the customers to whom, buyers can sell the product.[36] As the benefit of the Regulation can only be withdrawn prospectively,[37] it provides legal certainty and operates as an important safe harbour for a large group of vertical

---

[28] In such circumstances, the administrative savings may outweigh the cost of small false positives and exceed the efficiencies that can be derived from moving to a more comprehensive antitrust analysis see A Jones and WE Kovacic, 'Identifying Anticompetitive Agreements in the United States and the European Union: Developing a Coherent Antitrust Analytical Framework' (2017) 62(2) *Antitrust Bulletin* 254.

[29] See eg A Jones and M de la Mano, 'Vertical Agreements under EU Competition Law: Proposals for Pushing Article 101 Analysis, and the Modernization Process, to a Logical Conclusion' in D Healey, M Jacobs, and RL Smith, *Research Handbook on Methods and Models of Competition Law* (Edward Elgar 2020).

[30] A rich literature explains that a number of vertical restraints, including RPM, territorial restrictions or selective distribution, may be used as mechanisms to allow suppliers to elicit optimal service levels (for example, presale services, quality certification and the building of brand reputation) and to counter free riding or designed to prevent retailers from lowering retail prices in circumstances where they simply attract customers from competing retailers, but without increasing output or the brand manufacturer's profits see eg P Ippolito, 'Resale price maintenance: empirical evidence from litigation' (1991) 34 Journal of Law & Economics 263, JC Cooper, LM Froeb, D O'Brien, and MG Vita, 'Vertical antitrust policy as a problem of inference' (2005) 23 International Journal of Industrial Organization 639, S Dutta and others, 'Vertical Territorial Restrictions and Public Policy: Theories and Industry Evidence' (1999) 63 Journal of Marketing 121, 122 ('our results suggest that efficiency arguments should play an important role in the public policy debate on vertical restraints'); F Lafontaine and ME Slade, 'Exclusive Contracts and Vertical Restraints: Empirical Evidence and Public Policy' in P Buccirossi, *Handbook of Antitrust economics* (MIT Press 2008) ch 11, but cf A MacKay and D Aron Smith 'The Empirical Effects of Minimum Resale Price Maintenance' http://home.,uchicago.edu/mackay/files/The%20Empirical%20Effects%20of%20MRPM.pdf.

[31] See n 17 above.

[32] See further discussion in sections 3.1.2 and 4.2 below.

[33] European Commission's Notice on agreements of minor importance which do not appreciably restrict competition under art 101(1) of the Treaty on the Functioning of the European Union (De Minimis Notice), C(2014) 4136 final.

[34] See n 15 above.

[35] Regulation 330/2010 [2010] OJ L102/1, art 3.

[36] ibid art 4. Certain restraints listed in art 5 are also not exempt but do not stop the block exemption from applying to the agreement if they can be severed from it or are compatible with art 101.

[37] See Regulation 1/2003 [2003] OJ L1/1, art 29 and reg 330/2010 [2010] OJ L102/1, recital 15 and art 6.

agreements whose efficiencies are presumed to offset any anti-competitive effects which might arise.

2.2.3 Agreements within a Single Economic Unit

Agreements between a parent and its subsidiary (where the subsidiary does not enjoy real autonomy in determining their course of action in the market)[38] and certain agency agreements[39] fall outside of Article 101 as a result of the single economic unit concept; they are treated as arrangements within a single undertaking and not joint conduct falling within the scope of Article 101.

2.2.4 Fuller Effects Analysis

It is only where these rules, or presumptions, do not apply that fuller analysis of the agreements impact on competition under Article 101(1) or (3) is required. Under the modernized regime this is a question for 'self-assessment'. One consequence, however, of the EU system's significant reliance on presumptions of illegality, legality, and safe harbours is that, although providing desirable legal certainty where applicable, little jurisprudence post-modernization, and guidance, has emerged to clarify the law in the scenarios where they do not apply.[40] Although case law on effects analysis does exist, it is sparse and now mainly relatively old; see in particular *Société Technique Minière v Maschinenbau Ulm GmbH (STM)*,[41] *Metro-SB Grossmärkte GmbH v Commission (Metro 1)*,[42] *Pronuptia de Paris GmbH v Pronuptia de Paris Irmgard Schillgallis (Pronuptia)*,[43] and *Delimitis*.[44]

   In *Delimitis*, dealing with a single branding agreement (in this case a beer supply agreement in which the buyer was induced to concentrate orders for beer with the supplier),[45] the Court indicates that the inquiry under Article 101(1) should focus on the question whether or not the agreement, alone or in conjunction with a network of similar agreements, would be likely to have an appreciable impact on the parameters of competition, allow the parties to foreclose the market to competitors, and exercise market power. A different approach is taken in cases dealing with intrabrand restraints; incorporated in, for example, exclusive distribution agreements granting each dealer an exclusive sales territory or perhaps allocating it an exclusive customer group (exclusive customer allocation), franchising agreements, or SDSs. In these latter cases greater weight has been attached to the importance of the structure of competition and undistorted competition in all market segments (including at the distributor level) than to their impact on interbrand competition. They thus reflect a greater suspicion of intrabrand restraints on rivalry between a supplier's dealers than on interbrand ones on rivalry between a supplier and its competitors, treating

---

[38] See eg Case C-73/95P *Viho Europe BV v Commission* EU:C:1996:405.

[39] See eg Case C-279/06 *CEPSA* EU:C:2008:485.

[40] In particular, since modernization the Commission has not adopted either an infringement decision involving an analysis of the restrictive effects of a vertical agreement, or a non-infringement decision or published a 'guidance letter'.

[41] Case 56/65 EU:C:1966:38.

[42] See n 20 above.

[43] ibid.

[44] Case C-234/89, EU:C:1991:91. See also Case 23/67 *Brasserie de Haecht v Wilkin* EU:C:1967:54.

[45] E.g. where the buyer is precluded from manufacturing, buying, marketing, and/or selling competing products or services (non-compete or non-competition obligations) or required to purchase a specific percentage or a specific amount of its requirements of a type of product from the supplier (quantity forcing or requirements contracts).

the former as restrictive of competition unless objectively necessary to achieve a legitimate objective—for example, the penetration of a new market, to prevent free riding, to encourage non-price competition between dealers, or to ensure the commercial success of a franchise agreement. Not only are these cases not entirely easy to reconcile with the general, modernized approach advocated in the Commission's Vertical Guidelines but they shed little light on the question of how certain vertical restraints—such as price parity and most favoured nation clauses (MFNs)[46]—should be assessed. Rather, a transparent structure for analysing and balancing the competitive harms and benefits of vertical arrangements has not developed.[47]

3 UK Jurisprudence

3.1 Vertical Agreements and the Competition Act

3.1.1 Overview

In line with the CMA's guidance and the EU approach, a majority of public enforcement in relation to vertical agreements has, since the withdrawal of the Verticals Exclusion Order, focused on vertical agreements[48] containing severe and established restrictions of competition by object—mainly RPM, online RPM, or other restraints on online selling. Many of these cases have resulted in the imposition of fines on infringing undertakings.

A number of UK cases have, however, also examined vertical arrangements involving restraints which are not 'established' object restraints. For example; price relationship agreements or contracts that reference rivals' prices—where a supplier requires a reseller to set the resale price of its product at a price related to the price set for a competitor's product; MFNs where the supplier constrains its ability to price discriminate amongst customers by promising to treat a customer no less favourably than other customers;[49] and, exclusivity provisions.

---

[46] See n 49 below. Relatively few cases at the EU level have focused on such restraints, but see COMP/39.847, *e-books* [2013] OJ C378/25 (proceedings concluded when five principal publishers agreed to terminate their agency agreements with Apple and offer other retailers the opportunity to end their agency agreements too), (see also Case CE/9440-11, *e-books* (1 December 2011, OFT investigation into e-books and arrangements closed on grounds of administrative priorities and in particular because the OFT considered the European Commission was well placed to arrive at a comprehensive resolution of this matter); AT40153 *Amazon* (28 July 2017), (the Commission accepted commitments to address concerns that certain clauses, especially MFN provisions, in distribution agreements between Amazon and e-book publishers, infringed art 102, rendering it more difficult for other e-book platforms to compete with Amazon see also n 102 below).

[47] This is in stark contrast to the relative advances that have occurred in the economic and legal assessment of vertical mergers and abuse of dominance (often involving the analysis of similar competitive effects) see Jones and de la Mano (n 29).

[48] Although there have been no UK cases involving the applicability of Chapter I to an agreement between a parent and its subsidiary, in OFTEL decision, *Vodafone* (5 April 2002), an issue arising was whether agreements entered into between Vodafone and its distributors that fixed the retail prices of pre-pay mobile phone vouchers were agency agreements. In the end, however, no decision had to be made on this point as Chapter I was found not to apply in this case on the basis that Vodafone was found to have acted not autonomously but pursuant to a regulatory obligation.

[49] For example, that it will not provide its products to other customers at lower prices (and/or if it does it will also reduce the price to that customer) (wholesale MFNs) or that it will not sell its products on the agent's platform at a price higher than on which it sells on other platforms or which it sells itself (retail MFNs or across platform parity agreements (APPAs)).

3.1.2 Resale Price Maintenance and Online Selling Restraints

A relatively large proportion of the OFT's early Chapter I decisions involved RPM, the only vertical restraint not covered by the Verticals Exclusion Order.[50] For example, in May 2002, the Director General of Fair Trading (DGFT) issued a decision finding that three undertakings had infringed the CA 1998 by entering into agreements for the supply of MEI automatic slack adjusters which incorporated RPM provisions.[51] The DGFT found that the Verticals Exclusion Order did not apply, and that the agreements appreciably restricted competition within the UK (thus, there was therefore no need to prove that this was their effect),[52] before imposing fines totalling £33,737. In addition, a fine of £4.95 million was imposed on *Hasbro*[53] for agreeing with its distributors that toys and games should not be sold below its list prices. In *Lladró Comercial SA*[54] the DGFT concluded that agreements containing provisions requiring retailers to inform the supplier of proposed discounts, allowing the supplier to repurchase discounted products, and prohibiting the advertising of discounts amounted to RPM which did not benefit from the Exclusion Order.[55] In *Toys & Games: Hasbro UK Ltd, Argos Ltd and Littlewoods Ltd*[56] and *Replica Football Kit*[57] much higher fines, totalling £22.65 and £18.6 million, respectively, were imposed for RPM (although both fines were reduced on appeal).[58] In each of these cases, however, the price fixing also had a much more serious horizontal price fixing component (a hub and spoke type agreement).[59] These cases are consequently discussed more fully in Chapter 2.

Since 2005, investigations have more frequently focused on online pricing or selling restrictions (perhaps filling a gap left by the European Commission which between 2005 and 2018

---

[50]   Land and Vertical Agreements Exclusion Order (n 6) arts 3 and 4.

[51]   DGFT Decision, *Price Fixing Agreements involving John Bruce (UK) Limited, Fleet Parts Limited and Truck and Trailer Components* (13 May 2002).

[52]   See especially ibid paras 35-37, 68–72, and 73–75.

[53]   DGFT Decision, *Agreements between Hasbro UK Ltd and distributors fixing the price of Hasbro toys and games* (28 November 2002). No fines were imposed on the distributors as Hasbro took the initiative for the agreement and the distributors had no choice but to accept the restrictive terms.

[54]   DGFT Decision, *Agreements between Lladró Comercial SA and UK retailers fixing the price of porcelain and stoneware figurines* (31 March 31 2003).

[55]   ibid para 107. No fine was imposed in this case however as Lladró had received a comfort letter from the European Commission that the agreement did not infringe art 101(1). As this letter had been issued on the basis that the agreement did not substantially affect trade between Member States it did not have any relevance to the question of whether the DGFT could proceed to an infringement decision or whether the agreement contained anticompetitive provisions.

[56]   DGFT Decision, *Agreements between Hasbro UK Ltd, Argos Ltd and Littlewoods Ltd fixing the price of Hasbro toys and games* (21 November 21 2003).

[57]   OFT Decision (1 August 2003).

[58]   Cases 1014 and 1015/1/1/03 *Argos Ltd and Littlewoods Ltd v OFT* [2005] CAT 13, upheld on appeal [2006] EWCA Civ 1318, Cases 1021/1/1/03 and 1022/1/1/03 *JJB Sports plc v Office of Fair Trading* [2004] CAT 17, aff'd *Argos Ltd and Littlewoods Ltd v Office of Fair Trading; JJB Sports plc v Office of Fair Trading* [2006] EWCA Civ 1318.

[59]   In the former, the OFT found an overall agreement between the three parties, comprised of two bilateral vertical price-fixing agreements (which themselves constituted infringements of the Act) concluded between Hasbro and Argos and Hasbro and Littlewoods, respectively. Although there was no evidence that Argos or Littlewoods had directly contacted the other, the OFT decided that each had agreed with Hasbro to adhere to recommended retail prices on the clear understanding that they would also be adhered to by the other, and confidential information was exchanged between them with Hasbro acting as their middleman. The Director thus found evidence of collusion between the three parties that had the common objective of fixing the price of Hasbro toys and games. Because of the serious nature of the infringement, the DGFT imposed penalties of £17.28 million and £5.37 million on Argos and Littlewoods, respectively. Hasbro, however, received no fine, reflecting 100 per cent leniency granted due to its cooperation with the OFT. See also Case CE/2464-03 *UOP desiccant* (8 November 2004) and eg Case CE/9161-09 *Distribution of Mercedes-Benz commercial vehicles (van)* (27 March 2013) and Case CE/3094-03 *Dairy* (10 August 2011).

stood back from enforcement of Article 101 in relation to vertical agreements).[60] Although e-commerce has rapidly transformed distribution and retailing methods and, arguably, can exacerbate free riding risks, especially where consumers rely on retail services—for example in the case of complex products, experience goods, or one off purchases of durable goods—the CMA has not treated online RPM differently from other cases of RPM. Rather, it is clearly concerned that e-commerce can enhance the effectiveness of RPM, especially by making monitoring easier. Its decisional practice thus establishes that it generally considers online RPM to constitute a serious infringement of the CA 1998 which is likely to attract fines, unless it is a small agreement between SMEs.[61] In a number of cases, however, fines have been reduced where firms have applied for leniency,[62] settled,[63] cooperated, or agreed to introduce competition law training or compliance programmes.[64] In some cases the CMA has found vertical agreements or concerted practices to exist based on policies announced by a supplier and accepted, or acquiesced in, by its retailers[65] (although the CMA has on occasions decided not to impose fines on retailers).[66]

In *Fender Musical Instruments*,[67] for example, the CMA imposed a £4.5 million fine on Fender following a finding that it had implemented and enforced a pricing policy designed to ensure that musical instrument resellers would not advertise or sell its guitars online below a specific minimum specified price (enforced through the sending of price lists, monitoring, including through the use of an auto-tracking software, and complaints) that breached Chapter I and Article 101. The CMA concluded that the agreement, which reduced downward pressure on online prices, reduced price competition and stabilized prices between resellers, increased the attractiveness of the Fender brand to resellers, and secured, maintained, or improved Fender's position in the market, appreciably restricted competition by object. In so finding the CMA stressed the importance of the internet as a retail channel and that price was one of the main factors on which resellers competed.[68] The facts and reasoning adopted in this case were very similar to those involved in *Casio Electronics*,[69] decided six months before it. In this case the CMA imposed a £3.7 million fine on Casio in

---

[60] The first vertical case decided after COMP/36.623, 36.820, and 37.275 *Peugeot* (5 October 2005) was Case AT/40.465 *Asus* (26 September 2018) IP/18/460.

[61] CA 1998, s 39(3) was applied in the cases of *Pride* and *Roma* (nn 71 and 72 below).

[62] The UK leniency system applies to RPM as well as to cartel arrangements; see OFT 1495 *Applications for leniency and no-action in cartel cases* (July 2013), para 2.3 https://www.gov.uk/government/publications/leniency-and-no-action-applications-in-cartel-cases and has been applied in a number of RPM cases; see eg *Toys and Games* (n 56); Case 50565-3 *Fender* (20 January 2020); Case 50343 *Light fittings* (3 May 2017); Case 50565-5 *Electronic drum sector* (29 June 2020).

[63] See eg Case CE/9857/14 *Ultra Finishing Ltd (Bathroom Fittings)* (10 May 2016); *Light fittings* (n 62) and *Electronic drums* (n 62); Case 50565-4 *Synthesizers and high-tech equipment* (29 June 2020) and Case 50565-6 *Digital keyboards and guitars* (17 July 2020) (fine of £278,945 for RPM).

[64] Especially where the firms are SMEs and appear to have limited knowledge of competition law. See eg *Ultra Finishing* (n 63) and Case CE/9856/14 *Foster Refrigerator UK (Commercial Refrigeration)* (24 May 2016).

[65] See eg n 74 and text below and Case T-41/96 *Bayer AG v Commission* EU:T:2000:242, aff'd Joined Cases C-2 and 3/01 P EU:C:2004:2. But see eg Case CP/1709-02 *Elite Greenhouses Limited*, where no RPM agreement was found.

[66] See eg Case 50230 *Ping* (n 16) and *Fender* and *Casio* (nn 67 and 69 below).

[67] Case 50565-3 (20 January 2020). On 26 March 2019, the CMA also fined Fender £25,000 for hiding documents during the investigation.

[68] ibid para 4.208.

[69] Case 50565-2 (1 August 2019). See also *Synthesizers and high-tech equipment* (n 63) (fine of around £1.5 million for provisions prohibiting advertising and selling online below minimum prices); *Electronic drums* (n 62) (fine of just over £4 million for RPM); *Digital keyboards and guitars* (n 63) (fine of £278,945 for RPM); *Light fittings* (n 62) (imposing fines totalling £2,763,000); *Ultra Finishing Ltd (Bathroom Fittings)* (n 63); and Case CE/9856/14 *Foster Refrigerator UK (Commercial Refrigeration)* (24 May 2016),)n 70 and text below. The CMA has also issued a number of advisory and warning letters alerting recipients to the illegal nature of RPM and prompting action

relation to its market-wide pricing policy, designed to ensure that resellers would not advertise or sell digital pianos or digital keyboards online below a specified price (also monitored through installed software).

In a series of cases the CMA has also dealt with restrictions on online advertising of prices; including *Foster Refrigerator UK (Commercial Refrigeration)*,[70] *Roma Medical Aids Ltd*,[71] *Pride Mobility Products Ltd*,[72] and *TGA Mobility Ltd*.[73] The latter was ultimately closed on administrative priority grounds after TGA removed the restrictions and agreed to introduce competition law training and a compliance programme. In *Foster*, the CMA concluded that a policy, which prohibited resellers from advertising Foster products below minimum advertised prices (both online and offline) amounted to RPM infringing Chapter I and Article 101. It found that an agreement or concerted practice between Foster and its resellers could be established in this case as the policy was clear, the policy was monitored and enforced with sanctions for non-compliance (in some cases through ceasing supply or closing accounts), and each reseller acquiesced to the policy by changing their online prices when requested to do so by Foster.[74] Further, that the agreement restricted competition by object. In so doing the CMA rejected, on the facts, Foster's argument that the object of the policy was not to restrict competition but to protect its brand and reputation by ensuring that dealers had the incentive to invest in the brand and pre—and post-sale services and to prevent misleading advertising. Rather, the evidence indicated that the purpose of the policy was to prevent discounting and maintain reseller margins and not to tackle unprofessional conduct.

In *Roma* the CMA also found that a restriction on online sales by certain retailers infringed the rules, an issue which also arose in the case of *Ping*.[75] In the latter keenly contested case, Ping was found to have infringed the Chapter I prohibition and Article 101 by introducing a policy which prevented retailers from selling its golf clubs online. The core issues arising in this case were whether the arrangements should be characterized as restrictive of competition by object and, if so, whether they were capable of satisfying the legal exception/exemption criteria set out in the CA 1998 and Article 101(3). Ping vociferously contended that its selective distribution arrangements did not infringe the rules. Rather, the policy was designed to protect its brand and confine sales to brick and mortar stores that could increase club quality and consumer choice by providing buyers with custom fitting, and to protect retailers from others free-riding on their efforts; the restraints on internet selling were thus justified because they pursued legitimate aims. Further, that given the high

---

to ensure compliance. See also eg Case 50523 *Heathrow Airport* (25 October 2018) (condemning a provision in a lease agreement between Heathrow and Arora preventing the latter from charging lower prices to non-guests for the T5 Sofitel car park than the equivalent rates from those charged elsewhere at Heathrow airport. Given that this protected Heathrow's car parking from price competition the parties were competitors and this was not a vertical agreement see also CAA decision in *East Midlands International Airport/Prestige Parking Ltd* (20 December 2016)).

[70] Case CE/9856/14 (24 May 2016).
[71] Case CE/9578-12 (5 August 2013).
[72] Case CE/9578-12 (27 March 2014). Although a claimant tried to bring a follow-on, opt-out collective action for damages on behalf of pensioners (see CA 1998, s 47B) who may have suffered harm as a result of the price restrictions, the action was ultimately withdrawn. See Case 1257/7/16 *Gibson v Pride Mobility Products Ltd*.
[73] Case 50469 (19 October 2017).
[74] See also eg *Ultra Finishing Ltd (Bathroom Fittings)* (n 63).
[75] Case 50230 (24 August 2017).

levels of interbrand competition, customers that wished to buy golf clubs without custom fitting could easily purchase a different brand.

The CMA, whose decision was upheld by both the CAT[76] and the Court of Appeal,[77] rejected this argument finding that prohibiting online sales is liable to restrict, and is by its very nature restrictive of, competition—eliminating a modern means of distribution incentivizing and enabling retailers to attract, and consumers to purchase, a product outside of their normal catchment area.[78] Further, the CMA rejected Ping's argument that the ban was either necessary—clubs could be, and were, sold online without a custom fitting—or proportionate to the commercial aim of promoting in-store custom fitting—other less restrictive, technically achievable and viable alternatives were available to meet Ping's legitimate objectives.

The reasoning of the CMA, the CAT, and the Court of Appeal differed and each presents difficulties in places.[79] Nonetheless, none of them was prepared to find that the objective and the context of the agreement—designed in this case to improve customer satisfaction and the appeal of Ping golf clubs—meant that the contractual ban on internet selling (a de facto territorial restraint) did not have as its object the restriction of competition. Consequently, the burden was not shifted to the CMA to establish a restrictive effect before justifications under the exemption criteria had to be proffered and considered. Rather, the approach adopted by the CMA and courts closely follows, without expressly acknowledging the internal market perspective, the hardline attitude towards territorial restraints and prohibitions, or limitations, on parallel trade between Member States set out by the Court of Justice in *Pierre Fabre*[80] and the European Commission in its Vertical Guidelines and other communications. Because such restraints impinge on market integration goals, they are almost invariably considered to be incompatible with EU competition law, irrespective of any efficiency or other justification for the agreement.[81] Indeed, eliminating these private obstacles to free movement is considered necessary to achieve the maximum possible level of EU market integration;[82] so adding 'an extra dimension to the analysis of vertical restraints'[83] in the EU.[84] The promotion of online sales is also considered to be 'extremely important for the internal market in Europe because it broadens the market, improves the choices for customers, and generally speaking, enhances competition';[85] online selling

---

[76] Case 1279/1/12/17 *Ping Europe Ltd v CMA* [2018] CAT 8 (although the CAT found that the CMA had erred in the law in some respects it nonetheless held that the agreement did restrict competition by object. However, it reduced the level of fine).

[77] [2020] EWCA Civ 13.

[78] Relying in Part II of its decision on the Court of Justice's and the opinion of Advocate General Mazac in Case C-439/09 *Pierre Fabre* (n 24).

[79] See eg Professor Pablo Ibanez Colomo's analysis of the CMA, CAT, and Court of Appeal rulings in Chillincompetition https://chillingcompetition.com/2018/05/15/on-the-cmas-ping-case-objective-justification-and-object-restrictions-under-article-1011-tfeu/.

[80] Case C-439/09 *Pierre Fabre* (n 24).

[81] See nn 23–27 and text above.

[82] Removal of non-tariff barriers is not sufficient for the full development of parallel trade, arbitrage and changes in distribution across Europe. For the complete success of economic integration it is necessary that producers, distributors and consumers, find it profitable to move towards the new market situation and not take actions to avoid or counteract the effects of the Single Market measures The elimination of barriers to trade may not achieve its objective if producers and/or distributors introduce practices contrary to integration.

[83] Green Paper on Vertical Restraints in EC Competition Policy, COM(96) 721, para 70.

[84] Companies have not been allowed to recreate private barriers between Member States where State barriers have been successfully abolished or to seal off territories.

[85] 'Interview with Dr Alexander Italianer, Director General for Competition, European Commission' @ theantitrustsource (April 2011) 1, 6.

can therefore be restricted only in exceptional circumstances.[86] Given the strong internal market impact on this line of cases, it is debatable whether it should be so influential on UK competition law (see further section 4).

In *BMW/Carwow*[87] the CMA also indicated that it was concerned about the impact on competition of BMW's decision not to allow dealers to list their cars on a new car comparison website, 'carwow': 'Online comparison tools can promote competition in many markets and help consumers make informed choices.'[88] However, in the light of its prioritization principles the CMA decided not to open a formal investigation after BMW UK informed the CMA of its decision to change its policy in order to allow its dealers to work with carwow and other internet-based new car portals.

3.1.3 Price Relationship Agreements and MFNs

No EU law yet sheds light on the question of how price relationship agreements should be analysed under Article 101.[89] Key questions arising include: (i) whether any such 'newer' vertical restraints or business practices, in particular ones which may resemble RPM, are sufficiently deleterious to be treated as a restriction by object; or (ii) whether, given the relative lack of experience with these provisions and their potential to give rise to efficiencies (by e.g. facilitating customer investment or market entry and/or reducing transaction costs), effects analysis should be conducted to ensure a fuller understanding of the clauses is accumulated and, if so, how that analysis is to be conducted.[90]

In *Tobacco*[91] the OFT controversially found that a series of agreements between two tobacco manufacturers and ten retailers, under which retailers agreed to set prices for tobacco products in accordance with set 'parity and differential' requirements relating to competing linked brands, restricted competition by object. Although it did not find horizontal or vertical price fixing (or other 'established' object restraints), it concluded relying on the Court of Justice's judgment in *T-Mobile Netherlands*[92] that the scope of object infringements should not be interpreted narrowly,[93] and that taking account of the nature, objectives and context of the agreements they were by their very nature injurious to competition. Further, and in spite of the complexity of the decision (which exceeded 700 pages), it imposed the largest aggregate fines it had levied in a single decision, totalling £225 million.

---

[86] See eg Pablo Ibáñez Colomo, 'Article 101 TFEU and Market Integration' (2016) 12 Journal of Competition Law & Economics 749.

[87] See https://www.gov.uk/government/news/bmw-changes-policy-on-car-comparison-sites-following-cma-action and n 25 above.

[88] Ann Pope, CMA Senior Director of Antitrust.

[89] See nn 40–46 and text above.

[90] See eg UK's Office of Fair Trading (OFT) and prepared by Laboratorio di Economia, Antitrust, Regolamentazione (LEAR), OFT 1438, 'Can "Fair" Prices be Unfair? A Review of Price Relationship Agreements' (September 2012); A Fletcher and M Hviid, 'Retail Price MFNs: Are they RPM "At Its Worst"' CCP Working Paper 14–15.

[91] Case CE/2596–03 *Tobacco* (15 April 2010). See eg A Jones and A Turati. 'The UK Tobacco Case: Restrictions by Object in Vertical Agreements' (2012) 3 Journal of European Competition Law and Practice 287.

[92] Relying on Case C-209/07 *Competition Authority v Beef Industry Development Society Ltd (BIDS)* EU:C:2008:643.

[93] Holding that an agreement could be regarded as having an anticompetitive object, where 'it has the potential to have a negative impact on competition. In other words, the concerted practice must simply be capable in an individual case, having regard to the specific legal and economic context, of resulting in the prevention, restriction or distortion of competition'. See Case C-8/08 *T-Mobile Netherlands BV v Raad van beestuur van de Nederlandse Mededingingsautoriteit* EU:C:2009:343, para 31.

Although the OFT's decision was set aside on appeal, the CAT did so on procedural grounds.[94] This meant that it did not have to rule on the substantive question of whether the OFT had correctly found the arrangements to be restrictive of competition by object. It seems unlikely nonetheless that this finding would have been upheld. Not only were key elements of the OFT's reasoning in its decision related to the theory of harm abandoned during the appeal hearings, but the OFT's statements on the breadth of the object category seemed out of line with EU case law. This latter view is now reinforced by the Court of Justice's subsequent, and important, judgment in *Groupement des cartes bancaires v Commission (CB)*.[95] In this case the Court stressed that because a finding that an agreement restricts competition by object exempts a claimant from its ordinary burden of demonstrating a restriction of competition, the category of object restrictions is a narrow one, confined to agreements which obviously harm the proper functioning of competition. No detailed market analysis should thus be conducted in object cases. If such an assessment is required, as would appear to be the case where a complex theory of harm is developed, that indicates that a fuller effects analysis is necessary.[96]

The OFT also took a robust view on object restraints in its *Hotel Online Booking*[97] investigation. In this case it adopted the provisional view that agreements between hotels (including the InterContinental Hotels Group) and Online Travel Agents (OTAs, Booking.com, and Expedia Inc), restricting each OTA's ability to discount the rate at which room only hotel accommodation bookings were offered to consumers, had as their object the restriction of competition in breach of the Chapter I prohibition and Article 101 (through limiting price competition between OTAs and hotels). Again, however, the suitability of applying object analysis to new restraints in this way was never fully tested, as the OFT did not adopt a final decision but instead accepted commitments from the parties to change their behaviour.[98] Although the case was remitted back to the CMA after the commitments were quashed, in the end the CMA closed the case on the grounds of administrative priorities.[99] By this time developments were occurring in other Member States, and within the European Competition Network, leading a number of Member States (but not all)[100] to allow the OTAs to retain narrow MFNs. These permitted the hotels to give OTAs parity in respect of rates and conditions published by the hotels online, but eliminated availability parity and price/condition parity against other

---

[94] Cases 1160–5/1/1/10 [2011] CAT 41. The CAT only set aside the Decision insofar as it applied to the appellants. This raised the difficult issue of how the annulment of a decision affected the position of the parties that entered into 'early resolution' agreements with the OFT and which elected not to appeal the Decision (could they continue to be found to have infringed the CA 1998 by entering an agreement with another party where the other party to the agreement had been found not to have committed such an infringement?). Although the Court of Appeal held that two companies that did not appeal the *Tobacco* decision could recover the fines imposed on them, on the basis that requirements of fairness and equal treatment had been breached (the OFT reached a settlement agreement with another party to the agreement whereby the penalty imposed was repaid with a contribution to interest) see *Gallaher Group Ltd v CMA* [2016] EWCA Civ 719. This judgment was reversed by the Supreme Court [2018] UKSC 25.

[95] Case C-67/13 P EU:C:2014:2204.

[96] See ibid paras 48–92 and eg L Peeperkorn, 'Coherence in the Application of Articles 101 and 102: A Realistic Prospect or an Elusive Goal?' (2016) 39(3) World Competition 389; and Jones, Sufrin, and Dunne (n 5) ch 5.

[97] Case CE/9320-10 (31 January 2014).

[98] 31 January 2014 (see CA 1998, s 31A).

[99] 16 September 2015 (it continued to monitor developments in the sector, however).

[100] See the Bundeskartellamt's decision (20 December 2013).

OTAs or through offline channels and allowed hotels to offer lower rates to, for example, loyal customers.[101]

In later cases a more nuanced approach has been adopted. In some cases investigations into price parity clauses have been closed[102] or conducted in conjunction with exclusivity provisions (see section 3.1.4 below) or within market studies or market investigations under the EA 2002 (see section 3.2 below). However, in November 2020, the CMA found that MFN clauses, or price parity clauses, by comparethemarket.com, providing that home insurance providers must not offer lower prices for insurance policies on other price comparison websites had an appreciable restrictive effect on competition and infringed the Chapter I prohibition and Article 101.[103] Following an analysis of the relevant market, the CMA concluded that the network of MFNs was likely to have led to higher home insurance prices. It reduced price competition between PWCs, lowered incentives for insurers to lower prices, restricted the ability of rival price comparison websites to expand (so maintaining or strengthening comparethemarket.com's market power) and reduced price competition between home insurers competing on price comparison websites. It also concluded that no evidence of pro-competitive efficiencies had been adduced which would meet the conditions of section 9 CA 1998 or Article 101(3) before imposing fines of £17,910,062 on comparethemarket.com to reflect the serious nature of the infringement and the need for deterrence.

3.1.4 Other Distribution Arrangements

A handful of cases have also raised the compatibility of exclusive distribution, single branding and exclusivity agreements with Article 101 and Chapter I.

In two early CA 1998 cases the OFT considered the application of Chapter I to exclusive distribution agreements but found that they were covered by the Verticals Exclusion Order which in both cases the DGFT decided not to withdraw.[104] In *ATG Media*[105] the CMA also investigated exclusivity conditions and MFNs in the market for live online bidding (LOB) platforms that allow bidders to bid in real time in a live auction taking place in an auction house. Complaints were made that ATG Media prohibited auction house customers from using a competing LOB auction platform that offered bidders a lower price, from offering more favourable terms to other platforms and imposed restrictions on their ability to advertise or promote services provided by other platforms. The CMA was concerned that the restraints foreclosed the relevant market by reinforcing entry and expansion barriers. The proceedings were closed, however, after ATG Media agreed for a period of 5 years to refrain from incorporating these clauses in its agreements.

---

[101] See N Varona and A Hernandez Canales, 'Online Hotel Booking' *CPI Antitrust Chronicle* (May 2015) and Report on the monitoring exercise carried out in the online hotel booking sector by EU competition authorities in 2016 http://ec.europa.eu/competition/ecn/hotel_monitoring_report_en.pdf.

[102] See eg Case CE/9692/12 *Amazon Retail* (1 November 2013) (CMA investigation closed on administrative priority grounds after Amazon ended its Marketplace price parity policy and informed third party sellers).

[103] See https://www.gov.uk/cma-cases/price-comparison-website-use-of-most-favoured-nation-clauses. The investigation was launched following the CMA's market study into digital comparison tools (September 2017) and continued even though soon after the launch comparethemarket.com contacted insurers to say it would no longer be enforcing the wide MFN clauses.

[104] See n 6 above. See also *Paroxetine* (n 8).

[105] Case 50408 (29 June 2017). See also *Street Furniture (Outside Advertising)* (17 May 2012), in which the OFT closed its investigation into the use of long exclusivity provisions in relation to outdoor advertising following assurances by the parties to change their behaviour.

Exclusivity clauses have also been considered by the UK courts in a number of private actions. For example, in *Calor Gas Ltd v Express Fuels (Scotland) Ltd & Anor*[106] the Scottish Outer House Court of Session had to consider the compatibility with competition law (Article 101(1)) of provisions in distribution agreements obliging dealers of Calor's cylinder liquefied petroleum gas (LPG) (i) only to purchase and sell Calor LPG and (ii) not to handle Calor cylinders once the contract was terminated. Calor claimed that Express Fuel had infringed the agreement, whilst the latter contended that the restraints infringed Article 101 and were void. Applying *Brasserie de Haecht, Delimitis*,[107] and *Neste Markkinointi Oy v Yotuuli Ky*[108] the Court found, given the significant share of the GB market enjoyed by Calor (of 50 per cent), the mature nature of the market and the nature and extent of the provisions, that the restraints foreclosed new entry and infringed Article 101:

> It is not difficult to understand that if a nationwide network of principal dealers is tied to the brand leader for at least five years, this will restrict competition, especially in a mature market. When the post-termination handling restrictions are added, the defenders' case becomes even more compelling, though I would have considered the vertical restraint as sufficient in itself to amount to non-compliance with Article [101(1)].[109]

Further, in *Socrates Training Ltd v The Law Society of England and Wales*[110] the CAT had to consider Socrates' claim that a requirement imposed by the Law Society that solicitors had to obtain certain mandatory training, exclusively from the Law Society, infringed both Chapters I and II CA 1998. In relation to Chapter I, the CAT found that the Law Society, in providing training, was an undertaking and that the arrangements between it and law firms constituted agreements between undertakings for the purposes of section 2.[111] Further, in line with its finding under Chapter II that the tying arrangement was abusive and not objectively justified, it held that the agreements restricted competition and did not satisfy the conditions of Article 101(3).

In *Agents' Mutual Ltd v Gascoigne Halman Ltd*[112] the CAT had to adjudicate on the question of whether certain rules imposed by Agents' Mutual Ltd when it opened a new online portal, OnTheMarket, for the sale of properties (in competition with Zoopla and Rightmove) were compatible with the CA 1998. The rules at issue prevented estate agents subscribing with it from subscribing with more than one other portal, restricted

---

[106] [2008] CSOH 13.

[107] See n 44 above.

[108] Case C-214/99 EU:C:2000:679.

[109] [2008] CSOH 13, para 35.

[110] Case 1249/5/7/16 [2017] CAT 10. See also eg Case 1298/5/7/18 *Achilles Information Ltd v Network Rail Infrastructure Ltd* [2019] CAT 20 (finding that a scheme instituted by Network Rail preventing Achilles from providing supplier assurance services in the GB had as its effect the restriction of competition. Further the exclusivity mandated by the schemes was not indispensable to health and safety goals and so was not objectively justified and did not meet the conditions for exemption. The CAT also held that, on the assumption that Network Rail had a dominant position in the market for the operation and provision of access to national rail infrastructure in GB, its conduct constituted an abuse of its dominant position. The critical issue considered under both provisions was whether the restriction on competition in a safety-critical industry was justified on health and safety grounds).

[111] *Socrates Training Ltd* (n 110) paras 89–92.

[112] Case 1262/5/7/16 (T) [2017] CAT 15 (transferred from the High Court 5 July 2016). The judgment was upheld on appeal [2019] EWCA Civ 24.

membership to full-service office-based estate or letting agents, and required members to promote only OnTheMarket and no other portals. Gascoigne Halman in this case argued that as the provisions restricted competition they were void and unenforceable; the One Other Portal rule in particular operated as a boycott and restricted competition by object. The CAT rejected the claim, concluding that Agents' Mutual Ltd did not have market power either in the property portals market, where it was a new entrant, or in the estate agents' market, where its Members accounted for only a small share of relevant purchase revenues. It held that the restraint was neither restrictive by object (applying *CB*), nor by effect. Rather, the rules provided mechanisms for an entrant to launch a new product and to break into the market.

The OFT, and CMA, have also provided some guidance on when distribution arrangements concluded during an emergency, or a period of crisis, might be compatible with UK competition rules. In *Memorandum of Understanding (MoU) on the supply of oil fuels in an emergency*,[113] the OFT decided that an agreement between the government, major oil companies, oil independents, road hauliers, and police and trade unions, allowing the government to direct the supplies of fuel to 'essential users' in a fuel crisis or shortage did infringe section 2(1) CA 1998 (by protecting supplies to defined users), but merited an exemption (in the end, the MoU was used as the basis for a public policy exclusion order).[114] In particular, the MoU improved the distribution of oil fuels during an oil fuel emergency and would benefit consumers who would profit from the priority given directly to essential users (those providing emergency services, maintaining public safety, or supplying food).

During the Covid-19 pandemic the CMA also made it clear that it is unlikely to enforce the CA against business cooperation—including horizontal or vertical arrangements—designed to ensure the supply and fair distribution of scarce products or services affected by the crisis to all consumers if: appropriate and necessary to avoid shortage or ensure security of supply; in the public interest; to the benefit of consumers; and, lasting no longer than necessary.[115] Further, in relation to section 9 the CMA set out its view that: conduct is likely to be efficiency-enhancing if: it ensures essential goods and services are made available to the public or an important sub-set of it; consumers are likely to get a fair share of the benefits if the arrangement mitigates shortages in supply; cooperation is likely to be indispensable where, in light of the circumstances and limited time available, the conduct can reasonably considered to be necessary, especially if it is temporary in nature; and, if competition remains possible and cooperation is limited to where it is necessary. Specific public policy exclusion orders affecting distribution arrangements were also made in the groceries[116] and dairy[117] sectors in relation to qualifying activity between groceries chain suppliers (covering both retailer and suppliers) and dairy producer suppliers (including both farmers and milk processors) designed to prevent or mitigate disruption caused by Covid-19 and notified to the Secretary of State.

---

[113] DGFT Decision Memorandum of Understanding on the Oil Fuels in an Emergency (25 October 2001).
[114] http://www.legislation.gov.uk/uksi/2012/710/made.
[115] See https://www.gov.uk/government/news/covid-19-cma-approach-to-essential-business-cooperation.
[116] See https://www.legislation.gov.uk/uksi/2020/369/made.
[117] See http://www.legislation.gov.uk/uksi/2020/481/made.

3.2 Vertical Agreements and the Enterprise Act

The market investigation provisions of the EA 2002, like the preceding monopoly provisions of the Fair Trading Act 1973 (FTA), have been used to investigate markets in which vertical agreements are prevalent, where access to the market appears to be foreclosed to new competitors, and where use of the CA 1998 is inappropriate (see further Chapter 6[118]). These provisions enable the CMA to concentrate on the market as a whole rather than the individual agreements concluded by each undertaking. In *New Cars*,[119] for example, the (then) Competition Commission (CC) investigated under the FTA a market in which suppliers operated selective and exclusive distribution agreements. Even though these agreements were permitted at that time by an EU block exemption, the CC concluded that these practices restricted innovation and choice, resulted in higher prices to private customers, and operated against the public interest. It concluded further that the adverse effects resulting from the combination of the practices specified were greater than the sum of adverse effects from each of the practices individually. Recommendations made to address the adverse effects identified culminated in The Supply of New Cars Order 2000.[120] This investigation took place prior to the adoption of Regulation 1/2003, which provides that national competition authorities must apply EU law, in addition to national competition law, to agreements affecting trade between Member States and cannot apply that national competition law more strictly than Article 101 (see Article 3(1)(2)). UK Guidance under the EA subsequently clarified that although Article 3(2) of Regulation 1/2003 does not prevent a market investigation reference, it would impact on remedies that could be imposed following it.[121]

More recently in *Private motor insurance*[122] the CMA conducted a market investigation into the supply or acquisition of private motor insurance. The CMA considered whether a range or practices, including the incorporation of price parity provisions in contracts between motor insurance providers and price comparison websites, had an adverse effect on competition. In relation to the price parity provisions, the CMA found that the use by the four large price comparison websites[123] of wide MFNs, prohibiting insurers from charging lower prices on other sales channels, softened price competition between the price comparison websites regarding their services to private motor insurance providers and were likely to: raise barriers to entry into the market; reduce innovation; raise commission fees; and result in higher private insurance premiums for consumers. Narrow MFNs (only prohibiting lower prices being offered on the insurer's website) were, in contrast, less likely to produce anti-competitive effects and would help to drive interbrand competition by reducing the possibility of free-riding by private motor insurance providers.

The CMA proposed a package of remedies to mitigate and prevent the adverse effects on competition identified in the market, including an order that use of wide MFNs by price comparison websites and private motor insurance providers be terminated and that the

---

[118] See also eg C Ahlborn and D Piccinin, 'Between Scylla and Charybdis: Market Investigations and the Consumer Interest' in B Rodger (ed), *Ten Years of UK Competition Law Reform* (Edinburgh University Press 2010).

[119] Cm 4660 (2000).

[120] SI 2000/2088.

[121] OFT511 *Market Investigation References* (March 2006), adopted by CMA in March 2014, para 2.12.

[122] 24 September 2014.

[123] Which had significant market power and faced no effective constraints.

parties do not adopt practices replicating the anti-competitive effects caused by the wide MFNs (and preventing lower prices being quoted on sales channels other than the PMI provider's website).[124]

4 The Future

4.1 Should UK Law Continue to Follow EU Law?

Since the end of the transition period on 31 December 2020, the UK has no longer been part of the EU competition system.[125] Although vertical agreements concluded in the UK which affect trade between Member States still need to comply with EU law, EU law is no longer applied by the CMA, EU law does not have supremacy over UK law and the CMA now has principal responsibility for investigating agreements that affect trade within the UK, irrespective of whether or not the Commission is doing so. Further, the Competition Statutory Instrument[126] amending the CA 1998 and the EA 2002 has come into force. Although this retains the EU block exemptions in UK law until their expiry (the Verticals block exemption expires on 31 May 2022), it does not seem likely that the EU exemptions will be retained beyond this point. Further, section 60 CA 1998 has been omitted and new section 60A allows for inconsistency, and divergence, between UK and EU law in defined cases, including where necessary to reflect developments in the forms of economic activity or generally accepted principles (or the application of principles) of competition analysis. Both of these developments mean that, over time, the UK has scope, should it wish to do so, to diverge from EU law and practice in this area.

The crucial matter considered in this section therefore is whether UK law governing vertical agreements should continue to follow EU law or whether, especially because some of the EU jurisprudence and practice remains for historical reasons rather overly-formalistic and influenced by particular EU law goals (including market integration), the opportunity should be seized for change. In particular, whether a more permissive approach could be followed—rooted more closely in economics and aligned more closely with the interests of competition and consumers—in the analysis of vertical agreements, especially those incorporating restraints on intrabrand competition.

A first question could be whether UK should return to its original approach, excluding vertical agreements other than those incorporating RPM from the Chapter I prohibition of restrictive agreements. It is submitted however that this would not be desirable as experience, and an established body of literature, suggests that vertical agreements do have the potential to produce anti-competitive effects even when concluded by firms which are not

---

[124] See Private Motor Insurance Market Investigation Order 2015 https://assets.publishing.service.gov. uk/government/uploads/system/uploads/attachment_data/file/453475/Private_Motor_Insurance_Market_ Investigation_Order_2015.pdf

[125] See Agreement on the Withdrawal of the United Kingdom of Great Britain and Northern Ireland from the European Union and the European Atomic Energy Community (the Withdrawal Agreement), art 126.

[126] See the European Union (Withdrawal) Act 2018, European Union (Withdrawal Agreement) Act 2020, the Competition (Amendment etc) (EU Exit) Regulations 2019 (22 January 2019) https://www.legislation.gov.uk/ uksi/2019/93/contents/made, and https://assets.publishing.service.gov.uk/government/uploads/system/uploads/ attachment_data/file/864371/EU_Exit_guidance_CMA_web_version_final_---2.pdf.

dominant.[127] A decision to exclude vertical agreements in this way would therefore create a risk that the systems would not be flexible enough to reach all potentially problematic vertical arrangements, capable of harming competition through for example, facilitating collusion on markets (especially oligopolistic ones), or foreclosing competitors and/or the penetration of new markets.

If vertical agreements are not excluded from the Chapter I prohibition then the basic structure for analysing vertical agreements set out in EU law, and on which UK law is modelled, would remain: with strong presumptions against agreements incorporating object restraints; rules of legality or safe harbours for de minimis agreements and agreements satisfying the conditions of any relevant block exemption; and, full analysis being reserved for more complex situations where the rules and presumptions do not apply.

It has been seen that although this system developed under Article 101 provides considerable legal certainty to firms entering into vertical agreements, some problems do arise from it. For example, because of the extremely strict approach towards object and 'hard-core' restraints the system does create error risks; a possibility that some agreements designed to ensure efficient distribution across the EU will be deterred (type I errors). In addition, because relatively few cases exist in which a full effects based analysis of a vertical agreement is conducted,[128] guidance is limited on the question of how it is determined whether a vertical agreement has as its effect the appreciable restriction of competition and/ or whether the agreement satisfies the four conditions of Article 101(3).[129] In particular, it is unclear when concerns manifest in the jurisprudence about restraints on rivalry and internal market integration prevail over analysis based on an assessment of the impact of the conduct on economic efficiency and the welfare of consumers in the EU. The lack of a clear framework for assessment has meant that it is difficult to know how new vertical models of distribution or vertical restraints emerging on online markets and platforms are to be assessed. Many of these practices are not dealt with in detail in the Commission's Vertical Guidelines and, although some proceedings have taken place at the national level, a clear picture has not yet emerged as to how EU competition law governs them.

A second question therefore is whether some gradual modifications to the EU framework should be adopted in the UK to address some of the shortcomings of EU law in this sphere. For example, should the strong presumption of illegality applicable to certain vertical agreements in EU law continue to be applied or tempered, should a UK specific verticals block exemption be adopted and should more detailed guidance on vertical agreements be developed?

---

[127] See eg WS Comanor, 'Vertical Price-fixing, Vertical Market Restrictions, and the New Antitrust Policy' (1984–1985) 98 Harvard LR 983, R Pitofsky, 'In Defense of Discounters: The No-frills Case for a Per Se Rule against Vertical Price Fixing' (1983) 71 Geo LJ 1487; P Rey and T Vergé, 'Resale Price Maintenance and Horizontal Cartel' CMPO Discussion Paper 02/047 (2004); A Fletcher and M Hviid, 'Broad Retail Price MFN clauses: Are They RPM "At Its Worst"' (2016) 81 Antitrust Law Journal 1; and T Cheng, 'A Consumer Behavioral Approach to Resale Price Maintenance' (2017) 12(1) Virginia Law & Business Review 1.

[128] Most competition agency decisions relating to vertical agreements have involved object infringements and firms seek where possible to rely on the safe harbour of the block exemption. Most EU 'effects' cases have therefore involved references from national courts in the course of private litigation,

[129] See eg O Brooks, 'Struggling with Article 101(3) TFEU: Diverging Approaches of the Commission, EU Courts, and Five Competition Authorities' (2019) 56(1) CMLRev 121.

4.2 Presumption of Illegality

One important issue is whether the strong presumption of illegality[130] currently applied to RPM, online RPM, territorial restraints, and online selling restraints should remain and whether it should be extended to other provisions—for example, certain (e.g., wide) MFNs or restraints on online selling. The answer to the former question depends upon an assessment of whether the UK wishes to remain bound by EU precedents influenced by single market objectives and/or whether the 'economics' alone provides sufficient justification for the approach in these cases. In relation to the latter it could be argued, that as the frequency and magnitude of positive or negative effects of newer, and especially online, vertical restraints remain relatively unexplored, the category of object restraints should not be expanded further than the current object restraints, established in both EU and UK case law. Indeed, in *comparethemarket.com* discussed in 3.1.3 above, the CMA did not find that wide MFNs had as their object the restricition of competition, but rather conducted an analysis of their effects before concluding that a serious infringement of the rules had been committed.

Application of the general EU principles laid out in relation to object restraints should therefore be applied cautiously and rigorously and would be less contentious in the future if a fuller and more realistic characterization process were conducted to determine if object analysis is appropriate in any individual case involving a vertical agreement. The rigidity of and problematic resort to an overly expansive object category could be mitigated if the UK authorities were more willing, even for agreements incorporating established vertical price and territorial restraints, to consider the purpose and the context of the agreement before concluding whether object or effect analysis is required. Indeed, EU case law (including CB)[131] makes it clear that horizontal cooperation agreements with the potential to have mixed effects on competition—even those containing price or output restraints—do not fall within the object category unless they do not truly concern, for example, joint research and development, production, or joint purchasing, but serve as a tool to engage in a disguised cartel. Logic, and case law, requires that a similar, robust 'characterization' exercise should be carried out in relation to vertical restraints: meaning that RPM and territorial restraints plausibly necessary to the pursuit of a legitimate pro-competitive objective should not be found to restrict competition by object. Further, new restraints should not be added to the object category unless theory or experience justifies a finding that the clauses and context reveal a high probability of anti-competitive effects.[132]

This important step would ensure that where, as in a case such as *Ping*, plausible efficiency justifications for an agreement exist, the CMA would be required to establish and consider actual or likely anti-competitive effects, as well as proffered pro-competitive justifications, prior to the practice being condemned.

---

[130] Although no absolute or per se rule applies against object restraints, it has been seen that a perception has been built that they are most unlikely to be compatible with art 101, even where it has been vociferously argued by parties that the restraints at issue were necessary to enable a supplier to penetrate a new national market, prevent free-riding and so increase competition, consumer choice and market integration.

[131] See n 95 above. See also eg Commission's Horizontal Cooperation Guidelines, paras 128, 160–161, and 205–206.

[132] See Jones and de la Mano (n 29) and Jones and Kovacic (n 28).

4.3 Verticals Block Exemption or Another Safe Harbour

Another question to be resolved is whether a UK specific verticals block exemption should replace the EU Verticals Regulation once it expires in 2022. Clearly the EU block exemption provides desirable legal certainty which is highly appreciated by businesses. An alternative to adopting UK block exemptions, however, could be to provide a safe harbour in another way, perhaps through Guidelines explaining that vertical agreements are unlikely, in the absence of object restraints or networks of agreements, to have restrictive effects if the parties to the agreement lack market power (proxied, for example, by market shares of 30 per cent). Although this latter approach would lack the same legal effect and force of an exemption valued by firms, it would have some advantages over the block exemption approach from a legal coherence perspective. First, one problem with the Verticals Regulation, which exempts agreements in case they restrict competition, is that they focus attention on the exemption criteria and, implicitly, indicate that an infringement of Chapter I (and Article 101) has occurred (or is likely to have occurred). Arguably this contributes to the lack of clarity shrouding the question of how Article 101(1), and Chapter I, analysis is to be conducted (see further 4.4 below), especially given that most agreements satisfying the conditions of the current Verticals block exemption are in fact highly unlikely to affect actual or potential competition to such an extent that a negative effect on prices, output, innovation, or the variety of quality of goods can be expected. Guidelines on the interpretation of section 2(1) would, in contrast, help to shed light on how effects analysis under Chapter I is to be conducted in the future. Secondly, Guidelines would be less rigid than block exemptions which provide an automatic exemption for vertical agreements that satisfy its conditions which can only be withdrawn prospectively, even if they incorporate restraints that were not specifically considered at the time of the drawing up of the exemption; for example, in relation to the current Verticals Regulation restraints on use of price comparison websites, online advertising, selling on the internet via a third party platform or market place,[133] or price parity provisions and MFNs. Even though the benefit of the block exemption can be withdrawn this can only be done prospectively, and is rarely a priority for a competition authority. In contrast, guidance under section 2 would give the CMA greater flexibility and scope to consider a new restraint and, if appropriate, address it in a decision.

4.4 Provision of Guidance

Another crucial matter is how guidance can be provided as to how agreements that are not presumed to be illegal or legal, or which do not benefit from a safe harbour, are to be appraised. This is crucial, as effective enforcement of the competition laws needs to ensure not only that breaches are halted, punished, and deterred,[134] but also that the law is developed and elucidated. If the breadth of the object category is more realistically limited and block exemptions abandoned, the CMA (and claimants in private litigation) might, more frequently, be required to analyse the actual or likely anti-competitive effects of vertical agreements before an agreement is condemned under Chapter I. Although concern about

---

[133] See *Coty* (n 25).
[134] And, where appropriate, victims compensated.

the open-textured nature of full antitrust analysis has often led decision-takers to shy away from adopting it, and an anxiety that it will become tantamount to a rule of per se legality (given the difficulty it presents for claimants) leading to type I errors, the UK administrative system provides a flexible forum for the CMA to develop an administrable and workable framework for an assessment of vertical restraints which need not be an expensive, excessively complex or time-consuming task. For example, the UK competition agency's experience with price parity agreements and MFNs under both the CA 1998 and the EA 2002 has allowed it over time to build experience in appraising their mixed effects. It also illustrates the dangers of applying object analysis to them, prior to that experience being developed. If progress is advanced in this way through close analysis and decisions, which are reviewed on appeal, it would allow the law to evolve and provide greater clarity to firms. Indeed, if the CMA were to bring a number of carefully targeted effect cases in this way, they could help to lift the perception of effects analysis being unmanageable and disorderly and shed greater light on how:

- anti-competitive effects in terms of parameters of competition can be identified under Chapter I (departing from the objective necessity test set out in many of the EU cases) i.e. whether the agreement is likely to enable or facilitate the exercise of market power through input or customer foreclosure or coordination; and
- how those anti-competitive effects can be balanced against pro-competitive effects demonstrated under section 9. For example, that the parties may enhance the ability of the firms to act pro-competitively for the benefit of consumers by internalizing double mark-ups, preventing free riding, encouraging investment in customer services, permitting a cost effective alternative to service contracts, facilitating market entry for new firms and brands, or otherwise aligning the incentives of the parties.

5 Conclusions

Since the adoption of the CA 1998 UK competition law has taken a hardline approach towards RPM. Although the withdrawal of the Verticals Exclusion Order meant that many more vertical agreements were brought within the ambit of Chapter I, the main focus of the OFT and the CMA has remained on RPM (and more recently online RPM) and other established object restrictions. Indeed, of the eighteen CA 1998 infringement decisions adopted in relation to vertical agreements between 2000 and March 2020, sixteen of these related to RPM (some with hub and spoke or more serious horizontal aspects), online RPM or restraints on online selling. (One of the others was a more problematic infringement decision involved complex, vertical price relationship arrangements but was annulled on appeal (*Tobacco*) and only the eighteenth, *comparethemarket.com*, involved a finding of restrictive effects on competition).

As many other vertical agreements concluded in the UK benefit from the de minimis principle of the safe harbour of the EU Verticals Regulation, relatively few other vertical agreements have been reviewed by the CMA or UK courts. Filling a lacuna left by the European Commission, however, the UK competition agency has taken interest in MFNs, especially when used in relation to platforms, examining them, both in the context of the CA 98 and the EA 2002 market investigation procedures. A handful of other vertical agreements containing exclusivity provisions have also been reviewed by the CMA and the UK courts in private enforcement actions.

Although the UK has greater flexibility than exists under EU competition law to examine networks of vertical agreements and new vertical practices closely under its market investigation provisions, the approach towards vertical agreements under the CA 1998 has to date been based on EU law and, in line with the principle of supremacy of EU law and former section 60 CA 1998, followed it closely and without deviation. Indeed, in *Ping* the UK authorities applied principles of EU competition law, even in circumstances where they are heavily influenced by the EU single market objective.

Post-Brexit, the UK authorities and businesses will no doubt be keen to ensure that UK competition law and policy remains closely aligned with EU competition rules which many firms will in any event need to continue to comply with. There is scope, however, over time for UK law to diverge from EU law if this is thought to be beneficial and necessary to improve law and policy. This chapter suggests that some helpful improvements could be made, to develop a more coherent framework for the analysis of vertical agreements under Chapter I CA 1998. In particular, it has proposed a more robust mechanism for identifying object restraints and much clearer guidance, set out by the CMA and developed through decisional practice, on the questions of how restrictive effects of vertical agreements should be identified under section 2 and balanced against identified efficiencies under section 9.

4

Exclusionary Abuses

*Renato Nazzini**

1 Introduction

This chapter discusses the application of the Chapter II prohibition of the Competition Act 1998, as well as Article 102 TFEU, to exclusionary abuses in the UK from 2010 to 2020.[1] After a first decade in which the Office of Fair Trading (OFT), the Competition Appeal Tribunal (CAT) and the UK courts decided a number of leading cases that, in certain respects, broke new ground,[2] this second decade involves a more cautious approach, certainly from the Competition and Markets Authority (CMA). Infringement decisions are rare and the approach seems cautious, strictly anchored to EU and UK precedents. The CAT and the courts have been more innovative, particularly in private enforcement cases, which do, however, constitute a minority of the cases brought in the English courts, which are (not surprisingly) primarily follow-on actions based on Commission infringement decisions.

In public enforcement, the CMA has closed a number of cases with commitments and published a few detailed case closure decisions, with the aim of providing guidance to business in difficult areas of the law, such as anti-competitive rebates. As in the first decade, pharmaceuticals have been under the spotlight. Regulated industries such as post and transport have also, not surprisingly, featured prominently in the list of infringement decisions. Given the paucity of interventions, however, it is difficult to discern significant enforcement trends in this context.

In its second decade, modern UK competition law continued a trend already clear in the first decade: the prohibition of abuse of dominance has been applied in a more economically robust and commercially reasonable way than it has been by the EU institutions, the Commission, and the EU courts, and in certain other Member States.[3] Following the end of

* Professor of Law, King's College London. I am grateful to Silvia Massaro, Luigi Calini, and Davide Canzano for their help.

[1] The United Kingdom's exit from the European Union is effective in the UK since 31 January 2020 (Exit Day). However, a key feature of the Withdrawal Agreement between the EU and the UK is that the UK entered a Transition Period from 31 January 2020 until 31 December 2020. During the Transition Period, EU law applied in the UK (except for certain specified provisions) and must also be interpreted and applied in the UK in accordance with the same methods and general principles as those applicable in the EU. Therefore, provisions of the EU treaties, EU regulations and other legislation which deal with EU competition law continued to apply in and to the UK during the Transition Period. Furthermore, during the Transition Period, the European Commission and the Court of Justice continued to have the powers conferred upon them by EU law in relation to the UK and natural and legal person residing or established in the UK. Accordingly, their jurisdiction during the Transition Period remained the same as it did before Exit Day. As a result, the practical implication of the UK leaving the EU did not occur on Exit Day, but rather at the end of the Transition Period. After the Transition Period, EU law ceased to apply in the UK.

[2] These are discussed in Renato Nazzini, 'A Welfare-based Competition Policy Under Structuralist Constraints: Abuse of Dominance and OFT Practice' in B Rodger and A MacCulloch (eds), *Ten Years of UK Competition Law Reform* (Dundee University Press 2010) 97–138.

[3] ibid.

Renato Nazzini, *Exclusionary Abuses* In: *The UK Competition Regime.* Edited by: Barry Rodger, Peter Whelan, and Angus MacCulloch, Oxford University Press. © The Contributors 2021. DOI: 10.1093/oso/9780198868026.003.0004

the Brexit transition period, this trend may become more pronounced, as UK law is free of the constraints of EU law.

This chapter is structured as follows. Section 2 deals with dominance. Section 3 deals with the test for abuse, focusing on retroactive rebates and bundled discounts, exclusion in multi-market settings, exclusivity, most favoured nation (MFN) and equivalent clauses, discrimination, and exclusionary abuses in the pharmaceutical sector. Section 4 concludes.

2 Dominance

2.1 General Approach

The assessment of dominance is the first, necessary step in any abuse of dominance case. There can be no abuse without dominance. What dominance precisely means—beyond the vague definitions of the EU courts[4]—and, above all, how it can be proven, continues to be somewhat controversial globally.[5]

The CMA considers dominance as coextensive with substantial and durable market power, or, at the very least, substantial and durable market power is a necessary and major element of the assessment of dominance.[6] This is demonstrated by the CMA's consistent approach to dominance, which relies on: (a) market definition and analysis of short-term competitive constraints—market shares are an indication of dominance but generally not conclusive proof of it and existing and potential short-term competition is generally closely scrutinized; (b) barriers to entry are almost invariably an element of the analysis even if market shares are high; (c) buyer power is also considered, whenever relevant; and, (d) evidence of market dynamics, entry and exit, profitability, and conduct is also seriously considered. The CMA has thus continued the approach of the OFT in the previous decade.

In *Certas Energy*, a commitments case, Certas Energy had entered into long-term exclusive contracts with filling stations in certain geographic areas where it was dominant on the market for the wholesale supply of road fuels to filling stations.[7] The CMA's assessment of dominance focused not only on very large market shares but also on access to 'important infrastructure', namely the Shell Street terminal and the Loch Carnan terminal, although access to the former was also granted to Certas Energy's competitor under undertakings in lieu of a merger refence previously provided to the OFT. Failure by customers to switch notwithstanding the contractual right to do so also evidenced dominance.[8]

---

[4] Case 27/76 *United Brands v Commission* EU:C:1978:22, para 65; see also Case 85/76 *Hoffmann-La Roche v Commission* EU:C:1979:36, para 38 and Case T-219/99, *British Airways v Commission* [2003] ECR II-5917, para 189.

[5] R O'Donoghue, 'Exploitative Abuses', ch 5 in this volume; A J Padilla, 'The Law and Economics of Article 102 TFEU' (2nd edn, Hart Publishing, 2013) ch 4; J Faull, A Nikpay, and D Taylor (eds), 'Faull & Nikpay: The EU Law of Competition' (3rd edn, Oxford University Press, 2014) ch 4; P Ibáñez Colomo, 'The Shaping of EU Competition Law' (Cambridge University Press, 2018) ch 4; R Whish and D Bailey, *Competition Law* (9th edn, Oxford University Press, 2018) ch 5; D Bailey, Laura E John (eds), *Bellamy & Child: European Union Law of Competition* (8th edn, Oxford University Press, 2018) ch 10.

[6] On the CMA's general approach to dominance see CMA Guidance, 'Abuse of a Dominant Position' (OFT402) para 4.11 and 'Assessment of Market Power' (OFT 415) para 2.9.

[7] CMA, Decision to accept binding commitments from Certas Energy UK Limited and DCC plc, *Western Isles Road Fuels* (24 June 2014) (*Certas Energy*).

[8] ibid para 3.19.

In *INDEXX*, the OFT closed an investigation concerning IDEXX Laboratories Ltd.[9] There was no finding of dominance, but the OFT believed that IDEXX might be dominant on the market for the distribution of in-clinic veterinary analysers and consumables by individual type of test in UK (in-clinic market) because of high market shares[10] combined with significant barriers to entry and/or expansion, barriers to customer switching[11] and relatively low levels of buyer power.[12] The OFT also considered that IDEXX might be the monopoly supplier of certain specialist external lab tests in the UK (specialist external lab market) due to its being the holder of European patents and/or having been granted exclusive licences concerning European patents for these tests.[13]

In *Flybe*, a case closure decision, the OFT adopted a standard route-by-route market definition approach in a case concerning alleged predatory entry by Flybe on the Newquay to London Gatwick route.[14] Given the absence of significant buyer power and regulatory barriers to entry, the OFT focused on market shares, slot availability, sunk costs, economies of scale and scope, and a short runway at Plymouth that required the use of smaller aircraft.[15]

A robust assessment of dominance was also undertaken by the Office of Communications (OFCOM) in *Royal Mail*. Notwithstanding the very high market share of the dominant undertaking at the relevant time, which was approximately 98 per cent of the bulk mail delivery market in the UK, OFCOM also considered that: (a) Royal Mail was an unavoidable trading partners for anybody wishing to operate in the market; (b) it had the power to change the terms of access unilaterally; (c) there were high barriers to entry; and, (d) access operators and customers did not have sufficient countervailing buyer power.[16]

In *Impulse Ice Cream*, the CMA closed its investigation into a suspected abuse of a dominant position by Unilever plc in the supply of single-wrapped impulse ice cream in the UK, as there were no grounds for action.[17] The CMA considered that there were reasonable grounds for suspecting that Unilever had a dominant position on this market because of its market share well in excess of 50 per cent, which engenders a presumption of dominance, and because of its 'significant assured based of sales due to the strength of some of its brands and freezer exclusivity requirements'.[18]

It is clear, therefore, that the CMA—in accordance with the economic approach adopted previously by the OFT—assesses dominance in light of all available evidence, which necessarily includes both static structural indicators, such as market shares, and dynamic elements, including barriers to entry and expansion, buyer power, and customers' and competitors' counterstrategies.

---

[9] OFT, No Grounds for Action Decision, *Alleged abuse of a dominant position by IDEXX Laboratories Limited* (OFT1387 (1 November 2011) (*IDEXX*).

[10] ibid para 5.8–5.10.

[11] ibid paras 5.11–5.29.

[12] ibid paras 5.30–5.31.

[13] ibid para 5.50.

[14] OFT, No Grounds for Action Decision, *Alleged abuse of a dominant position by Flybe Limited* (OFT1286, 5 November 2010) (*Flybe*).

[15] ibid paras 5.12–5.28 and 5.76–5.79.

[16] OFCOM, *Discriminatory pricing in relation to the supply of bulk mail delivery services in the UK* (CW/01122/01/14, 14 August 2018) (*Royal Mail*) paras 6.73–6.98. The finding of dominance was not challenged on appeal.

[17] CMA, No Grounds for Action Decision, *Investigation relating to supplies of impulse ice cream* (9 August 2017) (*Impulse Ice Cream*).

[18] ibid para 23.

2.2 Dominance in Pharmaceutical Markets

The analysis of dominance in pharmaceutical markets poses its own challenges. Patents and their the anticipated or actual expiry have a significant impact on potential or actual competition. Furthermore, the 'consumer' in pharmaceutical markets is a multi-faceted concept, comprising the patient, who uses the drug, the clinician, who chooses which drug should be prescribed, and the national health service, which often pays, in full or in part, for the drug.

In *Paroxetine*, the question was whether GlaxoSmithKline was dominant concerning its anti-depressant drug Seroxat. GlaxoSmithKline argued that other anti-depressants with equivalent therapeutic effect were in the same market. GlaxoSmithKline's market shares on the paroxetine market during the relevant period were 100 per cent in manufacturing and 60 per cent in the finished product market.[19] The CMA, while duly referring to the EU law presumption of dominance triggered by market shares greater than 50 per cent,[20] stated that market shares are an 'indication' of dominance 'especially relevant when the undertaking concerned has maintained a high market share over a long period of time and when its nearest competitors hold shares that are considerably lower'.[21] Nevertheless, the CMA went on to assess barriers to entry,[22] expansion,[23] and buyer power.[24] Concerning barriers to entry, GlaxoSmithKline held several patents for paroxetine, which, unless declared invalid or not infringed, allowed GlaxoSmithKline to start costly litigation against any generic entrant. This, plus the costs of developing generic paroxetine, influenced the durability of GlaxoSmithKline's substantial market power.[25] Furthermore, the CMA analysed market evidence of what happened following independent generic entry, finding that, before such entry, prices were some 90 per cent higher and profits were around 8.5 times higher.[26]

In *Remicade*, a case closure decision, the CMA considered a suspected abuse of a dominant position concerning a discount scheme applied by Merck Sharp & Dohme Limited's (MSD) for the supply of Remicade to the NHS.[27] The CMA proceeded on the basis that MSD enjoyed a dominant position in the market for the supply of infliximab, including both Remicade and biosimilar medicines (that is, medicines that are only similar, not identical, to the originator medicine), in England, focusing on three factors. First, the evolution of market shares, by both volume and value, indicated dominance. Prior to the introduction of biosimilar medicines, MSD was the monopoly supplier of infliximab with a 100 per cent share of the relevant market, which declined month on month after the expiry of the Remicade patent, to reach 67 per cent by volume and 78 per cent by value in February 2016.[28] Secondly, 'clinical caution'—as a result of biosimilar medicines being only similar, not identical, to the originator medicine, the lack of previous experience of using biosimilars, and the paucity of relevant clinical trial data—was a key barrier to entry and expansion. The NHS would therefore have continued to meet a significant proportion of its total infliximab

---

[19]   CMA, *Paroxetine* Case CE-9531/11 (12 February 2016) (*Paroxetine*) para 4.100.
[20]   ibid para 4.102, relying on Case C-62/86 *AKZO Chemie v Commission* [1991] ECR I-3359, para 60.
[21]   *Paroxetine* (n 19) para 4.103.
[22]   ibid paras 4.116–4.123.
[23]   ibid paras 4.112–4.115.
[24]   ibid paras 4.124–4.126.
[25]   ibid paras 4.116–4.123.
[26]   ibid para 4.111.
[27]   CMA, No grounds for Action Decision, *Remicade* (50236, 14 March 2019) (*Remicade*).
[28]   ibid paras 3.36–3.38.

demand through Remicade throughout the relevant period.[29] Finally, MSD's conduct was unlikely to be constrained by any countervailing buyer power.[30]

In *Reckitt Benckiser*, the OFT determined that Reckitt Benckiser was dominant in the market for the NHS supply of alginate and antacid heartburn medicines. High market shares, greater than 80 per cent at the material time, were held to indicate dominance in all but exceptional circumstances, especially when the competitors' market shares were significantly smaller and incapable of undermining Reckitt Benckiser's leading market position.[31] Notwithstanding this finding, the OFT assessed barriers to entry[32] and countervailing buyer power.[33] It believed that Reckitt Benckiser's dominance was indicated by the fact that it was able to withdraw the leading and most popular product in the relevant market without losing significant market share. This suggested that Reckitt Benckiser was in a position to disregard the wishes of its consumers and users, which is the hallmark of dominance.[34]

2.2.1 A Gloss on Market Definition in Pharmaceutical Markets

A 10-year overview of UK cases on exclusionary abuses would be incomplete without a discussion of the issue of market definition in *Paroxetine*. In the CAT, GlaxoSmithKline challenged dominance on the basis of an erroneous market definition.[35] The CAT referred to established case law regarding the definition of the relevant product market[36] and focused on demand-side substitutability.[37] The CMA's decision had found that there were other anti-depressants that could be considered equivalent to paroxetine from a therapeutic perspective. However, for the CMA, competition from these medicines in the same treatment area did not constrain GlaxoSmithKline, which was able to sustain anti-competitive prices until generic entry.[38] Therefore, the CMA's market definition included only paroxetine.

Concerning this ground of challenge, the CAT adopted a 'novel' approach. The CAT recognised that before generic entry became a real prospect, paroxetine was not part of a separate market and competed somewhat with other selective serotonin reuptake inhibitors.[39] However, that degree of competition 'pales into insignificance compared to the effect of generic paroxetine'.[40] Consequently, the CAT thought it was 'not illogical to find that, as a pharmaceutical product approaches the stage when generic entry becomes a realistic possibility, the generic product is then taken into account in determination of competitive constraints and thus market definition'.[41] Moreover, the CAT found that GlaxoSmithKline was exposed to competitive pressure from parallel importers. For the CAT, this supported the finding that the most significant 'competitive constraint on GlaxoSmithKline's Seroxat

---

[29] ibid para 3.35.
[30] ibid paras 3.39–3.41.
[31] OFT, *Abuse of a dominant position by Reckitt Benckiser Healthcare (UK) Limited and Reckitt Benckiser Group plc* (OFT1368, 12 April 2011) (*Reckitt Benckiser*) para 5.11.
[32] ibid paras 5.47–5.48.
[33] ibid para 5.51.
[34] ibid para 5.54.
[35] *Generics UK Limited v Competition and Markets Authority* [2018] CAT 4 (CAT judgment in *Paroxetine*) para 379.
[36] Case T-504/93 *Tiercé Ladbroke SA v Commission of the European Communities* [1997] ECR II-00923, para 81.
[37] CAT judgment in *Paroxetine* (n 35) paras 381–83.
[38] *Paroxetine* (n 19) para 4.111.
[39] CAT judgment in *Paroxetine* (n 35) para 402.
[40] ibid.
[41] ibid.

in economic terms came from paroxetine' and not from other anti-depressants.[42] Given the much stronger constraint exerted by generic paroxetine (even if the generic companies had not actually entered the market yet), the CAT upheld the CMA's market definition, albeit on a different basis.[43] To support this approach, the CAT mainly relied on the Commission Decision in *Perindopril*, where the Commission relied 'on the extent of the competitive constraint from the generic product, although generic companies were not yet on the market'.[44] However, given that the *Servier* case was under appeal, the CAT preferred to include this matter in its reference to the Court of Justice of the European Union (CJEU).[45] Notwithstanding this, before the CJEU, the CAT narrowed down the market definition question. The CAT explained that the question referred on market definition did not concern whether Seroxat competed with other anti-depressants having equivalent therapeutic effect. The question was limited to whether potential generic entrants should be included in the market definition when the patent on the molecule had expired but the original patent holder had another patent on the manufacturing process.[46] The CJEU's answer was that if the generic manufacturers can enter the market within a short period of time with sufficient strength to constitute a serious competitive constraint on the branded manufacturer, they must be included in the relevant market.[47] The mere fact that the branded manufacturer still holds a process patent does not rule out that generic products can be part of the same relevant market because a process patent does not mean that the generic products cannot be placed on the market as such a patent may be invalid or not infringed.[48]

More troubling is the CAT's conclusion that, before the expiry of the molecule patent, the market was wider and included Seroxat and other anti-depressants, whereas after the expiry of that patent, the market became limited to paroxetine. While any market definition exercise is facts-centric, this approach appears wrong in principle. If certain other anti-depressants exerted sufficient competitive constraint on paroxetine before the expiry of the main patent, they would continue doing so even after its expiry. That generic alternatives would be closer substitutes is quite obvious; but it does not mean that the other anti-depressants become irrelevant. Rather, the normal position would be that the market would, at that point, comprise branded and generic paroxetine and the other-anti-depressants that are substitutable for paroxetine. Generic paroxetine may be a closer substitute, but this does not exclude any other substitutes from the relevant market. Although it is correct that market definition may change over time, the reasons set out in the CAT's judgment are

---

[42] CAT judgment in *Paroxetine* (n 35) para 407.

[43] ibid paras 402–404.

[44] ibid para 406, relying on Commission Decision in Case AT.39612—*Perindopril (Servier)* (30/09/2016), appealed before the General Court in Case T-691/14, *Servier SAS and Others v European Commission* (at the time of the CAT's judgment the General Court had not yet ruled on the appeals). The General Court has partially annulled the Commission Decision on the basis that Servier's dominant position has not been demonstrated either on the market for perindopril or on the technology market, questioning the existence of an abuse of that position. Further appeals against the General Court's judgment are pending before the Court of Justice (under Joined Cases C-176/19 P and C-201/19 P).

[45] CAT judgment in *Paroxetine* (n 35) para 409.

[46] Case C-307/18 *Generics (UK) Ltd and Others v Competition and Markets Authority* [2020] ECLI:EU:C:2020:52 (CJEU judgment in *Paroxetine*) paras 125–26.

[47] ibid para 133.

[48] ibid paras 136–37.

unconvincing. The CMA's approach is the correct one: either equivalent molecules are the same market, or they are not. The answer does not depend on whether the allegedly dominant molecule faces generic entry.

2.3 Dominance and Platforms

The debate as to whether the approach to assessing dominance should change when the allegedly dominant undertaking is a digital platform is a heated one.[49] Some argue that the traditional tools for the assessment of dominance are inadequate and should be replaced by new ones.[50] Others emphasize the current analytical framework, solidly based on economic theory, is sufficient to capture the complexities of the analysis of dominance in digital markets.[51] The CMA had the opportunity to test its approach to dominance in digital markets in two commitments decisions.

In *ATG Media*, the CMA accepted binding commitments from ATG Media concerning suspected exclusionary and restrictive pricing practices, including most favoured nation provisions in respect of online sales.[52] ATG Media was the largest provider of live online bidding (LOB) platforms in the UK, including 'The Saleroom'—an arts and antiques platform. These platforms are used by auction houses to facilitate online live bidding without bidders having to attend in person. The CMA preliminarily concluded that ATG Media may be dominant on the relevant market.[53] It referred to substantial market power as a key element in the assessment of dominance, explaining that market power is a matter of degree[54] and without relying on any presumption of dominance. Rather, a range of case-specific factors were analysed such as ATG Media's high market share in the relevant market, the relative market positions of competing LOB auction platform services suppliers (which had significantly lower market shares than ATG Media), and ATG Media's own conduct.[55] The CMA relied on the views of market participants and the views set out in certain of ATG Media's internal documents.[56] The CMA also assessed barriers to entry and, in particular,

---

[49] C Caffarra, 'Follow The Money: Mapping Issues with Digital Platforms into Actionable Theories of Harm' in F Jenny, N Charbit (eds), *Competition Case Law Digest, A Synthesis of EU, US and National Leading Cases* (Concurrences, 2020) 329–43; D Coyle, 'Practical Competition Policy Implications of Digital Platforms' (2019) 82 Antitrust Law Journal 835; Sir P Roth, 'The Continual Evolution of Competition Law' (2019) 7 J Antitrust Enforcement 23; C Shapiro, 'Antitrust in a time of populism' (2018) 61 International Journal of Industrial Organization 714; A Ezrachi, M Stucke, *Virtual Competition: The Promise and Perils of the Algorithm-Driven Economy*' (Harvard University Press 2016); M Rato and N Petit, 'Abuse of Dominance in Technology-enabled Markets: Established Standards Reconsidered' (2013) 9 Eur Competition J 1. See also 'The World's Most Valuable Resource Is No Longer Oil, But Data' *The Economist* (6 May 2017); 'The Superstar Company: A Giant Problem' *The Economist* (17 September 2016).

[50] See eg L M Kahn, 'Amazon's Antitrust Paradox' (2017) 126 Yale Law Journal 564.

[51] See eg T J Muris, J E Nuechterlein, 'Antitrust in the Internet Era: The Legacy of United States v A&P', (2019) 54 Rev Ind Organ 651.

[52] CMA, *Decision to accept binding commitments offered by ATG Media in relation to live online bidding auction platform services* Case No 50408 (29 June 2017) (*ATG Media*).

[53] ibid para 3.13.

[54] ibid para 3.10, referring to the OFT's Guidance on Abuse of a dominant position (OFT402, December 2004), adopted by the CMA board, para 4.11.

[55] ibid para 3.11.

[56] ibid.

network effects on both sides of the market, that is, bidders and auction houses. The CMA considered that:

> the greater the number of registered bidders on a particular platform, the more attractive it is for an auction house to list its live auctions with that platform and, similarly, the greater the number (and quality) of auction houses listing live auctions on the platform, the more attractive it is for bidders to register with the platform. New entrants therefore have to invest in developing their platform and establishing a 'network' (ie a client base) of sufficient scale on both sides of the market.[57]

In *Epyx*, the CMA accepted commitments from Epyx following an investigation into a suspected abuse of a dominant position in the supply of vehicle service, maintenance, and repair (SMR) platforms in the UK.[58] The CMA expressed the preliminary view that Epyx was likely to have a dominant position in the market for the supply of SMR platforms in the UK.[59] The test was once again one of substantial market power.[60] Relevant to the CMA assessment was the weakness of actual competition as 'information from customers indicated that there are no alternative platforms which offer the same functionality, or access to such an extensive network of customers, as the SN [1link Service Network] platform'.[61] Buyer power was not a sufficient constraint because customers were unable to sponsor new entry due to Epyx's own exclusionary conduct.[62] Potential competitors would face a significant cost to establish a functional service and a sufficient network of repairers and customers while also having to overcome Epyx's exclusionary conduct.[63]

It seems that the CMA, while adapting the current framework to the specificities of digital markets, has remained firmly anchored to a concept of dominance as substantial and durable market power that gives the dominant undertaking the ability and incentive to harm competition. In digital markets, substantial and durable market power can be assessed by focusing on the platform's functionality, its market share and the degree of competitive pressure it faces from existing and potential competitors. This is, however, not the end of the matter. Barriers to entry should always feature in the analysis. Among barriers to entry, network effects are particularly significant, but the relevant question is always whether network effects contribute to the platform's dominance and cannot be overcome by competitors. This is a promising start. The CMA has clearly rejected the simplistic view that a larger platform equals to a competition problem and continues to analyse markets in the round based on all available evidence. It is hoped that—notwithstanding the populist pressure to do away with rigorous principles in favour of political intervention to 'remedy' the 'power' of digital platforms—the CMA will not abandon this path.

---

[57] ibid para 3.12.
[58] CMA, *Decision to accept commitments offered by epyx Limited and FleetCor Technologies, Inc., Supply of service, maintenance and repair platforms* (9 September 2014) (*Epyx*).
[59] ibid para 3.8.
[60] ibid para 3.5.
[61] ibid para 3.6.
[62] ibid.
[63] ibid para 3.7.

3 Legal Test for Abuse: Standard of Foreclosure and Efficiencies

3.1 Clarifying the Law on Retroactive Rebates and Bundled Discounts

The law on retroactive rebates and bundled discounts has been for the past three decades the battleground for the debate on the foreclosure standard in EU and UK law.[64] On one view, the law should rely on legal tests or presumptions that define clearly what rebates are allowed and what rebates are prohibited.[65] On another view, all above-cost rebates should be presumptively lawful and should be prohibited only if a competition authority or claimant proves that the discounts under review have genitive effects on competition.[66] The very concept of 'negative effects on competition' is also controversial. Is a likely foreclosure effect sufficient or should it be necessary to prove that the discounts foreclose as efficient competitors?[67] Or should even proof of likely consumer harm be required?[68]

The European Commission sought to clarify the issue in its Guidance on Article 102.[69] The Commission defines conditional rebates as rebates that reward customers for a particular purchasing behaviour.[70] Retroactive rebates apply the discount to all units purchased in the relevant period, below and above the threshold, once the threshold has been attained.[71]

---

[64] D Ridyard, 'Exclusionary Pricing and Price Discrimination Abuses under Article 82—An Economic Analysis' (2002) 23 ECLR 286; J Temple Lang and R O'Donoghue, 'Defining Legitimate Competition: How to Clarify Pricing Abuses under Article 82 EC' (2002) 26 Fordham Intl LJ 83, 91–115; A Heimler, 'Below-Cost Pricing and Loyalty-Inducing Discounts: Are They Restrictive and, If So, When?' (2005) 1 Competition Policy International 149; H G Kamann and E Bergmann, 'The Granting of Rebates by Market Dominant Undertakings under Article 82 of the EC Treaty' (2005) 26 ECLR 83; G Federico, 'When Are Rebates Exclusionary?' (2005) 26 ECLR 477; D Spector, 'Loyalty Rebates: An Assessment of Competition Concerns and a Proposed Structured Rule of Reason' (2005) 1 Competition Policy International 89; C Ahlborn and D Bailey, 'Discounts, Rebates and Selective Pricing by Dominant Firms: A Trans-Atlantic Comparison' (2006) 2 European Competition Journal 101; D Geradin, 'A Proposed Test for Separating Pro-Competitive Conditional Rebates from Anti-Competitive Ones' (2009) 32 World Competition 41; L Kjolbye, 'Rebates under Article 82 EC: Navigating Uncertain Waters' (2010) 31 ECLR 66; E Rousseva, *Rethinking Exclusionary Abuses in EU Competition Law* (Hart Publishing, 2010) 173–218; R Nazzini, *The Foundations of EU Competition Law: The Objective and Principles of Article 102* (OUP 2011) 233–42; N Petit, 'Intel, Leveraging Rebates and the Goals of Article 102 TFEU' (2015) 11 European Competition Journal 26; P Ibáñez Colomo, 'Post Danmark II, or the Quest for Administrability and Coherence in Article 102 TFEU' LSE Legal Studies Working Paper No 15 (2015) https://ssrn.com/abstract=2636407; P Ibáñez Colomo, 'Beyond the More Economics-Based Approach: A Legal Perspective on Article 102 TFEU Case Law' (2016) 53 Common Market L Rev 709; M Marinova, 'Should the Rejection of the as Efficient Competitor Test in the Intel and Post Danmark II Judgements Lead to Dismissal of the Effect-Based Approach' (2016) 12(2) ECJ 387; N Petit, 'Rebates and Article 102 TFEU: The European Commission's Duty to Apply the Guidance Paper' (2016) 2 CLPD 4l; P Akman, 'The Reform of the Application of Article 102 TFEU: Mission Accomplished' (2016) 81 Antitrust LJ 145; Daniel A Crane, 'Formalism and Functionalism in the Antitrust Treatment of Loyalty Rebates: A Comparative Perspective' (2016) Antitrust LJ 209; Jorge Padilla, 'Whither Article 102 TFEU: A Comment on Akman and Crane' (2016) 81 Antitrust LJ 223; M Kadar, 'Article 102 and Exclusivity Rebates in a Post-Intel World: Lessons from the Qualcomm and Google Android Cases' (2019) 10 Journal of European Competition Law & Practice 439; P Davis, 'As Efficient Competitor Test' in Frédéric Jenny, Nicolas Charbit (eds), *Competition Case Law Digest, A Synthesis of EU, US and National Leading Cases* (Concurrences, 2020) 79–96.

[65] See eg W Wils, 'The Judgment of the EU General Court in *Intel* and the So-called More Economic Approach to Abuse of Dominance' (2014) 37 World Competition 4.

[66] P Rey and J S Venit, 'An Effects-Based Approach to Article 102: A. Response to Wouter Wils' (2015) 38 World Competition 3; L Peeperkorn, 'Conditional Pricing: Why the General Court is Wrong in Intel and What the Court of Justice Can Do to Rebalance the Assessment of Rebates' (2015) 1 Concurrences 46.

[67] See eg K U Kuhn and M Marinova, 'The Role of the as Efficient Competitor Test after the CJEU Judgment in *Intel*' (2018) 4 CLPD 64.

[68] J M Jacobson, 'Exclusive Dealing, Foreclosure, and Consumer Harm' (2002) 70 Antitrust LJ 311.

[69] Communication from the Commission—Guidance on the Commission's enforcement priorities in applying Article 82 of the EC Treaty to abusive exclusionary conduct by dominant undertakings [2009] OJ C45/7.

[70] ibid para 37.

[71] ibid.

The Commission applies to such rebates the 'as efficient competitor' test, seeking to determine whether an effective price calculated by allocating all the discount to the contestable share of demand would be above or below a relevant cost benchmark.[72] The non-contestable share of demand is defined as 'the amount that would be purchased by the dominant undertaking in any event'.[73] The contestable share of demand is defined as 'the amount for which the customer may prefer to be able to find substitutes'.[74] The Commission envisages that, if the effective price is below the AAC of the dominant undertaking, the rebates will be capable of excluding equally efficient competitors.[75] If the effective price is above the AAC of the dominant undertaking but below its LRAIC, the Commission will investigate whether competitors have 'realistic and effective counter-strategies' to compete against the price schedule of the dominant undertaking. If they do not, the rebate will be considered capable of foreclosing an equally efficient competitor.[76] In addition to the price/cost analysis, the Commission also considers that an individualized volume threshold is more likely to be anti-competitive because it can be designed based on the non-contestable share of each customer. A standardized volume threshold may be too low for some customers and too high for others. However, a standardized threshold may approximate the requirements of most customers and thus have a foreclosure effect.[77] Finally, if the rebates are capable of foreclosing an equally efficient competitor, the Commission will examine whether the foreclosure will lead to consumer harm, applying the general framework in paragraph 20 of the Guidance.[78]

The Commission applied the above framework in *Intel*.[79] The Court of Justice allowed an appeal against the General Court's decision that upheld the Commission's decision. The Court of Justice reiterated that it is an infringement of Article 102 for a dominant undertaking to tie purchasers by an obligation or promise to buy from the dominant undertaking all of most or their requirements, whether or not the arrangements provides for the grant of a rebate. The same applies when this objective is achieved by the application of loyalty rebates.[80] However, when the dominant undertaking adduces evidence that its conduct is incapable of producing the alleged foreclosure effect, the Commission must assess the extent of the dominant position, the share of the market affected by the allegedly abusive practice, the conditions and arrangements for the granting of the rebates, their duration and their amount, and the existence of a strategy aimed at excluding as efficient competitors.[81] The analysis of foreclosure is also relevant to whether an allegedly exclusionary rebate scheme may be objectively justified by efficiencies that also benefit consumers.[82] When the Commission is required to undertake a full analysis of the rebate scheme, all the evidence relevant to foreclosure must be examined. The Court of Justice, therefore, set aside

---

[72] ibid para 41.

[73] ibid para 39.

[74] ibid.

[75] ibid para 44.

[76] ibid.

[77] ibid para 45.

[78] ibid para 20.

[79] *Intel* [2009] OJ C227/13, upheld on appeal in Case T-286/09 *Intel Corp v Commission* [2014] ECLI:EU:T:2014:547, appeal allowed in Case C-413/14 *Intel Corp v Commission* [2017] ECLI:EU:C:2017:632, case now pending before the GC for reconsideration.

[80] Case C-413/14 P *Intel Corp v Commission* [2017] ECLI:EU:C:2017:632, para 137.

[81] ibid paras 138–39.

[82] ibid para 140.

the judgment of the General Court that had not addressed Intel's arguments concerning the Commission's application of the as efficient competitor test.[83] The Court of Justice's judgment in *Intel* has been considered by some as a significant development towards a more thorough effects analysis of loyalty rebates.[84] Probably, the judgment seeks to establish a middle ground between a strict and formalistic prohibition of royalty rebates and a full, unstructured 'rule of reason' approach.[85] [86] It does not, however, endorse the as efficient competitor test. The reason why the judgment of the General Court was set aside was not that the application of the as efficient competitor test is a necessary requirement for a finding that loyalty rebates are unlawful. Rather, the Court of Justice held that, since the Commission had relied heavily on the as efficient competitor test in support of its finding of abuse and Intel had argued in its appeal that the application of the test by the Commission was seriously flawed, the General Court was bound to examine Intel's arguments. This is a rather narrower, if not obviously persuasive, basis on which the judgment was vitiated by an error of law.

It is interesting to consider how these European developments have been tracked in the United Kingdom, first, in the pre-*Intel* period, by focusing on the as efficient competitor test as the main tool for assessing the anti-competitive effects of loyalty rebates, then, in the post-*Intel* period, by following the more qualitative approach of the Court of Justice. Following the end of the Brexit transition period, EU law is no longer binding in the United Kingdom and the CMA and the UK courts are now able to develop their own legal tests and overall approach free from the constraints of EU case law. It may be, therefore, that UK law will revert to a more robust application of the as efficient competitor test and overall exclusionary effects based on all available evidence.

To illustrate the above, in the pre-*Intel* period, the OFT appeared committed to applying the as efficient competitor test to retroactive rebates. For instance, in the 2011 *IDEXX* case, the OFT analysed contracts containing conditional rebates and found that the effective price paid for the contestable share of demand was always above average avoidable costs (AAC). The OFT did not carry out a detailed assessment of whether the incremental price was below long-run average incremental costs (LRAIC) because it did not consider that the extent of the conduct was such that it would have a foreclosure effect.[87] This approach was clarified and refined in *Loyalty-inducing Discount Scheme*, where it was held that a retroactive rebate may be abusive when: (a) a customer is required or has a strong preference to buy certain units from the dominant undertaking ('assured base' or the 'non-contestable' share of demand); (b) there are, however, also units that the customer may buy from competitors ('contestable share' of the customer's demand or 'contestable sales'); and (c) the grant of the rebate or discount is conditional on the customer purchasing contestable units from the dominant company. Where the structure of the rebate scheme means that the price which a competitor would have to charge to compete for contestable units

---

[83] ibid paras 142–43.

[84] See eg DD Sokol, 'European Competition Law: Enforcement or Regulation after *Intel*'? (2017) 2 CPI Antitrust Chron 1; G Colangelo and M Maggiolino, '*Intel* and the Rebirth of the Economic Approach to EU Competition Law', (2018) 49(6) IIC 685.

[85] See eg A Boutin and X Boutin, 'The as Efficient Competitor Test: Back to Facts' (2018) 4 CLPD 51.

[86] For further commentary on the Intel judgment see, among others, P Colomo 'The Future of Article 102 TFEU after *Intel*' (2018) 9 Journal of European Competition Law & Practice 293; N Petit, 'The Judgment of the EU Court of Justice in *Intel* and the Rule of Reason in Abuse of Dominance Cases' (2018) 43 European Law Review 728.

[87] *IDEXX* (n 9) paras 6.30–6.31 and 6.34.

is below the dominant company's AAC, as a general rule the CMA is likely to consider that the rebate or discount scheme is capable of foreclosing even equally efficient competitors. Where the effective price remains consistently above the LRAIC of the dominant company, this would normally allow an equally efficient competitor to compete profitably notwithstanding the rebate/discount. In such circumstances the CMA is likely to consider that the rebate or discount is normally not capable of foreclosing in an anti-competitive way. Where the effective price is between AAC and LRAIC, the CMA is likely to investigate whether other factors suggest that entry or expansion even by equally efficient competitors is likely to be affected. Factors that may be considered are whether a competitor cannot employ effective counterstrategies—e.g., because there are long-term contracts in place and a lack of price transparency—or whether the customer is able to reduce its overall expenditure on the dominant company's products by increasing the volume of contestable sales it purchases from the dominant company.[88]

The OFT applied the AAC benchmark also to bundling of veterinary in-clinics analysers and consumables by IDEXX. The test was applied to samples of both bundles and individual products as well as to the tied product alone to determine whether a competitor supplying only the tied product would have to offer a price below AAC in order to persuade the customer to forgo the bundle. No price was below AAC. Furthermore, the OFT considered that competitors could, in any way, replicate the bundle or deploy effective counterstrategies.[89]

This approach effectively applies a predation analysis to rebate schemes by applying a price-cost test to the contestable share of demand or the relevant range of the contestable share that the customer is able and willing to purchase from a competitor. It is a logic and coherent application of the as efficient competitor test. Effectively, a loyalty rebate can be considered as nothing else and nothing more than targeted predation with simultaneous recoupment. Predation will always be targeted. Why incurring more losses than necessary? And it will always be carried out with the intention of recouping the losses. Otherwise it would be irrational self-harm. By a loyalty rebate, predation is targeted not at a particular customer but at the contestable share of demand. Recoupment is simultaneous because the profits sacrificed by granting the rebate are recouped by the higher overall profits that can be sustained thanks to the foreclosure effect of the rebate.[90]

In *Impulse Ice Cream*, a case decided shortly before the judgment of the Court of Justice in *Intel*, but after the judgment of the General Court in that case, the CMA appeared to have changed approach and adopted the three categories of rebate described in the judgment of the General Court which was set aside on appeal by the Court of Justice in *Intel*.[91] This was a

---

[88] CMA, Statement regarding the CMA's decision to close an investigation into a suspected breach of competition law in the pharmaceutical sector on the grounds of administrative priority, *Suspected loyalty-inducing discount scheme* (CE/9855-14, June 2015).

[89] *IDEXX* (n 9) paras 6.45–6.72.

[90] The analogy to predation is, of course, not perfect, not least because the 'losses' that the dominant undertaking incurs are only notional. Overall, the line of business in question remains profitable. On the pros and cons of applying a predation framework to loyalty rebates see Timothy J Brennan, 'Bundled Rebates as Exclusion rather than Predation' (2008) 4 J Comp L & Econ 335; G Federico, 'The Antitrust Treatment of Loyalty Discounts in Europe: Towards a More Economic Approach' (IESE Occasional Paper, OP-186, Feb 2011); S C Salop, 'Raising Rivals' Cost Foreclosure Paradigm, Conditional Pricing Practices and the Flawed Incremental Price-Cost Test' (2017) 81 Antitrust Law J:371; Pinar Akman, 'The Reform of the Application of Article 102 TFEU: Mission Accomplished' (2016) 81 Antitrust LJ 183. With specific regard to the debate in the U.S. see eg Sean P Gates, 'Antitrust by Analogy: Developing Rules for Loyalty Rebates and Bundled Discounts' (2013) 79 Antitrust LJ111; D W Moore and J D Wright, 'Conditional Discounts and the Law of Exclusive Dealing' (2015) 22 Geo Mason L Rev 1205.

[91] *Impulse Ice Cream* (n 17) paras 14–30.

much more formalistic approach, with the first two categories being effectively form-based prohibitions and the third a sort of general catch-all provision based on a vague test requiring the consideration of all the circumstances of the case; but, incidentally, we may ask, should one not look at all the circumstances of the case all the time?[92]

In *Remicade*, decided after the Court of Justice's *Intel* ruling, the CMA adopted a much broader approach, requiring an analysis all the relevant circumstances and expressly ruling out the application the as efficient competitor test[93] put forward in *Loyalty-inducing Discount Scheme*. Clearly, the CMA was following the approach of the Court of Justice in *Intel*. Still, the CMA made a couple of interesting points. It held that even if the dominant undertaking's strategy was intended to be exclusionary,[94] under the prevailing market conditions it turned out to be unlikely to have such an effect[95] and was, therefore, not abusive. This is important. While the point was, and is, clear as a matter of law,[96] excessive reliance on internal documents in recent times[97] has created the impression that the subjective intention of managers and employees of a company was a key factor in assessing abuse. Such evidence is, instead, just relevant evidence to be understood in its context; it can never replace an objective assessment of the impact of the conduct on the market. It is also noteworthy that the CMA distinguished in this decision the potential of the conduct under review to exclude competitors from the likelihood of exclusion. Conduct that has the potential to exclude but is unlikely to do so is not abusive.[98] As for actual effects, the CMA held that the likelihood of the dominant undertaking's conduct to produce anti-competitive effects should be assessed at the time when the conduct was implemented and not 'at some point after the allegedly abusive conduct had been in place'.[99] The distinction between potential and likely effects is welcomed as too often in EU-level jurisprudence the two tests are considered synonymous,[100] which is clearly wrong, as a matter of both language and policy and, it is submitted, also as a matter of law. However, it would have been desirable for the CMA to clarify that while the test is one of likely effects to be assessed at the time when the conduct was entered into and implemented—which can be, and generally is, a continuing period of time, that is, the entire period in which the rebates have been applied—actual effects are also relevant. If actual effects are proven, this strengthens the case of abuse as there is a strong inference that effects that occurred must have been likely when the conduct was

---

[92] On the General Court's *Intel* judgment see J Venit, 'Case T-286/09 Intel v Commission: The Judgment of the General Court: All Steps Backward and No Steps Forward' (2014) 10 European Competition Journal 203; Wils (n 65); R Whish, '*Intel v Commission*: Keep Calm and Carry On!' (2015) 6(1) Journal of European Competition Law and Practice 1; S Huijts, *Intel v Commission*: the AEC Test is Dead, Long Live the AEC Test, and Three Other Observations [2015] Comp Law 19; N Petit, '*Intel*, Leveraging Rebates and the Goals of Article 102 TFEU' (2015) 11 European Competition Journal 26.

[93] *Remicade* (n 27) paras 4.82–4.84.

[94] ibid paras 4.28–4.56.

[95] ibid paras 4.62–4.67.

[96] This follows from the case law that considers abuse as an 'objective' concept. What matters is, therefore, not the purely subjective intention of the dominant undertaking, but the objective impact of the conduct on the market: Case 85/76 *Hoffmann-La Roche v Commission* (n 4) para 91; Case 6/72 *Europemballage Corpn and Continental Can Co Inc Commission* EU:C:1973:22, para 226; more recently see eg Case C-280/08 P *Deutsche Telekom AG v Commission* EU:C:2010:603, para 174.

[97] See eg Case COMP/E-1/38.113—*Prokent-Tomra* (29 March 2006); Case COMP/C-3 /37.990—Intel (13 May 2009).

[98] *Remicade* (n 27) para 4.76.

[99] ibid para 4.78.

[100] Case C-23/14 *Post Danmark II* EU:C:2015:651, eg at paras 31, 35, 38, 49, 50, 67, 68, 69; see also Case T-201/04 *Microsoft v Commission* EU:T:2007:289, para 561.

implemented. By contrast, if actual effects did not materialise after the conduct has been applied for a certain period of time, this strongly suggests that anti-competitive effects were not likely in the first place, unless there is an alternative explanation for the lack of actual effects.

On loyalty rebates and bundled discounts, the UK authorities started the decade in a very good place: they applied the as efficient competitor test, broadly based on a predation framework, to assess whether these arrangements could have an exclusionary effect, while also considering all relevant circumstances, for example whether competitors could replicate the discount or bundle. However, they were then forced to play 'catch up' with the changing, wordy, and unclear EU-level jurisprudence from *Intel*. It is very much hoped that, after the Brexit transition period expires, UK law will revert to a clear, robust, and economically sound application of the as efficient competitor test, making a clear break with the forever nebulous, half-way house approach of the EU courts.

3.2 Exclusion in Multi-market Settings

A particularly complex question in the application of Article 102 is whether dominance, abuse, and anti-competitive effects can be in different markets.

The OFT sought to clarify the predation test in a multi-market setting in *Flybe*, a case concerning predatory entry in the aviation industry. The allegation was that Flybe was trying to exclude Air Southwest from the market. Having reached the conclusion that Flybe held a dominant position on the markets for routes from Exeter Airport to Jersey and Guernsey, the OFT proceeded to consider whether Flybe's entry on the different but related Newquay-London Gatwick route, where Air Southwest operated, was abusive.

The OFT noted that it is well-established that conduct on a related market may be an abuse where it is intended to strengthen an undertaking's dominant position, relying on the 'special circumstances' test in *Tetra Pak II*.[101] Following the Advocate General's opinion in *Tetra Pak II*, the OFT considered that whether there are 'special circumstances' that justify a finding of entry on a new market as an abuse of dominance was a question that had to be decided on a case-by-case basis, and that account must be taken of the supply and demand structure on the related markets, the product characteristics, the use by the dominant undertaking of its power on the dominated market in order to penetrate the related market, the market share of the dominant undertaking on the related market, and the degree of control exercised on the dominated market by the dominant undertaking.[102]

In the OFT's view, abusive conduct could be found on distinct but closely associated markets where the conduct in question is likely to protect or strengthen the position on the dominated market. In addition, or in the alternative, the OFT considered that there could be an abuse of dominance where conduct on a market distinct from the dominated market produces effects on the distinct market, provided that there are sufficiently proximate associative links between the respective markets.[103] Links must be stronger when

---

[101] Case C-333/94 P *Tetra Pak v Commission* [1996] ECR II-5951. Nazzini, *The Foundations of EU Competition Law* (n 64) 180–85.
[102] *Flybe* (n 14) paras 6.1–6.6.
[103] ibid para 6.14.

the anti-competitive effect occurs on the non-dominated market, whereas if the abuse strengthens the dominant position, links may be weaker.[104] Factually, there were sufficiently close links between the routes where Flybe was dominant and the route on which predatory entry was alleged to have occurred.[105] The OFT considered that, in undermining the prey's viability overall, Flybe would be expected to strengthen or protect its dominant positions on the Exeter Airport markets and that it would benefit from the diversion of passengers travelling to Jersey or Guernsey from Plymouth Airport. The OFT also considered that Flybe would be able to raise prices profitably on the Exeter Airports markets should Air Southwest exit so as to recoup any losses on the Newquay-London Gatwick route relatively quickly.[106]

To determine whether the conduct was predatory, the OFT applied the test set out in *AKZO*[107] and *Aberdeen Journals*.[108] However, the OFT noted that there was little case law dealing squarely with the question of what constitutes predation when launching a new product or service in a new market. There may be an important distinction to be made between pricing below cost when entering a new market and pricing below cost as the incumbent in order to deter a competitor. A different approach may be required so that dominant companies are not prevented from entering new markets.[109] On the facts, the OFT concluded that incurring a loss on entry during an initial period may be evidence of normal competition, rather than abuse, especially in the airline industry.[110] In assessing Flybe's costs and revenues, the OFT took AAC as the appropriate measure. Because the time period over which a route may become profitable will vary from route to route, the OFT focused on the period over which Flybe anticipated recovering AAC and considered whether this was a reasonable period in which to establish market presence on the route. The evidence indicated that the revenue generated on the Newquay-London Gatwick route was insufficient to cover AAC in the first year after entry. Revenue was forecast to catch up with AAC in the second year of the route's operation and to exceed AAC in year four. Internal documents from Flybe also demonstrated that it was aware that it would initially make losses on the Newquay-London Gatwick route.[111] The OFT then looked at Flybe's conduct on other routes as a benchmark for its conduct in this case. It found that the extent of losses projected on the Newquay-London Gatwick route in its first year of operation were on a similar scale to those incurred on other routes. The OFT concluded that the losses projected on the route for the first year could not be taken as conclusive evidence that Flybe had engaged in predation.[112]

The OFT then determined that, although Flybe had a plausible reason to attempt to eliminate the prey from the market,[113] it would have entered the Newquay-London Gatwick route anyway. Furthermore, it was not clear whether Flybe was capable of doing so, given the absence of strong barriers to entry. In May 2010, Air Southwest's owners put the airline

[104] ibid paras 6.7–6.15.
[105] ibid paras 6.54–6.96.
[106] ibid paras 6.56–6.71.
[107] ibid paras 6.17–6.20, relying on Case C-62/86 *AKZO Chemie v Commission* (n 20).
[108] *Aberdeen Journals Limited v Director General of Fair Trading* [2003] CAT 11.
[109] *Flybe* (n 14) paras 6.22–6.28.
[110] ibid paras 6.29–6.33.
[111] ibid paras 6.34–6.35.
[112] ibid paras 6.36–6.45.
[113] ibid paras 6.56–6.71.

up for sale and, in September 2010, it was announced that Air Southwest was to be sold to Eastern Airways (subject to regulatory approval). The OFT believed that the proposed sale and the apparent continuation of Air Southwest's services supported the conclusion that there were no particularly strong barriers to entry that would prevent the constraint currently imposed on Flybe by Air Southwest being replaced by another airline.[114]

The approach to multi-market abuses was further clarified by the CAT in *Achilles*, a private enforcement case. Achilles was a provider of supplier assurance services for critical industries in the UK and elsewhere. It had acted for a number of years as a provider of a rail industry qualification scheme and, from 2014 to 2018, was the operator of the Rail Industry Supplier Qualification Scheme (RISQS), a not-for-profit organization providing supplier assurance services for the UK rail sector. As of 2019, Network Rail, the owner and operator of most of the railway infrastructure in Great Britain, decided that, in relation to two key schemes for vetting of individuals and suppliers operating on Network Rail's managed infrastructure (key schemes'), vetting could be provided only by RISQS. Achilles complained that it had been excluded from the market and issued proceedings in the CAT claiming breaches of the Chapter I and the Chapter II prohibitions. The CAT ruled that Network Rail had infringed both prohibitions and ordered Network Rail to end the infringement.[115] The Court of Appeal rejected Network Rail's appeal against the CAT judgment.[116]

As the CAT trial was considered 'appropriate for expedition', the CAT heard the case on the assumption that Network Rail had a dominant position in the market for 'the operation and provision of access to national rail infrastructure in [Great Britain]'.[117] The anticompetitive effects occurred on the market for the provision of supplier assurance services in the British rail industry.[118]

The CAT applied a test of whether the relevant conduct was reasonably likely to have a serious or appreciable effect in the related market. More specifically, in conducting this assessment under Chapter II, the CAT referred to its effect analysis under Chapter I,[119] and articulated the following principles:

– at least in related market cases, to constitute an abuse, the conduct under review must lead to anti-competitive foreclosure on the related market and 'the effect on the related market must be more than de minimis (i.e. it is reasonably likely to have a serious or appreciable effect in the related market), at least in cases where the conduct is procompetitive in respect of the dominated market';[120]
– to gauge the restrictive effects of the allegedly anti-competitive conduct, one must carry out a detailed analysis of its effect on the relevant market(s);[121]

---

[114] ibid paras 6.72–6.87.

[115] *Achilles Information Limited v Network Rail Infrastructure Limited* (CAT judgment in *Achilles*).

[116] *Network Rail Infrastructure Limited v Achilles Information Limited* [2020] EWCA Civ 323 (CoA judgment in *Achilles*).

[117] CAT judgment in *Achilles* (n 115) paras 283 and 290; see also Order of the Chairman dated 22 October 2018, para 3.

[118] CAT judgment in *Achilles* (n 115) para 290.

[119] ibid para 285: 'There is a substantial overlap between the parties' respective cases under Chapter I and Chapter II and our conclusions under Chapter II largely flow from our conclusions in respect of Chapter I.' The CAT relied on *Socrates Training Limited v The Law Society of England and Wales* [2017] CAT 10.

[120] CAT judgment in *Achilles* (n 115) para 291. The CAT relied on the general principles for finding an abuse in 'related market' cases. See *Streetmap* (n 125 below) paras 96–98.

[121] CAT judgment in *Achilles* (n 115) para 121(3)–(4).

- the restrictive effects of the conduct should be considered by reference to a counterfactual situation;[122]
- without the 'RISQS-only rule', Achilles would have offered supplier assurance services in competition with RISQS 'at least for some time' and this would have produced pro-competitive effects in terms of lower prices and product differentiation;[123] and,
- prima facie abusive conduct may be objectively justified if 'the exclusionary effect is counter-balanced or outweighed by advantages that benefit consumers and if the conduct is proportionate' or, according to *Post Danmark I*,[124] relied upon by Roth J in *Streetmap*,[125] if the conduct is 'necessary for the achievement of those gains in efficiency and that it does not eliminate effective competition, by removing all or most existing sources of actual or potential competition'.[126]

On the facts, the CAT concluded that the RISQS-only rule did cause more than de minimis, and, therefore, appreciable foreclosure in a significant segment of the market for supplier assurance services in the British railway sector.[127] The CAT rejected Network Rail's argument that this restriction had 'no actual effect' given that the market 'would tip in favour of RISQS' anyway. For the CAT, it is "fundamentally not for Network Rail to make the decision for other buyers and suppliers that they would prefer RISQS to other supplier assurance services'.[128] The CAT also highlighted that the effects of Network Rail's conduct should be assessed by reference to a scenario where the RISQS-only rule 'never existed' rather than by the reference to the situation at the time of the judgment.[129] The CAT did not accept Network Rail's submission that 'there can be no abuse where the dominant company derives no competitive advantage from the alleged abusive conduct'.[130] Finally, the CAT dismissed Network Rail's arguments in support of objective justification, as the safety objective of RISQS-only rule could be met by less restrictive requirements and the RISQS-only rule did not generate cost efficiencies of a scale such to offset the loss of competition resulting from the rule.[131]

The Court of Appeal rejected Network Rail's appeal against the CAT judgment. Important points of principle arose in the appeal. First, on the test for anti-competitive foreclosure, the Court of Appeal referred to the discussion under the Chapter I prohibition. Therefore, the analysis and assessment of appreciability was imported, so to speak, wholesale from the Chapter I prohibition into the Chapter II prohibition. This approach endorses Roth J's approach in *Streetmap*.[132] While it may contradict the Court of Justice case law that there is

---

[122] ibid para 121(3)–(4).
[123] ibid para 150.
[124] Case C-209/10 *Post Danmark I* EU:C:2012:172, para 42.
[125] *Streetmap.eu Ltd v Google Inc and Others* [2016] EWHC 253 (Ch), [2016] All ER (D) 129 (Feb) at para 144 (Roth J).
[126] CAT judgment in *Achilles* (n 115) para 311.
[127] ibid para 292.
[128] ibid para 152.
[129] ibid para 153.
[130] ibid para 302. The CAT referred to Case T-128/98 *Aéroports de Paris v Commission* EU:T:2000:290, where the General Court did not accept the argument according to which there is not abuse if the dominant undertaking is not present in the affected market and has 'no interest in distorting competition on that market' and to *Arriva The Shires Ltd v London Luton Airport Operations Ltd* [2014] EWHC 64 (Ch), where Rose J agreed with the General Court's position in *Aéroports de Paris* that in order to find an abuse of dominant position 'it is not necessary for there to be some commercial benefit to be gained by the dominant undertaking from its conduct'.
[131] CAT judgment in *Achilles* (n 115) para 313.
[132] *Streetmap* (n 125) paras 96–98.

no appreciability requirement under Article 102 TFEU,[133] this will be irrelevant after the transition period expires and is, certainly, a welcome development towards a sounder, more economically robust application of the respective prohibition.

Secondly, the Court of Appeal upheld the CAT's conclusion that competition for the market is not necessarily sufficient to compensate for the loss of competition in the market. Network Rail's argument was that the RISQS's services are put out to tender periodically. Achilles, or anybody else, could, therefore, bid for the contract. Sufficient competition is, therefore, preserved. The CAT rejected this argument, holding that competition for the market does not 'justify or compensate for the elimination of competition in the meantime'.[134] This may or may not be correct on the facts and the Court of Appeal approached the issue by affording significant deference to the CAT's finding. The real question, however, which does not appear to have been fully aired in the case, and certainly not before the Court of Appeal, is whether there were compelling efficiency reasons why competition for the market should replace competition in the market. If not, one could conclude that competition in the market is superior, especially if the counterfactual is complete elimination of competition in the market for a significant period of time.

Thirdly, Network Rail argued that it did not benefit from the abuse. Therefore, there could not be any abuse of dominance. The only circumstance in which a dominant undertaking may be found guilty of an abuse even if it does not derive any benefit from the abusive conduct would be, according to Network Rail, when the dominant undertaking is an essential trading partner of the undertaking alleging abuse. Both the CAT and the Court of Appeal rightly rejected this argument, relying on *Aéroports de Paris*[135] and *Arriva The Shires Ltd*.[136] There is no requirement in the jurisprudence that the dominant undertaking must profit, or intend to profit, from allegedly abusive conduct. This conclusion is not only legally correct but sound in policy too. Competition law has the objective of protecting the competitive process to enhance long-term social welfare.[137] What matters is whether conduct harms the economy or not. Competitive harm does not become irrelevant because it was not motivated by profit maximization. This proposition, however, must come with an important caveat. The absence of any incentive to harm competition should, at the very least, raise suspicions of a competition authority or court in an individual case. If a dominant undertaking is harming another company without, however, being capable of deriving any resultant benefit, the anti-competitive effects of the conduct should be more closely scrutinized and any objective justification should be considered inherently more likely. It is not the legal test that changes, but the lack of any incentive to exclude may well make anti-competitive exclusion less likely and colour the way in which the remaining evidence in the case is assessed. Perhaps this was what Rose J was contemplating when she said in *Arriva The Shires Ltd* that 'the complete absence of any commercial gain on the part of the dominant undertaking may well be highly relevant in a particular case, for example on the issue of objective justification'.[138]

---

[133] Case 85/76 *Hoffmann-La Roche* (n 4) para 123 and Case C-23/14 *Post Danmark II* (n 100) paras 70–74.
[134] CAT judgment in *Achilles* (n 115) para 297.
[135] Case T-128/98 *Aéroports de Paris v Commission* (n 130).
[136] *Arriva The Shires Ltd* (n 130).
[137] Nazzini, *The Foundations of EU Competition Law* (n 64) 107–54.
[138] *Arriva The Shires Ltd* (n 130) para 99.

Purple Parking, *Streetmap.eu*, *Royal Mail*, and *Arriva The Shires Ltd* are also cases concerning multi-market abuses; they will be considered in the discussion on discrimination.

3.3 Exclusivity, MFNs, and Equivalent Clauses

Certain contractual arrangements such as exclusivity and MFN clauses may give rise to foreclosure effects by preventing competitors from having access to customers or suppliers. MFN clauses, in particular, have engendered much debate in the past decade, especially on digital markets.[139]

In *Epyx*, the OFT reached the preliminary view that Epyx was likely to be dominant in the market for supply, maintenance, and repair (SMR) platform services in the UK. The OFT expressed concerns that Epyx might have abused its dominant position due to certain provisions in its contracts with demand-side customers (fleet companies) and supply-side customers (vehicle repairers). On the demand side, Epyx's contracts: (a) contained use and development restrictions, requiring demand-side customers 'to process all service and maintenance transactions through' Epyx's platform and not to 'develop, use, market or support the sale' of any alternative systems; (b) provided for the obligation to pay a minimum annual fee, which was effectively a quantity commitment; and (c) were of long duration, typically between three to five years as a minimum period, to which notice periods applied. On the supply side, Epyx's contracts required its supply-side customers to process all of their SMR transactions with Epyx's demand-side customers through Epyx's platform. The OFT relied on the EU law foreclosure test of tendency or capability to foreclose,[140] but then went on to analyse more concretely the effects of the restrictions under review on switching and entry. In particular, the OFT noted that the restrictions prevented customers from trying and testing alternatives to the dominant undertaking and from facilitating new entry and entrants to achieve a minimum efficient scale.[141]

In *Certas Energy*, the CMA explained its approach to the analysis of exclusivity. Certas had entered into long-term exclusive contracts with filling stations in certain geographic areas where it was dominant on the market for the wholesale supply of road fuels to filling stations. Long-term exclusive contracts requiring customers to purchase all or significant parts of their demand from a single supplier may be exclusionary depending on their duration, market coverage, and the legal and economic context in which the contracts operate.[142] Any exclusionary effect may, however, be offset by efficiencies or the exclusivity 'may be objectively justified for other reasons, such as technical or commercial constraints and public interest considerations'.[143] Interestingly, the CMA appeared to require that

---

[139] Erik Hovenkamp, 'Platform Antitrust' (2019) 44 J Corp L 734; Jonathan B Baker and Fiona Scott Morton, 'Antitrust Enforcement against Platform MFNs' (2018) 127 Yale L J 2176; Amelia Fletcher and Morten Hviid, 'Retail Price MFNs: Are they RPM "at Its Worst"?' (2017) 81 Antitrust Law Journal 61. In the economic literature see eg Jonathan B Baker and Judith A Chevalier, 'The Competitive Consequences of Most-Favored-Nations Provisions' (2013) 27 Antitrust 20; Steven C Salop and Fiona Scott Morton, 'Developing an Administrable MFN Enforcement Policy' (2013) 27 Antitrust 15. See also the CMA's considerations on MFNs in the Final Report of its 'Digital Comparison Tools Market Study' (26 September 2017) (in particular, paras 4.90–4.101).

[140] *Epyx* (n 58) para 3.9.

[141] ibid paras 3.10–3.23.

[142] *Certas Energy* (n 7) para 3.20.

[143] ibid para 3.21.

exclusive contracts are not only capable but also likely to foreclose.[144] On the facts, the CMA's concerns related mainly to the long duration and the significant coverage of the contracts.[145] The case was closed with commitments.

In *ATG Media*, the CMA took the preliminary view that a platform dominant in the provision of LOB to auction houses had abused its dominant position by agreeing exclusivity clauses, MFN clauses, and prohibitions on promoting and advertising rival platforms with its customers. In particular, the CMA launched an investigation into three practices by ATG Media which it considered may breach competition law by preventing or discouraging its customers from using rival platforms, namely: (a) obtaining exclusive deals with auction houses, so that they do not use other providers; (b) preventing auction houses getting a cheaper online bidding rate with other platforms for their bidders—through MFN or price parity clauses; and (c) preventing auction houses promoting or advertising rival live online bidding platforms in competition with ATG Media.[146] The CMA considered that these practices may have prevented ATG Media's rivals from being able to compete effectively in the market and prevented consumers from getting a better deal for online bidding.[147] The CMA analysed the restrictions in question as giving rise to barriers to entry and expansion of rivals, especially given the network effects on the market, and, in relation to MFN clauses, as softening price competition. The case was closed with commitments.[148] The CMA's preliminary view, based, in particular, on ATG Media's internal documents, was that ATG Media used its market position to agree the restrictions described above with a targeted group of its auction house customers as part of a strategy to prevent certain rival LOB auction platforms from developing into effective competitors.[149]

The three cases above are all commitments cases and fall short of a full factual and legal analysis. Nevertheless, it is reasonably clear that the UK authorities analyse exclusivity and MFN clauses as exclusionary practices that are prohibited only if they have anti-competitive effects and, in particular, if they are likely to foreclose as efficient competitors or competitors that could become as efficient as the dominant undertaking but for the exclusionary conduct.

3.4 Discrimination

Discriminatory abuses may refer to two different types of abuse: (a) a purely exclusionary abuse whereby a dominant undertaking discriminates between itself and its competitors, thereby placing the latter at a competitive disadvantage; and (b) a market-distorting abuse whereby a dominant undertaking discriminates between two customers or suppliers, thereby placing one of them at a competitive disadvantage vis-à-vis the other. As regards both types of abuse, private and public enforcement cases have made significant contributions to clarifying this complex legal area.

---

[144] ibid paras 3.20 and 3.24.
[145] ibid paras 3.23–3.32.
[146] *ATG Media* (n 52) para 2.3.
[147] ibid para 3.14.
[148] ibid paras 3.14–3.16.
[149] ibid para 3.16.

In *Purple Parking*, a private enforcement case, the claimants, two operators of off-site car parks at Heathrow, complained that Heathrow Airport was abusing its dominant position by preventing them from meeting and greeting customers at a forecourt near the terminals, reserving this more attractive way of serving customers to itself. Heathrow Airport argued that, if its conduct amounted to an abuse at all, it could only be as an 'essential facility' case, where the facility was the airport premises, owned by Heathrow Airport, where the claimants wished to operate to meet and greet their customers. Therefore, to succeed, the claimants had to prove that the refusal to grant them access to the facility was capable of eliminating all competition.[150] The claimants, instead, argued that they were entitled to put the case as a discrimination case: Heathrow was applying dissimilar conditions to equivalent transactions with its trading partners, thereby placing them at a competitive disadvantage.[151] Mann J agreed with the claimants that the case could be put as a discrimination case even if the facilities that Heathrow Airport reserved for itself for the provision of meet and greet services could be described as 'essential'.[152] The list of abuses in Article 102 TFEU and section 18 of the Competition Act 1998 is not exhaustive. Furthermore, the EU case law applied different tests, not necessarily the 'essential facility' test,[153] to cases involving essential facilities, e.g., in margin squeeze cases in the telecoms industry.[154] This part of the judgment is, however, questionable. The point is not whether any case involving an 'essential facility' requires the application of the more stringent test of elimination of competition but that any case involving the refusal to license an intellectual property right or grant access or share another proprietary asset with a competitor requires a higher intervention threshold because of the impact that an obligation to share intellectual property rights or proprietary assets may have on incentives to invest. When this is the case, as a matter of policy and law, it is right that the threshold should be, and is, higher.[155] But there must be not only a proprietary asset in which the dominant undertaking has invested but also a refusal to share it.[156]

Concerning discrimination, the Court considered whether Heathrow Airport had applied dissimilar conditions to equivalent transactions, finding that it did.[157] It then went on to consider competitive disadvantage. The Court asked itself what would happen if the claimants had to operate from the car parks and only Heathrow Airport were left on the forecourts. The Court concluded that this would have an anti-competitive effect because

---

[150] *Purple Parking Limited and Meteor Parking Limited v Heathrow Airport Limited* [2011] EWHC 987 (Ch), para 76.

[151] ibid para 77.

[152] ibid para 105.

[153] Case 6/73 *Istituto Chemioterapico Italiano SpA and Commercial Solvents Corp v Commission* [1974] ECR 223; Case 311/84 *Centre Belge d'Etudes de Marché-Télémarketing (CBEM) v SA Compagnie Luxembourgeoise de Télédiffusion (CLT) and Information Publicité Benelux (IPB)* [1985] ECR 3261; Joined Cases C-241/91 P and C-242/91 P *Radio Telefis Eireann (RTE) and Independent Television Publications Ltd (ITP) v Commission* [1995] ECR I-743; Case C-7/97 *Oscar Bronner GmbH & Co KG v Mediaprint Zeitungsund Zeitschriftenverlag GmbH & Co KG* [1998] ECR I-7791; Case C-418/01 *IMS Health GmbH & Co OHG v NDC Health GmbH & Co KG* [2004] ECR I-5039; Case T-201/04 *Microsoft Corp v Commission* (n 100). In the literature see CI Nagy, 'Refusal to Deal and the Doctrine of Essential Facilities in US and EC Competition Law: A Comparative Perspective and a Proposal for a Workable Analytical Framework' (2007) 32 EL Rev 664; U Muller and A Rodenhausen, 'The Rise and Fall of the Essential Facility Doctrine' (2008) 29 ECLR 310; A Andreangeli, 'Interoperability as an "Essential Facility" in the *Microsoft* Case: Encouraging Competition or Stifling Innovation?' (2009) 34 EL Rev 584; E Rousseva, *Rethinking Exclusionary Abuses in EU Competition Law* (Hart Publishing, 2010) 81–132 and 412–16.

[154] *Purple Parking* (n 150) paras 98–103, relying on Case C-80/08 P *Deutsche Telekom AG v European Commission* [2010] ECR I-9555 and Case C-52/09 *Konkurrensverket v TeliaSonera AB* EU:C:2011:83.

[155] As argued by Heathrow Airport's counsel: *Purple Parking* (n 150) para 76.

[156] Nazzini, *The Foundations of EU Competition Law* (n 64) 258–73.

[157] *Purple Parking* (n 150) paras 134–40.

Heathrow Airport would become the only meet and greet operator, which would confer on it substantial advantages for customers. The claimants would no longer be able to compete on quality as they would not be able to offer the same service to their customers. The result would be an effective monopoly on the meet and greet service, and a serious risk to competition as far as the consumer is concerned. The customer would have only one product to buy. Heathrow Airport could charge monopolist prices. Those prices would be higher than the off-airport suppliers' current prices; and the meet and greet customers would have to pay those prices if they wanted that distinct product. This would operate to the detriment of the consumer who would be very likely to have to pay significantly higher, and unconstrained, prices for the forecourt meet and greet service [158] While, as explained above, one can question whether the Court should have applied a refusal to supply test in this case, the discrimination test, assuming it was applicable, was correctly understood. In particular, the analysis of competitive disadvantage is to be commended as the Court discussed not only the effect on competitors but also the effect on competition and, ultimately, on price.

In *Streetmap.eu v Google*, the claimant alleged that Google had abused its dominant position in general online search.[159] Streetmap's case was that, by displaying an image from Google Maps at the top of its search engine results page (SERP), and by relegating the link to Streetmap's service to a less prominent position on the page, Google had abused its dominant position under UK and EU competition law.[160] Although Streetmap advanced its claim in several alternative ways, Roth J considered that, on a proper analysis, Streetmap was really advancing what amounted to a claim of discrimination, by alleging that Google's conduct had placed competing online maps such as Streetmap's service at a competitive disadvantage.[161] Discriminatory abuses involve charging different prices or applying different conditions on customers in respect of an equivalent supply of products or services, without any objective justification. Discrimination is not, however, limited to this kind of conduct. As Roth J noted, the 'essence' of discrimination is treating like-products (or customers) in an unlike way.[162] Moreover, it is well-established that an undertaking that is dominant on one market can commit an abuse where the anti-competitive conduct in question takes effect on a different market, in which the undertaking is not dominant.[163]

Roth J held that, 'as a matter of principle', it may be abusive for a dominant company to leverage its power on a market in which it is dominant in order to promote its products on another market in which it is not dominant, thereby strengthening its position on that latter market.[164] Such conduct will, however, only constitute an abuse where the dominant undertaking's conduct has a foreclosing effect on its competitors. Determining whether this is the case requires careful consideration of the evidence, in its context.[165] Importantly,

---

[158] ibid paras 145–65.

[159] *Streetmap* (n 125).

[160] ibid para 50.

[161] ibid para 51. Roth J was unimpressed by Streetmap's suggestion that Google's conduct involved bundling or tying, including in the sense considered by what is now the General Court in Case T-201/04 *Microsoft v Commission* (n 100), concerning Microsoft's practice of pre-installing Windows Media Player on its Windows operating system. This is because Google users remained free to click on the links to third party providers' online maps without charge or any other particular burden, even though it was only Google Maps that benefited from having a clickable thumbnail.

[162] *Streetmap* (n 125) para 54.

[163] ibid para 59.

[164] ibid para 60.

[165] ibid para 61, referring to the European case law, eg Case C-549/10 P *Tomra Systems v Commission* EU:C:2012:221, para 18.

where foreclosure results from legitimate 'competition on the merits', there will be no abuse. What is required is 'anti-competitive foreclosure', whereby the dominant undertaking limits its competitors' ability to compete by depriving or hindering their access to essential inputs or customers. Input must be construed broadly and, in the instant case, Roth J held that the relevant input was 'the promotion afforded by display on the Google SERP; or put another way, display on the Google SERP is a form of access to customers'.[166]

Roth J also considered evidence of intent. Although the intention to pursue an anti-competitive strategy is not necessary to a finding of abuse, it may be a highly relevant consideration.[167] Having considered a range of contemporaneous evidence, the Roth J concluded that, while Google had expressly recognized that the introduction of the new Maps OneBox would drive more traffic to Google Maps, this was an expected consequence rather than a goal of the project. Google's intention was to improve its general search engine, by increasing user convenience and providing users with an instantly understandable result.[168]

Roth J observed that it was indisputable that the display of the thumbnail extract from Google Maps in response to geographical searches had improved the quality of Google's SERP. Roth J said:

> The unusual and challenging feature of this case is that conduct which was pro-competitive in the market in which the undertaking is dominant is alleged to be abusive on the grounds of an alleged anti-competitive effect in a distinct market in which it is not dominant. That is why much of the argument focused on alternative ways in which Google might have made this pro-competitive improvement without allegedly distorting competition in online maps.[169]

In considering whether (irrespective of any question of subjective intention) Google's conduct had the requisite anti-competitive effect, Roth J accepted that evidence of an actual effect on competition is not required before the court will make a finding of abuse. While the 'mere possibility' of anti-competitive foreclosure is not enough, it is sufficient if the claimant can show that the impugned conduct was 'reasonably likely to harm the competitive structure of the market'.[170] Importantly, however, Roth J noted that in determining that question, 'the court will take into account, as a very relevant consideration, evidence as to what the actual effect of the conduct has been'.[171] Furthermore, Roth J held that, in the particular circumstances, it was necessary to show that the effect in question is 'serious or appreciable'. Roth J recalled a number of Court of Justice authorities[172] which suggest that no de minimis threshold applies in abuse of dominance cases. However, those authorities concerned 'one market' cases (i.e. the relevant effect on competition was alleged to have occurred on the same market in which the undertaking was dominant). Differently, the

---

[166] *Streetmap* (n 125) para 63.

[167] ibid para 66.

[168] ibid paras 68–83.

[169] ibid para 84.

[170] ibid para 88. Roth J relied on the formulation adopted by the General Court in Case T-201/04 *Microsoft v Commission* (n 100) para 1089. He also recalled Case T-219/99 *British Airways v Commission* (n 4) para 293 and Opinion of AG Kokott in Case C-95/04 P *British Airways v Commission* [2007] ECR I-2331.

[171] *Streetmap* (n 125) para 89. Roth J relied on Case T-201/04 *Microsoft v Commission* (n 100) para 868.

[172] *Streetmap* (n 125) paras 93–95l and specifically Case 85/76 *Hoffmann-La Roche* (n 4) para 123; Case C-23/14 *Post Danmark II* (n 100) paras 70–74; and Case T-286/09 *Intel v Commission* (n 79) para 116.

alleged anti-competitive effect of Google's conduct was alleged to have occurred on a 'non-dominated' market. Roth J held that it would be especially 'perverse' to find that conduct which was clearly pro-competitive on the market in which the defendant holds a dominant position nonetheless contravened competition law because it had a non-appreciable effect on competition on a separate market.[173]

Accordingly, the question for the court was whether Google's conduct was reasonably likely to have a serious or appreciable effect on the market for online maps. Roth J regarded this question as 'the most difficult part of the case'.[174]

Roth J rejected Google's argument that its conduct had no effect on competition, finding it 'very relevant' that Google had itself expressed the view (in contemporaneous documents) that the new Maps OneBox would drive more 'traffic' to Google Maps.[175] The more difficult question was whether the effect in question was likely to be appreciable. This required a close analysis of a 'variety of data and metrics' which had been addressed, in particular, in the parties' economic evidence.[176] Roth J ultimately concluded that the introduction of the new Maps OneBox in 2007 was not reasonably likely to engender an appreciable anti-competitive foreclosure effect, essentially because any decline in Streetmap's users was not caused, or not caused to a significant extent, by the introduction of Maps OneBox but by the relative quality and strengths of the two services and competitive market dynamics.[177]

The fact that Google's conduct was not reasonably likely to have an appreciable effect on competition was enough to dispose of the allegation of an abuse.[178] However, Roth J also considered the question of objective justification, which had been heavily contested at the hearing. The key question here was whether there existed more proportionate alternatives by which Google could have achieved the improvements to its search engine which were attained by the display of a thumbnail map, but without placing Streetmap at a competitive disadvantage. Roth J ultimately rejected a number of alternatives advanced by Streetmap because they would have imposed a disproportionate additional burden and cost on Google, including those associated with having to introduce equivalent alternatives in any other EU markets in which Google holds a dominant position.[179]

In *Royal Mail*, a public enforcement case, the CAT upheld OFCOM's decision that Royal Mail abused its dominant position in the market for bulk mail delivery services in the UK by issuing contract change notices (CCNs) which introduced discriminatory prices. OFCOM had applied a test of reasonable likelihood of foreclosure but refused to apply the as efficient competitor test. The facts were that Royal Mail had introduced price changes to its two main price plans for access to Royal Mail's services so that a competitor wishing to compete with Royal Mail on an end-to-end basis would have to face higher prices than a competitor who had a more limited scale. Royal Mail had issued the relevant CCNs but, before the waiting period for implementation had expired, it withdrew them following the start of OFCOM's investigation.[180] OFCOM applied Article 102(c) TFEU and section 18(2)

---

[173] *Streetmap* (n 125) para 98.
[174] ibid para 99.
[175] ibid para 104.
[176] ibid para 107.
[177] ibid para 139. The reasoning of Roth J is particularly detailed on the issue of effect on competition; see paras 108–38.
[178] ibid para 141.
[179] ibid paras 142–76.
[180] *Royal Mail* (n 16) para 7.3.

(c) of the Competition Act 1998, thus treating the abuse as one of discrimination. In fact, the abuse was clearly exclusionary, carried out by way of a discriminatory pricing schedule. OFCOM found that the transactions for which different prices were proposed were equivalent,[181] that the discrimination was reasonably likely to have a foreclosure effect,[182] and that there was no objective justification.[183] Royal Mail's claim that the price discrimination was necessary to ensure the viability of the universal service obligation (USO) was deemed unsubstantiated because OFCOM had repeatedly found that the USO was not under threat.[184]

Two important points of principle arose in the appeal. First, whether a potentially abusive pricing schedule that had been announced but never actually implemented so that the prices in question never entered into effect and were never charged or paid could still constitute an infringement of Article 102 or the Chapter II prohibition. Secondly, whether OFCOM was required to carry out an as efficient competitor test to demonstrate that the pricing schedule under review would not allow a competitor as efficient as Royal Mail to be viable on the market. On both points, the CAT dismissed the appeal and upheld OFCOM's decision.

On the first point, the CAT held that the proper assessment of the relevant conduct was to ask, first, (a) whether the notified prices would have been discriminatory within the meaning of Article 102(c) TFEU or the Chapter II prohibition had they been charged; and, secondly, if so, (b) whether the price notification was likely to restrict competition and lacked objective justification.[185] The key issue was the latter. The CAT rejected Royal Mail's claim that the CCNs were merely preparatory acts. Rather, the CCNs were a formal, definitive, and public step necessary for the adoption of specific and detailed price and other changes to the relevant contracts with Royal Mail's customers. They were intended to, and did, cause customers to make appropriate changes to their activities, contractual and trading arrangements, and price schedules. The notice period was necessary to render this practicable. The publication of the CCNs had the express authority of the Royal Mail Board and senior management of Royal Mail Group and resulted from a process of internal discussions, consultation, and other market communications, as well as meetings and correspondence with Royal Mail's only competitor, Whistl.[186]

On the second point, the CAT held that as a matter of law or economics, it is not necessary to conduct an as efficient competitor test in all pricing cases. In *British Telecommunications PLC v Ofcom*, an appeal under the Communications Act 2003,[187] the CAT made clear that a price-cost test is not the only test under which the legality of the conduct of a dominant undertaking may be assessed.[188] Rather, in assessing whether an anti-competitive effect is likely, all the circumstances of a case must be examined and specifically whether the practice impairs buyers' freedom of choice, forecloses competitors, discriminates amongst counterparties, or strengthens the dominant position by distorting competition. Depending

---

[181] ibid paras 7.70–7.74.
[182] ibid paras 7.138–7.171.
[183] ibid paras 8.21–8.23.
[184] ibid para 8.18.
[185] *Royal Mail plc v Ofcom and Whistl UK Limited* [2019] CAT 27 (CAT judgment in *Royal Mail*), paras 308–309.
[186] ibid para 346.
[187] *British Telecommunications PLC v Ofcom* [2016] CAT 3.
[188] CAT judgment in *Royal Mail* (n 185) paras 472–73, relying on Case C-62/86 *AKZO Chemie v Commission* (n 20) para 70; Case C-209/10 *Post Danmark I* (n 124) para 25; Case C-23/14 *Post Danmark II* (n 100) paras 65–66 and 69–74; and Case C-52/09 *TeliaSonera Sverige* (n 154) para 28.

entirely on the facts of the case, it might be necessary in practice to use the as efficient competitor test to differentiate pricing conduct that is competition on the merits from that which is not. But if it is not necessary to do so, then the case law does not impose an obligation in principle to use the as efficient competitor test.[189] In the CAT's view, this position has not changed following the *Intel* judgment.[190] The CAT agreed with OFCOM that, in the particular circumstances of this case, the concept of a competitor as efficient as Royal Mail was not appropriate for reasons of scale of entry and because of the advantages and disadvantages that have accrued to Royal Mail due to its universal service provider status.[191] This approach is correct. The as efficient competitor test cannot be applied on the assumption that all competitors must be at least as efficient as the dominant undertaking. Particularly on markets characterized by strong entry barriers, network effects, or significant economies of scale, exclusion may be rational and effective precisely because it prevents competitors from becoming as efficient as the dominant undertaking. It would be absurd to rule out, or limit, the application of the abuse of dominance prohibition on these markets where it is most needed. It is, therefore, necessary to take a dynamic view of the as efficient competitor test, as OFCOM and the CAT did in this case.[192]

Unlike *Purple Parking*, *Streetmap*, and *Royal Mail*, which were cases involving exclusionary discrimination, *Arriva The Shires Ltd*[193] was a case of market-distorting discrimination, that is, discrimination that does not foreclose competitors of the dominant undertaking but distorts competition on a market on which the dominant undertaking provides an input but is not itself active.[194] Arriva The Shires Ltd used to operate a long-standing bus service connecting the airport of London Luton to London Victoria pursuant to a concession agreement with Luton Operations. In 2013, Luton Operations, instead of automatically renewing the agreement with Arriva The Shires Ltd, decided to grant the right to operate the Luton-Victoria route via a tender process. The contract was thereby secured by National Express, one of Arriva The Shires Ltd's competitors. The new concession agreement granted National Express (a) 'an exclusive right to run a coach service between the airport and much of central London for the next seven years, subject to an exception for a service operated by easyBus using smaller vehicles' and (b) the right of first refusal over the operation of other services on routes between the Airport and other destinations in London. Arriva The Shires Ltd claimed that Luton Operations abused its dominant position in the market for the 'grant of rights to use the Airport land and infrastructure' by way of: (a) discriminating against Arriva The Shires Ltd in the course of the tender process; (b) granting National Express an exclusive right to operate the bus service between Luton Airport and London Victoria for seven years; (c) discriminating in favour of easyBus, given the exemption to the exclusivity rule granted to this bus operator only. Rose J found that, while Arriva The Shires Ltd had not been discriminated in the tender process,[195] the introduction of the contested terms in the new concession constituted an abuse of dominant position for the purposes of the Chapter II prohibition as it seriously distorted competition among bus operators.[196]

---

[189] CAT judgment in *Royal Mail* (n 185) para 490.
[190] ibid paras 473–74, discussing paras 133 and 134 of Case C-413/14 P *Intel v Commission* (n 80).
[191] CAT judgment in *Royal Mail* (n 185) paras 532–48.
[192] Nazzini, *The Foundations of EU Competition Law* (n 64) 240–42.
[193] *Arriva The Shires Ltd* (n 130).
[194] On this distinction see Nazzini, *The Foundations of EU Competition Law* (n 64) 248–55.
[195] *Arriva The Shires Ltd* (n 130) paras 85, 92, and 93.
[196] ibid para 130.

Rose J found that the grant of an exclusive right to operate the Airport-Victoria route for seven years had an anti-competitive effect in that other bus operators are prevented to compete with the exclusive right holder.[197]

Rose J considered that the anti-competitive effects of the licence agreement were made more serious by a number of factors:

- the exclusivity was granted for a long period of time, affecting competition also in the future;[198]
- the grant of the right of first refusal was intentionally granted to shield National Express from competition from other bus operators. This additional protection was not justified because 'there was no real uncertainty about the level of continuing demand for the service; the infrastructure and marketing for the route were effectively already in place';[199] and,
- the exemption granted to easyBus even after October 2015 (i.e. after the expiry of the easyBus concession existing at the time of the tender) unjustifiably favoured this operator, placing 'other coach operators at an obvious competitive disadvantage in the downstream market'.[200]

Rose J excluded that Luton Operations' conduct was objectively justified because the reason behind the grant of the exclusive right to National Express (and related anti-competitive clauses) was not the lack of available space for alternative operators. Luton Operations wanted to protect National Express from competition from other bus operators and—as a result—maximise the fees it could earn from the license agreement.[201]

3.5 Exclusionary Abuses in the Pharmaceutical Sector

As in the previous decade, in 2010-2020 the UK authorities have continued focusing on the pharmaceutical markets, bringing both excessive pricing cases and exclusionary cases. The focus in this chapter is on exclusionary abuses.[202]

In *Reckitt Benckiser*, the OFT held that Reckitt Benckiser had abused its dominant position in the market for the NHS supply of alginate and antacid heartburn medicines by withdrawing and delisting NHS presentation packs of Gaviscon Original Liquid (the Withdrawal). The effect of the Withdrawal was that only Gaviscon Advance Liquid remained on the market. Gaviscon Original Liquid was off patent and had generic competition. Gaviscon Advance Liquid was, at the time of the Withdrawal, still patented and had, therefore, no generic competition. Consequently, general practitioners, when searching for a Gaviscon product in their IT system, would only find Gaviscon Advance Liquid, for which there was no generic alternative. This would lead their writing a prescription for the branded drug, which could not be substituted by the pharmacist with a generic alternative

---

[197] ibid para 106.
[198] ibid para 121.
[199] ibid para 123.
[200] ibid para 128.
[201] ibid paras 131–65.
[202] On excessive pricing cases see R O'Donoghue, 'Exploitative Abuses', ch 5 in this volume.

('closed prescription'). General practitioners would, thus, not write prescription for the generic product ('open prescriptions'). In this way, sales of generics, which were still available and were equivalent to Gaviscon Original Liquid, a more successful Reckitt Benckiser's product than Gaviscon Advance Liquid, were hindered. [203] The OFT relied heavily on internal documents to prove that Reckitt Benckiser's strategy was anti-competitive and would have been loss-making but for the exclusion of generic competition.[204] The OFT applied a test of tendency or capability to foreclose and concluded that it was reasonable to expect that the Withdrawal would hinder the development of generic supply of alginates and antacids by prescription in the UK. At the time of the Withdrawal, it was reasonable to expect that, if NHS packs of Gaviscon Original Liquid were withdrawn, general practitioners that searched for NHS packs of a liquid Gaviscon product would find only Gaviscon Advance Liquid, against which only closed prescriptions could then be issued. It was therefore reasonable to expect that, as a result of the Withdrawal, significantly fewer open prescriptions would be written than would have otherwise been the case following the publication of the generic name corresponding to Gaviscon Original Liquid. There would therefore be significantly less scope for pharmacies to choose between competing suppliers. It was, therefore, reasonable to expect that suppliers would have less incentive to compete on price to persuade pharmacies to dispense their medicines.[205]

In *Paroxetine*, GlaxoSmithKline entered into a set of agreements with three generic manufacturers that provided for substantial transfers of value by GlaxoSmithKline to them, their right to distribute certain quantities of GlaxoSmithKline's paroxetine in the UK, and their delayed entry in the UK market with their own independent generic version of paroxetine. Two agreements were settlements of ongoing litigation, whereas with respect to the agreement with IVAX there was no pending litigation. The CMA decided that GlaxoSmithKline had abused its dominant position by entering into the agreements. The agreements were also held to infringe the Chapter I prohibition and Article 101 TFEU,[206] with the exception of the agreement between GlaxoSmithKline and IVAX, which fell under the Vertical Exclusion Order and was, therefore, excluded from the application of the Chapter I prohibition,[207] and, furthermore, unlikely to have an anti-competitive object or effect and thus not subject to Article 101 TFEU.[208]

On appeal to the CAT, a number of questions were referred to the Court of Justice concerning both the prohibition of anti-competitive agreements and abuse of dominance.

In answering the questions referred, the Court of Justice noted that the same conduct may constitute an infringement of both Article 101 and Article 102 TFEU. Interestingly, the Court appears to say that the reason for the parallel application of both prohibitions is that they pursue different objectives and the harm caused by an infringement of Article 101 may

---

[203] *Reckitt Benckiser* (n 31) paras 6.8–6.29.

[204] ibid paras 6.29, 6.42, and 6.119.

[205] ibid paras 6.147–6.152.

[206] The focus in this chapter will be on the exclusionary abuses. For an analysis of the Chapter I and Article 101 infringement see R Whish, 'Horizontal Agreements', ch 2 in this volume.. P Ibáñez Colomo, 'Pay-for-Delay and the Structure of Article 101(1) TFEU: Points of Law Raised in Lundbeck and Paroxetine' (2019) 10 Journal of European Competition Law & Practice 591; Sven Gallasch, 'Debunking the Pay for Delay Myth: Pay for Delay Settlements Are No Ordinary Patent Settlements' (2016) 15 Competition LJ 89; Samantha Zakka, 'Pay-for-Delay Decisions: Are They Truly Restricting Competition' (2017) 1 Eur Competition & Reg L Rev 276.

[207] Competition Act 1998 (Land and Vertical Agreements Exclusion) Order 2000, SI 2000/310.

[208] CMA, Paroxetine investigation, *Case closure summary in respect of the IVAX-GlaxoSmithKline agreement* (CE9531/11, 10 August 2016).

not be the same as the harm caused by an infringement of Article 102. Under Article 101 the contracts are assessed individually, whereas under Article 102 there may be additional competitive harm to the competitive structure of a market in which, because of the dominant position of the branded manufacturer, the degree of competition is already weakened.[209]

As regards the test for abuse, the Court set out some established principles. First, the fact that an undertaking is in a dominant position does not prevent it from protecting its own commercial interests if they are attacked. Even a dominant undertaking has the right to take such reasonable steps as it deems appropriate to protect its commercial interests.[210] Secondly, the exercise of an exclusive right linked to an intellectual property right, such as the conclusion of settlement agreements to terminate litigation concerning a patent, falls within the scope of an intellectual property right. Therefore, the exercise of such a right in itself does not constitute an abuse of the dominant position.[211] Thirdly, however, even the exercise of an intellectual property right may be abusive when the purpose of the conduct is to strengthen the dominant position of the party engaging in it and to abuse that position, for example when such conduct is intended to deprive potential competitors of effective market access.[212] Fourthly, when the intention of a dominant manufacturer of a branded drug is to protect its own commercial interests, in particular by defending its patents, and to guard itself against the competition of generic medicines, that alone does not justify resorting to practices that fall outside the scope of competition on the merits.[213]

The Court then went on to discuss the principles applicable to pay-for-delay agreements. It said that, for such agreements to be characterised as abusive, they must be capable of restricting competition, that is, of having an exclusionary effect. That assessment must be undertaken having regard to all the relevant facts surrounding that conduct.[214] In this case, the CMA and the CAT considered that the set of settlement agreements concluded on the initiative of GlaxoSmithKline were part of an overall strategy and had, if not as their object, at least the effect of delaying the market entry of generic medicines containing the active ingredient paroxetine that had earlier entered the public domain. The direct consequence of that entry would have been an appreciable reduction in GlaxoSmithKline's market share and in the sale price of its originator medicine.[215]

The Court of Justice observed that the contract-oriented strategy under review constitutes, in principle, a practice that impedes the growth of competition in the market of a medicine containing an active ingredient that is in the public domain to the detriment of the national health systems.[216] The anti-competitive effects of such a contract-oriented strategy are liable to exceed the anti-competitive effects inherent in the conclusion of each of the agreements that are part of it. That strategy has a significant foreclosure effect on the market of the originator medicine, depriving the consumer of the benefits of entry into that market of potential competitors manufacturing their own medicine and, therefore, reserving that market directly or indirectly to the manufacturer of the originator medicine

---

[209] CJEU judgment in *Paroxetine* (n 46) paras 146–47.
[210] ibid para 149.
[211] ibid para 150.
[212] ibid para 151.
[213] ibid para 152.
[214] ibid para 154, relying on judgments in Case C-52/09 *TeliaSonera Sverige* (n 154) paras 64–68 and Case C-413/14 P *Intel v Commission* (n 80) para 138.
[215] CJEU judgment in *Paroxetine* (n 46) para 155.
[216] ibid para 156.

concerned.[217] It is immaterial in this regard that the IVAX agreement was entered into not to settle existing court proceedings but to avoid the bringing of such proceedings. It was also immaterial that the strategy was abusive that the IVAX Agreement could not have been penalised under national competition law or that it might have led to substantial savings for the national health system.[218] It is possible that the IVAX Agreement might have generated, taken together with the Alpharma and/GUK Agreements, cumulative effects from parallel restrictive agreements that were liable to strengthen GlaxoSmithKline's dominant position, and, therefore, that GlaxoSmithKline's strategy was abusive within the meaning of Article 102 TFEU.[219] There is no requirement to establish that the dominant undertaking has an anti-competitive intent. However, evidence of intent may be taken into account to determine that a dominant position has been abused.[220]

The Court of Justice also observed that it is open to a dominant undertaking to provide justification for behaviour that is liable to be caught by the prohibition under Article 102 TFEU, in particular by establishing that the exclusionary effect produced by its conduct may be counterbalanced, or outweighed, by advantages in terms of efficiency that also benefit consumers.[221] It is for the dominant undertaking to show that: (a) the efficiency gains offset any likely negative effects on competition and the interests of consumers in the affected markets; (b) those gains have been, or are likely to be, brought about as a result of that conduct; (c) such conduct is necessary for the achievement of those efficiency gains; and (d) it does not eliminate effective competition, by removing all or most existing sources of actual or potential competition. Therefore, an undertaking must do more than advance vague, general and theoretical arguments or rely exclusively on its own commercial interests.[222]

Whether a practice that may be subject to the prohibition laid down in Article 102 TFEU is justified requires, inter alia, a weighing of the favourable and unfavourable effects on competition of the practice concerned, which requires objective analysis of its market effects. Consideration of the efficiency gains of the practices cannot depend on the objectives that may have been pursued and, therefore, on whether those practices result from deliberate intention or are only fortuitous or accidental.[223] The fact that the financial implications of the IVAX agreement that are favourable to the national health system may have been accidental cannot ensure that, for that reason alone, such financial implications are excluded from the weighing of favourable and unfavourable effects on competition of the practice. Those financial implications must be duly taken into account in assessing whether they do constitute efficiency gains that may arise from the conduct under examination and, if so, whether they offset the adverse effects that that conduct is capable of having on competition and the interests of consumers in the market affected.[224] Such weighing of effects should be carried out in light of the specific characteristics of the practice and, in particular, of the fact that

---

[217] ibid para 157.

[218] ibid paras 158–60.

[219] ibid para 161.

[220] ibid paras 162–64, relying on Case C-549/10 P *Tomra Systems and Others v Commission* EU:C:2012:221, paras 20, 21, and 24.

[221] CJEU judgment in *Paroxetine* (n 46) para 165, relying on Case C-209/10 *Post Danmark I* (n 124) paras 40 and 41.

[222] CJEU judgment in *Paroxetine* (n 46) para 166, relying on Case C-209/10 *Post Danmark I* (n 124) para 42.

[223] CJEU judgment in *Paroxetine* (n 46) paras 167–69, relying on the case law on the objective nature of the concept of abuse, ie Case 85/76 *Hoffmann-La Roche* (n 4) para 91; and Case C-170/13 *Huawei Technologies* EU:C:2015:477.

[224] CJEU judgment in *Paroxetine* (n 46) para 170.

the demonstrated favourable effects resulting from the IVAX Agreement are significantly less than those which would have arisen upon the independent market entry of a generic version of Seroxat following a successful outcome for IVAX in the patent proceedings.[225]

At present, the case is still pending before the CAT, following the preliminary ruling of the Court of Justice.

4 Conclusions

In the second decade of the Competition Act 1998, the UK competition authorities and courts have continued a trend of applying the Chapter II prohibition and Article 102 TFEU in a sophisticated and commercially reasonable way, while being constrained by EU law.

The assessment of dominance continues to be robust and, as such, constitutes an important screen to avoid false positives. The CMA considers dominance as coextensive with substantial and durable market power, or, at the very least, substantial and durable market power is a necessary and major element of the assessment of dominance. This is demonstrated by the CMA's consistent approach to dominance, which relies on the following elements: (a) market definition and analysis of short-term competitive constraints; (b) market shares as an indication of dominance but generally not conclusive proof of it; (c) close scrutiny of existing and potential short-term competition; (d) assessment of barriers to entry, even when market shares are high; (e) analysis of buyer power, whenever relevant; and (f) evidence of market dynamics, entry and exit, profitability, and conduct. The CMA has thus continued the approach of the OFT in the previous decade.

As regards the abuse tests, the CMA has sought to clarify the law on retroactive rebates and did so by helpfully applying the as efficient competitor test in a structured and robust way in *IDEXX* and *Loyalty-inducing Discount Scheme*. However, after the EU-level judgments in *Intel*, the CMA had to change its approach to follow the less economically robust jurisprudence of these courts in *Impulse Ice Cream*, decided after the judgment of the General Court, and *Remicade*, decided after the judgment of the Court of Justice. It is hoped that following Brexit the CMA will feel free to revert to its earlier approach.

Exclusion in multi-market settings is, notoriously, a complex area of the law because the abuse or the anti-competitive effects, or both, occur on a market other than the market on which the undertaking concerned is dominant. *Flybe* and *Achilles* have clarified the law to a certain extent, together with discrimination cases such as *Purple Parking, Streetmap.eu, Royal Mail*, and *Arriva The Shires Ltd*. At least two elements are worth noting here. First, the closeness of the links between related markets. When anti-competitive conduct occurs on a related market, but the anti-competitive effect is felt on the dominant market because the conduct strengthens or protects the dominant position, the links between the dominant market and the related market can be weaker. In reality, while this is how the OFT out the issue in *Flybe*, it is probably better to understand this analysis in the sense that the strengthening or maintenance of dominance is a sufficiently strong link that may render a closer analysis of other links between the two markets superfluous. However, when both the conduct and the effects occur on the related market, the links between the dominated market and the

---

[225] ibid para 171.

related market must be particularly strong. In the author's view, this means that dominance must enable the anti-competitive conduct and the anti-competitive effect to occur. In the absence of such a link, there would be a risk that conduct by a dominant undertaking in any market could be an abuse of dominance even if it has nothing to do with the undertaking's dominant position. This would be contrary to the text of the Chapter II prohibition and Article 102 TFEU, which only prohibit an abuse *of* a dominant position, not any abuse *by* a dominant undertaking. Secondly, the case law has clarified that, when the anti-competitive effect occurs on a market other than the dominated market, the anti-competitive effects must be appreciable. This is logical. While it is possible to comprehend—although, in the author's view, sill not possible to justify—the EU case law that an anti-competitive effect on the dominated market need not be appreciable, because on that market competition is already weakened given the presence of the dominant undertaking, there is no reason whatsoever to prohibit even slight, insignificant anti-competitive effects on markets where the undertaking in question is not dominant.

In a number of cases, the CMA has examined exclusivity-type of arrangements and engaged in detailed analysis of the market to verify whether the clauses under review had anti-competitive effects. While there are occasional references to low thresholds of the foreclosure standard such as capability or tendency to foreclose, it appears that on the facts the CMA has applied a test of likelihood to foreclose an as efficient competitor.

In three discrimination cases, *Purple Parking*, *Streetmap.eu*, and *Royal Mail*, the English courts developed a principled approach to exclusionary discrimination characterised by a toning down of the element of whether dissimilar prices or conditions are applied to equivalent transaction and a detailed analysis of whether competitors are foreclosed and whether this leads to a negative effect on price and output. In *Arriva The Shires Ltd*, Rose J applied the test for market-distorting discrimination, focusing on the element of competitive disadvantage among undertakings operating in a market on which the dominant undertaking provides an input but is not present. These cases demonstrate that the prohibition of discriminatory abuses can be applied in an economically robust and commercially reasonable way and that requiring proof of anti-competitive effects does not make the application of the prohibition excessively difficult. Especially now that the transition period has expired, it is hoped that UK law will move further away from the formalistic way in which the prohibition of discriminatory abuses is applied in EU law.

Finally, public enforcement clearly had a focus on the pharmaceutical sector. *Paroxetine*, in particular, clarified important issues concerning pay-for-delay abuses. The Court of Justice, in particular, explained that a set of agreements that infringe Article 101 may also infringe Article 102 if they bring about an additional, distinct harm, over and above the harm cause by each agreement. Pay-for-delay agreements are to be assessed as ordinary exclusionary abuses with a focus, therefore, on their foreclosure effect. The circumstance that such agreements involve a patent dispute and that they may be in settlement of ongoing or contemplated litigation do not appear to play any significant role in the analysis. These cases, however, are highly fact specific. It remains to be seen how the CAT will rule on the appeals, following the preliminary ruling by the CJEU.

In conclusion, in its second decade, modern UK competition law continued a trend already clear in the first decade: the prohibition of abuse of dominance is applied in a more economically robust and commercially reasonable way than it is by the EU institutions, the Commission, and the EU courts, and in certain other Member States. Now that the Brexit transition period has expired, this trend may become more pronounced, as UK law will free itself of the constraints of EU law.[226] However, there is a risk that EU law may be replaced by an even more serious threat to sound competition policy: populist interventionism and political motivations in competition enforcement. Whether this threat will materialize, it is too early to say.

---

[226] Section 60 of the Competition Act 1998 requires UK judicial and administrative authorities to apply UK competition law consistently with EU principles. After the end of the Brexit transition period on 31 December 2020, section 60 of the Competition Act 1998 will be repealed: see Competition (Amendment etc.) (EU Exit) Regulations 2019/93 Pt 2 reg 22. The UK authorities would, therefore, be free to apply UK law without being constrained by EU law, going forward. Retrospectively, for issues still governed, *ratione temporis*, by EU law or UK law before the end of the Brexit transition period, a new s 60A will apply, broadly, to the same effect as the old section 60.

5

Exploitative Abuses

Robert O'Donoghue QC

1 Introduction

Cases of pure unfair pricing are rare in competition law. Authorities find them difficult to bring and are, rightly, wary of casting themselves in the role of price regulators. Generally, price control is better left to sectoral regulators, where they exist, and operated prospectively; ex post price regulation through the medium of competition law presents many problems.[1]

These salutary comments by the Competition Appeal Tribunal (CAT) in *Phenytoin*[2] might give the overall impression that any review of the treatment of exploitative abuses under the Competition Act 1998 (CA 1998) over the last two decades would be laconic in nature. This impression might also be fortified by the fact that, at the EU level, it is difficult to think of very many cases where the *only* issue was an excessive price. Most cases have additional elements or reflect predominant concerns other than excessive pricing, including: (1) cumulative abuses, where excessive price is often a consequence of exclusionary conduct;[3] (2) issues of parallel trade or market integration;[4] or (3) legal monopolies.[5] This has led one distinguished commentator to state, with some justification, that the EU Courts have 'not yet condemned a particular pricing practice, in a free and unregulated market, as amounting to unfairly high and exploitative prices and thus constituting an infringement of Article [102]'.[6] Indeed, the most comprehensive recent analysis by the Commission led it to *reject* an excessive pricing complaint in a way that was thought to make it practically difficult to pursue future cases.[7]

However, bucking this trend, exploitative abuses have featured surprisingly strongly under the CA 1998 (usually of course applied in parallel with Article 102 TFEU). Moreover, it is clear that these issues remain firmly on the agenda of the UK competition authority, the Competition and Markets Authority (CMA). In addition to the fact that the CMA is now looking again at the *Phenytoin* case, following the setting aside of the CMA's abuse findings by the CAT,[8] whose judgment was largely upheld by the Court of Appeal,[9] the CMA has

---

[1] *Pfizer Limited and Others v Competition and Markets Authority* [2018] CAT 11, para 3.
[2] ibid.
[3] Case 27/76 *United Brands v Commission* EU:C:1978:22.
[4] Case 226/84 *British Leyland Plc v Commission* [1986] ECR 3263 and Case 26/75 *General Motors Continental NV v Commission* [1975] ECR 1367.
[5] Case 395/87 *Ministère Public v Tournier* [1989] ECR 2521 and Joined Cases 110/88, 241/88, 242/88 *Lucazeau v SACEM* [1989] ECR 2811.
[6] See N Wahl, 'Exploitative High Prices and European Competition Law: A Personal Reflection' in Swedish Competition Authority, *The Pros and Cons of High Prices* (2007) 62 http://www.konkurrensverket.se/globalassets/english/research/the-pros-and-cons-of-high-prices-14mb.pdf.
[7] Case COMP/A.36.568/D3 *Scandlines Sverige AB v Port of Helsingborg* Commission Decision of 23 July 2004 and Case COMP/A.36.568/D3 *Sundbusserne v Port of Helsingborg* Commission Decision of 23 July 2004.
[8] *Pfizer Limited and Others v Competition and Markets Authority* (n 1).
[9] *Competition and Markets Authority v Pfizer UK Limited and Others* [2020] EWCA 339.

Robert O'Donoghue, *Exploitative Abuses* In: *The UK Competition Regime*. Edited by: Barry Rodger, Peter Whelan, and Angus MacCulloch, Oxford University Press. © The Contributors 2021. DOI: 10.1093/oso/9780198868026.003.0005

several other pending proceedings in the pharmaceutical sphere where excessive pricing abuses are the only, or main, allegations. In short, for the foreseeable future, investigations of exploitative abuses are here to stay under UK competition law.

This chapter synthesizes the main decisional practice and case law arising under section 18 of the CA 1998 over the last twenty years (section 2). It then seeks to distil these cases into a set of coherent principles, as well as identifying areas where the decisional practice and case law are unclear, have not yet addressed particular issues in detail, or are arguably incorrect (section 3). A short conclusion is then set out (section 4).

2 The Decisional Practice and Case Law

2.1 CAT Cases/Appeals in CAT Cases

2.1.1 Napp

The earliest case under the CA 1998 concerning exploitative abuse is *Napp*.[10] Napp, a pharmaceutical company, was the first to launch a sustained release morphine product (MST) in the United Kingdom, where it held a patent on the drug until 1992. In the market for MST, there are two customer segments: the community (or general practitioner) segment and the hospital segment. Approximately 85–90 per cent of the market was supplied by wholesalers to community pharmacies to be used by patients as prescribed by their primary care physicians, while the remainder was purchased directly by hospitals from manufacturers to be used for in-patient care, as prescribed by hospital doctors or specialists. However, the community segment was to some extent 'captive', since the brand of MST prescribed in the hospital segment was almost invariably prescribed in the community segment due to patient familiarity, etc. Napp had market shares in excess of 90 per cent in both segments. The Office of Fair Trading (OFT) decided that Napp enjoyed market dominance because of those high market shares and the existence of considerable barriers to entry. The OFT also found Napp's pricing policies for MST to be both predatory and excessive. Napp's practice of pricing the drug at a very low level in the hospital segment was ruled predatory and its pricing at a high level in the community segment was ruled excessive. On appeal, the CAT upheld these findings.

A number of aspects of *Napp* bear mention. First, it was not a case of 'pure' exploitation. The primary abuse was abusively low prices in the hospital segment which, once captured, then allowed abusively high prices in the community segment. Indeed, the OFT made clear that absent the predation aspect of the case, it would not have pursued the excessive pricing issues on their own.[11]

Secondly, the OFT and CAT took a wide and inclusive approach to the question of benchmarks against which to assess Napp's prices, using a 'predominance of evidence' approach. This included: (i) comparison with competitors' prices; (ii) comparison over time; (iii) comparison between the hospital and community segments; (iv) Napp's export prices;

---

[10] Case CA98/2/2001 *Napp Pharmaceuticals Holdings Ltd and Subsidiaries*, Decision of Director General of Fair Trading on 30 March 2001, on appeal *Napp Pharmaceutical Holdings Limited and Subsidiaries v Director General of Fair Trading* [2002] CAT 1 (*Napp*).

[11] ibid para 364.

(v) Napp's profits on community versus hospital; and, (vi) comparing Napp's margins with its competitors. The CAT noted that assessing unfair pricing is 'rarely an easy task'[12] but that one needed to look at 'relevant comparators'.[13] Indeed, even if there was 'some differential' in respect of Napp's export prices and its challenged domestic UK prices, that was still not a good reason to exclude them as a comparator.[14]

Thirdly, the CAT considered arguments by Napp concerning the 'dynamic' aspect of its pricing. Napp sought to justify its high prices for MST in the community segment by reference to the importance of ex ante uncertainty in the pharmaceutical industry and dynamic competition. It argued that prices in a dynamically competitive market would allow recovery of past investments in R&D and promotion over the life cycle of the product as a whole. This dynamic provides pharmaceutical firms: 'with the appropriate incentive to invest in such R&D, education, training, and promotion to the extent that consumers collectively are willing to fund such investment. Any such competitive price will take account of the *ex ante* uncertainty as to whether a particular product will succeed.'[15]

The CAT was unimpressed with this point, at least on the facts of *Napp*. It noted that:

Napp's original investment in MST was made in the early 1980s in launching and promoting a product which, at the time, represented an important innovation. [However,] Napp has provided no figures as to what that initial investment was. In the absence of any indication to the contrary, we would expect that initial investment to have been recouped long ago.[16]

Finally, there was an interesting issue in that many of Napp's prices were regulated under a voluntary government/industry agreement known as the Pharmaceutical Price Regulation Scheme (PPRS). Napp argued that it was engaged in 'portfolio pricing' in that, with regulation, some products would have low/no profitability and others would have much higher returns, leading to a balanced 'portfolio' pricing overall. The CAT disagreed, noting that 'it is not appropriate ... to take into account the reasonableness or otherwise of its profits on other, unspecified, markets comprised in some wider but undefined "portfolio" unrelated to the market in which dominance exists'.[17]

2.1.2 Albion Water

Albion Water involved two separate but related allegations of an exclusionary margin squeeze and exploitative excessive price, leading to two separate CAT judgments.[18] Dŵr Cymru (Welsh Water) was an effective monopolist supplier subject to sectoral regulation. For certain retail customers, the market was open to competition. The case concerned the price for the partial treatment and transmission of non-potable water through an existing pipeline to a large paper factory on the North Wales coast, which was a major user of

---

[12] ibid para 392.
[13] ibid para 394.
[14] ibid para 395.
[15] ibid para 354.
[16] ibid para 407.
[17] ibid para 413. See also para 417, where the CAT went on to stress that 'in the case of many pharmaceutical products, the expiry of a patent leads to competitive (often generic) market entry ... In the present case, however, Napp has maintained both the price of MST and an exceptionally high market share for many years'.
[18] *Albion Water Limited v Water Services Regulation Authority* [2006] CAT 36 (*Albion Water I*) and *Albion Water Limited v Water Services Regulation Authority* [2008] CAT 31 (*Albion Water II*).

non-potable water supplied through that part of the water pipe network belonging to Dŵr Cymru. For the use of the system, in March 2001, Dŵr Cymru proposed to charge Albion an access price for partial treatment and common carriage of that non-potable water of 23.2 p/m^3. Albion complained that the access price was so excessive as to amount to an abuse of a dominant position. The sectoral regulator, the Water Services Regulation Authority, rejected Albion's complaint. However, on appeal, the CAT found that the access price was indeed abusive.

A number of aspects of the case bear emphasis. First, like *Napp*, the case was not only, or even mainly, concerned with excessive pricing. The excessive pricing findings in *Albion Water II* followed the finding of a margin squeeze in *Albion Water I*. The fact of Dŵr Cymru's vertical integration—and the two abuses on related markets—was a critical component in the finding of excessive pricing. In particular, at paragraphs 234–35 the CAT noted that the fact that the case concerned two vertically related markets was central to its conclusions:

> If, as envisaged by the Guidance (OFT 422), common carriage is to be an important means of introducing competition to the water industry, it is neither possible nor desirable to divorce the economic value of common carriage from the fact that this is a vertically integrated market. In contrast to the position in Scandlines, where the dominant firm (the owner of the port of Helsingborg) was not present on the downstream ferry services market, in this case, Dŵr Cymru is not only present on the upstream market for the transportation of non-potable water for supply to industrial customers in the geographical area served by the Ashgrove system, but is also active in the downstream market for the supply of non-potable water to industrial customers in that area. Whereas in the upstream market, Albion and Dŵr Cymru act as customer and supplier, Albion and Dŵr Cymru are actual or potential competitors in the downstream market. An excessive upstream price charged by a vertically integrated dominant undertaking to customers which are also its competitors in a downstream market may have an exclusionary effect.
>
> Where, as here, the functions of treatment, distribution and retailing of water are carried out within the same company – Dŵr Cymru, two kinds of prices are set: retail prices for services supplied to its own customers, and access prices for the use of its infrastructure. A crucial factor in determining the economic value of common carriage is the margin between the two prices set by Dŵr Cymru. The CAT has already found that Dŵr Cymru imposed an unlawful margin squeeze on Albion.

Secondly, the CAT was careful to identify the various distinctive features of the case:

- The case concerned the supply of non-drinking water to a paper mill in Wales where Dŵr Cymru was the incumbent supplier and Albion succeeded in winning the business. In retaliation, when Albion sought a common carriage price (a form of wholesale access) under the First Access Price, Dŵr Cymru proposed very high prices. Thus, the case at its core was about Dŵr Cymru using its monopoly pricing to exclude its only downstream retail rival. That was the main focus, not excessive pricing.
- Albion was the only company to enter the water undertaker sector since privatization in 1989.[19]

---

[19] *Albion Water I* (n 18) para 7.

- Cost justification was the only way in which prices were set for water under the regulatory regime. As the CAT noted, 'the principal issue ... is the justification for the "distribution" cost element of the First Access Price, found by the Director to be 16 p/m³'.[20] All parties agreed that the case turned on a cost-price approach.
- The 'policy' questions arising out of the failed liberalization of the market were central to the case. It noted that the exclusion of the only market entrant since 1989 (the date of liberalization) 'are matters which the Tribunal views with serious concern, particularly against the background of recent policy to encourage competition in the water industry'.[21]

Thirdly, it was an unusual case because, on the facts, the CAT was compelled to ignore comparators or benchmark prices because it was 'impossible' to identify any. The CAT expressly found that to be the case: 'there is no substitute for the service of the transportation and partial treatment of water here in question ... It is therefore impossible to compare the level of the common carriage price charged by Dŵr Cymru with that of direct competitors because there are none'. [22]

Finally, the abuse was rather obvious. Albion paid 3 p/m³ to buy the water and had to pay Dŵr Cymru the First Access Price of 23.2 p/m³, and resell the water to the retail customer (the Welsh paper mill) where Dŵr Cymru's price was 26 p/m³.[23] Its best price was therefore above Dŵr Cymru and nearly all of this 'cost' to Albion was accounted for by Dŵr Cymru's access price. Albion was paying almost 8 times as much to have the water carried as it was for the water itself.

2.1.3 Phenytoin

In *Phenytoin*, the CMA imposed its highest ever fine on a single undertaking by fining Pfizer £85 million for an excessive pricing abuse in a decision rendered in late 2016.[24] The abuse findings were overturned by the CAT and its findings largely confirmed by the Court of Appeal,[25] with the result that the case has been remitted to the CMA, which is continuing to (re)investigate.

The case concerned phenytoin sodium, a treatment available in identical tablet and capsule form as an anti-epilepsy drug (AED). Epilepsy is a relatively common condition in the UK, affecting circa 400,000 people, who often require life-long treatment. Around 48,000 patients are stabilized on phenytoin sodium. Although it was an old drug long out of patent, the CAT accepted that phenytoin sodium is a 'useful and effective treatment for a significant number of patients'.[26] Phenytoin sodium is marketed in two chemically identical formulations in the United Kingdom: (i) capsules and (ii) tablets. There are also a large number of other AEDs routinely prescribed to patients in the United Kingdom. Until 2012, Pfizer manufactured and marketed phenytoin sodium capsules. In 2012, it transferred the marketing authorization for the product to Flynn, but retained control of the manufacturing

---

[20] ibid para 14.
[21] ibid para 11.
[22] *Albion Water II* (n 18) para 256.
[23] *Albion Water I* (n 18) para 8.
[24] Case CE/9742-13 *Phenytoin* (7 December 2016).
[25] *Pfizer UK Limited and Others v Competition and Markets Authority* (n 1), on further appeal *Competition and Markets Authority v Pfizer UK Limited and Others* (n 9).
[26] *Pfizer UK Limited and Others v Competition and Markets Authority* (n 1) para 412.

process, in order to ensure supply continuity for patients. NRIM is the other phenytoin so-dium capsule manufacturer, having entered the market in 2012. Teva, and a range of other undertakings, manufacture and/or supply the tablet form of phenytoin sodium.

Pfizer's phenytoin sodium pricing was historically included in the PPRS, a regulated drug pricing scheme for clusters of branded drugs. Under the PPRS, Pfizer's phenytoin sodium had over time become loss-making or only marginally profitable. Pfizer therefore sought to put the product on a more stable long-term footing by taking it out of the PPRS. The basic idea was to take it out of the PPRS by debranding it and then relaunch as a generic product at a revised higher price. Since Pfizer was, at the time, inexperienced in generic products (it is an originator company in the main), it sought assistance from third parties who special-ized in marketing generics. One such company was Flynn and the parties reached supply and related agreements in 2012. Under these arrangements, Pfizer would set a supply price to Flynn and Flynn would then market the products setting its own separate price down-stream. The actual supplies commenced in around September 2012.

The new Pfizer/Flynn capsule prices would be benchmarked against the Teva tablet price, since it was understood that the Teva price was effectively set by the Department of Health. Between 2005 and 2007, the price of a pack of Teva tablets rose significantly to £113.62 (for a packet of 28 tablets).[27] In or around October 2007 the Department of Health requested a meeting with Teva and asked Teva to reduce the price of the tablets. The evidence of Mr Beighton (who at the relevant time was a senior Teva individual) at trial—which was found to be 'broadly credible' by the CAT[28]—was that the Department of Health rejected Teva's offer of a price reduction to £40 and asked for a new price at £30. Teva agreed, and reduced the price accordingly.

Under Pfizer's revised pricing arrangements agreed with Flynn in 2012, Pfizer charged Flynn roughly half, on average, of the Teva tablet price. For example, taking the 100mg dose, Pfizer's price to Flynn was £35–40 and Flynn's price to its customers was £50–60, whereas the equivalent reimbursement price paid for the Teva tablet was around £90. However, the new prices for the capsules were very considerably higher than the prices which applied under the PPRS. The price charge by Flynn was circa 2,600 per cent higher than the old Pfizer price under the PPRS and Pfizer's price was just over half of that, so also a substantial increase.

2.1.3.1 CMA Decision

The CMA's analysis proceeded according to the two main limbs of the seminal *United Brands* judgment, namely whether (i) the difference between the costs actually incurred and the price actually charged is excessive, and, if so, (ii) a price has been imposed which is either unfair in itself or when compared to competing products.[29]

On the first limb of *United Brands*, the CMA applied the following steps in its approach. It first set out its general approach to the calculation of costs.[30] It then calculated the direct and indirect costs actually incurred by Pfizer.[31] It added to that (cost) figure a reasonable

---

[27]   ibid para 209.
[28]   ibid para 74.
[29]   Case 27/76 *United Brands v Commission* (n 3) para 250.
[30]   Decision of the Competition and Markets Authority Unfair pricing in respect of the supply of phenytoin so-dium capsules in the UK (Case CE/9742-13), 16 December 2016 (Decision), paras 5.27–5.57.
[31]   ibid paras 5.58–5.77.

rate of return. The CMA's preferred measure of return would have been return on capital employed (ROCE). But this measure had limitations due *inter alia* to the fact that Pfizer did not have production lines (and therefore capital investment) dedicated solely to its phenytoin sodium products.[32] Instead the CMA used a return on sale (ROS) measure for a reasonable rate of return.[33] Using ROS, the CMA found that 6 per cent is a reasonable rate of return.[34] This was based mainly on the circumstance that there is a 6 per cent ROS target level under the PPRS, a voluntary regulated scheme for branded products.[35] The CMA also said that it is 'informative' to look at the internal total profit margins of the UK company, Pfizer Limited, for the period from 2009 to 2013.[36]

The CMA then compared the resulting cost plus figure with the prices actually charged by Pfizer. This yielded an 'excess' ranging from 29 per cent (25 mg), 100 per cent (50 mg), 690 per cent (300 mg), and 705 per cent (100 mg).[37] It concluded that all four percentages were 'excessive' within the meaning of the first limb of *United Brands*, based primarily on the level of excess but also supplemented by other factors (e.g. that the prices have prevailed for four years, excesses considered in other cases).[38] The CMA then applied what it calls a 'sensitivity analysis' to the allocation of Pfizer's common costs, which results in significant downwards and upwards variations in the levels of excess for the four product dosages.[39]

On the second limb of *United Brands*, the CMA applied the following steps in its analysis: (It considers 'economic value' and concludes that it is no more than cost plus, i.e. there are no non-cost related factors that increase 'economic value' above the cost plus level identified by the CMA.[40] The main reasons given for this conclusion were as follows:[41] (i) the characteristics of phenytoin sodium capsules, and in particular that they are an 'old' drug.

There has been no change in Pfizer's costs justifying a price increase; (ii) phenytoin sodium capsules were sold much more cheaply before by Pfizer within the PPRS framework.

The NHS is not 'readily willing' to pay a premium.

The CMA concluded that each of Pfizer's four phenytoin sodium capsule supply prices is 'unfair in itself' based on:[42] (i) the 'substantial disparity' between Pfizer's supply prices and 'economic value'; (ii) competitive conditions did not function in a manner likely to produce a reasonable relationship between price and economic value; (iii) Pfizer's supply prices had an adverse effect on the end-customer, the NHS; and (iv) 'additional context' including the fact that historically (pre-divestment) the reimbursement price for Pfizer's capsules had been much lower, the fact that Pfizer's supply prices for phenytoin sodium capsules in the UK are materially higher than the price of Epanutin capsules in other EU Member States, and (iii) that one of the reasons why Pfizer made an agreement with Flynn was to avoid or reduce so-called 'pharmacopolitical risk', i.e. reputational damage.

---

[32] ibid paras 5.80–5.83. The Decision does state, however, that the CMA carried out some assessment of returns on capital as a 'cross-check' on ROS (para 5.84).

[33] ibid para 5.84.

[34] ibid para 5.86.

[35] ibid paras 5.93 ff.

[36] ibid para 5.89.

[37] ibid Table 5.8.

[38] ibid para 5.127 ff.

[39] ibid Table 5.9.

[40] ibid para 5.262.

[41] ibid paras 5.267–5.338.

[42] ibid paras 5.350–5.452.

The CMA went on to consider whether the Pfizer supply prices are unfair compared to competing products within the meaning of the second limb of the *United Brands* test, and concludes that there are no meaningful comparator products.[43] The CMA specifically rejected the arguments that NRIM's phenytoin sodium capsule product and parallel imports of Pfizer/Flynn phenytoin sodium capsules are relevant comparators.[44] It also considers that the reimbursement price of phenytoin sodium tablets is not a meaningful comparator.[45]

2.1.3.2 CAT Judgment

On appeal, the CAT quashed the CMA's Decision, insofar as it related to abuse, on a number of different—but independent—bases. Having heard the evidence and submissions at trial, the Tribunal identified a number of legal and factual errors in the CMA's approach and Decision.

First, the CMA erred in its assessment of the legal test in *United Brands*.[46] *United Brands* establishes that—in order to be unlawful—the price of the product must bear 'no reasonable relation' to its 'economic value'. The CAT held that, it is necessary to identify a benchmark price (or range) 'that would have pertained in circumstances of normal and sufficiently effective competition', using the evidence available.[47] The CMA had not done this. It rejected all the available methodologies by which an excessive price might be identified and relied exclusively on a Cost Plus approach. This was an error because Cost Plus in isolation is not: 'a sufficient method for establishing the excess if other methods are available … [the CMA] cannot simply choose the method of calculating the excess that was most favourable to establishing an infringement, to the exclusion of other methods'. [48]

Secondly, the CMA erred when applying its Cost Plus method in any event. The CAT held—after hearing the oral evidence of the witnesses and experts at trial—that the CMA's reliance on the 6 per cent ROS in the Pharmaceutical Pricing Regulation Scheme 'PPRS) was flawed. Only 'limited weight' could be placed on the that figure.[49] It should not be relied upon as a proper basis for 'confirming, far less determining' a reasonable rate of return in this case.[50]

Thirdly, the CMA erred by failing to gather sufficient evidence to place the product in its proper context. The CMA's refusal to make comparisons with other products or other companies, and failure to even place phenytoin sodium in the context of the other products produced by Pfizer and Flynn, led to the result that it had failed to put the prices 'in their commercial context during the relevant period'.[51]

Fourthly, the CMA erred in law when it applied limb 2 of the test in *United Brands* (unfairness). Consistent with its narrow (acontextual) approach under limb 1, the CMA erred in concluding that it could rely on only one of the tests identified by the Court of Justice for assessing unfairness. It only asked whether the price was 'unfair in itself' and concluded

---

[43] ibid paras 5.479.
[44] ibid paras 5.491 ff.
[45] ibid paras 5.496 ff.
[46] Case 27/76 *United Brands v Commission* (n 3).
[47] *Pfizer UK Limited and Others v Competition and Markets Authority* (n 1) para 310.
[48] ibid para 314.
[49] ibid para 333.
[50] ibid para 339.
[51] ibid para 318.

that it did not need to consider whether it was unfair by reference to comparator products.[52] This was an error of law.

Fifthly, the CAT held that the CMA had failed to conduct an adequate assessment of the relevant comparators. As well as arguing that it did not need to consider comparators (in law), and that the tablet was a poor comparator,[53] the CMA argued—as a fallback point—that it had considered the tablet in any event (and rejected it). The CAT rejected that submission. It recognized that the CMA enjoyed a 'wide margin of appreciation',[54] and that it had given 'some consideration' to tablets. However, it held that the CMA's investigation was inadequate.[55] Much the same position applied regarding the other AEDs.

Sixthly, the CMA erred as to the consequences of patient 'dependence' on phenytoin sodium when considering economic value. As set out in the judgment, phenytoin sodium has a Narrow Therapeutic Index ('NTI'), with the result that care should be taken when switching patients between formulations of the same drug. Pfizer's medical expert's evidence at trial was that 'the clinical risks of switching phenytoin formulations are small'.[56] The CAT held that the CMA had exaggerated the lack of switching in the Decision, and that there was a degree (even if limited) of switching between Flynn and NRIM (another capsule manufacturer).[57] The CAT also found that the CMA had erred when it held that the demand side value of phenytoin was zero once patients were stabilized on the product.[58] As a result, the CMA had understated the economic value of the product.

2.1.3.3 Court of Appeal Judgment

In its appeal against the CAT judgment, the CMA raised four main grounds of appeal.

First, it raised an issue which concerns the alternative fairness tests in paragraph 252 of *United Brands*. In particular, the issue was whether the two alternative tests—which say that a price can be excessive 'in itself' or by reference to 'competing products'—are self-contained 'true' alternatives, <u>or</u>, simply two examples of evidential tests which might (individually or collectively) be used in a particular case (as the CAT found and as recorded in paragraph 443(5) of its judgment). This in turn raised issues concerning (a) the nature and extent of the evidential burden upon defendant undertakings and the duty of competition authorities fairly to evaluate evidence adduced by such undertakings. In particular, whether an authority must evaluate the evidence submitted by a defendant undertaking, there is an obligation on the authority to perform a 'full investigation' of that evidence in all cases; or, whether the nature and extent of the duty to evaluate varies and is affected by the nature of the evidence before the authority.

This ground of appeal was unsuccessful. On the narrow legal point, the Court of Appeal concluded that the CMA's approach in the Decision to the effect that the 'in itself' and 'competing products' tests were 'true alternatives' in the sense that if the CMA relied upon one alternative to find abuse then it had no obligation in law to evaluate other prima facie evidence that prices were fair adduced by a defendant undertaking was wrong, and that

---

[52] ibid para 362.
[53] ibid paras 380–83.
[54] ibid paras 294(1), 392, 444.
[55] ibid para 389.
[56] ibid para 122.
[57] ibid para 150.
[58] ibid para 415.

the CAT was right to say that the 'in itself' and 'competing products' tests were not strict alternatives.[59]

But in reaching this conclusion the Court of Appeal also made a number of wider points about whether and to what extent the CMA was proactively obliged to consider evidence from comparable products. Its essential findings were that: (i) there is no single method or 'way' in which abuse might be established and competition authorities have a margin of manoeuvre or appreciation in deciding which methodology to use and which evidence to rely upon; (ii) depending upon the facts and circumstances of the case a competition authority might therefore use one or more of the alternative economic tests which are available; (iii) there is however no rule of law requiring competition authorities to use more than one test or method in all cases; (iv) in analysing whether the end price is unfair a competition authority may look at a range of relevant factors including, but not limited to, evidence and data relating to the defendant undertaking itself and/or evidence of comparables drawn from competing products and/or any other relevant comparable, or all of these; (v) if a competition authority chooses one method (e.g. Cost Plus) and one body of evidence and the defendant undertaking does not adduce other methods or evidence, the competition authority may proceed to a conclusion upon the basis of that method and evidence alone; and, (vi) if an undertaking relies, in its defence, upon other methods or types of evidence to that relied upon by the competition authority then the authority must fairly evaluate it.[60]

Secondly, the CMA raised the issue of whether a competition authority is required to use a hypothetical benchmark price or range of prices as part of its evaluation of whether an actual price is excessive or whether non-price benchmarks such as cost or other related benchmarks such ROS and ROCE as sufficient. Ground 2 of the CMA's appeal was allowed, but on a very narrow basis. As Green LJ explained, there was some ambiguity as to precisely what the CAT had held in respect of a benchmark price:

> It is not entirely clear what the Tribunal was referring to when it used the expression 'hypothetical' price. If this was intended to refer to an artificially constructed price, then I agree with the CMA and the Commission. But it might well be that the Tribunal was referring simply to the exercise of calculating a benchmark ROS or ROCE and/or the exercise of looking to external comparators" (emphasis in original).[61]

Green LJ said he agreed with Pfizer's and Flynn's submission that 'all that is required is that there be 'a' benchmark or standard against which to measure excess or fairness'.[62] Thus, while Ground 2 was allowed, the finding of the Court was, in context, more of a clarificatory nature (the Court repeatedly notes that it is not entirely clear whether its analysis differs from that of the CAT).

The CMA's third Ground of Appeal addressed the relevance of comparator evidence. It focused upon the existence of a 'margin of manoeuvre' or discretion for competition authorities and whether, assuming it exists, it serves to limit the jurisdiction of the CAT to reject findings or conclusions which amount to judgment calls of the authority. It also raised

---

[59] *Competition and Markets Authority v Pfizer UK Limited and Others* (n 9) para 117.
[60] ibid para 97.
[61] ibid para 120.
[62] ibid para 122.

the issue of the limits of the powers of the CAT, including the question of materiality. The CAT found that the CMA had committed various errors of fact or assessment. As noted above in the description of the CAT's findings, the main errors were: (i) the CMA placed too much reliance on the 6 per cent ROS contained in the PPRS regulatory scheme; (ii) the CMA's reliance on Cost Plus was too theoretical, owing more to a theoretical concept of idealized or near perfect competition, than to the real world; (iii) the CMA relied only on headline price differences between the UK and other EU Member States, taking not account of the effects of differences in regulation on pricing or differences in purchasing power; (iv) the CMA placed undue emphasis on the point that Pfizer's and Flynn's prices vastly exceeded the historic prices that applied under the PPRS; and (v) the CMA was wrong to conclude that the identical phenytoin sodium tablet product sold by other companies was not a good comparator for Pfizer's phenytoin sodium capsules, and had not sufficiently investigated this issue.

The Court of Appeal essentially concluded that it saw no error of law in the CAT's conclusions in this regard, most of which were either purely factual points or points of assessment that the Court of Appeal could see no error of law. However, in rejecting this ground of appeal, the Court of Appeal made a number of interesting wider findings.

First, it reiterated that the appeal to the CAT in CA 1998 cases is an appeal 'on the merits' and engaged principles of fundamental rights due to the quasi-criminal nature of fines in competition law cases. Green LJ summarized these principles as follows:

> From case law it is possible to draw various conclusions about the role of judicial bodies in relation to the margin of appreciation of a competition authority: (i) for a (non-judicial) administrative body lawfully to be able to impose quasi-criminal sanctions there must be a right of challenge; (ii) that right must offer guarantees of a type required by Article 6; (iii) the subsequent review must be by a judicial body with 'full jurisdiction'; (iv) the judicial body must have the power to quash the decision 'in all respects on questions of fact and law'; (v) the judicial body must have the power to substitute its own appraisal for that of the decision maker; (vi) the judicial body must conduct its evaluation of the legality of the decision 'on the basis of the evidence adduced' by the appellant; and (vii), the existence of a margin of discretion accorded to a competition authority does not dispense with the requirement for an 'in depth review of the law and of the facts' by the supervising judicial body. [63]

Secondly, the Court of Appeal held that, notwithstanding the first point, the jurisdiction of the CAT is not unfettered.[64] The appeal is not a *de novo* hearing but takes the decision as its starting, middle and end point. The appellant must identify the decision under appeal and set out why it is in error. The Grounds must set out the 'extent' to which the decision 'is based on an error of fact or was wrong in law': see CAT Rule 9(4)(d) (SI 2015/1648). Whilst it can hear evidence, including fresh evidence not before the CMA, and make findings of both fact and law, the right to adduce new evidence cannot be abused: see CAT Rule 21(2).

---

[63] ibid para 140.
[64] ibid para 141.

Thirdly, the Court of Appeal held that the materiality of an error may be important.[65] The CAT should interfere only if it concludes that the decision is wrong in a *material* respect. Whether an error is material will be a matter of judgment for the CAT. The Court of Appeal offered some further guidance on materiality:

First, materiality is not an exact science. The Tribunal might be able to do no more than conclude that an error might make a difference to the final outcome or to some significant component thereof; certainty might not be possible. An error of fact or law might not be material to the ultimate question (breach or no breach) but could be material to some significant aspect of the Decision such as duration of the breach, or geographical spread, or the number of customers or consumers affected etc. These might be relevant to penalty or remedial directions.

Second, there is no fixed list of errors that the Tribunal might consider material. Case law indicates that the following might be relevant: failing to take account of relevant evidence; taking into account irrelevant evidence; failing properly to construe significant documents or evidence; drawing inferences of fact from evidence about relevant matters which are illogical or unjustified; failing adequately or sufficiently to investigate an issue that the Tribunal considers to be relevant or potentially relevant to the analysis ...

Third, it is consistent with a merits appeal for the Tribunal, even having heard the evidence, to conclude that the approach taken by the CMA and its resultant findings are reasonable in all the circumstances and to refrain from interfering upon that basis. If the Tribunal considers that the findings of the CMA are reasonable it might be difficult to say that any findings that it arrives at which differ from those of the CMA are material ... Because the Tribunal has a full merits jurisdiction and can hear fresh evidence there could of course arise circumstances where the Tribunal finds that on the evidence before the CMA it arrived at a reasonable conclusion but on the basis of the new evidence before the Tribunal the CMA's conclusions were nonetheless wrong. Such cases may be rare, but the possibility necessarily arises because of the power of the Tribunal to receive and assess fresh evidence.

Fourth, I would expect that in a judgment the Tribunal would set out its reasoning on the materiality of errors so found. If the Tribunal annulled a decision upon the basis of an error that was very slight or de minimis and/or gave no reasoning to justify the annulment that might be considered an error of law, subject to an appeal.[66]

Finally, the CMA's fourth ground of appeal concerned the meaning and effect of the expression '*economic value*' as that phrase is used in paragraph [250] of *United Brands*. It focused upon whether the test is a legal or economic test; whether it is the same as or different to other components of the test; whether it is capable of taking account of demand side factors; and, whether a competition authority has a margin of manoeuvre or appreciation in relation to the evaluation of 'economic value' which the CAT should respect.

The critical CAT finding in this regard was as follows:

The CMA was criticised by the parties for not considering patient benefit although it did indeed describe, in broad outline in the Decision, the nature of epilepsy and phenytoin's role in its treatment. The CMA has not, however, contested the evidence of Professor Walker and has, in effect, conceded that phenytoin remains a useful and effective treatment for a significant number of patients. That being so, we find the outright rejection of any value at all to patients surprising. The CMA seems to have placed some reliance on the age of the drug, which is irrelevant in therapeutic terms. We think there is clearly some economic value to be derived from the therapeutic benefit to patients of phenytoin capsules.[67]

The Court of Appeal dismissed this ground of appeal, essentially on the basis that the CAT's findings in this regard were mainly factual in nature and not made in legal error:

The CMA objects that the Tribunal found that the CMA attributed a nil value to patient benefit as economic value whereas, in fact, it was analysed as part of the Cost Plus test carried out by the CMA. I agree that demand side factors may be capable of generating economic value but on a fair reading of the Judgment the Tribunal was not saying that the CMA failed to address its mind to the issue and for that reason ignored economic value. It was saying that having addressed itself to the issue (as part of CostPlus) it had failed adequately to take account of evidence that there might be 'some' (albeit unspecified) value to be attributed to patient benefit, and that the reasons given by the CMA for rejecting patient benefit as relevant (namely dependency) was itself an issue of fact and degree (and not principle) and did not mean that the CMA could ignore relevant evidence. The Tribunal articulated the issue in the following manner: 'The question is whether the CMA was correct, on the facts of this case, to exclude from its calculation of Pfizer's and Flynn's economic value all factors other than those that formed part of the Cost-Plus calculation' (Judgment paragraph 411). To the extent that it is argued that the findings made by the CMA fell within its margin of appreciation and that the Tribunal should not have interfered I do not repeat the conclusions at paragraphs [128]–[134] above which apply here. At base this was a finding by the Tribunal on the evidence and that specific finding is not challenged in this appeal.[68]

The Court of Appeal did, however, raise the issue of materiality in this connection:

There is a brief analysis in the Judgment of materiality. In an ideal world it might have been fuller. The nub of the reasoning was that: the undertakings had raised a series of challenges to the methodology adopted by the CMA; the Tribunal identified a series of individual errors in that methodology; the Tribunal itself was not in a position to conduct a review of these matters; they went to relevant parts of the test for abuse; they could individually and/ or cumulatively be material but the Tribunal was not in a position to form any conclusions about this. The CMA does not however argue that read fairly the Judgment discloses that the Tribunal ignored materiality altogether or applied illogical or irrational reasoning or

[67] *Pfizer UK Limited and Others v Competition and Markets Authority* (n 1) para 412
[68] ibid para 166.

that the reasoning was so lacking in detail as to amount to an error of law. Nor does it argue that the undertakings themselves failed altogether to adduce evidence on materiality as part of their evidential burden and that in such circumstances the Tribunal should have found that the errors were immaterial. There are no grounds of appeal which raise such matters. At base therefore, the criticism of the CMA is one of *fact* and, as such, outside the scope of the statutory right of appeal. Such criticisms must necessarily therefore fail.[69]

2.2 High Court Cases/Appeals from High Court Cases

Exploitative abuses have also been a reasonably strong feature of High Court judgments (and appeals) under the CA 1998. In the same way as most CAT exploitative abuse cases have concerned pharmaceutical cases, most High Court cases have also had a common theme: horse racing.

The first case was *Victor Chandler*.[70] It case concerned access to, and the pricing of, horse racing data compiled by the British Horseracing Board. This database included a collection of information accumulated over many years by way of registration of informa-tion supplied by owners, trainers and others concerned in the racing industry, the names and other details of over one million horses, tracing back through many generations, and details of registered owners, racing colours, registered trainers, and registered jockeys. The contents of the database and, in particular, the pre-race data were valuable, particularly for bookmakers.

A bookmaker, VCI, alleged that the British Horseracing Board was abusing its dominant position in the race data by setting prices for the pre-race data which were 'manifestly ex-cessive' in relation to the cost of generating that data. Following from this it is said that the British Horseracing Board is abusing its dominant position to force bookmakers, including VCI, to enter into an agreement to license the pre-race data at these excessive prices. These claims were both a defence to the British Horseracing Board's claim for payments under the British Horseracing Board/VCI Agreement, in support of their existing counterclaim for restitution of payments previously made and as the basis of an additional counterclaim for injunctive relief (restraining continuation of the abuse) and damages.

The narrow issue before the High Court (Laddie J) was whether an amendment to the pleadings should be permitted to raise the exploitative abuse issues. On the facts, the High Court found that the (draft) pleading was so defective that permission to amend should be refused. However, it made a number of findings of wider interest on the question of exploit-ative abuse.

It rejected the argument that 'where a dominant undertaking charges prices greatly in ex-cess of the cost of production, this is in principle an abuse of its dominant position'. Laddie J responded to this contention as follows:

> Even before one considers the case law, it appears that this approach is based on a number of doubtful propositions. It assumes that in a competitive market prices end up covering only the cost of production plus the cost of capital. I am not convinced that that is so. Sometimes

---

[69] ibid para 169 (emphasis in original).
[70] *BHB Enterprises v Victor Chandler (International) Limited* [2005] EWHC 1074.

the price may be pushed much lower than this so that all traders are making a very small, if any, margin. Sometimes the desire of the customer for the product or service is so pressing that all suppliers, even if competing with one another, can charge prices which give them a much more handsome margin. In other words, even when there is competition, some markets are buyers' markets, some are sellers'. I do not see that there is any necessary correlation between the cost of production and the cost of capital and the price which can be achieved in the market place. Furthermore, the question is not whether the prices are large or small compared to some stable reference point, but whether they are fair.

In addition, this rule breaks down as soon as one applies it in the real world. What happens if there are only a few customers? Must the cost of production, including all research and development, be recovered from them? If so, does that mean that the price varies depending on the number of customers one has? Does it also mean that the price must go down once all the research and development costs have been recovered? Does it mean that traders cannot increase the price if they engage in successful advertising campaigns which whet the consumer's appetite? If Mr Turner's proposition were correct, it would mean that for most fashion products (clothes, cars, perfumes, cosmetics, electronics and so on) the prices charged would be deemed to be unfair. Indeed, it must follow that if the price of a product differed significantly in a single market or between markets in different locations, one must assume that, at best, one set of customers is getting the fair price and all the ones being charged more are being charged an unfair price. This would be so even though no trader occupies a dominant position.[71]

Laddie J also warned for a degree of realism about a proposition that prices that materially exceed costs should be abusive and held that *United Brands* does not support such an approach:

I do not accept that this supports the proposition advanced on behalf of VCI. On the contrary it appears, particularly from the paragraph 252 of the judgment, that all the ECJ was saying was that comparing prices with costs determines the profit margin. Once that has been achieved it is necessary to go on to the next stage to determine whether the price is unfair. What it did not do was suggest that high prices or high margins are the same as unfair prices. Indeed, were Mr Turner right, it seems to me that the law reports would be full of cases where undertakings in dominant positions would have been found guilty of abuse by simply charging high prices. As Mr Vaughan says, the reality is that there are no such cases.[72]

Shortly after *Victor Chandler*, the Court of Appeal in *ATTHERACES* overturned an excessive pricing finding made by the High Court in respect of the British Horseracing Board pre-race data.[73] The context was somewhat different in that ATTHERACES supplied overseas bookmakers with a broadcast and data service (pre-race and race data) covering horseracing from British racecourses. One of the claims was that the price at which the British Horseracing Board supplied ATTHERACES with horseracing data was

---

[71] ibid paras 48–49.
[72] ibid para 51.
[73] *ATTHERACES Ltd & Anor v The British Horse Racing Board & Anor* [2007] EWCA Civ 38.

excessive. In overturning the High Court, the Court of Appeal made a number of important findings on the concept of 'economic value':[74] (i) the economic value of a product cannot be what in market terms is what it will fetch, since, otherwise, excessive prices could never be found; (ii) but nor on the other hand does it follow that whatever price a seller in a dominant position exacts or seeks to exact is an abuse of a dominant position; (iii) the essential question was whether the British Horseracing Board was seeking to charge ATTHERACES a price 'substantially more than the economic value of the pre-race data;' (iv) exceeding a cost plus benchmark is a necessary, but in no way a sufficient, test of abuse of a dominant position; (v) there is no reason why the economic value of the product should not be its value to the purchaser rather than cost plus; (vi) economic theory recognizes the relevance of externalities to price; and (vii) in the case at hand the money which ATTHERACES received from overseas bookmarkers purchasing its services reflected the value of the data to them, which in turn depended on the attractiveness and integrity of British racing; in other words, the British Horseracing Board had produced a positive externality which had benefited ATTHERACES, and should be paid by ATTHERACES for doing so.

The other important point to emerge from *ATTHERACES* is the notion that there is no single test for excessive pricing:

213. As already noted, the Commission's decision in *Scandlines* supports the view that the exercise under Article 82, while it starts from a comparison of the cost of production with the price charged, is not determined by the comparison. This in itself is sufficient to exclude a cost + test as definitive of abuse. Mr Roth accepts that there is no single methodology or litmus test of abuse: the court has a choice of methods, but not an unlimited one. His contention is that the judge has gone outside the admissible limits of method in coming to his conclusion. Mr Hollander, also contending that the choice of methodology is for the court, defends both the choice made by the judge and the way he has implemented it.

. . .

218. For all the above reasons we conclude that, in holding that the economic value of the pre-race data was the cost of compilation plus a reasonable return, the judge took too narrow a view of economic value in Article 82. In particular, he was wrong to reject BHB's contention on the relevance of the value of the pre-race data to ATR in determining the economic value of the pre-race data and whether the charges specified by BHB were excessive and unfair.[75]

The final High Court case to date was *Humber Oil.*[76] In that case, Associated British Ports owned and operated the port of Immingham on the south bank of the river Humber.

---

[74] ibid paras 203–218.

[75] ibid paras 213, 218.

[76] *Humber Oil Terminals Trustee v Associated British Ports* [2011] EWHC 352. Another case is *Ineos Vinyls Ltd v Huntsman Petrochemicals (UK) Ltd* [2006] EWHC 1241 (Ch), where excessive pricing claims were also rejected (see in particular para 248).

Humber Oil Terminals Trustee operated an oil terminal under a lease. When negotiations for the statutory renewal of a lease between Associated British Ports and Humber Oil Terminals Trustee broke down, Humber Oil Terminals Trustee issued proceedings claiming an abuse of dominance by Associated British Ports by, inter alia, demanding, in the course of negotiations, abusively high prices for the continued provision of facilities, and seeking court orders for such rent.

Associated British Ports succeeded in striking out the competition claims. The High Court rejected the contention of Humber Oil Terminals Trustee that 'to propose, in the course of negotiations, prices which are excessive was of itself and without more abusive conduct within s. 18 or Article 102'.[77]

As the court put it 'any element of compulsion which might arise from the dominant position of the proposer is negatived by the jurisdiction of the Court, in the absence of agreement, to assess the rent or price on the basis of a statutory formula which necessarily excludes any ransom element'.[78] On this basis, the court held that, until the defence of Associated British Ports to the claim for a new tenancy succeeds, the competition claim did not arise, and if the defence did succeed, there would be 'bound to be further negotiations in which Associated British Ports is willing to participate'.[79] The court found in any event, that even if the competition claim were a present issue and there would likely be no further negotiations, there was 'no proper pleading of the anti-competitive effect of what is alleged'.[80]

3 Distillation of the Core Principles

3.1 The Court of Appeal's Summary in *Phenytoin*

In *Phenytoin* the Court of Appeal conveniently summarized what it sees as the core principles as respects excessive prices. Lord Justice Green stated as follows:

> I would draw the following general conclusions from the case law about the test to be applied:
>
> (i) The basic test for abuse, which is set out in the Chapter II prohibition and in Article 102, is whether the price is 'unfair'. In broad terms a price will be unfair when the dominant undertaking has reaped trading benefits which it could not have obtained in conditions of 'normal and sufficiently effective competition', i.e. 'workable' competition.
> (ii) A price which is 'excessive' because it bears no 'reasonable' relation to the economic value of the good or service is an example of such an unfair price.

---

[77] *Humber Oil Terminals Trustee* (n 76) para 33.
[78] ibid para 33.
[79] ibid para 47.
[80] ibid para 48.

(iii) There is no single method or 'way' in which abuse might be established and competition authorities have a margin of manoeuvre or appreciation in deciding which methodology to use and which evidence to rely upon.

(iv) Depending upon the facts and circumstances of the case a competition authority might therefore use one or more of the alternative economic tests which are available. There is however no rule of law requiring competition authorities to use more than one test or method in all cases.

(v) If a Cost-Plus test is applied the competition authority may compare the cost of production with the selling price in order to disclose the profit margin. Then the authority should determine whether the margin is 'excessive'. This can be done by comparing the price charged against a benchmark higher than cost such as a reasonable rate of return on sales (ROS) or to some other appropriate benchmark such as return on capital employed (ROCE). When that is performed, and if the price exceeds the selected benchmark, the authority should then compare the price charged against any other factors which might otherwise serve to justify the price charged as fair and not abusive.

(vi) In analysing whether the end price is unfair a competition authority may look at a range of relevant factors including, but not limited to, evidence and data relating to the defendant undertaking itself and/or evidence of comparables drawn from competing products and/or any other relevant comparable, or all of these. There is no fixed list of categories of evidence relevant to unfairness.

(vii) If a competition authority chooses one method (e.g. Cost-Plus) and one body of evidence and the defendant undertaking does not adduce other methods or evidence, the competition authority may proceed to a conclusion upon the basis of that method and evidence alone.

(viii) If an undertaking relies, in its defence, upon other methods or types of evidence to that relied upon by the competition authority then the authority must fairly evaluate it.[81]

3.2 Comment and Critique

The above guidance is obviously useful to a certain extent, albeit much of what is set out is either uncontroversial or does not actually take matters very far. There are myriad issues which could be discussed in detail. But the main points of practical importance are five-fold.

First, there is a fundamental threshold question as to when intervention concerning excessive pricing is justified. This issue has a number of related facets. In the first place, there is a pragmatic point that in many markets, including many competitive markets, it is trite to

---

[81] *Competition and Markets Authority v Pfizer UK Limited and Others* (n 9) paras 97–98. For the CAT's summary of the relevant principles (which is in most material respects similar), see *Pfizer Limited and Others v Competition and Markets Authority* (n 1) paras 442–44. The main difference is that the Court of Appeal was, if anything, stricter than the CAT on the competition authority's duty to consider exculpatory evidence, holding that 'if an undertaking relies, in its defence, upon other methods or types of evidence to that relied upon by the competition authority then the authority must fairly evaluate it' (para 97(viii)) and that it was only where 'a competition authority chooses one method (e.g. Cost-Plus) and one body of evidence and the defendant undertaking does not adduce other methods or evidence' that the 'competition authority may proceed to a conclusion upon the basis of that method and evidence alone' (para 97(vii)).

observe 'high' prices. For example, most luxury good pricing bears no relationship at all to cost, but is based on the 'aura' that the brand creates. Bottled water is also enormously profitable, particularly when it is not spring water but treated mains water. [82] High-end smartphones and other smart devices are also enormously profitable in many cases, and the same is also true of accessories in such closed 'ecosystems'.[83] There is, accordingly, a practical question about overreach into normal commercial relations if intervention as respects excessive prices occurs merely where prices are perceived to be appreciable above production costs (plus a reasonable return).[84] This also has an economic component. Most economists would agree that there is no need to intervene over excessive pricing unless the market in question has insurmountable barriers, since the market will self-correct without intervention.[85] This point is not merely made out of caution or self-restraint for its own sake, but reflects a more important insight that, if prices are regulated downwards because they are 'excessive' but capable of self-correction, then competition could itself be <u>reduced</u> as entry is <u>deterred</u>. The reason is that firms who ex ante would have been incentivized to enter at 'high' prices are deterred from doing so by the prospect of *ex post* intervention requiring prices to be proximate to costs of production plus a reasonable return. More generally, neither courts

---

[82] For discussion see eg P Gleick, 'The Myth and Reality of Bottled Water' in P Gleick and others (eds), *The World's Water: The Biennial Report on Freshwater Resources* (Island Press 2004). https://www.wipo.int/publications/en/details.jsp?id=4230&plang=EN.

[83] See J Dedrick and K L Kraemer, 'Intangible Assets And Value Capture In Global Value Chains: The Smartphone Industry' World Intellectual Property Organisation Economic Research Working Paper No. 41 (and in particular Tables 9 and 10) https://www.wipo.int/publications/en/details.jsp?id=4230&plang=EN.

[84] See J Davies and J Padilla, 'Excessive Intervention? Should Competition Authorities Take on Excessive Pricing Cases in Markets with No Barriers to Entry?' *Compass Lexecon Expert Opinion* (July 2019) https://www.compasslexecon.com/wp-content/uploads/2019/06/CL_Expert_Opinion_Excessive_Pricing_July-2019.pdf. See also J Davies and J Padilla, 'Another Look at the Role of Barriers to Entry in Excessive Pricing Cases' (2019) 37 Revista de Concorrência e Regulação 15.

[85] Various authors argue that entry is unlikely to correct high prices. See eg A Ezrachi and D Gilo, 'Are Excessive Prices Really Self-correcting?' (2009) 5(2) Journal of Competition Law and Economics 249; D Gilo, 'Excessive Pricing by Dominant Firms, Private Litigation, and the Existence of Alternative Products' in N Charbit and S Ahmad (eds), *Frédéric Jenny Liber Amicorum* (Concurrences, 2018). They rightly point that a firm considering entry must consider how profitable the market will be not before, but *after*, it has entered. If this price is enough to reward the entrant for the costs and risks it undertakes, entry will occur; if not, then no entry will occur. Post-entry prices will be set by competition, so might be unaffected by the incumbent's initial price, in which case that price will not affect entry at all. Therefore, the argument goes, higher prices do not encourage entry, and government intervention is thus justified and need not deter entry either. However, as other authors explain, this claim is not enough in itself to justify their policy conclusion, as it rests upon narrow assumptions about what information is conveyed by pricing. First, the dominant firm may not be able to recover some of the customers lost to the entrant, since the entrant can enter with long-term contracts. Secondly, economic theory shows that the incumbent may not find it optimal to cut prices post-entry but rather to accommodate the entrant. This is especially true if the entrant enters with a relatively small scale, or when the entrant sinks considerable production costs before competition starts. Thirdly, the incumbent may not be willing to fight the entrant by cutting prices if the entrant's exit is unlikely to return prices to their pre-entry levels due to, for example, buyer power. Finally, on a practical level, where an experienced market operator makes entry projections based on past experiences, it is surely reasonable to have regard to such plans, even if they would also need to take account of post-entry factors. Furthermore, as an observable factual matter, high prices do seem to cause entry. Studies of several industries have demonstrated that more profitable markets lead to faster entry and that incumbents sometimes engage in 'limit pricing:' keeping prices down to deter entry, possibly because entrants might believe the incumbent's price conveys information about its cost and demand. Lower prices can deter entry by signaling low costs and/or low demand, and 'excessive prices' would, conversely, attract entry. See Davies and Padilla, 'Excessive Intervention?' (n 84). Furthermore, ex post studies of merger decisions tend to show that entry responds to high prices. Hence, the simple intuition that high prices encourage entry seems, therefore, to be correct, even if the mechanisms by which it does so require more economic analysis than might be expected. Since higher prices do attract entry, then regulatory action to reduce prices may in fact have the perverse effect of deterring or delaying entry. See eg KPMG LLP, 'Entry and Expansion in UK Merger Cases: An Ex-Post Evaluation' (April 2017) https://assets.publishing.service.gov.uk/government/uploads/system/uploads/attachment_data/file/606693/entry-and-expansion-in-uk-ex-post-evaluation-kpmg.pdf.

nor competition authorities are rate-setting agencies, and it must be recalled that all price regulation would require on-going monitoring to be effective at all.[86]

But it can be argued with some force that this issue is not (merely) a point of economics or policy but is a hard-edged legal point. The starting point is Advocate General Wahl's comment in *Latvian Copyright* that:

> [a] price cannot easily be set significantly above the competitive level where the market is not protected by high barriers to entry or expansion. Otherwise, as mentioned above, the market should, in principle, be able to self-correct in the short to medium term: high prices should normally attract new entrants or encourage existing competitors to expand. That is why—as stated in the beginning of this Opinion—I am convinced that *unfair prices under Article 102 TFEU can only exist in regulated markets, where the public authorities exert some form of control over the forces of supply and, consequently, the scope for free and open competition is reduced*. Obviously, the higher and longer-lasting the barriers created by the legislature, the more a dominant undertaking should be able to exercise its market power.[87]

The CJEU did not directly pick up on this issue in its judgment. But the CJEU's *Intel* judgment held that 'competition on the merits may, by definition, lead to the departure from the market or the marginalisation of competitors that are less efficient and so less attractive to consumers from the point of view of, among other things, price, choice, quality or innovation'.[88] From this, one can extrapolate a principle that: (i) a price that allows equally efficient firms to enter is not contrary to Article 102 and (ii) conversely, a price which deters equally efficient entry is inconsistent with the purpose of CA 1998/Article 102. It is also clear that the judgment in *Intel* is not a 'flash in the pan'—the principle outlined above has been repeated in subsequent cases such as *MEO*.[89] There is also domestic case law support. In *Napp*, the CAT noted that 'a price is excessive and an abuse if it is above that which would exist in a competitive market and where it is clear that high profits will not stimulate successful new entry within a reasonable period'.[90] Finally, in *Phenytoin*, the Court of Appeal stated as follows:

> Where there are no material barriers to entry high prices can act as a magnet to entry which, in due course, drives prices down. Many markets are thus self-correcting. In the absence of entry barriers regulatory intervention can risk prolonging a monopoly situation by blocking efficient signals which would otherwise promote market entry. A belief in market forces ' ... is often bolstered by the (perceived high) likelihood of regulatory failure, a risk which is compounded in the case of price regulation'.[91]

Secondly, there is some confusion as to the role that Cost Plus methodologies should play in the analysis. In recent pharmaceutical cases such as *Phenytoin* it is fair to say that the CMA

---

[86] In *Phenytoin*, the duty to notify the CMA of price changes lasted for 10 years (albeit the decision was overturned on appeal, for other reasons).
[87] Case C-177/16 *Latvian Copyright* EU:C:2017:286, para 48 (emphasis added).
[88] Case C-413/14 P *Intel v Commission* EU:C:2017:632, para 134.
[89] Case C-525/16 *MEO-Serviços de Comunicações e Multimédia* EU:C:2018:270, para 31.
[90] *Napp* (n 10) para 390, citing the OFT's own decision.
[91] *Competition and Markets Authority v Pfizer UK Limited and Others* (n 9) para 104.

has placed Cost Plus at the centre of its analysis and that the level of excess above Cost Plus was considered important if not decisive in that case. But it is important to be precise about the role of Cost Plus. In a narrow literal sense, all Cost Plus does is give *one* measure of the profitability level of the product/service in question.[92] Whether it involves any more than this requires care and precision.

There may be sectors where prices are not really a function of cost at all. The obvious case is artistic or other creative works. A hit song does not necessarily cost any more to make than an obscure one. Another example is pharmaceutical products where, outside of regulation, pricing tends to be value-based (including therapeutic value or quality of life) and successful products will also have to cover the (usually high) costs of unsuccessful ones.

There are many markets, including competitive markets, where prices are substantially above costs without this circumstance alone suggesting that a price is excessive. As the Court of Appeal observed in *ATTHERACES*: 'Where profit is obtainable, the margin of profit will be as great as the market will yield, reflecting such factors as elasticity of demand. Thus, even a hypothetically competitive market may yield a rate of profit above, as well as below, the reasonable margin represented by cost [plus].'[93] Perhaps more trenchantly, in *Victor Chandler* the High Court said:

> Even before one considers the case law, it appears that this approach is based on a number of doubtful propositions. It assumes that in a competitive market prices end up covering only the cost of production plus the cost of capital. I am not convinced that that is so. Sometimes the price may be pushed much lower than this so that all traders are making a very small, if any, margin. Sometimes the desire of the customer for the product or service is so pressing that all suppliers, even if competing with one another, can charge prices which give them a much more handsome margin. In other words, even when there is competition, some markets are buyers' markets, some are sellers'. I do not see that there is any necessary correlation between the cost of production and the cost of capital and the price which can be achieved in the market place. Furthermore, the question is not whether the prices are large or small compared to some stable reference point, but whether they are fair.[94]

There are markets, usually regulated, where prices are strongly correlated with cost. Thus, in *Albion Water* the CAT accepted that cost justification was the only way in which prices were set for water under the regulatory regime: 'the principal issue ... is the justification for the "distribution" cost element of the First Access Price, found by the Director to be 16p/m³.'[95] Indeed, all parties agreed that the case turned on a cost-price approach. But it would be wrong to argue from this particular, largely regulatory, context to the more general notion that there is something fishy about a price not being closely correlated with cost.

---

[92] It is important to emphasize that it is just one measure. For example, in an industry with high fixed costs held in common across two or more products, what account, if any, is taken of those common costs can have an enormous bearing on the level of cost and the figure to which plus is added.

[93] *ATTHERACES Ltd & Anor v The British Horse Racing Board & Anor* (n 73) para 208.

[94] *BHB Enterprises v Victor Chandler (International) Limited* (n 70) para 48.

[95] *Albion Water I* (n 18) para 14.

Accordingly, Cost Plus is neither necessary nor sufficient. The Court of Appeal put it well in *ATTHERACES*:

> [United Brands] did not say that the economic value of a product is always ascertained by reference to the cost of producing it plus a reasonable profit (cost [plus]), or that a higher price than cost [plus] is necessarily an excessive price and an abuse of a dominant position. The court was indicating that one possible way ('inter alia') of objectively determining whether the price is excessive and an abuse is to determine, if the calculation were possible, the profit margin by reference to the selling price and the cost of production.[96]
>
> But, to the extent that [it is argued that] to make charging above cost [plus] the principal criterion of abuse of a dominant position, we do not agree. Exceeding cost [plus] is a necessary, but in no way a sufficient, test of abuse of a dominant position.[97]

Thirdly, there is some confusion following *Phenytoin* as to whether and to what extent the CMA must pro-actively go out obtain evidence or benchmarks to support its findings. For example, Green LJ noted that: 'At base the CMA has a duty to conduct a fair evaluation of all the evidence before it. What this means in a given case is impossible to say in advance and will depend upon the facts of the case. A degree of proactivity might be needed, in some cases, but not in others'.[98] Later, he noted:

> the authority has a duty to conduct a fair evaluation of the evidence. It has a margin of manoeuvre or discretion in how it goes about meeting this obligation. This might, depending upon the facts, involve the taking of proactive steps, such as the issuance of requests for information to third parties, but it will not inevitably do so. The extent of the duty will be affected by the nature, extent and quality of the evidence adduced by the defendant undertaking which has an evidential burden. The fact that upon an appeal the Tribunal might review the evaluation is not a factor which affects the nature and extent of the prior duty imposed upon the competition authority.[99]

Then, in the same judgment, the Chancellor noted that: 'it may well be prudent for the CMA to make its own investigations, but it is not under a legal duty to do so. If the CMA wrongly ignores evidence of comparators, and those comparators turn out to be relevant or important, their analysis will fail at the CAT. In my judgment, the suggestion of an obligation in every case to conduct any investigation is not warranted in law'.[100]

A number of clarificatory remarks are in order. In the first place, the competition authority bears the legal burden of proof. If an element is missing, its conclusions obviously cannot be sustained. Secondly, where the competition authority relies on certain evidence that, it considers, supports a finding of unlawful unfair pricing, but the defendant puts forward prima facie credible evidence tending to suggest the price is not unfair, it is clear that that evidence must at least be *considered* by the competition authority: not to do so is, at least, procedurally unfair. Whether more than that is required may depend on the nature of

---

[96] *ATTHERACES Ltd & Anor v The British Horse Racing Board & Anor* (n 73) para 118.
[97] *ATTHERACES Ltd & Anor v The British Horse Racing Board & Anor* (n 73) para 209.
[98] *Competition and Markets Authority v Pfizer UK Limited and Others* (n 9) para 113.
[99] ibid para 116.
[100] ibid para 273.

the information and its availability. For example, in *Phenytoin*, a major issue was the comparison of the price charged for Pfizer's capsules with the identical third party tablet products. Information on competitors' costs was obviously not available to Pfizer (it would be illegal for the third party to disclose it). So it seems obvious that the competition authority should both obtain and evaluate such information. Similarly, there must be questions of realism versus theory in the case at hand. For example, if the relevant market analysis shows that all firms approach pricing using a particular benchmark that the competition authority takes no real account of, the competition authority relying on some theoretical or other non-market benchmark not actually applied by any undertaking in the market may look incongruous and inapposite. As Green LJ stated in *Phenytoin*, 'the counterfactuals of greatest practical value are often those drawn from real life, as opposed to some hypothetical model'.[101] Finally, if the competition authority either leaves out of account entirely, or takes into account but conducts a perfunctory assessment, particular evidence and/or benchmarks that could be material to the conclusions on unfair pricing, that may itself be a legal error on appeal to the CAT. Whether it is or not will of course depend on inter alia the nature of the evidence, its probative force compared to the other evidence, and whether and to what extent it was reasonably available to the CMA or appellant.

Fourthly, as with other areas of competition law, unfair pricing will inevitably have to grapple with its application to two-sided markets, particularly of course digital platforms. The key characteristic of a multi-sided platform is that it intermediates to match the interests of two or more distinct, non-competing groups of users.[102] For example, a search engine competes to acquire 'eyeballs' (or attention) from users searching for information, e.g. on products, on one market side and to then match those users to vendors or advertisers on the other side who have services or products to sell. This gives rise to a 'chicken and egg' problem of balancing the respective interests of the two user groups.[103] For example, if a search engine has too many ads, and not enough relevant information, users would switch off, which in turn would make it less interesting as an outlet for advertisers.

This also has significant implications for pricing in two-sided markets. Usually, one side will pay zero or next to nothing whereas the other will pay a 'high' price which monetizes the value of the users from the other side.[104] It is difficult to get the price 'just right' in a multi-sided market. Setting a price on one side that is too high will reduce the number of customers on both sides of the platform. Setting a price on one side that is too high will reduce the number of customers on both sides of the platform. Platforms will thus choose their price structure considering both the price elasticity of each side as well as the magnitude of the externalities or network effects linking both sides. Hence, the profit maximizing

---

[101] ibid para 121.
[102] See M Katz and J Sallet, 'Multisided Platforms and Antitrust Enforcement' (2018) 127 Yale Law Journal 2142; J Tirole, *Economics for the Common Good* (Princeton University Press 2017), and in particular ch 14; and D S Evans, 'Governing Bad Behaviour by Users of Multi-Sided Platforms' (2012) 2(27) Berkeley Technology Law Journal 1201.
[103] See B Caillaud and B Jullien, 'Chicken & Egg: Competition among Intermediation Service Providers' (2012) 34(2) RAND Journal of Economics 309.
[104] See M Armstrong, 'Competition in Two-sided Markets' (2006) 37(3) RAND Journal of Economics 668; A Hagiu and J Wright, 'Multi-sided platforms' (2015) 43 International Journal of Industrial Organisation 162; P Belleflamme and M Peitz, *Industrial Organisation: Markets and Strategies* (2nd edn, Cambridge University Press 2015); and P Belleflamme and M Peitz. 'Platform Competition: Who Benefits from Multi-homing?' University of Mannheim Working Paper (2017).

price on one side may fall below its marginal cost. It may be zero or even negative. This presents particular challenges for unfair pricing, and can create enormous complexities in practice. But the key basic insight is that one cannot simply consider pricing on one side of the market.

Finally, what the CA 1998 cases show is the enormous value of the 'merits' appeal system, live evidence of fact and expert evidence, cross-examination, and judicial probing. The OFT/CMA track record before the CAT remains impressive. But those rare defeats which have occurred underline the value of the merits-based appeal system, and reveals the dangers of recent calls for a shift to something less than a merits appeal. Most notably, in *Phenytoin*, expert medical evidence on epilepsy and phenytoin sodium and factual evidence on the Department of Health's efforts to reduce phenytoin sodium prices was central to the CAT entertaining doubts on key aspects of the case and remitting the matter back to the CMA for further investigation. Indeed, if there is one area in which judicial review is probably most crucial of all, it is unfair pricing given the serious concerns over false positives and price regulation.

4 Conclusions

The treatment of unfair pricing under the CA 1998 has been one of its undoubted success stories. In seminal cases such as *Napp, Albion Water, Phenytoin*, and *ATTHERACES*, the competition authorities and courts have applied a rigorous factual, economic, and legal approach to this sensitive and difficult area, whilst showing considerable appreciation of the real-world or commercial issues that would arise in practice through over-deterrence. Testimony to this lies not only in the quality and depth of the analysis in the individual decisions and judgments themselves but, perhaps more importantly, in the fact that these seminal cases have been exported, with approval, the world over at both the EU level[105] and in jurisdictions as diverse as Israel, South Africa, Hong Kong, etc.[106] Indeed, the EU Commission's unusual intervention in *Phenytoin* was made on the express basis that the case could have EU-wide implications, as well as implications for the Commission's own pending cases. As noted at the outset, the CMA has a surprisingly large number of excessive pricing cases still on its docket. So it seems safe to predict that the next twenty years of the CA 1998 on unfair pricing are likely to be as vibrant as its first twenty years. This continued vitality speaks for itself.

---

[105] See eg in Case C-177/16 *Latvian Copyright* EU (n 86) Advocate General Wahl refers extensively to cases such as *Napp* (n 10).

[106] See eg Case 70/CAC/Apr07 *Mittal Steel South Africa Limited v Harmony Gold Mining* [2009] ZACAC 1, para 48 (referring to *Napp* (n 10)). For Israel see T Solomon and I Achmon, 'Excessive Pricing in Israel: How to Deal with A "Hot Potato"'? (2017) 8 Journal of European Competition Law & Practice 660 (discussing inter alia the impact of recent UK excessive pricing cases on practice and policy in Israel).

6

'Jack of All Trades, Master of None': The Ever-increasing Ambit of the Market Investigation Regime

Christian Ahlborn and Will Leslie[*]

1 Introduction

Much has changed in the ten years since the first iteration of this chapter.[1] The unique market investigation regime established by the Enterprise Act 2002 ('EA 2002') has gone from strength to strength. The Office of Fair Trading (OFT) and, its successor, the Competition and Markets Authority (CMA) have conducted ten market investigations during the second decade (with a further investigation ongoing).[2] The Competition Appeal Tribunal (CAT) has ruled on twelve applications for judicial review. The Enterprise and Regulatory Reform Act 2013 (ERRA 2013) reformed the regime's institutional framework and expanded its substantive scope. The CMA has also issued an array of soft-law guidance to supplement the rules themselves. All have shed more light on the regime's mechanics and intended scope.

However, in substance, much has remained the same since 2010. The substantive boundaries of the regime remain unclear. There is a continued juxtaposition between the ostensibly broad powers conferred by the market investigation regime and the CMA's exercise of self-restraint. The response of the Courts, most notably the CAT as the court responsible for reviewing the CMA's decisions in the first instance, has been to check the regime in some cases and reinforce its powers in others; but so far there have been no answers to the more fundamental questions on the scope of the regime.[3] Meanwhile, new proposals for reform would further broaden the regime and confer greater enforcement powers on the CMA.[4]

[*] The authors are competition lawyers at Linklaters. They are very grateful to Marvin Berkel for his research assistance and to Helen Crossley, John Davies, and Miguel de la Mano for their thoughtful comments. All views expressed are, however, solely those of the authors.
[1] Christian Ahlborn and Daniel Piccinin, 'Between Scylla and Charybdis: Market Investigations and the Consumer Interest' in Barry J Rodger (ed), *Ten Years of UK Competition Law Reform* (Dundee University Press 2010).

[2] We use 'CMA' to denote both the CMA (following its formation in April 2014) and both of its predecessor organizations, the OFT and the Competition Commission. The law is stated as of 31 October 2020. See also Professor Richard Whish, 'New Competition Tool: legal comparative study of existing competition tools aimed at addressing structural competition problems with a particular focus on the UK's market investigation tool', Expert Report prepared for the European Commission kd0420573enn.pdf (europa.eu).

[3] Section 179 of the EA 2002 makes provision for review of decisions under Pt 4 of the EA 2002.

[4] See eg the propositions made by the chair of the CMA, Andrew Tyrie, to the Secretary of State for Business, Energy and Industrial Strategy on 21 February 2019 https://assets.publishing.service.govuk/government/uploads/system/uploads/attachment_data/file/781151/Letter_from_Andrew_Tyrie_to_the_Secretary_of_State_BEIS.pdf accessed 30 June 2020.

Christian Ahlborn and Will Leslie, *'Jack of All Trades, Master of None': The Ever-increasing Ambit of the Market Investigation Regime*
In: *The UK Competition Regime*. Edited by: Barry Rodger, Peter Whelan, and Angus MacCulloch, Oxford University Press.
© The Contributors 2021. DOI: 10.1093/oso/9780198868026.003.0006

Section 2 sets out a brief summary of the revised market investigation regime. Section 3 provides an overview of the market studies and investigations undertaken in the last ten years as well as the judicial reviews that have been sought from 2010 onwards. Section 4 describes the trends in enforcement and evolution of the regime. Sections 5 to 7 set out key issues that have arisen from the CMA's market investigations in the last decade. Section 8 gives an outlook on future developments and section 9 concludes.

2 The Market Investigation Regime

While the substantive core of the market investigations regime has not changed since its inception, the ERRA 2013 broadened the scope of the regime and altered its institutional framework, both directly and indirectly. The changes to the market investigation regime (and, indeed, the wider UK competition regime) were, in part, driven by internal and external criticism. In particular, the National Audit Office's 2010 review of the UK competition regime found that there were significantly fewer market investigation references than envisaged, in large part due to the reticence of regulators to make market references.[5]

2.1 Background

The market investigation regime remains an unusual policy instrument. It is not, however, entirely *sui generis*. It emerged from the UK's Fair Trading Act provisions which gave the then Monopolies and Mergers Commission (MMC) the power to investigate 'complex' monopoly situations.[6] Such situations occurred where independent firms had an aggregate market share of at least 25 per cent and whose conduct prevented, restricted, or distorted competition. The MMC's procedural powers bore significant similarities to the current market investigation regime, with the Director General for Fair Trading and the Secretary of State for Trade and Industry entitled to refer potential infringements to the MMC for investigation.

The MMC's ability to intervene in 'complex' monopoly situations was, however, far more limited than the power conferred under the market investigation regime that was established by the EA 2002. As Sir Jeremy Lever summarized on the advent of the UK's Competition Act 1998 (CA 1998), the complex monopoly provisions were typically used to regulate industry-wide vertical supply arrangements, such as brewery—pub 'beer ties'.[7] Furthermore, the MMC did not possess its own remedial powers but made recommendations to the Secretary of State.[8] The market investigation regime was, however, intended to have wider reach and powers. It empowered the then Competition Commission to investigate any market where it appeared that competition may be restricted 'by the structure of a market (or any aspect of its structure)' and the ordinary competition powers were not sufficient.[9] The Explanatory Notes cite non-collusive oligopoly specifically as an example of

---

[5] National Audit Office (NAO), *Review of the UK's Competition Landscape* (22 March 2010) 24.

[6] The MMC was replaced by the Competition Commission in 1999, which was replaced by the CMA in 2014.

[7] Jeremy Lever, 'The Development of British Competition Law: a Complete Overhaul and Harmonisation' WZB Discussion Paper, No FS IV 99-4.

[8] ibid.

[9] Explanatory Notes to the Enterprise Act 2002, para 292.

circumstances which the new market investigation instrument would be able to address.[10] Furthermore, the Competition Commission was also empowered to impose a wide range of remedies to address any concerns as well as make recommendations to the UK government.[11] As the CAT summarized in *BAA*, the market investigation regime confers 'enormous powers' on the CMA.[12]

In contrast to the period from 1998 to 2010, there has been no significant upheaval of the UK's wider substantive competition regime over the last ten years.[13] There has, however, been significant institutional reform, manifested most prominently in the creation of the CMA. More subtly, the CMA's pursuit of market investigations focused on 'demand-side' features over the last decade has tested the boundaries of a competition policy tool which remains ill-defined.

2.2 Institutions and Procedure

The two-stage process of market studies and market investigations and the route of appeal by way of judicial review are largely the same as was introduced under the EA 2002. There have been, however, a number of significant institutional and procedural reforms that have altered the way in which the regime operates. The most significant change was the merger of the OFT and the Competition Commission (CC) into one unified institution, the CMA, on 1 April 2014.[14] This made the CMA responsible for making the vast majority of market investigation references pursuant to an initial market study, as well as conducting the investigations themselves.

The CMA continues, however, to keep the two processes (largely) separate. On completion of a market study and issuance of a market investigation reference by the CMA board, the CMA's market study team hands over to the market investigation team and the Inquiry Group, who are responsible for conducting the market investigation under the auspices of the Panel, usually appointed by the Panel Chair.[15] The CMA allows, however, for some degree of case team continuity for operational efficiency. The partial separation reflects the aim for the market investigation to involve a 'fresh pair of eyes' (similar to the merger regime), and to avoid the Inquiry Group prejudging the outcome of the market investigation.[16]

2.2.1 Phase 1: Market Studies and Market Investigation References
Notwithstanding the significant procedural change wrought by the ERRA 2013, the routes for initiating a market investigation remain the same: both the CMA and the sectoral regulators (the latter in their respective sectoral domains) may conduct market studies and

---

[10] ibid.

[11] ibid para 320.

[12] *BAA Limited v Competition Commission* [2009] CAT 35, para 117 https://www.catribunal.org.uk/sites/default/files/1110_BAA_Judgment_21.12.09.pdf accessed 30 June 2020.

[13] Ahlborn and Piccinin (n 1).

[14] Enterprise and Regulatory Reform Act 2013 (EA 2002) s 25.

[15] CMA, Market Studies and Market Investigations: Supplemental guidance on the CMA's approach (revised 2017) para 1.25 (CMA3 revised).

[16] CC, Guidelines for market investigations: Their role, procedures, assessment and remedies (April 2013) para 22, para 156 (CC3 revised).

make market investigation references.[17] The Secretary of State retains a reserve power to make ordinary and cross-market references in limited circumstances.[18]

The ERRA 2013 has, however, overhauled the market study framework to put the CMA's initiation of market studies on a firmer statutory footing. Prior to the ERRA 2013, market studies were a less codified market review which often preceded a market investigation reference. Now when the CMA conducts a market study that may result in a market investigation reference, such a study must be conducted in accordance with the statutory framework set out in consolidated Chapter 1 of the EA 2002. This imposes time limits for the conduct of the study as well as an obligation to determine whether to make a market reference.[19] However, despite the new statutory framework for market studies, the CMA may still procedurally make a market investigation reference without conducting a market study.[20]

The CMA or the Sectoral Regulators 'may' make a market investigation reference where they have reasonable grounds for suspecting that: 'any feature, or combination of features, of a market in the United Kingdom for good or services prevents, restricts or distorts competition in connection with the supply or acquisition of any goods or services in the United Kingdom or part of the United Kingdom.'[21] As such, the CMA and Sectoral Regulators have discretion in determining whether to refer a market. When making such a determination, the CMA's guidelines on market investigation references set out four criteria:

(i) whether it would be more appropriate to deal with the competition issues with the CMA's antitrust enforcement powers;
(ii) whether 'undertakings in lieu' that can address the competitive problems identified by the CMA can be agreed;
(iii) the scale of the competition problems identified; and
(iv) the availability of remedies and the value of a market investigation report.[22]

The CMA and the Sectoral Regulators must also consult on their decision regarding whether to refer the market for investigation or not and must give reasons for any such decision.[23]

No later than the issuance of a market investigation reference, the Secretary of State may also issue a public interest intervention notice. Where a public interest intervention is in force, the CMA must submit any market study report to the Secretary of State instead of publishing it or, where pursuant to section 169 EA 2002 the CMA is consulting to make a market reference, must provide a document containing the CMA's decision and its reasons.[24] Following receipt of the market study report or the relevant reasoned document, the Secretary of State determines whether to make a full or partial public interest reference, provided the CMA has decided to make a reference on competition grounds

---

[17] On concurrency see ch 10 below.

[18] EA 2002, s 132.

[19] The CMA continues to have the power to open a general market study into markets without issuing a market study notice to which the formalities introduced by the ERRA 2013 do not apply.

[20] EA 2002, s 131(1).

[21] ibid.

[22] OFT, Market investigation references: Guidance about the making of references under Part 4 of the Enterprise Act (March 2006) (OFT511).

[23] EA 2002, s 172.

[24] ibid ss 141, 144.

(i.e. a market investigation reference cannot be taken forward on public interest grounds alone).[25]

2.2.2 Phase 2: Market Investigations

Following a market investigation reference, the CMA has eighteen months to determine whether any 'feature' gives rise to an adverse effect on competition (shortened from twenty-four months under the ERRA 2013). This period may be extended by a further six months in special cases.[26] If the CMA identifies one or more features that give rise to adverse effects on competition, the CMA must accept final undertakings or make a final order within six months of publication of the market investigation report (subject to a potential four-month extension in special circumstances).[27]

When a market investigation reference has been made, the Panel Chair of the CMA appoints at least three, although usually between four to six CMA panel members, to form an inquiry group to conduct the market investigation.[28] The CMA panel members are not involved in market studies or in reference decisions in an effort to ensure their impartiality.[29] The market investigation 'terms of reference' must identify the goods or services to which the feature or combination of features concerned relates[30] and may be limited to certain suppliers, customers, or regions. The Inquiry Group is bound by the terms of reference, unless the terms are subsequently amended by the CMA board.[31]

Where a public interest reference has been made, the CMA must prepare a report setting out its conclusions on both competition and public interest issues.[32] Where the Secretary of State is required to decide on public interest considerations in relation to any features having adverse effects on competition, the CMA must provide the report to the Secretary of State.[33] The Secretary of State then has ninety days to decide on whether to make adverse public interest findings and, if so, whether to accept any undertakings or make any orders that seem appropriate to remedy the adverse effects on the public interest.[34]

2.2.3 Enforcement Powers and Remedies

If the CMA identifies one or more features having an adverse effect on competition, it is under a duty to take such action as it considers 'reasonable and practicable' to remedy the adverse effects on competition *and* remedy any detrimental effects on customers insofar as they have resulted from, or may be expected to result from, the adverse effect on competition.[35]

---

[25] The only grounds for a public interest referral are national security as of 1 May 2020. The Secretary of State may, however, amend this list by Order.

[26] EA 2002, s 137(2A); CMA3 (n 16) para 3.6.

[27] EA 2002, s 138A.

[28] CMA, Rules of procedure for merger, market and special reference groups (corrected November 2015) para 6.1 (CMA17); and CC3 (revised) para 46.

[29] CMA17, para 6.2(b), CC3 (revised) (n 16) para 22, para 156.

[30] EA 2002, s 133.

[31] ibid s 133; OFT511 (n 22) paras 3.13 ff.

[32] EA 2002, s 142.

[33] ibid ss 146 and 146A.

[34] ibid s 146(3).

[35] ibid s 138.

The CMA has wide powers to accept undertakings or impose orders to address any adverse effects on competition identified in a market investigation. The CMA's Market Investigation Guidelines classify remedies as either 'structural' or 'behavioural', identifying four broad types.[36]

    (i) Divestitures, notably the divestment of businesses or assets (structural remedy);
    (ii) Intellectual property remedies, notably the licensing or assignment of IP (structural remedy);
    (iii) Enabling measures, which remove obstacles to competition (behavioural remedy); and
    (iv) Controlling outcomes, which limit the effects of significant market power (behavioural remedy).

The CMA may also make recommendations to regulatory bodies, such as the Sectoral Regulators, or the government, to take action needed to address any findings of adverse effects on competition. This may occur where the regulatory framework itself is hampering competition. The CMA cannot order regulatory or legislative changes intended to rework the regulatory framework within which firms operate, hence the need to issue recommendations. The CMA may also make recommendations where it is more practicable or otherwise preferable to do so.

When determining which of the different possible remedial actions to impose or to recommend, the CMA has to take into account their effectiveness and practicability, their timing, their reasonableness and proportionality, and the focus of the proposed remedies.[37]

2.2.4 Judicial Review

Section 179 of the EA 2002 provides that any aggrieved person may seek review in the CAT of any decision of the CMA or relevant Secretary of State in relation to a market investigation reference or potential market investigation reference. It is therefore possible to challenge the CMA's or Secretary of State's decision as to whether or not to refer a market for investigation, the CMA's findings following a market investigation, or any remedies agreed or imposed following a market investigation. Aggrieved parties may also challenge a sectoral regulator's decision to refer, or not to refer, a market for investigation under their concurrent powers.

Section 179 of the EA 2002 does not cover decisions by the CMA and the Sectoral Regulators on whether to exercise their powers to conduct market studies pursuant to section 5 of the Act.

The CAT applies the principles and standard of judicial review to any challenge to a market investigation reference or potential market investigation reference. The CAT does not, therefore, conduct a 'full merits review' of the relevant decision. This is in keeping with the standard of judicial review for merger control decisions but lower than a 'merits review'

---

[36] CC3 (revised) (n 16) para 320.
[37] ibid.

standard for CA 1998 cases.[38] Any challenge to the CAT's judgment thereafter is before the Court of Appeal (subject to permission to appeal being granted either by the CAT or the Court of Appeal).[39]

2.3 Substantive Provisions

The substantive heart of the market investigations regime remains section 134(1) EA 2002 which, following a market investigation reference, requires the CMA to decide whether: 'any feature or combination of features, of a market in the UK for goods or services [which] prevents or distorts competition in connection with the supply or acquisition of any goods or services' (an adverse effect on competition 'AEC').[40] The definition of 'feature' is broad, encompassing the structure of the market concerned or any aspect of that structure; any conduct of one or more persons who supply or acquire goods or services in the market concerned or any conduct relating to the market concerned of customers or any person who suppliers or acquires goods or services. The inclusion of customer 'conduct' broadens the scope of the regime beyond conventional competition policy issues (which focus on supply-side issues) to include more complex behavioural consumer issues (i.e. demand-side issues). Where the CMA concludes that there is such an adverse effect on competition, it is under a duty to determine whether it or others should take any action to remedy, mitigate or prevent the adverse effect on competition.[41]

While the ERRA 2013 had no impact on the core of the market investigation regime, it made a number of additions. The ERRA 2013 introduced 'cross-market references', which enable the CMA to investigate multiple markets simultaneously.[42] Cross-market references do not change the substantive test for an AEC but enable the CMA to investigate multiple markets where the relevant feature or features occur. The ERRA 2013 also expanded the residual public interest powers. The regime already empowered the relevant Secretary of State to intervene prior to initiation of a market investigation where it considers specified public interest considerations are germane to the market in question.[43] Prior to the reform the Competition Commission would investigate the competition issues while the Secretary of State would investigate the relevant public interest consideration. This so-called 'restricted public interest' referral remains.[44] However, the ERRA 2013 introduced the option for a 'full public interest reference' which enables the relevant Secretary of State to require the CMA to not only investigate the competition issues but also the public interest issues as well as the possible remedies.[45] In both cases, the Secretary of State and the CMA are limited to assessing public interest considerations insofar as they apply to the features that may give rise to an AEC. Broadening the power of the CMA was intended to harmonize the market investigation regime and the

---

[38] David Bailey, 'The Early Case Law of the Competition Appeal Tribunal' in Barry J Rodger (ed), *Ten Years of UK Competition Law Reform* (Dundee University Press 2010).

[39] EA 2002, s 179(6) and (7).

[40] OFT511 (n 22).

[41] EA 2002, s 138(2).

[42] ibid s 131(2A).

[43] ibid s 153.

[44] The Competition Commission was the predecessor of the CMA; see section 2.2.

[45] EA 2002, s 140A(7)(a).

merger regime and enable a more holistic view on the competition and the public interest issues.[46]

The cross-market reference and public interest references have however only academic relevance so far. No *cross-market references* have been made in the six years since their introduction. This is not entirely surprising as cross-market reference were not expected to be used often.[47] However, the absence of any such reference is likely driven by difficulties in defining the scope of cross-market investigations, particularly the firms potentially affected, sufficiently early in the process. Similarly, as of 2 July 2020 no public interest references— whether restricted or full—have been launched since the advent of the market investigation regime in 2002. Furthermore, the list of public interest considerations remains limited to 'national security' considerations despite the UK government having the power to expand this list by order.[48]

2.4 Policy Goal

The policy goal of the ordinary market investigation regime remains consumer welfare (with knock-on positive effects on the UK's productivity).[49] While the concept of an AEC tracks, in part, the legal test for a Chapter I CA 1998 infringement, its objective is, however, inherently broader, capturing all features that 'prevent, restrict or distort competition'. In so doing, the regime in practice empowers the CMA to intervene where there is any 'market failure'. The counterfactual for establishing a market failure is 'a well-functioning market' but does not impose a concept of idealized competition.[50]

The policy goal of the regime has, however, been muddied by the introduction of the public interest test where the reference is either a partial or full public interest reference. Where the Secretary of State makes either type of public interest reference, the CMA must also form a view on public interest considerations insofar as they also apply to markets where the CMA has found an AEC. The inclusion of the public interest test has so far not been relevant in practice as no public interest references have been made and national security remains the single public interest ground for intervention.[51] There has, however, been an increasing use of public interest references in the context of UK mergers. Seven such references have been made in the last decade, heralding a potentially greater willingness on the part of the UK government to exercise these powers.[52]

---

[46] Explanatory Notes (n 9) para 264.

[47] A Coscelli and A Horrock, 'Making Markets Work Well: The UK Market Investigations Regime' (2014) 10(1) CPI https://www.competitionpolicyinternational.com/making-markets-work-well-the-u-k-market-investigations-regime/ accessed 30 June 2020.

[48] EA 2002, s 153.

[49] OFT, Market Studies: Guidance on the OFT approach (June 2010) para 2.11 (OFT519). See also the UK White Paper 'Productivity and Enterprise: a world class competition regime' on the role of the market investigation regime in driving improvements in productivity https://assets.publishing.service.govuk/government/uploads/system/uploads/attachment_data/file/265534/5233.pdf.

[50] CC3 (revised) (n 16) para 320.

[51] EA 2002, s 153.

[52] There were five public interest intervention notices: BskyB/ITV; LloydsTSB/HBOS; Global Radio Holdings Ltd/GMG Radio Holdings Ltd; Hytera Communications Corporation Ltd/Sepura plc; Gardener/Nothern and two Special public interest intervention notices Lockheed Martin/Stasys; Atlas Elektronic/Qinetiq.

Finally, as outlined in section 8, the CMA has plans afoot to revise the policy goal by removing the need for any 'adverse effect on competition' such that the CMA could intervene in any market where a feature is sufficiently likely to cause consumer harm.

3 Overview of the Last Ten years

3.1 Stage 1: Market Studies

The CMA has conducted twenty-six market studies since 2010.[53] These market studies covered a range of markets from school uniforms to statutory audit services. In addition, the CMA has conducted a range of studies (often in the guise of research or calls for information) in markets including the supply of medicines and short-term car rentals without a formal market study.[54] These less formal studies covered ad hoc issues (e.g. the review of medicine shortages in the UK) or collaborations with other European authorities (e.g. pan-EU review of contractual provisions in short term car rental). The number of studies has in broad terms, remained consistent in comparison to the thirty-three market studies conducted between 2002 and 2010.

The CMA accepted undertakings in lieu of a market investigation reference in one instance, *Extended Warranties on Domestic Electrical Goods*, which was one fewer than between 2002 and 2010.[55] In 2017, the CMA also decided not to refer the *Digital Comparison Tool Services* market study for further investigation because the potential consumer harm could be adequately addressed by making recommendations.[56] However, the CMA subsequently opened a CA 1998 investigation on the back of the study against one market participant.[57]

Since 2010, eleven market investigation references have been made. Of these, seven market investigation references arose from prior market studies, three were made by sectoral regulators (*Investment Consultancy Management Services*,[58] *Supply and Acquisition of Energy*,[59] and *Movies on Pay-TV*[60]) and one investigation was opened off the back of a

---

[53] Excluded from the market studies are calls for information and super-complaints that did not result in a market study and less formal studies and investigations into markets.

[54] Examples include: *Scottish legal services research* (2020), *Commercial use of consumer data (call for information)* (2015), *Car rental in the UK* (2015), *Public transport* (2015), *Competition in passenger rail services in GB* (2016), *Supply of medicines* (2015), *Competition and regulation in higher education in England* (2015), *Commercial use of consumer data (call for information)* (2015).

[55] OFT, '*Extended Warranties on Domestic Electrical Goods—Final decision on Market Investigation Reference*' (June 2012) https://webarchive.nationalarchives.govuk/20140402172800/http://oft.govuk/shared_oft/markets-work/OFT1417dec_Extended_warrant1.pdf accessed 30 June 2020.

[56] CMA, *Digital Comparison Tool Services market study—Final Report* (26 September 2017); see in particular s 5 https://assets.publishing.service.govuk/media/59c93546e5274a77468120d6/digital-comparison-tools-market-study-final-report.pdf accessed 30 June 2020.

[57] CMA opened Chapter I investigation on 27 September 2017, sending a statement of objections against BGL (Holdings) Limited, BGL Group Limited, BISL Limited (BISL), and Compare The Market Limited on 2 November 2018.

[58] FCA, '*Investment Consultancy Services—Terms of reference*' (14 September 2017) https://www.fca.org.uk/publication/market-studies/final-decision-market-investigation-reference.pdf accessed 30 June 2020.

[59] Ofgem, '*Supply and Acquisition of Energy—Terms of reference*' (21 July 2014) https://www.ofgem.govuk/sites/default/files/docs/2014/06/state_of_the_market_-_decision_document_in_ofgem_template.pdf accessed 30 June 2020.

[60] Ofcom, '*Movies on Pay-TV—Terms of reference*' (4 August 2010) https://www.ofcom.org.uk/__data/assets/pdf_file/0017/72008/pay-tv-movies-decision.pdf accessed 30 June 2020.

preceding inquiry by the House of Lords Economic Affairs Select Committee (*Statutory Audit of Large Companies*). This was broadly in line with the number of market investigations (9) in the period from 2002 to 2010 but was a significant increase in the number of references from sectoral regulators (1), taking into account the National Audit Office's criticism of the paucity of such references prior to 2010.[61] The CMA and the Secretary of State have not, however, made use of the new powers conferred under the ERRA 2013 to make cross-market references or public interest references with none made following implementation of the revised regime.

Finally, the CMA issued its first penalty decision for a firm failing to provide the necessary information by the required deadline in the market study into *Online Platforms and Digital Advertising in the UK*.[62]

3.2 Stage 2: Market Investigations

As set out above, the CMA has conducted ten market investigations over the last ten years with one, *Funerals and Crematoria Services*, ongoing.[63] Table 6.1 provides a summary of the investigations.

The CMA has only accepted one undertaking in lieu of making a market investigation reference (*Extended Warranties on Domestic Electrical Goods*).[64] This is not surprising; the CMA's guidance outlines the difficulties of accepting undertakings in lieu of market reference, not least due to the potential need to engage with multiple firms on the basis of a preliminary analysis of the AECs and suitable remedies.[65]

Of the nine cases where the CMA has imposed remedies since 2010, only two cases involved structural (divestment) remedies: *Aggregates*,[66] where two different firms had to divest different types of production facilities and *Private Healthcare*,[67] where HCA International had to divest a private hospital (albeit the divestiture was quashed on judicial review and subsequently dropped by the CMA on remittal).[68] In the other seven cases, the CMA imposed a range of behavioural remedies encompassing market-opening measures through removing barriers to entry, expansion or switching (*Retail Banking*)[69] or transparency enhancing measures based on the disclosure and publication of information (*Payday Lending*)[70] or a remedy requiring compulsory audits (*Private Motor Insurance*).[71] Remedies seeking to control market outcomes include the

---

[61] National Audit Office, Review of the UK's Competition Landscape (18 March 2010) https://www.nao.org.uk/wp-content/uploads/2010/03/0910_competition_landscape.pdf accessed 30 June 2020.

[62] CMA, '*Online Platforms and Digital Advertising in the UK—Penalty notice under section 174A of the Enterprise Act 2002*' (10 January 2020) Case MA/50777/19 https://assets.publishing.service.govuk/media/5e21e70be5274a6c38aae2bc/Penalty_notice_Non-confidential.pdf accessed 30 June 2020.

[63] *Funerals and crematoria services* market investigation opened on 28 March 2019, supposed to close by 27 September 2020 but got extended by six months to 27 March 2021 due to the outbreak of the virus Covid-19 referred to as *Funerals*.

[64] *Extended Warranties* (n 55).

[65] OFT511 (n 22) paras 2.21 and 2.25.

[66] CMA, *Aggregates* (see Table 6.1 and n 186 below).

[67] CMA, *Private Healthcare* (see Table 6.1 and n 184 below).

[68] *HCA International Ltd v CMA* (see Table 6.1 and n 185 below).

[69] CMA, *Retail Banking* (see Table 6.1 and n 180 below).

[70] CMA, *Payday Lending* (see Table 6.1 and n 182 below).

[71] CMA, *Private Motor Insurance* (see Table 6.1 and n 183 below).

Table 6.1 Market investigations (2010–2020)

Market investigation	Start Date	End Date	Size of market[a]	Type of remedy
Funerals[b]	March 2019	March 2021	£ 2 bn	n/a
Investment Consultancy Management Services[c]	September 2017	December 2018	£ 0.6 bn	Behavioural
Retail Banking[d]	November 2014	August 2016	£ 10.6 bn	Behavioural
Energy[e]	June 2014	June 2016	£ 35 bn	Behavioural
Payday Lending[f]	June 2013	February 2015	£ 2.8 bn	Behavioural
Private Motor Insurance[g]	September 2012	September 2014	£ 11 bn	Behavioural
Private Healthcare[h]	April 2012	April 2014	£ 6.7 bn	(Structural)[i], behavioural
Aggregates[j]	January 2012	January 2014	£ 1.4 bn	Structural, behavioural
Statutory Audit Services[k]	October 2011	October 2013	£ 2 bn	Behavioural
Movies on Pay TV[l]	August 2010	August 2012	£ 4 bn	No remedies imposed
Local Bus Service[m]	January 2010	December 2011	£ 4.1 bn	Behavioural

[a] Market sizes are taken from the final reports of the respective market investigations.

[b] CMA, *Funerals—Terms of reference* (28 March 2019) https://assets.publishing.service.govuk/media/5c9ba414e5274a527e52389d/Terms_of_reference.pdf accessed 30 June 2020.

[c] CMA, *Investment Consultancy and Fiduciary Management Services—Final Report* (12 December 2018) referred to as *Investment Consultancy Services* https://assets.publishing.service.govuk/media/5c0fee5740f0b60c8d6019a6/ICMI_Final_Report.pdf accessed 30 June 2020.

[d] CMA, *Retail Banking Market Investigation—Final Report* (9 August 2016) https://assets.publishing.service.govuk/media/57ac9667e5274a0f6c00007a/retail-banking-market-investigation-full-final-report.pdf accessed 30 June 2020.

[e] CMA, *Supply and Acquisition of Energy Market Investigation—Final Report* (24.06.2016) referred to as *Energy* https://assets.publishing.service.govuk/media/5773de34e5274a0da3000113/final-report-energy-market-investigation.pdf accessed 30 June 2020.

[f] CMA, *Payday Lending Market Investigation—Final Report* (24.02.2015) https://assets.publishing.service.govuk/media/54ebb03bed915d0cf7000014/Payday_investigation_Final_report.pdf accessed 30 June 2020.

[g] CMA, *Private Motor Insurance—Final Report* (24 September 2014) https://assets.publishing.service.gov.uk/media/5421c2ade5274a1314000001/Final_report.pdf accessed 30 June 2020.

[h] CMA, *Privately-Funded Health Care Market Investigation—Final Report* (02 April 2014) referred to as *Private Healthcare* https://assets.publishing.service.govuk/media/533af065e5274a5660000023/Private_healthcare_main_report.pdf accessed 30 June 2020.

[i] The CAT quashed the decision with regard to HCA's divestment of hospitals and referred the case back to the CMA for a renewed analysis see: Case 1228/6/12/14 *HCA International Ltd v CMA* [2014] CAT 23 https://www.catribunal.org.uk/sites/default/files/1228-30_AXA_HCA_FIPO_Judgment_CAT_23_231214.pdf accessed 30 June 2020.

[j] CMA, *Aggregates, Cement and Ready-Mix Concrete Market Investigation—Final Report* (14 January 2014), referred to as *Aggregates* https://assets.publishing.service.govuk/media/552ce1d5ed915d15db000001/Aggregates_final_report.pdf accessed 30 June 2020.

[k] CMA, *Statutory Audit Services for Large Companies—Final Report* (18 April 2019) referred to as *Statutory Audit Services* https://assets.publishing.service.govuk/media/5cb74577e5274a7416b64f01/final_summary_report.pdf accessed 30 June 2020.

[l] CC, *Movies on Pay-TV—Final Report* (2 August 2012) https://assets.publishing.service.govuk/media/5519492940f0b614040001ca/main_report.pdf accessed 30 June 2020.

[m] CC, *Local Bus Services Market investigation—Final Report* (20 December 2011) https://webarchive.nationalarchives.govuk/20140403001219/http://www.competition-commission.org.uk/assets/competitioncommission/docs/pdf/inquiry/ref2010/localbus/pdf/00_sections_1_15.pdf accessed 30 June 2020.

introduction of price caps (*Local Bus Services*)[72] and *Energy*[73]) and supply commitments. Regulatory remedies are mostly recommendations to the government or regulatory bodies such as the reduction of barriers to entry that exist because of existing laws or regulatory actions (*Energy (2016)*[74]). The CMA does not have the power to enforce the recommendations it makes to government or regulatory bodies, and in practice few are implemented in full.

3.3 Judicial Review: The CAT

The increased number of challenges heard by the CAT (and beyond) since 2010 are one of the biggest changes relative to the period 2002–2010. Until 2010, six challenges were adjudicated by the CAT. In the last decade, there have been twelve challenges including three subsequent appeals to the Court of Appeal.

Parties have challenged a range of aspects of the market investigation regime in connection with a reference or possible reference.[75] The following cases have involved challenges before the CAT with the *BAA Airports Market Investigation* and, in particular, the *Private Healthcare Market Investigation* spawning multiple challenges:

  (i)   *Beer and Pub Market* (CAMRA Super-Complaint)[76]
 (ii)   *BAA Airports Market Investigation*[77]
(iii)   *Newspaper and Magazine Distribution*[78]
 (iv)   *Extended Warranties on Domestic Electrical Goods*[79]
  (v)   *Aggregates*[80]
 (vi)   *Private Healthcare*[81]
(vii)   *Groceries.*[82]

---

[72] CC, *Local Bus Services* (see Table 6.1 and n 189 below).

[73] CMA, *Energy* (see Table 6.1 and n 181 below).

[74] ibid.

[75] EA 2002, s 179.

[76] Case 1148/6/1/09 *Campaign for Real Ale v OFT* [2009] https://www.catribunal.org.uk/sites/default/files/1148_CAMRA_Summary_30.12.09.pdf accessed 30 June 2020.

[77] Case 1110/6/8/09 *BAA Limited v CC* (n 12) https://www.catribunal.org.uk/sites/default/files/1110_BAA_Judgment_21.12.09.pdf accessed 30 June 2020 and Case 1185/6/8/11 *BAA Limited v CC* [2011] https://www.catribunal.org.uk/sites/default/files/1185_BAA_Judgment_CAT_3_010212.pdf accessed 30 June 2020.

[78] *Association of Convenience Stores and National Federation of Retail Newsagents v OFT* [2012] Case 1191/6/1/12 https://www.catribunal.org.uk/sites/default/files/1191_ACS_NRFN_Judgment_CAT_27_241012.pdf accessed 30 June 2020.

[79] Case 1203/6/1/12 *John Lewis v OFT* [2012] https://www.catribunal.org.uk/sites/default/files/1203_John_Lewis_Judgment_CAT_7_280313.pdf accessed 30 June 2020.

[80] Case 1223/6/8/13 *Hanson Quarry v CC* [2013] and Case 1222/6/8/13 *Lafarge Tarmac v CC* [2013] https://www.catribunal.org.uk/sites/default/files/1222_Lafarge_Notice_311013.pdf accessed 30 June 2020.

[81] Case 1228/6/12/14 *AXA PPP Healthcare Limited v CMA* [2015] CAT 5(https://www.catribunal.org.uk/sites/default/files/1228_AXA_PPP_Judgment_CAT_5_130315.pdf; Case 1229/6/12/14 *HCA International Ltd v CMA* [2014] CAT 23. https://www.catribunal.org.uk/sites/default/files/1228-30_AXA_HCA_FIPO_Judgment_CAT_23_231214.pdf; Case 1230/6/12/14 *Federation of Independent Practitioner Organisations v CMA* [2015] CAT 8 https://www.catribunal.org.uk/sites/default/files/1230_FIPO_Judgment_CAT_8_290415.pdf; Case 1218/6/8/13 *BMI Healthcare Limited v CMA (I)* [2013] CAT 24 https://www.catribunal.org.uk/sites/default/files/1218_BMI_Judgment_021013_1.pdf; Case 1220/6/8/13*BMI Healthcare v CMA (II)* [2013] https://www.catribunal.org.uk/sites/default/files/1220_BMI_Notice_091013.pdf all accessed 30 June 2020.

[82] Case 1301/6/12/18 *B&M European Value Retail v CMA* [2018] https://www.catribunal.org.uk/sites/default/files/2019-05/1301_B%26M_Judgment_CAT_13_130519.pdf accessed 30 June 2020.

Of the challenges, two concerned challenges by parties on whom the CMA had imposed inter alia, structural remedies (*BAA Airports* and *Private Healthcare*). *Private Healthcare* also saw other parties challenge the CMA's decision to impose a behavioural remedy in one area, and the CMA's failure to impose a remedy in other areas; as well a judicial review on a procedural issue relating to access to file midway through the investigation. *Lafarge Tarmac* and *Hope Construction Materials* also started the judicial review process in relation to *Aggregates* but ultimately withdrew their application for review. Two parties challenged the CMA's decision not to make market investigation references (*Newspaper and Magazine Distribution* and *Beer and Pub Market*). Finally, interested parties also challenged remedies in previous market investigations (*Extended Warranties on Domestic Electric Goods* and *Groceries*). Table 6.2 summarizes the applications for judicial review.

On balance, the CMA has successfully defended most challenges, winning ten of the twelve cases. The exception is *Private Healthcare*, where the CMA lost one of the four challenges brought before the CAT and, in addition, effectively admitted defeat in a second challenge by requesting that the CAT allow the CMA to withdraw one of its findings of

Table 6.2 Market investigation and market study challenges (2010–2020)

Market investigation judicial reviews	Date of Decision	Grounds of review	Outcome
B&M European Value Retail (*Groceries*)	May 2019	Procedural Irrationality Illegality	Dismissed Dismissed Dismissed
FIPO (Court of Appeal) FIPO (*Private Healthcare*)	July 2016 April 2015	Procedural Irrationality Procedural Illegality	Dismissed Dismissed Dismissed
HCA (Court of Appeal)	May 2015	Procedural Illegality	Dismissed Dismissed
HCA (*Private Healthcare*)	December 2014	Procedural Irrationality Illegality	Successful (partly)[a] Dismissed Dismissed
AXA (*Private Healthcare*)	March 2015	Procedural Illegality	Dismissed Dismissed
BMI (I) (*Private Healthcare*)	October 2013	Procedural	Successful
John Lewis (*Extended Warranties*)	March 2013	Procedural Illegality	Dismissed Time-barred
ACS (*Newspaper*)	October 2012	Irrationality Illegality	Dismissed Dismissed
BAA (Court of Appeal) BAA (*BAA 2011 report*)	July 2012 February 2012	Illegality Irrationality Illegality	Dismissed Dismissed Dismissed

[a]The CAT quashed the decision with regard to HCA's divestment of hospitals and referred the case back to the CMA for a renewed analysis see: Case 1228/6/12/14 *HCA International Ltd v CMA* (n 73).

an AEC due to manifest procedural errors and order a remittal to the CMA for fresh consideration.[83]

4 Trends in Market Investigations

The market investigation regime has been described as the 'archetypal example' of a 'fully hybridized approach to market supervision' spanning competition policy, consumer policy, and regulation.[84]

The conventional competition toolkit regulates agreements between undertakings, unilateral conduct on the part of firms with significant market power and mergers between undertakings. The core of antitrust and merger control therefore is the regulation of market power, whether its creation, strengthening or exploitation. These policy instruments share three salient, common characteristics:

   (i)   the subjects of the instruments are firms active in the markets under scrutiny (i.e. the rules only regulate the conduct of firms in the market);[85]
   (ii) the relevant firms have engaged in a clearly defined 'act' (i.e. an agreement, unilateral conduct or a transaction); and
   (iii) the act is likely to have anti-competitive effects either proven (antitrust / mergers) or presumed (object infringements/cartels).

The market investigation regime has, however, a far wider scope than conventional competition policy. Sir John Vickers described the regime as follows: 'What is unusual in the UK regime is a system where markets can be investigated and remedies applied, which can change market conditions very significantly, even though no one has broken any prohibition in the law.'[86] The market investigation regime empowers the CMA to investigate whether any 'feature' of the market distorts competition and any public interest considerations, even if these 'features' are not related to market power. The concept of such features enables the CMA to look at almost any market failure. In stark contrast to the conventional competition instruments, the CMA may assess all three market dimensions: the conduct and structure of the firms supplying the market (the supply-side), the firms and end-consumers acquiring the relevant products in a market (the demand-side) and the market's regulatory framework (i.e. the state's actions). Further, the CMA is not limited to investigating anti-competitive 'acts' but may review any source of competitive 'harm'. To this end, the CMA's *Market Investigation Guidelines* identify a range of competitive 'harms' as the potential focus of market investigations ranging from unilateral harm through to barriers to entry / expansion and poor consumer response.[87] The common thread between the market investigation

---

[83] [2014] CAT 23 (n 81).

[84] Niamh Dunne, 'Between Competition Law and Regulation: Hybridized Approaches to Market Control' (2014) 2 Journal of Antitrust Enforcement 225 (emphasis added).

[85] EU law does, however, contain rules regulating anti-competitive state action, notably the state aid rules and Article 106 TFEU. For more see also Julio Baquero Cruz, *Between Competition and Free Movement: The Economic Constitutional Law of the European Community* (Hart Publishing 2002).

[86] Enterprise and Regulatory Reform Bill Deb 21 June 2012 col 81.

[87] CC3 (revised) (n 16) paras 117 ff.

regime and conventional competition policy is thus the need for anti-competitive effects (using a consumer welfare standard).

This mandate enables the CMA to pursue an extremely broad range of potential market failures. The CMA may investigate 'oligopoly' problems where firms' uncoordinated parallel conduct is not caught by conventional competition policy but which nevertheless falls within the scope of recognized competition 'problems' ('extended competition policy'). Beyond this, the CMA may also investigate market failures linked to the behaviour of the demand side absent any link to conduct on the part of firms active in the market ('consumer policy'). Finally, the CMA may also investigate anti-competitive state action where regulation is distorting competition in the market. The market features subject to the market investigation regime can thus be categorized as follows:

(i) conventional competition features;
(ii) extended competition features;
(iii) consumer policy; and
(iv) state action.

Market investigations, however, investigate markets, not these specific features. Accordingly, market investigations frequently scrutinize multiple features testing whether the features in isolation or in aggregate are producing market outcomes falling short of those that would be delivered by a 'well-functioning market'.[88] State action, for example, has never been the sole AEC identified in a market investigation.

4.1 Conventional Competition Cases

The 'overlap' between the CMA's conventional competition tools and the market investigation regime raises the risk of regulatory arbitrage where the CMA uses the market investigation regime to circumvent the limitations of its conventional competition tools. The CMA recognizes this risk. Its guidance provides that the CMA will first consider whether any feature may involve an infringement of the CMA's conventional competition tools and will only consider a market investigation reference where/when:

(i) it has reasonable grounds to suspect that there are market features which prevent, restrict or distort competition, but not to establish a breach of the CA 1998 prohibitions;
(ii) an action under the CA 1998 has been or is likely to be ineffective for dealing with the adverse effect.

---

[88] CC3 (revised) (n 16) para 320; see also Stephen Littlechild, 'The CMA Energy Market Investigation, the Well-functioning Market, Ofgem, Government and Behavioural Economics' (2015) 11 European Competition Journal 574.

Of the CMA's eleven market investigations, two were primarily focused on concerns that would also fall within the scope of the CMA's conventional competition tools:

- *Private Motor Insurance;*[89]
- *Movies on Pay-TV.*[90]

While the *Private Motor Insurance* investigation spanned consumer policy and extended competition policy, the key remedy was a prohibition on private motor insurers and price comparison websites using 'wide' MFNs or provisions with similar effects.[91] MFNs in this context were a vertical restriction on the distribution of motor insurance and hence fell within the scope of Chapter I CA 1998 as well as Article 101 TFEU. The CMA's pursuit of 'wide' MFNs under the market investigation regime was also curious given that other European competition authorities were actively pursuing them under conventional antitrust policy in parallel.[92] The CMA did not address the potential overlap with its CA 1998 powers in its reference as vertical restraints had not been specifically identified in the market study as giving rise to a potential AEC.

In *Movies on Pay-TV*, the market investigation more squarely fell within the scope of conventional competition policy. The Competition Commission's investigation focused on whether Sky's control of the rights to distribute movies from the six largest Hollywood studios (and other studios), due to its market power in the retail pay-TV market, was adversely affecting competition in the market.[93] The theory of harm was that access to movie content was a 'significant' factor in consumers selecting a pay-TV provider and Sky's control meant that other pay-TV providers could not compete effectively. The theory of harm was thus a de facto abuse pursuant to Article 102 TFEU whereby Sky was allegedly refusing to supply or only supplying on disadvantageous terms access to an important input to the benefit of its own retail pay-TV business.[94]

4.2 Extended Competition Cases

The CMA has also continued to use the market investigation regime as a tool to address competition concerns that cannot easily be addressed under its conventional competition tools, including the exploitation of significant market power, oligopolistic markets (notably parallelism) and unmerited barriers to entry and expansion. The following cases, in particular, focused heavily on wider competition issues:

- *Private Healthcare;*[95]
- *Aggregates;*[96]

---

[89] CMA, *Private Motor Insurance* (n 71).
[90] CC, *Movies on Pay-TV* (see Table 6.1 and n 188 below).
[91] CMA, *Private Motor Insurance* (n 71) paras 12.17 ff.
[92] See eg the German Competition Authority, Decision B 6–46/12; French Competition Authority, Decision 15-D-06; Italian Competition Authority Decision dated 21 April 2015; Swedish Competition Authority, Decision 596/2013 (15 April 2015).
[93] CC, *Movies on Pay-TV* (n 90) paras 9 ff.
[94] See eg *Cross-border access to pay-TV* (Case AT. 40023) Commission Decision (7 March 2019).
[95] CMA, *Private Healthcare* (n 67).
[96] CMA, *Aggregates* (n 66).

- *Statutory Audit Services;*[97]
- *Local Bus Services.*[98]

The most notable cases were *Private Healthcare, Aggregates,* and *Local Bus Services,* where the CMA focused heavily on existing levels of concentration raising competition concerns. This comes to the fore in *Local Bus Services,* where the Competition Commission found AECs arising from high levels of concentration and bus operators 'avoiding competing with other operators in "Core Territories".'[99] Similarly, in *Aggregates,* the CMA found that the combination of 'barriers to entry, transparency, homogeneous products, vertical integration and multi-market contacts' reduced competition in the setting of high levels of concentration.[100]

Since its *Private Healthcare* market investigation there has been a sharp decline in 'extended competition' cases. While market investigations post-2014 have contained elements of extended competition policy, such issues no longer appear at the forefront of the CMA's investigations. This is a significant change. It is one, moreover, which is all the more surprising given concerns within and outwith the antitrust community around the potential deleterious effects of increased levels of market concentration.[101] That said, the reduction can in part be attributed to the evolution of Article 101 TFEU and Chapter I CA 1998 to address information sharing practices that often underpin parallelism in oligopolistic markets.[102] However, this only addresses part of the picture, notably omitting the drop off in cases such as *Private Healthcare,* which centred on the risk of exploitative conduct by firms with market power.

4.3 Consumer Policy

In contrast, the most notable trend in the CMA's market investigations in the last ten years has been the increased focus on demand-side behavioural issues as cause of market failings. While the Competition Commission had looked at consumer policy issues in a number of cases prior to 2010, the CMA increasingly put consumer policy at the centre of its market investigations. This is particularly accentuated in the latter half of the decade: from 2014 onwards, all five of the CMA's market investigations have focused heavily on consumer-facing markets where market failure stems from the behaviour of consumers (i.e. on the demand-side):

---

[97] CMA, *Statutory Audit Services* (see Table 6.1 and n 187 below).
[98] CC, *Local Bus Services* (n 72) paras 50 ff.
[99] ibid.
[100] OFT (n 65).
[101] Nicole Rosenbom, 'Increased Market Power: A Global Problem That Needs Solving?' Oxera Agenda (2019) https://www.oxera.com/wp-content/uploads/2019/01/Increased-market-power.pdf accessed 30 June 2020; Francisco Beneke and Mark-Oliver Mackenrodt, 'Artificial Intelligence and Collusion' (2019) 50 International Review of Intellectual Property and Competition Law 109 https://link.springer.com/article/10.1007/s40319-018-00773-x#citeas accessed 30 June 2020.
[102] Ariel Ezrachi and Maurice E Stucke, 'Sustainable and Unchallenged Tacit Collusion' (2019) 16 Oxford Legal Studies Research Paper 217 https://papers.ssrn.com/sol3/papers.cfm?abstract_id=3282235 accessed 30 June 2020; Virgílio Pereira, 'Algorithm-driven Collusion: Pouring Old Wine into New Bottles or New Wine into Fresh Wineskins?' (2018) 39(5) ECLR 212.

- *Funerals;*[103]
- *Investment Consultancy Services;*[104]
- *Retail Banking;*[105]
- *Supply and Acquisition of Energy;*[106]
- *Payday Lending.*[107]

The trend is no coincidence. Alex Chisholm (the CMA's CEO from 2013 to 2016) observed that market investigations 'reflecting the insights and techniques of behavioural economics' are increasingly important to the CMA's work.[108] The CMA has embraced the use of behavioural economics to identify concerns on the demand side (consumer behaviour) and design appropriate remedies.

The CMA's focus on demand-side market features comes through particularly strongly in the CMA's flagship market investigations into *Energy*, *Retail Banking*, and *Investment Consultancy Services*. In all three, the CMA identified AECs based on 'weak customer response' to price and quality or 'low levels of engagement by some customers'. While the *Retail Banking* and *Energy* market investigations concerned end-customers, it is notable that the CMA found similar concerns in *Investment Consultancy Services* where the customers were pension schemes, charities, insurance companies and endowment funds.

The CMA imposed remedies in all three investigations. In *Retail Banking* and *Energy*, the remedies focused on solving the demand-side concerns through greater information, mechanisms to facilitate switching and greater transparency over products. The CMA also imposed a temporary price cap for pre-payment customers.[109] In *Investment Consultancy Services*, the CMA's remedies package was more ambitious—de facto transforming a market based on relationship contracting into a tendering market. In particular, the CMA introduced a remedy which required pension trustees to conduct a competitive tender for first time awards of fiduciary management mandates for 20 per cent + of their scheme assets and imposed a separate remedy mandating fiduciary management providers to provide significantly greater transparency on their fee structures.

4.4 State Action

Another evolution of the market investigation regime has been a greater focus on aspects of the regulatory and legislative framework which may give rise to AECs. While none of the market investigations to date has been primarily focused on state action as the source of potential AECs, the CMA has identified features of the regulatory framework as adversely affecting competition in a number of investigations and, furthermore, proposed a number of

---

[103] CMA, *Funerals* (n 63). See also n 178 below.
[104] CMA, *Investment Consultancy Services* (see Table 6.1 and n 179 below).
[105] CMA, *Retail Banking* (n 69).
[106] CMA, *Energy* (n 73).
[107] CMA, *Payday Lending* (n 70).
[108] Alex Chisholm, 'Reflections on the UK Competition and Markets Authority and Wider Global Trends' (2016) 4 Journal of Antitrust Enforcement 274.
[109] The UK government subsequently intervened to impose a wider price cap for all customers on standard variable and default tariffs based on a dissenting opinion from the Panel overseeing the *Energy* market investigation;

regulatory changes as a means of remedying the AECs identified. The CMA's lack of powers to require the state to implement specific measures means, however, that these take the form of recommendations.

The CMA recommended legislative and regulatory changes in the following cases:

- *Investment Consultancy Services;*[110]
- *Acquisition and Supply of Energy;*[111]
- *Retail Banking;*[112]
- *Payday Lending;*[113]
- *Private Healthcare;*[114]
- *Private Motor Insurance;*[115]
- *Statutory Audit Services;*[116]
- *Local Bus Services.*[117]

Of these, the CMA's *Energy* market investigation saw the most far-reaching recommendations for overhauling the regulatory framework. While the big six enjoy unilateral market power which they exploited through pricing policies, the CMA did not find evidence of coordination in the retail market. The CMA explicitly linked three findings of adverse effects on competition in the retail market to the regulatory regime including Ofgem's introduction of a ban on more complex tariffs. However, the CMA went further and identified 'a lack of robustness and transparency in regulatory decision-making' and 'industry code governance' as both having adverse effects on competition. In particular, the CMA concluded that poor coordination between Ofgem and the then Department for Energy and Climate Change (DECC) was hampering efficient regulation. To address its concerns, the CMA made a series of recommendations including amendments to primary legislation to alter Ofgem's statutory objectives and duties, proposals to 'recalibrate' the relationship between Ofgem and the DECC, and an overhaul of primary legislation to give Ofgem greater powers in administering the licence regime for energy (including the exceptional right to directly modify the industry codes).

5 Market Investigations and the Rise of Behavioural Economics

The rise of behavioural economics has had the most marked impact on the market investigation regime over the last decade.[118] While the previous iteration of this chapter speculated in its conclusion that consumer policy issues would feature less frequently in market

see https://assets.publishing.service.govuk/government/uploads/system/uploads/attachment_data/file/683926/ cma-energy-market-investigation-government-response.pdf.

[110] CMA, *Investment Consultancy Services* (n 104).
[111] CMA, *Energy* (n 73).
[112] CMA, *Retail Banking* (n 69).
[113] CMA, *Payday Lending* (n 70).
[114] CMA, *Private Healthcare* (n 67).
[115] CMA, *Private Motor Insurance* (n 71).
[116] CMA, *Statutory Audit Services* (n 97).
[117] CC, *Local Bus Services* (n 72).
[118] Littlechild (n 89); Maurice E Stucke, 'How Can Competition Agencies Use Behavioural Economics?' (2014) 59(4) The Antitrust Bulletin 695; Mike Walker, 'Behavioural Economics: the Lessons for Regulators' (2017) 13(1)

investigations in the future, the reverse has occurred.[119] Indeed, over the last five years, the CMA's market investigations have focused almost entirely on consumer policy issues. This is almost entirely attributable to the use of behavioural economics which has, in particular, underpinned the CMA's flagship market investigations into *Energy* and *Retail Banking*.[120] The focus of attention on consumer policy issues is even greater in terms of the size of the markets: these two investigations alone concerned markets collectively worth more than £44 billion in revenues, making up more than half the total value (by revenues) of the markets investigated between 2010 and 2020.

This focus and, more specifically, the inclusion of behavioural economics is in keeping with the broad scope of the market investigation regime. The focus over the last five years to the near exclusion of other policy issues does, however, mark a shift from the legislative expectations in 2002. The inclusion of behavioural economics meanwhile is entirely novel. When the EA 2002 introduced the market investigation regime, its Explanatory Notes specifically cited parallel conduct in the context of a non-collusive oligopoly as the example of the sort of market failures that the market investigation regime was intended to pursue.[121] Consumer behaviour was only mentioned insofar as consumers (as well as suppliers) may suffer from information asymmetries.[122] Consumers' behavioural biases did not feature.

While the insights of behavioural economics have enriched our understanding of how consumers and, in turn, markets work, their use raises three substantive issues which we address after a brief summary of the role of behavioural economics in market investigations.[123]

5.1   The Role of Behavioural Economics in Market Investigations

While behavioural economics emerged as part of mainstream economic theory some time ago, UK competition regulators first began incorporating behavioural analysis from the late 2000s in tandem with a wider upsurge in interest from the UK government.[124] Indeed, the UK's so-called Nudge Unit has been an international leader in the use of behavioural economics by governments. The OFT published an influential paper on the role of behavioural economics in competition policy in 2010 and behavioural economics had become sufficiently embedded in competition policy to merit inclusion in the Competition Commission's revised *Market Investigation Guidelines (2013)*.[125] The UK government also fostered the drive towards greater use of behavioural economics with the government's first

European Competition Journal 1; Pete Lunn, *Regulatory Policy and Behavioural Economics* (OECD Publishing 2014) 30 ff.

[119]   Ahlborn and Piccinin (n 1) 196.
[120]   Bruce Lyons, Nicola Mazzarotto, 'Behavioural Economics in Competition Policy Enforcement for Financial Product Markets' (2018) 14 Competition Law Journal 141.
[121]   Explanatory Note (n 9) para 292.
[122]   ibid.
[123]   Walker (n 119); Stucke (n 135 below).
[124]   Littlechild (n 89), also shown by the set-up of the Behavioural Insights Team, the so-called *nudge unit* in 2010 which was part of the UK's government until it became a social purpose limited company in 2014. The FSA (as it then was) and OFGEM were the first regulators to use or refer to behavioural concepts in 2008; see also Walker (n 119).
[125]   OFT, 'What Does Behavioural Economics Mean for Competition Policy?' OFT1224, March 2010 CC3 (n 16) paras 271 ff.

strategic steer in 2015 calling on the CMA to look at 'consumer behaviour' when assessing the functioning of markets.[126]

What is meant by behavioural economics?

Behavioural economics starts from the premise that consumers' behaviour does not conform to that of a *homo economicus* (i.e. a rational agent). As Daniel Kahneman, the Nobel Prize winning economist, summed up: 'Rationality is logical coherence—reasonable or not. Econs are rational by this definition but there is overwhelming evidence that Humans cannot be.'[127] Individuals instead exhibit certain behavioural patterns that are sufficiently consistent across society that they are not cancelled out on an aggregated basis.[128]

This runs counter to the assumption underpinning classical economic theory (including much of antitrust economics) that market actors act rationally. However, the fact that markets did not always behave 'rationally' had long been shown.[129] As Lord Currie observed, the key practical insight from behavioural economics is that 'consumers are not just not neoclassically rational, *but that they are predictably so*'.[130] The ability to link shortcomings in market performance to certain types of consumer behaviour is what is required for the CMA to identify market failures which have an adverse effect on competition. Absent this ability, any interest in behavioural economics would be a largely academic question.

To this end, the revised 2013 *Market Investigation Guidelines* incorporated behavioural biases as a cause of 'poor consumer response' (i.e. demand-side consumer policy issues that could be addressed under the market investigation regime). The Guidelines identify four broad types of consumer bias within which there are a range of different specific biases:

(i) processing power biases: where customers struggle to make the correct choice due to inability to process all of the relevant information (also known as bounded rationality biases);

(ii) framing biases: where customers' choices are skewed by how the relevant choices are presented;

(iii) time inconsistency biases: where customers' choices are skewed by errors on calculating their relative needs now and in the future; and

(iv) loss aversion biases: where consumers typically value something more once they have owned it than before they own it.

These types of bias have, in one guise or another, underpinned 'features' which the CMA has identified as giving rise to poor consumer response.

---

[126] Department for Business, Energy & Industrial Strategy, *The Government's Strategic Steer to the Competition and Markets Authority* (July 2019) https://assets.publishing.service.govuk/government/uploads/system/uploads/attachment_data/file/481040/BIS-15-659-government-response-governments-strategic-steer-to-the-competition-and-markets-authority.pdf accessed 30 June 2020.

[127] Daniel Kahneman, *Thinking, Fast and Slow* (Penguin 2011) 410.

[128] Dan Ariely, *Predictably Irrational: The Hidden Forces that Shape Our Decisions* (Harper Collins 2008).

[129] See eg Andrew Lo, *Adaptive Markets: Financial Evolution at the Speed of Thought* (Princeton University Press 2017) 75 ff.

[130] David Currie (CMA Chairman), 'Homo economicus and Homo sapiens: The CMA experience of behavioural economics' Speech at a New Zealand Commerce Commission public lecture (21 April 2015) (emphasis added) https://www.govuk/government/speeches/david-currie-speaks-about-the-cma-experience-of-behavioural-economics accessed 30 June 2020.

5.2 The Tension between Competition Policy and Consumer Policy

The first issue is that the use of behavioural economics over the last five years has revealed a tension between the promotion of competition policy and consumer policy within the market investigation regime. At its simplest level, this tension occurs because the object-ives of competition policy and consumer policy sometimes conflict. Competition policy seeks to ensure competitive markets whereas consumer policy seeks to protect the interests of consumers.[131] These two objectives are frequently symbiotic: competition policy seeks, after all, to promote consumer welfare. However, this is not always the case.

Promoting competitive markets does not, in the first instance, necessarily serve (all) con-sumers' interests. The CMA's Chief Economist observed, for example, that the UK energy market was highly competitive from a conventional competition perspective but delivered sub-optimal market outcomes due to behavioural issues: 'engaged' customers benefitted from intense competition; but 'unengaged' customers did not.[132] More competition can in-deed exacerbate some behavioural issues rather than solve them.[133] Ezrachi and Stucke have recently coined the term 'choice overload' for scenarios where consumers make economic-ally poor choices due to facing too many options.[134] In this scenario consumer policy may thus be best served by *less* competition or, at the very least, a different sort of competition.[135]

Addressing behavioural issues and promoting consumer policy can likewise run counter to promoting competitive markets. The premise of the market mechanism is that firms are incentivized to compete for customers and customers are incentivized to identify firms' of-fering the best products. Engineering a 'competitive' outcome for all customers undermines the incentives for one side of the market—consumers—to drive competition. Furthermore, solutions to some behavioural concerns may even disadvantage 'engaged' customers to the benefit of 'unengaged' customers. For example, reducing choice may drive better outcomes for unengaged customers but is potentially detrimental for 'engaged' customers.[136]

The practical consequence of the tension is that the market investigation regime is a cockpit for highly-political trade-offs between different policy objectives. In the first in-stance, the CMA has to balance the preservation of free markets versus the benefits of regulation. Put bluntly, the CMA has to answer the question of how far people should be protected from themselves. The CMA may also have to make an even more politicized trade-off between the interests of different customer groups where, for example, 'engaged' consumers may stand to lose out from intervention on behavioural grounds to the benefit of 'unengaged' consumers. This can be done on a utilitarian basis. However, what if one group

---

[131] OECD, 'The Interface between Competition and Consumer Policies' *Policy Roundtables* (5 June 2008).

[132] Walker (n 119).

[133] OFT, *Consumer behavioural biases in competition—Final Report* (May 2011) para 1.11.

[134] Barry Schwartz, *The Paradox of Choice: Why More Is Less*' (Harper Perennial 2004); Maurice E Stucke, Ariel Ezrachi, 'The Curious Case of Competition and Quality' (2015) 3(2) Journal of Antitrust Enforcement 227; Adi Ayal, 'Harmful Freedom of Choice: Lessons from the Cellphone Market' (2011) 74 Law and Contemporary Problems 91; Judith Mehta, Robert Sugden, 'Making Sense of Complex Choice Situations' in Behavioural Economics in Competition and Consumer Policy (2013) ESRC University of East Anglia http://competitionpolicy. ac.uk/documents/8158338/8193541/CCP+economics+book+Final+digital+version+-+colour.pdf/30214557-cace-4b0b-8aac-a801bbde87bc accessed 30 June 2020.

[135] Benjamin Scheibehenne, Rainer Greifeneder, and Peter M Todd, 'Can There Ever Be Too Many Options? A Meta-analytic Review of Choice Overload' (2010) 37 Journal of Consumer Research 409; Maurice E Stucke, 'Is Choice Always Good?' (2013) 1(1) Journal of Antitrust Enforcement 162.

[136] Walker (n 119).

of consumers is disproportionately poorer than the other: should the CMA give greater weight to protecting those less well-off? The CMA's Chief Economist has suggested that this may be the case, stating that the CMA 'might have to go ... towards a "harder" paternalism'.[137] The market investigation regime thus assumes a significantly more political complexion than conventional competition policy on its own. The CMA's proposals for reform of the market investigation would further embed this into the regime (see section 8 on *Future Developments* below).

This poses two difficulties which the CMA must address. First, the CMA is not necessarily equipped to make such choices. While competition policy also involves trade-offs between different parameters of competition (e.g. price and non-price competition; allocative and dynamic efficiencies), these trade-offs occur within an established utilitarian framework based on consumer welfare. In contrast, the combination of competition and consumer policy in the market investigation regime requires the CMA to mediate between a wider range of trade-offs which encompass issues of both efficiency and equity. Weighing up the balance between the role of the market and regulation and mediating between the different interests of groups within society is normally the role of legislators. The CMA is, however, ill-equipped to make value judgements on the organization of society. As the Competition Commission found in *Groceries*, it was not for the market investigation regime to address 'broader public policy issues' raised during the investigation, such as 'social cohesion' and the 'environmental impact of the groceries supply chain', which are the responsibility of the 'relevant government agencies or departments'.[138] Secondly, even if the CMA were well-equipped, there is a tension between being an ostensibly apolitical body which nevertheless ends up—inadvertently or otherwise—making political decisions. Whereas legislators are answerable to the electorate for their decisions, the CMA has no direct accountability.

5.3 Behavioural Economics and the Dangers of Reimagining Markets

The second issue is the potential complexity of remedies needed to address behavioural issues and the consequential risk of underestimating the adverse effects of intervention. As the CMA's Chief Economist wryly observed shortly after the *Energy* and *Retail Banking* market investigations: 'One of the things that we have certainly learnt is that remedies that are obviously the sensible solution to the relevant competition problem do not always work.'[139] The potential complexity of behavioural remedies stems from fact that behavioural issues are often not 'competition' problems per se but regulatory problems. While behavioural biases can lead to an 'adverse effect on competition' (i.e. a negative effect on consumer welfare), behavioural 'problems' are not directly or indirectly caused by the market power of the firms in the market. Instead, the problems stemming from behavioural biases are not exacerbated by 'more' or 'less' competition but by *how* competition takes place. Problems driven by behavioural biases are thus often a problem of wider market failure rather than a

---

[137] ibid.
[138] Competition Commission, *Groceries—Final Report* (30 April 2008), para 9 https://webarchive.nationalarchives.govuk/20140402235418/http://www.competition-commission.org.uk/assets/competitioncommission/docs/pdf/non-inquiry/rep_pub/reports/2008/fulltext/538.pdf accessed 27 July 2020.
[139] ibid.

problem of competition (i.e. something which the competitive process cannot solve). This has two implications. In the first instance, the broader scope of potential concerns beyond a failure of 'competition' necessitates a wider universe of remedies. In the second instance, the solutions must often dictate *how* markets function—or impose alternatives if the market is deemed incapable of delivering the desired outcomes—rather than simply facilitating an increase in competition.

This complexity poses practical difficulties. Such difficulties are, to some degree, inherent to behavioural concerns. The more complex trade-offs often involved in behavioural concerns translate, in turn, into more complicated trade-offs for determining effective remedies. This is not always true: competition concerns around defaults may, for example, be addressed with behavioural commitments mandating choice. Such concerns are, however, pertinent where remedies seek to re-engineer significantly the 'how' of the competitive process. The more intrusive the remedy the more likely it will be to have unintended and negative consequences. The unintended consequences of complex remedies are well illustrated in *Energy* where the CMA found that Ofgem's imposition of simplified tariff structures—introduced as a behavioural measure to stop energy companies 'confusing' customers—had in fact reduced competition.[140]

The lesson is accordingly that more complex behavioural remedies merit careful consideration and caution. But while the CMA has previously favoured more limited behavioural remedies in the past, the *Energy, Retail Banking* and *Investment Consultancy* market investigations display a greater willingness to intervene with remedies designed to alter the competitive process. In *Investment Consultancy*, for example, the CMA imposed a duty on pension trustees (the customers) to switch to a tender model for fiduciary management contracts of a certain size.[141] Furthermore, in *Energy*, the CMA concluded that the market was incapable—at least in the short term—of delivering a sufficiently optimal outcome, and imposed a temporary price cap on the pre-paid part of the market.

5.4 Appropriate Scope of Behavioural Economics

The third issue is the application of the principles of behavioural economics to intermediate markets where the 'consumers' are firms rather than individuals. This occurred in *Investment Consultants* which focused on an intermediate market where the consumers were corporate pension trustees.

On the one hand, this raises a mechanical question of the theoretical and empirical basis for applying behavioural economics on intermediate markets. The work underpinning the use of behavioural economics in competition policy is primarily focused on the 'predictable irrationality' of individuals.[142] The use of behavioural economics has thus been principally used in markets facing end-consumers. This is also intuitive. As Kahneman observes: '[organisations] are better than individuals when it comes to avoiding errors, because they naturally think more slowly and have the power to impose orderly procedures.'[143]

---

[140] CMA, *Energy* (n 73).
[141] *Investment Consultancy Services* (n 104) 20.
[142] Kahneman (n 128) 417.
[143] ibid.

More fundamentally, its use in intermediate markets raises a profound question on the purpose of competition policy. The basic premise of markets and competition policy is that the process of rivalry between firms seeking to win customers' business creates incentives for firms to meet customers' current and future needs as efficiently as possible. As Fatas and Lyons put it succinctly: 'firms failing to identify their best option will be less successful ... and replaced by those that do.'[144] The market mechanism thus addresses behavioural biases by favouring firms that are successful at overcoming any potential putative biases. By intervening to address demand-side issues in intermediate markets, the market investigation regime calls this fundamental principle into question.

Furthermore, assuming that behavioural economics does have a role to play in intermediate markets, a practical concern is where the line should be drawn.[145] Put differently, do all firms exhibit behavioural biases or only some, and for those that do, which deserve protection? Equally, are firms 'behavioural' in all or only some of their activities? The CMA's *Investment Consultants* market investigation analysed the decision-making of pension trustees who are decision-makers for pension schemes but are often unpaid lay people. This is perhaps a grey zone. However, the same logic arguably applies to the distinction between SMEs and large companies: the former suffer from a range of constraints that may make them less equipped to overcome potential behavioural issues, whereas large companies have greater resources to overcome behavioural biases. In short, where do behavioural biases stop and conventional competition rules begin?

6 Market Investigations and the Rule of Law

A question also arises whether the breadth of the market investigation regime as applied by the CMA over the last decade complies with the principles of the rule of law. This question can be seen through the prisms of both fundamental rights and economic efficiency.

Questions concerning the market investigation regime and the rule of law are not novel. Dunne has previously raised questions around the regime's legitimacy and compliance with the rule of law.[146] Unpicking the concept, there are two broad principles that are particularly pertinent for the regime. First, the law must be accessible and, insofar as possible, intelligible, clear and predictable. As the ECHR stipulated in *Sunday Times*, 'a norm cannot be regarded as 'law' unless it is formulated with sufficient precision to enable the citizen to regulate his conduct'.[147] Secondly, questions of legal right and liability should ordinarily be resolved by application of the law and not the exercise of discretion. This is not absolute but requires that 'no discretion should be unconstrained so as to be potentially arbitrary. No discretion may be legally unfettered'.[148] Lord Mance distilled these two principles as the 'idea of certainty' in a 2011 lecture.[149]

---

[144] Enrique Fatas, Bruce Lyons, 'Behavioural Economics in Competition and Consumer Policy' in ESRC CCP, *Behavioural Economics* in *Competition and Consumer Policy* at 29, 32 http://competitionpolicy. ac.uk/documents/8158338/8193541/CCP+economics+book+Final+digital+version+-+colour.pdf/ 30214557-cace-4b0b-8aac-a801bbde87bc.

[145] See eg Mark Armstrong and Steffen Huck, 'Behavioral Economics as Applied to Firms: A Primer' CESifo Working Paper Series No 2937 (February 2010) on the applicability of behavioural economics to firms.

[146] Dunne (n 85).

[147] *Sunday Times v United Kingdom* (1979) 2 EHRR 245, 271, para 49.

[148] Tom Bingham, *The Rule of Law* (Penguin 2011) 56.

[149] Lord Mance, '*Should the Law Be Certain?*' The Oxford Shrieval Lecture, Oxford (11 October 2011) https:// www.supremecourt.uk/docs/speech_111011.pdf accessed 30 June 2020.

The need for 'certainty' is, furthermore, also a question of economic efficiency.[150] As Lord Mance recognized, in addition to being a legal principle protected by the European Convention of Human Rights, the rule of law is a public good and, accordingly, undermining it has deleterious economic consequences.[151] Put concretely, firms' and investors' incentives to develop new products and invest are reduced in jurisdictions where the rule of law is weaker as their return on investment is less predictable.[152] This is of course akin to the debate concerning over—and under—enforcement of competition law.

Yet while competition law and the market investigation regime are inherently complex, the latter is still remarkable in the breadth of its powers. And two aspects of the regime over the last decade—taken together—call into question whether it achieves the correct balance between ensuring effective competition and protecting the rule of law.

6.1 Conventional Competition Issues and Regulatory Arbitrage

The first aspect has been the blurring of the line between the subject matter of market investigations and the CMA's competition powers under Chapter I and Chapter II CA 1998. As outlined above, the CMA's guidelines provide that the CMA should only make a market investigation reference in relation to conventional competition issues where the market investigation regime is the more appropriate regulatory instrument. However, in *Private Motor Insurance*, the CMA used the market investigation regime to address 'wide' MFNs which other European regulators and, indeed, subsequently the CMA itself, addressed under conventional competition instruments.[153]

The *Private Motor Insurance* market investigation assessed a range of issues including the use of so-called 'wide' MFN provisions in contracts between private motor insurers and price comparison websites gave rise to adverse effects on competition. As MFNs were not the focus of the market study underpinning the market investigation reference, the CMA did not address whether a market investigation reference would be appropriate in light of its CA 1998 powers. However, once MFNs had become a key theory of harm by the time of the CMA's provisional findings, the CMA still did not question the appropriateness.[154] The issue came to a head as the parties under investigation contended that any remedies would breach the EU law principle that national competition law could not prohibit agreements which complied with Article 101 TFEU on competition grounds. The CMA then tied itself in knots to justify why wide MFNs were not in principle eligible under the EU's Vertical Block Exemption Regulation (VBER).[155]

The CMA's use of the market investigation regime to address wide MFNs was in sharp contrast to other European regulators and subsequently its own approach. The French, German, Italian, and Swedish competition authorities all addressed the use of wide MFNs

---

[150] ibid.

[151] As the historian E P Thompson wrote in an essay accompanying *Whigs and Hunters: The Origin of the Black Act* (Allen Lane 1975), calling the rule of law 'an unqualified human good'.

[152] United Nations Global Compact, '*Business for the Rule of Law Framework*' United Nations (June 2015).

[153] CC, *Private Motor Insurance market investigation—Provisional findings report* (17 December 2013); the European Commission coordinated investigations in the online hotel booking sector by the French, Swedish, and Italian competition authorities (15 December 2014).

[154] ibid paras 9.1 ff.

[155] ibid.

in similar contexts under Articles 101 and 102 TFEU (and recognized in principle that wide MFNs stood to benefit from the VBER).[156] Even more pertinently, the CMA subsequently took a different approach in its *Digital Comparison Tools* market study.[157] The market study's subject matter included the use of wide and narrow MFNs in multiple markets where digital comparison tools are used. The CMA concluded, however, that a market investigation was not needed to address MFNs because the provisions could be tackled under the CMA's existing powers.[158]

It is thus hard to reconcile *Private Motor Insurance* with the CMA's position that market investigations should only be used where the Competition Act would be ineffective. Leaving the procedural issue aside, it challenges the 'certainty' of the market investigation regime.[159] In the first instance, the standard for intervening under the market investigation regime is lower. There is no need to demonstrate, in particular, an anti-competitive agreement or, in the case of Chapter II CA 1998, significant market power. Firms are thus faced with two different 'competition' standards for the same conduct whereby compliance with competition law per se is not necessarily sufficient. By the same token, the CMA has an incentive to favour market investigation references over action under the CA 1998 given the lower legal standard. An incentive exacerbated by the lower standard of review for market investigations (judicial review) than for CA 1998 cases (full merits review). While *Private Motor Insurance* may be the exception that proves the rule, the CMA should remain vigilant against blurring its market investigation and Competition Act powers.

6.2 Insufficiently Weak Judicial Oversight?

The second aspect is whether the breadth of the market investigation regime is compatible with the relatively weak judicial oversight which, in relation to challenges on substance, requires that CMA's decision to be irrational or unlawful.[160]

The standard of judicial review is not a novel feature of the market investigation regime and is also common to the UK's merger control regime. However, the most striking features of the challenges to the market investigation regime over the last decade are the CMA's success record and the lack of head-on challenges to the CMA's substantive findings. In *Aggregates*, for example, none of the firms challenged the Competition Commission's finding of adverse effects on competition despite the imposition of significant structural remedies on two firms. BAA likewise did not challenge the substance of the Competition Commission's findings which mandated the break-up its airport franchise, contesting only whether the report was vitiated by apparent bias and the proportionality of the timeframe for implementation of the remedies.[161] *Private Healthcare* marked the sole successful

---

[156] Will Leslie, 'Online Booking Platforms, MFNs and the Vertical Block Exemption: the Need for Certainty' (2018) 39(7) ECLR 330.

[157] CMA, *Digital Comparison Tools* (n 56).

[158] CMA, *Digital Comparison Tools Market Study—Update Paper* https://assets.publishing.service.govuk/media/58da7afce5274a06b000003c/dct-update-paper.pdf accessed 30 June 2020.

[159] The case also exposes a lacuna in the market investigation regime. While the CMA considers the appropriateness of referrals at the time of the reference, the market investigation is not limited to the features identified as potentially problematic.

[160] Case 1229/6/12/14 *AXA PPP Healthcare Limited v CMA* (n 82) para 43.

[161] Case 1110/6/8/09 *BAA Limited v CC* (n 78) para 6 ff.

substantive challenge but this stemmed from a manifest factual error in the CMA's assessment rather than a challenge to the CMA's substantive reasoning.[162]

This is, however, unsurprising given the legal standard. As the CAT succinctly summarized in *AXA v CMA*:

> We are dealing with a challenge by way of a statutory form of judicial review, not with an appeal on the merits. *A review court or tribunal will be slow to find that an evaluative judgment of the nature in issue here, made by an expert regulatory body after careful assessment of the relevant evidence, as here, was irrational or unlawful.*[163]

The judicial review standard, in short, militates against substantive challenges—given the burden of demonstrating manifest error—and incentivizes challenges to the CMA's 'process' for decision-making and the proportionality of any remedies imposed. The consequence is, however, that the market investigation regime is comprised of a triad of features which limit legal certainty: the breadth of the regime, the CMA's discretion to determine the markets to investigate and limited judicial oversight. The comparison with the UK's merger control regime exposes the lack of balance. While both regimes share the judicial review standard for challenges to the CMA's decisions, the UK merger control regime has, in contrast, a precise scope and limited CMA discretion: first, there must be a precisely defined positive act—a notifiable transaction—and, second, the CMA may only investigate where the notifiable transaction satisfies the jurisdictional turnover or share of supply tests.[164]

While the CMA's self-restraint in applying the market investigation regime managed the inherent tension between the powers conferred and the rule of law, the CMA's interventionist approach over the last decade raises a question mark over whether the settlement is sustainable in the longer term.

7 Other Policy Issues

Beyond the issues raised in relation to the CMA's competition and consumer policy cases, the last ten years have seen a number of cross-cutting issues that have shed more light on the regime as a whole.

7.1 Territorial Limitations

Of these, the territorial limitations of the market investigation regime and what this means for the CMA's selection of market investigations is increasingly coming to the fore. Given that firms and markets increasingly do not respect borders, a key facet of competition instruments is whether they empower competition authorities to impose remedies with

---

[162] Case 1228/6/12/14 *HCA International Limited v CMA* (n 68) para 13.
[163] Case 1229/6/12/14 *AXA PPP Healthcare Limited v CMA* (n 82) para 43 (emphasis added).
[164] On mergers see ch 7 below.

extraterritorial effect.[165] As with conventional competition enforcement, a market investigation is most likely to involve remedies with extraterritorial effects where:

1) The relevant market is UK-wide (or narrower) but one or more of the supply-side firms is exporting the goods or services into the UK.
2) The relevant market is wider than the UK (i.e. the supply-side firms are providing the relevant goods or services on a wider than UK basis).

However, remedies for such markets do not axiomatically result in extraterritorial effects: this depends on the nature of the remedies and of the market in question. Structural remedies, for example, are more likely to have extraterritorial effects given they often require the divestment of business units that have pan-national operations. Conversely, while behavioural remedies are less likely to have extraterritorial effects (as they can be limited to business conducted in the UK), the practical effects depend on the firm's business model; where firms provide products or services on a pan-national or even global basis—as is the case in the online world—adjustments for ostensibly national remedies can be impractical.

Consistent with the UK conventional competition policy instruments, the market investigation regime has, in principle, extraterritorial effect: there is no restriction on the CMA imposing remedies on firms domiciled outside of the UK or, indeed, remedies which have potential effects outside of the UK (provided that they address the adverse effects in the UK).[166] There are, however, legal and practical limits on the CMA's powers. Remedies must be *'reasonable'* and practical overreach runs the risk of firms treating the UK as a 'special case'. The CMA's guidance on the criteria for launching a market investigation takes this into account, providing that a market investigation is unlikely to be justified in the context of markets broader than the UK where: 'any remedy for the UK (which would be all that was available under the Act) would have no discernible impact on the way the market operated even in the UK'.[167] The subtleties of the territorial reach of the market investigation regime did not pose issues in the first six years given the 'domestic' flavour of the Competition Commission's investigations. This has changed. In particular, the CMA's *Statutory Auditing Study*, *Online Platforms and Digital Advertising Study*, and *Statutory Auditing Market Investigation* have given insight into how the CMA manages the legal and practical limitations of the regime.

On the one hand the CMA has recognized the limitations of the regime addressing global firms and global markets. In the 2019 *Statutory Audit* market study the CMA assessed the appropriateness of breaking up the big auditing firms (i.e. a structural remedy). The CMA concluded, however, that this was only practicable if the split created 'two international networks in each instance, i.e. *the remedy could only work if applied internationally*'.[168] The CMA went further in its *Online Platforms and Digital Advertising Study*, concluding in its interim report that a market investigation reference was not appropriate given that the potential structural and behavioural remedies were not practicable in light of the global nature

---

[165] OECD, 'Roundtable on the Extraterritorial Reach of Competition Remedies' (20 November 2017) https://one.oecd.org/document/DAF/COMP/WP3(2017)4/en/pdf accessed 30 June 2020.
[166] Enterprise and Regulatory Reform Act 2013, s 25(3).
[167] OFT511 (n 22) para 2.30.
[168] CMA, *Statutory audit services* (n 97) para 8.8 (emphasis added).

of the businesses. The CMA observed that it needed 'to be pragmatic about what changes could efficiently be pursued unilaterally by the UK'.[169] On the other hand, the CMA has also recognized the opportunity to use market investigations as an instrument for standard setting. When deciding to make a market investigation for *Statutory Audit* in 2013, the OFT rebutted the challenge that a market investigation would 'interfere' with the parallel development of EU legislation on the grounds that the market investigation could 'assist' with the consideration of proportionate and appropriate remedies across the EU.[170] In other words, the Competition Commission's proposals could act as 'standard setting' for the EU as a whole.

The CMA, and the OFT and Competition Commission before it, thus adopted a sensibly pragmatic approach. The territorial limitations do, however, have practical ramifications for those markets which the CMA can most usefully pursue. These may be increasingly at odds with the UK government's expectations. The CMA's most recent strategic steer singles out digital markets as a focus.[171] Given that digital markets are frequently those which have global scope, the CMA may increasingly become confronted with the territorial limitations of the market investigation regime.

7.2 Back to the Future: The Introduction of a Public Interest Test

A further issue is the curious expansion of the public interest reference under the ERRA 2013. While no public interest reference, restricted or full, has been made since its introduction in 2014, its introduction exposes a facet of legislative thinking around the market investigation regime and the role of the CMA.[172]

The use of a public interest test is not new.[173] Prior to the introduction of the Enterprise Act 2002, the UK's merger control regime applied an entirely 'public interest' test under the Fair Trading Act 1973.[174] The explanatory notes to the ERRA 2013 state that the revisions bring the test into line with the public interest test contained in the UK's merger control regime.[175] Furthermore, the circumstances in which the public interest test is relevant remains narrow: public interest considerations can only be taken into account where there is also an AEC. As such, the ERRA did not create an autonomous instrument for intervening in markets on solely public interest grounds.

Yet, leaving the logic of ensuring consistency and its limited role aside, the question of 'why' the market investigation regime needs a public interest component still remains. The effect of the ERRA 2013 reform is to reinstitute the CMA's role in assessing public interest issues alongside its competition functions. When the EA 2002 was introduced, one of the

---

[169] CMA, *Online Platforms And Digital Advertising—Interim Report* (18 December 2019), para 91.

[170] OFT, *Supply of Statutory Audit Services for Large Companies—Terms of reference* (October 2011) https://assets.publishing.service.govuk/media/532ad1f8ed915d0e60000307/oft1357MIR.pdf accessed 30 June 2020.

[171] Department for Business, Energy & Industrial Strategy (n 141).

[172] On the broader issues of the lack of democratic legitimacy and the independence of competition authorities in the context of enforcing broader policy objectives see e.g. John Davies, 'Means and Ends in Competition Law Enforcement' in Nicholas Charbit and Sonia Ahmad (eds), Liber Amicorum Frédéric Jenny, Vol I (Concurrences 2019) 217–19.

[173] Stephen Wilks, *'In the public interest: In the Competition Policy and the Monopolies and Mergers Commission* (Manchester University Press 1999).

[174] Fair Trading Act 1973, s 84.

[175] Explanatory Notes (n 9) para 264.

'advantages' of the new regime encapsulated by the CA 1998 and the EA 2002 administered by the OFT and the Competition Commission was that it focused solely on competition matters. The narrower focus on competition issues also facilitated the conferral of enhanced remedial powers under the regime. So, while the expansion of the CMA's 'public interest' function may be largely academic, it challenges the theological settlement of competition policy.

8 Future Developments

Finally, the market investigation regime continues to evolve. Given the current circumstances, it would be bold to make predictions on its future scope and use. That said, while there is no proposed legislation altering the regime, there is a range of proposals for reform which would have a significant bearing on the scope of the regime. The most eye catching are contained in a letter from the former Chairman of the CMA to the Secretary of State at the beginning of 2019.[176] While the letter contains proposals for reforming the entire UK competition regime, it contains a specific set of proposals for reform of market investigations, notably:

(i)   replacing the need to show 'adverse effects on competition' with 'consumer detriment' as threshold for intervention;

(ii)   reinforcing 'interim measures' so that CMA can take action during the market study phase;

(iii)   introducing an ability to accept undertakings in lieu of a reference at any stage; and

(iv)   conferral of fining powers on the CMA to sanction firms for failing to comply with remedies.

While the latter three proposals are primarily procedural measures designed to 'speed up' the administrative process, the first proposal has understandably garnered significant attention as a significant expansion of the regime's scope. This is in some ways surprising: the CMA's use of behavioural economics in the last five years has already pushed the boundaries of the regime with interventions focused on consumer policy issues that have only a limited link to the process of competition. As such, the reform would arguably be incremental with the CMA having already blurred the line between 'AEC' and 'consumer detriment' as the substantive test for intervention. Yet the reform would formally remove the boundaries of the regime and empower the CMA to intervene to address *any* concerns which cause consumer harm. Given that almost any regulatory weakness can be framed as harming consumer welfare, the boundary between the CMA and legislators in relation to economic policy would be significantly reduced with the main difference being the 'remedies' available. This, in turn, would force the CMA to make a greater range of trade-offs between different policy objectives and consumer groups with the concomitant problems outlined in section 5 above. So, while it remains to be seen whether the UK government will take all,

---

[176] Tyrie (n 4).

some or none of these proposals forward, the direction of travel indicates that, if anything, the substantive issues over the breadth of the regime are likely to increase.

9 Conclusions

The market investigation regime remains a highly flexible policy instrument. The last decade has served to reinforce its scope: the ERRA 2013 put the regime's procedural frame-work on a firmer statutory footing while the CAT's and the Court of Appeal's judgments largely upheld the CMA's findings.

The economic and political context has, however, changed. The NAO's 2010 report criti-cizing the regime, in particular, the sectoral regulators' reticence to make market references marked a watershed. Following 2010, two of the CMA's largest market investigations—*Energy* and *Retail Banking* stemmed from references by sectoral regulators. The regula-tory pendulum also undoubtedly swung towards greater intervention during the period with the CMA willing to contemplate far greater levels of intervention. The consequence is that the CMA has exercised less self-restraint in the last decade. Furthermore, rather than employing it sparingly as a policy tool, the CMA has used the regime to address all manner of alleged sins. In so doing, firms, consumers and practitioners have been left wondering what the regime is intended to tackle, apart from 'everything'. That said, the CMA's initi-ation of market investigations has dropped off since 2014 with nine references between January 2010—December 2014 but only two references in the period until December 2019. Whether this indicates a change of heart or merely a regulatory pause is unclear.

In short, the market investigation regime does indeed provide the CMA with 'extraor-dinary' powers but it remains to be seen whether the CMA has decided what it wants to do and how often it wants to use them.

7

UK Merger Control

Finely Tailored but Time for a New Suit?

David Reader

1 Introduction

The UK merger control regime under the Enterprise Act 2002 (EA 2002) has attracted wide praise for the transparency and predictability it affords stakeholders through its robust competition-based assessment of mergers, carried out by a specialist independent competition authority. This stands in stark contrast to the framework that preceded it under the Fair Trading Act 1973, which prescribed a broad public interest test that, in the hands of a ministerial decision-maker, returned opaque and inconsistent outcomes across numerous cases.[1] Further legislative and procedural refinements over the past two decades have also afforded enhanced powers to the competition authority and delivered a more streamlined assessment process for merging parties.

The regime is not without its quirks and controversies, however. The UK's continued use of a voluntary notification system is an increasingly rare sight among mainstream merger control frameworks,[2] and while it is ostensibly business-friendly, the enforcement powers that reinforce it are anything but. A limited role also endures for politicians to have the final say on mergers raising specific public interest concerns which, although invoked sparingly, has still produced decisions that have brought the integrity of the UK's competition-based approach into question and aroused suspicion of political bias. And with increasing regularity, cases involving foreign bidders for UK companies have captured the interest of the wider British public and renewed the debate on what some suggest is an overly permissive approach to foreign takeovers under the EA 2002.[3]

The UK's socio-political climate is now far-removed from anything feasibly envisaged by the drafters of the EA 2002 regime, and immediate challenges now present themselves in the form of Brexit, the broader rise of nationalist sentiment, and mergers in digital markets. While trite to suggest that the UK regime once again finds itself at a 'fork in the road' (in terms of whether or not to persevere with its voluntary notification system),[4] or a 'crossroads' (regarding how it confronts the inevitable increase in cases after Brexit),[5] the signs

---

[1] Stephen Wilks, *In the Public Interest: Competition Policy and the Monopolies and Mergers Commission* (MUP 1999) 226–27.

[2] Only three countries within the OECD currently utilize a voluntary regime, following Chile's move to a full mandatory system in 2017; OECD, 'Local Nexus and Jurisdictional Thresholds in Merger Control' (Background paper by the Secretariat, 10 March 2016) 9.

[3] Lord Michael Heseltine, *No Stone Unturned: In Pursuit of Growth* (Independent Report, BIS 2012) para 5.106.

[4] Peter Freeman, 'UK Merger Control: Where Do We Stand?' (2010) 9(1) Comp Law 26, 26.

[5] Nigel Parr and Catherine Hammon, 'UK Merger Control at a Crossroads' (2017) 16(1) Comp Law 13.

David Reader, *UK Merger Control* In: *The UK Competition Regime*. Edited by: Barry Rodger, Peter Whelan, and Angus MacCulloch, Oxford University Press. © The Contributors 2021. DOI: 10.1093/oso/9780198868026.003.0007

point towards a proverbial 'spaghetti junction' of options for responding to these emerging challenges.

This chapter reflects on the evolution and performance of UK merger control under the EA 2002 and contemplates its capacity to respond to contemporary challenges. Section 2 presents an initial primer for the discussion, remarking on the origins of the regime and its initial 'bedding down' period. Section 3 revisits the UK's main efforts to fine-tune the regime under the Enterprise and Regulatory Reform Act 2013 (ERRA 2013) and the 'missed opportunities' of this reform package. Section 4 takes an empirical glance at the trends and performance indicators of merger enforcement under the EA 2002, with a particular focus on the impact of the ERRA 2013 reform package. Section 5 explores the agenda for further reform and examines the merits of confronting new challenges with further refinement (tailored adjustments) or more revolutionary reform (a new suit). Section 6 offers concluding remarks and highlights the residual public interest regime and the UK's approach to digital mergers as solid candidates for more extensive reform.

2 Merger Control under the Enterprise Act 2002: A Primer

2.1 Removing Politicians and Reaffirming Competition

The present-day merger control framework under the EA 2002 is unrecognizable from the UK's initial regime, formalized under the Monopolies and Mergers Act 1965. This legislation introduced a broad public interest test by which to scrutinize mergers,[6] with an independent competition authority tasked with investigating the merger before making a recommendation to a government minister, the Secretary of State for Trade, who would then make a final decision on whether or not to permit the transaction. This arrangement of a broad public interest test and ministerial decision-making was to continue under the revised provisions of the Fair Trading Act 1973, albeit with some efforts made to assign widely-framed criteria to the public interest test.[7] The reason for maintaining a broad public interest test under the 1973 Act has been attributed to the government, at the time, attempting to give effect to a number of conflicting political discourses,[8] which—almost inevitably—resulted in a mergers regime that was opaque and unpredictable.[9]

A further change in political discourse, namely towards a neoliberal approach to merger control,[10] brought an end to the practical application of the broad public interest test in 1984, when the so-called 'Tebbit doctrine' confirmed that mergers in the UK were to be assessed purely on the basis of their effect on competition.[11] As of 20 June 2003, the essence of the Tebbit doctrine had been captured under the EA 2002, formally adopting an economic

---

[6] Monopolies and Mergers Act 1965, s 6(2)(ii).

[7] Fair Trading Act 1973, ss 84(1)(a)–(e).

[8] Hubert Buch-Hansen, 'The Political Economy of Regulatory Change: The Case of British Merger Control' (2012) 6(1) Regulation & Governance 101, 110.

[9] Andrew Scott, Morten Hviid, and Bruce Lyons, *Merger Control in the United Kingdom* (OUP 2006) 1.08.

[10] ibid 115.

[11] This policy change was announced by Norman Tebbit MP in the Commons; HC Deb 5 July 1984, vol 63, cols 213-14W. In practice, the enhanced focus on competition criterion meant the other public interest criteria were almost completely ignored by the competition authority; see eg Charlie Weir, 'The implementation of merger policy in the U.K. 1984–1990' (1993) 38 Antitrust Bull 943, 962; and Barry J Rodger, 'Reinforcing the Scottish "Ring-fence": A Critique of UK Mergers Policy vis-a-vis the Scottish Economy' (1996) 17(2) ECLR 104, 112.

test for merger review, the substantial lessening of competition (SLC) test,[12] which remains in place to this day. The Act also sought to depoliticize the assessment process—and thereby make decision-making more predictable to businesses[13]—by removing the vast majority of decision-making powers from the Secretary of State and reassigning them to two independent competition authorities, the Office of Fair Trading (OFT) and the Competition Commission (CC). These agencies operated as part of a two-phase merger review process, with the OFT performing an initial Phase 1 investigation and under a duty to refer any problematic mergers (i.e. those raising a realistic prospect of an SLC) to the CC for a further in-depth Phase 2 investigation.[14] Following its investigation, the CC would then publish a final Phase 2 decision on whether the case raised SLC concerns and, based on this, would exercise its powers to permit, prohibit or impose remedies on the merger. Moreover, the decisions of both the OFT and CC would—for the first time—be subject to judicial review before a specialist judicial body, the Competition Appeal Tribunal (CAT).

Supplementing these pro-business institutional reforms was the UK's renewal of a voluntary system of notification, meaning there would be no legal requirement for parties to notify their merger to the OFT and no penalty for completing a merger that had not been issued with a clearance decision. These features collectively aimed to facilitate a regime that avoided undue burden on businesses,[15] while also renewing efforts to pursue a strict competition-based approach under the EA 2002. The notable exception to this was the Act's retention of a residual power for the Secretary of State to intervene and assume the decision-making role in mergers that raise specific public interest concerns.[16] While 'national security' was the only public interest ground originally prescribed under the EA 2002, this has since been joined by further grounds relating to media plurality and the presentation of news (in 2003), stability of the UK financial system (in 2008), and public health emergencies (in 2020). A brief account of the early controversies of the public interest provisions is presented in section 2.2.3, below, but as an initial comment, their application has been limited, despite the headlines they so often attract.

2.2 The Initial 'Bedding Down' Period

2.2.1 Interpreting the OFT's 'Duty to Refer' to Phase 2

As with merging parties seeking to challenge a referral decision, the EA 2002 afforded interested third parties the legal recourse to apply to the CAT for a review of a case where the OFT decided to *not* make a referral to Phase 2.[17] Indeed, such third party actions proved a key catalyst in affording the courts an early opportunity to interpret the outer limits of the OFT's duty to refer. Most (in)famous was the *IBA Health* case, in which the CAT originally

---

[12] Specifically, the EA 2002 Act prohibits any merger that 'has resulted, or may be expected to result, in a substantial lessening of competition' within the relevant market; see eg EA 2002, ss 35(1)(b) and 36(1)(b), which express this wording in the context of Phase 2 investigations.

[13] Department of Trade and Industry, *A World Class Competition Regime* (White Paper, CM 5233, 2001) paras 5.4 and A4.4.

[14] Enterprise Act 2002, ss 22(1)(b) and 33(1)(b); applying to completed and anticipated mergers respectively.

[15] Freeman, 'UK Merger Control' (n 4) 27.

[16] EA 2002, s 42(2).

[17] A consequence of this has been the common practice of the Phase 1 decision-maker publishing decisions that seek to clarify its reasoning to all interested parties, rather than just the merging parties; Richard Whish and David Bailey, *Competition Law* (9th edn, OUP 2018) 936–937.

interpreted the OFT's duty to refer as a 'two-part test' where the OFT should only decide *not* to refer when: (i) it is satisfied that there is no expectation of an SLC arising from the merger, and (ii) it is satisfied that there is no credible possibility that the CC would reach a different conclusion.[18] This interpretation was overturned by the Court of the Appeal which, while accepting that the OFT had adopted too high a threshold, held that the referral duty was to be read according to its ordinary meaning under the EA 2002.[19] Nevertheless, a further third party action, in the case of *UniChem*,[20] saw the CAT overturn another non-referral decision on the basis that, *inter alia*, the OFT had not sought input from interested third parties. Collectively, these decisions have been said to establish a lower standard of proof for referral than had originally been anticipated by the OFT,[21] thereby increasing the likelihood of referrals, particularly in marginal cases.[22] The OFT itself expected to refer up to twice as many annual cases as a result of this case law,[23] but these predictions never materialized in practice (see section 4.3).

The updated *Merger Assessment Guidelines* of 2010 confirmed that—drawing on the Court of Appeal's judgment in *IBA Health*—the OFT was to apply a 'realistic prospect' threshold at Phase 1, compared to the CC, which would use a 'balance of probabilities' standard of proof at Phase 2.[24] The authorities articulated this lower 'realistic prospect' standard as a duty to refer when there is either: (i) a belief that the merger 'is more likely than not to result in an SLC', or (ii) a belief that the likelihood is 'greater than fanciful' but below 50 per cent.[25] While this second standard afforded the Phase 1 decision-maker 'a wide margin of appreciation in exercising its judgement',[26] the CAT's ruling in *Celesio* dismissed the notion that the Phase 1 decision-maker should *always* refer when the likelihood of an SLC is greater than fanciful.[27] The OFT's duty to refer was not absolute under the EA 2002, however, and merging parties whose transaction raised competition concerns could benefit from such 'get-outs' as qualifying for the *de minimis* exception, demonstrating countervailing customer benefits or, as discussed in section 3.2.3 below, agreeing to undertakings in lieu of a reference.[28]

2.2.2 The Concept of 'A Relevant Merger Situation'

Prior to the enactment of the EA 2002, some commentators expressed concern that the new mergers regime would create a more burdensome clearance process for businesses, especially if the competition authorities sought to flex their newfound (regulatory) muscles, or if

---

[18] *IBA Health Ltd v OFT* [2003] CAT 27, para 192.

[19] *OFT v IBA Health Ltd* [2004] EWCA Civ 142, para 38.

[20] *UniChem v OFT* [2005] CAT 8.

[21] Although, perhaps not as low as some had predicted, including those who feared the OFT would make a referral simply because time constraints did not allow for a 'full and proper assessment' of a merger at Phase 1; Shaun Goodman, 'Steady as She Goes: the Enterprise Act 2002 Charts a Familiar Course for UK Merger Control' (2003) 24(8) ECLR 331, 344.

[22] David Went, 'Recent Developments in UK Merger Control: Establishment of Solid Foundations for the New Regime' (2007) 28(12) ECLR 627, 627.

[23] See eg Parr's observations on the OFT's Annual Plans around this time; Nigel Parr, 'Merger Control in the Wake of IBA Health' (2007) 6(4) Comp Law 282, 294.

[24] CC and OFT, *Merger Assessment Guidelines* (CC2(Revised) and OFT1254 (September 2010) para 2.2.

[25] ibid para 2.6.

[26] ibid.

[27] *Celesio AG v OFT* [2006] CAT 9, para 74.

[28] On these and other 'escape routes' see Stephen Kon and Amanda Butler, 'UK: How to Escape Phase II Investigations in the Context of Mergers' (2012) 3(1) JECL & Pract 88.

a trend emerged of third parties making frequent—potentially vexatious—applications for judicial review.[29] Close attention was therefore paid to the *types* of transactions that would fall to be captured by the provisions, which had previously been determined by an 'assets test' under the Fair Trading Act 1973.[30] Ultimately, the legislators chose to limit the scope of the OFT's and the CC's decision-making powers to apply only to transactions that had created—or were expected to create—a 'relevant merger situation'.[31] A relevant merger situation is created where two or more enterprises have 'ceased to be distinct',[32] and *one* of two jurisdictional tests are satisfied; namely, either: (i) the UK turnover of the target/acquired firm exceeds £70 million (the turnover test), or (ii) the merger would result in the merging parties supplying (or, as the case may be, acquiring) 25 per cent or more of a particular good or service in the UK (the share of supply test).[33] Furthermore, in cases where a merger had already been completed, the OFT would only be able to make a Phase 2 referral within 4 months of (i) the merger being completed or (ii) the material facts of the merger entering the public domain (the four-month rule).[34]

The practical implication of these jurisdictional thresholds has been that the vast majority of mergers taking place in the UK are not captured by the EA 2002, meaning that— even if the review process itself were found to be onerous for businesses—a relatively low proportion of deals would need to endure it.[35] While a party to the EU, the UK was also subject to the jurisdictional turnover thresholds of the EU Merger Regulation (EUMR),[36] which would result in some large-scale cross-border mergers (which also possessed a UK dimension) being reviewed only by DG Competition (DG COMP), rather than the UK authorities, as part of the 'one-stop shop' facilitated under the EUMR.

2.2.3 The Residual Public Interest Regime: A Test of the EA 2002's Integrity

A notable omission from the Hansard debate of the Enterprise Bill was a meaningful engagement with the goals of merger control, with discussions instead being driven by a primary vision of creating certainty and transparency for businesses.[37] The public interest test had been a 'cornerstone' of UK competition policy since time immemorial,[38] yet the EA 2002 had significantly limited the scope of its application and afforded it formal status as a mere 'exception' to the default competition-based test. Nonetheless, retaining some scope for political intervention on public interest grounds was seen as a necessity within the new

---

[29] Niamh McCarthy, 'Proposed New UK Merger Regime' (2002) 5 IBLJ 603, 611.

[30] Fair Trading Act 1973, s 64(1) (now repealed). Satisfying this test would result in the creation of a 'merger situation' qualifying for investigation.

[31] EA 2002, ss 22(1)(a) and 33(1)(a) at Phase 1, and ss 35(1)(a) and 36(1)(a). Note, however, that establishing the existence of a relevant merger situation forms part of the review process itself and, as such, mergers found not to meet this criterion may still be subject to a Phase 1 and, potentially, Phase 2 investigation.

[32] ibid s 23(1).

[33] ibid ss 23(1)(b) and 23(2)–(4).

[34] ibid s 24(1).

[35] The level of the thresholds themselves represents something of a compromise between the government and the Confederation of British Industry to capture a similar number of annual cases to that of the assets test under the FTA73; Ruchit Patel, 'BIS Reforms to the UK Merger Regime: an Opportunity Missed?' (2012) 11(2) Comp Law 139, 145–46.

[36] Council Regulation (EC) 139/2004 on the control of concentrations between undertakings (EU Merger Regulation) [2004] OJ L24/1, art 1.

[37] Barry J Rodger, 'UK Merger Control: Politics, the Public Interest and Reform' (2000) 21(1) ECLR 24, 25, and 28.

[38] ibid 25.

regime and, aside from the named public interest grounds listed under section 58,[39] the Secretary of State was also afforded the power to add or remove a public interest ground from this list by virtue of section 58(3). Officially, this broad power was intended as a 'necessary safeguard' to provide flexibility in unforeseen circumstances,[40] so that 'very exceptional case[s] can be dealt with appropriately'.[41] A more cynical interpretation is that section 58(3) represents a symptom of the legislators' failure to consult on the wider aims of UK merger control, thus kicking the can down the road by enabling the Secretary of State to introduce new grounds, subject to limited parliamentary approval via a statutory instrument.[42]

The Secretary of State first exercised the powers contained in section 58(3) at the height of the 2007–2008 financial crisis, doing so in order to introduce a new public interest ground for upholding 'the stability of the UK financial system'.[43] This new financial stability ground enabled the government to force through a 'rescue merger' involving Lloyds TSB's purchase of HBOS in 2008. As a result, the government acted contrary to a recommendation by the OFT to refer the merger to a Phase 2 investigation, on the basis that the merger was likely to create an SLC in the UK markets for personal current accounts, mortgages and SME services.[44] *Lloyds/HBOS* remains, to date, the only occasion where the EA 2002's public interest provisions have been exercised 'positively' to permit an otherwise anti-competitive transaction. At the time, however, the case raised fundamental questions regarding the UK's continued commitment to a competition-based approach to mergers,[45] and further criticism of the political involvement in the regime after the merged entity ultimately required a government bailout at a cost of £17bn to the UK taxpayer.[46]

As of June 2020, when 'public health emergencies' became the EA 2002's fourth public interest ground (and the second to be introduced via the section 58(3) power),[47] the Secretary of State had issued a public interest intervention notice (PIIN) on only 20 occasions under the EA 2002,[48] demonstrating—with hindsight—that *Lloyds/HBOS* did not bring about a lasting departure from the UK's competition-based approach to merger review. While the inaugural use of section 58(3) could well have established a platform for the introduction of further public interest grounds and more frequent political interventions,[49] the severe costs to consumers and taxpayers in the aftermath of *Lloyds/HBOS* has acted to highlight 'the importance of restricting political interventions on public interest grounds to exceptional circumstances in specific industries'.[50] This enduring commitment to the

---

[39]   Which were 'national security' (s 58(1)) and, as introduced by the Communications Act 2003 shortly after the EA 2002 came into force, 'media plurality and presentation of news' (ss 58(2A)–(2C)).

[40]   HL Deb 15 October 2002, vol 639, col 801.

[41]   HL Deb 18 July 2002, vol 637, col 1466.

[42]   EA 2002, s 42(8)(b).

[43]   Enterprise Act 2002 (Specification of Additional Section 58 Consideration) Order 2008.

[44]   OFT, *Anticipated acquisition by Lloyds TSB plc of HBOS plc* (Report to BERR Secretary, 24 October 2008). See also: Andreas Stephan, 'Did Lloyds/HBOS Mark the Failure of an Enduring Economics-based System of Merger Regulation?' (2011) 62(4) NILQ 539, 544.

[45]   Martin McElwee, 'Politics and the UK Merger Control Process: The Public Interest Exceptions and Other Collision Points' (2010) 9(1) Competition Law Journal 77.

[46]   Stephan (n 44) 548.

[47]   Enterprise Act 2002 (Specification of Additional Section 58 Consideration) Order 2020.

[48]   There have been 12 interventions on national security grounds, 7 for media plurality, and 1 for financial stability.

[49]   McElwee (n 45) 88.

[50]   Stephan (n 44) 541. For further comment on how 'financial stability' may represent one of only a very limited number of justifiable public interest exceptions see Bruce Lyons, 'Competition Policy, Bailouts, and the Economic Crisis' (2009) 5(2) CPI 25.

competition-based approach comes in spite of repeated calls for successive governments to make greater use of the public interest powers in order to protect domestic firms from unwanted foreign takeovers; this is considered in section 5.2, below.

2.2.4 A 'New Era' or 'More of the Same'?

Opinion is split as to whether the EA 2002 heralded a 'new era' or a mere codification of the increasingly competition-based merger regime that preceded it during the final years of the Fair Trading Act 1973.[51] De facto political decision-making had been on the decline throughout the Tebbit doctrine era, with the Secretary of State only deviating from the competition authority's recommendation in 0.75 per cent of cases during the 1990s, and not deviating at all in the four years leading up to the EA 2002.[52] The broader public interest criteria had lost its relevance under the Tebbit doctrine and, in its place, the competition authorities were well on their way to engaging with sophisticated theories of harm and adopting new concepts, such as 'SLC', 'material influence' and 'share of supply'.[53] These terminologies were all commonplace in merger reviews by the end of the last century. The impact of the EA 2002 might therefore be seen as serving more of a symbolic value in terms of formally endorsing a predictable competition-based approach which places its faith in the decision-making of independent authorities. Indeed, this itself sent a clear and reassuring message to businesses that they need not fear a return to the 'dark ages' of the old public interest regime.

A more optimistic interpretation points to the significant improvements that the EA 2002 has delivered to transparency (by requiring the competition authorities to publish guidance documents and reasoned decisions)[54] and to accountability within the decision-making process.[55] Deterrence also stood to benefit from the regime's enhanced transparency as parties could now turn to the guidance and past decisions of the competition authorities in order to self-assess the risk of their deal resulting in an SLC—therefore, enabling merging parties to amend the strategy of their deals accordingly.[56]

3 Fine-tuning and 'Missed Opportunities' under the ERRA 2013

3.1 A Merger Regime for Growth

By 2011, the merger regime under the EA 2002 had come through its 'bedding down' period and had independently been assessed as 'world class' for its legal and procedural effectiveness, in a report commissioned as part of a government consultation on competition reform.[57] That same consultation sought views on how to create a 'stronger' merger regime,

---

[51] Some commentators felt the EA 2002 charted a familiar course to that of the previous regime; see Goodman (n 21) and McCarthy (n 29). However, Graham described it as 'a significant new era'; Cosmo Graham, 'The Enterprise Act 2002 and Competition Law' (2004) 67(2) MLR 273, 288.

[52] Goodman (n 21) 332.

[53] ibid 333 and 335–39; and Peter Freeman, 'Competition Policy in the UK: Lessons from the Past Decade' (2011) 10(4) Comp Law 251, 257.

[54] EA 2002, ss 106 and 107, respectively.

[55] Graham, 'The Enterprise Act 2002 and Competition Law' (n 51) 274 and 288.

[56] Freeman, 'UK Merger Control' (n 4) 26.

[57] The UK regime ranked second worldwide, behind the US; Department for Business, Innovation and Skills, *A Competition Regime for Growth: A Consultation on Options for Reform* (Consultation document, March 2011) para 1.5.

which the government suggested could be achieved through new powers to shore up the voluntary notification system and further measures to streamline the review process. The result of the consultation and subsequent legislative scrutiny was the ERRA 2013, which ushered in the most substantial changes to the EA 2002 regime to date. While the reforms were mainly of procedural refinement and strengthening, a significant institutional change was also realized.

On 1 April 2014, when the OFT and the CC were abolished—or, effectively merged—under the ERRA 2013,[58] the newly established Competition and Markets Authority (CMA) inherited the Phase 1 and 2 roles of its predecessors. In an effort to maintain separation between the phases, the CMA board is now responsible for decision-making at Phase 1, while an independent Inquiry Group (comprising between three to five members selected from the CMA Panel of independent experts) oversees the Phase 2 investigation and decision-making. The CMA has largely adopted the guidelines of its predecessors and has proceeded to update and publish new guidelines since its establishment.

This merging of the merger decision-makers presented new opportunities for the single CMA to realize procedural efficiencies, particularly by allowing a proportion of staff from Phase 1 to proceed on to the Phase 2 investigation, thereby facilitating knowledge transfer and minimizing duplication between the phases.[59] Numerous commentators, however, expressed concern about the impact that this new institutional set-up would have on independence between the phases, with many noting the heightened potential for confirmation bias under the single authority model.[60] The business community was itself apprehensive about the perceived loss of 'a fresh pair of eyes' at Phase 2, seeking assurances from the CMA that its case teams would be able to 'consider cases from a new perspective and higher legal threshold' at Phase 2.[61] Others noted the practical difficulties involved in preventing Phase 1 preconceptions from trickling through to the Phase 2 investigation, leading to an increased likelihood of an SLC being concluded at Phase 2,[62] despite the higher standard of proof attributed to Phase 2 decision-making. In practice, there is evidence that a significant minority of Phase 1 staff tend to cross over to Phase 2,[63] but the CMA has sought to reduce the risk of confirmation bias by ensuring key decision-makers (namely, inquiry chairs and panel members) are always different at Phase 2.[64]

Related to confirmation bias, there is also a risk that resourcing considerations may enter into the decision-making of the CMA board when deciding whether or not to make a referral to Phase 2. Pre-ERRA 2013, Wilks describes a 'tense' relationship between senior members of the OFT and the CC, partly resulting from the OFT making frequent spates of reference decisions that left the CC with a difficult caseload to manage.[65] As a separate

---

[58]   Enterprise and Regulatory Reform Act 2013, s 26.

[59]   CMA, *Mergers: Guidance on the CMA's jurisdiction and procedure* (CMA2, January 2014) para 10.8.

[60]   See eg Ali Nikpay and Deirdre Taylor, 'The New UK Competition Regime: Radically Different or More of the Same?' (2014) 5(5) JECL & Pract 278, 279; and Bola Ajayi, 'The Competition and Markets Authority: A More Effective Merger Control Authority?' (2014) 13(3) Comp Law 223, 224.

[61]   Ajayi (n 60) 224.

[62]   Nikpay and Taylor (n 60) 279.

[63]   In a sample of cases in 2015, the NAO observed between 29–44% of CMA staff involved in a Phase 1 investigation being transferred across to the Phase 2 investigation upon referral; National Audit Office, *The UK competition regime* (Report by the Comptroller and Auditor General, HC 737, 5 February 2016) para 2.22.

[64]   ibid.

[65]   Stephen Wilks, 'Institutional Reform and the Enforcement of Competition Policy in the UK' (2011) 7(1) ECJ 1, 5.

body, the OFT had little awareness of how a referral decision would impact upon the CC's resources, meaning the risk of such considerations influencing its Phase 1 decision was remote. Under the CMA model, however, housing the Phase 1 and Phase 2 decision-makers within the same authority created a holistic awareness of the resource implications of a Phase 2 referral. Objectively, the CMA model therefore creates a greater risk of resourcing considerations entering into the Phase 1 decision process, albeit informally.[66] However, in practice, there has been very little evidence to suggest that either resourcing considerations or confirmation bias are at play in the CMA's decision-making (see section 4.4).

Aside from the major institutional reforms, the broader workings of merger control were left relatively untouched by the ERRA 2013. Notable changes were, however, made to the powers of the CMA to impose and enforce interim measures, along with a series of new statutory time limits aimed at streamlining the review process.

3.2 Fine-tuning under the ERRA 2013

3.2.1 New Powers for the CMA to Order Interim Measures to Halt Integration

A notable trade-off of the business-friendly environment facilitated under the UK's voluntary notification system is the potential for parties to choose not to notify an anti-competitive merger and, instead, press ahead with completing the transaction. While the majority of these completed mergers were detected by the OFT's mergers intelligence function (see section 4.1, below) and consequently called in for investigation, the OFT—and the CC at Phase 2—faced numerous difficulties when seeking to halt further integration between the parties and, where necessary, in seeking to reverse integration after a finding of an SLC (i.e. 'unscrambling the eggs').[67] Two matters of particular concern in the pre-ERRA 2013 era were: (i) where parties had taken pre-emptive action (integration ahead of formal clearance) to such an extent that it limited the possibility of effective remedies being proposed, and (ii) where parties continued to take pre-emptive action while an investigation was ongoing, thereby presenting the OFT with a moving target that threatened to prejudice its investigation by rendering its reference decision and proposed remedies outdated after further integration had taken place.[68]

While the OFT did not possess direct powers to prevent parties completing a merger during an investigation, it could nonetheless implement so-called 'hold-separate' measures in the form of initial undertakings (IUs) agreed with the merging parties, which would limit the extent to which the parties could further integrate their businesses.[69] The OFT also had the power to impose hold-separate measures via an initial enforcement order (IEO), but this power was never utilized in practice and 'merely acted as a lever which encouraged acquirers to offer IUs'.[70] Yet, despite having these powers in its arsenal, the OFT faced significant challenges when seeking to agree IUs with the merging parties, who could—and

---

[66] Nikpay and Taylor (n 60) 279.

[67] Patel provides a list of 11 completed mergers that required 'unscrambling' pre-ERRA 2013, most of which act to illustrate the practical difficulties of implementing remedies after partial-integration; Patel (n 35) 149–50.

[68] Tom Heideman and Ajal Notowicz, 'Interim Orders in UK Merger Control: an Interim Verdict' (2016) 37(7) ECLR 264, 264.

[69] EA 2002, s 71 (now repealed). A roughly equivalent power at Phase 2 enabled the CC to impose 'interim undertakings' on parties once a referral has been made but before a Phase 2 decision had been published; s 80(2).

[70] Heideman and Notowicz (n 68) 264.

often would—continue to integrate their businesses right up to the point where the IUs were agreed and the hold-separate order took effect.[71] This opportunity for further integration meant the parties to completed mergers had little incentive to agree IUs with any haste, and certainly not before agreeing exceptions (derogations) to the hold-separate measures.[72] Moreover, in order to accept IUs or impose an IEO, it was first necessary for the OFT to establish the creation of a relevant merger situation,[73] an evidential threshold that posed further delays to the OFT's efforts to combat pre-emptive action.

An important milestone of the EA 2002's 'bedding down' period in this context was the CAT's 2006 decision in *Stericycle*,[74] which—while concluding that the CC had acted reasonably in appointing a hold-separate manager to ensure the merged parties remained operationally separate during its investigation—criticized the OFT for being slow and unclear when agreeing IUs with the parties.[75] This ruling enabled the competition authorities to become more familiar and assured with the use and (considerable) extent of their powers to impose interim measures to combat pre-emptive action,[76] and coincided with the OFT's issuing of more hold-separate orders to completed mergers at Phase 1.[77] However, the OFT's reliance on the IU route still placed it at the mercy of parties' willingness to agree to undertakings—the need for reform was therefore apparent.

The ERRA 2013 removed the ability of the parties to negotiate IUs at Phase 1 and, in its place, introduced new powers for the CMA to (absent any agreement with the parties) impose 'interim measures orders' on the parties in order to halt integration. These can take the form of either: (i) an IEO at Phase 1,[78] or (ii) an 'interim order' at Phase 2,[79] and parties can only seek derogations from an order *after* it has come into effect and only with the prior consent of the CMA. Moreover, these interim measures orders could—for the first time—be applied to both completed *and* anticipated mergers. The threshold for imposing an interim measures order was also lowered, departing from the need to demonstrate a relevant merger situation and now requiring only reasonable grounds for suspecting that firms have ceased to be distinct or that they soon would be.[80] These reforms enhanced the ability of the CMA to suspend pre-emptive action and to bring it to an end more swiftly. In terms of 'unscrambling the eggs', the ERRA 2013 also afforded a clear statutory basis to the CMA's unwinding powers, which are now available at both Phase 1 and Phase 2.[81] Finally, as a means of reinforcing these changes, the CMA was allocated further powers to impose administrative penalties on parties that fail to comply with interim measures orders.[82]

---

[71] Tamara Todorovic, 'The Reform of the UK Merger Regime in the Enterprise and Regulatory Reform Act 2013—Not Much to Shout About' (2013) 12(3) Comp Law 338, 348.

[72] Department for Business, Energy and Industrial Strategy (BEIS), *Competition law review: post implementation review of statutory changes in the Enterprise and Regulatory Reform Act 2013* (July 2019) 84.

[73] EA 2002, ss 71(3) and 72(3)(a) (now repealed).

[74] *Stericycle International LLC v Competition Commission* [2006] CAT 21.

[75] Went (n 22) 629–30.

[76] Peter Freeman, 'Stericycle: A Lifeline for the UK's Voluntary Merger Control Regime?' (2007) 6(4) Comp Law 298, 305.

[77] The OFT agreed IUs in 4% of completed mergers reviewed in 2004, 7% in 2005, 12% in 2006, and 46% in the first 8 months of 2007; Went (n 22) 630.

[78] EA 2002, s 72(2).

[79] ibid s 81(2).

[80] ibid s 72(1)(b).

[81] ibid ss 72(3B), s80(2A), and 81(2A).

[82] ibid s 94A; a penalty of up to 5% aggregate worldwide turnover. The CMA expressly refers to this power as a deterrent to parties seeking to 'undermine to effectiveness' of interim measures; CMA, *Interim measures in merger investigations* (CMA108, 28 June 2019) para 1.10.

In light of these extended enforcement powers, greater risks now loom over parties that choose not to notify a merger that is capable of raising competition concerns, which may prompt firms to revisit their deal strategies.[83] This is indicative of a stricter approach to non-notified mergers, which now face the onerous task of complying and negotiating derogations from the interim measures order.[84] The introduction of powers to impose interim orders on *anticipated* mergers, in particular, raised eyebrows given the voluntary nature of the UK regime;[85] although, the CMA was quick to clarify that it only intends to impose interim measures on anticipated mergers in rare situations where there is concern over pre-emptive action.[86] Other commentators have also suggested that the clearer statutory scope the CMA now has to unwind integration post-ERRA 'waters down to some extent the voluntary nature' of the regime.[87]

There is credibility to claims that the voluntary regime 'has almost become mandatory and suspensory in practice' as the CMA has shown itself to be increasingly willing to use its enhanced powers to prevent firms integrating while an investigation is ongoing.[88] A government review of the impact of the ERRA 2013 reforms observed that, in its first four years, the CMA issued 100 IEOs (approximately 40 per cent of Phase 1 cases) and 92 of those cases involved completed mergers.[89] IEOs are now 'routinely imposed' in completed mergers reviewed by the CMA and, more recently, there is a growing trend of cases where IEOs are being imposed in anticipated mergers.[90] As of June 2018, the CMA has also started to use its powers to fine parties for a breach of interim orders and, in February 2019, used its unwinding powers for the very first time.[91] This points towards the CMA adopting a stricter approach to non-compliance with procedural rules but also, as the CMA has itself stated, a 'significantly increased' ability to use interim measures to prevent consumer detriment arising out of pre-emptive action by parties.[92]

3.2.2 Statutory Time Limits for Streamlining the Review Process

While the EA 2002 had attempted to limit the burden that the review process posed to merging parties, the speed of the process had been ranked second-worst in a government peer review of eight merger regimes in 2007.[93] In response, the ERRA 2013 attempted to strike a 'Goldilocks' model at Phase 1, where straightforward cases could be quickly disposed of and problematic mergers were referred swiftly on to Phase 2.[94] The reforms sought to achieve this by introducing a blanket deadline of forty working days after the launch of the Phase 1 investigation for the CMA board to decide whether or not to issue a referral.[95] Significantly,

[83] Nikpay and Taylor (n 60) 280.

[84] Alan Davis and Marguerite Lavedan, 'Merger Control in the UK Utilities Sector' (2016) 21(2) Util LR 59, 62.

[85] Ajayi (n 60) 228.

[86] CMA Guidance 2014 (n 59) Annex C5. This clarification is retained in the updated guidance; CMA *Interim measures guidance* (n 82) para 2.15.

[87] Nikpay and Taylor (n 60) 279.

[88] Paul Johnson, 'Brexit: the Implications for EU and UK Merger Control' (2016) 15(3) Comp Law 131, 136.

[89] BEIS Competition Law Review (n 72) 84.

[90] Mark Jephcott and Ruth Allen, 'The CMA Steps up Enforcement of Procedural Merger Control Rules: Key Lessons from Recent Cases' (2020) 19(1) Comp Law 10, 11.

[91] ibid 12–13.

[92] BEIS Competition Law Review (n 72) 85.

[93] National Audit Office, *Review of the UK's Competition Landscape* (22 March 2010) para 5.8 and fig 13.

[94] Peter Freeman, ' "Beware the Ides of March": The Government's Proposed Competition Reforms' (2012) 8(3) ECJ 563, 568.

[95] EA 2002, s 34ZA. Prior to the ERRA 2013, 'straightforward' cases (ie non-completed cases notified via a Merger Notice) were subject to a 20-working day Phase 1 timetable, with the possibility of a 10-working day

the reforms also afford discretion to the CMA over when to, in effect, 'start the clock' on the Phase 1 investigation, which comes about when the CMA accepts the Merger Notice it has received from the parties.[96] The CMA will only accept the Notice once it is satisfied that it has sufficient information to launch an investigation.[97] While the revised time limit has been described as 'rather generous',[98] the reforms were widely interpreted as bringing discipline to the Phase 1 timetable, particularly as the forty-working day deadline had long been an administrative aim of the OFT, albeit not one that generated the level of pressure associated with a statutory requirement.[99]

This added pressure on the CMA at Phase 1 did in fact prompt a number of commentators to suggest that, rather than streamlining the review process, the reforms would actually have the opposite effect in practice.[100] As statutory time limits 'inevitably increase the pressure on case teams', it was predicted the CMA would be less eager to exercise its discretion to 'start the clock' at the earliest opportunity, or may have a greater incentive to exercise its powers to 'stop the clock' more frequently.[101] In other words, by affording discretion to the CMA over when to 'start the clock' on a Phase 1 investigation, the effect might actually be a longer period of pre-notification discussions,[102] particularly in light of the significantly higher information requirements imposed on parties submitting the statutory Merger Notice.[103]

Further amendments to the statutory timetable at Phase 2 also sought to bring about a streamlined process, most notably by imposing a twelve-week deadline for the CMA Panel to accept final undertakings or to make a final order following an infringement decision.[104] No such deadline had previously existed and was intended to reduce the limbo period faced by parties to the most problematic mergers, especially as the CC had notoriety for being inconsistent in how long it took to reach a resolution.[105] As with Phase 1, this timetable was also made subject to 'stop the clock' measures of up to 6 weeks where a 'special reason' exists for doing so, or for an indefinite period if the parties fail to comply with an information request that the CMA has issued under its section 109 powers.[106] In practice, the ERRA 2013 revisions to the review timetable appear to have had the intended effect of streamlining the formal investigatory process, although doubts remain over the resulting impact this has had on the duration of pre-notification discussions (see section 4.5).

3.2.3 Unlocking the Potential for 'Undertakings in Lieu' at Phase 1

An evidently beneficial change brought about by the ERRA 2013 has been its revisions to the timetable for offering and accepting undertakings in lieu of a reference (UILs). Prior to

---

extension under special circumstances. Other cases (ie completed mergers that had not been notified) were not subject to a statutory time limit for review but, rather, an informal administrative timetable of 40 working days.

[96] ibid s 34ZA(3).
[97] ibid s 96(2A).
[98] Freeman, 'Beware the Ides of March' (n 94) 568.
[99] Todorovic (n 71) 342.
[100] See eg Patel (n 35) 152, Nikpay and Taylor (n 60) Todorovic (n 71) and Ajayi (n 60).
[101] Nikpay and Taylor (n 60) 279.
[102] Todorovic (n 71) 342.
[103] Ajayi (n 60) 226.
[104] EA 2002, s 41A(1).
[105] Nikpay and Taylor (n 60) 279.
[106] EA 2002, ss 41A(2) and (3) respectively.

the ERRA 2013, there had been no statutory timetable to dictate when parties should offer UILs to the OFT, merely that they were to be submitted at some stage before the OFT tabled its Phase 1 decision. The OFT would then consider whether to accept the UILs having determined that the merger invoked its duty to refer. This created numerous problems for the merging parties who, lacking a reasoned final decision on the specific ways their transaction raised SLC concerns, were forced to second-guess the Phase 1 decision by referring to, for example, the OFT's initial issues letter.[107] OFT guidance also specified—at regular intervals—the need for UILs to be 'clear-cut' in terms of their ability to remedy the competition concern in question,[108] a standard which may have prompted some parties to propose UILs that exceeded the invasiveness of the remedies they would ultimately have faced at Phase 2.[109]

Under the ERRA 2013 reforms, parties now have 5 working days following the tabling of a Phase 1 decision in which to offer UILs,[110] while the CMA has until 10 working days after the decision to notify the parties of whether the proposed UILs might be acceptable.[111] The introduction of this five-working day window for parties to offer UILs—and, more importantly, the parties' ability to see the CMA's decision first[112]—'allow for more targeted and effective undertakings', thereby improving the parties' chances of avoiding a Phase 2 reference.[113] In contrast, Todorovic also suggests that, whilst transparency is achieved by allowing parties to see the Phase 1 decision before offering UILs, the five-day time limit could actually result in more Phase 2 referrals if there is insufficient time for the parties to interpret the decision and formulate agreeable UILs.[114] The practical impact of these refinements under the ERRA 2013 reforms are considered in section 4.2, below.

3.3 A Missed Opportunity for Radical Change?

Taken as a whole, the ERRA 2013 reform package for merger control represents a fine-tuning of the procedures that underpin the broader substantive vision of the EA 2002 legislators. A government review of the impact of the ERRA 2013 observed numerous positive outcomes; most notably, improvements to the timeliness and predictability of decisions and to the implementation of remedies.[115] However, some commentators suggest opportunities for more radical change to the mergers regime were missed under the ERRA 2013, especially concerning the viability of the UK's voluntary notification system.[116]

[107] Todorovic (n 71) 342.
[108] OFT, *Mergers: Exceptions to the duty to refer and undertakings in lieu of reference guidance* (OFT1122, December 2010). This standard is replicated under the CMA's revised guidance; CMA, *Mergers: Exceptions to the duty to refer* (CMA64, December 2018) para 34.
[109] Kon and Butler (n 28) 93. It is widely accepted that the EA 2002 drafters had not foreseen this possibility.
[110] EA 2002, s 73A(1).
[111] ibid s 73A(2). A final decision on whether to accept the UIL proposal should be arrived at within 50 working days, subject to a possible forty-working day extension under special circumstances (eg to find an upfront buyer); ss 73A(3)–(4).
[112] Ajayi (n 60) 228.
[113] Nikpay and Taylor (n 60) 279.
[114] Todorovic (n 71) 343. The author does, however, note that the limited timeframe may act as an incentive for parties to proactively preparing UIL proposals earlier in the Phase 1 process.
[115] Although, the government acknowledges that non-statutory improvements to the CMA's procedures have also contributed to these successes; BEIS Competition Law Review (n 72) 3.
[116] See eg Patel (n 35) 153; Freeman, 'Beware the Ides of March' (n 94) 572; and Karman Gordon and Christopher Hutton, 'An Opportunity Missed: the Proposed Reforms to the UK Competition Regime' (2012) 8(2) CLI 49, 49.

Despite aiming to minimize unnecessary red tape for merging parties, the voluntary notification system—and, more specifically, the lack of a mandatory system has been described as a weakness of the UK regime.[117] Peter Freeman, Chairman of the CAT and a vocal advocate of the UK's adoption of a mandatory regime during the pre-ERRA 2013 consultation period, suggested that mandatory notification may be a necessity if firms routinely avoid pre-notification as a deliberate means of getting their deal through.[118] The prospect of some potentially anti-competitive mergers escaping review was indeed one of the key drivers of proposals to reform the voluntary regime, as outlined in the government's consultation.[119] The BIS Consultation proposed three options: a *full mandatory* notification system (for £5 million UK and £10 million worldwide turnover), a *hybrid mandatory* notification system (requiring parties to notify where the target firm's turnover exceeds £70 million, and allowing the CMA to call in mergers that satisfy the share of supply test), and retaining the *voluntary* regime alongside stronger hold-separate powers.[120]

Proposals to introduce a mandatory regime were met with hostility from most respondents to the government consultation,[121] many citing its propensity to subject firms to higher administrative costs and others expressing confidence in the mergers intelligence function of the CMA (in terms its ability to detect potentially anti-competitive mergers that are not notified).[122] A minority of respondents in favour of adopting a mandatory notification system pointed to numerous potential benefits including, inter alia, its ability to avoid the risk of non-notified firms taking irreversible pre-emptive action (e.g. where parties exchange sensitive business information), and how it removes the four-month period of uncertainty after completion where the competition authority could still make a referral.[123] Ultimately, however, the government decided that the 'most proportionate response' was to retain and strengthen the voluntary regime, as a mandatory system 'would increase costs to both business and the CMA'.[124]

For some, this decision marked a missed opportunity to radically alter the UK notification procedure in order to combat the threat of non-notified mergers head-on. Freeman, for example, was unconvinced by the government's reasoning for its decision—namely, on the basis that a mandatory regime was inconsistent with its deregulation agenda—and suggested further thought should have been afforded to the *form* the regime would take.[125] Others were sceptical that the government could robustly conclude that the problem of mergers going 'under the radar' was insignificant, as its impact assessment had concluded,[126] without first conducting a quantitative analysis of the potential harm that undetected anti-competitive mergers pose to the economy,[127] going as far as to suggest that

[117] Wilks 'Institutional Reform' (n 65) 5.

[118] Freeman, 'UK Merger Control' (n 4) 27. Some suggest Freeman's calls for a mandatory regime likely contributed to its appearance in the consultation document; Parr and Hammon (n 5) 14, fn 10.

[119] Patel (n 35) 140.

[120] Department for Business, Innovation and Skills, *A Competition Regime for Growth: A Consultation on Options for Reform* (Consultation document, BIS 2011) para 4.6.

[121] Cosmo Graham, 'The Reform of UK Competition Policy' (2012) 8(3) ECJ 539, 551.

[122] Patel (n 35)142.

[123] ibid 141.

[124] Department for Business, Innovation and Skills, *Growth, Competition and the Competition Regime: Government response to the consultation* (BIS 2012) para 5.8.

[125] Freeman, 'Beware the Ides of March' (n 94) 568.

[126] Department for Business, Innovation and Skills, *A Competition Regime for Growth: A Consultation on Options for Reform (Impact Assessment)* (BIS 2012) para 48.

[127] Patel (n 35) 145–46 and 153.

the government may have 'implicitly tolerated' missed mergers because, among other things, they are typically smaller transactions with limited potential for anti-competitive impact.[128]

4 Enforcement Trends under the EA 2002

The UK merger regime under the EA 2002 has now undergone a sustained period of evolution, most significantly through an initial 'bedding down' period and a package of procedural and institutional reforms under the ERRA 2013. To determine the impact that this evolution has had in practice, we can look to outcomes data to detect trends in enforcement activity. The CMA now publishes transparency data on merger review outcomes on its website,[129] providing a comprehensive statistical resource relating to mergers investigated by the UK competition authorities since April 2004. The observations in this section draw on 16 years of statistical data covering the reporting years from 2004–2005 to 2019–2020. For the most part, the analysis utilizes the methodologies of previous empirical studies of the UK merger regime undertaken in Parr (2010)[130] and Robert (2017),[131] and updates these studies based on the most recent data available at the time of writing.[132]

4.1 A Higher Rate of Enforcement, But Not All Is as It Seems

The 'rate of enforcement' denotes the proportion of mergers reviewed by the competition authority that ultimately lead to some form of intervention, be this in the form of UILs at Phase 1, or remedies and prohibitions at Phase 2.[133] A higher rate of enforcement is indicative of a statutory regime with a low threshold for finding infringement,[134] and enforced by a competition authority that adopts a stringent approach to interpreting and executing its statutory remit. Conversely, a lower rate implies a regime that adopts a high standard of proof for satisfying the SLC test (or one where the parties have a credible opportunity to argue a defence). Other specific variables, such as the level of resources at the authority's disposal and the statutory timeframe it has to conduct investigations, can also have a bearing on the rate of enforcement.

---

[128] ibid 143.

[129] CMA, 'Merger inquiry outcome statistics' (*Gov.uk*, first published: 7 May 2014) www.gov.uk/government/publications/phase-1-merger-enquiry-outcomes accessed 1 August 2020.

[130] Parr uses data collected between 1999 and 2008 and, in doing so, draws insights on the initial impact of the EA 2002 on merger enforcement; Nigel Parr, 'The Competition Commission, Merger Control and the SLC test' in Barry J Rodger (ed), *Ten Years of UK Competition Law Reform* (Dundee University Press 2010).

[131] Robert uses data from 2007 to 2016 to draw insights on the potential impact that the CMA and the ERRA 2013 reforms had on various aspects of enforcement; Gavin Robert, 'Three Years of CMA Merger Control: a Statistical Review' (2017) 3 Comp Law 211.

[132] The above-mentioned studies were repeated to test for accuracy, before the updated CMA data was incorporated. Any errors are the author's own.

[133] Within the scope of 'interventions', Robert also includes mergers that were abandoned after a referral to Phase 2. This, he suggests, demonstrates the burden parties attribute to Phase 2 investigations and how a referral decision (regardless of the Phase 2 outcome) is 'itself a significant form of regulatory intervention'; Robert (n 131) 212–13. The logic of this is convincing and, as such, this chapter adopts the same definition of 'intervention'.

[134] Namely, a regime where the standard of proof for finding an SLC is low and there are very few defences available to the merging parties.

Table 7.1 Rate of Merger Enforcement under the EA 2002 (2007–2020)

	2007–2008 to 2013–2014 (OFT/CC)	2014–2015 to 2019–2020 (CMA)	2007–2008 to 2019–2020
Notifications less 'out of scope'	497	367	864
Phase 1 remedy	35	41	76
Phase 1 remedy as a % of notifications less 'out of scope'	7.0%	11.2%	8.8%
Phase 2 remedy	17	18	35
Prohibition	6	4	10
Withdrawal post-Phase 2	14	11	25
Total Phase 2 enforcement	37	33	70
Total Phase 2 enforcement as % of notifications less 'out of scope'	7.4%	9.0%	8.1%
Total enforcement	72	74	146
Total enforcement as a % of notifications less 'out of scope'	14.5%	20.2%	16.9%

Adapted and updated from 'Table 2' of Parr (n 130) 214.

The institutional change from the OFT/CC model to the CMA model has presented intriguing opportunities to observe changes in the enforcement rate before and after 1 April 2014, when the CMA took the reins. Between 2007 and 2020, the average enforcement rate under the EA 2002 has been 16.9 per cent (Table 7.1);[135] that is to say, roughly one in six mergers reviewed by the competition authorities have resulted in the imposition of either UILs, remedies or prohibitions. The rate of enforcement has also witnessed a small but notable increase under the CMA's stewardship, from 14.5 per cent in the OFT/CC era, to 20.2 per cent in the CMA era. Indeed, the CMA's enforcement rate between 2015 and 2020 is 23.4 per cent, just shy of one in four mergers, which is significantly higher than any other period in the regime's history.

A likely contributor to this is the 'more targeted approach' that the CMA has taken towards identifying mergers that require investigation, which has benefited enormously from renewed investment in its mergers intelligence function.[136] The CMA's Mergers Intelligence Committee is tasked with detecting non-notified mergers that raise competition concerns, thereby allowing the CMA board to open 'own initiative' investigations which typically equate to anywhere between a quarter and a third of all annual UK merger

---

[135] This figure is a percentage of the total number of investigations that were ultimately found to fall within the jurisdiction of the EA 2002. It excludes mergers that the CMA data refers to as 'found not to qualify' (i.e. do not create a relevant merger situation), as the competition authorities do not have the ability to enforce these mergers in any case; Robert (n 131) 212.

[136] Andrea Coscelli, 'The First Year of the CMA' (British Institute of International and Comparative Law, London, 30 April 2015) 4.

enforcement.[137] Rather than indicating a tougher approach by the CMA, a higher rate of enforcement may therefore denote a more effective screening mechanism (where transactions that raise little or no suspicion of an SLC—or which are unlikely to meet the jurisdictional thresholds—are not recommended for a formal Phase 1 investigation). This is supported by the CMA statistics, which show a sharp and consistent decline in the number of Phase 1 investigations where a relevant merger situation was ultimately found not to exist (this was true in 21.6 per cent of OFT investigations, compared with only 4.4 per cent of investigations conducted by the CMA). The knock-on effect of this is that the CMA's Phase 1 caseload, at least in terms of formal investigations, is markedly lower than its predecessor, despite initially showing a willingness to launch more investigations.[138] Between 2004 and 2014, the OFT tabled an average of 111 Phase 1 decisions each year, whereas the figure is sixty-four decisions per year for the CMA between 2014 and 2020.

4.2 A False Dawn for Undertakings in Lieu?

Figure 7.1 shows that main contributor towards the CMA's initial enforcement rate (between 2015 and 2018) was the imposition of remedies at Phase 1, i.e. agreeing UILs with the merging parties. This demonstrates the early success of the reforms to the Phase 1 timetable under the ERRA 2013, particularly regarding the opportunity parties now have to read the CMA board's Phase 1 decision before proposing UILs. Robert suggests that this initial revival in UILs may also be explained by (i) parties' fear of confirmation bias within the new single authority model (with UILs offering an appealing alternative to a repeat performance at Phase 2), and (ii) by a policy shift whereby the CMA became more open to resolving

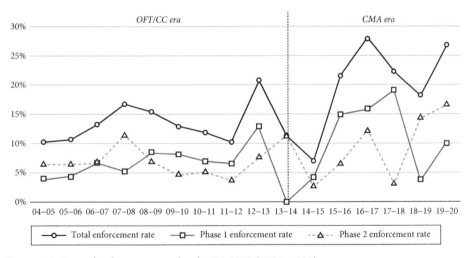

Figure 7.1 Rate of enforcement under the EA 2002 (2004–2020).

---

[137] For an excellent first-hand account of this function see Simon Chisholm and Tom Heideman, 'The Decision to Investigate Mergers in the United Kingdom's Voluntary Regime' (2017) 13(4) JCL&E 637.

[138] The CMA tabled 83 Phase 1 decisions in its first year, compared to 65 by OFT in its final year; Alastair Chapman, Sarah Jensen and Michael Caldecott, 'UK Antitrust Reform: The CMA's First Year' (2015) 29 Antitrust 61, 62.

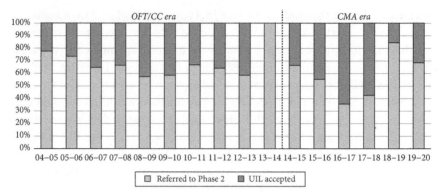

Figure 7.2 Outcomes of Phase 1 decisions raising SLC concerns (2004–2020), excl. abandoned cases.

investigations at Phase 1 in order to reduce the burden on parties and their employees.[139] However, Figure 7.1 also illustrates how the Phase 1 enforcement rate has returned to something resembling pre-CMA levels in more recent times and, during the 2018–2020 reporting periods, the CMA board made exactly three times more Phase 2 referrals than UILs (Figure 7.2). While there have been signs of a greater propensity by the CMA to accept (or at least contemplate) UILs, this may yet prove to be a false dawn.

4.3 The Likelihood of Referral Remains Unchanged under the CMA

As mentioned above, the early cases of *IBA Health* and *UniChem* arguably had the effect of lowering the standard of proof for Phase 2 referrals, meaning 'marginal cases' were at an increased risk of being referred. Parr (2010) observes evidence of this in 2004 and 2005, the period immediately following the *IBA Health* case, when references increased to their highest level under the EA 2002.[140] This period still represents the highest frequency of referrals in the EA 2002 regime's history (Figure 7.3) and, given that the number of referrals was in decline for several years after this period, it has been suggested that the OFT was taking an extra cautious approach to its duty to refer during this time,[141] presumably in an effort to avoid further third party litigation.

The period from 2004 to 2005 does not, however, represent an unusually high *rate* of referral (14.3 per cent of qualifying cases) when considered alongside the OFT's average referral rate (12.9 per cent between 2004 and 2014). In fact, the final two years of the OFT's existence both witnessed higher rates of referral; 18.2% (2012–2013) and 15.1 per cent (2013–2014). Equally, while the CMA makes comparably fewer references each year on average (9.2 referrals p.a.) compared to the OFT era (11.2 referrals p.a.), it too displays a marginally higher rate of referral when one considers the total number of qualifying cases it investigates (see Table 7.2).

---

[139] Robert (n 131) 215.
[140] Parr (n 130) 206–207.
[141] ibid.

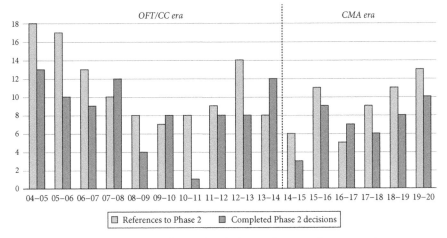

Figure 7.3 References to Phase 2 and completed Phase 2 decisions (2004–2020).
Adapted and updated from 'Figure 1' of ibid 207.

Table 7.2 Likelihood of Phase 2 Referral under the EA 2002 (2007–2020)

	2007–2008 to 2013–2014 (OFT enforcement)	2014–2015 to 2019–2020 (CMA enforcement)	2007–2008 to 2019–2020
Notifications	601	384	985
Out of scope	104	17	121
Notifications less 'out of scope'	497	367	864
Phase 2 referrals	64	55	119
Phase 2 referrals as a % of notifications less 'out of scope'	12.9%	15.0%	13.8%

Adapted and updated from 'Table 1' of Robert (n 131) 213.

As noted in the table, the Phase 2 referral rate across the EA 2002's enforcement history stands at 13.8 per cent, a slightly less than one-in-seven chance of any given merger
being referred. This rate is relatively high compared to referral rates in other regimes but,
as Robert observes,[142] this can also be explained by the ability of the UK's voluntary regime
to 'handpick' the non-notified mergers that have the potential to raise competition concerns, while disregarding the mergers that are very unlikely to raise any concerns. It is not,
therefore, necessarily the case that a given merger is more likely to be referred in the UK,
despite the referral rate increasing slightly from 12.9 per cent in the OFT era, to 15 per cent
under the CMA's reign. Of course, the notable alternative to making a referral is accepting
UILs and, in 2016–2017, the Phase 2 referral rate dropped to an all-time EA 2002 low of 8.8

---

[142] ibid 213.

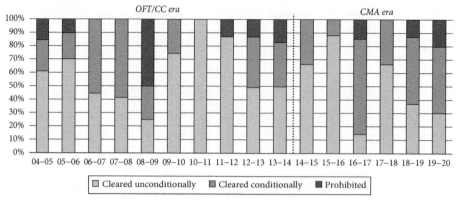

Figure 7.4 Completed merger decisions by outcome (2004–2020).
Adapted and updated from 'Figure 2' of Parr (n 130) 207.

per cent, as the CMA (and merging parties themselves) began to see UILs as a more viable option post-ERRA 2013 (see Figure 7.2, above). Yet with the CMA accepting fewer UILs between 2018 and 2020, referral rates have witnessed a resurgence; 21.7 per cent of qualifying mergers were referred to Phase 2 in 2019–2020, a higher percentage than any seen under the EA 2002.

4.4 No Evidence of Confirmation Bias within the CMA Model

The 'merging' of the Phase 1 and Phase 2 decision-makers under the ERRA 2013 prompted initial concern that bias would enter into the merger assessment process by virtue of the single authority set-up (see section 3.1, above). The first concern is that, within a single authority, the CMA board may have an incentive to consider resource allocations before deciding whether or not to refer a merger for in-depth investigation by the CMA Panel. As the previous sub-section notes, the rate of referral has actually increased slightly under the single authority arrangement, meaning there is no evidence to suggest resource considerations are weighed against the duty to refer.[143]

The second concern related to the risk of confirmation bias between the phases, i.e. that initial thinking and conclusions at Phase 1 would, following a referral, cross over to Phase 2 and influence the CMA Panel's final decision. Robert (2017) proposes a simple test for confirmation bias; namely, by determining whether a Phase 2 referral 'inevitably' leads to remedies or prohibitions in an excessively high proportion of Phase 2 decisions.[144] Given that the CMA board's duty to refer is subject to a lower standard of proof than the CMA Panel's ultimate infringement decision,[145] 'it can only be expected that there will be more cases referred to Phase 2 than cases which ultimately lead to an SLC finding', meaning a significant proportion of cases should receive unconditional clearance at Phase 2 (assuming

---

[143] This logic is proposed in ibid.
[144] Robert (n 131) 217.
[145] See section 2.2.1 above.

Table 7.3 Testing for Confirmation Bias between the Phase 1 and 2 Decision-makers (2007–2020)

	2007–2008 to 2013–2014 (OFT/CC)	2014–2015 to 2019–2020 (CMA)	2007–2008 to 2019–2020
Notifications less 'out of scope'	497	367	864
Phase 2 referrals	64	55	119
Total Phase 2 enforcement	37	33	70
Phase 2 unconditional clearance	30	21	51
Unconditional clearance as % of Phase 2 referrals	46.9%	38.2%	42.9%

Adapted and updated from 'Table 3' of Robert (n 131) 217.

confirmation bias is not present).[146] Under the OFT/CC framework, 46.9 per cent of all Phase 2 referrals were cleared unconditionally, compared with 38.2 per cent of referrals to the CMA Panel (Table 7.3). Both of these figures are sufficiently far above 0 per cent to reject the suggestion that confirmation bias has been an inherent problem under the EA 2002 regime; although, the marginal decline of unconditional clearances under the single authority model may arouse concern in the business community. However, Figure 7.4 illustrates how the unconditional clearance rate has varied significantly during the CMA's tenure, from a high of 88.9 per cent in 2015–2016, to a low of 14.3 per cent a year later in 2016–2017. This lack of consistency again acts to corroborate the suggestion that there is no ingrained conformation bias within the CMA's decision-making process.

As a separate point, the relatively high rate of unconditional clearances in 2014–2015 and 2015–2016 (by the CMA's standards, at least) might be seen to indicate a period where the new authority struggled to manage the workload presented by a stricter Phase 1 time limit following the ERRA 2013 reforms—the suggestion being that the CMA board was more likely to refer 'marginal' cases to Phase 2 in order to meet the forty-working day statutory deadline. However, as section 4.3 touches on, referral rates during this period were in keeping with the levels observed under the OFT, suggesting the CMA has been perfectly able to carry out thorough Phase 1 assessments within the post-ERRA 2013 time limit.

4.5 A Streamlined Regime, But Questions over Pre-Notification Discussions

Since the introduction of the revised statutory time limits (referred to in section 3.2.2, above), the CMA has succeeded in meeting the Phase 1 and Phase 2 deadlines in all of its investigations.[147] This compares favourably to the pre-ERRA 2013 period, which saw numerous instances where the OFT exceeded the forty-working day administrative deadline

---

[146] Robert (n 131) 217.
[147] BEIS Competition Law Review (n 72) 74.

on non-notified mergers at Phase 1,[148] and where the CC was inconsistent in the time taken to accept final undertakings in the period following a Phase 2 infringement decision.[149] In the first four years of the CMA's existence, the average duration of a Phase 1 investigation was 34.8 working days, suggesting the CMA often completes its investigation well in advance of the forty-working day statutory deadline.[150] This points towards an overall quicker formal review process post-ERRA 2013.

However, commercial lawyers have expressed concern over the interpretation of these figures,[151] noting that they do not take account of the 'informal' element of the review process—namely, the pre-notification discussions—which several commentators had predicted could take longer as a result of the stricter deadlines introduced by the ERRA 2013.[152] Some respondents to the government's post-implementation review of the ERRA 2013 reforms claimed to observe an increased tendency of CMA case teams to use the pre-notification discussions to ask questions that would have traditionally been asked during the formal Phase 1 investigation which, they suggest, may be a case of the CMA delaying 'starting the clock' in order to manage its workload.[153] Former Chairs of the Mergers Intelligence Committee at the OFT and the CMA have also confirmed that the ERRA 2013 has had the effect of widening the scope of questions that parties are asked during pre-notification and has led to an increase in the number of information requests.[154] The government review estimates that approximately 60 per cent of CMA merger investigations were launched after pre-notification discussions, and that these discussions extend to a mean average of 33.5 working days (and a median of 29 working days); although, it is conceded that this may underestimate the full extent of the pre-notification period, as the date at which parties first contact the CMA is not publicly available.[155]

Delays in 'starting the clock' cannot, however, be solely attributed to suggestions of more extensive questioning by the CMA during pre-notification discussions. Much also depends on the speed of the parties themselves in terms of responding to information requests with the level of detail that is demanded of them.[156] Indeed, an NAO audit of the UK competition regime revealed that many merging parties 'valued having early discussions with decision-makers',[157] which contradicts the suggestion that the CMA has extended pre-notification discussions for its own ulterior motives.

5 Emerging Challenges and the Agenda for Further Reform

While the fundamental traits of the EA 2002 survived the ERRA 2013 reform package, successive governments have demonstrated a desire to keep the UK merger control regime

---

[148] NAO 2016 (n 63) 38 (Figure 17).
[149] Nikpay and Taylor (n 60) 279.
[150] BEIS Competition Law Review (n 72) 74. A greater proportion of 'less complex' cases (ie cases that do not require an issues/review meeting) are being reviewed in fewer than 35 days, increasing from 23% in 2014–15 to 91% in 2017–18; (n 72) 75.
[151] ibid 75.
[152] See eg Todorovic (n 71) 342 (referred to in section 3.2.2 above).
[153] BEIS Competition Law Review (n 72) 75–76.
[154] Chisholm and Heideman (n 137) 654.
[155] BEIS Competition Law Review (n 72) 76.
[156] ibid 77.
[157] NAO 2016 (n 63) 9.

under review. Indeed, just two years after the CMA came into existence, the government began consultations on further options for reform, which included the potential to realize further efficiencies and cost savings in the short term by integrating parts of Phases 1 and 2 of the review framework and, in the longer term, to consider the merits of adopting a 'single decision-maker' approach.[158] While these proposals have yet to come to fruition, emerging challenges continue to influence the agenda for reform, some of which are already influencing how the regime operates in practice. The government's 2019 *Competition Law Review* suggests further reforms are 'likely' needed for the CMA to effectively handle the larger number of multi-jurisdictional mergers in the post-Brexit era, which will be considered as part of the much-anticipated Competition Green Paper.[159] Unwanted foreign takeovers have also been in the government's crosshairs since the EU Referendum result, and recent revisions look set to be followed by more fundamental change under the National Security and Investment Bill.[160] Moreover, the CMA's approach to mergers in the digital sector will undoubtedly remain on the policy agenda in the coming years, and legislative reform may well be a necessary policy response.

5.1 Managing the Post-Brexit Caseload

The UK's departure from the EU removes the application of the 'one-stop shop' for merger clearances, previously available to transactions that meet both the UK and EU jurisdictional thresholds (so-called 'dual capture' mergers). This will present a more expensive and procedurally onerous approval process for many businesses, and require the CMA to duplicate much of the work undertaken by DG COMP in merger investigations.[161] In practice, the additional filing requirement in the UK is unlikely to have a meaningful impact on 'mega-mergers' that already meet the jurisdictional thresholds of multiple regimes,[162] but the prospect of other cross-border mergers facing two separate investigations (in the UK and the EU) may act to disincentivize merger activity in the UK, especially if the respective decisions of the CMA and DG COMP prove to diverge on a regular basis.[163]

The CMA has long been braced for a 'hard' or 'no deal' Brexit outcome and, as such, has proceeded to invest in the appointment of new staff, many of whom will be assigned to reviewing an estimated 50 additional Phase 1 cases a year.[164] In an effort to manage this extra workload and mitigate the effects on the CMA's resources, it has been suggested that policy-makers—and the CMA itself—may invoke the expertise of sector regulators on a more routine basis in order to conduct 'quick' assessments of mergers taking place in particular markets.[165] Evidently, however, more drastic change is necessary if the CMA is to

---

[158] Department for Business, Innovation and Skills, *Options to refine the UK competition regime: A consultation* (May 2016) paras 27–31 and 41.

[159] BEIS Competition Law Review (n 72) 3.

[160] National Security and Investment HL Bill (2019–21) 165.

[161] Richard Whish, 'Brexit and EU Competition Policy' (2016) 7(5) JECL & Pract 297, 297.

[162] Johnson (n 88) 134.

[163] Martin Rees and Cathal Flynn, 'Effect of a British Exit from the EU on Competition Law Enforcement in the UK' (2015) 21(3) Int TLR 67, 68.

[164] Barney Thompson, 'UK Competition Watchdog Braced for Jump in Workload after Brexit' *The Financial Times* (5 February 2019) www.ft.com/content/9fd79e72-12a7-11e9-a581-4ff78404524e accessed 1 September 2020. It is anticipated that roughly five cases per year will be referred to Phase 2.

[165] Johnson (n 88) 136.

effectively manage the resources it allocates to merger reviews. The independent Penrose Report, published in early 2021, called for changes that would permit the CMA to accept legally-binding undertakings from merging parties *before* the end of a Phase 1 or 2 investigation, where 'the answers and solutions are clear early on'.[166] The government has itself conceded that the increased responsibility on the CMA to deal with large-scale mergers suggests 'a need for wider reform' and, in particular, a requirement to 'work in parallel with other jurisdictions, including the EU, [which] may require changes to current procedures' under the EA 2002.[167]

A bilateral agreement between the UK and EU—and, more specifically, between the CMA and DG COMP—is one option for facilitating this cooperation and would act to create more consistency and alignment between assessment outcomes.[168] Alternatively, some have suggested a 'partial remedy' would be for the UK to adopt a review timetable that aligns more closely to the EUMR's,[169] or a 'more complete solution' of adopting a system of mandatory notification that would allow both the CMA and DG COMP to start their investigatory clocks at similar times.[170] In an open letter to the Secretary of State in 2019, the then Chairman of the CMA, Lord Tyrie, called for a mandatory notification regime and standstill obligations for mergers above a certain threshold, in place of the existing interim measures under the voluntary regime.[171] Such proposals are likely to form part of the government's forthcoming Competition Green Paper and, while the UK's voluntary notification system was passionately defended during consultations leading up to the ERRA 2013, Brexit undoubtedly moves the goal posts on the debate. The informality of the UK notification system provides the CMA with a greater degree of freedom over the type and, in turn, number of cases it calls in,[172] but this freedom does not extend to disregarding any merger it deems to have a realistic potential of resulting in an SLC. Here, there is a fine balance to be struck between the resources allocated to the CMA's mergers intelligence function and to its Phase 1 case teams; adequate investment in the former remains critical for as long as the UK continues to endorse a system of voluntary notification. An unfortunate reality is that, short of infinite time and resources, the CMA's procedural aims (of efficiently identifying and reviewing potentially harmful mergers) may need to take priority over substantive norms (e.g. a business-friendly approach to notification, a fresh pair of eyes at Phase 2, etc).

5.2 Resisting the Rise of Nationalist Sentiment

Outside the jurisdiction of the EUMR, the UK government will also have greater freedom to intervene in large cross-border mergers on public interest grounds. Prior to Brexit, the government would have to request jurisdiction to review the public interest element of an

---

[166] John Penrose, *Power to the People: Stronger Consumer Choice and Competition so Markets Work for People, Not the Other Way Around* (Independent Report, BEIS 2021) 17.

[167] BEIS Competition Law Review (n 72) 89.

[168] Parr and Hammon (n 5) 21.

[169] Leigh M Davison, 'Envisaging the Post-Brexit Landscape: an Articulation of the Likely Changes to the EU–UK Competition Policy Relationship' (2018) 39 Liverpool LR 99, 115; and Parr and Hammon (n 5).

[170] Davison (n 169) 115–16.

[171] Letter from Lord Tyrie to the Secretary of State for Business, Energy and Industrial Strategy (21 February 2019).

[172] Peter Roth, 'Competition Law and Brexit: the Challenges Ahead' (2017) 16(1) Comp Law 5, 7.

EU-level merger under Article 21(4) EUMR. This provision affords Member States the opportunity to assume competence over mergers that raise 'legitimate national interest' concerns, which include public security, media plurality and prudential rules (as part of a non-exhaustive list). Significantly, the European Commission will only consider granting an Article 21(4) request if the merger itself does not arouse suspicion of creating a significant impediment to effective competition (SIEC).[173] This negative application (meaning Member States will never be permitted to clear an anti-competitive merger on legitimate interest grounds), combined with the Commission applying a traditionally narrow interpretation to what constitutes a 'legitimate national interest',[174] has so far acted to temper the UK's ability to intervene in large-scale European mergers involving 'crown jewel' firms based in the UK.[175]

While the limited scope of Article 21(4) proved a hindrance to the UK's pursuit of public interest interventions, it also provided 'an important safeguard against protectionism and undue political intervention',[176] which a post-Brexit UK is no longer subject to. Brexit opens up opportunities for the UK to use its public interest powers under the EA 2002 to block (or extract undertakings from) mergers that have been approved by DG COMP and, more alarmingly, the opportunity for the UK to permit (on public interest grounds) a merger that DG COMP has blocked (on competition grounds), assuming that the EU aspects of the merger can be 'carved-out of the wider transaction'.[177] The shackles of the EUMR are being removed at a time when public opinion of foreign investment and takeovers, in particular, is at an all-time low and calls for economic protectionism are becoming increasingly audible.[178]

As such, with greater freedom to intervene and to propose new public interest grounds under section 58(3) EA 2002, the Secretary of State may well find themself under pressure to exercise these powers where a foreign bidder (or an unpopular domestic bidder) seeks to acquire a popular or lucrative domestic firm. Some fear that it would only take a single interventionist Secretary of State to, in essence, repoliticize the UK merger regime, which 'would be a field day for the lobbying and public relations industry'.[179] Moreover, section 58(3) requires only secondary legislative approval for new public interest grounds to be enacted, denying Parliament the opportunity to rigorously scrutinize provisions that—collectively—stand to have a significant impact on the perceived certainty and transparency of the merger regime. Additional safeguards to prevent the Secretary of State being unduly lobbied would go some way towards mitigating the risk of an influx of new public interest grounds under the EA 2002.[180]

---

[173] European Commission, 'Community Merger Control Law' (1990) Bulletin of the European Communities, Supplement 2/90, 24.

[174] Michael Harker, 'Cross-border Mergers in the EU: the Commission v the Member States' (2007) 3(2) ECJ 503.

[175] eg Pfizer's failed approach for AstraZeneca reportedly saw the Commission ready to reject an Article 21(4) request from the UK, which was seeking to protect the UK science base; David Reader, 'Pfizer/AstraZeneca and the Public Interest: Do UK Foreign Takeover Proposals Prescribe an Effective Remedy?' (2014) 10(1) CPI Antitrust Chronicle 1.

[176] Bruce Lyons, David Reader, and Andreas Stephan, 'UK Competition Policy Post-Brexit: Taking Back Control while Resisting Siren Calls' (2017) 5(3) JAE 347, 356.

[177] Parr and Hammon (n 5) 22.

[178] Alison Jones and John Davies, 'Merger Control and the Public Interest: Balancing EU and National Law in the Protectionist Debate' (2014) 10(3) ECJ 453, 492.

[179] John Vickers, 'Consequences of Brexit for Competition Law and Policy' (2017) 33(1) Oxford Review of Economic Policy S70, S75.

[180] Lyons, Reader, and Stephan (n 176) 358.

As early as 2018, the government had begun to legislate for greater powers to intervene in mergers that raise national security concerns,[181] namely by amending the share of supply test and lowering the turnover test threshold from £70 million to £1 million for mergers involved in (i) the dual use and military use sector, (ii) parts of the advanced technology sector, and—as of July 2020—(iii) artificial intelligence, (iv) cryptographic authentication, and (v) advanced materials.[182] The scope of these provisions is potentially vast, capable of capturing 100 or more additional cases each year, by government estimates.[183] Given the relevance of these sectors and technologies to the government's Industrial Strategy, in which the Business Secretary is tasked with targeting companies to invest in specific UK sectors,[184] an evident conflict of interest arises. One can envisage the absurd scenario where the Secretary of State undertakes a national security assessment of a foreign takeover in the advanced technology sector, while simultaneously negotiating with other parties to invest in the same sector.[185] Such a scenario undermines the Business Secretary's quasi-judicial decision-making role in public interest cases and cannot be allowed to materialize in practice.

Given the prevalent role that national security review is set to play in the post-Brexit era, it is also critical that the concept of 'national security' does not lose the specific meaning intended for it by the drafters of the EA 2002; as was close to being the case in *Melrose/ GKN*, where the Secretary of State faced pressure from various politicians and stakeholders to block the acquisition of an Armed Forces supplier.[186] The definition that the EA 2002 ascribes to 'national security' is notably narrower than that of many other developed countries. For instance, when a foreign takeover is reviewed on national security grounds in the US, it is not uncommon for authorities to take account of industrial policy considerations in order to limit foreign ownership in economically important sectors. Under the EA 2002, there is no such scope for the Business Secretary to consider industrial policy concerns when reviewing a merger on national security grounds. While Parliament had initially struggled to identify a precise definition for 'national security' in debates around the Enterprise Bill,[187] Hansard debate reveals the definition to be closely aligned to protecting the personal safety and security of citizens,[188] rather than any form of economic security. Lord Sainsbury confirmed this by remarking that any intervention on the grounds of 'economic security' (to protect e.g. an asset that is 'essential to large parts of the British

---

[181] David Reader, 'Extending "National Security" in Merger Control and Investment: A Good Deal for the UK?' (2018) 14(1) CLI 35.

[182] EA 2002, s 23A (as amended).

[183] The government estimated 'fewer than 100 transactions per year' would be captured by the initial reforms, while it expects an 'additional 16 cases' to arise from the 2020 reforms; see Department for Business, Energy and Industrial Strategy, *National Security and Infrastructure Investment Review* (Green Paper, 2017) para 154; and HL Secondary Legislative Scrutiny Committee, *21st Report of Session 2019-21* (HL Paper 96, 9 July 2020) para 6.

[184] HM Government, 'Industrial Strategy: Building a Britain Fit for the Future' (White Paper, Cm 9528, 2017) 190.

[185] Reader (n 181) 49. For proposals on mitigating the potential for political bias here see 49–51.

[186] David Reader, 'Why "National Security" Concerns are Unlikely to Impede the Melrose/GKN Takeover' *Competition Policy Blog* (8 February 2018) https://competitionpolicy.wordpress.com/2018/02/08/why-national-security-concerns-are-unlikely-to-impede-the-melrose-gkn-takeover accessed 1 September 2020.

[187] Enterprise HC Bill (2001–02) 115. The Bill's sponsor commented that 'national security is like an elephant: one knows it when one sees it'; Enterprise Bill Deb 30 April 2002, col 356.

[188] Section 58(2) explicitly acknowledges that 'national security' includes 'public security' within the meaning of Article 21(4) EU Merger Regulation (which has been interpreted as relating to mergers with connections or contractual ties to the military or to the maintenance of public health).

economy') would require the Secretary of State to propose a new public interest ground using their powers under (what is now) section 58(3).[189]

Further fundamental reform has been tabled under the National Security and Investment Bill, which—while not limited to acquisitions that create a relevant merger situation—stands to supersede the national security public interest procedure under the EA 2002.[190] If enacted, the Bill would establish a mandatory notification requirement for acquirers seeking to invest in one of (a proposed) 17 key sectors,[191] as well as powers for the Secretary of State to call in unnotified investments up to five years after the transaction was completed.[192] So as to provide flexibility to respond to unforeseen security risks, the government has deliberately omitted a definition for 'national security' under the Bill—although, on Second Reading, the Business Secretary sponsoring the Bill clarified:

> These powers are narrowly defined and will be exclusively used on national security grounds. The Government will not be able to use these powers to intervene in business transactions for broader economic or public interest reasons, and we will not seek to interfere in deals on political grounds.[193]

While the very existence of a national security review procedure may have the effect of reducing foreign investment into the UK, an overtly expansive and aggressive review procedure could inflict irreputable damage on the UK's ability to attract 'welcome' investment, as well as that which is unwanted.[194] This is the risk the government takes in choosing not to narrow the definition of 'national security', nor to adopt the intended meaning ascribed to national security under the EA 2002. However, the statements of the Business Secretary during the Second Reading indicate a definition that does not entirely depart from the EA 2002 and that, critically, does not treat pursuits of economic policy as being within the scope of 'national security'. Nonetheless, the expansive breadth of the Bill and the license it affords the Secretary of State to call in investments retrospectively has raised legitimate concerns regarding the knock-on effect on foreign investment, in particular.[195]

5.3 Rising to the Challenge Presented by Digital Mergers

Understanding and assessing the dynamic theories of harm associated with mergers in the digital sector is among the hottest topics for any competition authority at present.[196] One of

---

[189] HL Deb 18 July 2002, vol 637, col 1490.

[190] NSI Bill (n 160) sch 2.

[191] Department for Business, Energy and Industrial Strategy, *National Security and Investment: Sectors in Scope of the Mandatory Regime* (Consultation document, November 2020) 5.

[192] NSI Bill (n 160) cls 1–2.

[193] National Security and Investment Bill Deb 17 November 2020, vol 684, col 210.

[194] John Fingleton, 'Mergers and the Public Interest: a Wolf in Sheep's Clothing?' *Fingleton Associates* (16 October 2018) https://fingleton.com/news/mergers-and-the-public-interest-a-wolf-in-sheeps-clothing accessed 1 August 2020.

[195] John Fingleton, 'Britain must rethink its "national security" law' *Financial Times* (23 January 2021) https://www.ft.com/content/8606231f-5660-4553-a263-31b16faf4071, accessed 1 February 2021.

[196] On competition law and digital markets see Liza Lovdahl Gormsen, 'Competition Law and the Digital Economy in the UK and Beyond', ch 14 in this volume.

the main theories relates to so-called 'killer acquisitions',[197] where a large digital firm purchases a 'younger', smaller start-up firm that has yet to realize its potential in the market, with the purpose of removing it as a potential future competitor. These younger firms may have the potential to innovate their products and services to such an extent that they will one day amount to exerting competitive pressure on large incumbent firms, thereby incentivizing firms to compete to deliver the most innovative experience to consumers.[198] But if a young firm is acquired by large established firm in the same market or an adjacent market, the young firm will lose the opportunity to one day rival the incumbent and to enhance consumer choice. Realizing this, young firms and new entrants may themselves be disincentivized from bringing new products to market, mindful that their efforts to innovate will be short-lived if it automatically renders them a takeover target.[199] The effect is an overall loss of innovation (and incentives to innovate) in a highly concentrated market, meaning the digital economy fails to reach its full potential.[200]

In the UK, the policy debate in this area has been largely shaped by two seminal reports published in 2019; the government-commissioned *Report of the Digital Competition Expert Panel* (hereafter, 'the Furman Report'),[201] and the CMA-commissioned *Lear Report*.[202] Both reports were critical of what they observed as under-enforcement of mergers in digital markets by the UK competition authorities; the Furman Report suggesting that 'false negative' approvals may have taken place as a result of no digital mergers being blocked under the EA 2002,[203] and the Lear Report even suggesting a tendency of the authorities to err towards under-enforcement in order to avoid over-enforcement.[204] The Lear Report also describes significant M&A activity among the Big Tech players and how they most often (in 60 per cent of mergers) acquire young firms of four years old or less.[205]

Each report makes its own recommendations to detect harmful mergers in the sector and to improve overall enforcement. Among the most prominent of the Furman proposals is to legislate in order to introduce a 'balance of harms' test for digital mergers under the EA 2002, which would require the CMA to take into account 'the scale as well as the likelihood of harm in merger cases involving potential competition and harm to innovation'.[206] Believing the traditional SLC test to present too high a threshold for the CMA to effectively consider dynamic theories of harm, the balance of harms approach 'would mean mergers being blocked when they are expected to do more harm than good'. The Lear Report, on the other hand, recommended placing greater emphasis on the value of transactions in an effort to screen for problematic deals; where the price paid by the acquiring firm is unexplainably high for a young firm, the motives of the acquirer should be questioned to determine whether the merger is intended to kill off emerging competition.[207]

---

[197] For an insightful overview see Chris Pike, 'Start-ups, Killer Acquisitions and Merger Control' (2020) OECD Background Note DAF/COMP(2020) 5.

[198] See eg Kiran Desai, 'Changes for the Digital Economy—Merger Control' (2019) 3(2) CoRe 122, 126.

[199] Eleni Gouliou and others, 'Merger Control in Dynamic Markets' (2020) 19(1) Comp Law 30.

[200] ibid 127.

[201] Digital Competition Expert Panel, 'Unlocking digital competition' (Independent report (Furman Report), HM Treasury 2019).

[202] Lear, *Ex-post Assessment of Merger Control Decisions in Digital Markets: Final report* (Independent report prepared for the CMA (Lear Report), May 2019).

[203] Furman Report (n 201) para 3.43.

[204] Lear Report (n 202) para I.148.

[205] ibid para I.150.

[206] Furman Report (n 201) 10.

[207] Lear Report (n 202) para I.154.

In a speech to mark the publication of the government's *Competition Law Review*, the Business Secretary said of killer acquisitions:

> When a big pharma company buys the minnow with a promising molecule for a spectacular sum is it helping to get a valuable product to market or is it taking out potential competition against something it has on its own lab-bench? In the first case, a merger authority should OK the deal. In the second, in my view, it should say no.[208]

The analogy holds true for mergers in digital markets but presents a notable practical difficulty in terms of the competition authority's ability to establish the motives of the acquiring party. The CMA sought to establish this motive for the first time in the case of *PayPal/iZettle* which, while ultimately found not to be a killer acquisition, demonstrates the lengths that the CMA is prepared to go to in accessing and reviewing internal documents in order establish the underlying rationale for the merger and what justifies the value paid by the acquiring firm.[209]

In response to the Furman and Lear Reports, the Chief Executive of the CMA initially claimed that the authority's merger control toolkit was 'fit for purpose' in terms of addressing concerns related to killer acquisitions in the digital sector.[210] He did, however, appreciate a need for the CMA to rebalance its approach to enforcement and, potentially, to subject powerful companies to greater scrutiny, especially where entry barriers are high and competition is essentially 'for' the market, rather than 'within' it. A year later, while reaffirming its belief that the current merger regime is 'largely fit for purpose', the CMA confirmed that it was 'considering the need for legislative changes' to ensure it has the right tools to prevent consumers being harmed by digital mergers.[211] In October 2020, the Chief Executive announced that the CMA was considering advising the government to create a 'parallel merger regime' for digital mergers that would potentially be subject to mandatory notification and a lower standard of proof under the SLC test.[212] It was anticipated this special parallel regime 'could also accommodate a separate assessment of non-competition concerns such as data protection'.[213] This parallel regime is set to come to pass in 2021, when a new Digital Markets Unit (DMU) within the CMA will be tasked with enforcing a statutory code of conduct for digital platforms who possess 'strategic market status'.[214] The DMU stands to derive significant enforcement powers from the Code, including 'powers to suspend, block and reverse the decisions of tech giants', as well as powers to impose compliance orders and fines for non-compliance.[215]

---

[208] Greg Clark, 'Competition Rules Must Continue to Evolve' Speech to Social Market Foundation, London, 18 July 2019).

[209] Stephen Smith and Matthew Hunt, 'Killer Acquisitions and PayPal/iZettle' (2019) 18(4) Comp Law 162.

[210] Andrea Coscelli, 'Competition in the digital age: reflecting on digital merger investigations' (OECD/G7 Conference on Competition and the Digital Economy, Paris, 3 June 2019).

[211] CMA, *Online platforms and digital advertising market study: Final report* (1 July 2020) para 10.31.

[212] It is anticipated that this regime would apply to firms who are deemed to have 'strategic market status'; Andrea Coscelli, 'Digital Markets: Using our Existing Tools and Emerging Thoughts on a New Regime' (Fordham Competition Law Institute 47th Annual Conference on International Antitrust Law and Policy, Virtual Conference, 9 October 2020).

[213] ibid.

[214] HM Government, 'New competition regime for tech giants to give consumers more choice and control over their data, and ensure businesses are fairly treated' Press release (27 November 2020).

[215] ibid.

The introduction of the DMU will act to reassure the CMA of its ability to address the challenge of digital mergers under a prescriptive Code that is reinforced by enhanced enforcement powers. The approach will also require more 'imagination' going forward,[216] including through further engagement with the non-price effects of mergers.[217] However, some of this refinement risks stretching the EA 2002 provisions beyond their means in ways that may not be readily accommodated under the new statutory Code. For example, while the SLC test allows for the consideration of dynamic competition, this does not tie in well with the 'robust' measures that competition authorities usually deploy.[218] A substantive test akin to the 'balance of harms' test proposed by the Digital Competition Expert Panel, or a lower evidential threshold to allow the CMA to accept more uncertainty when considering counterfactuals as proposed by the Lear Report, may offer a more workable approach. Equally, a value-based jurisdictional test would improve the chances of capturing killer acquisitions, especially given these young firms are far less likely to meet the turnover or share of supply thresholds under the EA 2002.[219] The prospect of non-competition concerns being considered within a parallel merger regime is perhaps the most revolutionary of these proposals. Any departure from the EA 2002's strict competition-based approach would first require a meticulous impact assessment, but there is merit in affording the CMA the ability to holistically address merger-specific issues of privacy and data protection within a limited range of merger cases.

6 Conclusion

The evolution of the UK merger regime under the EA 2002 has largely been one of fine tuning, either in response to judicial review rulings, public consultations or independent expert reports on emerging issues. These are positive traits of a regime that has shown itself to be proactive in its efforts to identify and respond to its weaknesses, while maintaining the EA 2002's original vision of a rigorous competition-based approach with minimal political involvement. What the regime needs to improve upon is evaluating the practical impact of its reforms. The ERRA 2013 reform package has been praised for streamlining the review process and unlocking the potential for parties to offer reasoned UILs—but both conclusions are premature and, in particular, further understanding of the nature and duration of pre-notification discussions is required.

Tailored adjustments have delivered a regime that, for the most part, provides a transparent, consistent and business-friendly review process, while also affording the CMA extensive powers to halt integration and to penalize parties for non-compliance with interim measures. The CMA's role is critical and, going forward, funding and resource management will greatly influence the early performance of UK merger control in the post-Brexit era. Further procedural refinements (e.g. converging closer to the EUMR review timetable) may well be necessary to aid the CMA's transition towards a significantly larger caseload, and calls to depart from the voluntary notification system should remain on the back burner

---

[216] Sir Peter Roth, 'The Continual Evolution of Competition Law' (2019) 7(1) JAE 6, 23.
[217] Peter Wantoch and others, 'Non-price Effects of Mergers' (2019) 18(2) Comp Law 73.
[218] Roth (n 216) 23.
[219] ibid 24.

until the extent of the CMA's task is fully appreciated. In any case, if the CMA continues its recent trend of showing a firm hand to non-notified completed merger, the business community will ultimately come to see the UK as administering a quasi-mandatory regime.

As a consequence of Brexit and a general rise in nationalist sentiment, the Secretary of State now risks being put under greater pressure to intervene in mergers—and, in particular, foreign takeovers—on public interest grounds and to introduce new public interest grounds using the section 58(3) power. While objectively legitimate interests may well be pursued under this power,[220] expanding the scope and application of the public interest exceptions is a slippery slope and, once the Secretary of State blocks or permits one merger, it establishes an expectation that other interventions are also justifiable. Policy-makers cannot allow an excessive use of section 58(3)—or an overly interventionist application of the new National Security and Investment regime—to take merger control back into the dark ages of the broader public interest regime under the Fair Trading Act 1973. *Lloyds/HBOS* should act as a lasting reminder of the pitfalls of political intervention and, in order to preserve the primacy of the competition-based approach, safeguards are needed to prevent the Secretary of State being unduly lobbied to make an intervention.

The CMA has been confident of tailoring its approach to digital mergers using its existing toolkit and will benefit from the new enforcement powers in the arsenal of the DMU going forward. It remains to be seen whether the SLC test is able to accommodate fully dynamic theories of harm under a more 'imaginative' approach, or whether it is worth investing in a 'new suit' in the form of a revised substantive test or a lower standard of proof for digital mergers. Introducing a value-based jurisdictional test for digital mergers may prove a useful starting point in terms of enhancing the CMA's powers to call in potential killer acquisitions for review. From its pre-legislative origins, the EA 2002 merger regime has been a twenty-year work-in-progress, and while its greatest challenges undoubtedly lie ahead, responsible governance and effective enforcement may yet extend its shelf life.

---

[220] Holmes, for example, advocates the introduction of "sustainability and climate change" as a named public interest ground; Simon Holmes, 'Climate change, sustainability and competition law in the UK' (2020) 41(8) ECLR 384, 392.

8

Unfinished Reform of the Institutions Enforcing UK Competition Law

*Bruce Lyons**

1 Introduction

Institutions are where decisions are made. They frame how decisions are made and determine who makes them. Some of these decisions are strategic, such as the allocation of resources and prioritization of cases. Other decisions are case specific and adjudicative (e.g. merger prohibition or finding abuse of dominance). Legislation may detail the powers of decision and the broad organizational structure in which they are made, but much remains dependent on the internal institutional culture. Institutions provide the foundation on which a competition regime can either build solidly or crack and subside. Foundations must be appropriate to the structure of competition law being built, and in the UK that structure has changed fundamentally since 1998. The institutions have also changed, but too little attention has been placed on how the changes in competition law require complementary changes in the institutions.

It is easy to list the organizational changes of the last two decades. The Monopolies and Mergers Commission (MMC) became the Competition Commission (CC) in 1999 following the Competition Act 1998 (CA 1998); an independent Competition Appeals Tribunal (CAT) was established in 2003 following the Enterprise Act 2002 (EA 2002), and the Office of Fair Trading (OFT) and the CC merged to become the Competition and Markets Authority (CMA) in 2014 following the Enterprise and Regulatory Reform Act 2013 (ERRA 2013).[1] There were also new competition powers and reorganizations for the specialist sector regulators. The overall effect was to raise the penalties for transgressing competition law at the same time as the competition agencies were taking the power of decision away from the elected Secretary of State.[2]

* The author would like to thank the editors and particularly Amelia Fletcher and Mike Walker for insightful comments on an earlier draft. All opinions and errors are solely those of the author.

[1] Membership of the EU has also affected the UK institutions, particularly since 2004 with powers to enforce Articles 101 and 102 TFEU under Regulation 1/2003 (although the European Commission retained the power to return a case to Brussels), and participation in the European Competition Network (ECN). More recently, the European Union (Withdrawal Agreement) Act 2020 allows the UK to investigate mergers and antitrust issues which affect multiple Member States, which were previously reserved for the European Commission.

[2] The relevant Secretary of State is the head of the 'business' ministry, which was the Department of Trade and Industry (DTI, 1970-2007), Department for Business, Enterprise and Regulatory Reform (2007-09), Department for Business, Innovation and Skills (BIS, 2009-16), and Department for Business, Energy and Industrial Strategy (BEIS, since 2016).

Bruce Lyons, *Unfinished Reform of the Institutions Enforcing UK Competition Law* In: *The UK Competition Regime*. Edited by: Barry Rodger, Peter Whelan, and Angus MacCulloch, Oxford University Press. © The Contributors 2021. DOI: 10.1093/oso/9780198868026.003.0008

The aim of this chapter is to understand not just the organizational changes set out above, but the ways of working, conventions, appointments, decision-making procedures, and safeguards that give the organizational skeleton its functionality. It is these factors, alongside any formal rules and organizations, that North would consider the institutions of the UK competition regime.[3] Regulatory agencies and formal rules can be created, renamed, and redesigned by political fiat, but operational decisions remain strongly influenced by the continuing culture:

> Institutions typically change incrementally rather than in discontinuous fashion ... Although formal rules may change overnight as a result of political or judicial decision, informal constraints embodied in customs, traditions, and codes of conduct are much more impervious to deliberate policies.[4]

So, it is necessary to delve back to their origins to understand the current UK institutions, their strengths, and their weaknesses.

In section 2, I set out what matters in institutional design and how success should be measured. Section 3 provides a short history of the very different institutional cultures in the competition agencies inherited from the twentieth century. Section 4 highlights how the new century brought a new economic approach to competition policy alongside the new powers of remedy, penalty, and decision in the CA 1998 and the EA 2002. I examine how these were addressed in the OFT, the CC, and the CAT. Section 5 considers the compromise embodied in the contrasting institutional cultures within the newly merged CMA brought about by ERRA 2013. In section 6, I highlight the very substantial new challenges for the CMA going forward from 2020, examine the CMA's own flawed agenda for reform, and suggest a more robust way forward. Section 7 concludes.

2 What Matters in Institutional Design and Performance?

An effective institutional arrangement cannot simply pick-and-mix because changing one part of that system has ramifications elsewhere. There is no research that identifies a uniquely optimal system, but there is a consensus amongst scholars of the features that matter.[5]

---

[3] Douglass C North, *Institutions, Institutional Change and Economic Performance* (CUP, 1990).

[4] ibid 6.

[5] See William E Kovacic, 'Rating the Competition Agencies: What Constitutes Good Performance?' (2009) 16 Geo Mason L J 903; Michael J Trebilcock and Edward M Iacobucci, 'Designing Competition Law Institutions: Values, Structure, and Mandate' (2010) 41 Loy U Chi L J 455; Eleanor M Fox, 'Antitrust and Institutions: Design and Change' (2010) 41 Loy U Chi L J, 473; Philip Lowe, 'The Design of Competition Policy Institutions for the 21st Century—The Experience of the European Commission and DG Competition' Competition Policy Newsletter, European Commission (2008) 1; Eleanor M Fox and Michael J Trebilcock, *The Design of Global Law Institutions: Global Norms, Local Choices* (OUP, 2013) Introduction; Joshua Wright and Angela Diveley, 'Do Expert Agencies Outperform Generalist Judges? Some Preliminary Evidence from the Federal Trade Commission' (2012) 1 Journal of Antitrust Enforcement 1; Frédéric Jenny, 'The Institutional Design of Competition Authorities: Debates and Trends' in Yannis Katsoulacos and Frédéric Jenny (eds), *Competition Law Enforcement in the BRICS and in Developing Countries. Legal and Economic Aspects* (Springer 2016) 1.

2.1 Mandate

Competition authorities are given a *range of responsibilities* and legislation to implement. They also have advisory and advocacy duties. The portfolio of legal instruments usually includes powers concerning agreements between firms, the behaviour of a single firm (or group of firms) with market power, and mergers. UK competition law also provides for market investigations with strong potential remedies including the ability to cap prices or order a firm to be broken up. Consumer law enforcement and, prospectively, the review of state aid are also the CMA's responsibility, and sector regulators have both direct regulatory powers and concurrent powers for competition enforcement. There is a basic organizational trade-off between clear focus on a range of activities requiring similar skills (e.g. analysis of the competitive effects of business strategies, or industry knowledge), as against resource-sharing and coordination across a wider, more diverse range of responsibilities (e.g. competition and consumer protection).

Competition authorities are also given overarching goals in the form of *legal duties*. For example, there may be a primary duty to act in the public interest, or to promote competition, or to protect consumers. Sparse legal wording is open to interpretation, so the agency may choose to express its mission in language that helps its staff focus on priorities, or which is better understood by other stakeholders. For example, the CMA's mission is to make markets work in the interests of consumers, businesses and the economy.[6] The mission can be influential in prioritizing cases, motivating staff and gaining public support.

A third dimension of their mandate is the extent to which a competition authority is allowed to make decisions without *reference to the minister*.[7] Even when a minister is not the decision-maker, politicians can exert general influence through budget setting, parliamentary scrutiny, the approval of senior appointments (and, importantly, reappointments), and informal pressure (e.g. conversations between the agency head and the minister). The degree of independence of those making first instance decisions is greatly enhanced if their continuation in that role cannot be influenced by the determinations they make. This can be achieved by either appointment until retirement or fixed term appointments without possibility of renewal.

2.2 Organizational Design and Decision-making

The institutions of any competition regime frame a wide range of different types of decision, including: budget allocation; case selection; case investigation and analysis; first instance determination of whether business behaviour is anti-competitive and, if so, what fines and/ or remedies to apply; and appeal/review of contested determinations. The way these decisions are organized can have a profound effect on both the efficiency and the fairness of a competition regime.

---

[6] See section 5.1.1.

[7] Politicians are often happy to reduce their operational workloads and shift responsibility for decisions that may be unpopular with certain interest groups. For evidence that political independence enhances the quality of a competition regime see Christel Koop and Chris Hanretty, 'Political Independence, Accountability, and the Quality of Regulatory Decision-Making' (2018) 51(1) Comparative Political Studies 38.

Trebilcock and Iacobucci identify three organizational models in which these decisions are made.[8] The bifurcated agency model has two specialized agencies, each with investigative resources, the first focusing on case selection ('phase 1'), and the second completing the investigation and adjudicating ('phase 2'). This was the UK structure for markets and mergers with the OFT and CC prior to ERRA 2013. The integrated agency model brings case selection, investigation and adjudication under one roof, as with the CMA (also with the OFT for CA 1998 prohibitions). Both agency models are naturally inquisitorial, with the adjudicating body aiming to adopt a balanced view. In contrast, a bifurcated judicial model has a specialized investigative agency, which brings each case for adjudication by an independent tribunal or court. This prosecutorial system is periodically proposed as an alternative model for UK competition enforcement, with the CMA taking cases to the (renamed) CAT for first instance decisions.[9]

Cross-examination in court provides the characteristic challenge to evidence and analysis in a prosecutorial system. An inquisitorial system must build challenge into its own decision-making processes, and provide access for the parties to the decision-maker. A lone decision-maker can act decisively and with speed, but he or she can find it difficult to shift from an initial position. Group decision-making is not necessarily better if its members are of unequal status in a hierarchy, or if all have a similar perspective, or if the same individuals are involved at successive stages of case determination and so vulnerable to confirmation bias.[10] A group with a greater diversity of skills and experience is more likely to start from different positions and has a greater need to debate and test positions.

2.3 Rights of Appeal

Parties subject to an adverse determination must have the right of review or appeal. The right of third-party appeal provides a check on under-enforcement. A central issue is the degree of scrutiny conducted by the appeal court or tribunal. Judicial review addresses the lawfulness of the decision—whether it is illegal, irrational, procedurally inappropriate or disproportionate. A merits appeal additionally addresses the correctness of the decision—it is less deferential to the first instance decision, and the appeals body may substitute its own determination.

The level of review/appeal is a matter of common law, the Human Rights Act 1998, and legislation (e.g. the CA 1998 requires merits review for the prohibitions).[11] There are generally two sets of factors to be balanced.[12] First, the seriousness of the consequences of the

---

[8] Trebilcock and Iacobucci (n 5). See also Michael Trebilcock and Edward Iacobucci, 'Designing Competition Law Institutions' (2002) 25 World Competition 361, 372–80.

[9] See Department for Business, Innovation and Skills (BIS), *A Competition Regime for Growth: A Consultation on Options for Reform* (March 2011); Renato Nazzini, 'A Reform Too Few or a Reform Too Many: Judicial Review, Appeals or a Prosecutorial System under the UK Competition Act 1998?' (2021) Journal of Antitrust Enforcement, forthcoming 1.

[10] See Damien J Neven, 'Competition Economics and Antitrust in Europe' *Economic Policy* (October 2006)741; William E Kovacic and James C Cooper, 'Behavioral Economics and Its Meaning for Antitrust Agency Decision Making' (2012) 8 JL Econ & Pol'y 779. The latter discuss the evidence and foundations of confirmation bias, which Neven labels 'prosecutorial bias'.

[11] Nazzini (n 9). The right to a fair trial is enshrined in art 6 of the European Convention for the Protection of Human Rights (1950), brought into effect in the UK by the Human Rights Act 1998. On this issue see ch 9 below.

[12] A review on merits 'will accord appropriate respect to the decision of the lower court. Appropriate respect will be tempered by the nature of the lower court and its decision-making process. There will also be a spectrum

first instance decision. This includes fines and remedies affecting property-rights (e.g. price controls, divestiture/break-up of a firm), as well as the reputational damage associated with quasi-criminality. Secondly, the expertise, processes, and independence of decision-making behind the first instance determination, especially relative to that of the appeals body.

2.4 Evaluation of Performance

Performance appraisal is a prerequisite for understanding how a competition regime can be improved. The problem is how to do this systematically. It is easy enough to write down a list of theoretically desirable indicators: elimination of consumer detriment; appropriate choice of cases for precedent; speed, efficiency and consistency of decisions; procedural fairness and rights of defence; quality of decisions and robustness to appeal; deterrence achieved by the above; and effective advocacy. It is another matter to appraise success in these dimensions. A number of indicators have been proposed.

The number of decisions is suggestive, not least because decisions are necessary for precedent and deterrence, but this conveys nothing about each decision's quality or wider importance.[13] The number of successful appeals may appear to provide a negative indicator of the quality of individual decisions, but this is fundamentally biased—prohibitions are more likely to be appealed than clearances, and weak agencies do not take controversial decisions. Careful ex-post reviews of individual cases are useful indicators, but they are expensive to conduct and provide no cross-organizational comparisons.[14] Similar problems affect other case-centric measures of performance.

An alternative methodology is to focus on the institution as a whole and its coherence along the dimensions set out in sections 2.1-2.3. This approach facilitates greater sensitivity to the less quantifiable nuances of institutional design, but it can only identify broad lessons given the range of dimensions of design and the international diversity of institutions.[15]

Further insight at the institutional level can be gained through peer assessment of reputation. Kovacic explains the benefits:

"Perceptions of a competition agency's quality directly influence judicial decisions about whether to defer to the agency's positions, legislative decisions about the agency's budget and statutory authority, the willingness of companies to comply with laws entrusted to the agency's enforcement, and the agency's ability to hire and retain capable staff. A competition agency that enjoys an excellent brand is also likely to inspire citizen confidence in government by showing that public institutions truly 'work'.[16]

of appropriate respect depending on the nature of the decision of the lower court which is challenged'. *Dupont de Nemours v Dupont* (2003) EWCA Civ 1368, para 94.

[13] W E Kovacic, H Hollman, and P Grant, 'How Does your Competition Agency Measure Up?' (2011) 7(1) European Competition Journal 25.

[14] The CMA conducts an externally validated annual impact assessment of its work, based on the estimates of consumer benefit it calculates for each completed case. See section 5.3.

[15] The most detailed study along these lines compare nine different jurisdictions using criteria of efficiency and fairness. See Fox and Trebilcock (n 5).

[16] William Kovacic 'Rating the Competition Agencies: What Constitutes Good Performance?' (2009) Geo. Mason L Rev 16:4, 903.

Each of the above approaches has weaknesses, but together they become persuasive so I draw on each in the following sections appraising the UK institutions.

3 Institutional Cultures Inherited from the Twentieth Century

3.1 The 'Monopolies Commission' and Restrictive Practices Court

Fox argues that '[a] jurisdiction's first design is its most important design'.[17] The UK's first competition agency was the Monopolies and Restrictive Practices Commission (MRPC).[18] It was established in 1949 to investigate and report on the public interest of any monopolies or restrictive practices referred to it by the Secretary of State, who would then decide on action in the light of the report. It was fundamentally an investigative body, writing reports with recommendations for the minister to decide.

The MRPC consisted of a panel of members with a chairman who was primus inter pares in decision-making. Both were appointed by the Secretary of State. Members sat as a group and were all part-time. The chairmen from 1954 to 1993 were all Queen's Counsel, but the members included people from business, finance, public sector and universities.[19] The institutional longevity of this decision-making structure was such that half a century later, members were 'recognisably similar people, doing a recognisably similar job, to their predecessors appointed in 1949'.[20] They were, in today's parlance, part of the gig economy, paid at a modest rate, only for the days they attended meetings, and providing a remarkably cheap source of expertise and experience.

The MRPC rapidly established an investigative procedure that was to cover all types of case. This included: the members attending site visits and informal discussions; a fact-finding stage and a formal clarification hearing with the main parties; reflection and analysis to establish a provisional view of the public interest; communicating this in writing to the parties and inviting written responses, with a further hearing to discuss these; followed by a full report. Reports were published in full, subject to excisions for business confidentiality. Apart from the public interest test, these institutional procedures remain substantially unchanged in the markets and mergers directorate of the CMA seventy years on.

The public interest was loosely defined: 'The Commission shall take into account all matters which appear to them in the particular circumstances to be relevant'.[21] The interpretation of public interest was decided afresh in each case with no constraint of precedent and no issuance of guidance.

In the 1940s, there was no strong presumption against either monopolies or restrictive practices, which had been seen as helpful for coordination during the crisis of the Second World War—indeed, it was a period of monopoly creation under public ownership (i.e.

---

[17] Eleanor M Fox, 'Antitrust and Institutions: Design and Change' (2010) 41(3) Loyola University Chicago Law Journal 473.

[18] For the history of the MRPC and its successors in the twentieth century, I draw heavily on Stephen Wilks, *In the Public Interest: Competition Policy and the Monopolies and Mergers Commission* (Manchester UP, 1999).

[19] A civil servant at the grade of Under-Secretary helped design procedures and oversee the staff support.

[20] Wilks (n 18) 2.

[21] Fair Trading Act 1973, s 84.

nationalization). Over the years, the public interest test became interpreted more narrowly on competition, but it lasted formally throughout the twentieth century.

As the problems with cartels and other restrictive practices became apparent, the 1956 Restrictive Trade Practices Act established a Restrictive Practices Court (RPC) to adjudicate on them. They were not per se illegal, but they had to be registered and a new Registrar of Restrictive Trade Agreements could take them to the RPC. The requirement to register harmless agreements made the system administratively burdensome.[22] Furthermore, the Secretary of State could exempt agreements and the RPC had no power to impose penalties other than for contempt of court.

The MRPC was renamed the Monopolies Commission (MC) in 1956, when it lost its role in restrictive practices, and then the Monopolies and Mergers Commission (MMC) in 1973, eight years after its mandate was extended to include reporting on the public interest of mergers.[23] Similarly to monopolies, the Secretary of State referred mergers for investigation, the MMC wrote its report and made recommendations, then the Secretary of State was determinative on remedies and prohibitions.[24] Looking forwards in this institutional story, the MMC would become the CC and continue with its established inquisitorial approach, panel of independent members and group decision-making.

The post of Registrar and the RPC set the seeds for two new institutional lines that emerge as the OFT and the CAT. The Registrar was a personalized role, albeit with a small staff to advise him and, if he could not cajole firms into dropping an agreement, he could refer the agreement to the RPC for determination. The individual Registrar, with only advisory and referral powers, would evolve into the pre-CA 1998 DGFT supported by OFT staff. The RPC sat, when needed, as a three-person group including a senior judicial appointment and lay members who had business or economics expertise. The character of this decision-making group is to be found in today's CAT, although the RPC was not an appeals body.

3.2 The OFT and Sector Regulators

The birth of the Office of Fair Trading (OFT) in 1973 was in economically chaotic times.[25] In the same year, the Counter-Inflation Act set up a separate (and larger) Price Commission to try to control prices whilst inflation was rising to over 25 per cent pa. Political attention in 1973 was also directed at UK accession to the EU. The government wanted to shed some burdensome operational responsibilities from the Secretary of State and the business ministry (then named the DTI). Consideration had been given to various organizational models, including extending the mandate of the MC, but eventually it was decided to create

[22] The European Commission would find much the same problem with Article 101 until the reform of Regulation 17/62 in 2003.

[23] Monopolies and Mergers Act 1965. In 1980, it was given a further role in investigating the efficiency of nationalized industries, which helps explain why it later became the appeals body for firms subject to decisions by the post-privatization sector regulators.

[24] The European merger regulation No 4064/89 limited the MMC's role in merger control to mainly domestic mergers from 1990. By this time, 'monopoly' was defined broadly to be either a single firm with at least 25 per cent share of supply, or parallel conduct by oligopolists (known as 'complex monopoly').

[25] Established under the Fair Trading Act (1973). See Wilks (n 18) ch 6, and Sir Gordon Borrie's valedictory reflections on his 16 years as DGFT in his 'Annual Report of the Director General of Fair Trading' (OFT 1991).

the new role of Director-General of Fair Trading (DGFT), to be supported by a civil service staff in the form of the OFT.

The DGFT had duties relating to the economic interests of consumers and to competition.[26] The consumer portfolio ranged from licensing debt collectors to liaising with trading standards officers, and it took up 50 per cent more resources than competition.[27] The competition portfolio included absorbing the role of the Registrar and advising the Secretary of State on whether to refer a merger to the MMC. The OFT also took over from the Secretary of State/DTI in horizon-scanning and initiating monopoly references, though the Secretary of State retained a veto. The OFT was further responsible for implementing remedies recommended by the Secretary of State.[28]

The DGFT was appointed by the Secretary of State on renewable 5-year terms, so the system encouraged cooperation between the DGFT and Secretary of State through the DTI. It became the practice to negotiate with businesses about their restrictive agreements, rather than challenge them before the RPC. One result was the lack of published evidence or reasoning, and so also the lack of precedent or guidance for firms. The same negotiated approach developed for mergers, with divestments in lieu of a reference to the MMC.[29]

As the privatization of public utilities proceeded through the 1980s and 1990s, it became necessary to regulate the non-competitive elements of the market. This led to the establishment of a series of sectoral regulators, starting with the Office for Telecommunications in 1985. They were set up with Director Generals and in the image of the DGFT/OFT. Their roles included setting price controls and revising licence conditions (initially issued by the Secretary of State). They could also make merger and monopoly references to the MMC, which additionally advised on appeals in relation to their regulatory decisions.[30]

3.3 Inherited Institutional Cultures

The second half of the twentieth century established the deep-rooted decision-making cultures into which the three major pieces of legislation of the last two decades would be fitted. The MMC was unable to initiate its own inquiries but had a powerful tradition of reporting by independent groups. The OFT and sector regulators were established under single person Director Generals, with competition powers mainly to refer to another body for determination, and a closer relationship with the Secretary of State. The Secretary of State/ DTI was not involved in investigations but retained widespread powers to overrule both the DGFT and MMC. The RPC was required only on the few occasions when the DGFT and businesses could not agree on restrictive agreements. The substantive test for all was whether business practices were against the public interest. If they were found to be so, firms faced no significant penalty beyond being told to stop.

---

[26] Fair Trading Act 1973, Pt 1 s 2.
[27] OFT Annual Report 1991, Appendix K,.83. The first two DGFTs were lawyers, including Sir Gordon Borrie QC who was a consumer protection lawyer and held the post from 1976 to 1992.
[28] To give a sense of relative scale, the OFT had 400 staff in 1990, the MMC had volatile staff numbers but never more than 120, and the Price Commission had 500–600 in the late 1970s.
[29] See Borrie (n 25) 10; Peter Freeman, 'Better to Travel Hopefully than to Arrive? The Reform of UK Competition Law 1991-2016' Zeeman Lecture at Regulatory Policy Institute, Oxford (2016).
[30] See Wilks (n 18) 255.

4 The Competition Test and New Powers of Decision: Institutional Implications of CA 1998 and EA 2002

The turn of the millennium brought a burst of reform in competition law, both in the UK and across Europe. Two transformative Acts, the CA 1998 and the EA 2002, brought about three fundamental changes. First, public interest was replaced explicitly by competition as the substantive test for appraising restrictive practices, monopolies and mergers. This necessitated a much sharper focus on the economic analysis. Secondly, anti-competitive agreements and the abuse of a dominant position were prohibited, and significant penalties were introduced for firms in breach of a prohibition. Third, the OFT and MMC became determinative, including for the new markets regime, with the Secretary of State withdrawing from case decisions other than for narrowly defined and rare public interest exceptions. The institutions needed to evolve to take proper advantage of these changes.

4.1 The Rise of the Economic Approach

While the interpretation of 'public interest' is naturally a political decision, anti-competitive effects lie in the more technical realm of economic analysis. In the 1980s, the development of a game-theoretic analysis of competitive interactions had provided a rigorous framework that could incorporate details of the market.[31] New microdata and econometric techniques in the 1990s showed how the theory could be used to interpret economic evidence.[32] Further interaction between academics (and their newly trained students) with competition practitioners in the 2000s facilitated the development of practical tools and guidance. Senior legal scholars in the USA had prepared the way for a more economic approach to competition analysis and the US agencies were early adopters. The intellectual conditions were right for institutions in the UK and Europe to follow suit.[33]

Influential appointments of academic economists to lead the UK institutions confirmed the central role of economic analysis. In 1998, Derek Morris became the first competition economist appointed chairman of the CC, and in 2000, John Vickers was appointed DGFT. Their immediate successors were also competition economists.

4.2 The OFT

The core change brought about by CA 1998 was the move from absence of a formal presumption against restrictive agreements or monopoly practices, to the formal prohibitions against anti-competitive agreements (Chapter I) and abuse of dominance (Chapter II), to mirror TFEU Articles 101 and 102. Penalties for breach of the prohibitions were potentially

---

[31] See eg Jean Tirole, *The Theory of Industrial Organization* (MIT Press, 1988); Massimo Motta, *Competition Policy: Theory and Practice* (CUP, 2004).

[32] See Bruce Lyons (ed), *Cases in European Competition Policy: The Economic Analysis* (CUP, 2009).

[33] A further conduit was the rise of specialist economic consultancies, which grew rapidly in the late 1990s. See Damien J Neven, 'Competition Economics and Antitrust in Europe' (2006) 48 Economic Policy741. For a discussion on the quantification of the rise of economic effects over legal form in the EU see Pablo Ibanez Colomo and Andriani Kalintiri, 'The Evolution of EU Antitrust Policy: 1966-2017' (2020) 83(3) MLR 321.

substantial (up to 10 per cent of turnover), and there were new rights of private action for damages, which further raised the consequences of an adverse determination. European legal precedent was added to a mix that would inevitably become more litigious. A key aim was that the prohibitions should encourage firms to act competitively ex ante (i.e. to enhance deterrence), rather than wait for ex post investigations.

The DGFT was charged with enforcing the new prohibitions and became the first-instance decision-maker.[34] The RPC was abolished. This created a single stage of investigation with a single person determination in relation to prohibitions with high penalties, so merits appeals were legislated to provide some balance to this lack of safeguards. Appeals were to be heard by a new specialist appeals tribunal, the Competition Commission Appeals Tribunal (CCAT). The OFT retained its dual consumer and competition roles, alongside its mission 'to make markets work well for consumers'.[35]

The EA 2002 took a formal step towards more dispersed decision-making by abolishing the role of DGFT. The OFT became a corporate entity led by a chief operating officer (CEO), chairman, and strategic board. Although formally made by the Secretary of State, senior appointments were subject to a process overseen by the Commissioner for Public Appointments, including open advertisement and transparent interviewing. Stated aims for the Board were to appoint only those with expertise relevant to competition or consumer protection, and to enhance the voice of business and consumers. Consumer groups were also given a statutory role in being able to make 'super-complaints' which required a formal response from the OFT.

Nevertheless, there remained a lack of transparency in the OFT. For the prohibitions, case initiation, investigation, and decisions were all in the hands of staff. No separation was introduced between the decision to issue a Statement of Objections (SO) and the first-instance decision. Hearings were not routine and apparently not always attended by the decision-maker. For many years, the identity of the decision-maker was not even disclosed.

EA 2002 distanced the Secretary of State from merger referrals by giving the OFT a duty to refer potentially anti-competitive mergers to the CC, though the OFT could alternatively accept undertakings in lieu of a reference. The OFT was able to conduct market studies which would be the main route to using its new power to refer a market to the CC for a full investigation.[36] Finally, the EA 2002 introduced personal penalties in the form of potential incarceration under a criminal cartel offence and the disqualification of directors. This was to prove something of a poisoned chalice by greatly complicating the pursuit of cartels.

4.3 The CC

The CA 1998 gave the MMC yet another new name, the Competition Commission (CC). It was to have internal separation of two panels of members from which decision groups could be selected: reporting members would consider merger and market references, as

---

[34] The sector regulators were given concurrent powers to enforce the CA 1998 prohibitions.

[35] This mission was repeated prominently at the beginning of each OFT Annual Report, including its final report for 2013–2014 (HC27). Andrew Motion, then Poet Laureate and Professor of Creative Writing at UEA, once suggested to me that it would sound better if it was 'to make markets work wonderfully'!

[36] The sector regulators were given concurrent powers to refer a market in their own sectors to the CC for investigation.

well as regulatory appeals; and the CCAT members would consider appeals in relation to OFT decisions. The reporting side of the CC continued to apply the public interest test and report to the Secretary of State on mergers and monopolies. The 'monopoly' provisions of Fair Trading Act 1973 were retained, although the prohibition of abuse of a dominant position was intended to take much of the caseload.[37]

The EA 2002 returned substantive consistency in the substantive test across the institutions by replacing public interest with competition tests for mergers and market investigations. The latter replaced 'monopoly' references. The CC also became determinative on both the finding of an adverse effect and the choice of appropriate remedy—the Secretary of State was taken out of case decision-making other than for minor public interest exceptions. The CC became accountable to Parliament through its annual review and scrutiny by select committees, and it was required to publish guidance on its approach to merger and market investigations. In its casework, it was given stronger powers to demand information and witnesses, and it was required to meet statutory timetables. It had to consult parties who might be adversely affected by its proposed decisions, which meant publishing provisional findings and a list of remedies under consideration. Its determinations were subject to judicial review by the newly separated CAT.

The modus operandi of the CC remained very close to that of its predecessors. Each case was decided by a group of four or five members, typically including a lawyer, an economist, an accountant/finance person, and a former public sector or business executive. The group was involved early in the investigation, approving work streams, reading all the evidence submitted (apart from raw data and highly technical reports), sometimes commenting on draft staff working papers, deciding the outcome and remedies, and approving the provisional and final reports. The group attended site visits and held hearings with all main parties both early and later in the proceedings. This gave several opportunities for open discussion between the group of decision-makers and the senior management of the firms under investigation (almost always including the CEOs). The extent of involvement by the group in the details of the investigation (e.g. commenting on draft technical working papers) potentially compromised the separation of investigation and first instance determination.

All members, including the chairman, were formally appointed by the Secretary of State following an open process overseen by the Commissioner for Public Appointments. All were appointed for a maximum of eight years and with no possibility of renewal. EA 2002 brought the promise to appoint only those with expertise relevant to competition.[38]

4.4 The CAT

Whereas CA 1998 had created the CCAT within the CC, EA 2002 reinforced its independence with organizational separation as the renamed CAT. The CAT is headed by a president and there is a panel of chairmen who are either judges or QCs. These judicial appointments are made by the Lord Chancellor on the recommendation of the Judicial Appointments Commission following an open competition. In the tradition of the RPC, either the

---

[37] The CC continued to publish around two monopoly reports each year (much the same as in the second half of the 1990s) until the new markets regime of the EA 2002 became operational.

[38] In 2004, there were 41 reporting members.

president or a chairman sits with two ordinary members in a panel of three to adjudicate. Like the CC's reporting members, the ordinary members of the CAT are recruited in open competition according to the guidelines of the Office of the Commissioner for Public Appointments, subject to formal appointment by the Secretary of State.[39] In fact, many of the latter are former members of the CC, and they have similar attributes, including expertise in competition economics and business. Administrative support is provided by a small Competition Service, which has no capacity for further investigation.

The CAT exercises judicial review of contested decisions in relation to mergers and markets, and merits appeals in relation to the CA 1998 prohibitions determined by the OFT and concurrent regulators. It has additionally collected appeals roles in relation to a wide range of other regulatory decisions, including merits appeals for Ofcom's 'significant market power' decisions. Appeals in relation to fines and penalties are also adjudicated on merits. The CAT further makes first-instance decisions in relation to damages. Initially only for follow-on claims, the Consumer Rights Act 2015 extended its jurisdiction to private actions and gave it power to grant injunctive relief.

CA 1998 appeals are conducted in an adversarial manner before the CAT. This created a difficult switch of approach in the context of a merits appeal following an inquisitorial approach to the first-instance decision. In addition to the written evidence, there are oral hearings where witness evidence is often considered persuasive because of the ability to cross-examine.[40] Decisions are quick compared to, say, appeals at the EU level.[41] CAT decisions can (with permission) be appealed to the Court of Appeal.

4.5 Performance of the OFT and the CC

In a 2010 review of the first ten years of CA 1998, Bloom identified a number of problems and possible causes.[42] There were too few infringement decisions and they took too long. There was excessive focus in the OFT on a small number of high impact cases whereas a larger number and wider mix of cases might better promote deterrence. A high turnover of skilled staff and consequent loss of experience left the OFT vulnerable relative to stronger teams defending firms. A NAO report also emphasized problems with skilled staff retention and recruitment, especially at the level of case handlers.[43] It was a highly competitive recruitment market with better remuneration offered by law firms and economic consultancies. Nevertheless, the CAT substantially upheld all the appeal decisions sufficient to warrant fines, even if those fines were mostly reduced. Two infringements without fines were successfully appealed[44] and one OFT non-infringement decision was also

---

[39] In 2019, there were 27 ordinary members of the CAT.

[40] See Dinah Rose and Tom Richards, 'Appeal and Review in the Competition Appeal Tribunal and High Court' (2010) 15(3) Judicial Review 201; Marcus Smith, 'Standards of Review and Appeal in Cases before the Competition Appeal Tribunal' (2012) 11 Competition LJ 169.

[41] For example, the CAT appeal in Pfizer Phenytoin had a 13-day trial and the judgment was published 18 months after the contested decision. By way of comparison, the Intel appeal before the European General Court took five years. See Paul Gilbert, 'What's the Appeal' CPI Antitrust Chronicle (November 2018)

[42] Margaret Bloom is a former Director of Competition Enforcement at the OFT; Margaret Bloom, 'The Competition Act at 10 Years Old: Enforcement by the OFT and the Sector Regulators' (2010) 9 Competition LJ 141.

[43] NAO report in 2009 HC127 Session 2008–09 https://www.nao.org.uk/wp-content/uploads/2009/03/0809127es.pdf.

[44] The Racecourse Association and Others v Office of Fair Trading; The British Horseracing Board v Office of Fair Trading, (Case Nos 1035/1/1/04 and 1041/2/1/04) [2005] CAT 29, [2006] CompAR 99. MasterCard UK Members

overturned.[45] The latter resulted in an OFT preference for case closures over formal 'no grounds for action' decisions, so losing the opportunity for argued precedents.

In 2006, the OFT restructured internally from one based on legal instruments to one based on markets.[46] This change may have further encouraged the use of 'easier' market studies instead of CA 1998 enforcement. A total of forty-five market studies were conducted by the OFT in the ten years from 2003 to 2012, but there were only four infringements of the Chapter II prohibition in CA 1998. Criminalization also delayed civil cartel cases as any criminal case had to be finalized before civil enforcement could proceed. Similarly, sector regulators preferred to use their regulatory powers instead of the prohibitions. Meanwhile, each of France, Germany, and Italy were making five times more enforcement decisions than the UK, and UK decisions took significantly longer.[47]

The CC remained dependent on the OFT providing work. It was making an average of fifteen merger decisions per annum in the period from 2004 to 2008, but this dropped to six per annum in the period from 2008 to 2010. With no market investigation references in 2008 or 2009, this created a serious work insufficiency problem.[48] Nevertheless, one case was to have a major long-term influence on wider expectations about market investigations, and not just on the particular market under investigation. BAA had been created by privatizing ready-made state airport monopolies in London and Scotland. It had no significant rivals, and entry was impossible. It had regulated prices and demonstrably poor quality. The CC's market investigation resulted in the break-up of the airport monopolies in both regions.[49] It was a successful structural intervention in a market with highly specific characteristics, but it was destined to raise expectations of structural interventions in markets with very different characteristics.

As discussed in section 2.4, case numbers are a very imperfect measure of performance, and peer reputation is a relevant qualitative indicator. The most comprehensive and widely read set of internationally comparable star ratings is published by GCR.[50] The maximum rating is 5-stars. Figure 8.1 shows that the OFT averaged 4¼-stars over the period from 2006 to 2013. The CC achieved the maximum 5-stars alongside the highest rated US agencies and DG Competition, only dropping to 4½-stars in the year before its abolition as an independent agency.

Forum Ltd and Others v Office of Fair Trading Supported by The British Retail Consortium (Case Nos 1054/1/1/05, 1055/1/1/05, 1056/1/1/05) [2006] CAT 14, [2006] CompAR 595.

[45] Case No 1044/2/1/04 *ME Burgess, JJ Burgess and SJ Burgess (trading as JJ Burgess & Sons) v Office of Fair Trading and W Austin & Sons, Harwood Park Crematorium Ltd, The Consumers' Association* [2005] CAT 25, [2005] CompAR 1151. A further CA 1998 decision by Ofwat was also overturned: (Case Nos 1046/2/4/04, 1034/2/4/04(IR)) [2006] CAT 36, [2007] CompAR 328; and *Albion Water Ltd v Dŵr Cymru Cyfyngedig (Water Services Regulation Authority intervening)* [2008] EWCA Civ 536, [2009] 2 All ER 279.

[46] DG Competition had made a similar change in 2004.

[47] See the formal consultation that preceded ERRA 2013: BIS (n 9).

[48] Merger references partially recovered to 11 per annum from 2011 to 2013, and the flow of markets references returned to normal. See section 5.2 for judicial review of markets cases.

[49] 'BAA airports market investigation' (2009) https://webarchive.nationalarchives.gov.uk/20140402170709/http://www.competition-commission.org.uk/our-work/directory-of-all-inquiries/baa-airports/final-report-and-appendices-glossary.

[50] Global Competition Review, *Rating Enforcement* (various years) https://globalcompetitionreview.com/edition/1001376/rating-enforcement-2019.

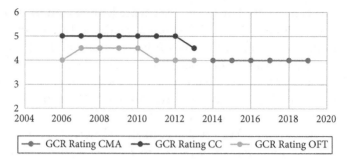

Figure 8.1 International Reputation of OFT, CC, and CMA.

5 Compromise(d) Merger: the ERRA 2013 and the CMA

The government set out three objectives in motivating its 2011 consultation on further re-forms: to improve the robustness of decisions and strengthen the regime; to support the competition authorities in taking forward high impact cases; and, to improve speed and predictability for business.[51] With these objectives in mind, the ERRA 2013 brought about the most substantial organizational change since the creation of the OFT. The OFT and CC were merged to form the Competition and Markets Authority (CMA).

There were also significant strengthening of the merged organization's powers and meas-ures to speed up investigations. These included: a range of enhancements to investigation powers and interim measures for CA 1998 investigations; sector regulators were required to consider the use of their concurrency powers before using their licence enforcement powers, with the CMA being given a leadership role in promoting this;[52] statutory time limits were introduced for the mergers and the markets regimes; a change to the criminal cartel offence; and, there was a new power for the Secretary of State to request the CMA to investigate a specified public interest issue in a market investigation.[53]

5.1 CMA Design

5.1.1 Mandate
The CMA was given a primary duty 'to promote competition, both within and outside the United Kingdom, for the benefit of consumers'.[54] This was developed by the board to set out a new mission: 'The CMA makes markets work well in the interests of consumers, busi-nesses and the economy'.[55] This appeared to presage a wider focus than the old OFT mission

---

[51] BIS (n 9).

[52] The ERRA 2013 gives the CMA a coordinating role in CA 1998 concurrency, including the ability to de-cide whether a sector regulator or the CMA should lead on an enforcement case. The UK Competition Network (UKCN) provides the forum for strategic dialogue, promotion of enforcement cooperation and capabilities, advo-cacy and case activity. United Kingdom Competition Network (UKCN) Statement of Intent https://www.gov.uk/government/publications/uk-competition-network-statement-of-intent. On concurrency, see ch 10 below.

[53] Most of these are discussed in depth in other chapters of this book.

[54] ERRA 2013, s 25(3).

[55] See CMA13 'Vision, values and strategy for the CMA' January 2014. This mission is repeated prominently alongside its primary duty at the front of every CMA annual report.

only 'to make markets work well for consumers', but there is little evidence of any wider emphasis on 'businesses and the economy'.

The CMA is constituted as a Non-Ministerial Department, much like its predecessors and has independence to prioritize its own activities and use of resources. It is directly accountable to the Public Accounts Committee, and is set the Treasury target to achieve £10 of measured consumer benefits for every £1 of its costs. The CMA's strategic direction is set by a board consisting of a chairman, a CEO and other senior CMA executives, and non-executive directors formally appointed by the Secretary of State. The appointments process is overseen by the Commissioner for Public Appointments. Board members are appointed for fixed terms but can be reappointed without limit.[56]

The board determines resource allocation and decision processes. The Secretary of State feeds into this by issuing a non-binding Ministerial Strategic Steer outlining the government's strategic priorities for the CMA.[57] While this may look like overtly political interference, it is probably better interpreted as providing transparency in the inevitable line of communication between government and an important public body. It would be more worrying if private discussions were influential in case selection and determinations. The first chairman of the CMA, David Currie, was a highly experienced regulatory economist. The second, Andrew Tyrie, had an early career as an economist, then spent twenty years as an influential backbench MP prior to his appointment. It is difficult for an outsider to know the extent to which this political background affected the relationship between the CMA and the Secretary of State.

The range of consumer responsibilities previously held by the OFT was reduced (e.g. credit licensing and anti-money laundering was transferred to the FCA, and Local Trading Standards Services became the [under-funded] lead enforcers of consumer protection legislation), but the CMA retains a leadership role in issuing guidance and taking on key consumer cases.[58] Thus, the CMA was designed to focus more clearly on competition law, but it retains the link with consumer law. This is helpful given the growing awareness that consumers do not always act with classic rationality and effective competition policy needs to take account of 'behavioural' consumers.

5.1.2 Organizational Design and Decision-making

The Board decides on opening market studies and references for full market investigation. Other case decisions are made in ways inherited from the OFT and the CC, and this has determined the internal structure of the CMA. It is split into two delivery directorates whose executive directors sit on the Board. The enforcement directorate continues the OFT mandate on cartels, CA 1998 prohibitions, and consumer protection, with each section headed by a senior director. The markets and mergers directorate brings together the OFT's first phase role and the CC's second phase role, with separate senior directors for markets and mergers. Most staff working on cases and projects work flexibly across directorates. There is also a separate general counsel with legal service, and a chief economic adviser with

---

[56] This contrasts with appointments in line of descent from the CC (including the CMA panel members and panel chair), which are non-renewable.

[57] For the most recent steer see BEIS, 'The Government's Strategic Steer to the Competition and Markets Authority' (July 2019).

[58] The sector regulators also have consumer enforcement powers. Citizens Advice provides consumer advocacy, education, and advice.

separate office. Both attend board meetings in a non-voting capacity. Carrying over from the CC's reporting members, there is a CMA panel including a panel chair. Two panel members, normally including the panel chair, sit as non-execs on the board.

Decision-making in each CMA directorate follows different processes inherited from the OFT and CC. For CA 1998 cases, the OFT had made a belated move to replace individual decision-makers with case decision groups (CDGs) and appointed a procedural officer. Both were put on a statutory footing by the ERRA 2013. Other changes were improved transparency in identifying decision-makers and greater internal challenge at key stages of case development.

Following intelligence about a possible competition issue (e.g. whistle-blowing or a complaint) and the application of prioritization principles, a case may be passed to the *enforcement directorate*. CA 1998 cases are then developed in two stages with the same investigation team but separate decision-makers.[59] If a case is opened, a case team is allocated to direct the investigation and a Senior Responsible Officer (SRO) is nominated to oversee and decide provisionally whether there has been an infringement. If so, a Statement of Objections (SO) is issued and, if the parties do not accept the infringement and reach a settlement, a three-person CDG is appointed to oversee the second phase, attend any oral hearing and make the final determination. The SRO cannot be a member of the CDG but continues to work with the case team. The CDG may be entirely CMA staff, or include one or possibly two panel members.[60] The CMA's lack of a fully independent decision group stands in contrast to the leading concurrent regulators. Ofgem and the FCA both have fully independent expert panels to determine CA 1998 cases presented by internal staff.[61]

CMA CDGs are appointed by the Case and Policy Committee (CPC). This consists of eight CMA executives plus two Panel Members (more specifically, inquiry chairs). It is chaired by the CEO and accountable to the Board. Its terms of reference include 'advising teams on legal, economic or policy issues arising from individual cases and projects ... promoting consistency of the CMA approach and application of policy across all cases, projects and tools.' In addition to appointing CDGs to determine CA 1998 investigations (including infringement, no grounds for action and penalty decisions), it considers the proposed decisions of a CDG, and provides advice and recommendations on any policy, legal or economic issues the CDG should consider further before finalizing its decision. It further approves decisions of senior staff on the use of commitments or settlements in CA 1998 investigations.

This suggests that the CPC is highly influential in individual cases. Its membership is dominated by the top of the executive hierarchy and in direct line of management of any staff appointment to a CDG. The careers of staff members on a CDG thus depend on the CPC. Furthermore, they may be dependent on the SRO who wrote the SO. A further distortion is that the CPC chooses the legal instrument used to address a suspected competition issue (e.g. consumer enforcement or antitrust enforcement or, on approval by the

---

[59] 'Competition Act 1998: Guidance on the CMA's Investigation Procedures in Competition Act 1998 Cases' (18 January 2019) CMA8.

[60] The published decision on *Phenytoin* Case CE/9742-13 reveals that there were only two members of the CDG; one was a panel chair and the other a staff economics director.

[61] For Ofgem's Enforcement Decision Panel see 'Ofgem Enforcement Guidelines' (2017). The CAA also uses the Ofgem EDP. For the FCA's Competition Decisions Committee see 'Corporate Governance of the Financial Conduct Authority' (March 2020).

Board, market study), and in doing so it may be influenced by the greater independence of decision-making by a group determining a market investigation.

Case development and decision-making in the *mergers and markets directorate* largely carries over from the CC. The two phases of decision-making in merger and market investigations are retained, with the first phase being conducted by staff and the second phase being conducted by independent groups chosen from Panel Members. Referral for a phase 2 market investigation is made by the Board, while merger referrals are by a single decision-maker. A significant difference brought about by the CMA is the continuity of investigation staff across phases 1 and 2, which can be efficient but it reinforces the importance of independent decision groups. Groups require a two-thirds majority for adverse findings. Panel Members continue to adjudicate on regulatory appeals. The role of CC chairman is reduced to that of Panel Chair who selects each case group from the Panel Members.

In short, there was little design in the creation of the CMA—the OFT and CC were simply squeezed together. Of course, this was a low risk consensus adaptation in the short run, and it provided a non-disruptive transitional arrangement, but it is not a coherent institutional design.[62] The CMA's proposals for reform (discussed below) suggest a desire to move closer to the OFT's executive institutional culture.[63]

5.2 CMA Performance

On its formation, the CMA was granted an additional £12m to expand its competition work, but it was again beset by staffing problems. Prior to the merger, the OFT had around 650 staff, of which around 150 were in credit licensing and anti-money laundering. The CC employed around 160. The CMA employed 653 at the end of 2014 and a similar number over the next four years. However, that simple arithmetic misses the staff turnover and loss of morale during the transition. The OFT's permanent workforce dropped to 477 and the temporary workforce rose to nearly 200 in the year prior to the merger. Staff recruitment and retention was made particularly difficult by the simultaneous expansion of competition units in sector regulators. In the two years from 2013 to 2014, nearly forty staff left the OFT/CC/CMA for a sector regulator, half to the FCA which offered higher salaries, and the rest spread across seven other regulators. Experienced senior staff were a particular loss.[64]

There has been a modest increase in the number of CA 1998 decisions. The OFT averaged only two infringement findings per annum, with twelve in the five-year period 2000-04, ten in 2005–2009, and ten in 2010–2014. [65] Sector regulators chipped in with a couple

---

[62] In 1996, Sir Gordon Borrie had already expressed concerns: 'I am not too keen on joining the OFT and MMC together because they have different cultures and the more questioning, partisan, activities of the OFT are not naturally combined with the necessarily more cautious, impartial and judicious approach of the MMC. Yes, you can combine in one body the roles of investigator, prosecutor and judge, but justice does need to be seen to be done.' Quoted by Wilks (n 18) 322.

[63] As of mid-2020, none of the eleven board members was previously associated with the CC. The panel chair and additional non-exec panel member were both first appointed to the panel only in September 2018.

[64] Source: OFT, CC and CC annual report and accounts.

[65] Source: author's count of cases from the CMA cases website https://www.gov.uk/cma-cases?case_type%5B%5D=ca98-and-civil-cartels&case_state%5B%5D=open and (for pre-2010) Bloom (n 42). These exclude private actions. For simplicity, I refer to calendar years when the data refers to financial years finishing the following April. For greater detail see Barry J Rodger, 'Application of the Domestic and EU Antitrust Prohibitions: an Analysis of the UK Competition Authority's Enforcement Practice' (2020) 8 Journal of Antitrust Enforcement 86.

more over the fifteen years but more often they found no grounds for action. There was a step change from 2015 to 2019, with the CMA finding five and six infringements in 2016 and 2017, although it averaged only two per annum for the other three years, and the regulators chipped in with an average one per annum between them. In addition, the CMA and regulators have reached five settlements. Overall, the number of infringement or settlement findings by the CMA and concurrent regulators has risen from two per annum to an average of five per annum. The time taken to complete CA 1998 investigations has also been halved.[66]

This is a positive achievement, but it remains an internationally small number of enforcement cases, which has consequences. It severely limits precedent, which is important both for firms (clarification, guidance and deterrence), and for the CMA itself (experience, identification of pitfalls and methodology). The latter is highlighted by the fact that the CMA has found only one Chapter II excessive pricing infringement, and on appeal the CAT remitted the case due to the CMA's incomplete analysis of the excessiveness of price (Phenytoin).[67] Unwisely, the CMA took the CAT's judgment to the Court of Appeal and substantially lost, which delayed the opening of the remittal by a full two years.[68] The only other Chapter II (also Chapter I) infringement finding by the CMA was for exclusionary conduct (Paroxetine), which was also appealed.[69] The CAT's judgment on that case has been delayed due to questions being referred to the CJEU. The CMA has been more successful with Chapter I appeals, other than in the level of fines.[70]

For mergers, there was a higher propensity to accept undertakings in lieu of a reference than in the ten years before the CMA. If we define merger interventions as either phase 1 undertakings in lieu of a reference or referral for phase 2, the share of phase 1 settlements rose from 32 per cent pre-CMA to 43 per cent in the period from 2014– to 2019. This is consistent with reaching outcomes more quickly. There has been no discernible impact on the number and distribution of phase 2 outcomes . In terms of workload, and given that the CMA has no control over merger activity, the flow of qualifying mergers for consideration has also been remarkably steady at around sixty or seventy per annum. The time taken for both merger review and the markets regime have been reduced, which owes more to statutory time limits than to the creation of the CMA per se.

For markets, phase 1 activity had been around 4 per annum at the OFT, but this has fallen to 2 per annum under the CMA.[71] The CMA inherited five open phase 2 cases from the CC, including one remittal, but it has only opened four phase 2 investigations in six years itself. Two of those (domestic energy and retail banking) followed phase 1 collaboration between the OFT and sector regulators, and another (investment consultants) was referred by the

---

[66] BEIS 'Competition Law Review: post implementation review of statutory changes in ERRA13' (April 2019).

[67] *Unfair pricing in respect of the supply of phenytoin sodium capsules in the UK*, Case CE/9742-13 [2016]. *Flynn Pharma Ltd and Flynn Pharma (Holdings) Ltd v Competition and Markets Authority; with Pfizer Inc. and Pfizer Limited v Competition and Markets Authority (Phenytoin)* [2018] CAT 11 7

[68] Case No: C3/2018/1847 and 1874 [2020] EWCA Civ 339. The author had no role in this case but the gap in the CMA's reasoning (reliance on margins to the exclusion of a natural comparison of the price of capsules and tablets) was clear even before the non-confidential decision was published, let alone the CAT judgment. See blog by Farasat Bokhari and Bruce Lyons at https://competitionpolicy.wordpress.com/2016/12/16/pfizer-and-flynn-how-are-excessive-prices-for-generic-drugs-possible-and-should-competition-authorities-do-more-about-exploitative-pricing/.

[69] CMA, *Paroxetine* (Case CE-9531/11, 12 February 2016).

[70] See eg *Ping Europe Limited v Competition and Markets Authority* [2018] CAT 13.

[71] Own calculations based on CMA website https://www.gov.uk/cma-cases?case_type%5B%5D=markets.

FCA in 2017. The funerals market reference in 2019 is the only phase 2 market investigation generated entirely under the CMA's own initiative.

The energy and banking investigations were opened almost simultaneously in the first few months of the CMA in 2014. This was a substantial and possibly damaging workload for the new organization. Earlier that year, the CC/CMA had published two final reports each of which included structural remedies (divestitures). The structural remedy proposals in one (private healthcare) did not survive an appeal with remittal,[72] and potential appeal of the other (aggregates) was overtaken by negotiations to push a much bigger Europe-wide merger through the European Commission in Phase 1.[73] No new markets work was opened in 2015, and of the eight market studies opened from the start of 2016 to mid-2020, only one (funerals) led to a phase 2 market investigation.[74] There appears to be impatience with fully-evidenced investigations by independent groups of Panel Members, who have typically chosen behavioural remedies over structural remedies, usually for the very good reason that the identified competition failures were due to features of the market other than the number of firms.[75]

The CMA's 10:1 consumer benefits to costs target set by H M Treasury has not been helpful. If the target means anything, failure to meet it would result in substantial budget cuts and the debilitating loss of skilled staff. This creates insidious distortions. It is difficult to measure the value of deterrence or precedent, so has created undue pressure for large scale investigations arguably at the expense of more socially beneficial case choice. It shifts focus away from cartels (which are typically in small markets) and the abuse of dominance (which is typically an exclusionary abuse without immediate price effects), and may help explain why the CMA conducts so few enforcement cases.[76] Beyond case selection, the target adds pressure on CMA staff for adverse findings and promotes measurable interventions.

The CMA has an important advocacy role in promoting competition between firms. In 2018, it commissioned a survey of 1,200 UK businesses to test how its message was getting across. Only 3 per cent of respondents could name the CMA as the official body responsible for enforcing competition law in the UK.[77] When prompted with a list of possible answers, 49 per cent said the OFT, 15 per cent said the CC, and 14 per cent said the CMA. This suggests more could be done in raising business awareness. It further suggests that there is

---

[72] 'Private healthcare market investigation: Final report' (2 April 2014) CC; 'HCA International Limited v Competition and Markets Authority' CAT Case 1228/6/12/14, in which the CMA accepted its mistakes in data analysis, and the CAT quashed both the finding of an adverse effect of competition in Central London and the divestiture remedy. The CMA's Remittal final report, without any divestiture remedy, was published 17 months after its original final report.

[73] 'Aggregates, cement and ready-mix concrete market investigation: Final report' (14 January 2014) CC. For the European merger see European Commission Case M.7252 *Holcim/Lafarge* (15 December 2014).

[74] In addition, there was one response to a super-complaint (on the loyalty penalty). The flow of market investigations from the regulators is likely influenced by a preference for the use of regulatory powers. To complete the picture of caseload, the average number of consumer enforcement cases per annum remained essentially unchanged compared with the OFT at around 25 per annum. On market investigations see ch 6 above.

[75] As noted in section 4.5, the *BAA* case was a monopoly structure, which is rare to find in market investigations. See section 6.2.2 for an expression of this impatience.

[76] The CMA's own estimated average annual consumer savings relative to costs (2017-20) show that competition enforcement (CA 1998 outcomes) covered just under 50 per cent of costs, whereas market studies and market investigations alone covered over nine times costs; *CMA Impact Assessment* (14 July 2020) CMA121.

[77] 'Competition law research 2018' a report by ICM on behalf of the Competition and Markets Authority https://www.gov.uk/government/publications/uk-businesses-understanding-of-competition-law.

a danger in confusing businesses, let alone consumers, with too many institutional name changes.

Finally, the CMA's international reputation is very good, but it is some way from being world leading. As Figure 8.1 shows, the CMA inherited the OFT's 4-star rating and has been stuck at 4 stars ever since. In 2019, France, Germany, and the US FTC were given the elite 5-star rating. Australia, the European Commission, Japan, South Korea, and the US DOJ were rated at 4½ stars, and Brazil was alongside the CMA on 4 stars.

6 The Case for Institutional Reform

6.1 Five New Twenty-first Century Challenges

Five very substantial new challenges add further pressure for CMA reform.

6.1.1 Loss of Public Faith in Markets
There has been a public and political loss of faith in markets to deliver the best outcome for consumers.[78] At the turn of the millennium, there was a strong political consensus on the benefits of competition. Competitive markets would provide consumers with what they wanted at the lowest feasible price, and provide the right incentive for innovation and productivity growth. The consensus went further to agree that the promotion of competition was a technical matter best left to experts. Politicians could then focus on wider policy. The 2008 banking crisis and bailouts, and the subsequent years of austerity and recession, shook faith in capitalism and failures in financial markets have affected faith in product markets.[79] A particular concern has been the unfairness of some pricing practices, especially those disproportionately affecting 'vulnerable' consumers. There has further been an international rise in economic nationalism, leading to pressures for public interest interventions. This makes the CMA's role in competition enforcement and advocacy both harder and more important.

6.1.2 Digital Markets and Dominant Platforms
The digital economy, especially the dominant digital platforms, create a major challenge. Digital markets have many characteristics that are also found in more traditional market settings (e.g. network effects, cross-network externalities, continuous marginal innovation, drastic Schumpeterian innovation, high fixed/low marginal costs, global reach, big data accumulation, targeted advertising, potential for price discrimination). However, there is a major qualitative difference in that so many of these characteristics are combined in digital settings and their effects are exacerbated by personalized data. Furthermore, digital technology can be used globally without transport costs, marginal costs are often close to zero, and a very small number of platforms have become both first-choice access points for

---

[78] See eg James Kirkup, 'Better Regulators, Fairer Markets' Social Market Foundation (2019); Maurice E Stucke and Ariel Ezrachi, *Competition Overdose: How Free Market Mythology Transformed Us from Citizen Kings to Market Servants* (Harper Collins, 2020).

[79] For example, Maurice E Stucke, 'Reconsidering Antitrust's Goals' (2012) 53 BCL Rev 551 http://lawdigitalcommons.bc.edu/bclr/vol53/iss2/4.

time-constrained consumers and the core route-to-market for many suppliers. The result has been dominant digital platforms, even at the global level.

The CMA has been taking measures to address the digital challenge. Its mandate in consumer law is important for tackling issues that might otherwise fall in a gap between competition and consumer laws. It made clear that it wanted new powers and lobbied with the slogan that the 'UK has an analogue system of competition and consumer law in a digital age'.[80] Provoked by the independent Furman inquiry on digital competition, it conducted a market study into online platforms and digital advertising. It leads a Digital Markets Taskforce operating jointly with the Information Commissioner's Office and Ofcom. In November 2020, a permanent Digital Markets Unit was announced by the government, to be located in the CMA. Its role includes to develop and enforce a code of conduct for digital platforms designated as having 'strategic market status'.

6.1.3 Brexit Including Scrutiny of State Subsidies

Brexit brings a step change in the CMA's workload as it takes on international mergers and antitrust cases previously dealt with in Brussels. DG Competition has averaged 95 'significant' mergers per annum since 2014, where 'significant' is defined for this purpose as requiring a Phase 1 investigation that does not qualify for the simplified procedure. If only a third of these have an impact on the UK market, this would be a 50 per cent increase in the CMA's caseload and include mergers of a much greater scale and complexity than domestic mergers, so effective workload will be higher still.[81]

The required increase in CA 1998 cases is of an even greater magnitude. How well placed is the CMA to take on an abuse of dominance case against any of the digital giants? The CMA has published just two Chapter II decisions since its formation six years ago, both in 2016, both for pharmaceuticals, and both found wanting in the CAT. Meanwhile, the European Commission undertook sixty Art.102 investigations, including twenty-seven decisions in the same period. These include cases against US-based Intel, Google, Amazon and Qualcomm, which would be in the CMA's remit post-Brexit. Tools go rusty if unused, so there must be a question mark against the CMA's experience and ability to challenge potential abuse by internationally dominant firms. The loss of cooperation and information sharing within the European Competition Network (ECN) is an additional problem, particularly with confidential information in Chapter I cases, as it will be a major impediment to investigations involving precisely the international firms and cartels previously investigated by DG Competition on behalf of the UK.

The CMA's enforcement directorate was provisionally given the additional task of investigating state aid (i.e. subsidies that may distort competition). At the time of writing (June 2020), this was a highly contentious issue and the CMA's role would remain

---

[80] Chairman and CEO Foreword to the Annual Plan 2020/21. On competition law and digital markets see ch 14 below.

[81] The 50 per cent increase is identical to the CMA's own estimate in its Annual Plan for 2020/21. It may turn out to be an underestimate given recent CMA interpretation of its jurisdiction. For example, in 2020 the CMA prohibited the merger of two US airline booking software firms whose UK sales were to a single airline, BA. 'Anticipated acquisition by Sabre Corporation of Farelogix Inc.: Final report' (9 April 2020). Meanwhile, the European Commission is becoming more active in monitoring foreign ownership of strategic assets and there are proposals to extend merger review to appraise the distortionary effects of acquisitions by foreign state-owned or state-subsidized firms: https://trade.ec.europa.eu/doclib/docs/2020/march/tradoc_158676.pdf; https://ec.europa.eu/competition/international/overview/foreign_subsidies_white_paper.pdf. If the UK follows suit, that would be additional work for the CMA.

unclear until a trade deal (if any) was agreed with the EU.[82] Prior to the Covid-19 emergency, the EC investigated around 500 state aid cases per annum, with only twenty-five of those relating to UK subsidies. Political opinion on both left and right is becoming more interventionist, so contentious spending is likely to rise. Additionally, 'repatriated' EU spending broadens the potential for granting aid (e.g. agriculture, regional, infrastructure). Devolution of spending decisions within the UK raises politically sensitive issues of intra-UK monitoring and review (e.g. Scotland, Wales, Northern Ireland, and English cities/regions). State aid is the most political and time-consuming activity in DG Competition.[83] Even if the workload will be relatively lower for the CMA, it has the potential to be particularly contentious as London does not benefit from the distance between Brussels and most Member States.

The government's allowance for all Brexit-related issues was a £20 million per annum increase the CMA's budget to around £90 million. The CMA has used this to expand its staffing from 640 at the end of March 2018 to 853 a year later, making it larger than DG Competition.[84] At least in part in preparation for its likely UK internal market and subsidy roles, the CMA established regional offices in Edinburgh, Belfast, and Cardiff.

6.1.4 Covid-19 Pandemic

The Covid-19 pandemic has had significant market effects. Both demand and supply have been subject to major shocks, with resulting price swings, some of which are the natural operation of competition. In the longer term, supply adjustments leading to exit may raise concentration and market power. Some of the biggest winners of the Covid-19 induced change in consumption patterns are the global digital platforms, reinforcing digital market concerns.

The CMA established a Covid-19 taskforce to monitor issues. Price rises trigger public scrutiny even if they are the result of competitive supply and demand, so careful advocacy

---

[82] By the time of proof reading (early February 2021), there had been three major Brexit-related developments that affect the CMA and the CAT: (1) The UK Internal Market Act 2020 establishes a new Office for the Internal Market (OIM) within the CMA. The OIM will conduct an annual review of the functioning of trade within the UK internal market and, if requested by one of the devolved administrations, provide non-binding expert advice on the potential regional economic impact of proposed regulations made by another. This will feed into political decision-making on whether the UK internal market is compromised. (2) The EU–UK Trade and Cooperation Agreement 2020 (TCA) includes detailed provisions on subsidy control (the new name for state aid control) as a condition for UK access to the EU internal market in goods. For a succinct summary of the relevant provisions, see Bruce Lyons and Andreas Stephan, 'State Aid Control' in *Brexit and Beyond* (UK in a Changing Europe, 2021) Brexit-and-Beyond-report-compressed.pdf. (3) The Secretary of State subsequently opened a consultation on 'Subsidy Control: Designing a New Approach for the UK' (BEIS, February 2021) with a view to legislation. The scope includes both the UK internal market and external obligations under the TCA. A wide range of possible roles is under consideration for the 'independent body', from pre-award information and advice to public authorities, through systemic or individual post-award reviews, to enforcement powers (eg to order amendment or withdrawal of a subsidy, or to initiate judicial proceedings). Although the CMA was asked in 2018 to prepare for a major role in state aid control, and readied a Senior Director for State Aid in the enforcement directorate, the consultation suggests there are also non-CMA alternatives under consideration for the 'independent body'. The consultation seems clearer that the CAT will be the default legal forum and that the appeal standard should be judicial review for decisions made by either public authorities or the independent body.

[83] On a simple count of case decisions during the decade 2010-19, the Commission made 123 antitrust/cartel decisions, 3,401 merger decisions and 4,281 state aid decisions. Although this case count is unweighted by case complexity, state aid cases are rarely straightforward and the number count excludes both the height of the financial crisis and the Covid-19 emergency measures.

[84] If the CMA is funded for the OIM and subsidy control roles discussed in n 82, and if the DMU is funded for, say, 200 staff, the CMA could well double its 2018 size by 2022.

is necessary to control expectations and highlight what can and what should not be done.[85] Much of the CMA's Covid-19 response applied consumer law (e.g. for refunds), but it did launch four investigations related to suspected charging of excessive and unfair prices for hand sanitizer products under Chapter 2 of CA 1998.[86] Within a month, it had dropped three of the cases, and the fourth was dropped two months later. Since then, price gouging has disappeared from the headlines and no further cases have been opened. It is difficult to judge whether this was due to effective market forces or the demonstration that the CMA was willing to get tough.

The government introduced some direct measures that had the effect of suppressing competition law enforcement. Merger legislation was amended to add a new public interest of maintaining capability to combat a public health emergency. This may be pro-competitive if it prevents opportunistic acquisitions of, say, a vaccine supplier, but it would be the opposite if used to support a bid to create a national champion.[87] Crisis cooperation agreements may have a short-term role but they forge connections between firms that are hard to let go after the immediate crisis.[88] The failing firm defence in mergers may be invoked but it will be hard to assess.[89]

6.1.5 Climate Change

Climate change has finally reached prominence in the national policy agenda. The CMA's 2019/20 annual plan listed four strategic priorities: protecting vulnerable consumers; improving trust in markets; digital competition; and economic growth and productivity. 'Supporting the transition to a low carbon economy' was added to the list for the first time in the 2020/21 plan. The CMA proposed cautious first steps to develop an understanding of how climate change goals affect markets, and action to protect consumers from misleading 'green' claims. It has recently used climate change for case prioritization.[90] The CMA may be pushed to adapt further, possibly to include an evaluation of climate externalities as part of the competition analysis where this is likely to be relevant. Examples might include a merger that would eliminate high carbon production but reduce capacity, or a research agreement between horizontal rivals to develop a green technology. In post-Brexit state aid control,

---

[85] The Financial Times (17 May 2020) reported that the CMA has asked BEIS for 'emergency time-limited legislation' to prevent 'price gouging'. This was in response to a spike of consumer complaints about products with suddenly increased demand, including hand sanitizers. Shortly afterwards (21 May 2020), a CMA Covid-19 Taskforce update revealed that the spike in price complaints in late March and early April had dropped to a negligible level by May, with the overwhelming number of ongoing complaints relating to holiday and flight refunds.

[86] *Hand Sanitiser Products: Suspected Excessive and Unfair Pricing*, Case reference: 50924. It separately reported that hand sanitizer was the worst case of suspected 'price gouging' with the median reported complaint to the CMA being for a 400 per cent price increase: Update on the work of the CMA's Taskforce, Published 3 July 2020; https://www.gov.uk/government/publications/cma-coronavirus-taskforce-update-3-july-2020/update-on-the-work-of-the-cmas-taskforce.

[87] Urgent exceptions, like Lloyds/HBOS during the banking crisis, can be forced through in haste then regretted at leisure; Bruce Lyons and Minyan Zhu, 'Compensating Competitors or Restoring Competition? EU Regulation of State Aid for Banks During the Financial Crisis' (2012) 13 Journal of Industry, Competition and Trade 39..

[88] For example, the Secretary of State signed The Competition Act 1998 (Dairy Produce) (Coronavirus) (Public Policy Exclusion) Order 2020. The CMA's position is set out in CMA, *Approach to Business Cooperation in Response to COVID-19* (25 March 2020) CMA118. For an international perspective see OECD, *Co-operation between competitors in the time of COVID-19* (26 May 2020).

[89] The difficulties are illustrated by Amazon/Deliveroo where the failing firm defence was first accepted by the CMA, then rejected, but the merger was still allowed; https://www.gov.uk/cma-cases/amazon-deliveroo-merger-inquiry.

[90] In December 2020, the CMA opened a market study into electric vehicle charging.

it would be straightforward to accommodate aid to reduce carbon emissions, although it might be politically delicate similarly to penalize aid for carbon intensive sectors (e.g. air-lines). However, vigilance will be necessary because the best climate policy instruments are regulation and taxation, and only very exceptionally might reduced competition be an ap-propriate part of the mix. There is also a danger that additional objectives (e.g. inequality, labour market issues) may be added in the future, which would be an effective return to the public interest and undermine the legitimacy of CMA determinations as an expert body.[91]

6.2 CMA's Own Proposals for Reform: The Tyrie Letter

In early 2019, chairman of the CMA Andrew Tyrie sent a letter[92] to the then Secretary of State Greg Clark requesting new powers to allow it to act quickly and with reduced oversight by the CAT.[93] Two motivations were given: 'First, the growth of new and rapidly-emerging forms of consumer detriment, caused in part by the increasing digitalisation of the economy, requires more rapid intervention, and probably new types of intervention ... Second, there are increasing signs that the public doubt whether markets work for their benefit.'

The Tyrie letter makes eight proposals, but three get to the heart of the CMA as an in-stitution: (i) 'consumer interest' to replace competition as the CMA's 'overriding statutory duty'; (ii) new powers to impose legally binding interim remedies during a phase 1 market study, which would also 'enable the CMA more effectively to influence the conduct of those businesses whose practices raise concerns, without the need for formal work in the form of market studies or market investigations.'; and, iii) a more limited standard of review for CA 1998 cases.

6.2.1 The Consumer Interest as an Overriding Statutory Duty
The OFT's mission to 'make markets work well for consumers' captured both the funda-mental importance of competitive markets and the regulator's focus on who markets should benefit. The regulator's job was to ensure that consumers have a competitive range of oppor-tunities to choose from, and then leave them to make their own choices. Cutting out the role of markets/ competition and fast-tracking to 'the consumer interest' risks a wide-ranging and paternalistic determination of what is the consumer interest. This echoes the language and problems of previous 'public interest' tests. There is a worrying absence of any discus-sion in the Tyrie letter of how the consumer interest will be determined. What exactly is the consumer interest other than in relation to what the market provides and consumers

---

[91] Maarten Pieter Schinkel and Leonard Treuren, 'Green Antitrust: Friendly Fire in the Fight against Climate Change' in S Holmes, D Middelschulte and M Snoep (eds), *Competition Law, Climate Change & Environmental Sustainability* (Concurrences, 2021). See also Simon Holmes, 'Climate Change, Sustainability, and Competition Law' (2020) 8 Journal of Antitrust Enforcement 354.

[92] Since this chapter was drafted, Lord Tyrie has announced his resignation as chairman of the CMA as from September 2020 (i.e. after only three years in post). Tyrie was the sole signatory of the letter to the Secretary of State. Nevertheless, his letter says: 'The proposals are the product of careful consideration by senior CMA staff, and discussion at Executive and Board level', so it must be presumed that the letter remains CMA policy. This section draws on the author's CCP blog published on 7 March 2019 https://competitionpolicy.wordpress.com/2019/03/07/why-the-cma-is-wrong-in-its-proposals-for-reform-and-what-should-be-done-instead/.

[93] https://www.gov.uk/government/publications/letter-from-andrew-tyrie-to-the-secretary-of-state-for-business-energy-and-industrial-strategy (accessed 21 February 2019).

choose? The great concern is that consumer interest becomes whatever the CMA deems it to be.[94]

Nevertheless, it is potentially problematic that the CMA's primary duty in the ERRA 2013 is to promote competition for the benefit of consumers, and this exclusive role of supply-side competition underplays the CMA's role in consumer law. Markets may be distorted on the demand-side if consumers are, for example, uninformed or misled despite (or even because of) fierce competition.

6.2.2 Anticipated Use of Interim Measures in the Markets Regime

Phase 2 market investigations provide the CMA with uniquely strong powers to intervene in markets where firms are not suspected of illegal practices. Market investigations have been used recently to promote competition through demand-side remedies which help consumers become better informed and better able to switch suppliers (e.g. energy, retail banking). It is reasonable to observe that the markets regime can be a lengthy process and that interim measures would be helpful in fast moving markets. However, in line with the proposed change is statutory duty, the letter proposes to extend the powers of a market investigation to include *either* competition *or* the interests of consumers.

The aim seems to be to incentivize firms to cooperate before a market study has to be opened, and the arbiter of consumer interest will tell them what to do. Tyrie writes:

> Weighing on the minds of management in deciding whether to cooperate with the CMA would be the alternative: direct intervention, in the form of legally-binding require-ments ... Many of these exchanges would occur in private. Early public communication of problems in markets, and sources of consumer detriment, could also encourage improve-ments to behaviour .... Legal protections may also be required to ensure that the CMA is adequately protected from defamation liability [17–18].

This reveals an impatience with formal market investigations and the loss of executive con-trol once independent panels have been appointed. A Consumer Interest Authority, pos-sibly guided by focus groups, media or political opinion, could decide which firms and in which markets pricing and other business strategies should be controlled—without the ne-cessity for either an investigation or an objective definition of consumer interest.[95] In the absence of clear principles to guide business compliance, firms would be left to wait for a tap on the shoulder from the Consumer Interest Authority.

6.2.3 Limited Standard of Review for CA 1998 Enforcement Cases

The CMA complains that the CAT's merits reviews of its CA 1998 determinations are lengthy and over-burdensome, so should be replaced by judicial review (or a similar standard). The letter shows no appreciation of why determinations by staff-led CDGs from its enforcement directorate face a different standard of review to determinations by groups of independent Panel Members in its markets and mergers directorate. As discussed in

---

[94] The proposal also looks odd in the context of the CMA's own revised mission to make markets work well in the interests of consumers, businesses, and the economy. See section 5.1.1.

[95] There is even a suggestion that the markets regime may be made 'simpler and more effective' by removing phase 2 market investigation; see (n 93) 18.

section 2.2, the independence of decision-making behind the first instance determination should be a key factor in setting the appropriate standard of review.

A second factor is the seriousness of the consequences of the CMA's determination. For these, it is less clear that that there is more at stake from a civil breach of the CA 1998 prohibitions, than there is, at least potentially, from some of the remedies that may be imposed by market investigations. Breach of the prohibitions can result in a substantial fine, though fines rarely make a substantial dent in the financial health of the firm. Associated damages can also be high, though damages are intended only to return an ill-gotten gain. The quasi-criminality of breaching a prohibition can also be reputationally damaging, as well as being important under HRA 1998. While there are no fines following a market investigation, the range of potential remedies can have a very significant financial effect (e.g. price controls or the break-up of a firm). These can be imposed despite the absence of any breaches of the law. Such remedies are a major challenge to property rights, arguably requiring greater safeguards than fines following quasi-criminality.

Overall, there is a case for clarifying and rationalizing the standards of review for CMA determinations, but this should not be done piecemeal and without reform of CMA decision-making.

6.3 Coherent Institutional Reform for the CMA

There are very serious challenges facing the CMA. It needs to have the institutional strength and confidence to restore public faith in markets and to address the turbulent competition landscape of digital markets, Brexit, pandemic, and climate change.

The CMA has been very active in thinking about some of these new challenges, as well as appreciating the significance of behavioural consumers. Its portfolio of responsibilities, including leadership in consumer law alongside competition, is helpful for integrating the supply-side of markets (competition) and the demand-side (consumers). The skill set of the CMA also makes it the most appropriate institutional arrangement for reviewing the market effects of state aid, but there is no disputing the fact that proper execution of this role would test the relationship between the CMA and Secretary of State. Finally, on its mandate, it would be helpful to have a more appropriate primary duty, not for ungrounded 'consumer interest', but 'to promote effectively competitive markets for the benefit of consumers' or a similar wording that would be more inclusive of consumer law and additional post-Brexit role.

Unfortunately, the current institutional narrative told by the CMA is to blame 'new forms of business behaviour' and the CAT appeals process for weaknesses in its own performance. It requests new powers at the same time as its current powers are under-used. It seems happiest operating through less formal market studies, making recommendations for regulation or actions for implementation by other bodies. Such recommendations eschew the requirement for rigorous evidence gathering, and avoid using the CMA's statutory powers with risk of the associated appeals processes. This is not healthy for an institution charged with implementing competition law. What should be done?

One alternative would be to change the system fundamentally from the current inquisitorial approach to one in which the CMA prosecutes cases before the CAT. This was seriously considered for CA 1998 cases in the review prior to the ERRA 2013 and has been proposed by Nazzini as a response to the CMA's concerns in the Tyrie letter.[96] It would be a completely new approach to case choice and development, and undoubtedly take many years to bed down. This would be a huge distraction from the current challenges, and it would leave unjustifiable differences between the prohibitions and merger and market investigations. Furthermore, there is no convincing evidence that a prosecutorial system would be a superior arrangement to a well-designed inquisitorial system. It would be better to reform the current, compromise and compromised institution. It would be different if the current system was completely broken, but that is not the case.

Much of the problem derives from the way the CMA squeezed together the OFT and CC. If it had been designed from scratch, there would be a common approach to decision-making across the enforcement and markets and mergers directorates. The current differences are a historical artefact. In cases requiring similar economic analysis, and with similar effects on consumers and firms, there is no good reason to have different decision structures according to legal instrument.[97] From this perspective, the challenge is to draw on the best of the two institutional traditions to create a common approach to determining cases.

All non-cartel first instance determinations under CA 1998 and EA 2002 should be made by groups drawn exclusively from the independent panel, with a mix of backgrounds including law and economics. For full independence, panel members should continue to be appointed for fixed terms without possibility of renewal. Each decision group should be selected independently by the panel chair, who should not be a member of an executive committee, particularly of the CPC which initiates cases.

While this arrangement looks like the current decision-making for phase 2 mergers and market investigations, there should be a qualitative change in the distance between the decision group and investigation staff. Prior to the CMA, there were separate staff investigation teams in the OFT for phase 1 and in the CC for phase 2. One of the aims of creating the CMA was to allow staff continuity for speed and efficiency of investigations. However, the institutional arrangements did not change sufficiently to balance the increased potential for confirmation bias. This requires a greater element of staff challenge by the decision group, and a reduced level of the group's control of the investigation. This applies equally to CA 1998 and EA 2002 cases.[98]

Parties should continue to have access to decision groups in hearings and, if appropriate, on site visits. Decision groups should be able to revise the first phase SO, or theories of harm for second phase mergers and market investigations, and request further evidence gathering or analysis from CMA staff. They should not be involved in the production of technical working papers but should fully consider and, if necessary, challenge CMA staff analysis. The current openness and publication of non-confidential evidence, analysis and decisions should be preserved.

There should similarly be a greater separation between the Panel and senior executive staff. Neither the panel chair nor panel members should sit on the Case and Policy

[96] BIS (n 9); Nazzini (n 9).

[97] Price-fixing and market-sharing cartels are an exception because such agreements are per se illegal even if they have no economic effects.

[98] While this is close to Nazzini's option 2 (see (n 9) 30), he offers this only hypothetically as a contrast to the staff dominated CDGs. He does not mention the current independent CMA Panel, or decision-making in the mergers and markets directorate. He only says, in passing, that EA 2002 determinations are subject to judicial review because they 'do not involve a finding of liability but are of a regulatory or administrative nature'; Nazzini (n 9) 4.

Committee. A purely executive CPC would continue with its current role except it should withdraw from involvement once it has referred a case to the panel chair to select a phase 2 decision group. The common approach to phase 2 decision-making across directorates would result in a more neutral choice in case selection and legal instrument to address an identified competition problem. This would pave the way for a legislative change to remove the requirement for merits appeals in CA 1998 cases, other than for the level of fines, which do not lend themselves to remittal.[99] The depth of review should then flex with the degree of regulatory intervention and penalty. The CMA board might continue to decide on opening market studies and references for full market investigation, but any panel member on the board, including the panel chair, should withdraw from all such case-specific discussions.

Finally, the distortionary Treasury target should be suspended pending the development of a credible methodology to estimate the value of the CMA's casework for precedent-setting and deterrence, and the value of its wider advocacy. Both accountability and best-practice would be better achieved by requiring investigated firms to cooperate beyond case decisions, by collecting and providing information required for ex post reviews of interventions and marginal clearances.

7 Conclusion

The OFT and the CC's predecessors were established at a time when their roles were essentially advisory for the minister's determination, and few business practices were necessarily unlawful. There was consequently little role for appeals. Despite these common features, each institution was established at a different time and with very different decision-making. The DGFT was an executive decision-maker while the CC's predecessors were in the spirit of a Royal Commission with a group leading an investigation and coming to a collective decision. Institutions evolve but they remain hostages to their historical roots.

CA 1998 and EA 2002 were transformative in the roles and responsibilities of the OFT and CC. Competition replaced public interest as the substantive test across the body of competition law. Anti-competitive agreements and the abuse of dominance were prohibited for the first time, and significant penalties for breach were introduced. The OFT and the CC became determinative, with the Secretary of State withdrawing from case determinations. The CAT provided an essential safeguard in the form of review for disputed decisions. The OFT, in particular, was slow to change its decision-making structures as its powers switched from being advisory and without firms being liable to penalties, to becoming determinative and with substantial financial liability for firms.

ERRA 2013 then squeezed the OFT and the CC together into one organization, the CMA, with the CC emerging in the markets and mergers directorate. Staff were combined, but there was no fundamental attempt to design an integrated approach to decision-making. The independence of CDGs in the enforcement directorate remains deeply compromised. The CMA also faces new challenges beyond its control. It needs to find the institutional strength and confidence to restore public faith in markets and to address the turbulent competition landscape of digital markets, Brexit, pandemic, and climate change.

---

[99] A similar point was made in the Furman review of digital markets; *Unlocking Digital Competition: Report of the Digital Competition Expert Panel* (2019) Recommended Action 14.

The CMA's response in the form of the Tyrie letter has been to request replacement of promotion of competition with an overriding consumer interest, to have new powers to threaten interim measures to cajole firms into doing what the CMA believes is in the consumer interest (without having to conduct an investigation), and to reduce the level of review by the CAT for enforcement decisions.

I have argued that the CMA needs to reform its own processes first. It is not necessary to go as far as taking determinations away from the CMA and requiring prosecution before the CAT, whose decisions would be subject to review in another court. Much could be achieved by the enforcement directorate adopting the independent expert group decision-making currently used in the mergers and markets directorate, and creating more distance between such groups and staff investigators. Further reform of the Case and Policy Committee would more clearly separate first and second phase decisions and reduce distortions in the choice of legal instrument. It would only then be appropriate to rationalize the standard of review by the CAT. Despite numerous reorganizations and name changes, seventy years of history confirm how slowly institutional ways of working and decision-making procedures evolve. These straightforward proposals draw naturally on what has worked well in the past and would create a robust institutional foundation on which to build for a challenging future.

9

Human Rights and the UK Competition Act

Public Enforcement and Due Process

Arianna Andreangeli

1 Introduction

The entry into force of the Competition Act 1998 (CA 1998) marked a sea change in the way in which competition law is applied in the UK: it created an independent agency, responsible for the investigation and sanctioning of anti-competitive behaviour on the basis of the application of legal standards contained in the Act. However, since the new competition authority acts as 'police, prosecutor and judge' in respect of allegations of restrictive behaviour and can impose significant financial penalties, important questions have arisen as to whether this new set-up complies with basic human rights safeguards, such as the right to a fair trial. The adoption of the Human Rights Act 1998 (HRA 1998) made these issues even more compelling. The HRA 1998 transposed the European Convention on Human Rights (ECHR) into UK law, including those principles enshrined in Article 6's right to a 'fair trial' that had been held to be applicable also to administrative proceedings affecting, respectively, the determination of a criminal charge and of rights and obligations.

The purpose of this chapter is to discuss the approach adopted in the UK towards questions of human rights compliance by the competition enforcement structures, with a particular focus on the role of the Competition Appeal Tribunal (CAT) and of its powers of review on the merits. The chapter will examine the nature of competition proceedings in light of Article 6 of the ECHR and, on that basis, discuss any resultant implications for the fairness standards that are relevant to them. Thereafter, it will analyse the relevant UK case law and will identify the approach adopted by the CAT and the appellate courts to questions of standard of proof of competition infringements and of review of any decisions adopted by the Competition and Markets Authority (CMA). It will be argued that, while the recognition that these cases have a 'criminal nature' does not justify the wholesale extension of all the safeguards that the Convention reserves to criminal cases tried before the ordinary courts, it nonetheless means that the investigated parties are entitled to some basic protections that Article 6 ECHR enshrines. In this specific context, the chapter will explore the tribunal's powers of review of infringement decisions and will suggest that at the root of the conferral to the CAT of a power of scrutiny 'on the merits' is the need to ensure that the public enforcement proceedings disciplined by the CA 1998 and the Enterprise Act 2002 (EA 2002) are 'human rights-proofed'.

This chapter will conclude with some reflections on the future of the CAT as the specialized court for competition cases and will argue that, while the demands of effectiveness in the application of the competition rules cannot be overlooked, maintaining the tribunal's

Arianna Andreangeli, *Human Rights and the UK Competition Act* In: *The UK Competition Regime*. Edited by: Barry Rodger, Peter Whelan, and Angus MacCulloch, Oxford University Press. © The Contributors 2021. DOI: 10.1093/oso/9780198868026.003.0009

rigorous review role for competition decisions is indispensable for the purpose of ensuring compliance with human rights standards and for the continuing integrity and reputation of the UK competition framework.

2 Competition Enforcement and Human Rights Observance in the UK—'Criminal in Nature' and Its Implications

2.1 From a Registration-based to an Enforcement-based Structure: The Competition Act 1998 and Its Implications

The impact of the CA 1998 on the UK competition framework is discussed elsewhere.[1] At this stage, it suffices to recall that the Act introduced a framework where an independent agency, now the CMA, is responsible for the application of the prohibition of anti-competitive arrangements and of the abuse of dominance. The CMA acts as 'police, prosecutor and judge' and its decisions are subject to appeal before the CAT. It acts impartially and in light of objective legal standards that necessitate strong investigative powers as well as the deployment of expert knowledge. These reforms have led to a stronger, more effective, and more impartial system for the application of the competition rules in the UK. In particular, the adoption of the integrated agency model is fully consistent with a commitment to making the assessment of restrictive practices an economic and legal matter, as opposed to an issue of political nature.

However, these changes have had significant consequences for the continued observance of fairness and due process principles, since they confer upon the competition agency pervasive investigative and sanctioning powers. It is submitted that these issues were even more relevant at the time of entry into force of the CA 1998, due to the enactment in the same year of the HRA 1998, whose objective was to incorporate the ECHR into UK law.[2] As is well known, until 1998 the UK, while being a founding member of the Council of Europe and a major influence in the drafting and stipulation of the Convention itself, had not transposed its rights into domestic law. In addition, the Convention had a limited role in the UK courts' adjudication: while they accepted the existence of a presumption that domestic law should be interpreted in conformity with the ECHR obligations, they restricted this approach to cases in which there was a 'genuine ambiguity' as to how domestic law should be construed to avoid a departure from the Convention's obligations.[3]

Against this background, the enactment of the HRA 98, by which the ECHR rights were eventually transposed into UK law, brought about extremely significant changes in the way in which human rights are protected.[4] As was aptly put by the House of Lords in *Re McKerr*, the Act 'create[d] domestic rights expressed in the same terms as those contained in the

---

[1] See ch 8 above.

[2] See inter alia David Pannick, 'Principles of Interpretation of Convention Rights under the Human Rights Act and the Discretionary Area of Judgment' [1998] *Public Law* 545; Nicholas Bamforth, 'Parliamentary Sovereignty and the Human Rights Act' [1998] PL 572; Francesca Klug, 'Incorporation through the Front Door' [2001] PL 654.

[3] See *R (Brind) v Secretary of State for the Home Department* [1991] 1 AC 696, 748 (Bridge LJ). See inter alia Michael Supperstone and Jason Coppel, 'Judicial Review after the Human Rights Act' (1999) 3 EHRLR 301, 302–03.

[4] 'Rights Brought Home—The Human Rights Bill', presented to Parliament by the Secretary of State for the Home Department, by Command of Her Majesty, October 1997, CM3782, 3 https://assets.publishing.service.gov.uk/government/uploads/system/uploads/attachment_data/file/263526/rights.pdf.

Convention',[5] thereby allowing the courts to provide effective legal remedies to individuals, while at the same time respecting the sovereignty of Parliament.[6] The Act imposes an obligation on all public bodies to exercise their functions compatibly with the ECHR rights. According to section 3, courts and tribunals must 'strive to avoid incompatibility between the ECHR and domestic legislation'.[7] This obligation, which applies to the interpretation of primary and delegated legislation, means that the latter must be read in a way that is fully consistent with the Convention, so as to afford the rights enshrined therein effective protection.[8] Issuing a declaration of incompatibility occurs exceptionally when the domestic courts cannot read the legislation in conformity with the ECHR without '[d]oing such violence to the statute as to make it unintelligible or unworkable'.[9]

In this context, it is argued that thanks to the HRA 1998 the ECHR provides the benchmark against which observance of human rights must be measured in regards to any aspects of the exercise of public powers by UK authorities, with the courts playing a pivotal role in securing its observance.[10] It is, however, equally clear that, especially in more recent years, the role of the common law as a source of human rights guarantees has reared its head, so to speak, in the practice of the UK courts. In *R (Guardian News and Media Ltd) v City of Westminster Magistrates' Court*, for instance, Toulson LJ recognized the common law as 'flourishing' in the context of fundamental rights protection.[11] Although it was acknowledged that the case law of the European Court of Human Rights (ECtHR) seemed to 'be leading in the same direction' as the common law, the decision to allow the appeal brought by *The Guardian* against a decision denying access to court documents was rooted not on Article 10 of the ECHR but on the established common law principle of open justice.[12] A broadly similar approach seemed to prevail also in *Osborn*, which concerned the right to an oral hearing: it was held that failure to afford such a hearing would go against the common law requirements of fairness, as well as infringing Article 6 of the ECHR.[13]

On this basis, commentators argued that, without going so far as to recognize explicitly its 'primacy' over the Convention, the UK courts have appeared to champion the role of the common law as a source of constitutional rights.[14] Thus, on the one hand it was recognized that the UK courts are obliged to give effect to the Convention rights, as embodied in the HRA 1998 and that 'if development of the common law [was] called for, this development should ordinarily be in harmony with the UK's international obligations'.[15] On the other hand, however, it is also clear that the analysis of the ECHR should not be the exclusive source of authority for the determination of those rights that both the Convention and the common law provide.[16] As the UK Supreme Court held in *UNISON*, fundamental

---

[5] [2004] UKHL 12, para 63 (Lord Hofmann). See Anthony Lester, 'Human Rights and the British Constitution' in Jeffrey L Jowell and Dawn Oliver (eds), *The Changing Constitution* (7th edn, OUP 2011) 77.

[6] Lester (n 5) 79.

[7] ibid 80.

[8] ibid 81.

[9] *R v Lambert* [2001] 2 AC 545 585 (Lord Hope).

[10] See Lord Derry Irvine of Lairg, 'The Impact of the Human Rights Act: the Executive, Parliament and the Courts' [2003] PL 308.

[11] [2012] EWCA Civ 420, para 88 (Toulson LJ).

[12] ibid; see also para 91. For comment see Christina Lienen, 'Common Law Constitutional Rights: Public Law at a Crossroads?' [2018] PL 649, 653 ff.

[13] *Osborn v Parole Board* [2013] 3 WLR 1020, para 113 (Reed LJ). See Lienen (n 12) 654.

[14] Lienen (n 12) 653.

[15] *A v Secretary of State for the Home Department* [2005] UKHL 71, para 27 (Bingham LJ).

[16] ibid.

entitlements such as the right of access to justice, are not 'European imports', but have been long embedded in the constitutional law of the UK and find their justification in the fact that the UK is built on the respect for the rule of law.[17]

In light of the foregoing analysis, it may be concluded that the enactment of the HRA 1998 marked a significant change in the way in which human rights are protected in the UK, to the extent that it made express and enforceable the ECHR rights before the courts, thus increasing legal certainty and enhancing the respect of the Convention obligations. It is, however, clear from more recent case law that the common law remains equally important in the identification of relevant human rights standards. In particular, the *UNISON* decision emphasizes the observance of the rule of law as a powerful justification for relying on this source in the determination of the scope of these rights.[18] The next section will outline the meaning of the right to a fair trial as it applies to competition cases.

2.2 Defining the Benchmark: The Right to a Fair Trial and 'Criminal in Nature' Infringements—Article 6 ECHR and the Judicial Scrutiny of Competition Cases

2.2.1 Administrative Decisions and the European Convention: What Is 'Criminal' or 'Civil'? What Is 'Fair'?

The previous section summarized the key features of the development of human rights protection in the UK and argued that, thanks to the HRA 1998, the ECHR plays a significant role in this context, along with an 'emboldened' common law. This section will explore the meaning of Article 6 ECHR, which enshrines the right to a fair trial, and will concentrate on how this provision has been interpreted by the Strasbourg Court in the context of those infringements that, while being defined as 'administrative' by domestic law, fall nonetheless within the scope of the Convention. On that basis, it will explore how the approach adopted in this context becomes significant for the public enforcement of competition law.

As is well known, Article 6(1) of the Convention states that in the 'determination of civil rights and obligations or of a criminal charge' everyone enjoys the right to a fair and public hearing before an 'independent and impartial tribunal, established by law'. The case law of the ECtHR indicates that the notions of 'criminal charge' and 'determination of civil rights and obligations' must be determined in light of the Convention and not just in light of national law, although national law can provide a useful starting point.[19] Thus, in relation to a definition of 'criminal charge', the nature of the prohibition being infringed, and in particular whether the latter was of general application and in the public interest, the gravity of the alleged infringement and the severity of the sanctions that could be inflicted for it are relevant in this assessment.[20] In addition, the fact that the sanctions pursue an aim which is

---

[17] *R (UNISON) v Lord Chancellor* [2017] UKSC 51, paras 64, 67–69.
[18] See ibid eg paras 86–89. For commentary see inter alia Jo Eric Khushal Murkens, 'Judicious Review: The Constitutional Practice of the UK Supreme Court' (2018) 77(2) CLJ 349, 367–68; see also Tim Eicke, 'Speaking in UNISON: Access to Justice and the Convention' (2018) 1 EHRLR 22, esp 24–25.
[19] See *Engel and Others v Netherlands* App no 5100/71 (1979-1980) 1 EHRR 647, para 81.
[20] ibid.

both deterrent and punitive can indicate that a certain prima facie 'disciplinary' or 'regulatory' infringement is actually 'criminal in nature'.[21]

A similar approach has also been adopted in respect of the notion of 'determination of civil rights and obligations'.[22] For this purpose, what is relevant is whether 'a dispute (contestation)' exists 'over a "right" which can be said, at least on arguable grounds, to be recognised under domestic law'. This 'contestation' can concern the existence of a right as well as the way in which it should be exercised, must be 'genuine and serious', and the outcome of the proceedings in issue must be 'directly decisive for the right in question'.[23] Once it has been determined that prima facie administrative proceedings are in fact, respectively, 'civil' or 'criminal' for ECHR purposes, the question arises as to their compliance with the fairness standards enshrined in Article 6(1).

On this point, it should be emphasized that, according to the ECtHR, the 'integrated agency' model, with its non-judicial approach to the investigation and decision-making in matters that are 'criminal' for the purpose of the Convention, is not necessarily incompatible with Article 6(1). In *Albert and Le Compte* the ECtHR acknowledged that '[i]n many member States of the Council of Europe, the duty of adjudicating on disciplinary offences is conferred on [inter alia] jurisdictional organs of professional associations'. On that basis, it excluded, on the one hand, that '[e]ven in instances where Article 6 para. 1 (art. 6-1) is applicable, conferring powers in this manner does not in itself infringe the Convention'. On the other hand, however, the Court found that:

in such circumstances the Convention calls at least for one of the two following systems: either the jurisdictional organs themselves comply with the requirements of Article 6 para. 1 (art. 6-1), or they do not so comply but are subject to subsequent control by a judicial body that has full jurisdiction and does provide the guarantees of Article 6 para. 1 (art. 6-1)[24]

In light of this decision, therefore, what is relevant is the possibility for the investigated party to have access to a 'proper', impartial, and independent court which is competent to scrutinize all aspects of the decision, both in fact and in law.[25] As to the meaning of 'fair' in these cases, the Court has accepted that, even when a prima facie 'administrative offence' is found to be 'criminal in nature', there may be legitimate justifications for limiting the reach of certain due process entitlements which would be essential in 'full' criminal cases tried in court, such as the entitlement to an oral hearing[26] or the right to remain silent.

The ECtHR has recognized therefore that what represents a 'fair trial' should be commensurate in scope to the nature of the legal framework in which it was invoked.[27] In this context, the rationale for any restriction and in particular whether the latter was motivated

---

[21] ibid para 82. See also inter alia *Ezeh and Connors v United Kingdom* App no 39665/98 (2004) 39 EHRR 1, para 86.

[22] See *Zander v Sweden* App no 14282/88 (1994) 18 EHRR 175, para 27.

[23] ibid para 22.

[24] *Albert and Le Compte v Belgium* App nos 7299/75 and 7496/76 (1983) 5 EHRR 533, para 29.

[25] See eg *Menarini Diagnostics v Italy* App no 43509/08 (ECHR 27 September 2011) para 63 http://hudoc.echr.coe.int/eng?i=001-146341.

[26] *Jussila v Finland* App no 73053/01 (2007) 45 EHRR 39, paras 42–43.

[27] See eg *John Murray v United Kingdom* App no 19731/91 (ECHR 8 February 1996) paras 47, 50–51 http://hudoc.echr.coe.int/eng?i=001-57980.

by reasons of public interest and the broader legal framework in which it is imposed should be taken into account.[28] Consequently, the entitlements that characterize this notion can be subject to limits so long as, in the specific case, these limits are appropriately counterbalanced by other procedural safeguards.[29]

The question of what standard of proof administrative authorities charged with determining 'criminal charges' for the purpose of Article 6 ECHR must satisfy to establish the existence of the infringement of which the investigated undertaking is accused provides a good example of this assessment. In *Steel* the ECtHR acknowledged that Article 6 ECHR does not lay out any specific requirements as to the standard of proof applicable to the determination of civil disputes as opposed to criminal or 'quasi-criminal' offences, but that this is a matter which lies within the power of appreciation of the contracting states.[30] What the Convention requires, however, is that proceedings aimed at the determination of 'criminal charges' be 'fair', having regard to the case as a whole, of which the burden and standard of proof represent but one aspect.[31] Thus, the Court took the view in several decisions that to fulfil the requirements of Article 6 ECHR an offence should be proved on the basis of the '[c]oexistence of sufficiently strong, clear and concordant inferences or of similar unrebutted presumptions of fact', providing that appropriate safeguards are in place to protect the rights of the accused.[32]

As the ECtHR held in *Albert and Le Compte*, the intensity of the Court's review powers is critical to ensuring the compliance of administrative proceedings concerning, respectively, the determination of civil rights and obligations or of criminal charges with the Convention requirements. The question is whether the notion of 'full review' concerning all matters of fact and of law requires that the court reviewing the legitimacy of these administrative decisions demands the competent judicial authorities to scrutinize administrative decisions on their merits, without being limited by specific grounds of review, and to substitute their own judgment to that of the administrative agencies.[33]

In relation to 'civil matters', the ECtHR held in, for instance, the *Bryan* decision that the judicial review remedy, available to the applicant before the High Court to challenge a planning notice, was sufficient to guarantee respect of his right to a fair trial. It was found that this remedy, while being only 'on points of law', allowed the Court to scrutinize whether the decision had been taken in reference to 'irrelevant factors' or on the basis of insufficient evidence or 'perverse or irrational … inferences of fact'.[34] The judgment in *Grande Stevens v Italy* addresses similar questions in relation to an administrative decision concerning a 'criminal' matter.[35] The Court found that the administrative stage of these proceedings

---

[28]   *O'Halloran and Francis v United Kingdom* App no 15809/02 (2008) 46 EHRR 21, paras 55–57.

[29]   ibid. See also inter alia *Condron v Austria* App no 35718/97 (ECHR 2 May 2000) para 56 http://hudoc.echr.coe.int/eng?i=001-58798.

[30]   See inter alia *Steel and Morris v United Kingdom* App no 24838/94 (ECHR 23 September 1998) para 70.

[31]   See eg *Salabiaku v France* App no 10589/83 (1991) 13 EHRR 79 paras 26–30.

[32]   See inter alia *Bouyid v Belgium* App no 23380/09 (2016) 62 EHRR 32 para 82; see also *Jalloh v Switzerland* App no 54810/00 (2007) 44 EHRR 20, para 67.

[33]   See eg Arianna Andreangeli, 'Toward an EU Competition Court: "Article 6 Proofing" Antitrust Proceedings before the Commission?' (2007) 30(4) W Comp 595; also more generally Julian Rivers, 'Proportionality and Variable Intensity of Review' (2006) 65(1) CLJ 174; (mutatis mutandis) Csongor Istvan Nagy, 'EU Competition Law's Fair Trial Revolution: Too Much Ado about Nothing?' (2016) 37(6) ECLR 232; Renato Nazzini, 'Judicial Review after KME: an Even Stronger Case for a Reform that Will Never Be' (2015) 40 (4) EL Rev 490.

[34]   *Bryan v United Kingdom* App no 19198/91 (1996) 21 EHRR 342, paras 44, 47. Cf *Kingsley v UK* App no 35605/97 (2001) 33 EHRR 13, paras 54–60.

[35]   App no 18640/10 (ECHR 4 March 2014) paras 99–101 http://hudoc.echr.coe.int/eng?i=001-141794.

lacked key procedural safeguards such as the possibility for the investigated parties to have access to the investigating officers' reports, which formed the basis of the agency's final decision and to attend the only oral hearing allowed under domestic law.[36] On this basis alone, the Court found an infringement of Article 6 ECHR.[37] As to the powers enjoyed by the reviewing court in the course of the judicial phase of the case,[38] the Court observed that the Turin Court of Appeal '[h]ad jurisdiction to rule, in respect of both law and fact, on whether the offence ... had been committed, and was authorised to set aside the decision'.[39] It could also examine the proportionality of the sanctions imposed and could reduce them if it found that they were not appropriate in light of the nature of the unlawful conduct.[40]

In light of the foregoing analysis it can be concluded that Article 6 of the ECHR applies not merely to civil or criminal cases that are heard before national courts, but also to the adoption of prima facie administrative decisions that, owing to the substance and nature of their subject matter, are 'civil' or 'criminal' in nature. While the Convention allows similar cases to be decided in a non-judicial manner, it nonetheless requires the observance of certain basic fairness standards. It was shown that in this context the nature and intensity of the review powers exercised by the courts responsible for deciding on the lawfulness of administrative decisions are especially important. The next section will consider how these principles affect the compliance of competition decision-making with the Convention; in particular, it will be examined whether the functioning of the procedural framework enshrined in the CA 1998 for the investigation and sanctioning of anti-competitive arrangements and abuses of dominance conforms with the notion of 'fair trial' provided in Article 6(1) ECHR.

2.2.2 Article 6(1) ECHR and Competition Cases in the UK

The previous section outlined the approach taken by the ECtHR in respect of the applicability of Article 6 of the Convention to proceedings which, while dealing with matters substantively 'civil' or 'criminal', are conducted by administrative authorities. The purpose of this section is to discuss the implications of the applicability of Article 6(1) of the Convention to proceedings aimed at the detection and sanctioning of prima facie infringements of Chapter I and Chapter II of the CA 1998. Should these proceedings be regarded as being aimed at the determination of 'criminal charges' within the scope of the ECHR? And if this is the case, is it compatible with the Convention to entrust the investigation and decision-making to administrative authorities, albeit subject to the review/appeal before a fully fledged, independent court?

In relation to the nature of alleged antitrust infringements, the ECtHR has consistently taken the view that what constitutes a 'criminal matter' should not be determined solely on the basis of the relevant domestic law.[41] The nature of the prohibition, and in particular whether the latter was of general application and in the public interest, the gravity of the alleged infringement and the severity of the sanctions that could be inflicted for it are relevant in this assessment.[42] In addition, the fact that the sanctions pursue an aim which is both

[36] ibid paras 117–18.
[37] ibid para 122.
[38] ibid paras 138–39.
[39] ibid para 149.
[40] ibid.
[41] ibid; see also *Öztürk v Germany* App no 8544/79 (1984) 6 EHRR 409, paras 37 ff.
[42] *Engel and Others v Netherlands* (n 19) para 81.

deterrent and punitive can indicate that a certain prima facie 'disciplinary' or 'regulatory' infringement is actually 'criminal in nature'.[43]

In *Société Stenuit v France*, the now-defunct European Commission on Human Rights took the view that because the rules prohibiting anti-competitive agreements were aimed at pursuing a public interest, their infringement was of a serious nature and the sanctions that the competent authorities could impose were, by reason of their magnitude, both deterrent and punitive.[44] The position taken in *Stenuit* was reaffirmed more recently in the *Menarini* decision.[45] The application concerned whether the Italian system for the application of the rules prohibiting cartel behaviour and abuse of dominant position complied with the Convention's standards of 'fair trial'. As in the UK and EU contexts, Italian competition law adopted an 'integrated agency' model, with the Autorità Garante per la Concorrenza ed il Mercato (AGCM) responsible for the investigation and sanction of unlawful conduct. The decisions of the AGCM are subject to review before the administrative courts, namely the Tribunale Amminstrativo Regionale (TAR) of the Lazio region and, on appeal on points of law only, the Consiglio di Stato.[46]

In its judgment the ECtHR considered whether proceedings before the AGCM (and, upon a challenge against its decision, before the administrative judges) were 'criminal' in nature for Convention purposes. In accordance with the approach adopted in *Engel*, the Court looked at how the infringement in question was classified in domestic law, at its nature, and at the gravity and nature of the sanction that the AGCM could impose. Importantly, it was emphasized that these three conditions were 'alternative' and not 'cumulative'.[47] Thus, for the Convention to be applicable, it is sufficient that one of them is met. Nonetheless, the Court held that, if the application of one of the criteria was not conclusive, the other would have to be fulfilled in order for Article 6(1) to become relevant.[48]

In light of the foregoing, the judgment observed that while infringing the competition rules was not a criminal offence, the rules involved pursued 'societal interests of a general nature, normally protected by the criminal law'. In addition, the sanctions that the AGCM could impose aimed to deter future breaches and therefore had a punitive essence.[49] The Court observed that financial penalties could not be swapped with or accompanied by sanctions affecting the personal freedom of the individuals involved in anti-competitive behaviour.[50] Nonetheless, it took the view that, owing to the size of the potential financial penalties, their function could only be defined as repressive and aimed at punishing further unlawful conduct.[51] On that basis, the ECtHR concluded that allegations of cartel behaviour or of abuses of dominance should be treated as a 'criminal charge' for the purpose of the ECHR.[52] In light of the similarities between the Italian competition legislation and the CA

---

[43] ibid para 82. See also *Ezeh and Connors v UK* (n 21) para 86.

[44] App no 11598/85 (ECHR 30 May 1991) (1991) ECC 41, paras 60–64.

[45] *Menarini Diagnostics* (n 25) paras 38–42. For commentary see inter alia Bruno Nascimbene, 'Fair Trial and the Rights of Defence in Antitrust Proceedings before the Commission: a Need for Reform?' (2013) 38(4) EL Rev 573; Mario Siragusa, 'The ECtHR Judgment in Menarini Srl v Italy and Its Implications for Private Enforcement of EU Competition Law' (2012) 5(4) GCLR 129; Igor Nikolic, 'Full Judicial Review of Antitrust Cases after KME: a new Formula of Review?' (2012) 33(12) ECLR 583.

[46] Law No 287 of 10 October 1990; see esp arts 10 ff.

[47] *Menarini Diagnostics* (n 25) para 38.

[48] ibid.

[49] ibid para 40.

[50] ibid para 41.

[51] ibid para 42.

[52] ibid; see also para 44.

1998, in terms of the public interest they seek to protect and of the institutional enforcement mechanisms as well as substantive approach they adopt, it can be concluded that Article 6 of the ECHR is equally applicable to proceedings concerning allegations of behaviour infringing Chapters I and II of the CA 1998. Just as with the Italian legislation, the CA 1998 pursues public interests of a broad societal nature and targets behaviour of a serious nature. Furthermore, the financial penalties that the CMA can impose on undertakings that have engaged in anti-competitive behaviour can be of such a significant level that they perform both deterrent and punitive functions.

In light of the foregoing, the next question is whether the ECHR requirements are satisfied where these matters are dealt with by an 'integrated agency'—namely an agency combining investigating and decision-making functions—such as the CMA. In the *Stenuit* decision, cited above, the European Commission on Human Rights observed that the applicant had been able to seek the judicial scrutiny of a ministerial decision imposing fines adopted on recommendation from the Competition Commission before the Conseil d'Etat.[53] It also found that, prima facie, the court enjoyed the power to review in full the decision itself, including the imposition of penalties.[54] However, it held that in the case at hand, this review had not occurred: the Conseil d'Etat had rejected the challenge solely on the ground that the minister, acting upon opinion of the Competition Commission, had acted on the basis of law and that, in any event, the charges made against the applicant were not 'criminal in nature'.[55] Thus, it had not ruled on the merits of the allegations that had led to the decision and the financial penalties in question.[56]

Against this background, and in light of the approach adopted in the *Grande Stevens* decision discussed in section 2.2.1 above, it is suggested that the central issue in ascertaining compliance of competition proceedings with the ECHR is the scope of the powers of judicial scrutiny of the decision adopted by the relevant competition authority: is the competent court able to carry out a sufficiently pervasive examination of the impugned decision? In other words, what does it mean in this context that the court competent for the scrutiny of the decision should enjoy the power to rule on all matters of fact and of law that were relevant in the finding of an infringement?[57] This issue was eventually addressed by the ECtHR in the *Menarini* decision.[58] Unlike in the *Grande Stevens* decision cited above, a competition decision adopted by the Italian competition authority could be challenged before the TAR for Lazio. The ECtHR therefore had to examine the question as to whether the nature and scope of the powers exercised by the appellate court were consistent with the Convention requirements.

The Court of Human Rights observed that in Italian law jurisdiction on the merits, in the context of the review of administrative acts, represented an exception to the general rule that the administrative courts could only review the legal aspects of an administrative decision but could not substitute its own assessment of the merits of the case to the conclusions of the competition authority if the decision was annulled.[59] Competition

[53] *Société Stenuit* (n 44) paras 69, 71.
[54] ibid para 72.
[55] ibid para 71.
[56] ibid paras 72–73.
[57] See *Albert and Le Compte* (n 24) para 29.
[58] *Menarini Diagnostics* (n 25).
[59] ibid 6–7.

decisions were subject to a 'legitimacy review'; however, the administrative judge could exercise control on the merits in respect of the size of the sanction imposed by the AGCM, as a result of which it could reduce and even quash the penalty imposed on the appellant.[60]

The Strasbourg Court examined the nature of the scrutiny exercised by the TAR in the case at hand. It observed that the judge had examined all the legal aspects of the decision and scrutinized how the Italian competition authority had exercised its discretionary powers in the adoption of the decision, especially in relation to its technical aspects.[61] In addition, in accordance with its full jurisdictional powers in this context, the Tribunal could examine the adequacy of the sanction to the nature of the offence and if necessary, alter its amount.[62] Thus, the ECtHR concluded that, while the Consiglio di Stato was not competent to 'remake' the TAR's decision regarding whether there had been an infringement, its powers complied with the requirement of 'full jurisdiction' in respect of profiles of fact and law, enshrined in Article 6 ECHR.[63]

In light of the foregoing analysis, it is suggested that, for the purpose of ensuring compliance with the Convention, decisions concerning cartel and abusive behaviour adopted by 'integrated agencies' must not necessarily be subject to a full review on the merits, entailing the power of the competent court to substitute its own view to that of the agency, if the latter is found to have acted unlawfully. However, it is vital that the review outlined in the *Menarini* ruling should have actually occurred in the case at hand to ensure compliance. This point was made very forcefully by one of the judges in that case, who in his dissenting opinion argued that while Italian law expressly conferred these powers upon the TAR, the administrative court had actually not engaged fully with the matters of fact and law arising from the impugned decision. In his view, therefore, the requirements of fairness embedded in the ECHR had not been complied with.[64]

It can be concluded, therefore, that the ECHR does not require the contracting states to subject the finding of infringements of their competition rules to the authority of judicial bodies, but allows them to choose to entrust this function to non-judicial bodies, such as expert administrative authorities independent of government and endowed with the necessary expertise. However, it demands that the decisions adopted by these bodies be subject to a 'full review' of facts and law, entailing a consideration of the accuracy of the facts, of the correct application of the law, and of the way in which the competition agency had exercised its discretion, especially on the basis of expert knowledge, in reaching its conclusions. Moreover, this control should have occurred in practice in a specific case; thus, it is submitted that if an appeal was rejected, for instance, on the basis of formal arguments, Article 6 ECHR would not be complied with.

---

[60] ibid 7, para C.
[61] ibid para 64 of the Italian translation provided by the Ministry of Justice https://hudoc.echr.coe.int/eng#{%22docname%22:[%22\%22CASE%20OF%20A.%20MENARINI%20DIAGNOSTICS%20S.R.L.%20v.%20ITALY\%22%22],%22documentcollectionid2%22:[%22GRANDCHAMBER%22,%22CHAMBER%22],%22itemid%22:[%22001-146341%22]}.
[62] ibid.
[63] ibid para 67; see also para 63.
[64] *Menarini Diagnostics* (n 25) paras 7–8 of the dissenting opinion (Pinto de Albuquerque J).

3 United Kingdom Competition Proceedings Put to the Human Rights Test—Article 6 and the Competition Appeals Tribunal

3.1 A 'Fair Trial' in the UK—Between the Common Law and the ECHR: Summary Remarks

The previous section discussed the impact of Article 6(1) ECHR on proceedings concerning allegations of cartel or abusive behaviour in accordance with the case law of the ECtHR. It was argued that while the Convention allows contracting states to entrust these proceedings to an 'integrated' administrative agency, it nonetheless demands the observance of stringent standards concerning the standard of proof of an infringement and, perhaps most importantly, the scope and intensity of the judicial scrutiny that courts must exercise on competition decisions. This section will move on to a brief analysis of the notion of due process as has been developed by the UK courts, both in the context of the common law and of the ECHR, paying particular attention to areas where non-judicial authorities are responsible for deciding upon 'criminal' matters, within the meaning of the Convention.

The scope of this chapter does not permit a detailed consideration of the human development of the right to a fair trial in the UK.[65] It is, however, indispensable to recall that a number of rights that collectively contribute to ensuring the fairness of civil or criminal proceedings have been enshrined in the common law and as such therefore predate the ECHR.[66] In *Ex p. Witham*, for instance, it was held that the right to access to the courts found its roots in the common law, and could be regarded as being a 'constitutional right' even though the UK lacks a written constitution.[67] As such, therefore, it could only be abrogated or limited in its reach by an act of Parliament and the courts were therefore competent to ensure its observance against attempts on the part of the executive to interfere with it without a statutory basis.[68]

Other aspects of what may be regarded as falling within the concepts of a 'fair trial' and a 'fair procedure' have also been recognized as being rooted in the common law. The right to an impartial tribunal, for instance, was recognized as 'sacred' by the House of Lords in *Dimes v Grand Junction Canal Co* and as such as embedded in the essence of justice, and that it should entail not only actual impartiality but also an appearance thereof.[69] The right to be presumed innocent until guilt has been established is another feature of a fair trial that shares this common law origin. In *R (Lyons)* the House of Lords took the view that the right to remain silent belonged to the 'collection of rules and principles' that all together made up what a 'fair trial' is and that are enshrined first and foremost in the common law.[70] Importantly, their Lordships accepted that the UK had undertaken to secure the rights

---

[65] See Roger Masterman, 'Determinative in the Abstract? Article 6(1) and the Separation of Powers' (2005) 6 EHRLR 628; mutatis mutandis Samuels, 'The Planning Process and Judicial Control' [2007] JPL 1570; Robert Thomas, 'A Different Tale of Judicial Power: Administrative Review as a Problematic Response to the Judicialisation of Tribunals' [2019] PL 537; Ian Leigh, 'Taking Rights Proportionately; Judicial Review, the Human Rights Act and Strasbourg' [2002] PL 265.

[66] See generally Dawn Oliver, 'Common Values in Public and Private Law and the Public/private Divide' [1997] PL 630; also John Laws, 'Is the High Court the Guardian of Fundamental Constitutional Rights?' [1993] PL 59.

[67] *R (Witham) v Lord Chancellor* [1998] QB 575, 581.

[68] ibid 585.

[69] [1852] 10 ER 301, 315 (Campbell LJ). For commentary see Geoffrey A Flick, 'Impartiality and the Administrative Process in Common Law Nations' (1977) 5 West S U L Rev 45, 47–48.

[70] *R v Lyons, Parnes, Ronson, Saunders* [2002] UKHL 44, para 30 (Hoffmann LJ).

enshrined in the ECHR and that, as a result, the judiciary had an obligation to interpret the common law in a way that was consistent with the Convention.[71] As was forcefully held by Lord Hoffmann, the ECHR had long 'exerted a persuasive and pervasive influence on judicial decision making' in the UK, inter alia, by 'bearing on the development of the common law'. However, it was concluded that the question of whether the accused's right to a fair trial and in particular to whether the presumption of innocence had been infringed should have been answered exclusively in light of that 'collection of rules and principles' that belonged to '[t]he common law'.[72]

The enactment of the HRA 1998, to the extent that it reproduced the right to a fair trial contained in the Convention in UK law, had a significant impact on the reach of these protections. Giving evidence before the UK Parliament Joint Committee on Human Rights, Amos expressed the view that the enactment of the HRA 1998 had consolidated this 'immeasurable' contribution by providing a clear pathway for individuals who wished to seek protection of Convention rights before the UK courts.[73] It was emphasized that as a result of the duty imposed on national courts to 'act compatibly with Convention rights when developing the common law',[74] many due process rights had been confirmed and strengthened. This was the case, for instance, for the right not to incriminate oneself and the right to legal assistance at all stages of criminal proceedings.[75]

It is observed that a similar trajectory could be seen in respect of the development of several safeguards of fairness in the context of administrative decision-making. Just as with the criminal process' procedural standards mentioned above, several procedural rights were embedded by the common law in administrative decision-making and later confirmed and reinforced as a result of the impact of the HRA 1998. The requirement that an administrative decision-maker should be unbiased, in accordance with the natural justice principle *nemo judex in causa sua*, and that the principle that both parties should be heard have both been considered essential for the observance of basic rules of natural justice in the course of administrative decision-making.[76] The common law has also influenced significantly the standards governing the judicial scrutiny of administrative decisions affecting the rights of individuals: in the *Alconbury* decision the House of Lords took the view that the common law had 'developed specific grounds for the review of administrative acts' and that these principles ensured a degree of control over the legitimacy of these decisions that was sufficient to remedy the lack of an independent decision-maker.[77]

The influence of the ECHR, before as well as after the enactment of the HRA 1998, has been significant in confirming and in many cases reinforcing many of these safeguards in the context of administrative proceedings aimed at the determination of 'criminal charges'. The protection of the right of prisoners to be heard in the course of disciplinary

---

[71] ibid para 27.

[72] ibid paras 30, 31.

[73] Valerie Amos, 'Evidence Given to the UK Parliament Joint Committee on Human Rights, Twenty Years of the Human Rights Act Inquiry' (HRA0019) http://data.parliament.uk/writtenevidence/committeeevidence.svc/evidencedocument/human-rights-committee/20-years-of-the-human-rights-act/written/89739.html.

[74] ibid.

[75] Dimitrios Giannoulopoulos, 'What Has the European Convention on Human Rights Ever Done for the UK?' (2019) 1 EHRLR 1, 8.

[76] See *Kanda v Malaya* [1962] AC 322, 337–38; see also more recently *R (Hawthorne) v Police Ombudsman for northern Ireland* [2018] NIQB 5, paras 104, 114.

[77] *R (Alconbury Developments and Others) v Secretary of State for the Environment, Transport and the Regions* [2003] AC 295, paras 49, 135.

proceedings is an apt example of the mutual influence existing between the common law and the Convention in ensuring the right of individuals to a fair hearing throughout the proceedings and not just in their judicial segment.[78] On other occasions, however, the impact of the Convention has revealed that common law standards were not sufficient to meet the ECHR requirements.

For instance, in the *Ezeh and Connors* decision, another judgment related to procedural rights in prison disciplinary inquiries,[79] the Strasbourg Court held that even though natural justice did not require the applicant to have legal representation, Article 6(1) ECHR demanded that she be given access to a lawyer in the course of those disciplinary proceedings as a result of which her sentence could have been increased.[80] It was emphasized that the position adopted hitherto on this issue was no longer tenable, once the 'criminal' nature of the offence against prison discipline was recognized.[81] The rules of natural justice had, therefore, to be 'read up' in light of the obligations arising from the ECHR, which instead extended the right to consult a lawyer in proceedings that had a 'criminal nature'.[82]

In light of the foregoing analysis, it may be concluded that the common law has played a significant role in embedding a number of procedural fairness standards in the way in which non-judicial proceedings that affect civil rights or the determination of criminal matters. In this context, the ECHR has both confirmed existing safeguards and increased standards of protection of these procedural rights.[83] The next section will consider the question of the extent to which the observance of Convention standards, arising from the HRA 1998, has influenced the nature and structure of competition proceedings after the enactment of the CA 1998.

3.2 UK Competition Proceedings Put to the ECHR Test:
The *NAPP* Judgment

The previous section sketched out the standards of protection of the right to a 'fair hearing' in the UK and highlighted how this important safeguard has been shaped by the common law, as well as being influenced by the ECHR. The purpose of this section will be to address the question of how the framework for the enforcement of Chapters I and II of the CA 1998 by the CMA 'scores' under the ECHR rules. It is necessary to bear in mind that the Convention does not go so far as to require that all matters falling within the scope of Article 6(1) ECHR be subject to the decision-making authority of judicial bodies, thereby allowing administrative authorities to adopt decisions affecting civil or criminal matters.[84] However, the Convention does require that these decisions be subject to the scrutiny of a proper court enjoying the power to review it in all its aspects of fact and law. Accordingly,

---

[78] See inter alia *R (Smith) v Parole Board and R (West) v Parole Board* [2005] UKHL 1, para 35 (Lord Bingham); see also para 74.

[79] *Ezeh and Connors v UK* (n 21) para 86.

[80] ibid paras 120–30; see also para 88; see also judgment of 15 July 2002, handed down by Chamber (2002) 35 EHRR 28, paras 105–106.

[81] See *Ezeh and Connors* (n 21) para 104; see also Grand Chamber (n 80), paras 103–108.

[82] See inter alia Lienen (n 13) 654.

[83] See inter alia Giannoulopoulos (n 75) 7–8. See also mutatis mutandis Mark Elliott, 'Has the Common Law Duty to Give Reasons Come of Age Yet?' [2011] PL 56, 64, 67.

[84] See s 2.2.2 above.

this section will focus on the nature of the powers of review enjoyed by the CAT vis-à-vis infringement decisions adopted by the CMA in relation to cartel and abusive behaviour under both the EU and UK prohibitions.

As was illustrated earlier, the ECtHR held in *Grande Stevens* and *Menarini* that limited forms of judicial scrutiny of competition decisions, such as the review of these measures only 'on points of law', are not going to ensure observance of Article 6 of the Convention. Although Article 6 was not read as far as requiring the reviewing court to substitute its views to those of a competition authority in the event of the annulment of a competition decision, it certainly demands that the former be empowered to engage in the scrutiny of all aspects of the decision, including a consideration of the manner in which the competition agency had exercised its discretionary powers and its ability to conduct complex technical assessments.[85]

How do these principles 'play out' in the framework for the application of the rules prohibiting collusive or abusive behaviour in the UK? While the remit of this chapter does not allow an examination of the jurisdiction of the CAT, it is indispensable to remember that this tribunal enjoys a number of jurisdictional powers vis-à-vis the CMA and a number of sector regulators.[86] Among these functions is the power to hear appeals brought against decisions finding an infringement of the CA 1998 rules prohibiting collusive practices or the abuse of a dominant position (and the equivalent EU law prohibitions under Articles 101 and 102 of the Treaty on the Functioning of the European Union (TFEU)). According to paragraph 3 of Schedule 8 to the CA 1998, the CAT can not only 'confirm and set aside' the impugned decision, but can also 'give such directions, or taken such steps' and 'take any other decision' that the CMA could have taken itself in relation to the subject matter of the case. Against this background, the question is whether the nature and intensity of these powers of judicial scrutiny meet the ECHR requirements. This question was addressed by the CAT in the *Napp* appeal case: this was the first opportunity for the new (at the time) CAT to hear an appeal brought against an Office of Fair Trading (OFT) decision finding an infringement of the CA 1998. Accordingly, it can be regarded as something of a 'test' as to the compatibility of the regime introduced in 1998 with, among others, the human rights principles of a 'fair hearing', enshrined in Article 6 of the ECHR. In its infringement decision, the OFT had found that Napp had abused its dominant position on the market for the supply of certain painkilling drugs.[87]

On appeal, the infringing company, Napp Pharmaceuticals, made a number of allegations concerning the compatibility of the decision and of the proceedings with its entitlement to a 'fair and public hearing' and to the presumption of innocence. It also claimed that since competition cases were 'criminal in nature', the existence of an infringement should have been established 'beyond reasonable doubt'.[88] The applicant also took exception to the way in which the CAT should have exercised its powers of review on the merits and in particular its ability both to allow and examine additional evidence, including evidence

---

[85] See *Menarini Diagnostics* (n 25) paras 63, 67.

[86] For an analysis of the role of the CAT see David Bailey, 'Early Case-Law of the Competition Appeal Tribunal' in Barry Rodger (ed), *Ten Years of UK Competition Law Reform* (Dundee University Press 2010) ch 2.

[87] *Napp Pharmaceutical Holdings v Director General for Fair Trading* [2001] Comp AR 1; for commentary see eg Mark Furse, 'Caught Napping: DGFT and Napp Pharmaceutical Holdings Ltd' (2001) 22(10) ECLR 477; more generally see inter alia Barry Rodger, 'Early Steps to a Mature Competition Law System' (2002) 23(2) ECLR 52.

[88] *Napp Pharmaceutical Holdings Ltd & Others v DGFT* [2002] ECC 13, paras 89, 94 (*Napp 4*).

provided by the respondent.[89] The CAT addressed these pleas in an interim decision and, in that context, had to consider whether competition proceedings were 'criminal in nature'.[90] It was held that the nature of the penalties—both 'deterrent and punitive'—indicated that allegations of collusive or abusive behaviour belonged to the 'criminal sphere'.[91] On that basis, the judgment considered the general question of the compliance of UK competition investigations with Article 6 ECHR. The tribunal acknowledged that the CA 1998 had established an integrated agency framework for the detection and sanction of competition infringements. It took the view that the Act had introduced '[a]n administrative procedure before the Director, followed by a full judicial determination of the merits of the Director's decision, with the Tribunal being vested ... with the power to take any decision the Director could have taken'.[92]

The interim decision observed that, while the investigated parties enjoyed a number of procedural rights vis-à-vis the OFT's predecessor (the Director General for Fair Trading (DGFT)), it could not be said that the administrative stage of these 'composite proceedings' complied with Article 6 of the Convention.[93] Nonetheless, the Tribunal took the view, in accordance with the *Albert & LeCompte* judgment of the ECtHR that it was the judicial segment that secured compliance with the right to a fair trial: '[t]he Act looks to the judicial stage of the process before this Tribunal to satisfy the requirements of Article 6 of the ECHR'.[94] On that basis, the CAT proceeded to discuss, albeit in brief, the question of whether the nature of the powers of appeal it enjoyed vis-à-vis a competition decision conformed to the Convention.[95] It was observed that the CAT enjoyed full powers of review on the merits in the determination of appeals against competition infringement decisions; this was sufficient, in the tribunal's view, to 'legitimately correct any unfairness' that might have affected the adoption of the administrative decision, without necessarily having to quash the impugned decision.[96]

The tribunal added that, for this purpose, the CA 1998 and the CAT rules of procedure should have been interpreted so as to allow the appellant to place before the tribunal not only the evidence that it had already adduced before the DGFT, but also fresh evidence, including new material substantiating different arguments as to why the decision should be annulled and remade.[97] In the CAT's view, because the appellant had no possibility of examining witnesses before the DGFT, the demands of due process could be fully satisfied only before the tribunal itself, where the appellant could cross-examine witnesses against it before a full court.[98] However, the judgment excluded that the same approach could be extended to the DGFT's submissions on appeal. In the CAT's view, the competition agency 'should normally be prepared to defend the decision' under challenge, on the basis of the evidence adduced to support the decision's conclusions.[99] The tribunal emphasized that the infringement decision was a legally binding act crystallizing the DGFT's position as to

---

[89] *Napp Pharmaceutical Holdings Ltd & Others v DGFT* [2002] ECC 3, para 58 (*Napp 3*); see also para 80.
[90] ibid para 71.
[91] *Napp 4* (n 88) para 99.
[92] *Napp 3* (n 89) para 74.
[93] ibid para 75.
[94] ibid para 76.
[95] ibid paras 77 ff.
[96] ibid para 77.
[97] ibid para 78.
[98] ibid.
[99] ibid para 79.

the truth of the allegations made against the appellant.[100] Thus, to allow the competition authority to adduce new evidence and make new arguments on appeal would render the case against the appellant a 'moving target' and thereby jeopardize the right to challenge the decision itself.[101]

At the same time the CAT made clear that this 'presumption' against the DGFT making a 'new case' in the course of an appeal was not absolute. In its view, the need to deal with cases 'justly' and in particular to ensure the overall fairness of the appellate process might justify allowing the competition agency to respond to a new report put before the CAT by the appellant, in support of its challenge against the decision.[102] Another circumstance in which the tribunal could consider exercising its discretion and allow new evidence is where there are third party interventions on the part of, for example, competitors. It was suggested that, provided that the latter have been 'closely involved', their position should be a relevant factor in this assessment.[103]

In the judgment on the merits the CAT took the opportunity to draw a number of important conclusions from the analysis contained in its interim decision.[104] It started by reiterating that in the course of the appeal process Napp was entitled to, among other safeguards, 'the right to a fair and public hearing within a reasonable time by an independent and impartial tribunal established by law'.[105] The appellant also enjoyed a 'kernel' of other rights, such as the right to the presumption of innocence and to access evidence, including witnesses relied upon by the OFT, so as to be able to question and refute them in parity with the competition authority.[106]

The CAT, however, excluded that the finding that competition cases were 'criminal in nature' could be stretched as far as to mandate that the DGFT prove its finding of an infringement beyond reasonable doubt.[107] It was observed that the ECHR and the HRA 1998 had not required any particular standard of proof for criminal or civil cases.[108] Accordingly, the tribunal took the view that this matter was left to the appreciation of the contracting states, who retained the ability both to choose as to how to classify offences and to discipline issues such as the burden and standard of proof applicable to them.[109]

The judgment went on to explain that the seriousness of the allegations made against NAPP had significant implications for how the 'preponderance of probabilities' standard should be interpreted in the particular case. The tribunal confirmed that 'the more serious the allegation, the more cogent should be the evidence before the court' that the 'charge' against the investigated undertaking is ascertained on the preponderance of the probabilities.[110] On this basis, it was held that, in establishing that the appellant had engaged in collusive practices or in an abuse of a dominant position, it was incumbent on the OFT to provide 'strong and convincing evidence' of the existence of a suspected infringement of the CA 1998. In the CAT's view, it would be 'difficult to imagine' that a decision imposing

---

[100] ibid.
[101] ibid para 80.
[102] ibid paras 82–83.
[103] ibid para 84.
[104] *Napp 4* (n 88) para 98.
[105] ibid.
[106] ibid.
[107] ibid para 100.
[108] ibid para 102.
[109] ibid para 104.
[110] ibid para 107.

a financial penalty on an undertaking for having breached the CA 1998 would be upheld if there was 'a reasonable doubt ... or if it were less than sure that the decision was soundly based'.[111]

Thus, in order to meet this standard of proof, it would be incumbent on the competition agency to provide '[s]trong and compelling evidence, taking account of the seriousness of what is alleged, that the infringement is duly proved, the undertaking being entitled to the presumption of innocence, and to any reasonable doubt there may be'.[112] While the CAT excluded that there should be an 'intermediate' standard of proof for competition offences, it affirmed that, in order to fulfil the rules on due process enshrined in Article 6 ECHR, the 'preponderance of the probabilities' benchmark should have been applied in the individual case, bearing in mind the fact that the investigated undertaking was liable to significant financial penalties.[113]

The importance of the interim decision adopted in *NAPP* cannot be understated. The CAT articulated a powerful human rights justification for its powers of review on the merits. As was illustrated earlier, once the criminal nature of competition cases had been recognized, it would have been difficult to reconcile limited forms of judicial scrutiny, such as ordinary judicial review remedies, with the Convention requirements applicable to competition decisions.[114] The CAT, therefore, read the ECHR requirement of 'full jurisdiction' over all matters of fact and of law as requiring the widest possible power of scrutiny, embracing not just the legality of the impugned decision but also its merits. It is added that the approach adopted in the judgment in comment has equal impact after the reforms of the framework for the application of the CA 1998 that were introduced in 2013. The Enterprise and Regulatory Reform Act 2013 created the CMA, which combines the functions of the OFT and of the Competition Commission.[115] Just as the OFT, the CMA combines investigative and decision-making functions in relation to allegations of collusive and abusive practices and therefore retains the same characteristics as integrated agency as those of the OFT, in accordance with the CA 1998.[116] The next section will explore more recent case law of the UK courts, with a view to examining how this approach has been developed in judicial practice.

3.3 Competition Enforcement, Human Rights, and Judicial Scrutiny—A Settled Question?

The previous section discussed the *Napp* judgments and argued that in that decision the CAT constructed a compelling justification of the scope of its own jurisdiction on the basis of the demands of human rights protection stemming from the HRA 1998.[117] As was argued by one of the chairs of the CAT, Marion Simmons QC,[118] conferring upon the tribunal these

---

[111] ibid para 108.

[112] ibid para 109.

[113] ibid; see also para 107.

[114] See eg Lucile Sheppard Keyes, 'Antitrust at Last in Britain: the UK Restrictive Practices Act' (1956–57) 25 Geo Wash L Rev 627, 630, 637.

[115] See Enterprise and Regulatory Reform Act 2013, ss 29 ff.

[116] ibid ss 39 ff.

[117] *Napp 4*, paras 76–77.

[118] Marion Simmons QC, speech given at the conference 'Competition Litigation in the EU: Where Do We Stand?' (3 February 2006).

extensive powers of scrutiny and, in appropriate cases, the power to 'remake' the OFT decision, acts as an indispensable 'human rights proofing' factor for preserving the integrity of
the rights of the investigated parties to be heard 'fairly', in accordance with the Convention,
as incorporated in UK law by means of the HRA 1998.

In the *Argos* judgment the Court of Appeal acknowledged that the function of the CAT's
review on the merits jurisdiction was to ensure compliance with Article 6 of the ECHR.[119]
Lloyd LJ, speaking for the Court, stated that the CAT's powers had to be distinguished from
those of other courts that are responsible for the scrutiny of competition infringement decisions, such as, inter alia, the EU General Court: whereas the latter does not examine any
new evidence and its review powers are limited to the subject matter of the decision, the
CAT can receive fresh evidence from the appellant who seeks to contest a finding that collusion or an abuse of a dominant position have been committed.[120] In the Court of Appeal's
view, since that evidence was likely to be different from the evidence gathered by the OFT in
its original investigation, only the CAT could have reached a decision on the existence of an
infringement and on any penalty being imposed on the appellant.[121] That the CAT should
adopt this approach was all the more important in respect of the scrutiny of the sanctions
imposed by the OFT on the appellant: it was held that, according to Article 6(1) of the
ECHR, 'an undertaking penalised by the Director is entitled to have that penalty reviewed
ab initio by an independent and impartial tribunal' on the basis of the tribunal's own assessment of the gravity of the infringement and in light of all the evidence brought before it.[122]

The issue of compliance with the Convention was re-examined more generally in *HCA
International v Competition and Markets Authority*.[123] In that judgment, the Court of
Appeal, albeit in an *obiter dictum*, confirmed the CAT's assessment of this question, and
took the view that '[w]here the area is a specialised one', such as in competition enforcement,
Article 6 required the '[c]ombination of fair treatment by the administrative body and the
availability of judicial review'.[124] Importantly, the Court pointed out that the co-existence of
these two requirements would be indispensable in all cases where it was regarded as 'appropriate to allow the administrative body a substantial margin of appreciation'.[125]

The *Flynn Pharma and Others* appeal, concerning a decision finding an abuse of a dominant position in the form of unfair pricing, further elaborated on these issues.[126] The Court
of Appeal emphasized once again the 'criminal law' nature of competition law, and on that
basis held that the tribunal's 'merits jurisdiction ... flow[ed] from important legal considerations relating to the rights of defence and access to a court, under fundamental rights such
as Article 6 of the Convention'.[127] The judgment acknowledged that a competition authority
such as the CMA enjoyed a margin of appreciation when it came to evaluating the evidence
with a view to making a finding of infringement and to quantifying a penalty to be imposed
on the responsible undertakings. However, it expressed the view that the existence of this

---

[119] *Argos and Others v OFT* [2006] EWCA Civ 1318, para 17 (Lloyd LJ).
[120] ibid para 272.
[121] ibid.
[122] ibid para 499. See also most recently *Kier Group Plc and Others v OFT* [2011] CAT 3, eg para 27; see also
para 74.
[123] [2015] EWCA Civ 492.
[124] ibid para 49.
[125] ibid.
[126] *Competition and Markets Authority v Flynn Pharma Ltd and Others* [2020] EWCA 339.
[127] ibid para 136.

margin did not 'dispense with the requirement for an in-depth review of the law and of the facts' by the court competent for hearing the appeal.[128] On this specific point, Mr Justice Green, consistently with the approach adopted in *Argos*, confirmed that a 'necessary connection' existed 'between a full merits hearing and Article 6' of the Convention.[129] While the CMA should be afforded a certain degree of appreciation as regards the fact and evidence before it, in light of the relevant legal principles, this margin of discretion should not have been used by the CAT as a ground for avoiding an in-depth review of the law and the facts at the basis of the impugned decision.[130] Accordingly, Mr Justice Green concluded that moving away from the standard of review on the merits in what are, for ECHR purposes, 'criminal proceedings' would no longer ensure compliance with the Convention, since no other form of scrutiny would be consistent with the requirement of 'full jurisdiction' enshrined in Article 6(1).[131]

The recent decision in *Gibson* confirmed the CAT's willingness to engage with human rights questions.[132] That judgment concerned an application for collective opt out proceedings lodged against a company active on the market of mobility appliances that had been found responsible for price fixing. The applicant, acting for an open class of victims, sought to rely on the new section 47B of the CA 1998.[133] However, the defendants argued that since the infringement had occurred before the entry in force of this new provision, the applicant should be precluded from doing so as it would have been an unlawful interference with the defendants' right to enjoy their property, in accordance with the Convention. The tribunal rejected this argument.[134] It acknowledged that the remedy sought by the applicant had only come into existence with the Consumer Rights Act 2015, whereas the infringements had occurred in 2010 and 2011. However, the tribunal held that the cause of action, namely the claim for liability brought against the defendants, had its basis in the CA 1998 and thus predated the enactment of the 2015 legislation.[135] Accordingly, the tribunal rejected the plea that the claim constituted an unlawful interference with the defendants' property rights.[136] In its view, section 47B had been adopted in the area of social and economic policy, with a view to serving the interests of both the victims of collusive behaviour and the broader society, by 'establishing a redress mechanism for violations of competition law'.[137] On that basis, it was concluded that, while the legislation in question interfered with the applicant's right to the peaceful enjoyment of property, it nonetheless struck an appropriate balance between Pride's rights under Article 1, Protocol 1 to the ECHR and the legitimate interests of the community at large.[138] In the CAT's view, 'the latter covers in particular the victims' of restrictive or abusive behaviour, who are able to claim redress for their injuries. In addition, section 47B serves a broader societal objective, by 'establishing an effective redress mechanism' for the consequences of anti-competitive behaviour.[139]

---

[128] ibid para 140.
[129] ibid para 136.
[130] ibid para 138.
[131] ibid paras 137, 140.
[132] *Dorothy Gibson and Others v Pride Mobility* [2017] CAT 9.
[133] ibid paras 5–6.
[134] ibid para 36.
[135] ibid; see also para 35.
[136] ibid para 44.
[137] ibid; see also para 45.
[138] ibid para 44.
[139] ibid.

In light of the above analysis, it is suggested that respect for human rights and in particular for the right to a fair hearing is now accepted as the justification for the introduction of the powers of review on the merits that the CAT enjoys in scrutinizing decisions finding an infringement of Chapters I and II of the CA 1998. As was illustrated in section 3.1 above, owing to the 'criminal' nature of these cases, compliance with Article 6(1) ECHR could not have been secured only by way of a limited form of judicial scrutiny, such as an action for judicial review. 'Something more' was required to meet the Convention requirements, and in this context the UK legislature opted for allowing the CAT to examine all aspects of a competition decision and to take a number of decisions concerning the appeal. As is provided by paragraph 3 of Schedule 8 to the CA 1998, the tribunal, in annulling the CMA decision, can remit the matter to the agency, revoke or alter any penalty imposed on the applicant, or 'give such directions' and 'make any decisions that the CMA could have made'.

Thus, in appropriate circumstances, the CAT is empowered to substitute its own appreciation of the facts and evidence of the case to that of the competition authority, on the basis of the grounds and evidence provided in the notice of appeal. On this specific point, a comparison can be drawn with the powers of judicial scrutiny that the CAT enjoys vis-à-vis the CMA's merger decisions. In these cases, the tribunal's jurisdiction is limited by the ordinary rules governing judicial review, in accordance with section 120(4) of the EA 2002. The same form of scrutiny is available for decisions concerning market investigation references, in light of Article 179(4) EA 2002. It is suggested that, owing to the 'civil' nature of merger and market investigation decisions,[140] a judicial review remedy provides sufficient protection to the right to a fair hearing of the undertaking concerned, on the ground that, while not permitting the tribunal to replace with its own findings those contained in the impugned decision, it nonetheless allows for a sufficiently scrupulous scrutiny of the decision itself.[141]

Against this background, it is argued that the choice made in the CA 1998 can be seen as the expression of the legitimate exercise of the UK's margin of appreciation in securing the respect of Article 6 of the Convention.[142] It is acknowledged that over the years there have been numerous calls for the reform of the jurisdiction and appeal role of the CAT in the UK competition law enforcement framework: in this context, the review on the merits was regarded as one of the targets of these calls for reform. In 2013, for instance, the UK Government Department for Business, Innovation and Skills argued for the replacement of review on the merits with a more limited form of scrutiny in relation to decisions concerning the infringement of Chapter I and Chapter II of the CA 1998.[143] These proposals called for the creation of a judicial review-type remedy aimed at challenging a competition decision on the basis of five 'focused grounds' of review.[144] Three of these grounds concerned the observance of procedural rules and the accurate statement of the facts of specific cases; the other two, instead, pertained to the way in which the CMA had exercised its

---

[140] See n 24 above and accompanying text.

[141] See eg *Bryan* (n 34) paras 44, 47; see also *R (Alconbury)* (n 77) para 135.

[142] *Menarini Diagnostics* (n 25) para 62. See also mutatis mutandis *Valico Srl v Italy* App no 70074/01 (ECHR 21 March 2006) esp Part B.2 http://hudoc.echr.coe.int/eng?i=001-110210

[143] Government Department for Business, Innovation and Skills, 'Streamlining Competition and Regulatory Appeals: Options for Reform' BIS/13/876 (19 June 2013) https://www.gov.uk/government/uploads/system/uploads/attachment_data/file/229758/bis-13-876-regulatory-and-competition-appeals-revised.pdf.

[144] ibid paras 3.19–3.20, 3.27. For comment see eg Arianna Andreangeli, 'The Changing Structure of Competition Enforcement in the UK: the Competition Appeals Tribunal between Present Challenges and an Uncertain Future' (2015) 3(1) J of Antit Enf 1, 23 ff.

discretionary powers, in particular in relation to the assessment of relevant evidence.[145] At the basis of this proposal was a concern for 'filtering' what the government referred to as 'groundless appeals'[146] and for making the tribunal's adjudicatory process more streamlined and more focused on reviewing a decision, as opposed to purportedly allowing a rehearing of the case.[147]

The UK government argued in its consultation paper that the 'flexibility' typical of a judicial review-type action would have allowed the tribunal to focus its scrutiny on issues of fairness and on compliance of the decision with human rights standards, thus ensuring appropriate accountability of the CMA's action.[148] In this specific context, the UK government pointed to the ECtHR's decision in *Menarini Diagnostics* to argue in favour of introducing this more limited form of appeal.[149] It was acknowledged that the general action for judicial review would not have been sufficient to comply with Article 6 ECHR in relation to the imposition of financial penalties.[150] Nonetheless, the consultation paper proposed introducing 'focused grounds of appeal', leading to greater latitude in the scrutiny of certain aspects of a competition decision, on the ground that it would meet the Convention requirements while at the same time maintaining the accountability of the CMA and protecting the rights of the applicant undertakings.[151]

It is acknowledged that the proposals outlined above were not given any further consideration. However, it is legitimate to query why they were seen as necessary by the UK government, especially taking into consideration the rather cautious approach that the CAT itself has been adopting in the exercise of this aspect of its jurisdiction.[152] It is also argued that the proposals only focused on the tribunal's scrutiny powers in light of concerns for efficiency in adjudication and of a preoccupation with, purportedly, protecting the CMA's ability to shape its own enforcement agenda without becoming unduly risk averse owing to the 'threat' of the CAT's exercising its powers of review on the merits.[153]

It should be noted that similar calls for abolition of the power of review on the merits from the CAT's jurisdiction made another appearance more recently. In his letter to the then Business Secretary, Lord Tyrie, the chair of the CMA called for, among other proposals for reform, radical reform of the CAT in a number of respects.[154] In relation to procedural issues, he called for the tribunal to go back to the mainly paper-based, tightly managed regime that had originally been envisaged when the CAT had been created and therefore for new rules designed to restrict the admissibility of new evidence and the reliance on oral

---

[145] Government Department for Business, Innovation and Skills (n 143) paras 4.16 ff.

[146] ibid para 4.12.

[147] ibid 'Executive summary' 4 and paras 3.28–3.31. See also Andreangeli, 'The Changing Structure of Competition Enforcement in the UK' (n 144) 25.

[148] Government Department for Business, Innovation and Skills (n 143) paras 4.18–4.21.

[149] ibid para 4.49.

[150] ibid paras 4.55–4.56.

[151] ibid paras 4.62–4.63.

[152] See eg (ex multis and mutatis mutandis) *Hutchinson 3G Ltd v OFCOM* (non-price control matters), App no 1083/3/3/07 (ECHR 20 May 2008) [2008] CAT 12, esp para 164. See also more generally *Lloyd v McMahon* [1987] AC 625, 642–46 (Lawton LJ), 715–16 (Templeman LJ). For commentary see inter alia Andreangeli, 'The Changing Structure of Competition Enforcement in the UK' (n 144) 24–25.

[153] Government Department for Business, Innovation and Skills (n 143) paras 1.4–1.7, see also paras 1.13–1.14, 3.31, and 4.28.

[154] Lord Tyrie, Letter to Greg Clark MP, Secretary of State for Business, Enterprise and Industrial Strategy (21 February 2019) https://assets.publishing.service.gov.uk/government/uploads/system/uploads/attachment_data/file/781151/Letter_from_Andrew_Tyrie_to_the_Secretary_of_State_BEIS.pdf.

witnesses.[155] In relation to the scope of the tribunal's jurisdiction, Lord Tyrie called for the abolition of the review on the merits powers and the introduction of a limited remedy based only on a few, well-defined grounds for review, to be exercised in accordance with judicial review standards.[156] In his opinion, these two reforms would ensure the quicker resolution of appeal cases and make them better suited to the demands of investigating more complex and wider-ranging cases, especially after Brexit.[157]

It is not clear whether these specific proposals made by the chair of the CMA will actually make their way onto the statute book. In addition, it is acknowledged that after the *Menarini* decision the ECtHR seems to have endorsed a more 'in-context' and, therefore, a relatively more flexible approach to the question of how Article 6 ECHR should be respected.[158] Nonetheless, it is submitted that restricting the tribunal's realm of adjudication only to deciding in light of a set of well-defined grounds could actually deprive it of the flexibility which is recognized as being inherent to the appeal mechanism and which has allowed the UK courts to engage in the extensive scrutiny of public measures to accommodate the demands of human rights protection.[159]

In light of the foregoing analysis, it may be concluded that the demands of compliance with human rights standards provide a powerful justification for the conferral on the CAT of powers of scrutiny on the merits vis-à-vis competition decisions: this is so, especially when the latter entail a financial penalty, the criminal nature of allegations of collusive practices, or of the abuse of a dominant position which underpins the existence of this remedy. It is acknowledged that with *Menarini* judgment the ECtHR seemed to suggest a more flexible view of what represented a 'fair hearing' in competition cases, as a result of which on the merits scrutiny might not be inevitable to avoid censure under the Convention. However, it is also suggested that any reform of the jurisdiction of the CAT should be treated with caution, in consideration of the importance of the CAT's role as the ultimate guarantor of the fairness of competition enforcement proceedings in the UK and of the potentially unpredictable consequences that limiting or 'focusing' the judicial review remedy might have on the effectiveness of the scrutiny exercised over CMA decisions.

4 Conclusions

The creation of a sanction-based framework centred on an integrated agency has led to greater effectiveness in promoting and protecting competition in the UK and a more expert, evidence-based approach to decision-making.[160] However, the reform of UK competition law in 1998 raised the question of the extent to which proceedings concerning alleged infringements of Chapters I and II of the CA 1998 were compatible with standards of human rights protection. The conferral upon the CAT of powers of review on the merits emerged as

---

[155] ibid 34–35.
[156] ibid 36.
[157] ibid.
[158] See n 79 above and accompanying text. See also Andreangeli 'The Changing Structure of Competition Enforcement in the UK' (n 144) 27.
[159] See mutatis mutandis *R v Haddock* [2006] HRLR 40, paras 63–64; for commentary see Andreangeli, 'The Changing Structure of Competition Enforcement in the UK' (n 144).
[160] Kirsty Middleton, 'Reform of UK Competition Law' (1998) 8 Scot L Times 47, 50.

perhaps the strongest safeguard of the right to a fair hearing of investigated undertakings, in line with the requirement of 'full jurisdiction' enshrined in the *acquis* of the ECtHR.

It is acknowledged that the ECtHR seems to have shifted towards a more 'flexible' approach to questions of fairness in competition proceedings, as demonstrated by the 2011 *Menarini* judgment. Indeed, it emerges from the debate leading to the creation of the CMA and, lately, from the calls made by the current CMA chair in 2019 that this approach was taken as the basis for renewed pleas for reform of the CAT's power to review on the merits. However, any future reform of the tribunal's jurisdiction should be approached with caution. As was argued in section 3.3 of this chapter, reverting from a review on the merits approach to a 'focused grounds' review or even to the traditional judicial review remedy could not only raise pressing questions of human rights compliance, but also hinder the very function of the appellate courts which, especially with a 'focused' remedy, might no longer be able to rely on the flexibility of ordinary administrative law remedies, which are regarded as vital to secure a sufficient degree of protection of human rights.

In light of this analysis, it may be concluded that, as it turns twenty, the UK competition enforcement regime retains its reputation as an effective yet fair framework for the detection and sanctioning of anti-competitive behaviour. It is acknowledged that its future is to an extent uncertain, especially in light of the impact of Brexit for its future performance. However, it is argued that the existence of strong fairness safeguards and in particular of the role of the CAT as an effective review court should be regarded as a strength for the system, as opposed to being seen as a 'threat' to the supposed effectiveness of the CMA.

10

Concurrency

Niamh Dunne

1 Introduction

This chapter discusses the UK's distinctive 'concurrency' regime for the enforcement of competition law by sector regulators alongside the Competition and Markets Authority ('CMA'). The regulated sectors within the regime account for about a quarter of the UK's GDP, and the products concerned comprise essential goods and services that touch almost every household and business.[1] Yet despite its expansive scope of application, and a history that predates the Competition Act 1998 (CA 1998) by more than a decade, concurrency has been slow to deliver on its promise to replace economic regulation with competition in these markets. This prompted efforts to 'enhance' concurrency within the Enterprise and Regulatory Reform Act 2013 (ERRA 2013), which sought both to encourage regulators to make greater use of their concurrent powers, and to give the CMA a more formal leadership role in assisting them to do so.[2] Yet the jury remains out as to whether these formal enhancements to concurrency will enhance effective enforcement in practice—and, indeed, whether simply increasing the number of antitrust cases is an appropriate measure of well-functioning competition in the regulated sectors.

The chapter is structured as follows. Section 2 traces the origins of the concurrency regime, from its piecemeal beginnings in the context of early privatization and liberalization efforts to today's greatly expanded and more formalized framework. Section 3 details the ERRA 2013 reforms, which seek to give greater priority to competition enforcement in regulated sectors. Section 4 considers the progress of concurrent enforcement under this enhanced regime. It provides an account of the functioning of the concurrency arrangements twenty years after the entry into force of the CA 1998, and surveys the individual enforcement records of sector regulators. Section 5 steps back to offer an assessment of the concurrency regime as a whole. Section 6 concludes briefly.

2 The Origins and Evolution of Concurrency

The early history of the concurrency regime has been discussed elsewhere,[3] but in short, the arrangements stem from the recommendations of the influential Littlechild Report, which

---

[1] Competition and Markets Authority, *Annual Report on Concurrency 2020* (CMA119) (15 April 2020) (CR2020), para 2.

[2] Explanatory Notes to the Enterprise and Regulatory Reform Act 2013, para 370.

[3] See eg Giorgio Monti, 'Utilities Regulators and the Competition Act 1998' in Barry J Rodger (ed), *Ten Years of UK Competition Law Reform* (Dundee University Press 2010), Colm O'Grady and Liam Maclean, 'Concurrency Past, Present, and Future: Too Many Cooks?' (2014) 13 Competition Law Journal 163 (2014), Jon Stern, 'Sectoral Regulation and Competition Policy: The UK's Concurrency Arrangements—An Economic Perspective' (2015) 11

Niamh Dunne, *Concurrency* In: *The UK Competition Regime*. Edited by: Barry Rodger, Peter Whelan, and Angus MacCulloch, Oxford University Press. © The Contributors 2021. DOI: 10.1093/oso/9780198868026.003.0010

preceded the privatization of British Telecommunications.[4] The Report was published on the cusp of a wide-ranging (and enduring) experiment in market liberalization and privatization in the UK, which was to become one of the defining pillars of Thatcherism. Its author, Stephen Littlechild, was strongly of the view that economic regulation was an inherently temporary form of market control, which could and should be superseded as competition increased within liberalized/privatized sectors. The Report thus recommended that sector regulators should be equipped with antitrust enforcement powers alongside any economic regulatory functions also granted to them, with the latter used merely to 'hold the fort' until effective competition emerged.[5] This approach was adopted within the Telecommunications Act 1984, which granted the newly-created sector regulator, Oftel,[6] the capacity to apply the Fair Trading Act 1973 and Competition Act 1980 specifically to telecommunications undertakings. The then Secretary of State for Trade was nonetheless reluctant to dilute the powers of the Office of Fair Trading (OFT) and the Monopolies and Mergers Commission (MMC), which resulted in a compromise arrangement of concurrency: the existing competition agencies would retain their enforcement jurisdiction alongside that granted to the new regulator.[7] Equivalent concurrent powers were later extended to the newfound regulators for energy, rail, airports, and water, as privatization and liberalization were extended across the British economy.

The concurrency regime involves two distinct, albeit complementary, layers of concurrent—or parallel—enforcement within regulated markets. The basic premise is that individual sector regulators are empowered to apply the competition rules within their respective areas of market supervision. This power is held concurrently with the continuing jurisdiction of the competition agencies—at first the OFT and MMC, later the Competition Commission, and now the CMA—over anti-competitive conduct in regulated markets. Simultaneous enforcement by multiple agencies against the same behaviour is, however, not permitted. Secondly, the competition enforcement powers granted to the regulators typically overlap with their sector-specific powers to control the market behaviour of regulatees. Accordingly, the same behaviour may be susceptible to a disposition under either field of law; although, under the ERRA 2013, competition enforcement should take priority where this delivers an equally appropriate outcome.[8]

The concurrency regime is portrayed as a uniquely British institutional arrangement for competition enforcement,[9] reflecting a deep and unwavering commitment to the social value of open and competitive markets. Indeed, for most regulators, their concurrent powers sit alongside an explicit overarching duty to promote competition within their

---

Journal of European Competition Law & Economics 881, and previously by this author, Niamh Dunne, 'Recasting Competition Currency under the Enterprise and Regulatory Reform Act 2013' (2014) 77 Modern Law Review 254.

[4] Stephen Littlechild, 'Regulation of British Telecommunications' Profitability: Report to the Secretary of State' Department of Industry (February 1983).

[5] ibid para 4.11.

[6] Oftel's functions, including its concurrent enforcement powers, were inherited by the Office of Communications in 2003.

[7] Discussed by Stern (n 3) 887.

[8] See text accompanying n 35 below.

[9] See eg Cosmo Graham, 'UK: The Concurrent Enforcement by Regulators of Competition Law and Sector-Specific Regulation' (2016) 7 Journal of European Competition Law & Regulation 407, 407. Contrast, however, Stern (n 3), who argues that the UK experience with concurrency is unique only to the extent that it is both highly formalized and applies across broad swathes of the regulated sectors.

respective regulatory spheres.[10] Yet the passage of the CA 1998 changed radically the nature of the competition powers available to sector regulators. Prior to the CA 1998, the powers exercised concurrently by regulators and the OFT were essentially quasi-regulatory, centred around the ability to make references to the MMC to investigate 'monopoly situations'[11] and 'anticompetitive practices'.[12] Neither the OFT nor regulators had the capacity to make determinations upon alleged antitrust violations, while the remedial framework was highly politicized, relying upon ministerial involvement and assent.[13] The CA 1998, by contrast, effectively incorporated the EU law prohibitions on anti-competitive coordination and abuse of dominance directly into UK law, to the extent that the suspect conduct 'may affect trade within the United Kingdom'. Enforcement of the Chapters I and II prohibitions against anti-competitive agreements and abuse of dominance, respectively, was, moreover, to be 'exercised concurrently' by the OFT and specified sector regulators within their respective spheres.[14] Despite some initial unease about extending this law enforcement-type role to regulators,[15] arguments premised on sectoral expertise, the functional overlap between economic regulation and antitrust enforcement, and the desirability of preserving the 'status quo', ultimately proved compelling.[16] Thus, as the UK competition framework as a whole saw a paradigm shift under the CA 1998, later complemented by the Enterprise Act 2002 (EA 2002) which reconfigured the market investigation reference 'MIR) procedure,[17] so the concurrency regime evolved in tandem.

The movement from a quasi-regulatory paradigm to a law enforcement-oriented approach in line with the EU exemplar did not, however, result in a corresponding increase in the intensity or effectiveness of competition enforcement within regulated markets. In anticipation of potential disputes over jurisdiction between concurrent enforcers, a set of Concurrency Regulations on the allocation of jurisdiction were drawn up.[18] These were supplemented by a Concurrency Working Party to provide a vehicle for multilateral interactions,[19] and by frequent bilateral communications.[20] Yet, despite plentiful discussion of concurrency in the early years of the modernized framework,[21] little enforcement actually occurred either in respect of the CA 1998 prohibitions or the MIR procedure. In practice, the OFT deferred to regulators within the latter's areas of expertise,[22] whereas the regulators themselves tended to prefer their direct regulatory powers over competition enforcement

---

[10] See eg section 3(2)(b) of the Telecommunications Act 1984; section 4AA of the Gas Act 1986; section 3A of the Electricity Act 1989; section 2 of the Water Act 1991; section 4 of the Railways Act 1993; section 2(4) of the Transport Act 2000; and section 1E of the Financial Services and Markets Act 2000. Pursuant to section 62(3) of the Health and Social Care Act 2012, the health care regulator exercises its functions merely 'with a view to preventing anticompetitive behaviour'.

[11] Fair Trading Act 1973, ss 50 and 52–55.

[12] Competition Act 1980, ss 2–10.

[13] Fair Trading Act 1973, ss 56 and 88, and Competition Act 1980, ss 9–10.

[14] CA 1998, s 54.

[15] See eg *Competition Bill [HL] Bill 140 of 1997-1998*, House of Commons Research Paper 98/53 (1998) 49–53.

[16] Discussed in Dunne (n 3) 260–61.

[17] EA 2002, Pt 4.

[18] The Competition Act 1998 (Concurrency) Regulations 2004, SI 1077/2004.

[19] Office of Fair Trading, *Concurrent Application to Regulated Industries* (2004) para 3.9.

[20] ibid para 3.3.

[21] In a piece reflecting upon ten years of enforcement under the CA 1998, Monti notably contrasted the considerable efforts that had been expended to avoid problems like inconsistency and duplication arising in concurrent enforcement practice, with the very limit efforts made towards *actually* enforcing the competition rules in the regulated sectors: see *supra* n.3.

[22] OFT (n 19) para 3.13, and Department for Business, Innovation and Skills, *A Competition Regime for Growth: A Consultation on Options for Reform* (2011), para 7.6.

against market problems within their concurrent jurisdiction.[23] Numerous reasons have been advanced to explain this consistent preference for regulation: from the comparative ease and certainty of applying regulatory powers compared with the complexity of the new competition rules;[24] to the shorter timeframe and resource requirements for such interventions;[25] and a concern that a type of regulatory myopia may have caused regulators to undervalue the potential contribution of competition law.[26] The upshot, in any event, was a chronic and much criticized absence of antitrust enforcement in regulated sectors: meaning that, quite paradoxically, the presence of multiple agencies with overlapping enforcement jurisdiction resulted in *less* rather than more enforcement in practice. It is this apparently contradictory outcome which prompted the enhancements introduced by the ERRA 2013, discussed in the next section.

Yet alongside the substantive deepening of the concurrency regime represented by the CA 1998, EA 2002, and ERRA 2013, there has also been a broadening in its scope of application. Concurrency was initially conceived in the context of an economy-wide campaign of privatizing formerly state-owned monopoly providers in the utility sectors. The past decade, however, has seen its extension into regulatory areas that extend far beyond this archetype. First, under the Health and Social Care Act 2012, concurrent powers were granted to Monitor, the regulator for health services, now incorporated into the umbrella organization NHS Improvement ('NHSI'). The work of NHSI is notable insofar as its enforcement jurisdiction applies primarily to foundation and NHS trusts in public ownership, rather than the privatized playing-field of other regulators within the concurrency regime. Secondly, following significant regulatory reforms in the wake of the Global Financial Crisis,[27] concurrent powers were similarly conferred on the newly-created Financial Conduct Authority (FCA) and Payment Systems Regulator (PSR). This latter development extends concurrency in the opposite direction, namely to the activities of entities that, by and large, have always been in private ownership, yet where there is increasing concern about the negative public interest implications of uncompetitive market structures.[28]

Concurrent competition powers are thus today held by nine regulators, which operate across the UK unless otherwise specified: namely, the Civil Aviation Authority (CAA), which regulates airport operation and air traffic services; the Office of Communications (Ofcom), which regulates broadcasting, electronic communications and postal services; the Gas and Electricity Markets Authority (Ofgem), which regulates electricity and gas in Great Britain; the FCA, which regulates financial services; the PSR, which regulates payment systems; NHSI, which regulates healthcare services specifically in England; the Office of Rail and Road (ORR), which regulates railway services; the Water Services Regulation Authority (Ofwat), which regulates water and sewerage services in England and Wales; and

---

[23] Discussed critically in Department of Trade and Industry (DTI), *Concurrent Competition Powers in Sectoral Regulation. A Report by the Department of Trade and Industry and HM Treasury,* URN 06/1244 (2006), and National Audit Office (NAO), *Review of the UK's Competition Landscape. Review by the Comptroller and Auditor General* (2010).

[24] DTI (n 23) paras 4.21–4.24 and 4.29.

[25] ibid paras 4.25–4.28, and NAO (n 23) para 2.9.

[26] House of Lords Select Committee on Regulators, 1st Report of Session 2006–2007, *UK Economic Regulators,* Vol I: Report HL Paper 189-I (2007), para 6.41.

[27] See, in particular, the Financial Services Act 2012.

[28] Competition and Markets Authority, 'Baseline Annual Report on Concurrency (CMA24) (1 April 2014) (Baseline Report), paras 258–64.

the Northern Ireland Authority for Utility Regulation (NIAUR), which regulates electricity, gas, water and sewerage services in Northern Ireland.[29]

3 'Enhancing' Concurrency: The Enterprise and Regulatory Reform Act 2013

The preceding section described how the bold legislative move of extending full competition enforcement powers to specified regulators under the CA 1998 and EA 2002 proved less spectacular in practice, as regulators were perceived to under-enforce these competition tools by preferring to resolve problems through regulatory intervention. Frustration with regulator inaction found expression in the Coalition Government review of the UK competition framework, commenced in 2011, which examined options for strengthening domestic competition policy to improve economic growth.[30] Despite a growing chorus of sceptical voices regarding the effectiveness of the concurrency regime, the starting point of the consultation was the necessity to retain but also enhance the existing arrangements.[31] Although respondents were not universally convinced,[32] a critical mass of support confirmed the Government's decision to revive rather than replace the concurrency regime.[33] This culminated in sections 51 to 53 of the ERRA 2013, which together seek to ensure that all relevant agencies pull their weight in terms of competition enforcement in the regulated sectors.

The reforms introduced by the ERRA 2013 broadly comprise three strands: an obligation for regulators to prioritize competition enforcement over their sector-specific powers to the greatest extent possible; various innovations designed to involve the newly-created CMA more centrally in the concurrency regime, including granting it enforcement priority in defined circumstances; and a—to date, unexercised—'nuclear option',[34] whereby repeated failure by a regulator to exercise its concurrent competition powers may result in those powers being removed permanently.

First, and most straightforwardly, section 51(5) introduces an across-the-board statutory preference for competition enforcement over sector-specific regulation, achieved through modification of the underlying sectoral legislation creating concurrent jurisdiction for each regulator.[35] This has come to be known as the 'primacy provision'.[36] Specifically, prior to exercising certain defined regulatory powers in respect of behaviour also within the ambit of CA 1998, authorities are now required, first, to 'consider whether it would be more appropriate

---

[29] Taken from Competition and Markets Authority, *Annual Report on Concurrency 2019* (CMA107) (10 April 2019) (CR2019) 2, Table 1. The list of designated regulators is up-to-date as of 1 July 2020.

[30] See n 22 above.

[31] ibid ch 7.

[32] See eg Office of Fair Trading, *A Competition Regime for Growth: A Consultation on Options for Reform: The OFT's Response to the Government's Consultation* (OFT1335), para 6.1, discussed further in Department for Business, Energy and Industrial Strategy, *Competition law review: post implementation review of statutory changes in the Enterprise and Regulatory Reform Act 2013* (July 2019) 43.

[33] Department for Business, Skills and Innovation, *Growth, Competition and the Competition Regime: Government Response to Consultation* (March 2012) para 8.13.

[34] So described by Lord Whitty during House of Lords committee stage debate of what became the ERRA 2013: HL Grand Committee col 512 (18 December 2012).

[35] ERRA 2013, s 51(5) gives effect to Sch 14.

[36] See BEIS (n 32) 44.

to proceed under the Competition Act 1998'. To the extent that competition enforcement is deemed more appropriate, regulators are thereby prohibited from ('shall not') exercising their regulatory powers in respect of the matter. The determination of whether this threshold is met lies with each regulator; and the ERRA 2013 falls short of dictating the factors to be taken into account, or of imposing more prescriptive duties with respect to use by regulators of their competition powers.[37] In order to monitor compliance, however, information about any cases where concurrent competition powers were 'exercisable', but where a regulator considered 'that it was more appropriate for it to proceed by exercising functions other than those it has under [CA 1998]', must be detailed in an annual 'concurrency report', as explained below.[38] This requirement does not align precisely with the obligations introduced by Schedule 14, however, and so concurrency reports published to date provide information on both categories. Although many regulators were already subject to distinct sector-specific obligations to favour competition enforcement where possible,[39] Schedule 14 introduces an *explicit* standard shared across the regulated sectors,[40] together with more formalized reporting mechanisms. The objective, of course, is to encourage regulators to make greater use of their concurrent competition jurisdiction in circumstances where they might previously have preferred their more familiar regulatory powers, by requiring them, unambiguously, 'to turn their minds' to the possibility of competition enforcement in relevant circumstances.[41]

Secondly, although the primary thrust of the ERRA 2013 amendments is to encourage greater use of concurrent powers by regulators, the legislation introduces a series of measures designed to also secure greater involvement by the CMA in regulated sectors: either by assisting regulators in their enforcement activities, or by stepping in directly to enforce the rules. These are contained in section 51 and Schedule 4 of the ERRA 2013, and given expression in a statutory instrument, the Competition Act 1998 (Concurrency) Regulations 2014 (Concurrency Regulations).[42] Information-sharing between 'the CMA or any of the regulators' with respect to potential cases is authorized,[43] and these agencies are obliged to put in place 'arrangements for sharing' in respect of a broad spectrum of activities.[44] The latter are now reflected, in part, in the work of the UK Competition Network (UKCN), which replaces the Concurrency Working Party with a more formalized structure.[45] Explicit provision is made for secondments between agencies,[46] thus formalizing what had previously been a sporadic but generally well-regarded practice. Additionally, the CMA has been entrusted with the preparation of an annual report, 'containing an assessment of how the concurrency arrangements have operated during the year'.[47] Schedule 4 of the ERRA 2013 sets

---

[37] In line with a general reluctance among respondents to the consultation about imposing more prescriptive duties on regulators in this regard: see BIS (n 33) paras 8.14–8.18.

[38] ERRA 2013 Sch 4, , s 16(3)(c).

[39] See eg section 28(5) of the Gas Act 1986; section 25(5) of the Electricity Act 1989; section 55(5A) of the Railways Act 1993; and section 317(2) of the Communications Act 2003; discussed further in the Baseline Report (n 28) para 42.

[40] The Explanatory Notes to the Enterprise and Regulatory Report Act 2013, para 378 note that while most regulators already have an 'implicit requirement' to make such a determination prior to exercising their sector-specific regulatory powers, the Sch 14 amendments transform this into an 'explicit duty'.

[41] ibid.

[42] The Competition Act 1998 (Concurrency) Regulations 2014, SI536/2014.

[43] Concurrency Regulations, reg 3 Regulation 3,. This power is envisaged by ERRA 2013, s 51(4).

[44] Concurrency Regulations, reg 9.

[45] Discussed further in section 4.1 below.

[46] Concurrency Regulations, reg 10.

[47] ERRA 2013 Sch 4, s 16.

out the required contents of each report, and requires consultation with regulators in its preparation. The requirement of regular publicity appears to be intended to shed greater light on the previously somewhat murky operation of the concurrency regime, and in particular, to expose (and by consequence, require explanation for) evidence of systematic *under*-enforcement of their concurrent powers by regulators.[48]

The Concurrency Regulations also make provision for the apportionment of jurisdiction between the CMA and regulators should clashes arise. The starting point is a consensual process, whereby any agency that wishes to exercise jurisdiction must inform any other enforcer with concurrent jurisdiction, and can take the case only where the other(s) agree.[49] An approach of cooperation and consent is, moreover, precisely how the sharing of jurisdiction has played out in practice following the ERRA 2013 reforms, as discussed in the next section.[50] Yet the Concurrency Regulations make provision for potential disputes, with the CMA nominated to act as the ultimate decision-maker in cases of conflict. In particular, as foreseen by section 51(2), the CMA is now empowered, in essence, to 'take' competition enforcement cases from otherwise-willing sector regulators where it determines that to do so 'would further the promotion of competition, within any market or markets in the United Kingdom, for the benefit of consumers'.[51] The CMA is subject to certain procedural obligations if it intends to exercise this power,[52] but no provision is made for appeal against its decision-making, subject to the ordinary principles governing judicial review of administrative action. An analogy might thus be drawn with the sharing of jurisdiction between the European Commission and national competition authorities ('NCAs') under Regulation 1/2003, whereby each has full jurisdiction to enforce Articles 101 and 102 of the Treaty on the Functioning of the European Union, *unless and until* the Commission formally exercises its enforcement jurisdiction to the (temporary) exclusion of NCAs.[53] It was, however, correctly assumed that the CMA's power to commandeer competition cases unilaterally would rarely be used.[54] Parallel competition enforcement by multiple agencies is not permitted under the Concurrency Regulation, and in particular, 'double jeopardy' for defendants is ruled out expressly.[55]

Thirdly, there is the so-called 'nuclear option',[56] which envisages a worst-case scenario whereby a sector regulator persistently fails to exercise its concurrent powers effectively, despite its renewed statutory obligation to do so. In this case, sections 52 and 53 of the ERRA

[48] BEIS (n 32) 52, describes the purposes of the report as being to 'provide transparency and promote effective monitoring and evaluation of the impact of regulatory intervention in the regulated sectors'.

[49] Concurrency Regulations, reg 4.

[50] See also BEIS (n 32) 51, noting the perception on the part of regulators that the CMA was exercising its leadership role in this regard 'fairly' and CR2020, para 123, noting the continued smooth operation of the case allocation process.

[51] Concurrency Regulations, regs 5(4)(b) and 8(1)(a). The Regulations add a proviso in respect of the activities of Monitor (now NHSI), however, to the effect that the CMA must be satisfied that 'the case is not principally concerned with matters relating to the provision of health care services for the purposes of the NHS in England' (Regs 5(5) and 8(1)(b), Concurrency Regulations).

[52] ibid regs 5 and 8.

[53] See, in particular, arts 5 and 11(6) of Council Regulation 1/2003 of 16 December 2002 on the implementation of the rules on competition laid down in Articles 81 and 82 of the Treaty (OJ L 1/1, 4 January 2003); the operation of the Commission's power of pre-emption is discussed in detail in Case C-17/10 *Toshiba Corporation and Others v Úřad pro ochranu hospodářské soutěže* EU:C:2012:72.

[54] UKCN, *Statement of Intent* 6 https://www.gov.uk/government/publications/uk-competition-network-statement-of-intent.

[55] Concurrency Regulations, reg 6,.

[56] See n 34 above.

2013 together enable the Secretary of State, should (s)he consider 'that it is appropriate to do so for the purpose of promoting competition',[57] to make a 'sectoral regulator order' which removes a regulator's ability to apply the competition rules contained in the CA 1998 and/or EA 2002 concurrently. Where such an order is made, only the CMA would retain the power to apply competition law within the relevant sector.[58] Section 53 of the ERRA 2013 sets out a two-stage consultation procedure that must be followed by the Secretary of State prior to making an order, involving the affected regulator and related regulated providers, the CMA, in certain instances the devolved governments, and 'such other persons as the Secretary of State considers appropriate'. Section 52(6) of the ERRA 2013 moreover establishes that sectoral regulator orders are to be enacted under the affirmative resolution procedure for statutory instruments, thus requiring the approval of each House of Parliament.

Given the strong emphasis upon *enhancing* concurrent enforcement in the first instance under the ERRA 2013, it is unsurprising that sectoral regulator orders were envisaged as a last resort, which would be pursued only exceptionally. Since the power has been introduced, there has little public discussion of its possible use let alone any actual application of the power in practice.[59] This is despite the somewhat varied experiences of the different regulators under the enhanced regime. A cynical reading might thus dismiss the possibility of removal as, in effect, an antitrust example of 'big stick' policymaking: whereby the primary intention is never to actually deploy the nuclear option, but rather to focus the mind of regulators and thereby 'encourage' them to make more regular and effective use of their concurrent powers. Yet one may still have some qualms about the incursion it represents in terms of greater executive control over what is, at its core, a quasi-judicial role, even if exercise of the power appears to be more theoretical than likely in practice.[60]

4 Concurrency in Practice: Twenty Years after the Competition Act 1998

At the time of its creation, and acting on a 'strategic steer' from central government,[61] the CMA committed itself to five underpinning goals, the second of which is to 'extend competition frontiers'.[62] Included within this rubric is a need to 'ensure the application of competition law and policy in regulated sectors, working alongside and supporting sector regulators'.[63] This is consistent with the enhanced role envisaged for the CMA within the concurrency framework by the ERRA 2013, and the implicit wish to shed greater light on the workings of concurrency in practice. Indeed, the subtext of the ERRA 2013 reforms might be summed up as a perceived need to increase levels of 'proactive'[64] competition enforcement across the regulated sectors, whether by hook (by regulators directly) or by crook

---

[57] ERRA 2013, s 52(1).

[58] Under Regulation 1/2003 (n53), the European Commission had parallel jurisdiction to enforce the EU competition rules with respect to behaviour occurring within the UK which had an effect on interstate trade, a power that disappears with Brexit.

[59] BEIS (n 32) 52.

[60] See Dunne (n 3) 267.

[61] Department for Business, Innovation and Skills, *Competition Regime: Response to the Consultation on Statement of Strategic Priorities for the CMA* (1 October 2013).

[62] Competition and Markets Authority, *Vision, Values and Strategy for the CMA*, CMA13 (January 2014) 1.

[63] ibid. See also Baseline Report (n 28) para 45.

[64] Explanatory Memorandum to the Competition Act 1998 (Concurrency) Regulation 2014, (SI 536/2014) 7.1.

(by the CMA, where necessary). Twenty years after the concurrency arrangements were 'formalised' in the CA 1998,[65] and more than half a decade after their enhancement under the ERRA 2013, the remainder of this chapter considers whether the anticipated benefits of the concurrency arrangements are any closer to being realized in practice.[66]

The centrepiece of the enhanced concurrency regime is the publication by the CMA of an annual report detailing both its efforts and those of the designated regulators to apply the competition rules within regulated sectors. At the time of writing, six such documents have been produced, plus a 'baseline report' against which future developments are to be measured. These reports offer a comprehensive and admirably granular picture of how the enhanced regime is playing out in practice, and form the basis for much of this section. Further assessments of the revised arrangements have been provided by the National Audit Office (NAO)[67] and the Department for Business, Energy and Industrial Strategy (BEIS),[68] whose work similarly informs this discussion.

4.1 Concurrency in Practice: The Framework of 'Enhanced' Concurrency

As noted,[69] nine sector regulators hold concurrent enforcement powers, which may be exercised alongside equivalent powers held by the CMA in their respective areas of regulatory supervision. The regulators are empowered to apply the Chapter I and II prohibitions, and to conduct market studies and make MIRs under Part 4 of the EA 2002.[70] Moreover, regulators are not merely authorized to find infringements of the antitrust rules, but are also equipped with a swathe of procedural powers that enable them to conduct and conclude investigations, such as information-gathering, imposing interim measures and financial penalties, and settling cases with or without findings of infringement.[71] These powers mirror those available to the CMA in its competition enforcement capacity, although only the CMA is empowered to issue certain categories of guidance and to make the procedural rules which govern application of the CA 1998 prohibitions.[72] The CMA is also the only competition agency, alongside the Serious Fraud Office and the Crown Office and Procurator Fiscal Service, which is empowered to prosecute suspected breaches of the criminal cartel offence, with the result, *inter alia*, that it has been selected by UKCN members as the initial 'single port of call'[73] for all leniency applications relating to the regulated sectors.[74]

---

[65] So described by BEIS (n 32) 42.

[66] The period covered by this analysis runs from the creation of the CMA on 1 April 2014, to the end of the period covered by CR2020 (n 1), namely 31 March 2020.

[67] NAO, *The UK Competition Regime*, HC 737 (3 February 2016).

[68] See n 32 above.

[69] See n 29 above, and accompanying text.

[70] Regulators have arguably made more enthusiastic use of their powers under the latter, as detailed by the annual concurrency reports. The focus of this chapter, however, is enforcement (or otherwise) of the Part 1 prohibitions.

[71] Competition and Markets Authority, *Regulated Industries: Guidance on concurrent application of competition law to regulated industries* (CMA10) (March 2014) para 2.3.

[72] ibid para 2.4.

[73] Competition and Markets Authority, *Leniency applications in the regulated sectors. Consultation response* (3 November 2017) para 2.4.

[74] Competition and Markets Authority, *Information Note: Arrangements for the Handling of Leniency Applications in the Regulated Sectors* (3 November 2017).

A key aim of the ERRA 2013 was to place the interactions between the CMA and designated regulators on a more formal footing.[75] Although the CMA and regulators shared information and coordinated their activities prior to 2014, the enhanced arrangements under the ERRA 2013 have led to what is described as a 'step-change in the breadth and depth of cooperation' between these agencies.[76] Enhanced agency cooperation has occurred on both a bilateral and multilateral basis.

On the one hand, the CMA has entered into individual Memoranda of Understanding (MOUs) with each of the concurrent regulators.[77] The MOUs are intended to provide a detailed foundation for bilateral cooperation and coordination between the CMA and individual regulators,[78] albeit expressly on the basis that the documents 'are not intended to have legal effect'.[79] Each sets out what are termed the 'working arrangements'[80] for cooperation in the exercise by the CMA and regulators of their concurrent competition functions, including detailed principles on case allocation, information-sharing, and the pooling of resources and other means of more informal support. Quarterly bilateral meetings are held at working level between the CMA and each of the concurrent regulators, with further ad hoc contacts as necessary.[81] This includes cross-participation in staff development training, and policy support work, for instance in the context of market studies.[82]

The UKCN, on the other hand, forms the lynchpin of multilateral collaboration between regulators and the CMA. It has, as noted, replaced the Concurrency Working Party, which provided a similar albeit less well-developed vehicle for interaction between concurrent enforcers prior to the enhanced concurrency regime.[83] Described variously as a 'forum'[84] and an 'alliance',[85] the creation of the UKCN was agreed jointly by the concurrent enforcers as a means by which to give further effect to the enhanced cooperation requirements of the ERRA 2013 and the Concurrency Regulations.[86] Its mission is 'to promote competition for the benefit of consumers and to prevent anti-competitive behaviour, both through facilitating the use of competition powers and the development of pro-competitive regulatory

---

[75] Graham (n 9) 408.

[76] Competition and Markets Authority, *Annual Report on Concurrency 2018* (CMA79) (April 2018, CR2018) para 49.

[77] These are *Memorandum of understanding between the Competition and Markets Authority and the Payment Systems Regulator* (22 December 2015); *Memorandum of understanding between the Competition and Markets Authority and the Gas and Electricity Markets Authority* (18 January 2016); *Memorandum of understanding between the Competition and Markets Authority and the Northern Ireland Authority for Utility Regulation* (18 January 2016); *Memorandum of understanding between the Competition and Markets Authority and the Office of Communications* (2 February 2016); *Memorandum of understanding between the Competition and Markets Authority and the Civil Aviation Authority* (9 February 2016); *Memorandum of understanding between the Competition and Markets Authority and the Office of Rail and Road* (9 February 2016); *Memorandum of understanding between the Competition and Markets Authority and the Water Services Regulation Authority* (23 February 2016); *Memorandum of understanding between the Competition and Markets Authority and NHS Improvement* (1 April 2016); and *Memorandum of understanding between the Competition and Markets Authority and the Financial Conduct Authority* (7 August 2019).

[78] CMA, *Regulated Industries* (n 71) para 3.6.

[79] According to point 2 of each MOU.

[80] According to point 1 of each MOU.

[81] First reported in Competition and Markets Authority, *Annual Report on Concurrency 2015* (CMA43) (1 April 2015, CR2015) para 11; see also Competition and Markets Authority, *Annual Report on Concurrency 2017* (CMA63) (28 April 2017, CR2017), para 37.

[82] CR2018 (n 76) paras 41–42.

[83] CR2015 (n 81) para 11.

[84] CMA, *Regulated Industries* (n 71) para 3.16.

[85] So described on the UKCN website at https://www.gov.uk/government/groups/uk-competition-network.

[86] UKCN (n 54) 2.

frameworks'.[87] Its statement of intention thus commits it to six priority areas, which inform its work, both 'individually and collectively'. These are: strategic dialogue between agencies; enforcement cooperation to ensure consistent application of competition law; enhancing enforcement capabilities; sharing best practice; building expertise and supporting individual advocacy efforts; and cooperating to produce the annual concurrency reports.[88]

The activities of the UKCN are detailed in the concurrency reports. These include regular meetings of network members at various levels, from agency heads to officials at working level;[89] the organization of workshops and other events to develop competition expertise among members;[90] and discussion of cross-cutting problems, such as resourcing, information-gathering, and leniency.[91] Consistent with the greater emphasis on sharing of staff reflected in the Concurrency Regulations, the UKCN has agreed a set of 'secondment principles',[92] which supplement the specific arrangements in each MOU. Much like the European Competition Network ('ECN') on the EU-wide level, the body appears to be a particularly effective vehicle for discussion and sharing of best practice and 'lessons learned' in enforcement activity.[93] Discrete research projects have been pursued under its aegis, most importantly a wide-ranging investigation into consumer-facing remedies, jointly led by the CMA and FCA.[94] The 2018 concurrency report lavished praise on that enterprise, both as a specific instance of knowledge generation, but also, more generally, as a means of 'fostering the UK's competition concurrency regime'.[95] Finally, in the run up to EU exit, the UKCN functioned as a vehicle for Brexit preparations, through which the CMA liaised with other concurrent enforcers about likely changes to the enforcement framework and policy guidance.[96]

4.2 Concurrency in Practice: Case Allocation

The meat of the concurrency regime is the exercise of their concurrent powers by the sector regulators; our focus is the distinctive power to apply the UK and EU prohibition rules. The ERRA 2013 enhancements were designed, in large part, to increase levels of competition enforcement in the regulated sectors, and the early evidence suggests that they have succeeded in doing so—albeit, given the low starting point, absolute levels of enforcement remain low. In this subsection, we consider the tricky preliminary question of who actually takes competition cases in the regulated sectors; in the next, we trace the contours of enforcement activity by the various regulators within the enhanced concurrency regime.

As noted in section 2, the OFT's approach to concurrent enforcement prior to the ERRA 2013 reforms was one of almost total deference to regulators, who in turn were perceived

---

[87] ibid.

[88] ibid 3–4.

[89] CR2015 (n 81) para 11, and CR2017 (n 81) para 33.

[90] CR2017 (n 81) para 33, and CR2020 (n 1) paras 141–42.

[91] CR2017 (n 81) para 33, and CR2018 (n 76) paras 35 and 38.

[92] See United Kingdom Competition Network, *Secondment Principles* (31 March 2017): https://www.gov.uk/government/publications/ukcn-secondment-principles.

[93] CR2018 (n 76) para 35.

[94] See Competition and Markets Authority and Financial Conduct Authority, *Helping people get a better deal: Learning lessons about consumer facing remedies* (1 October 2018); and discussion in CR2018 (n 76) para 39.

[95] CR2018 (n 76) para 39.

[96] CR2019, paras 247–50, and CR2020 (n 1) para 146.

to underuse their available competition powers. A clear objective of the enhanced regime was to reduce the number of viable competition cases that were, as a result, falling through the cracks of the enforcement framework. Thus, the initial question of case allocation has taken on extra importance, insofar as the implicit rule of thumb that preceded the ERRA 2013 reforms—in essence, always defer to regulators—is no longer adequate. Regulators continue to perform the lion's share of enforcement in regulated sectors, but the CMA has ramped up its own levels of activity, and, indeed, it will be suggested in section 5 that enhanced cooperation means that, increasingly, a strict demarcation between discrete concurrent enforcers no longer makes sense.

As noted, under the Concurrency Regulations, case allocation is conceived of as an essentially consensual process, centred on discussion and compromise.[97] While this starting point must be viewed against the CMA's new power to 'take' cases from regulators in appropriate circumstances,[98] the absence of any need to do so thus far suggests that this consensual vision is largely playing out in practice. General principles on case allocation in concurrent cases are set out in the CMA's guidance.[99] These follow the approach, already in place prior to the ERRA 2013 enhancements, of granting jurisdiction to the agency deemed 'better or best placed'[100] to pursue a case. This, moreover, mirrors the ECN approach of allocating enforcement jurisdiction on the basis that an authority is 'well placed' or 'better placed' to apply the EU competition rules.[101] This determination is made taking account of, *inter alia*, the comparative sector knowledge of the regulator and the CMA; any prior experience in dealing with either the undertakings or market problems involved; and a potential desire to set a market-wide precedent through generalist agency enforcement.[102]

The default assumption, pre-ERRA 2013, was that regulators would take any case falling within their areas of sectoral expertise, unless there were specific factors which rendered the OFT better placed to do so.[103] The CMA's guidance, by contrast, is more ambivalent, steering clear of any explicit prioritization of regulators over the CMA itself.[104] Nonetheless, in the period since the entry into force of the ERRA 2013, the majority of cases have indeed been pursued by regulators. The exceptions are worth considering, however, for what they tell us about the circumstances in which the CMA may be perceived to have an enforcement advantage even within a regulator's sector of expertise.

The *Heathrow Airport/Arora Group* case involved price-fixing for airport parking facilities: specifically, a tenant's covenant which prevented a hotel operator from charging prices for non-hotel guests that were cheaper than those charged at other car parks at Heathrow. Opened by the CMA in December 2017, the investigation resulted in an infringement decision in October 2018. It saw a fine of £1.6 million for one defendant (the airport operator), and full immunity under the CMA's leniency policy for the other (the hotel operator).[105] At first glance, the decision to assign jurisdiction to the CMA rather than the CAA

---

[97] Concurrency Regulations, reg 4.

[98] ibid. See n 51.

[99] CMA, *Regulated Industries* (n 71) paras 3.21–25.

[100] CMA10 (n 71) para 3.22; see also Office of Fair Trading, *Concurrent application to regulated industries* (OFT405), (December 2004) para 3.13.

[101] Case allocation within the ECN is determined in line with the European Commission's *Notice on cooperation within the Network of Competition Authorities* (OJ C101/43, 27 April 2004).

[102] ibid.

[103] OFT405 (n 100) para 3.13.

[104] CMA10 (n 71) para 3.22.

[105] See Case 50523 *Conduct in the transport sector (facilities at airports)*, Decision of 25 October 2018.

seems curious, since the regulator had investigated and sanctioned similar conduct at East Midlands International Airport less than two years previously.[106] Yet a concern at the outset in the Heathrow case was whether the full extent of the anti-competitive behaviour would fall within the scope of the CAA's (limited) concurrent jurisdiction.[107] That is, although the suspect behaviour nominally fell within the scope of 'airport operation services'—one of two discrete areas in respect of which the CAA holds concurrent powers—it was anticipated that the investigation might uncover issues that would reach beyond this, thus going beyond the scope of the CAA's enforcement jurisdiction.[108] As such, the decision for the CMA to pursue the case represents a pragmatic acknowledgment of the benefit of having a generalist competition enforcer with economy-wide jurisdiction, in circumstances where anti-competitive behaviour may spread across various market segments, not all of which fall within the control of the sector-specific regulator.

A second example arose in the energy sector. Here, an investigation into a suspected breach of the Chapter I prohibition by price comparison websites that offered energy tariff comparisons in relation to paid online search advertising was opened by Ofgem in October 2015. Subsequently, however, it was formally transferred to the CMA under the procedure specified in the Concurrency Regulations.[109] The concern at issue was rather more awkward than that in the *Heathrow Airport* case, however: namely, fears about the regulator's perceived impartiality. These arose from prior contracts between Ofgem staff and staff of some of the defendants, which had occurred before the investigation had commenced, and which related to Ofgem's own procurement of search advertising. The concern, ultimately, was that this perceived lack of impartiality might provide good grounds to challenge the investigation process or its outcome.[110] This example might thus be seen as a salutary tale about the potential risks of mixing competition enforcement—in effect, a quasi-judicial activity that requires rigorous impartiality and avoiding any perception of bias—with the day-to-day business of sector regulation, which typically involves close ongoing relationships with market actors. Particularly in light of the exacting review to which competition decisions are subject by UK courts subsequently,[111] the case functions as a reminder that competition law enforcement and regulatory supervision are distinct activities that do not necessarily make comfortable bedfellows. The case had an even less satisfactory ending, moreover, when the investigation was closed by the CMA on the grounds of administrative priority several months later:[112] an outcome already anticipated and proffered as an (eventually unpersuasive) reason to refuse transfer to the CMA in the circumstances.[113]

---

[106] See discussion in n 163 below.

[107] Competition and Markets Authority, *Annual Report on Concurrency 2016* (CMA54) (28 April 2016, CR2016), para 76.

[108] CR2018 (n 76) para 62. Under section 68 of the Civil Aviation Act 2012, 'airport operation services' are defined narrowly to include only certain services 'provided *at* an airport' (emphasis added). The provision of car park services at a hotel *adjacent to* an airport could, therefore, conceivably fall outside the scope of the CAA's concurrent powers.

[109] Gas and Electricity Markets Authority, *Formal Notice of Transfer* (13 June 2016) https://www.ofgem.gov.uk/system/files/docs/2016/06/formal_notice_of_transfer_14_june_2016.pdf.

[110] CR2017 (n 81) para 204.

[111] An example is the scrutiny directed at the Commission Commission's *BAA Airports Markets Investigation*, which involved allegations of apparent bias on the part of one panel member: see *BAA v Competition Commission* [2010] EWCA Civ 1097.

[112] Competition and Markets Authority, *Statement regarding the CMA's decision to close an investigation into a suspected breach of competition law by some price comparison websites that offer energy tariff comparisons in relation to paid online search advertising on the grounds of administrative priorities* (October 2016).

[113] As discussed in Ofgem's *Formal Notice of Transfer* (n 110).

A third exception, more readily foreseen by the CMA's guidance on case allocation, arose in respect of the FCA's concurrent jurisdiction over the financial services sector. Again, it involved the activities of a price comparison website, the prominent *comparethemarket.com* tool, in respect of its advertising and sale of home insurance products. Here, the allegation was that the defendant had entered into anti-competitive agreements, specifically the use of illegal 'most favoured nation' (MFN) clauses.[114] Although the FCA had concurrent jurisdiction insofar as the case involved the provision of financial services, it was allocated to the CMA on the basis both of its experience of considering MFN clauses across a range of sectors, and of the potential broader competition policy implications of the investigation, in terms of the development of precedent for the treatment of MFN clauses generally.[115] Thus, in effect, the case was treated as an example of a recurrent economy-wide competition problem which arose in that instance in a regulated sector, rather than as a problem that was specific to its regulated context. The CMA's investigation resulted, in November 2020, in a formal finding of breach of the Chapter I prohibition and Article 101 TFEU, with a fine of more than £17 million imposed on the defendant website operator. The infringement decision notes that the CMA engaged the FCA 'in formal concurrent review of both the Statement of Objections and the present Decision'.Infringement Decision was published on 19 Nov 2020 – CMA Decision, Case 50505, Price comparison website: use of most favoured nation clauses, 19 November 2020..[116]

The CMA launched a second investigation into alleged anti-competitive agreements in the financial services sector in November 2018. Subsequent concurrency reports have been uncharacteristically unforthcoming about the reasons behind this allocation of jurisdiction.[117] Thus, one can only speculate why, despite the FCA's now proven ability to bring Chapter I infringement cases,[118] the CMA was considered 'better placed': whether a practical consideration, like resource constraints, or a more formal one, like the FCA's inability to pursue criminal prosecutions.

The CMA has also taken two cases in the private healthcare sector, instead of the nominal concurrent regulator, NHSI. These are, first, an investigation under Chapter I and Article 101 TFEU into price-fixing and information-sharing in the provision of private ophthalmology services, which resulted in an infringement decision and fine in August 2015[119]; and a Chapter I prohibition decision involving price-fixing for initial consultation fees for self-pay patients charged by ophthalmologists at Spire's Regency Hospital in Macclesfield, taken in July 2020.[120] Again, one finds little discussion of the rationale for awarding jurisdiction to the CMA in either instance. Yet, arguably, it is easier to guess at the reasoning here. On the one hand, NHSI's core mission is focused on the regulation of public healthcare, making it less obvious that it would be 'best placed' to adjudicate upon anti-competitive behaviour by private providers, even where the latter sell services to the public system. Indeed,

---

[114] CR2019 (n 29) para 39.

[115] CR2018 (n 76) para 62.

[116] Case 50505, *Price comparison website: use of most favoured nation clauses*, Decision of 19 November 2020, para 2.3. The case is discussed further in Chapter 3 of this volume on Vertical Agreements.

[117] CR2019 (n 29) para 40, and CR2020 (n 1) para 40.

[118] See n 170 below and accompanying text.

[119] Case CE/9784-13 *Conduct in the ophthalmology sector*, Decision of 20 August 2015. See also discussion in CR2015 (n 81) para 11.

[120] Case 50782-1, *Privately funded ophthalmology services*, Decision of 1 July 2020. See also discussion in CR2020 (n 1) para 42.

it is doubtful whether many of the entities that comprise the core regulatory focus of NHSI comprise 'undertakings' within the meaning of the competition rules at all. Non confidential Infringement decision published 1 July 2020 – CMA Decision, Case 50782-1, Privately funded ophthalmology services, 1 July 2020.[121] On the other, and perhaps more pertinently, NHSI sits awkwardly as a concurrent enforcer, and, as will be discussed in the next subsection, it is not obvious that its concurrent powers are working well in practice. Thus, it is unsurprising that it entrusts the pursuit of unambiguous anti-competitive behaviour to a less reticent enforcer. Nonetheless, NHSI has provided staff and technical assistance to support the CMA's enforcement activities.[122]

4.3 Concurrency in Practice: Enforcement Activity in Regulated Markets

Having considered those cases where regulators did not exercise their concurrent jurisdiction, we turn to those examples where they opted to do so. Our focus is the period following the entry into force of the enhanced concurrency arrangements,[123] which has seen a rise in both the number of investigations opened by regulators and their findings of infringement. The aim is to provide an indicative overview of the major contours of the more successful examples of completed enforcement activity, rather than a blow-by-blow account of all cases. A more probing analysis of the totality of enforcement efforts during the period follows in the next section.

Before considering the formal exercise of enforcement jurisdiction, however, it is useful to note a parallel increase in the use of 'soft' enforcement mechanisms in regulated sectors, namely advisory and warning letters.[124] Advisory letters are essentially educational, designed to inform firms about the existence of competition law and their obligations under these rules. Warning letters, by contrast, place firms 'on notice' of potential violations. The suspected breach, typically, falls below the required threshold of severity or significance so as to merit formal enforcement by the regulator concerned, meaning that the intention of the enforcer is, instead, to prompt greater—essentially voluntary—compliance by defendants.[125] It could be argued that such softer enforcement tools are more appropriate in regulated markets, where competition often takes a backseat to prescriptive regulatory interventions, and where market actors are more accustomed to being told what to do than what *not* to do. Yet many of the sectors within the concurrency regime have been subject to competition law for decades, so that arguments premised on a lack of awareness are less compelling. Advisory and warning letters at least have the advantage, nonetheless,

---

[121] Compare, for instance, the expansive approach taken by the UK's Competition Appeal Tribunal in *Bettercare Group Ltd. v The Director General of Fair Trading* [2002] CAT 7, with the greater caution of the European Court of Justice in Case C-205/03 P *FENIN v Commission* EU:C:2006:453. There is a notable disjuncture within the Health and Social Services Act 2012, between the health care regulator's general duty 'to [prevent] anti-competitive behaviour in the provision of health care services for the purposes of the NHS which is against the interests of people who use such services' (s 62(3)) and its apparently rather wider concurrent competition powers, which encompass 'the provision of health care services in England' more generally (s 72(2)).

[122] CR2017 (n 81) n 10.

[123] See n 66 above.

[124] CR2018 (n 76) para 7; CR2019 (n 29) paras 48–54; and CR2020 (n 1) paras 50–51.

[125] As explained, specifically in relation to the FCA's activities, in CR2016 (n 107) paras 182–83; see also CR2020 (n 1) para 50.

of providing a nominally constructive avenue for case disposition in circumstances where, even given the existence of multiple concurrent enforcers, it is impossible for agencies to pursue all alleged breaches to the fullest extent.

Turning to concrete enforcement activity, we start with those regulators who have seen greatest success in use of their concurrent power, before turning to those who have exhibited more reluctance in practice. Prior to the ERRA 2013 enhancements, Ofcom was the concurrent regulator with the greatest enforcement experience; yet it was also, arguably, the poster child for the frustrated ambitions of the regime. Ofcom formally launched 13 antitrust investigations under its concurrent powers in the period 2004-2013, yet none had resulted in findings of infringement.[126] There are multiple possible reasons for Ofcom's failures, and indeed one commentator has argued that its fault was an undue willingness to open unpromising investigations, rather than any unwillingness to bring promising ones to fruition.[127] Yet Ofcom's lack of enforcement success had not gone without criticism, and was prominent in discussions preceding the ERRA 2013 reforms.

During the period of enhanced concurrency, by contrast, Ofcom has taken two infringement decisions, both of which involve Royal Mail (the latter being the last major UK state-owned company to be privatized, in 2013). In August 2018, Ofcom found an abuse of dominance contrary to both the Chapter II prohibition and Article 102 TFEU, relating to discriminatory pricing practices designed to exclude Royal Mail's only significant competitor in the bulk mail delivery market, Whistl.[128] Specifically, Royal Mail increased its wholesale (access mail) prices in a manner which significantly increased costs for rival operators that intended to self-deliver part of their bulk mail business, compared with those who used Royal Mail for all bulk deliveries. The infringement decision put emphasis on internal documents which, it held, evidenced a 'deliberate strategy' to stamp out the nascent competition represented by Whistl's market entry. A substantial fine—£50 million—was imposed in response. The regulator's decision was appealed, unsuccessfully, to the Competition Appeal Tribunal (CAT),[129] with the defendant now seeking to take the case to the Court of Appeal.[130]

The second finding of infringement, involving anti-competitive agreements in the business parcel delivery sector, came in November 2019. Specifically, Ofcom found that Royal Mail had entered into a customer allocation arrangement with The Salegroup Limited, whereby neither company would offer parcel services to the other's business customers.[131] Whereas the Chapter II/Article 102 case was initiated on foot of a complaint to Ofcom by Whistl, here the case stemmed from a leniency application made by Royal Mail to the CMA. The application was shared with Ofcom as concurrent enforcer, and a fairly swift agreement was reached that the regulator should take the case.[132] On this occasion, Royal Mail avoided any fine for its breach of Chapter I/Article 101 TFEU, while its co-defendant received a

---

[126] Baseline Report (n 28) para 137.

[127] Pietro Crocioni, 'Ofcom's Record as a Competition Authority: An Assessment of Decisions in Telecoms' *EUI Working Papers* RSCAS 2019/93 (2019).

[128] CW/01122/01/14 *Discriminatory pricing in relation to the supply of bulk mail delivery services in the UK*, Decision of 14 August 2018. See also discussion in CR2019 (n 29) paras 42–44.

[129] *Royal Mail v Ofcom* [2019] CAT 27; see also CR2020 (n 1) paras 48–49.

[130] Initial permission to appeal was refused by in *Royal Mail v Ofcom* [2020] CAT 2.

[131] CW/01222/07/18 *Royal Mail Group Limited and The Salegroup Limited (trading as despatchbay.com)*, Decision of 14 November 2019.

[132] ibid A2.2–A2.5.

comparatively small penalty (£40,000) which included a 20% discount for settlement. This cooperation was also reflected in the speedy timeframe of the investigation: the case was concluded within eighteen months of the initial leniency application, compared with a four-and-a-half year time-lag between Whistl's complaint and Ofcom's finding of abuse.

Even the enhanced concurrency regime does not mean, however, that every investigation conducted by Ofcom during this period has resulted in findings of infringement. Two cases in the broadcasting sector, both closed without breach, are noteworthy. In February 2016, Ofcom closed a complaint alleging abuse of dominance by Sky Sports, on the basis that the remedy sought—access to Sky Sports channels on a non-reciprocal basis—had already been provided during the investigation. Thus, Ofcom held, the principal risks to the interests of consumers at stake had been addressed.[133] The case is notable insofar as it overlapped with Ofcom's regulatory role in mandating wholesale access to Sky Sports programming, an obligation that had been removed only a few months previously for essentially the same reasons as dismissal of the complaint.[134]

Secondly, in August 2016, Ofcom closed an investigation into alleged anti-competitive practices by the Premier League with respect to the licensing of broadcasting rights for football matches. Again, the case was closed on the basis that the defendant had increased significantly the number of matches available for live broadcast in the UK, a change which the regulator considered sufficient to address the competition concerns raised. Ofcom made explicit reference to consumer research it had carried out to understand the market concerned, which suggested that a more expansive remedy might, conversely, negatively affect football fans who prefer to attend matches in-person.[135] These 'split loyalties'—between fans who wanted greater numbers of televised matches, and those who would be inconvenienced by the disruption of live schedules—complicated the consumer welfare equation, thus rendering intervention less justifiable, or at least more risky, for Ofcom.

The second area to be granted concurrent powers was that of energy, now regulated by Ofgem. Prior to entry into force of the enhanced regime, Ofgem launched five antitrust investigations in the period 2005-2013.[136] Its case tally included one infringement decision—a finding of abuse of dominance by National Grid in the provision of domestic-sized gas meters[137]—and another to accept commitments in lieu of breach.[138] This approach, which combines resort to both infringement decisions and settlements as appropriate, has continued under the enhanced regime.

First, the infringement case: in May 2019, Ofgem imposed fines on three undertakings for their participation in an illegal market-sharing arrangement, contrary to the Chapter I prohibition, relating to the supply of gas and electricity to domestic customers.[139] The

---

[133] See Ofcom, *Complaint from British Telecommunications plc against British Sky Broadcasting Group plc alleging abuse of a dominant position regarding the wholesale supply of Sky Sports 1 and 2* https://www.ofcom.org.uk/about-ofcom/latest/bulletins/competition-bulletins/all-closed-cases/cw_01106; discussed in CR2016 (n 107) paras 95–97.

[134] See Ofcom, *Review of the pay TV wholesale must-offer obligation* (19 November 2015).

[135] CR2017 (n 81) paras 154–64.

[136] Baseline Report (n 28) para 256.

[137] Upheld in *National Grid Plc v GEMA* [2009] CAT 14, and [2010] EWCA Civ 114, albeit the fine was progressively reduced from the figure of £41.6 million imposed by Ofgem, to £30 million by the CAT, and £15 million by the Court of Appeal.

[138] Case 76/12 *Decision to accept binding commitments from Electricity North West Limited over connection charges*, Decision of 24 May 2012; discussed in Baseline Report (n 28) paras 254–55.

[139] *Infringement by Economy Energy, E (Gas and Electricity) and Dyball Associates of Chapter I of the Competition Act 1998 with respect to an anti-competitive agreement*, Decision of 29 May 2019.

cartel comprised two retail energy companies, and a third defendant, a business specialized in providing software and consulting services to the energy sector, which acted as facilitator. In short, the energy providers agreed not to actively target each other's existing customers, a non-competition arrangement enabled by software provided by the third defendant.

Several aspects of the case are noteworthy. The case was initiated by Ofgem upon receipt of 'information from anonymous sources', which, together with market-switching data, caused it to suspect a breach.[140] Throughout the investigation, moreover, Ofgem received 'unsolicited information' from a whistle-blower associated with one of the parties, nominally relating to breach by one defendant of its licence conditions, but which also had a bearing on the cartel investigation.[141] The latter, in particular, suggests a synergy between regulatory and antitrust enforcement that perhaps would not exist absent the concurrency regime—although, as the extended discussion of the whistle-blower material in the infringement decision illustrates, this brings its own risks.

The other interesting aspect was the comparative novelty and complexity of the issues raised. First, the retail defendants argued that they comprised a single undertaking, due to cross-links in the ownership and governance of each organization. This claim was ultimately rejected, but necessitated a detailed consideration of the concept of an undertaking and its application to the facts.[142] Secondly, the case involved the not-uncontentious cartel facilitation doctrine, whereby an undertaking not active in the cartelized market may nonetheless be held liable on the basis that it provided services to the direct cartelists.[143] Again, the decision provides a clear account of the law in this area and a plausible application of the legal principles, thus providing a counter-example to concerns regarding the ability of regulators to run effective, high-quality antitrust cases.

Ofgem has also, during the reference period, closed two cases on the basis of binding commitments. In November 2016, Ofgem closed its investigation into an alleged abuse of dominance by SSE, one of the 'big six' energy companies.[144] The investigation arose from suspect behaviour uncovered in the course of Ofgem's first review of competition in the retail energy market,[145] and concerned alleged anti-competitive conduct by SSE when providing non-contestable connection services. SSE offered a range of commitments— including on pricing, functional separation, training, and monitoring—which were accepted on the basis, *inter alia*, that these adequately addressed the regulator's concerns without the need for further resource-intensive investigation.

A second dominance investigation, involving access to cross-border intraday electricity trading platforms and related services, was similarly concluded in June 2019.[146] Here, the defendant, a power exchange, was alleged to have excluded other exchanges from participating in electricity trading auctions between Great Britain and Ireland. The commitments, in brief, required the defendant to open up its trading auctions, to provide regular progress

---

[140] ibid paras 3.2 and 4.2.

[141] ibid para 5.29.

[142] ibid paras 7.12–7.50.

[143] Established, most concretely, in Case C-194/14 P *AC-Treuhand* EU:C:2015:717; although see Advocate General Wahl's significant reservations in his Opinion in that case, EU:C:2015:350.

[144] *Notice of decision to accept binding commitments from SSE plc*, Decision of 3 November 2016; discussed in CR2017 (n 81) paras 200–203.

[145] Conducted jointly with the OFT and CMA; see *State of the Market Assessment* (27 March 2014).

[146] Ofgem, *Notice of Decision to accept binding commitments offered by EPEX Spot SE and EEX in relation to electricity wholesale trading activities* (18 June 2019).

reports, and to put in place a mandatory competition compliance programme for its staff. The case was notable, moreover, insofar as three agencies had concurrent jurisdiction—Ofgem, CMA, and NIAUR—while another NCA, Ireland's Competition and Consumer Protection Commission, was consulted during the investigation.[147]

In the period from 2005 to 2013, ORR formally launched three antitrust investigations,[148] and took one infringement decision, finding abuse of dominance by a freight rail operator through exclusionary and discriminatory practices.[149] During the reference period, it has not taken any further infringement decisions. In December 2015, nonetheless, ORR accepted commitments in lieu of a finding of breach in respect of an alleged abuse of dominance affecting deep sea container rail transport services. The defendant, Freightliner, agreed to prohibit all forms of exclusivity arrangements with customers, which the ORR considered would adequately create a more level playing field.[150] The commitments have been reviewed annually,[151] and, three years on, were considered to be working well; in particular, levels of competition in the sector were increasing.[152] A subsequent complaint against the same defendant, alleging a refusal to supply access to essential port infrastructure, was submitted and thus assessed under the ORR's regulatory powers. The complaint was ultimately rejected on the basis that the refusal was justified due to capacity constraints.[153]

Although Ofwat had several competition investigations ongoing when the enhanced regime came into force,[154] it had taken no infringement decisions.[155] The regulator moreover cautioned that competition remained 'in its infancy' in the sector.[156] This, arguably, continues to be the case, and as yet the water sector has seen no formal findings of breach.

Ofwat's most exacting investigation and outcome to date was that against Bristol Water, into allegations that the defendant water company abused its dominant position through exclusionary pricing structures which discriminated against self-lay organizations in the new water connections market. The case was concluded on the basis of binding commitments in lieu of a finding of breach.[157] Two aspects are noteworthy. First, various respondents to the market-testing process carried out before acceptance of the commitments criticized Ofwat for not being 'more assertive' (i.e. finding an infringement) in the case.[158] The regulator countered that the resources required to get to the stage where a credible infringement decision could be taken were disproportionate when compared with its incremental benefit, not least because the commitments adequately addressed the immediate problem.[159] Yet it might be queried whether a better-resourced agency, or one which placed greater value on developing antitrust precedent, would have treated this balancing exercise differently. The

---

[147] ibid para 3.2.

[148] Baseline Report (n 28) paras 368–70.

[149] *English Welsh and Scottish Railway Limited*, Decision of 17 November 2006.

[150] *Provision of Deep Sea Container rail transport services between ports and key inland destinations in Great Britain. Decision to accept commitments offered by Freightliner Limited and Freightliner Group Limited*, Decision of 18 December 2015; see also CR2016 (n 107) paras 277–84.

[151] CR2018 (n 76) para 404.

[152] CR2020 (n 1) paras 46–47.

[153] CR2017 (n 81) para 339.

[154] Detailed in the Baseline Report (n 28) paras 410–18.

[155] ORR had conducted and closed (in one instance on the basis of commitments in lieu) several in-depth competition investigations: see Baseline Report (n 28) paras 426–36.

[156] Baseline Report (n 28) para 406.

[157] *Decision to accept binding commitments from Bristol Water plc*, Decision of 23 March 2015.

[158] ibid para 4.5.

[159] ibid paras 4.6–4.13.

second aspect is that respondents also raised concerns about the wider market context, and in particular, fears that water companies other than the immediate defendant engaged in the same behaviour. In response, Ofwat noted, *inter alia*, the wide range of regulatory tools available to it beyond its competition powers, which could address the issue. Pointedly, however, it referenced its primacy obligation to explain why it had opted for antitrust intervention in that instance.[160]

A second prominent investigation involved an alleged margin squeeze by Anglian Water in the provision of water and sewerage services. In December 2015, however, Ofwat determined that there were no grounds for further action. Although it concluded, preliminarily, that the defendant may have engaged in a squeeze with respect to sewerage services, it took the view that any customer (that is, property developers) would wish to buy the two services as a combined bundle, so that it was more difficult to effect an anti-competitive impact by the squeezing of one service alone.[161]

The CAA has concurrent powers over two, fairly narrowly-drawn areas of aviation: airport operation services and air traffic services. Prior to the enhanced regime, the CAA had taken no antitrust cases: it received its concurrent powers over airport operation services only in 2013, and there was ambiguity about the extent to which the principal entities that provide air traffic control services in the UK constitute 'undertakings' under the competition rules.[162]

In December 2016, however, the CAA took its first (and to date, only) infringement decision, finding breach of the Chapter I prohibition stemming from a price-fixing agreement at East Midland International Airport (EMIA).[163] The case originated in a leniency application submitted by the operator of EMIA to the OFT in June 2013. The case was allotted to the CAA, on the basis that the alleged activity fell within both its concurrent jurisdiction and its casework priorities.[164] As noted, the behaviour resembled that in the later *Heathrow Airport* case,[165] involving a minimum pricing obligation which required a third party operator of car parking facilities, Prestige, not to undercut the prices charged by EMIA itself. Notably, however, although the CAA found a 'by object' infringement of Chapter I, and calculated indicative fines for each defendant, no fines were actually imposed, as EMIA benefited from full leniency, and Prestige had gone out of business in 2012.[166]

The CAA also opened an investigation in alleged abuse of dominance at the same facility, which remained ongoing at the time of the first infringement decision.[167] The dominance case was later closed on administrative priority grounds, on the basis that the relevant facts had already been sanctioned, and following a sector-wide review of surface access to UK airports which resulted in the issuance of advisory letters to relevant stakeholders.[168]

---

[160] ibid paras 4.31–4.36.

[161] *Fairfield Competition Act 1998 investigation decision summary*, Decision of 22 December 2015. See also discussion in Concurrency Report 2016, paras 351–61.

[162] Baseline Report (n 28) paras 120–21.

[163] CA98-001, *Access to car parking facilities at East Midlands International Airport* (CAP 1507), Decision of 15 December 2016.

[164] ibid paras 9–13.

[165] See n 105 above.

[166] Accordingly, under the applicable *OFT's guidance as to the appropriate amount of a penalty* (OFT423, September 2012), the statutory cap for the fine was zero, as the reference year was 2015: see CA 1998-001 (n 164) Appendix C.

[167] CR2017 (n 81) para 95.

[168] CR2018 (n 76) para 137.

The FCA received its concurrent enforcement powers in April 2015, a year after the entry into force of the enhanced regime. Unlike the more established concurrent regulators who took time to warm up to competition law, the FCA has made effective use of its powers right out of the blocks. In this regard, it may benefit from the more supportive (and perhaps also expectant) environment of the enhanced concurrency regime, but no doubt also benefits from being particularly well-resourced and thus at a technical advantage compared with peer regulators.[169]

The upshot is that the FCA's first formal decision under its competition powers, adopted in February 2019, involved both a finding of breach and fines.[170] Specifically, it found breaches of Chapter I and Article 101 arising from the strategic sharing of information between competing asset management firms in the context of an initial public offering. The case arose from a leniency application to the CMA, which subsequently allocated the case to the FCA.[171] Fines were imposed on two defendants, while the third benefited from full immunity. Of particular interest for our purposes is that, in parallel to the antitrust investigation conducted against the undertakings concerned, the FCA opened an investigation into, and subsequently issued a Decision Notice against, a specific *individual* in relation to the same conduct, under regulatory powers granted to it by the Financial Services and Markets Act 2000.[172]

As noted in the preceding section, two investigations in the financial services sector have been taken by the CMA in the parallel exercise of its concurrent powers. A third, involving alleged anti-competitive information exchange in the aviation insurance sector, was closed by the FCA when the investigation was taken over by the European Commission.[173]

The PSR is a subsidiary of the FCA, albeit an independent regulator, and thus treated separately for concurrency purposes. Like the FCA, the PSR received its concurrent powers in April 2015, when it became fully operational. As of 31 March 2020, it had one ongoing investigation, which had entailed, *inter alia*, several inspections under warrant at business premises in the UK.[174]

This brings us, more problematically, to those regulators without *any* enforcement experience.[175] At the time the enhanced regime entered into force, the NIAUR had not yet received any complaints which it considered to raise potential competition law issues, let alone opened any formal investigations under its concurrent powers.[176] The baseline report noted several differentiating features of Northern Ireland's regulated markets, including the region's small size,[177] and the fact that the water incumbent is the sole monopoly provider of both water and sewerage services.[178] The NIAUR received a complaint alleging a potential abuse of dominance in August 2016. Since, however, the complainant informed the regulator that it intended to purse private action through the CAT, no formal investigation was opened by either the NIAUR or CMA.[179] The NIAUR provided support to Ofgem

---

[169] NAO (n 67) para 1.26.
[170] CMP/01-2016/CA98 *Anti-competitive conduct in the asset management sector*, Decision of 21 February 2019.
[171] ibid paras 2.2–2.3.
[172] ibid paras 2.12–2.16.
[173] CR2018 (n 76) para 273.
[174] ibid para 355; see also CR2020 (n 1) para 41.
[175] CR2019 (n 29) para 23; CR2020 (n 1) did not disclose any new enforcement activity.
[176] Baseline Report (n 28) para 467.
[177] ibid para 439.
[178] ibid para 445.
[179] CR2017 (n 81) para 438.

in its abuse of dominance investigation relating to wholesale trading activities,[180] although did not exercise its concurrent enforcement jurisdiction directly.[181]

The position of the health services regulator, NHSI, is unique among the concurrent enforcers. What was then known as Monitor received its concurrent powers in April 2013, enabling it to apply the CA 1998 and EA 2002 competition powers to health service providers in England.[182] Yet, unlike other regulators, the agency does not have a duty to *promote* competition within its areas of jurisdiction, but rather is obliged to 'exercise its functions with a view to *preventing anticompetitive* behaviour in the provision of health care services'.[183] Moreover, not only are the large majority of healthcare providers in England part of the NHS and thus, essentially, owned and operated by the state;[184] they also compete, in principle, on the basis of quality of care rather than cost.[185] (It is difficult, however, to ignore more politically-oriented questions regarding the adequacy of public funding of the NHS.) NHSI also had the distinction of being the only regulator to escape the reach of the 'nuclear option' introduced by the ERRA 2013, meaning that it is largely immune from ministerial oversight of its (chronic under-) use of its concurrent powers.

At 1 April 2014, Monitor had received one 'potentially relevant' complaint, but decided that it would not be appropriate to use its competition powers.[186] As noted, the two cases that have arisen during the reference period were allotted to the CMA, and the various concurrency reports disclose an emphatic absence of concurrent activity by NHSI. It might reasonably be queried, therefore, whether it makes sense for NHSI to retain its concurrent powers (although, as discussed, the obvious path of removing its jurisdiction under a sectoral regulator order is formally unavailable). In February 2021, the Department of Health and Social Care issued a rather radical White Paper, which proposes to do away with many of the competition-focused reforms of the Health and Social Care Act 2012, including to 'remove NHS Improvement's specific competition functions and its general duty to prevent anti-competitive behaviour'.[187] Should this come to fruition, the CMA will presumably retain its jurisdiction to apply the Chapter I and II prohibitions to the provision of health care services—at least to the extent that the relevant providers qualify as 'undertakings' for these purposes.

5   Reflections on Concurrency

What should we make of this patchwork of experiences: hard enforcement, softer enforcement, and not-insignificant amounts of continuing *non*-enforcement? The enhancements introduced by the ERRA 2013 have, without doubt, strengthened the bones of the regime, but leave unresolved the determination of what 'effective' concurrent enforcement should,

---

[180]   See n 146 above.
[181]   CR2020 (n 1) para 125.
[182]   Health and Social Care Act 2012, ss 72 and 73.
[183]   Health and Social Care Act 2012, s 62(3)(emphasis added).
[184]   Baseline Report (n 28) para 303.
[185]   ibid para 302.
[186]   ibid para 339.
[187]   Department of Health and Social Care, *Integration and Innovation: Working Together to Improve Health and Social Care for All*, February 2021, para 5.43. The White Paper, conversely, proposes to remove the *CMA's* function to review mergers involving NHS foundation trusts (ibid).

and actually can, look like. This penultimate section considers general themes arising from operation of the enhanced concurrency regime, and reflects on its future prospects.

At the most basic level, the ERRA 2013 reforms have succeeded in prompting greater levels of enforcement—almost double the number of CA 1998 investigations have been opened by regulators annually in the first five years of the enhanced regime, compared with the preceding decade—but these remain low in absolute terms.[188] Yet this bare measurement—more cases, but still comparatively few—provides little indication of the success or otherwise of the concurrency regime. There is also a higher level question, as yet unanswered, of whether it makes sense to aggregate, in a fairly undifferentiated manner, the enforcement experiences of discrete regulators, each operating in different markets, under disparate regulatory regimes, and with varying levels of resources,[189] even if certain 'cross-cutting themes' can be identified.[190]

While concurrent regulators pursue relatively few cases, this is not out of step with the UK system as a whole, which has seen (often far) lower levels of enforcement than equivalent competition regimes in similarly-placed Member States.[191] Moreover, while the practice of concluding competition investigations in regulated sectors through consensual settlements without a finding of breach has been criticized as 'unhelpful',[192] it is consistent with the seemingly ever-greater use of commitment decisions within contemporary enforcement.[193] A particular problem is the perceived rigour of *ex post* scrutiny by UK courts, which has earned the jurisdiction a reputation as 'the best . . . in the world to defend a competition case'.[194] Shifting the balance of review more firmly in favour of enforcers is one (unsurprisingly contentious) proposal of the Furman Report on competition policy for the digital economy.[195] In the meantime, however, the concern is that fear of *ex post* disapproval of antitrust decision-making may render inexperienced regulators even more risk averse in the exercise of their competition powers.[196]

There is, moreover, considerable ambivalence about whether the bare number of investigations pursued provides an effective measurement of either the levels of effective competition, or of anti-competitive behaviour, in regulated sectors.[197] BEIS, surveying five years of enhanced concurrency, acknowledged the difficulty of determining whether persistent low levels of enforcement stem from *under*-enforcement by regulators *or* low levels of

---

[188] There were 2.7 cases per year, compared with 1.5 cases annually between January 2007 and March 2014: see BEIS (n 32) 45.

[189] NAO (n 67) para 1.26.

[190] CR2016 (n 107) paras 35–50.

[191] NAO (n 67) para 2.11, comparing Germany and France; also BEIS (n 32) 56–57. For an assessment of the past two decades of enforcement by the OFT/CMA, highlighting these agencies' 'disappointing track record' see Barry J Rodger, 'Application of the Domestic and EU Antitrust Prohibitions: an Analysis of the UK Competition Authority's Enforcement Practice' (2020) 8 *Journal of Antitrust Enforcement* 86.

[192] DTI (n 23) para 5.8.

[193] A practice well-established before the ERRA 2013: see European Commission, *Ten Years of Antitrust Enforcement under Regulation 1/2003: Achievements and Future Perspectives* (COM(2014) 453) of 7 July 2014.

[194] NAO (n 67) para 2.15.

[195] *Unlocking digital competition. Report of the Digital Competition Expert Panel* (March 2019) paras 3.128–3.141. See also *Letter from Andrew Tyrie, CMA Chair, to the Secretary of State for Business, Energy and Industrial Strategy* (21 February 2019), proposing inter alia a statutory 'consumer interest' duty binding upon courts that review competition decisions, and a lessening of the current 'full merits' review standard employed by courts in such cases. For discussion of these proposals see Renato Nazzini, 'A Reform Too Few or a Reform Too Many: Judicial Review, Appeals or a Prosecutorial System under the UK Competition Act 1998?' (2020) Journal of Antitrust Enforcement 1.

[196] NAO (n 67) para 2.15.

[197] CR2018 (n 76) para 46.

anti-competitive *behaviour* in regulated markets.[198] The report suggested three alternative explanations for the continuing absence of cases, but, tellingly, refused to endorse any due to an absence of evidence: the comparative ease and/or suitability of regulatory remedies to solve problems in regulated markets; the possibility that successful regulatory interventions *ex ante* largely remove the need for *ex post* enforcement; and the constraints of capacity and expertise faced by regulators.[199] These competing perspectives on concurrency merit closer examination.

The interrelationship between competition and regulation is a perennially complex question. The UK orthodoxy, in line with the underlying logic of the concurrency arrangements, is that competition and regulation are complementary rather than mutually exclusive phenomena.[200] Thus, a 'dual approach' to market supervision, combining both regulatory oversight and competition enforcement, is considered to be the optimal means by which to ensure outcomes that are both efficient and fair.[201] The baseline report thus contended that competition law and sector-specific regulation 'serve different, but compatible and consistent means for achieving the same fundamental, procompetitive outcomes'.[202] In this regard, much is made of the complementarity of the skills of the regulators and CMA in exercising their concurrent powers: one bringing detailed market knowledge, the other experience and expertise for the technical task of enforcement.[203] In its first concurrency report, the CMA suggested that the fact that the first two market investigations initiated by the new agency had been in the regulated sectors was 'not mere chance', but rather reflected both the inherently uncompetitive market structures often found in such sectors and the strong public interest considerations at stake.[204] Even if competition enforcement is an inexact measure of the health of the competitive process, moreover, such activity brings the benefit of publicity, with—ideally—attendant benefits of deterrence and compliance.[205] A lack of awareness of competition law among business characterizes the UK competition system as a whole,[206] and the historic absence of enforcement in some of the most high-profile (and politically salient) markets in the economy may explain this failing at least in part.

There is, however, some indication that the regulated market problems typically tackled through competition enforcement in other jurisdictions are simply not present in UK markets, largely as a result of the emphasis on achieving competitive outcomes already embedded within the sectoral regimes.[207] Thus, treating concurrency as an aspect

---

[198] BEIS (n 32) 42.

[199] ibid 49–50.

[200] Competition and Markets Authority, *Regulation and Competition: A Review of the Evidence* (CMA111) (January 2020) para 2.2. The inter-relationship between competition law and regulation is a topic addressed almost exhaustively in the literature: for a sample of perspectives, see David Newbery, 'The Relationship Between Regulation and Competition Policy for Network Industries' EPRG 0611 (March 2006), Giorgio Monti, 'Managing the Intersection of Utilities Regulation and EC Competition Law' (2008) 4 Competition Law Review 123, and Pablo Ibáñez Colomo, 'On the Application of Competition Law as Regulation: Elements for a Theory' (2010) 29 Yearbook of European Law 261.

[201] ibid CMA111 (n 1).

[202] Baseline Report (n 28) para 33.

[203] CR2017 (n 81) para 49; and CR2019 (n 29) para 16.

[204] CR2015 (n 81) para 17.

[205] NAO (n 67) para 2.12.

[206] ibid para 2.2.

[207] CR2017 (n 81) paras 41–45. Although contrast the more sceptical note of Stern (n 3) 897, who compares the pure competition focus of UK antitrust enforcement in recent decades with the continuing existence of the sectoral regulatory regimes, which imply an enduring absence of competition severe enough to raise public interest concerns.

of *competition* policy may be misguided; Stern argues that, instead, it should be seen as the 'coping stone' of the UK's strongly procompetitive system of sector-specific *economic regulation*.[208] It is impossible to ignore, furthermore, the significant influence that government policymaking has on competition dynamics in regulated markets, over and above enforcement activity under either the competition or sector-specific rules.[209] Thus, despite the almost sacrosanct assumption that competition law has an indispensable role to play within the UK's ever-more-competitive regulated sectors, it is unclear whether significantly greater levels of individual enforcement are necessary or possible.

The primacy provision nonetheless seeks to put competition law at the forefront of the market governance activities of sector regulators. The provision is considered to provide 'useful discipline' for regulators, which is now embedded in decision-making processes.[210] Its comparatively 'narrow phrasing' means that its practical scope of application is limited,[211] however, and the concurrency reports to date indicate that it is triggered only exceptionally. BEIS suggested that the primacy provision may, indeed, *over*-incentivize concurrent enforcement by regulators, as reflected by the comparatively high number of cases closed for reasons of administrative prioritization.[212] Yet, although there is evidence that the obligation may skew how regulators approach the determination of the optimal solution to certain market problems,[213] it is more difficult to establish that it does so at the expense of better regulatory outcomes in the alternative.

Merely hammering home the obligation to consider competition law is meaningless, of course, to the extent that regulators continue to lack (or, perhaps, perceive themselves to lack) the technical capacity and/or expertise to pursue enforcement effectively and successfully. Several years into the enhanced arrangements, the CMA surveyed regulators in order to understand the slow uptick in the number of cases being pursued. The survey revealed a general enthusiasm for concurrency among regulators, but also lingering doubts about their capacity to conduct such cases, despite the improved arrangements for information-sharing and support.[214] While this led to increased efforts by the CMA to ramp up technical support,[215] it chimes with long-standing concerns about both the feasibility and desirability of entrusting a complex law enforcement task to agencies whose primary focus and expertise lie in rather different fields. The case examples discussed in section 4 served to confirm but also, arguably, to belie some of these concerns.

As noted, the ERRA 2013 enhancements seek to involve the CMA more centrally and proactively in competition enforcement within regulated sectors. The CMA takes an explicit 'leadership' role within the concurrency framework, in order to promote consistency and quality in enforcement.[216] The NAO review suggested that this rather lopsided arrangement may prevent the concurrency regime, in particular the UKCN, from becoming 'a genuinely collaborative enterprise'.[217] Yet any fears that this essentially hierarchical

---

[208] Stern (n 3).

[209] ibid 910.

[210] BEIS (n 32) 51.

[211] ibid.

[212] ibid.

[213] See eg n 160 above.

[214] CR2017 (n 81) paras 44–47.

[215] ibid paras 48–49; by the following year, the CMA reported 'positive outcomes' from these efforts; see CR2018 (n 76) para 47.

[216] CMA10 (n 71) para 3.2; also CR2019 (n 29) para 19, and BEIS (n 32) 44.

[217] NAO (n 67) para 1.26.

arrangement might lead to an 'adversarial relationship' between the CMA and regulators have not materialized in its first years of operation.[218] As the enhanced regime matures, moreover, the strict binary implied by two parallel regimes of jurisdiction may indeed be disappearing: with more nuanced case allocation, sharing of expertise (across enforcement activity and beyond), and joint efforts to develop guidance and know-how.[219]

Thus, while enhanced cooperation unsurprisingly encompasses the parameters of the concurrency regime, it goes beyond its formal limits.[220] Competition assessment of mergers, for instance, lies solely within the purview of the CMA,[221] yet recent concurrency reports describe on-going collaboration with all sector regulators in the exercise of the CMA's merger control functions.[222] The CMA has also collaborated with smaller groups of regulators on projects that fall within the jurisdiction of multiple agencies, for example in drafting a response to the loyalty penalty super-complaint made by Citizens Advice;[223] its work on vulnerable consumers;[224] and the development of its digital market strategy.[225] Accordingly, as Whish notes, the concurrency regime today 'is about much more than the mere allocation of cases',[226] and indeed has fostered a much broader, generally 'constructive' relationship between the CMA and regulators.[227]

Finally, although nominally a parallel regime for competition enforcement, the concurrency arrangements comprise part of the broader UK competition framework, which is undergoing a series of shocks that may have significant impact upon how the rules are applied and evolve in future. First, there is the inescapable impact of Brexit. This will remove both the ability of the regulators to apply Articles 101 and 102 in their respective sectors, and contrariwise, the ability of the European Commission to enforce these rules (to the temporary exclusion of domestic enforcement[228]) in UK markets. Although there are fears that EU withdrawal might divert resources from competition enforcement by regulators,[229] it has alternatively been suggested that the CMA's greater workload may cause it to defer more readily to concurrent regulators.[230] Secondly, there is the changing contemporary landscape for competition enforcement generally, linked to increasing concern about the need for more rigorous control of the digital economy,[231] and a greater focus on the perceived fairness of market outcomes. Significant changes have been proposed,[232] which, if enacted, are likely to affect the concurrency regime. Indeed, these themes also permeate

---

[218] BEIS (n 32) 51.

[219] CR2018 (n 76) paras 47–49.

[220] Discussed in eg CR2019 (n 29) paras 13–16.

[221] There is a parallel regime for the review of media mergers on plurality grounds, while NHSI is required to conduct a risk assessment of certain transactions in healthcare.

[222] See eg CR2018 (n 76) paras 83–96; CR2019 (n 29) para 15; and CR2020 (n 1) paras 127–39.

[223] CR2019 (n 29) paras 172–78, and CR2020 (n 1) paras 94–96.

[224] As detailed in CR2019 (n 29) paras 234–36.

[225] CR2020 (n 1) paras 97–105.

[226] Richard Whish, 'The United Kingdom's "Enhanced Concurrency Regime"' (2018) 17 Competition Law Journal 63, 71.

[227] BEIS (n 32) 52.

[228] See n 53 above.

[229] CR2017 (n 81) para 47.

[230] Whish (n 226) 71.

[231] See n 195 above.

[232] The so-called Tyrie Proposals: see CMA Press Release, 'Reforms Proposed to Put Consumers at the Heart of UK Competition Regime' (25 February 2019) https://www.gov.uk/government/news/reforms-proposed-to-put-consumers-at-the-heart-of-uk-competition-regime and n 195 above. These are discussed in CR2020 (n 1) paras 11–13.

recent concurrency reports,[233] offering a reminder that, ultimately, the regime is concerned with securing effective enforcement of the ordinary competition rules.

6 Conclusion

'[T]he more competition there is, the less need there would be for regulation'.[234] It was in these uncompromising terms that the Littlechild Report set out, and set up, an essentially dichotomous relationship between the instruments of market control in the liberalized, privatized sectors. Almost four decades on, the inherent disposability of economic regulation is more disputable, yet the concurrency regime that the Report prompted remains intact and integral to the domestic competition framework. By any measure, the concurrency arrangements have been, at best, a qualified success: Stern appraised two decades of activity (albeit largely prior to the ERRA 2013 enhancements) as reflecting 'slow, steady and modest' gains.[235] Thus, the decision to double down on rather than dispense with concurrency in the ERRA 2013 might be viewed as the triumph of hope over experience—or perhaps, more cynically, as the persistence of ideology over evidence-based policymaking. Recent efforts indicate, however, that by hook or by crook, the concurrent regulators are becoming more enthusiastic enforcers, albeit within the constraints of their limited resources, their limited jurisdiction, and the complexity of the market circumstances that they encounter. While the paucity of countries that have followed the UK example suggests that the benefits of concurrent enforcement are not *entirely* self-evident in practice, the concurrency regime nonetheless remains a well-bolstered and vigorously defended, if somewhat curious, pillar of the ever-evolving UK competition system.

---

[233] On fairness see CR2018 (n 76) para 97; on the challenges posed by the digital economy, see CR2019 (n 29) para 21.

[234] Littlechild Report (n 4) para 4.13.

[235] Stern (n 3) 914.

11

The Emerging Contribution of Director Disqualification in UK Competition Law

*Peter Whelan**

1 Introduction

Competition law aims to ensure a competitive marketplace, with resultant consumer benefits. It can achieve this aim through sanctions designed to deter the occurrence of certain business practices that are harmful to competition. Deterrence is thus considered a significant enforcement objective for competition law,[1] with the result that 'the primary challenge facing all antitrust policy-makers is to devise a system of enforcement that achieves the optimal amount of deterrence'.[2] Modern UK antitrust enforcement is no exception. The enforcement powers granted under the Competition Act 1998 to the relevant UK competition authority (then the Office of Fair Trading (OFT); now the Competition and Markets Authority (CMA)) were designed so that the UK competition rules would 'no longer have an air of voluntariness about them': they were to be used to ensure that antitrust penalties would engender a deterrent effect on anti-competitive conduct.[3] Accordingly, one of the important principles underpinning UK competition policy is that a strong deterrent effect should exist regarding enforcement.[4] Over the years, this particular principle has been expressly endorsed by the UK legislature, the CMA and the courts.[5] Unsurprisingly, when the enforcement performance of the UK competition regime is assessed, it is done primarily on the basis of its deterrent effect.[6]

To achieve deterrence, the UK competition regime comprises both criminal and non-criminal (i.e. civil/administrative) elements. The criminal enforcement element (the 'UK Cartel Offence') focuses solely on cartels and only applies to individuals, who face up to five years imprisonment (and an unlimited fine) once convicted.[7] The criminal aspect

* Professor of Law, School of Law, University of Leeds. The author would like to thank Dr Konstantinos Stylianou (University of Leeds) for his comments on an earlier draft of this chapter. The usual disclaimer applies.

[1] On the possible objectives of competition law enforcement see UNCTAD, *Manual on the Formulation and Application of Competition Law*, UNCTAD/DITC/CLP/2003/4 (Geneva, 2004) 69–70.
[2] D Ginsburg, 'Costs and Benefits of Private and Public Antitrust Enforcement: An American Perspective' in A Mateus and T Moreira (eds), *Competition Law and Economics Advances in Competition Policy Enforcement in the EU and North America* (Edward Elgar Publishing 2010) 39.
[3] I Maher, 'Juridification, Codification and Sanction in UK Competition Law' (2000) 63(4) Modern Law Review 544, 558.
[4] Department of Trade and Industry, *A World Class Competition Regime*, CM 5233 (30 July 2001) [3.3].
[5] See Explanatory Notes to the Enterprise and Regulatory Reform Act 2013, [343]; Competition and Markets Authority, *CMA Impact Assessment 2018/19*, CMA110 (18 July 2019) [1.10]; and *Napp Pharmaceutical Holdings Limited v Director General of Fair Trading* [2002] CAT 1, [502].
[6] See E Morgan, 'Criminal Cartel Sanctions under the UK Enterprise Act: An Assessment' (2010) 17(1) International Journal of the Economics of Business 67; and C Veljanovski, 'A Statistical Analysis of UK Antitrust Enforcement' (2014) 10(3) Journal of Competition Law & Economics 711.
[7] See Enterprise Act 2002, s 188 (as amended).

Peter Whelan, *The Emerging Contribution of Director Disqualification in UK Competition Law* In: *The UK Competition Regime*. Edited by: Barry Rodger, Peter Whelan, and Angus MacCulloch, Oxford University Press. © The Contributors 2021.
DOI: 10.1093/oso/9780198868026.003.0011

of the regime will be examined elsewhere.[8] Suffice it to say that UK criminal antitrust enforcement has been underwhelming,[9] and that, despite the reform that took effect in 2014, this will undoubtedly remain the case for the foreseeable future.[10] The non-criminal aspect of UK competition law comprises administrative fines imposed upon companies and orders imposed (by courts) prohibiting individuals from acting as company directors for a specified time period. The non-criminal enforcement mechanisms are available for any type of infringement of the UK competition rules (i.e. those rules contained within Chapters 1 and 2 of the Competition Act 1998). The importance of non-criminal enforcement of UK competition law should therefore not be understated.[11]

Over twenty years have passed since the Competition Act 1998 entered into force. In that time, the number of jurisdictions with competition laws has grown enormously;[12] it currently encompasses over 130, with many keen to learn from more mature competition law regimes, such as the UK. With this context in mind, this chapter focuses on the non-criminal enforcement aspect of the UK competition regime. More specifically, it critically evaluates an enforcement mechanism that has been gaining in significance recently: director disqualification. To achieve this aim, the chapter comprises three substantive sections and a conclusion. In section 2, it establishes the normative role of director disqualification in the UK's armoury of non-criminal antitrust sanctions (i.e. its complementing of the deterrent function of corporate fines), following which it highlights their potential for performing this role effectively. In section 3, it outlines the legal basis for director disqualification within the UK, before evaluating its policy and enforcement practice to date. It then proceeds in section 4 to outline some of the insights that the UK director disqualification regime can provide to other jurisdictions. Ultimately, in section 5, it concludes that, on the basis of the promising, albeit nascent, UK experience to date, director disqualification should be seriously considered by jurisdictions wishing to operate a robust competition law regime.

2 The Rationale for Director Disqualification

This section examines the rationale underpinning director disqualification. It establishes the normative role of director disqualification in the UK's armoury of non-criminal antitrust sanctions (section 2.1), before critically evaluating its potential to perform this role effectively (section 2.2).

[8] See ch 13, A MacCulloch, 'The Quiet Decline of the UK Cartel Offence: A Principled Victory in the Face of Practical Failure'.

[9] See M Furse, 'The New Cartel Offence: "Great for a Headline But Not Much Else?"' (2011) 32(5) European Competition Law Review 223.

[10] See P Whelan, 'Section 47 of the Enterprise and Regulatory Reform Act 2013: A Flawed Reform of the UK Cartel Offence' (2015) 78(3) Modern Law Review 493.

[11] For a recent detailed assessment of UK competition law enforcement see B Rodger, 'Application of the Domestic and EU Antitrust Prohibitions: An Analysis of the UK Competition Authority's Enforcement Practice' (2020) 8(1) Journal of Antitrust Enforcement 86.

[12] See A Bradford, A Chilton, C Megaw, and N Sokol, 'Competition Law Gone Global: Introducing the Comparative Competition Law and Enforcement Datasets' (2019) 16(2) Journal of Empirical Legal Studies 411.

2.1 Its Normative Role in the Armoury of Non-criminal Antitrust Sanctions

For deterrence purposes, fines take central place in the UK antitrust armoury.[13] Like their counterparts,[14] the UK competition authorities have imposed significant levels of antitrust fines. In March 2020, for example, the CMA imposed fines totalling £3.4 million upon four companies for UK competition law violations.[15] The CMA's imposition of such fines has considerable levels of public support.[16] Although a growing literature on the failure of anti-trust fines to achieve optimal deterrence is evident,[17] faith in the deterrent aspect of such fines is not exactly misguided.[18] Key to their deterrent aspect is their 'ability to raise the expected cost of infringing activity'.[19] While not without their inherent drawbacks,[20] anti-trust fines have been found, empirically, to have some deterrent impact.[21] Rodger has found that there 'is certainly evidence from … interviews conducted in … various companies to support the view that the existence of fines in particular acts as a deterrent and motivates compliance efforts'.[22] In a study conducted for the OFT, interview data revealed that anti-trust fines were viewed as 'significant sanctions' in the pursuit of deterrence.[23] A later em-pirical study conducted for the same authority found that one of the most important tools for antitrust compliance was indeed fines.[24] More recent surveys of businesses have found that antitrust fines represent a very significant factor for antitrust deterrence.[25]

Fines though do not represent the complete picture regarding non-criminal competi-tion law enforcement in the UK. As noted above, its non-criminal aspect also comprises court orders imposed upon individuals prohibiting them from acting as company directors. Reflecting the traditional stance on the purpose of director disqualifications (i.e. protec-tion),[26] the latter enforcement mechanism was justified by the legislature on the basis of the

---

[13] See Competition Act 1998, s 36 (as amended).

[14] See C Beaton-Wells and J Clarke, 'Deterrent Penalties for Corporate Colluders: Lifting the Bar' (2018) 37(1) University of Queensland Law Journal 107, 110.

[15] See   https://www.gov.uk/cma-cases/pharmaceutical-sector-suspected-anti-competitive-agreements-and-conduct-50507-2#infringement-decisions.

[16] See A Stephan, 'An Empirical Evaluation of the Normative Justifications for Cartel Criminalisation' (2017) 37(4) Legal Studies 621, 641.

[17] See A Stephan, 'Cartels' in I Lianos and D Geradin (eds), *Handbook on European Competition Law: Substantive Aspects* (Edward Elgar Publishing 2013) 221–22.

[18] See ML Allain, M Boyer, and JP Ponssard, 'The Determination of Optimal Fines in Cartel Cases: Theory and Practice' (2011) 4 Concurrences 32; and Competition and Markets Authority, *The Deterrent Effect of Competition Authorities' Work: Literature Review* (7 September 2017) [4.39].

[19] C Jones, 'Deterrence and Compensation in New Competition Regimes: The Role of Private Enforcement' in R Whish and C Townley (eds), *New Competition Jurisdictions: Shaping Policies and Building Institutions* (Edward Elgar Publishing 2012) 171.

[20] See W Wils, 'Optimal Antitrust Fines: Theory and Practice' (2006) 29(2) World Competition 183.

[21] See P Buccirossi, L Cari, T Duso, G Spagnolo, and C Vitale, 'Deterrence in Competition Law', GESY Discussion Paper No 285 (October 2009) 19–22.

[22] B Rodger, 'Competition Law Compliance Programmes: A Study of Motivations and Practice' (2005) 28(3) World Competition 349, 358.

[23] Office of Fair Trading, *The Deterrent Effect of Competition Enforcement by the OFT—A Report Prepared for the OFT by Deloitte*, OFT 962 (November 2007) 71.

[24] Office of Fair Trading, *The Impact of Competition Interventions on Compliance and Deterrence: Final Report*, OFT 1391 (December 2011) 11.

[25] See R van der Noll and B Baarsma, 'Compliance with Cartel Laws and the Determinants of Deterrence—An Empirical Investigation' (2017) 13(2–3) European Competition Journal 336.

[26] See C Bradley, 'Enterprise and Entrepreneurship: The Impact of Director Disqualification' (2001) 1(1) Journal of Corporate Law Studies 53, 64–65; and Hansard, House of Commons, Session 1999–2000, Standing Committee B (7 November 2000) Col 119.

need to 'protect the public by disqualifying a person in consequence of ... her involvement in an infringement of competition law'.[27] This idea of protection has not been lost on UK competition officials. In March 2019, for example, the Executive Director, Enforcement, at the CMA, noted that the idea behind director disqualification is that it 'protect[s] the public from individuals who, in their business activities, are involved in anti-competitive practices – and [sends] a clear message about the personal responsibility that business people have for ensuring compliance with competition laws'.[28] As intimated by the idea of communicating a 'clear message' to directors, protection per se is not the only enforcement impact of director disqualification. An inherent aspect of such (protection-oriented) orders is their seeking of deterrence; after all, as acknowledged by Sir Andrew Park in Re Morija plc, '[p]artly a disqualification order or undertaking achieves its purpose of protecting the public by deterring other directors from misconduct which might lead to disqualification proceedings against them'.[29] Alongside firm-focused administrative fines, such orders thus have a *complementary role* to play in securing the *deterrence* of anti-competitive behaviour.[30] Not long after their addition to the statute books, this deterrent impact of director disqualification was emphasized in a survey conducted for the OFT, which found that '[w]hile the sanction has not yet been used, the threat ... is seen as a serious one by both lawyers and companies, and many thought that a greater use of this sanction would improve deterrence'.[31] The OFT expressly accepted this point and openly acknowledged that 'individual deterrence is ... important and that this in turn protects the public', with the result that the objectives of protection and punishment can be seen as 'complementary' to one another.[32] For it, Director Disqualification Order (DDOs) should be seen 'as an important sanction for deterring breaches of competition law. [They] impact on the individual responsible for the breach. They complement the OFT's power to impose financial penalties, which impact on the company and its shareholders'.[33]

The CMA has also appreciated the deterrent aspect of DDOs.[34] For it, the availability of DDOs for the violation of the UK competition provisions ensures that 'that individuals must take responsibility for ensuring that their businesses comply with competition law'.[35]

---

[27] Explanatory Notes to the Enterprise Act 2002, [437]. See also Department of Trade and Industry (n 4) [8.24].

[28] M Grenfell, 'UK Competition Law Enforcement: The Post-Brexit Future' Speech, City & Financial Global 'Future of UK Competition Law' Summit (11 June 2019) https://www.gov.uk/government/speeches/uk-competition-law-enforcement-the-post-brexit-future.

[29] Re Morija plc; Kluk v Secretary of State for Business and Regulatory Reform [2008] 2 BCLC 313, [33]. See also R Gorman, 'Disqualification of Directors' (2006) 1(2) Irish Business Law Quarterly 9, 10; and R Williams, 'Disqualifying Directors: A Remedy Worse than the Disease?' (2007) 7(2) Journal of Corporate Law Studies 213, 242.

[30] See Office of Fair Trading, Competition Disqualification Orders: Proposed Changes to the OFT's Guidance—A Consultation Paper, OFT 1111 (August 2009) [3.1] and [4.21]; and Competition and Markets Authority, Guidance on Competition Disqualification Orders, CMA 102 (6 February 2019) [4.8].

[31] Office of Fair Trading OFT 962 (n 23) [5.117].

[32] Office of Fair Trading, Director Disqualification Orders in Competition Cases: Summary of Responses to the OFT's Consultation and OFT's Conclusions and Decision Document, OFT 1244 (May 2010) [2.8].

[33] ibid [7.5].

[34] See eg Re Fourfront Group Ltd [2019] EWHC 3318 (Ch), [31] (noting that counsel instructed by the CMA has submitted 'that the court should bear in mind that the making of a competition disqualification order or the giving of a competition disqualification undertaking provides *not only enhanced protection* for the public from future harmful conduct by individuals who have demonstrated failures to comply (or to prevent compliance) with competition law in the past, but *also (importantly) serve as a general deterrent*, bringing home to individuals the jeopardy in which they place themselves if they fail to observe the required standards' (emphasis added)).

[35] Competition and Markets Authority, Annual Report and Accounts 2018/19 (18 July 2019) 10. See also 'Letter from Andrew Tyrie, CMA Chair, to the Secretary of State for Business, Energy and Industrial Strategy' (21 February 2019) 23.

The logic underpinning this stance is that, through facing the possibility of sanction (i.e. the loss of their ability to manage a business), directors are forced to use their available powers to ensure that their companies do not engage in competition law infringements.

2.2 Its Potential Effectiveness in its Complementary Deterrence Role

Director disqualification has numerous disadvantages. For example, it cannot be used against non-directors (actively) involved in their companies' anti-competitive activity; its deterrent effect depends upon how close the director is to retirement; and suitable indemnification by the company may be possible.[36] In addition, it may not be very effective in jurisdictions where relatively small companies or family-owned businesses are the norm. In such jurisdictions, a disqualified individual 'might still exercise control through having a family member act in their stead, thus limiting the deterrent effect of such measures'.[37] Moreover, unlike fines, when erroneously imposed it causes 'dead-weight loss' and not just welfare-neutral income redistribution.[38] Some have argued that disqualification may even 'lead to the exclusion of experienced and efficient managers from the conduct of companies'.[39] Furthermore, its deterrent effect depends upon whether directors believe that, following their granting by the courts, the orders will be enforced in practice.[40] One should understand here that DDOs can be difficult to enforce, not least when the individual concerned attempts to act as a consultant.[41] There is thus no doubt that director disqualification should neither be the sole nor the prime antitrust sanction. Indeed, corporate fines should always be a sanction for antitrust violations. Were it not so, firms would have the incentive to encourage their employees to violate competition law, to reduce or eliminate any monitoring activities, and/or to deal lightly with any employee transgressions.[42] Such fines, then, help to motivate competition compliance programmes within firms, thus contributing to antitrust deterrence.[43]

To appreciate its potential usefulness, however, one should understand that director disqualification operates best as a *complement* to corporate fines,[44] rather than as a sole or prime antitrust enforcement mechanism. Director disqualification should therefore be evaluated against that status. Whilst they are clearly not a panacea to the limitations of corporate fines

---

[36] W Wils, 'Is Criminalization of EU Competition Law the Answer?' in K Cseres, MP Schinkel, and F Vogelaar (eds), *Criminalization of Competition Law Enforcement: Economic and Legal Implications for the EU Member States* (Edward Elgar Publishing 2006) 86.

[37] P Massey, 'Criminalising Competition Law Offences: A Review of Irish Experience' (2012) 3(2) New Journal of European Criminal Law 153, 163.

[38] K Cseres, MP Schinkel, and F Vogelaar, 'Law and Economics of Criminal Antitrust Enforcement: An Introduction' in K Cseres, MP Schinkel, and F Vogelaar (eds), *Criminalization of Competition Law Enforcement: Economic and Legal Implications for the EU Member States* (Edward Elgar Publishing 2006) 10.

[39] E Combe and C Monnier, 'Why Managers Engage in Price Fixing? An Analytical Framework' (2020) 43(1) World Competition 35, 58.

[40] A Hicks, 'Director Disqualification: Can It Deliver?' [2001] Journal of Business Law 433, 441.

[41] A Stephan, 'Why Morality Should Be Excluded from the Cartel Criminalisation Debate' (2012) 3(2) New Journal of European Criminal Law 127, 134.

[42] See D Baker, 'The Use of Criminal Law Remedies to Deter and Punish Cartels and Bid-Rigging' (2001) 69(5–6) George Washington Law Review 693, 699.

[43] Rodger, 'Competition Law Compliance Programmes' (n 22) 358.

[44] They can also be a solid complement to imprisonment, at least with respect to cartels; see B Wardhaugh, 'Closing the Deterrence Gap: Individual Liability, the Cartel Offence and the BIS Consultation' (2011) 10(3) Competition Law Journal 175, 189.

(and specifically so concerning cartel activity, where a solid theoretical argument can be made that imprisonment is needed to secure optimal deterrence[45]), DDOs nonetheless have considerable potential for a deterrent-effect,[46] in that they can act as *sanctions* that are imposed upon individuals who ordinarily have significant power to control the market activity of their respective companies. The sanction effect should ensure that directors take on the responsibility for ensuring their companies' compliance with competition law;[47] it manifests itself in two ways: DDOs 'damage reputation and adversely affect career and earning potential.'[48] By fostering this (potentially 'severe'[49]) sanction effect, one thereby increases 'the incentives for ... directors to strengthen internal antitrust compliance structures.'[50] The result of this potential sanction is that directors 'cannot simply ignore infringements that are taking place, and so they must be more active in understanding the company's activities and ensuring that it is complying with the law.'[51] Consequently, DDOs can help to invigorate more effective governance within corporations.[52] Corporate culture, and whether legally-questionable conduct is acceptable within a given company, is 'generally determined at corporate level.'[53] Thus, corporate wrongdoing can often be understood as 'the expression of a corporate culture that tacitly condones, or at least tolerates, wrongdoing.'[54] By targeting directors, one acknowledges this reality and uses it to foster a culture of competition compliance.[55] In short, DDOs 'impact on—and therefore change the incentives of—individuals, not firms' and 'could therefore help to change boardroom culture and increase deterrence.'[56] The importance of such a strategy should not be underestimated,[57] especially given that the 'success of any antitrust programme is substantially linked to the creation and effective implementation of a compliance culture.'[58] Importantly too, by targeting directors, antitrust enforcement arguably becomes more effective and fairer: 'the prospect of personal liability is a more effective enforcement tool than corporate fines, which predominantly punish shareholders and leave those who are responsible for the day-to-day running of the company

---

[45]   See P Whelan, *The Criminalization of European Cartel Enforcement* (Oxford University Press 2014) ch 3.

[46]   See W Wills, *Efficiency and Justice in European Antitrust Enforcement* (Hart Publishing 2008) 583.

[47]   I Rose, 'Preparing for the Bribery Act 2010: Lessons from Competition Compliance' (2010) 9(3) Competition Law Journal 327, 332.

[48]   A Stephan, 'Disqualification Orders for Directors Involved in Cartels' (2011) 2(6) Journal of European Competition Law & Practice 529, 530.

[49]   J Aitken and A Jones, 'Reforming a World Class Competition Regime: The Government's Proposal for the Creation of a Single Competition and Markets Authority' (2011) 10(2) Competition Law Journal 97, 114.

[50]   Z Cronin, 'The Competitor's Dilemma Tailoring Antitrust Sanctions to White-Collar Priorities in the Fight against Cartels' (2013) 36(6) Fordham International Law Journal 1683, 1727.

[51]   A Khan, 'Rethinking Sanctions for Breaching EU Competition Law: Is Director Disqualification the Answer?' (2012) 35(1) World Competition 77, 93.

[52]   See Office of Fair Trading, *Drivers of Compliance and Non-Compliance with Competition Law—An OFT Report*, OFT 1227 (May 2010) [4.1.7].

[53]   D Geradin, A Layne-Farrar, and N Petit, *EU Competition Law and Economics* (Oxford University Press 2012) 409.

[54]   M Pieth and R Ivory, 'Emergence and Convergence: Corporate Criminal Liability Principles in Overview' in M Pieth and R Ivory (eds), *Corporate Criminal Liability: Emergence, Convergence, and Risk* (Springer 2011) 5.

[55]   Cf *In Re Blackspur Group plc and Others* [1998] BCC 11, 15 (Lord Woolf MR).

[56]   OFT 1244 (n 32) [1.2]. See also M Leppard, 'The Reform of the UK Competition Regime: What Can Be Learnt from France?' (2012) 11(3) Competition Law Journal 219, 227.

[57]   See Office of Fair Trading, *Company Directors and Competition Law—OFT Guidance*, OFT 1340 (June 2011) [1.2].

[58]   D Sokol, 'Cartels, Corporate Compliance and What Practitioners Really Think about Enforcement' (2012) 78(1) Antitrust Law Journal 203, 203. See also UNCTAD, *Strengthening Private Sector Capacities for Competition Compliance*, TD/B/C.I/CLP/39, Geneva (17 August 2016) [19].

comparatively unaffected'.[59] Moreover, provided immunity from disqualification is guaranteed to the directors of the first mover (i.e. the first undertaking to approach the authorities with evidence revealing the existence of the cartel), director disqualification can also bolster the effectiveness of the administrative leniency program, as it engenders further incentives for the board of an undertaking to apply early.[60] Finally, DDOs can be cheaper to administer than other personal sanctions (notably imprisonment),[61] which is a significant consideration when creating an optimal antitrust enforcement strategy.[62]

It has been argued that, to secure deterrence, *individual* sanctions are unnecessary regarding corporate wrongdoing.[63] The general argument is that corporate fines create 'an incentive for the corporation to monitor, detect, and prevent crimes committed by agents acting within the scope of their employment'.[64] Accordingly, if sanctions are imposed upon the infringing companies themselves, those companies (via their shareholders if necessary) will be incentivized to monitor actively their agents (including their directors) and to sanction them appropriately (e.g., through sacking) when they participate in prohibited activity, thereby deterring those agents from lawbreaking.[65] Imposing DDOs obviously runs counter to that argument. To advocate their use, one would therefore need to overcome such an argument, an exercise that can be completed with five points.

The first point is that the argument is very vulnerable to attack on the basis of two clear limitations facing a corporation that wishes to punish internally its infringing employees: (a) the ability of a company to discipline its employees is limited to both the impact of dismissal (itself undermined by the existence of alternative employment prospects) and the value of the director's personal assets;[66] and (b) the director may be aware that she will have left the firm by the time the infraction will be discovered.[67] Secondly, it is too simplistic to assume that in large corporations, where 'the relationship between management and the successive levels which exist in the corporate hierarchy become increasingly attenuated', the antitrust fine will 'be translated to subordinates with fluid efficiency', with the result that such fines may not fully manage to change organizational behaviour.[68] The third point is that, even when they face potential antitrust fines, companies may hesitate to punish transgressing employees (including directors) when they are discovered, as: (i) they may fear that firing employees or replacing directors too readily may create future recruitment difficulties; and

---

[59] C Kennedy-Loest, C Thomas, and M Farley, 'EU Public Procurement and Competition Law: The Yin and Yang of the Legal World' (2011) 7(2) Competition Law International 77, 79.

[60] A Riley, 'Outgrowing the European Administrative Model? Then Years of British Anti-Cartel Enforcement' in B Rodger (ed), *Ten Years of UK Competition Law Reform* (Dundee University Press 2010) 281. On leniency programmes and their potential for detecting cartels see eg C Leslie, 'Trust, Distrust, and Antitrust' (2004) 82(3) Texas Law Review 515, 639–46.

[61] See S B Farmer, 'Real Crime: Criminal Competition Law' (2013) 9(3) European Competition Journal 599, 610.

[62] See G Stigler, 'The Optimum Enforcement of Laws' (1970) 78(3) Journal of Political Economy 526, 526–27.

[63] See K Dau-Schmidt, 'Preference Shaping by the Law' in P Newman (ed), *The New Palgrave Dictionary of Economics and the Law: Vol 3* (Macmillan Reference Ltd 1998) 87.

[64] B Kobayashi, 'Antitrust, Agency, and Amnesty: An Economic Analysis of the Criminal Enforcement of the Antitrust Laws Against Corporations' (2001) 69(5-6) George Washington Law Review 715, 736.

[65] See W Page, 'Optimal Antitrust Remedies: A Synthesis' in R Blair and D Sokol (eds), *The Oxford Handbook of International Antitrust Economics: Vol 1* (Oxford University Press 2015) 264.

[66] AM Polinsky and S Shavell, 'Should Employees Be Subject to Fines and Imprisonment Given the Existence of Corporate Liability?' (1993) 13 International Review of Law and Economics 239, 255–56.

[67] See S Calkins, 'Corporate Compliance and the Antitrust Agencies' Bi-Modal Penalties' (1997) 60 Law and Contemporary Problems 127, 142.

[68] H Amoroso, 'Organizational Ethos and Corporate Criminal Liability' (1995) 17 Campbell Law Review 47, 58.

(ii) they may need the cooperation of those employees/directors to secure antitrust leniency from the authorities.[69] The fourth point is that to expect the company to discipline effectively its directors when the company's infringement is discovered ignores the fact that the interests of the directors and their company may well be fully aligned concerning antitrust law-breaking. When the antitrust sanctions to be imposed upon companies are sub-optimal, the targeting of directors of the company may become an attractive method of securing deterrence. By targeting directly 'the individual decision maker who is [ultimately] responsible for any violation',[70] they can impact upon that particular individual's cost/benefit analysis,[71] to move her towards antitrust compliance regarding their company's activities.[72] By targeting directors directly one can try to ensure that their incentives are not 'warped' and that they face 'the incentive to ensure compliance' with antitrust law.[73] Finally, when facing personal sanctions, directors will also be invested with a 'weapon' which they can use to resist any pressure applied by their 'superiors' in a corporate group to cause them to engage in anti-competitive behaviour,[74] a situation that is more likely to arise when corporate sanctions are sub-optimal. DDOs can thus be seen as a useful mechanism to resist any process of de-individualization that may occur in a corporate setting.[75]

3 The Development of the UK Approach to Direction Disqualification

This section outlines the development of the UK approach to the employment of director disqualification as an enforcement mechanism for the UK competition law provisions. It details the legal basis for the use of competition-focused director disqualification within the UK (section 3.1), before examining the specifics of the relevant enforcement practice to date (section 3.2).

3.1 The Legal Basis for Director Disqualification

DDOs as such have been part of English law since the early twentieth century.[76] Although throughout that century the potential scope of such orders would expand,[77] they would not expressly cover those situations where directors were involved in companies that engaged in a competition law violation.[78] This reality is somewhat ironic, given that the current

---

[69] F Wagner-von Papp, 'Compliance and Individual Sanctions in the Enforcement of Competition Law' in J Paha (ed), *Competition Law Compliance Programmes: An Interdisciplinary Approach* (Springer 2016) 139.

[70] R Blair, 'A Suggestion for Improved Antitrust Enforcement' (1985) 30(2) Antitrust Bulletin 433, 452.

[71] See Baker (n 42) 713.

[72] S Souam, 'Optimal Antitrust Policy under Different Regimes of Fines' (2001) 19 International Journal of Industrial Organization 1, 3.

[73] M Huffman, 'Incentives to Comply with Competition Law' (2018) 30 Loyola Consumer Law Review 108, 120.

[74] M Crane, 'Commentary: The Due Process Considerations in the Imposition of Corporate Liability' (1980) 1(1) Northern Illinois University Law Review 39, 45.

[75] See P Schultz, 'The Morally Accountable Corporation: A Postmodern Approach to Organizational Responsibility' (1996) 33(2) The Journal of Business Communication 165, 173.

[76] See *Official Receiver v Wadge Rapps & Hunt* [2003] UKHL 49, [32].

[77] See D Milman, 'Personal Liability and Disqualification of Company Directors: Something Old, Something New' (1992) 43(1) Northern Ireland Legal Quarterly 1.

[78] See Company Directors Disqualification Act 1986 (CDDA 1986), ss 2–8.

legislative framework for director disqualification was spawned, at least in part, to allow competitive forces a 'free rein' in the marketplace.[79] In 'a significant break with the past',[80] with the adoption of the Enterprise Act 2002 (EA 2002), the UK legislature expressly provided a legal basis for director disqualification to act as a complementary deterrent of antitrust violations.[81] The provision in question (section 204 EA 2002) came into force on 20 June 2003,[82] thereby inserting sections 9A to 9E into the CDDA 1986.[83] Section 9A provides that a court is *required* to issue a Competition Disqualification Order (CDO) against a director when two conditions are met (section 9A(1)): (a) when her company[84] commits a competition law violation (section 9A(2));[85] and (b) when her conduct as a director makes her 'unfit to be concerned in the management of a company' (section 9A(3)). Although not expressly stated, condition (b) ensures that the individual concerned must be a director of the company at the time that the infringement occurred.[86] The competition breach at issue can be a violation of either the Chapter 1 prohibition (anticompetitive agreements etc.) or the Chapter 2 prohibition (abuse of a dominant position) in the Competition Act 1998: CDDA 1986, section 9A(3). Following Brexit, violations of either Article 101 TFEU or Article 102 TFEU are no longer breaches of competition law for the purposes of CDDA 1986, section 9A(2).[87] In deciding whether the director is unfit to be concerned in the management of a company, the court must determine whether CCDA 1986, section 9A(6) applies to her (section 9A(5)(a)), which will be the case if, as a director of the infringing company,

(a) [her] conduct contributed to the breach of competition law mentioned in [section 9A(2)];[88]
(b) [her] conduct did not contribute to the breach but [she] had reasonable grounds to suspect that the conduct of the undertaking constituted the breach and [she] took no steps to prevent it;

[79] See S Wheeler, 'Directors' Disqualification: Insolvency Practitioners and the Decision-Making Process' (1995) 15(2) Legal Studies 283, 287–89.

[80] C Graham, 'The Enterprise Act 2002 and Competition Law' (2004) 67(2) Modern Law Review 273, 287.

[81] The CDDA 1986 applies to England, Wales and Scotland: CDDA 1986, s 24(1). An equivalent regime for (antitrust-based) director disqualifications in Northern Ireland exists due to the Company Directors Disqualification (Northern Ireland) Order 2002, Statutory Instrument 2002/3150 (NI 4), arts 13A–13E.

[82] The Enterprise Act 2002 (Commencement No 3, Transitional and Transitory Provisions and Savings) Order 2003, s 2(1).

[83] Technically, the orders imposed under s 9A CDDA 1986 are known as 'Competition Disqualification Orders'. Unless the context dictates otherwise, the terms 'Director Disqualification Orders' and 'Competition Disqualification Orders' are herein used interchangeably.

[84] A 'company' needs to be a company registered under the Companies Act 2006 or one that can be wound up under the Insolvency Act 1986, Pt 5: CDDA 1986, s 22(2). The CDDA 1986 also applies to building societies, incorporated friendly societies, NHS foundation trusts, registered societies, charitable incorporated organizations, further education bodies, and protected cell companies: ss 22A–22C and 22E–22H).

[85] The term 'director' includes a 'shadow director': s 9E(5) CDDA 1986. The CDDA 1986 does not distinguish between directors of private limited companies and those of public limited companies: A Rühmkorf and J du Plessis, 'The United Kingdom' in J du Plessis and JN de Koker (eds), *Disqualification of Company Directors: A Comparative Analysis of the Law in the UK, Australia, South Africa, the US and Germany* (Routledge 2017) 34.

[86] See M Frese, *Sanctions in EU Competition Law: Principles and Practice* (Hart Publishing 2014) 235.

[87] See Competition (Amendment etc) (EU Exit) Regulations 2019, Statutory Instrument 2019/93, Sch 1, para 1(2)(b).

[88] To establish (a), it is immaterial whether the director 'knew that the conduct of the undertaking constituted the breach': CDDA 1986, s 9A(7).

(c) [she] did not know but ought to have known that the conduct of the undertaking constituted the breach.[89]

In deciding on unfitness, the court may consider her 'conduct as a director of a company in connection with any other breach of competition law': CDDA 1986, section 9A(5)(b). The court cannot consider the factors specified in Schedule 1 to the CDDA 1986 (which concern matters regarding the unfitness of directors for other types of DDOs not related to competition law): CDDA 1986, section 9A(5)(c). The maximum duration of a CDO is fifteen years: CDDA 1986, section 9A(9).

The CMA cannot impose a CDO upon any individual; that power is only granted to the courts. Instead, it (just like the sectoral regulators,[90] which are subject to the same legal requirements) has the power to *apply* to the courts to seek a CDO: CDDA 1986, section 9A(10).[91] If the CMA has reasonable grounds for suspecting a breach of competition law, it may undertake an investigation to enable it to decide whether to apply for a CDO: CDDA 1986, section 9C(1).[92] If, on the basis of such an investigation, the CMA does indeed decide to apply for a CDO, before doing so it must: (a) give notice to the respective director; and (b) allow that person an opportunity to put forward representations.[93] At the hearing of the CDO application, the individual concerned has the right to appear, give evidence on her own behalf and call witnesses: CCDA 1986, section 16(1). The legislation also provides that the CMA 'shall appear and call the attention of the court to any matters which seem to [it] to be relevant, and may [itself] give evidence or call witnesses': CCDA 1986, section 16(3). The procedure involved is a civil one, with a standard of proof of 'on the balance of probabilities'.[94] If granted, the order will be for a specified duration and will prohibit the individual concerned from being a company director, acting as a receiver of company property, or being involved in 'in the promotion, formation or management of a company', unless she

---

[89] 'Conduct' includes omissions: CDDA 1986, s 9E(4). An 'undertaking' has the same meaning here as it does under the Competition Act 1998: CDDA 1986, s 9A(11).

[90] Namely, the Office of Communications, the Gas and Electricity Markets Authority, the Water Services Regulation Authority, the Office of Rail and Road, the Civil Aviation Authority, Monitor (now part of NHS Improvement), the Payment Systems Regulator, and the Financial Conduct Authority: CDDA 1986, s 9E(2). The Secretary of State can make regulations to coordinate the performance by the CMA and the sectoral regulators of their functions under s 9A: CDDA 1986, s 9D. On the issue of concurrency in UK competition law see ch 10 above.

[91] The court will be the High Court or, in Scotland, the Court of Session: CDDA 1986, s 9E(3). See, however, the Section 16 Enterprise Act 2002 Regulations 2015, Statutory Instrument 2015/1643, which enables 'the CMA and other parties to ask the High Court to transfer a dispute about the competition element of *a disqualification case* to the Competition Appeal Tribunal' (CAT) so that it is 'possible for all disputes about an infringement decision—[including] those arising in *a disqualification case* ...to be decided by the CAT at the same time or close together': Statement added by the Competition and Markets Authority in 2018 to the front page of Office of Fair Trading, *Director Disqualification Orders in Competition Cases an OFT Guidance Document*, OFT 510, Revised Version (June 2010) (emphasis added).

[92] That investigation will be subject to ss 26–30 of the Competition Act 1998, in line with how they apply for investigations under s 25 of that Act: CDDA 1986, s 9C(2).

[93] See CDDA 1986, ss 9C(3) and 9C(4). If any authorized body wishes to apply for an order under CDDA 1986, it must in any case give at least 10 days' notice of this fact to the director concerned: CCDA 1986, s 16(1).

[94] See, however, S Griffin, 'The Disqualification of Company Directors in the Management of Insolvent Companies' in J de Lacy (ed), *The Reform of United Kingdom Company Law* (Cavendish Publishing Ltd 2002) 206 (noting that 'because allegations made in the course of disqualification proceedings may invoke very serious insinuations of personal misconduct, the courts have occasionally failed to interpret the civil standard in its purest form, interpreting the provision as one whereby a director's culpability must be established at a standard which is reasonably conclusive of a finding of unfitness' and citing *Re Polly Peck International plc* [1994] 1 BCLC 574 and S Griffin, 'The Burden of Proof in Disqualification Proceedings' (1997) 18 Company Lawyer 24).

'has the leave of the court': CDDA 1986, section 1(a).[95] It will also prevent her from acting as an insolvency practitioner: CDDA 1986, section 1(b). If the order is breached, then the individual faces a criminal conviction, with penalties of up to 2 years imprisonment (if convicted on indictment), a fine, or both.[96] Any individual engaged in managing a company in violation of a CDO will be personally liable for the relevant debts of that company: CDDA 1986, section 15(1)(a). An official register of all DDOs is maintained by the Secretary of State: CCDA 1986, section 18(2).[97]

In amending the CDDA 1986, the Enterprise Act 2002 not only created the concept of a CDO, it also gave the statutory power to the CMA (and the sectoral regulators) to accept a 'disqualification undertaking' from an individual in lieu of applying for, or continuing an application for, a CDO: CDDA 1986, section 9B(2). The CMA can only accept such an undertaking if (a) it thinks that the individual is a director of company that has committed or is committing a competition violation, (b) it thinks that the individual's behaviour as a director renders her unfit to be concerned in the management of a company, and (c) the individual offers to provide a disqualification undertaking: CDDA 1986, section 9B(1). A Competition Disqualification Undertaking ('CDU') has the equivalent effect to a CDO,[98] has the same maximum duration as a CDO,[99] and engenders the same consequences for a breach as a CDO.[100] It too will be recorded in a register.[101] The individual concerned may offer a CDU at any time during a CMA investigation or the applicable court proceeding.[102] When a CDU is accepted by the CMA before court proceedings commence, it will not try to recover investigation costs from the director concerned.[103] If a CDU is offered during the CDO court proceedings and is accepted by the CMA, the proceedings will terminate, but the individual may be ordered to pay the CMA's legal costs.[104] The CMA will consider reducing the period of disqualification where the individual offering the CDU does so in terms acceptable to the CMA.[105] Whether it will do so—and the extent of any reduction—depends upon the point at which the individual concerned offers the CDU.[106]

3.2 Enforcement Practice to Date

Two relevant aspects of UK competition law enforcement practice concerning director disqualification should be emphasized. The first aspect is that, on two occasions, the UK

---

[95] The ability to seek 'leave to act' helps to ensure that the director disqualification regime respects the human rights of the individual concerned (in particular the right to respect for one's private and family life under art 8 of the European Convention on Human Rights): *Competition and Markets Authority v Martin* [2020] EWHC 1751 (Ch), [110].

[96] CDDA 1986, s 13(a). If the conviction is a summary one, then the convicted individual faces penalties of up to six months' imprisonment, a fine up to the statutory maximum, or both: ibid s 13(b).

[97] To search the register see https://www.gov.uk/search-the-register-of-disqualified-company-directors.

[98] CDDA 1986, s 9B(3). See also ibid s 9B(4), which allows for certain prohibitions under a CDU to be disapplied with the leave of the court.

[99] ibid s 9B(5).

[100] ibid ss 13 and 15.

[101] ibid s 18(2A)(b).

[102] CMA 102 (n 30) [3.4].

[103] ibid [3.5].

[104] ibid [3.6].

[105] ibid [3.7].

[106] ibid.

competition authorities (first the OFT and then the CMA) have seriously reflected on and finessed their guidelines on their director disqualification policy. The second aspect is that the CMA has, after a slow start, been successful in securing various director disqualifications, but has done so primarily via director disqualification *undertakings* rather than court orders.

3.2.1 The Refinement of the Guidelines on CDOs

Following the introduction of the CDO in June 2003, the OFT published guidance on how it would generally approach the employment of its new director disqualification powers. The ensuing document did not provide commentary on CDO court procedure and declined to speculate on future CDO court decisions.[107] In the interests of transparency, however, it detailed the five-step procedure that it would adopt to determine whether to apply for a CDO. The five steps required it to:

(1) consider whether an undertaking which is a company of which the person is a director has committed a breach of competition law

(2) consider whether a financial penalty has been imposed for the breach

(3) consider whether the company in question benefited from leniency ...

(4) consider the extent of the director's responsibility for the breach of competition law, either through action or omission [and]

(5) have regard to any aggravating and mitigating factors.[108]

These guidelines were in place until 2010, when, following a public consultation, they were revised slightly to maximize the deterrent effect of the OFT's approach to CDOs.[109] Up until the consultation, its CDO enforcement experience had been almost non-existent. By May 2010, the OFT had 'not used its CDO powers to date for a number of reasons - for example because the conduct in question pre-dated the CDO power, because the relevant individuals benefited from immunity from CDOs under the leniency regime, or because of a lack of evidence'.[110] Despite this discouraging background, the OFT continued to develop its CDO policy. The resultant revised guidance maintained the five-step procedure, but introduced important changes that can reasonably be supported on deterrence grounds.[111] The first change removed the self-imposed condition that, before applying for a CDO, the OFT would need to ensure that a breach of competition law was already proven in a relevant antitrust decision or judgment.[112] From 1 June 2010 onward, the guidance provided that, in 'exceptional cases', the OFT could apply for a CDO without a prior decision or judgment establishing the necessary breach of competition law.[113] The second change involved removing the (again) self-imposed requirement that the director's company be fined for a competition law infringement prior to the making of an application for a CDO.[114] With the amendment to the guidance, the OFT would be required to consider the nature of the

---

[107] Office of Fair Trading, *Competition Disqualification Orders—Guidance*, OFT 510 (2003 Version) [1.1].

[108] ibid [4.2].

[109] See OFT 1111 (n 30) [1.4].

[110] OFT 1244 (n 32) [2.6].

[111] OFT 510 (Revised Version) (n 91).

[112] OFT 510 (2003 Version) (n 107) [4.6].

[113] OFT 510 (Revised Version) (n 91) [4.7].

[114] OFT 510 (2003 Version) (n 107) [4.10].

competition law violation alleged, and in doing so, it would be 'more likely to consider CDO applications to be appropriate in cases involving more serious breaches', which would include 'those in which a financial penalty has been imposed'.[115] Other notable changes concerned the interaction of the leniency programme with the CDO regime. Specifically, the guidelines were changed to allow the OFT to apply for a CDO against a director of a company that has been granted either immunity or leniency when that individual (a) has 'been removed or otherwise ceases to act as a director of a company owing to [her] role in the breach of competition law in question and/or for opposing the relevant application for leniency'; or (b) has not cooperated within a leniency/immunity process.[116] The final notable change concerned the requirement to consider the extent of the director's responsibility for the breach of competition law. Under the original guidelines, a hierarchy of conditions existed, whereby (i) the OFT would be *likely to apply* for a CDO against a director who has been directly involved in the breach', (ii) the OFT would be *quite likely to apply* for a CDO against a director whom it considers improperly failed to take corrective action against the breach', and (iii) the OFT would *not rule out applying* for a CDO against a director whom it considers, taking into account that director's role and responsibilities, to have failed to keep ... herself sufficiently informed of the company's activities which constituted the breach of competition law'.[117] The revised guidelines abolished that hierarchy. Henceforth, '[i]n all cases' the OFT would consider whether the director falls within any of the three categories just noted (i.e. (i) to (iii)), and where it finds 'sufficient evidence of conduct falling into one or more of these categories', it would be 'likely' to take forward a CDO application.[118]

When the CMA fully replaced the OFT on 1 April 2014, its Board adopted the OFT's (2010) guidelines on CDOs.[119] These guidelines remained in force until 6 February 2019,[120] when, following another public consultation,[121] new guidelines were adopted. These latest guidelines (*Guidance on Competition Disqualification Orders*[122]) streamlined the CDO application process and updated it in line with recent CMA experience concerning director disqualification.[123] Two particular changes are noteworthy.[124] Arguably, the most

---

[115] OFT 510 (Revised Version) (n 91) [4.11].
[116] See ibid [4.14]. The first exception noted evidently accepts that a 'director' for the purposes of a CDO application does not need to be a *current* director of the infringing company, a situation that in the earlier years of the development of the CDO regime was at least open to question; cf E O'Neill and E Sanders, *UK Competition Procedure: The Modernised Regime* (Oxford University Press 2007) 420.
[117] OFT 510 (2003 Version) (n 107) [4.16] (emphasis added).
[118] OFT 510 (Revised Version) (n 91) [4.17]–[4.18].
[119] See https://www.gov.uk/government/publications/competition-disqualification-orders.
[120] Admittedly, on 4 June 2018, the CMA withdrew [4.10] of the guidelines, a provision which operated to prohibit the CMA from applying for a CDO whilst the decision or judgment on the breach of competition law at issue remained subject to an appeal. This technical change was implemented due to the impact of the Section 16 Enterprise Act 2002 Regulations 2015, Statutory Instrument 2015/1643.
[121] See Competition and Markets Authority, *Revised Guidance on Competition Disqualification Orders: Consultation Document*, CMA 93 (26 July 2018).
[122] CMA 102 (n 30).
[123] CMA 93 (n 121) [1.3].
[124] Other (more technical) changes included a number of those related to the procedure and content of a 'Section 9C Notice' under the CDDA 1986; see: Competition and Markets Authority, *Revised Guidance on Competition Disqualification Orders: Response to Consultation*, CMA 103 (6 February 2019) [2.9]–[2.18]; and CMA 102 (n 30) [5.2]. The interaction of CDOs and CDUs with 'no-action' letters in the context of the enforcement of the criminal Cartel Offence under s 188 of the Enterprise Act 2002 was also explained: CMA 102 (n 30) [4.16]–[4.18]. Most importantly, the guidelines state that, '[p]rovided the applicable conditions have been met, the CMA will not apply for a CDO against any beneficiary of a no-action letter in respect of the cartel activities specified in that letter': ibid [4.18]. The approach to 'no action' letters had of course been detailed for a number of years in separate guidance;

significant change was the abandonment of the five-step process that had existed, in two different guises, since 2003. It was felt that the steps involved had become more restrictive than was desirable (not to mention legally necessary) and had created a false impression that all of the respective steps would have the same significance in each case.[125] Instead of a five-step process, the new guidelines merely outline some of the principles and factors that will guide the CMA when deciding whether to undertake an investigation into a director and whether to seek disqualification. The overarching approach is one where, before taking a decision on director disqualification, the CMA will consider 'the facts and circumstances of each individual case, the evidence available and the public interest in the disqualification of the director'.[126] The factors that it will consider include: whether the director's company has breached competition law; the nature, seriousness and duration of the competition violation and its consumer impact; the undertaking's behaviour during the CMA's investigation; and any previous antitrust violation committed by the undertaking. To evaluate whether the individual concerned is indeed unfit to be concerned in managing a company, the CMA will also consider '[t]he nature and extent of the director's responsibility for, or involvement in, the breach, whether by act or omission'.[127] In line with section 9 CDDA 1986, the CMA will therefore consider whether

> the director's conduct contributed to the breach of competition law;
>
>   the director's conduct did not contribute to the breach of competition law but [she] had reasonable grounds to suspect that the undertaking's conduct constituted a breach and took no steps to prevent it; or
>
>   the director did not know but ought to have known that the undertaking's conduct constituted a breach.[128]

Any direct or indirect involvement by the director in previous antitrust infringements is mentioned as a potentially relevant factor,[129] as is her conduct during the CMA investigation.[130] The deterrent impact of the CDO in the market subject to the competition infringement is also relevant.[131] In line with the new (less restrictive) approach, the principles and factors noted in the document are expressly acknowledged as being non-exhaustive, so that the CMA will retain 'full discretion when deciding whether to investigate the conduct of a director, to apply for a CDO, or to accept a CDU'.[132] The guidelines also contained a novel statement on the impact that a director's cooperation can have on the CDO sought and/or the CDU accepted, when that director has not benefited from leniency.[133] Specifically, when

---

see Office of Fair Trading, *Applications for Leniency and No-Action in Cartel Cases: OFT's Detailed Guidance on the Principles and Process*, OFT 1495 (July 2013).

[125] CMA 93 (n 121) [3.3]–[3.4].
[126] CMA 102 (n 30) [4.3].
[127] ibid [4.5].
[128] ibid.
[129] ibid [4.6].
[130] ibid [4.7].
[131] ibid [4.8].
[132] ibid [4.9].
[133] The approach adopted in June 2010 with respect to leniency and DDOs was retained in the latest guidelines; see ibid [4.11]–[4.14]. For a recent case in which this approach was applied see https://www.gov.uk/government/news/3-directors-of-office-fit-out-firms-disqualified.

the director has failed to qualify for leniency, the CMA can consider 'the extent to which [she] has provided material assistance and co-operation to the CMA in its investigations' when deciding whether to apply for a CDO and, 'if so, whether such co-operation merits a reduction in the period of disqualification either in the form of a CDU or a recommendation to the court when it is making a CDO'.[134]

3.2.2 The CMA's Reliance Upon Director Disqualification Undertakings

Following the introduction of the CDO, there was noticeable optimism within the OFT concerning the potential impact that their embryonic policy on director disqualification would engender.[135] Over the ensuing years, its competition officials were keen to emphasize publicly that director disqualification could operate effectively as a complementary antitrust deterrent, alongside either criminal or administrative antitrust sanctions.[136] During that time, the OFT demonstrated that it was content to impose significant fines upon undertakings that had engaged in competition violations.[137] By contrast, the enforcement mechanism of director disqualification was viewed as being 'significantly underused',[138] to put it mildly. After a very slow start, it is only in the last four years that UK competition officials have been implementing a policy of genuinely considering the seeking of director disqualifications in every case revealing a UK competition law violation. As the Director of Litigation at the CMA has noted, the current policy is that the CMA considers 'whether to pursue director disqualification *in all cases* where competition law has been broken—scrutinising the responsibility of individual directors to see whether they contributed to the breach, or had reason to suspect it but failed to stop it, or ought to have known about it'.[139] Nevertheless, the CMA has mainly managed to secure CDUs, rather than CDOs, against directors. This is not to say, however, that the CMA is uncomfortable seeking CDOs from the courts. Indeed, two applications were made recently (26 March 2020) by the CMA to the High Court of Justice, Business and Property Courts to secure CDOs, but in that case both of the individuals eventually provided CDUs (both for 6.5 years) to the CMA and the applications were withdrawn.[140] This outcome was not a novel development. In fact, the same phenomenon occurred a year earlier, when on 30 April 2019, two months after the (very first) issuing of proceedings by the CMA in the High Court which was aimed at the securing of two DDOs, one of the individuals concerned offered a (5-year) CDU.[141] Importantly, on 3 July 2020, the

---

[134] CMA 102 (n 30) [4.15].

[135] See M Bloom, 'Key Challenges in Enforcing the Competition Act' (2003) 2(2) Competition Law Journal 85, 93.

[136] See S Blake, 'Criminal and Civil Cartel Enforcement: Issues and Challenges for Advisors and Authorities—Perspective of the Authority' (2008) 7(1) Competition Law Journal 9, 10–11.

[137] See A Jones and D Trapp, 'Penalties under the Competition Act 1998: March 2000 to March 2010' (2010) 9(2) Competition Law Journal 228.

[138] C O'Grady and L Maclean, 'Concurrency Past, Present, and Future: Too Many Cooks' (2014) 13(2) Competition Law Journal 163, 173.

[139] J Radke, 'Director Disqualification: An Increasing Risk', Competition and Markets Authority Blog (22 May 2019) https://competitionandmarkets.blog.gov.uk/2019/05/22/director-disqualification-an-increasing-risk (emphasis added). See also Institute of Risk Management and Competition and Markets Authority, *Competition Law Risk: A Short Guide* (10 September 2020) https://www.gov.uk/government/publications/competition-law-risk-a-short-guide/competition-law-risk-a-short-guide (providing that the CMA 'now consider[s] whether to pursue director disqualification in all cases where competition law has been broken').

[140] See Competition and Markets Authority, 'Estate Agent Directors Disqualified for Roles in Illegal Cartel' (15 June 2020). For access to the CDUs see https://www.gov.uk/cma-cases/residential-estate-agency-services-in-the-berkshire-area-director-disqualification.

[141] See https://www.gov.uk/cma-cases/residential-estate-agency-services-in-the-burnham-on-sea-area-director-disqualification.

CMA was successful in obtaining its first—and, at the time of writing, its only—CDO, when in the High Court, Insolvency and Companies Court Judge Jones disqualified Mr Michael Martin from being a company director for a period of 7 years.[142] Two CDO applications are currently pending in the Northern Ireland High Court,[143] whilst one such application is pending in the High Court of Justice, Business and Property Courts.[144] To date though, whilst the CMA is prepared to issue CDO proceedings in the courts, the enforcement of competition law via director disqualification has depended primarily upon the willingness of directors to engage with the CMA and to decline, ultimately, to take their chances in court. To be clear, it is true that, in the *Marine Hoses* case, Judge Rivlin imposed periods of director disqualification on the three convicted defendants of seven, five, and seven years respectively.[145] That case, however, was a criminal one, where the defendants pleaded guilty to the commission of the UK Cartel Offence.[146] Therefore, the orders that were imposed involved reliance upon section 2 CDDA 1986,[147] and not section 9A. The same can be said for the (seven-year) DDO that was imposed on 15 September 2017 upon Barry Cooper, after he pleaded guilty to the commission of the criminal Cartel Offence.[148] These two cases therefore involved the imposition of non-competition-related DDOs rather than CDOs as such; so, whilst the existence of those specific orders may have some deterrent effect,[149] it does not contribute to the CMA's record concerning sections 9A and 9B CDDA 1986.

At present (September 2020), the CMA has obtained 1 CDO and 18 CDUs in seven different cases, with two of those CDUs relating to the same individual.[150] This enforcement effort has been expended only very recently (see Figure 11.1). The first CDU was accepted in December 2016. Although none were accepted in 2017, from 2018 onwards there is a steady rise in the number of such undertakings. By 2019, the CMA was clearly ramping up its enforcement of competition law through the use of director disqualification.[151] In that year alone, it secured 9 director disqualifications, which was three times the total number of CDUs it had secured in the previous 16 years of the life of the CDU procedure. This focus on CDUs is likely to continue, not least because of their advantages to the CMA in terms of cost and time.[152] In the first nine months of 2020, the CMA has already secured six such undertakings in addition to its first CDO.

---

[142] See *Competition and Markets Authority v Martin* (n 95).

[143] See https://www.gov.uk/cma-cases/supply-of-precast-concrete-drainage-products-director-disqualification (Eoin McCann and Francis McCann).

[144] See https://www.gov.uk/cma-cases/suppliers-of-antidepressants-director-disqualification (Pritesh Sonpal).

[145] See *R v Whittle, Brammar and Allison*, Sentencing Remarks, Crown Court at Southwark (11 June 2008).

[146] While the terms of imprisonment were appealed by the defendants, their disqualification orders were not; see *R v Whittle, Brammar and Allison* [2008] EWCA Crim 2560. This fact has led MacCulloch to argue that CDOs may therefore 'constitute a much less effective deterrent; perhaps because imprisonment would effectively end a career, or it may be that CDOs are not, in reality, a significant hindrance to future earnings': A MacCulloch, 'The Cartel Offence' in B Rodger (ed), *Ten Years of UK Competition Law Reform* (Dundee University Press 2010) 291.

[147] Section 2(1) of the CDDA 1986 allows the sentencing court in a criminal case to impose a DDO on a director who is found guilty (whether on indictment or summarily) of committing an indictable offence 'in connection with the promotion, formation, management, liquidation or striking off of a company'.

[148] *R v Cooper*, Unreported, Crown Court at Southwark (15 September 2017). See also https://www.gov.uk/cma-cases/criminal-investigation-into-the-supply-of-products-to-the-construction-industry.

[149] See B Rusch, 'Risk Modelling and Antitrust Risk Assessment in Light of UK Cartel Enforcement Policy' (2014) 13(1) Competition Law Journal 107, 116–117.

[150] The full list of CDUs is contained below in Annex 11.1, which also provides the respective details on their acceptance dates, duration, individuals concerned, their underlying antitrust investigations, and the types of infringement at issue.

[151] The CMA was certainly enthusiastic to underscore that particular message; see Radke (n 139).

[152] See N Kar, R Walker, and G David, 'Competition Disqualification Orders and the Lessons Which Can Be Learned from the Insolvency Context' (2011) 10(4) Competition Law Journal 306, 318.

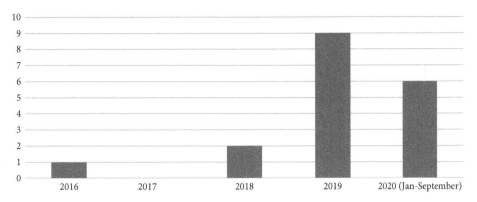

Figure 11.1 Number of CDUs Obtained by the CMA Per Year (2016 to September 2020)

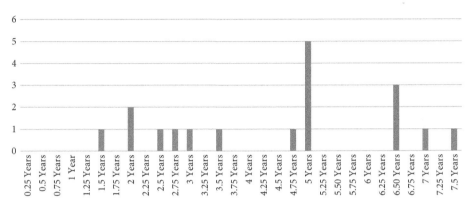

Figure 11.2 Number of CMUs Accepted by the CMA by Duration

Depending on the circumstances, the CMA will insist upon relatively significant periods of time for the disqualification itself. From analysing the specifics of the CDUs, one can calculate the average length of the disqualification to be just over 4.5 years, a figure that, arguably, is not far off the average length of the four disqualifications imposed to date by the *criminal* courts for the commission of the UK Cartel Offence (*viz.*, 6.5 years). As implied by Figure 11.2, the CMA does not adopt a 'one-size-fits-all' approach, although the 5-year director disqualification has been popular. The spread of the agreed durations of the CDUs reasonably suggests that the CMA is genuinely prepared to consider, on a case-by-case basis, the variety of factors that may be relevant in determining the duration of disqualification that best serves its underlying rationale.

Given the CMA's primary focus on (voluntary) CDUs and the detail typically found in the actual undertakings accepted, one might expect little to no litigation concerning such undertakings. That has indeed been the case, with one exception: in the *Design, Construction and Fit-Out Services* case, two individuals who had accepted CDUs later sought (under section 17 CDDA 1986) and received 'leave to act' from the courts.[153] The CMA stated that

---

[153] See *Re Fourfront Group Ltd* [2019] EWHC 3318 (Ch). For the order itself see https://assets.publishing.service.gov.uk/media/5e00b2ebe5274a33f13b25c8/Fourfront_Group_-_Sealed_Order.pdf. For a critique of the case see D Deba, D Wylde, and S Tang, 'By Your Leave: The English High Court Gives Guidance on When Directors

it welcomed 'the court's finding that permission to continue acting as a director is not a formality and should not be given readily' and underscored 'the judge's comment that he did not easily reach this decision'.[154] It was also keen to point out the limited nature of the court's order: '[i]mportantly the underlying director disqualifications remain in place. While they apply the two directors may not take on the directorship of any other company. The court's permission is conditional and relates only to certain companies in the Fourfront Group'.[155] Despite this ruling, and irrespective of the (reasonable) criticism that there has arguably been insufficient enforcement of UK competition law,[156] directors of UK companies should take seriously the CMA's attitude towards directors of companies that have breached competition law. As Annex 11.2 reveals, the CMA has yet to secure a director disqualification in relation to an abuse of dominance infringement. This will clearly need to change to ensure adequate deterrence of unilateral abuses of market power. Nonetheless, the current situation is not out of kilter with the 'official line' of competition enforcers concerning director disqualification.[157] Given the number of CDUs secured in a short period of solid enforcement action, the recent granting of the first CDO, and the fact that the criminal Cartel Offence is practically inactive,[158] it seems that in very recent years Graham's early prediction has arguably come to fruition: that director disqualification has become 'a stronger weapon' than criminal cartel sanctions in securing antitrust deterrence.[159]

4 The UK Regime as an Insightful Example for Other Jurisdictions

Following a slow start, in recent years the UK has become one of the few jurisdictions to rely significantly upon director disqualifications to enforce competition law.[160] However unintended as an outcome, it has become a point of interest for jurisdictions keen to improve the deterrent impact of their competition regimes.[161] Even commentators in countries with a mature competition regime (e.g., the US) have noticed the UK's approach and

---

Subject to Competition Disqualification Orders May Obtain Limited Permission to Act' (2020) 19(1) Competition Law Journal 1.

[154] Competition and Markets Authority, *CMA Statement on Design, Construction and Fit-Out Services Director Disqualification* (10 December 2019) https://www.gov.uk/government/news/cma-statement-on-design-construction-and-fit-out-services-director-disqualification.

[155] ibid.

[156] See R Whish, 'The National Audit Office's Report on the UK Competition Regime: How Well Is the Regime Performing?' (2016) 15(4) Competition Law Journal 197, 198; and Rodger, 'Application of the Domestic and EU Antitrust Prohibitions' (n 11).

[157] See A Coscelli, 'Closer to Consumers—Competition and Consumer Protection for the 2020s', Speech delivered by the Chief Executive of the CMA, at Policy Exchange (25 February 2020).

[158] Not only has the enforcement of the UK Cartel Offence been rather dismal to date, there have been no 'open' criminal cartel cases since 15 September 2017; see https://www.gov.uk/cma-cases?case_type%5B%5D=criminal-cartels.

[159] Graham (n 80) 288.

[160] Other jurisdictions that can impose DDOs for competition law violations include eg Australia, Lithuania, Mexico, Slovenia, Sweden, and Russia; see: G Lusty, 'Refining the Anti-Cartel Toolkit: Complements to Corporate Fines' (2010) 9(3) Competition Law Journal 338, 348; and OECD, *Sanctions in Antitrust Cases*, DAF/COMP/GF(2016)6, Paris (14 October 2016) 34.

[161] See S Muralidharan and C Deshpande, 'Scope for Intersection Between Antitrust Laws and Corporate Governance Principles Vis-À-Vis Cartels Deterrence in India' (2016) 9 NUJS Law Review 93, 135 (arguing that India should follow the UK approach to director disqualification).

are keen to see if it would work at home.[162] The above-detailed development of both the UK regime and the CMA's enforcement policy allow one to present insights that can be useful to those jurisdictions. These insights concern both effectiveness (section 4.1) and legitimacy (section 4.2).

4.1 Effectiveness

It would be easy to argue that the CMA's almost 20-year record on director disqualification is quite underwhelming and that, therefore, the UK has little to offer observers about how to use it to ensure *effective* antitrust enforcement. After all, the criticism that director disqualification was completely underused in the past is valid, and, although enforcement efforts have ramped up, the CMA has managed to obtain only one CDO from the courts. Clearly, there are a number of effectiveness-related challenges that remain to be met by the CMA. For example, it only persuaded a single judge of the necessity and appropriateness of imposing a CDO upon a specific individual. Despite its successes with CDUs, it has thus not fully created a credible threat of effective court action concerning director disqualification.[163] The natural result is a lack of concrete knowledge concerning the general factors and circumstances that the courts would consider relevant when evaluating the 'unfitness' of the individual to act as a director on the basis of her link to breaches of competition,[164] as well as concerning general judicial attitudes towards the appropriate duration of CDOs.[165] Public knowledge of these general factors, circumstances and attitudes is needed to achieve a solid threat to underpin the efforts to deter anti-competitive behaviour. In addition, appropriate Chapter 2 infringements have yet to be relied upon by the CMA to create a firm threat of director disqualification with respect to (clearly unlawful) unilateral conduct.[166] The CMA needs to continue to increase the number of CDUs and, very importantly, to seek (and obtain) more CDOs, if it is to genuinely increase the deterrent impact of personal sanctions for the violation of UK competition law.[167] Consequently, it needs to receive 'significant additional investment of investigative resources', as was in fact called for almost ten years ago.[168] The current author does not deny this reality. It is very likely that the CMA

---

[162] See Huffman (n 73) 111; S W Wailer, 'Corporate Governance and Competition Policy' 18(4) George Mason University Law Review 833, 866; and D Ginsburg and J Wright, 'Antitrust Sanctions' (2010) 6(2) Competition Policy International 19.

[163] See S Caliskan, 'Individual Behaviour, Regulatory Liability, and a Company's Exposure to Risk: The Deterrent Effect of Individual Sanctions in UK Competition Law' (2019) 10(6) Journal of European Competition Law & Practice 386, 390.

[164] See S Caliskan and S Oner, 'Individual Sanctions of Competition Law: A Comparison between the UK and Turkey' (2019) 28(1) European Review 154, 161–62.

[165] See, however, Kar and others (n 152) 135–136 (noting that the courts could rely upon the three-tier approach to seriousness adopted in *Re Sevenoaks* [1991] Ch 164, 174). The judge that imposed the sole CDO to date in fact adopted such an approach; see *Competition and Markets Authority v Martin* (n 95) [112].

[166] Not all instances of abuse of dominance should lead to the imposition of sanctions, particularly where the abuse at issue is a very novel one; see M Eben, 'Fining Google: A Missed Opportunity for Legal Certainty?' (2018) 14(1) European Competition Journal 129. See also OFT 1244 (n 32) [7.2] (noting the comment that it received that '[i]t would be a step too far to apply for a CDO in a case involving a novel infringement and where a director did not know of the breach').

[167] J Galloway, 'Securing the Legitimacy of Individual Sanctions in UK Competition Law' (2017) 40(1) World Competition 121, 154.

[168] J Ellison, 'Individual Deterrence and Competition Disqualification Orders' (2011) 10(1) Competition Law Journal 65, 65.

would not deny it either, particularly given its readiness to refine its director disqualification policy in acknowledgement of underperformance and ineffectiveness.

Such a critical stance, though, should not lead one to ignore the significance of the case study on director disqualification presented by the UK competition regime. A sole focus on the above-noted criticisms would be a slight disservice to the CMA's evident (albeit only recent) drive to ensure effectiveness in this context; more importantly, it would miss an important effectiveness-focused insight that can be gained from the UK regime, one that concerns the conceptualization of the behaviour that should underpin director disqualification. Indeed, the development of the UK regime has highlighted the importance of deciding on the type of individual conduct that is relevant to the seeking of a director disqualification. Wisely, the UK legislation does not allow director disqualification merely on the basis of a proven competition violation by the director's company: it also requires proof that the director's conduct makes her unfit to manage a business. This important additional element provides (welcome) scope to evaluate the director's link with the competition violation, and particularly so when decisions on applications for CDOs are made. This scope is welcome as it allows one to craft disqualification policy in a manner that maximizes its potential to in-centivize compliance.

Initially, that potential was not in fact maximized by the UK competition authority. In articulating its original policy on DDOs, the OFT largely confined itself to pursuing those directors who had displayed some direct link with the competition breach: in its self-imposed hierarchy of conduct, the OFT implied that it would be significantly less interested in seeking DDOs against those directors who did not participate directly in the infringement than those who did. Furthermore, whilst those who failed to take corrective action following a breach were 'quite likely' to be subject to a CDO application, this course of action was not enthusiastically endorsed concerning directors who failed to keep up with their companies' activities (i.e. it was not 'ruled out', a stance that hardly displays fer-vour for action). This approach was highly criticized at the time, with Hughes, for example, arguing that

> [i]t is not clear why the OFT seems willing to circumscribe its potential use of the dir-ector disqualification procedure for competition law infringements. Its guidelines seem inconsistent both with the textual content and general aims of the CDDA and with the duty of care which may be expected of a director under English company law. Fuller use of the CDDA where competition law breaches have occurred could affect perceptions of the director's general duty of care, perhaps requiring a greater respect for competition law compliance.[169]

The OFT's initial approach here undeniably incentivizes directors to remain ignorant of their companies' competition compliance record and efforts, rather than encouraging them personally to become proactive in seeking competition compliance through reliance upon their powers as directors. What is required instead, then, is an approach that incentivizes directors to use their best efforts to secure competition compliance.

---

[169] P Hughes, 'Directors' Personal Liability for Cartel Activity under UK and EC law: A Tangled Web' (2008) 29(11) European Competition Law Review 632, 645.

Clearly, a strict liability approach should not be advocated here, where (following legislative change) a director is susceptible to disqualification merely on the basis of her company's competition law violation. That approach goes too far. It would disincentivize talented individuals who wish to do all that they can to ensure competition compliance from becoming directors in the first place: the potential stigma associated with disqualification might put them off,[170] given that it could be imposed irrespective of their own exceptional conduct in attempting to ensure compliance. As 'disqualification should not deter qualified people from service' but instead should 'cleanse boards of the very people who permitted antitrust law violations to occur',[171] strict liability can be too far-reaching. On this basis, at least some link between the conduct of the director and the breach of competition law—a link over which the director has some control—should be present as a required condition of disqualification. This is where negligence can come in, with disqualification only occurring when the director has at least been remiss with respect to her control activities related to incentivizing compliance within the company. A negligence-based rule of liability 'invariably' can also be relied upon to encourage *efficient* enforcement on the basis that, by taking due care, a director will avoid all liability, with the result that any increase in her effort and resources to meet that level of care will never increase the director's expected liability.[172] In other words, '[a] negligence standard has the virtue of signalling to actors, ex ante, what level of precautions will, if taken, secure immunity from conviction [i.e. from a DDO]. By guaranteeing non-conviction in this way, the ... law creates a powerful incentive for actors to take reasonable precautions'.[173] Given that DDOs attempt to achieve their deterrence impact through the incentivizing of directors to take competition compliance seriously and that the negligence standard is a solid communicator of the level of action needed, that standard provides a workable minimal link between the disqualified director's conduct and the breach of competition law.

For its part, the OFT eventually accepted that it was unwise to restrict itself in the way that it did concerning the behaviour of directors, and it abolished the conduct-focused hierarchy that it had imposed upon itself in 2003. Thankfully, it could do so without violating any rule contained within the CDDA 1986. That legislative framework merely ensured that, before deciding on whether to seek a CDO, the OFT would be best advised *to consider* at the very least whether the director 'ought to have known that the conduct of the undertaking constituted the breach'; indeed, in the absence of that circumstance, it remained possible that the court would not find the individual to be unfit to manage a business. Importantly though, that legislative framework did not provide any instruction on the impact that such a consideration should have on the OFT's decision; thus, the authority could itself decide on the weight to give it. The lesson that other jurisdictions should take from the OFT's abandonment of its earlier approach is that, although reliance on a less direct link between the director's conduct and the infringement brings risk in that a court may fail to see the

---

[170] For evidence that DDOs can involve stigma see A Walters, 'Bare Undertakings in Disqualification Proceedings: A Postscript' (2002) 23(4) Company Law 123, 123.

[171] J Markham, 'The Failure of Corporate Governance Standards and Antitrust Compliance' (2013) 58(3) South Dakota Law Review 499, 537.

[172] J Arlen, 'The Potential Perverse Effects of Corporate Criminal Liability' (1994) 23(2) Journal of Legal Studies 833, 862. Employing negligence as a minimum requirement of a director's conduct underpinning disqualification would also improve the legitimacy of enforcement and not just its efficiency/effectiveness; see s 4.2.1 below.

[173] AP Simester, 'Is Strict Liability Always Wrong?' in AP Simester (ed), *Appraising Strict Liability* (Oxford University Press 2005) 30.

significance of that indirect link in practice,[174] it also 'extends the scope of behaviour that is likely to attract an application for a CDO', thereby facilitating 'a significant increase in the number of CDO applications', and with that an increase in deterrence, provided the enforcer devotes in an efficient manner 'significant additional resources to CDOs'.[175] Of course, given the number of CDOs to date, the CMA arguably still requires those additional resources.

4.2 Legitimacy

Competition enforcement must be legitimate in addition to effective. When perceived by stakeholders as legitimate, the enforcement of the UK competition law provisions becomes more readily acceptable as an important regulatory activity, to the benefit of the credibility of the CMA and the acceptability of its work. Ensuring both legality and the adherence to constitutional requirements is imperative to ensure legitimacy.[176] Due to its inherent link to legitimacy though, *fairness*, in particular, also becomes a vital consideration; this is because 'departure from the community's standards of fairness can undermine the legitimacy of the regulatory system and weaken the perceived obligation to comply with law'.[177] The UK director disqualification regime evidently was designed to ensure procedural fairness (and therefore legality and adherence to UK constitutional requirements),[178] but this is not the distinctive aspect that should be noted. Instead, in the interests of potential transferability, one should highlight the elements in the disqualification regime that help to secure substantive fairness, such as the inherent ability of enforcers to link the requirements for disqualification to the director's culpability (section 4.2.1) and the transparency of the CMA's policy and enforcement practice (section 4.2.2).

4.2.1 Director Disqualification and Culpability

The underlying purpose of director disqualification is to protect the public. The deterrence effect comes from the fact that, in protecting the public from errant directors, a sanction is created that disincentivizes others from engaging in similar behaviour. Thus, director disqualification is not about punishment as such;[179] it does not seek a retributive outcome. Nonetheless, for fairness and therefore legitimacy reasons, one should not ignore the concept of culpability when seeking director disqualifications. Even if director disqualification merely aims to protect the public (and therefore does not *require* proof of culpability), it would nevertheless be in the interests of competition enforcement to ensure that such disqualification does not occur absent at least a *minimal* level of culpability. The consequences of a disqualification for an individual could well be severe. If the severity of such an outcome

---

[174] See Ellison (n 168) 75–76.

[175] ibid 75.

[176] For an example of when constitutional requirements (namely, in Hungary) can completely scupper an attempted introduction of director disqualification for breaches of competition law see P Mezei, '"Wanted: Antitrust Criminals"—Criminalisation of Cartel Law with a Special View to Hungary' (2011) 2(2) New Journal of European Criminal Law 160, 173.

[177] R Jones, 'Law, Norms, and the Breakdown of the Board' (2006) 92 Iowa Law Review 105, 148–49.

[178] See eg the specified notice requirements and rights of the defence in CDDA 1986, ss 9C(3), 9C(4), and 16(1) and CMA 102 (n 30) [5.2].

[179] Cf. R Baldwin, 'The New Punitive Regulation' (2004) 67(3) Modern Law Review 351, 352 (viewing director disqualification as a move towards 'punitive regulation').

cannot be generally accepted on the basis of *some degree* of blameworthy behaviour, then one creates scope for the introduction of (perceptions of) unfairness and therefore (perceptions of) illegitimacy into the process. This outcome would be particularly likely when the ' "business enterprise" perspective on company law' is valued, as that approach 'sees the director as a taker of business risks, subject to a company law that respects and enables his/her freedom to manage', with the result that 'interference with the right to direct a limited liability company is only merited where culpability is present'.[180] To be clear, the point here is not that culpability should be proven to justify disqualification as punishment per se, but rather that culpability—as a *limiting* principle—can constrain efforts to seek disqualification, to the benefit of legitimacy.

What is noteworthy about the UK CDO regime is that, although protection is the underlying aim, the requirements that need to be proven to obtain a CDO provide sufficient scope for a limiting culpability principle to be applied. The relevant element is the requirement to prove that the individual is 'unfit' to be concerned in the management of a company. In considering that element, the court must consider the (culpability-focused) circumstances in section 9A(6), CDDA 1986: whether the individual's conduct contributed to the breach of competition law; if it did not, whether the individual had reasonable grounds to suspect the breach and failed to take preventative steps; or whether she should have known of the conduct underpinning the breach. There is no legal statement that culpability is actually required. However, two consequences can flow from the legislative statement of the relevant considerations. The first is that the courts have *the potential* to implement a constraining principle of culpability: judges can highlight, when refusing an order (or when imposing an order of very limited duration), that they have done so on the basis of the circumstances in section 9A(6). There have been no decisions on CDOs by the courts that expressly address this specific point, and so whether the courts would be receptive to the idea of implementing a constraining principle of culpability is yet to be seen.[181] It has to be said that courts have in the past displayed a willingness to consider culpability factors when determining the duration of a DDO.[182] One should note too that, with respect to the single CDO that has been granted to date, it is clear that the judge in that case was clearly content to take into account the culpability of the individual concerned when deciding on the duration of the disqualification.[183] There is potential therefore for the constraining principle of culpability to take effect in practice with respect to the duration of any disqualification at the very least. The second consequence is that the CMA has been influenced by the factors

---

[180] V Finch, 'Disqualifying Directors: Issues of Rights, Privileges and Employment' (1993) 22(1) Industrial Law Journal 35, 36.

[181] One should note that in the one case where a CDO has been imposed, the director in question was clearly aware of the competition law violation at issue: *Competition and Markets Authority v Martin* (n 95) [7] and [99]. Therefore, Judge Jones was obviously not faced with a situation where culpability on behalf of the individual concerned was lacking. In addition, where the Crown Court has been prepared to impose DDOs under s 2 CDDA 1986 for (criminal) cartel law violations, those violations inevitably involved 'dishonest' conduct, as a result of the wording in the relevant offence (s 188 of the Enterprise Act, as it was prior to 1 April 2014).

[182] See eg *Re Westmid Packing Services Ltd, Secretary of State for Trade and Industry v Griffiths and others* [1998] 2 BCLC 646, 655.

[183] See *Competition and Markets Authority v Martin* (n 95) [117] (noting that the duration chosen 'reflects the findings of knowledge ... and Mr Martin's responsibility as a director for the actions of Berrymans. However, it also takes into consideration that he was not at the forefront of the organization and implementation of the cartel even though which is important, he could and should have taken steps to stop it'), [119] (noting the existence of 'misconduct' on Mr Martin's behalf) and [122] (noting that the duration of the CDO was influenced by 'the seriousness of the findings of misconduct').

in section 9A(6) when adopting its enforcement policy. Specifically, it will consider such factors when deciding whether to apply for a CDO.[184] By going further and ensuring that it would *only* seek CDOs from the courts when a circumstance in section 9A(6) is present, the CMA too can implement a principle of culpability to the benefit of legitimacy. In previous policy documentation, the OFT in effect committed itself to such a position. Specifically, it stated that in reforming its policy, it would ensure that '[i]f a director has taken reasonable steps to ensure compliance in the company (including asking questions and making enquiries where appropriate), then that director will not fall foul of the "ought to have known" standard'.[185] The potential result here, then, is that a 'compliance' defence can be fashioned either by the courts or, perhaps more effectively, through express CMA policy.[186] The point is that when such a defence is not present (and a CDO is imposed), there will be at least some culpability (negligence) on behalf of the individual concerned, which bolsters the fairness of the (potentially severe) outcome. By having the intrinsic ability to implement a compliance defence, then, the UK regime has inherent potential to foster its legitimacy.

4.2.2 Transparency of CMA Policy and Practice

Whilst the current CMA record on director disqualifications can undoubtedly be criticized, the same cannot be said for its efforts to ensure that its disqualification policy is transparent and well understood. Guidance on the operation of director disqualification has been present since its introduction. This guidance has been revised significantly in response to both criticism and the authority's increased experience. Revisions were made after robust public consultations involving the publication in various publicly-available documents of questions for stakeholders, draft guidance (where applicable), summaries of responses, and positions ultimately adopted. Although the OFT/CMA did not implement changes on the basis of a simple majority of responses, it certainly gave the impression that suggestions and concerns were taken seriously, reflected upon and taken into account when appropriate to do so. The OFT/CMA has been prepared to depart from its proposals when convincing arguments have been made against them.[187] It has also made a solid effort to rationalize any changes that it has adopted with credible arguments, including when any changes have been made with some degree of opposition from consultation respondents. These actions have injected a commendable degree of transparency into policy creation, to the benefit of legitimacy in competition enforcement.

The CMA has also actively ensured that its (recent) enforcement practice concerning the seeking of director disqualification orders and, more frequently, its acceptance of director disqualification undertakings is publicized appropriately so that directors can take notice and, consequently, take steps in their respective companies to ensure competition compliance. Numerous speeches by CMA officials have underlined the CMA's performance on director disqualification and have highlighted the importance of this

---

[184] CMA 102 (n 30) [4.5]. In addition, and importantly, the CMA will also consider the individual's conduct during its investigation, another factor that provides some scope for allowing culpability to influence the process: ibid [4.7].

[185] OFT 1244 (n 32) [6.20].

[186] One should note here that corporate compliance programmes can lead to a reduction in antitrust fines imposed upon undertakings by the CMA; see P Henty and R Ashmore, 'Competition Authorities and Compliance Programmes: Cooperation and Enforcement' (2015) 14(2) Competition Law Journal 127.

[187] See eg OFT 1244 (n 32) [5.27]–[5.30].

enforcement mechanism. Press statements and news releases accompany case developments and copies of actual CDUs are posted online, with links to them in their respective news reports on the CMA website. Likewise, a link to the sole judgment imposing a CDO was posted on the CMA's news article that reported on the respective judgment.[188] The CMA has also created its own blog, which frequently reports on its practice on director disqualifications.[189] The CMA has therefore adhered rigidly to the spirit of its own written policy, namely that: '[t]he CMA will publish CDOs and CDUs on the relevant pages of its website and will make announcements, including informing media organisations, at key stages during a case such as the issue of court proceedings, the acceptance of a CDU and the making of a CDO'.[190] This transparent approach is well conceived and very important: for deterrence to work, it is obvious that the subjects of the legal sanction at issue need to be aware of it; indeed, it is trite to state that 'an unknown law' will have 'no impact in itself'.[191] The only legally-required publicity measure is the maintenance of a register of disqualified directors. That is obviously insufficient to communicate the existence of potential director disqualification to shape future behaviour. Other jurisdictions that are considering introducing director disqualification for breaches of competition law should learn from the impressive efforts of the CMA to create publicity surrounding their enforcement practice.[192] Competition advocacy also has a role to play. One can see from two surveys conducted in the UK that public support for director disqualification for cartel activity has grown considerably over the years, which could be due, at least partially, to the increasingly intense competition advocacy of the UK authorities. In 2007, out of the 1,219 (representative) individuals surveyed in the UK, only 48% felt that director disqualification would be an appropriate legal response to cartel activity.[193] In a later (2014) survey, that figure had risen to 75%, this time with 2,509 (representative) respondents.[194] Of course, this does not imply that the CMA should become complacent in its transparency and publicity efforts: although there is no discernible public opposition to the use of director disqualification, the authorities should continue to educate stakeholders on their appropriateness and fairness. To the extent that it can do so, the UK competition regime will grow in terms of legitimacy.

5 Conclusion

The enforcement of UK competition law is deterrence-focused and comprises both criminal and non-criminal elements. This chapter critically evaluates a particular non-criminal enforcement mechanism that has been gaining increasing importance lately: the use of

---

[188] See https://www.gov.uk/cma-cases/residential-estate-agency-services-in-the-burnham-on-sea-area-director-disqualification.

[189] See eg https://competitionandmarkets.blog.gov.uk/2019/05/22/director-disqualification-an-increasing-risk.

[190] CMA 102 (n 30) 12.

[191] L Friedman, *Impact: How the Law Affects Behaviour* (Harvard University Press 2016) 13–14.

[192] One future example here might possibly be Finland; see eg *Criminalisation of Cartels and Bid Rigging Conspiracies—Note by Finland*, DAF/COMP/WP3/WD(2020)5 (25 May 2020) [9]–[10].

[193] A Stephan, 'Survey of Public Attitudes to Price-Fixing and Cartel Enforcement in Britain' (2008) 5(1) Competition Law Review 123, 133.

[194] Stephan, 'An Empirical Evaluation of the Normative Justifications for Cartel Criminalisation' (n 16) 642.

director disqualification. The normative role of director disqualification for competition purposes was established as complementing the deterrent function of corporate antitrust fines, a role for which it is relatively well designed. If employed correctly, director disqualification has the potential, at relatively low cost, to incentivize directors to use their corporate powers to try to achieve competition compliance in their firms. Since 2003, the UK competition authorities have had the powers to seek CDOs from the courts. To date those authorities have obtained only one of those orders. This clearly needs rectifying if director disqualification is to be an effective deterrent of anti-competitive behaviour. That said, in recent years the CMA has been successful in obtaining a relatively significant number of CDUs from individuals who have acted as directors for companies that breached competition law. The CMA is increasing its experience in this context and, following reflection, public consultation and refinement efforts, it has at its disposal a well-constructed set of guidelines concerning director disqualification. The enforcement practice on director disqualification for UK competition violations is in a nascent state, but it arguably has potential to fulfil very effectively its identified role.

Other jurisdictions can learn from the policy and legal specifics of the UK director disqualification regime. This chapter only had the space to emphasize three pertinent lessons. The first one noted was that the UK regime demonstrates the importance of choosing the correct link between the conduct of the director and the breach of competition law. The competition authority should not confine itself to pursuing those directors who had displayed some direct link with the competition breach. In emphasizing a less direct link, a negligence standard is preferable to strict liability in that it, *inter alia*, creates a clearer message regarding the specific efforts that are needed to avoid disqualification. The second lesson is that there is good reason to allow for culpability of the director to influence the decision whether to apply for a CDO and/or the courts' decision concerning that application: it helps to ensure that the director disqualification regime is perceived by stakeholders to be legitimate. The final lesson concerns the commendable effort of the UK competition authorities to inject transparency into both the creation and refinement of enforcement policy and the operation of decisional practice, a process that also improves legitimacy. Director disqualification should be seriously considered by jurisdictions that wish to operate a robust competition law enforcement regime. Those jurisdictions would be advised to take on board the specific lessons that the UK regime has to offer in terms of both effectiveness and legitimacy.

Annex 11.1: CDUs Obtained by the CMA[195]

Acceptance Date	Individual	Duration	Case	Infringement
21/08/2020	Robin Davies	2 years	*Nortriptyline Investigation*	Chapter 1 CA 1998 (and Article 101 TFEU)
15/06/2020	Neal Mackenzie	6.5 years	*Residential Estate Agency Services in the Berkshire Area*	Chapter 1 CA 1998
15/06/2020	Stephen Jones	6.5 years	*Residential Estate Agency Services in the Berkshire Area*	Chapter 1 CA 1998
04/06/2020	Amit Patel	5 years	*Nortriptyline Investigation*	Chapter 1 CA 1998 (and Article 101 TFEU)
04/06/2020	Amit Patel	5 years	*Fludrocortisone Acetate Tablets*	Chapter 1 CA 1998
04/03/2020	Philip Hallwood	7 Years	*Nortriptyline Investigation*	Chapter 1 CA 1998 (and Article 101 TFEU)
31/07/19	Sion Davies *Leave to act later granted by the courts	1.5 years	*Design, Construction and Fit-Out Services*	Chapter 1 CA 1998
31/07/19	Aki Stamatis *Leave to act later granted by the courts	2 years and 9 months	*Design, Construction and Fit-Out Services*	Chapter 1 CA 1998
31/07/2019	Clive Lucking	4 years and 9 months	*Design, Construction and Fit-Out Services*	Chapter 1 CA 1998
10/05/2019	Oliver Hammond	2 years	*Design, Construction and Fit-Out Services*	Chapter 1 CA 1998
10/05/2019	Trevor Hall	2.5 years	*Design, Construction and Fit-Out Services*	Chapter 1 CA 1998

Continued

Continued

[195] Copies of all of the CDUs in this table can be found via the following link: https://www.gov.uk/cma-cases?case_type%5B%5D=competition-disqualification.

Acceptance Date	Individual	Duration	Case	Infringement
10/05/2019	Robb Simms-Davies	5 years	*Design, Construction and Fit-Out Services*	Chapter 1 CA 1998
30/04/2019	Graham Thompson	5 years	*Residential Estate Agency Services in the Burnham-on-Sea Area*	Chapter 1 CA 1998
26/04/2019	Philip Michael Stacey	7.5 years	*Supply of Precast Concrete Drainage Products*	Chapter 1 CA 1998 (and Article 101 TFEU)
26/04/2019	Robert James Taylor Smillie	6.5 years	*Supply of Precast Concrete Drainage Products*	Chapter 1 CA 1998 (and Article 101 TFEU)
10/4/2018	Julian Frost	3 years	*Residential Estate Agency Services in the Burnham-on-Sea Area*	Chapter 1 CA 1998
10/4/2018	David Baker	3.5 years	*Residential Estate Agency Services in the Burnham-on-Sea Area*	Chapter 1 CA 1998
01/12/2016	Daniel Aston	5 years	*Online Sales of Posters and Frames*	Chapter 1 CA 1998

Annex 11.2: CDOs Obtained by the CMA

Imposition Date	Individual	Duration	Case	Infringement
3 July 2020	Michael Martin	7 years	*Residential Estate Agency Services in the Burnham-on-Sea Area*	Chapter 1 CA 1998

12

Private Enforcement in the UK

Effective Redress for Consumers?

Barry J Rodger

1 Introduction

In this chapter I will analyse developments in private enforcement of competition law in the UK over the last twenty years. The chapter demonstrates the radical transformation in the UK competition law landscape by describing and assessing the shift from a fully public enforcement system to an environment in which competition litigation and the exercise of competition law rights is playing an increasingly significant role. The core research question is: to what extent do the statutory, institutional and case law developments in the UK and corresponding mechanisms, incentives, and levers to encourage private litigation adequately facilitate effective consumer redress for competition law infringements? The chapter will assume that the benefits of the availability of private enforcement are recognized, in terms of both deterrence and compensatory functions.[1] Competition law creates rights and obligations and it is also clear that price-fixing cartels in particular can produce direct detrimental effects on a wide range of consumers in society who pay more for their goods and services than in a cartel-free competitive marketplace.

First, the chapter will briefly reflect on legal and institutional developments over the twenty year period to create a modern UK competition law.[2] Secondly, a brief systematic analysis of the case law over that period is presented, allowing us to reflect on various particularly significant issues: the procedural rules on limitation; the binding effect of National Competition Authority (NCA) and Commission decisions; effective disclosure mechanisms; the existence of a specialist court/tribunal; the availability of compensatory damages awards; the specific mechanisms instituted in relation to collective redress; and finally, the funding of private enforcement actions. A detailed discussion of these aspects will allow for a rigorous and coherent analysis of the extent to which the UK system provides for effective consumer redress and how it compares with the model of US private antitrust enforcement in the twenty years since its introduction and evolution.[3] Moreover, the foregoing analysis

---

[1] See eg W Wils, 'Should Private Enforcement be Encouraged in Europe?' (2003) 26(3) World Competition 473; A P Komninos, 'Private Enforcement in the EU with Emphasis on Damages Actions' in I Lianos and D Geradin (eds), *Handbook on European Competition Law* (Edward Elgar Publishing 2013) 228–72.

[2] See B Rodger, 'UK Competition Law and Private Litigation' ch 3 in B Rodger (ed), *Ten Years of UK Competition Law Reform* (Dundee University Press 2010).

[3] It should be noted that limitations of space precluded analysis of *inter alia* two other significant issues in relation to competition law private enforcement:—the role of 'fault' (see eg K Havu, 'Fault in EU Law Damages Claims' (2015) 8 GCLR 1–15); and liability within corporate groups (see for instance C Kersting, 'Private Law Liability of the Undertaking pursuant to Art 101: consequences of Skanska (C-724/17) ECJ, 14 March, 2019' (2020) 13 GCLR 47).

Barry J Rodger, *Private Enforcement in the UK* In: *The UK Competition Regime*. Edited by: Barry Rodger, Peter Whelan, and Angus MacCulloch, Oxford University Press. © The Contributors 2021. DOI: 10.1093/oso/9780198868026.003.0012

will allow us to consider the extent to which the UK's withdrawal from the EU may have negative repercussions on the role of the UK courts in providing an adequate system for effective competition law consumer redress in the UK. The important role of consumers and respect for consumer rights is vital in a modern economy, and in light of the recent ruling of the Supreme Court in *Merricks v Mastercard*,[4] the chapter will draw conclusions on the maturity of the UK system of private enforcement and its suitability for and success in ensuring adequate consumer redress for competition law infringements.[5]

2 Key Legislative and Institutional Developments

2.1 UK Statutory Developments

Competition law and policy in the UK has been transformed in the last twenty years.[6] The Competition Act 1998 marked the start of the transformation[7] to a more legalistic, prohibition-based set of provisions with clear sanctions and remedies, although one should stress the ongoing significance of the retained (and revised) parallel system of market investigations under the Enterprise Act 2002.[8] The subsequent adoption of the Enterprise Act 2002 provided the Competition Appeal Tribunal (CAT) with a range of functions,[9] notably its role in relation to follow-on damages actions. Institutional mechanisms and bodies have been introduced (the follow-on damages action, the CAT itself, the opt-out collective proceedings mechanism) which have sought to facilitate private enforcement.

It was clearly intended that the prohibitions introduced by the Competition Act 1998 should be enforceable by means of private law actions through normal court processes. The Enterprise Act 2002 sought to facilitate private actions by introducing section 47A of the 1998 Act,[10] which made provision for the CAT[11] to award damages and other monetary awards where there was a finding by the relevant authorities of an infringement of the Chapters I or II prohibitions or Articles 101 or 102 of the Treaty on the Functioning of the European Union (TFEU).[12] Section 19 of the 2002 Act added section 47B to the 1998 Act, allowing damages claims to be brought before the CAT by a specified body on behalf of two or more consumers with claims in respect of the same infringement[13] —a form of 'consumer representative action'.

---

[4] See further below at 4.6.

[5] Of course there had been some earlier UK case law developments (see below at 3), primarily in relation to infringements of EU competition Law which the English courts considered as a breach of statutory duty. See notably *Garden Cottage Foods Ltd v Milk Marketing Board* [1984] AC 130; H Hoskins, 'Garden Cottage Revisited: The Availability of Damages in the National Courts for Breaches of the EEC Competition Rules' (1992) 6 ECLR 257; K M. Stanton, 'New Forms of the Breach of Statutory Duty' (2004) 120 LQR 324.

[6] See B Rodger and A MacCulloch (eds), *The UK Competition Act: A New Era for UK Competition Law* (Hart Publishing 2000); and Rodger (ed), *Ten Years of UK Competition Law Reform* (n 2).

[7] See S R M Wilks, *In the Public Interest: Competition Policy and the Monopolies and Mergers Commission* (Manchester University Press 1999).

[8] See C Ahlborn and D Piccinin, 'Between Scylla and Charybdis: Market Investigations and the Consumer Interest' in B Rodger (ed), *Ten Years of UK Competition Law Reform* (Dundee University Press 2010).

[9] See D Bailey, 'Early Case Law of the Competition Appeal Tribunal' in B Rodger (ed), *Ten Years of UK Competition Law Reform* (Dundee University Press 2010) ch 2.

[10] As introduced by s 18 of the Enterprise Act.

[11] For a fuller discussion of the CAT see Bailey (n 9).

[12] See M Furse, 'Follow-On Actions in the UK; Litigating Section 47A of the Competition Act 1998' (2013) 9(1) European Competition Journal 79.

[13] Section 47B(1) and (4).

Follow-on actions could, but were not required to, be brought before the CAT.[14] Stand-alone actions and non-monetary claims, prior to the Consumer Rights Act 2015 reforms,[15] could not be raised before the CAT. Given that claims against multiple parties often combine stand-alone and follow-on elements, such claims were outside the CAT's jurisdiction and had to be raised before the High Court.[16] Another rationale for a claim being raised before the High Court related to the fact that a CAT action could not be raised until all public enforcement appeal processes has been finalized.[17] The Consumer Rights Act 2015 made various amendments to the Competition Act regime as of 1 October 2015, to enhance the role of the CAT as the specialist forum for competition law disputes in the UK. In particular that legislation introduced an opt-out collective redress mechanism in relation to competition law infringements.[18] It is important to stress at the outset that this chapter focuses on developments in relation to private litigation involving UK competition law. Nonetheless, it is difficult to separate UK private competition law enforcement from the wider European context, in which there have been considerable developments which have impacted on the availability and success of remedies in competition litigation in the UK.

2.2 EU Law Developments

There have been a number of important developments over the last twenty-five years or more to encourage private enforcement of competition law, such as: the Commission Notice on Co-operation with the National Courts in 1993,[19] the ECJ's *Crehan* and *Manfredi* rulings,[20] and the introduction of Regulation 1/2003.[21] This trend culminated with the adoption of the Antitrust Damages Directive in 2014.[22] The Commission's focus in this area has been on damages actions.[23] The CJEU has also played a fundamental role in shaping the development of competition litigation across the EU in a range of preliminary rulings on rights and

---

[14] Section 47A(10) of the 1998 Act. See eg *Devenish Nutrition Ltd v Sanofi-Aventis SA (France)* [2007] EWHC 2394 (Ch) and [2008] EWCA Civ 1086 (CA).

[15] In force as of 1 October 2015, the Consumer Rights Act 2015 (Commencement No 3, Transitional Provisions, Savings and Consequential Amendments) Order 2015 SI 2015/1630.

[16] *Cooper Tire & Rubber Co v Shell Chemicals UK Ltd* [2010] EWCA Civ 864 (CA). See also, *Nokia Corporation v AU Optonics Corporation and Others* [2012] EWHC 732 (Ch) and *Toshiba Carrier UK Ltd and Others v KME Yorkshire Ltd and Others* [2011] EWHC 2665 (Ch). This may also arise where competition claims are combined in an action with non-competition law claims.

[17] *Emerson III* [2008] CAT 8 involving claims against parties who had appealed to the General Court.

[18] See A Andreangeli, 'The Changing Structure of Competition Enforcement in the UK: The Competition Appeal Tribunal between Present Challenges and an Uncertain Future' (2015) 3(1) JAE 1; A Robertson, 'UK Competition Litigation: From Cinderella to Goldilocks?' [2010] Competition Law Journal 275. See B Rodger, 'The Consumer Rights Act 2015 and Collective Redress for Competition Law Infringements in the UK: A Class Act?' (2015) 3(2) JAE 258.

[19] [1993] OJ C39/6.

[20] Case C-453/99 *Courage v Crehan* [2001] ECR I-6297; Case C-295/04 *Manfredi v Lloyd Adriatico Assicurazioni SpA* [2006] ECR I-6619.

[21] [1993] OJ L1/4.

[22] Commission Recommendation of 11 June 2013 on common principles for injunctive and compensatory collective mechanisms [2013] OJ L201/60. See also Directive 2014/104/EU of the European Parliament and of the Council of 26 November 2014 on certain rules governing actions for damages under national law for infringements of the competition law provisions of the Member States and of the European Union (Antitrust Damages Directive) [2014] OJ L349/1 (5 December 2014).

[23] See V Milutonivic, *Right to Damages Under EU Competition Law* (Kluwer Law International 2010). See B Rodger (ed), *Competition Law Comparative Private Enforcement and Collective Redress Across the EU* (Kluwer Law International 2014); cf Komninos (n 1).

remedies generally under EU law,[24] and specifically in relation to EU competition law.[25] EU law requires Member States to provide effective protection of rights granted under EU law to individuals against their violation by other individuals,[26] but the general principle, subject now of course to the Antitrust Damages Directive tenets of effectiveness and full compensation, has traditionally been that remedies for breaches of EU law rights are a matter for the national law.[27] The European Court's role and influence in relation to remedies for infringement of EU law was exemplified by its rulings in the *Crehan* and *Manfredi* cases in the English and Italian courts. As emphasized, the principle of the effectiveness of EU law rights is fundamental for national courts in dealing with claims (or defences) based on EU competition law and it also underpins the Antitrust Damages Directive[28] in the context of damages actions particularly in Articles 3 and 4 (the principles of effectiveness and equivalence). The effectiveness principle was re-emphasized in *Kone AG v OBB-Infrastruktur AG*.[29] The discussion of the availability of remedies in domestic legal systems for breach of EU competition law lies on the more general boundary between national procedural autonomy and the effectiveness or supremacy of EU law,[30] although the shift to recognition of the constituent elements of a damages claim as arising directly from EU Law in the recent case law[31] is consolidated by the provisions of the Directive.

In the UK, the Damages Directive Statutory Instrument—Claims in respect of Loss or Damage arising from Competition Infringements (Competition Act 1998 and other Enactments (Amendment) Regulations 2017 (Regulations) implemented the Directive.[32] The Regulations are applicable only in the context of competition law damages actions and make further revisions to the Competition Act 1998. The Regulations apply to any competition damages claim where there is an infringement of any of the UK and/or EU prohibitions without any requirement for parallel application of EU and national law in the proceedings. Article 22(1) of the Directive states that Member States shall ensure the national measures adopted under Article 21 to comply with the substantive provisions of the Directive 'do not apply retroactively' and Article 22(2) provides that they 'shall not apply to actions for damages for which a national court was seized prior to 26 December 2014'. Effectively, for the substantive provisions of the Directive, there will be a considerable lag before the implementing measures are effective and have any impact on competition damages actions before the UK courts. The only parts which are not covered by those restrictions are parts 6 and 7 relating to disclosure and use of evidence, deemed to be procedural

---

[24] See B Rodger, *Article 234 and Competition Law: An Analysis* (Kluwer Law International 2008).

[25] See for instance *Wyatt and Dashwood's European Union Law* (Hart Publishing 2014), particularly chs 7–9.

[26] Case 127/73 *BRT v SABAM* [1974] ECR 51.

[27] See Case 319/82 *Société de Vente de Ciments et Bétons de l'Est SA v Kerpen & Kerpen GmbH* ECLI:EU:C:1983:374, para 12. See more recently N Dunne, 'Antitrust and the Making of European Tort Law' (2016) 36(2) Oxford Journal of Legal Studies 366; O Odudu and A Sanchez-Graells, 'The Interface of EU and National Tort Law: Competition Law' in P Giliker (ed), *Research Handbook on EU Tort Law* (Edward Elgar Publishing 2017) ch 6.

[28] See N Dunne, 'The Role of Private Enforcement within EU Competition Law' (2014) 16 Cambridge Yearbook of European Legal Studies 143, 157 and 181–82 in particular.

[29] Case C-557/12, [2014] 5 CMLR 5; see also Case C-435/18 *Otis v Land Oberosterreich* EU:C:2014:1317.

[30] See eg G de Búrca, 'National Procedure Rules and Remedies: The Changing Approach of the Court of Justice' in J Lonbay and A Biondi (eds), *Remedies for Breach of EC Law* (Wiley 1997) 37; W van Gerven, 'Of Rights, Remedies and Procedures' (2000) CML Rev 501; W van Gerven, 'Harmonisation of Private Laws: Do We Need It?' (2004) 41(2) CML Rev 505.

[31] See eg Case C-274/17 *Vantaan Kaupunka v Skanska Industrial Solutions Oy* EU:C:2019:204 (14 March 2019).

[32] See HL, Hansard 2 March 2017 vol 779; B Rodger, 'United Kingdom' in B Rodger, M Sousa Ferro, and P Marcos (eds), *The EU Antitrust Damages Directive, Transposition in the Member States* (OUP 2018).

for these purposes, which apply to proceedings which began after the entry into force of the Regulations, i.e. 9 March 2017. It remains to be seen whether private means of redress will be further facilitated by the implementation of the Directive, or be discouraged by the departure of the UK from the European Union.

3 Overview of the UK Case Law

In this section we will merely give an overview of the UK case law, before we look at certain issues in more detail. Earlier research demonstrated a slow but significant increase in the rate of private enforcement cases through the 1970s, 1980s, and 1990s, relating to EU competition law[33] Overall, to 2010, there was limited private enforcement experience before the UK courts, including the CAT, and one would search in vain for a final judgment in a damages action. The follow-on procedure was not utilized as widely as anticipated. Research to May 2012 evidenced an increase in case law judgments, and anecdotal evidence is that there had been a considerable increase in private litigation over that ten year period to 2012, with the majority of cases settling,[34] and considerable ongoing litigation in the High Court in relation to a number of major international cartels.[35] In that period, prior to the CRA 15, claimants were not required to bring claims before the CAT, and non-monetary claims were specifically excluded from the ambit of the CAT's jurisdiction. Accordingly, there were important litigation strategy reasons why follow-on claims were not necessarily raised before the CAT.[36] In particular, in the early years the CAT was required to consider two key aspects related to the scope of its follow-on jurisdiction. The first related to the limitation rules before the CAT.[37] The second issue concerned the precise nature of the competition authority's findings and the consequences of those findings, potentially involving factually complicated determinations by the CAT, as evidenced by *Enron Coal Services Ltd (in Liquidation) v EWS Ltd*.[38] The follow-on mechanism before the CAT in the early years delivered some interesting and important judgments, clarifying various aspects of the process under the follow-on mechanism. However, given the number of infringement decisions by the relevant competition authorities, the follow-on procedure was not utilized as widely as expected. There was only one representative action raised prior to 2015 although the opt-in requirement clearly limited the impact of section 47B of the 1998 Act.[39]

Judgments at an interim stage are important indicators of the potential obstacles facing parties raising competition law issues during litigation and may be crucial in terms of litigative strategy and bargaining power. In reviewing the case law in 2012, the current author noted that there had been very few final substantive judgments, which may be more

---

[33] See n 5 above. See B Rodger, 'Competition Law Litigation in the UK Courts: A Study of All Cases to 2004 (Part I)' (2006) 27 ECLR 241; B Rodger, 'Competition Law Litigation in the UK Courts: A Study of All Cases to 2004 (Part II)' (2006) 27 ECLR 279; and B Rodger, 'Competition Law Litigation in the UK Courts: A Study of All Cases to 2004 (Part III)' (2006) 27 ECLR 341.

[34] See B Rodger, 'Private Enforcement of Competition Law, The Hidden Story: Competition Litigation Settlements in the UK 2000-2005' (2008) 29 ECLR 96.

[35] B Rodger, 'Why Not Court? A Study of Follow-on Actions in the UK' (2012) 1(1) Journal of Antitrust Enforcement 1.

[36] See 4.1 below.

[37] See Section 16 Enterprise Act Regulations 2015, discussed at 4.3 below.

[38] Case No 1106/5/7/08.

[39] See below at 4.6.

significant in developing a competition law culture.[40] Nonetheless, the profile associated
with the successful damages awards in *2 Travel Group PLC (in Liquidation) v Cardiff City
Transport Services Ltd*, and also *Albion Water v Dŵr Cymru Cyfyngedig*,[41] increased awareness of the possibility to seek redress for aggrieved parties, particularly before the CAT.
Subsequently the CAT has awarded damages in *Sainsbury's Supermarkets Ltd v Mastercard
Inc and Others*,[42] and there has been a first award of final damages by a UK court in a follow-
on cartel case in *Britned Development Ltd v ABB AB*.[43] Since the Consumer Rights Act the
rise in competition litigation has been evident,[44] and the increasing role of the CAT has
reflected the changes introduced, extending the scope of the CAT's jurisdiction[45] and limiting the significance of the distinction between stand-alone and follow-on actions in that
context at least. We can identify numerous strands in the overall pattern of the case law in
the UK: the continued significance of disputes and rulings in a range of important procedural issues such as limitation and discovery;[46] a recent increase in the number of claims
being raised before the CAT, including numerous applications to the CAT for Collective
Proceedings Orders (CPOs) under the new collective redress regime which allows for opt-
out (and opt-in) proceedings;[47] and, the number of stand-alone rulings in the last ten years
in relation to the abuse prohibition, both by the High Court and latterly also by the CAT.[48]
These cases shall be reviewed briefly here.

All of the five more recent court rulings on the abuse prohibition have concerned a dominant undertaking limiting access to a related or downstream market, and an assessment of
arguments to objectively justify those commercial decisions. Two of those cases have involved abusive behaviour by airport operators.[49] In *Purple Parking Ltd v Heathrow Airport
Ltd*,[50] Mann J held that the defendant airport operator had abused its dominant position
by changing existing arrangements to exclude, in effect, 'meet and greet' car park operators
from the airport terminal forecourts, while maintaining its own 'meet and greet' operations
there. It was stressed that commercial justification did not constitute an objective justification for such abusive behaviour, and the objective justification arguments based on security and congestion were rejected on the facts; it was clear that the airport operator was
motivated by an anti-competitive intent. In *Arriva The Shires Ltd v London Luton Airport
Operations Ltd*,[51] ATS had a concession agreement with the operator of Luton Airport
('Luton Operations') to carry passengers (over 1 million a year) on the 757 bus service
from the airport direct to London Victoria. Following a tender process, the concession was

---

[40] B Rodger, 'Competition Law Private Enforcement in the UK Courts: A Study of All Cases 2009-2012' (2013)
6(2) GCLR 55.
[41] See below at 4.5.
[42] Case 1241/5/7/15 (T) *Sainsbury's Supermarkets Ltd v Mastercard Inc and Others* [2016] CAT 11. See on appeal
[2019] EWCA Civ 1536 and [2020] UKSC 24.
[43] [2018] EWHC 2616 (Ch); appeal dismissed by CA, [2019] EWCA Civ 1840. Note, however, Smith J's comments in a costs ruling in the case [2018] EWHC 3142 (Ch) at para 12: 'In terms of expectation, BritNed was substantially the loser in this case, when measured by reference to its own Part 36 offer of €135 million.'
[44] See B Rodger, 'Competition Law Private Enforcement in the UK Courts: Case-Law Developments 2013-2016'
(2017) 10(3) GCLR 128.
[45] See Section 16 Enterprise Act Regulations 2015, discussed at 4.3 below.
[46] See eg *Granville Technology Group Ltd v Infineon Technologies AG* 25 Feb 2020 [2020] EWHC 415 (Comm).
[47] See eg Case 1282/7/7/18 *UK Trucks Claim Ltd v Fiat Chrysler*; Case 1289/7/7/18 *Road Haulage and Others v
Daimler AG* [2019] CAT 26.
[48] *Socrates Training Ltd v Law Society of England and Wales* [2017] CAT 10.
[49] In a Scottish context, see also *Arriva Scotland West Ltd v Glasgow Airport Ltd* [2011] CSOH 69.
[50] [2011] EWHC 987 (Ch).
[51] [2014] EWHC 64 (Ch).

awarded to a rival bus operator. The seven-year exclusive period awarded to the successful tender bid operator was deemed to be abusive. Rose J rejected the defendant's assertion that the dominant undertaking had to derive a competitive advantage or commercial benefit through the exclusionary conduct; for instance, by using its dominance in one market to improve its own position in a downstream market.[52] Clearly, Luton Operations were not active on the downstream bus services market, but they gained important commercial and financial advantages from the concession, which gave them a percentage of revenue earned by the bus operator. Rose J held that the grant of an exclusive right to the bus route for a lengthy period of seven years affected competition on that downstream market and was anti-competitive. As in *Purple Parking*, it was stressed that the objective justification de-fence was not available simply where a business decision was commercially rational. Both these cases demonstrate a robust approach to abusive conduct and a restrictive approach to defences based on the objective justification for dominant undertakings' business decisions. *Streetmap.EU Ltd v Google Inc*,[53] involved another alleged abuse of a dominant position involving the 'interaction of competition between online search engines and competition between suppliers of online maps'.[54] Basically the claimant contended that the preferential and prominent display of their own online map product restricted competition from com-peting suppliers of online maps. It was accepted for these purposes that Google held a dom-inant position in online search engines but there was considerable evidence to the effect that the Google Maps Onebox innovation had not had an appreciable effect in taking custom away from the claimant and was not reasonably likely to give effect to anti-competitive fore-closure. The two most recent final judgments on the abusive prohibition share a number of common elements: both are rulings by the CAT in private enforcement proceedings under the Chapter II prohibition, and also involve the Chapter I prohibition; both concern access to markets related to regulatory systems run by quasi-public body undertakings; and both involved failed attempts to use the objective justification defence where an abuse is prima facie established.

In *Socrates Training Ltd v the Law Society of England and Wales*,[55] the claimant, a training course provider brought proceedings against the Law Society in respect of the society's Conveyancing Quality Scheme. The scheme provided accreditation for solicitors' firms en-gaged in residential conveyancing, and incorporated mandatory training in mortgage fraud and anti-money laundering. The CAT rejected the Law Society's argument that no reason-able alternative to the mandatory training could be provided.[56] In *Achilles Information Ltd v Network Rail Infrastructure*,[57] Network Rail's operation of supplier assurance schemes, whereby potential suppliers seeking to work on its managed railway infrastructure could be approved only by the Railway Industry Supplier Qualification Scheme (RISQS) run by the Rail Safety and Standards Board, constituted (in addition to a breach of the Chapter I Prohibition) an abuse of a dominant position contrary to section 18. The conduct was not objectively justified (similarly in relation to the breach of chapter I) by the need to ensure

---

[52] See eg Case T-128/98 *Aéroports de Paris v Commission* [2000] ECR II-3939 and *SEL-Imperial Ltd v The British Standards Institution* [2010] EWHC 854 (Ch).

[53] [2016] EWHC 253 (Ch).

[54] ibid (Roth J) para 4.

[55] [2017] CAT 10.

[56] ibid para 168.

[57] [2019] CAT 20.

safety on the railway network because it was not impossible to achieve those aims without the RISQS-only rule.[58] The decision was upheld by the Court of Appeal early in 2020.[59]

The more recent case law suggests a lower level of deference to the legitimacy of rational business decisions (and their outcomes) when made by dominant undertakings, and a greater willingness to interfere with the sanctity of the principle of freedom to contract and exercise property rights. Moreover, the stand-alone cases form an important part of the competition law enforcement landscape where claimants may never have got beyond the application of the CMA's (or Regulators', eg ORR in *Achilles*) prioritization principles.

4 Specific Issues

This section of the chapter will address various core aspects of the private litigation architecture in the UK, and significant case law developments in these areas which are key to facilitating damages actions generally and consumer redress in particular.

4.1 Limitation Periods

The most significant procedural issue in practice, as evidenced by the considerable resultant litigation, concerns the application of the limitation rules in the competition law context.[60] Until the Consumer Rights Act reforms, the limitation rules before the CAT were distinctive from the 6 year limitation period for High Court claims, and they were also dependent on the post-infringement appeal process. There were numerous judgments focusing directly on time-bar issues by the CAT, for instance *Deutsche Bahn AG v Morgan crucible Company Plc and Others*.[61] Of course, for claims arising since 1 October 2015, the Consumer Rights Act revised the limitation regime, and section 47E of the Competition Act effectively applies the same rules in the CAT as those applicable in the High Court. However, for claims arising before 1 October 2015, there are transitional provisions in the 2015 Tribunal Rules 119(2)–(4).[62]

Generally, English law generally allows for a six-year limitation period.[63] There is special provision for postponement of the limitation period in case of fraud, concealment or mistake under section 32 of the Limitation Act 1980. In relation to secretive cartels in particular, section 32(1)(b) has potential relevance where 'any fact relevant to the plaintiff's right of action has been deliberately concealed from him by the defendant'. In such cases, the time limit will not run until the claimant has discovered the concealment or could have

---

[58] See paras 311, 313. This issue was not considered by the Court of Appeal.

[59] *Network Rail Infrastructure Limited v Achilles Information Limited* [2020] EWCA Civ 323.

[60] See B Rodger, 'Implementation of the Antitrust Damages Directive in the UK: Limited Reform of the Limitation Rules?' (2017) 38(5) ECLR 219–227.

[61] [2012] EWCA Civ 1055. See the earlier CAT ruling at [2011] CAT 16. *Deutsche Bahn AG and Others v Morgan Advanced Materials Plc* [2014] UKSC 24. P Akman, 'Period of Limitations in Follow-On Competition Cases: When Does a Decision become Final?' (2014) 2(2) JAE 389.

[62] See   http://competitionbulletin.com/2015/10/01/private-actions-the-cra-2015-giveth-and-the-2015-cat-rules-taketh-away/. See also Case 1240/5/7/15 *Deutsche Bahn AG and Others v Mastercard Inc and Others* [2016] CAT 13; *DSG Retail Ltd and Others v Mastercard Incorporated and Others* [2020] EWCA Civ 671 (CA), overruling the CAT's earlier determination [2019] CAT 5.

[63] Limitation Act 1980, s 2.

done so with reasonable diligence.[64] A related issue here is whether claimants would have sufficient information to substantiate their claim in court. Accordingly, the limitation rules generally cannot be viewed in isolation, and in the English litigation process the question has been effectively whether the claimant can (or should be able to) satisfy the 'statement of claim' test such that the claim would not be struck out for a failure to disclose reasonable grounds for bringing the claim.[65]

Those Limitation Act provisions were considered by the English courts in a competition law context in *Arcadia v Visa*.[66] It was held that the level of information published by the Commission in 2001 and 2002 in separate parts of the public enforcement process were sufficient for the claimants to establish the key ingredients of the claim. The Court of Appeal affirmed that none of the concealment issues raised by the appellant were sufficient to postpone the limitation period as they had sufficient facts to satisfy the statement of claim test.[67] Article 10 of the Antitrust Damages Directive provides for a specialized set of limitation (and prescription) rules, bringing significant change to the determination of the periods for competition damages actions in relation to infringements of both EU and UK competition law. The introduction of a five-year limitation period is relatively insignificant in itself. The most significant reform relates to when the limitation period begins to run—the so-called 'trigger point'. First, this will not take place until after the illegal activity has ceased. The second significant deviation from existing practice concerns the claimant knowledge requirements that trigger the limitation period. Paragraph 19(1) of the implementing Regulations states that the limitation or prescriptive period begins on the later of the day the infringement ceases or the claimant acquires knowledge of the infringement. The latter occurs when the claimant first knows or could reasonably be expected to know:

(a) of the infringer's behaviour;
(b) that the behaviour constitutes an infringement of competition law;
(c) that the claimant has suffered loss or damage arising from that infringement; and
(d) the identity of the infringer.

Moreover, despite suspensive provisions only existing in relation to proceedings before the CAT under the old CAT rules, the Directive provision in Article 10(4) on suspensive periods during and at the end of a competition authority investigation was effectively copied-out in paragraph 21 of Part 5 of the Regulations. This provision will be significant in practice given its application to investigations by the CMA, European Commission and other Member States' competition authorities.

The post-Directive rules certainly appear to recalibrate the procedural advantage in favour of claimants. It remains to be seen whether the constructive knowledge requirements will be retained or reviewed and revised post-withdrawal from the EU. Nonetheless, under Article 22 of the Directive, limitation is a substantive issue,[68] time-barred claims cannot

---

[64] See *Arcadia Group Brands and Others v Visa Inc and Others* [2015] EWCA Civ 883. In Scotland see Prescription and Limitation (Scotland) Act 1973, s 6 (and s 11(3)) and D Johnson, *Prescription and Limitation* (2nd edn, W Green/SULI, 2012).

[65] See *Arcadia v Visa* (n 64).

[66] ibid.

[67] See also *WH Newson Holding Ltd v IMI plc* [2015] EWHC 1676 (Ch) and [2016] EWCA Civ 773.

[68] P Kirst, 'The Temporal Scope of the Damages Directive: A Comparative Analysis of the Applicability of the New Rules on Competition Infringements in Europe' (2020) 16(1) European Competition Journal 97.

be revived post-implementation, and accordingly the revised limitation provisions will only apply where the elements of the infringement begin and the harm occurs, after the commencement of the implementing legislation. This was emphasized by the ruling in *Granville Technology Group Ltd v Infineon Technologies AG*,[69] a case concerning the application of the rules in the Limitation Act 1980 regarding the level of information in the public domain which would be sufficient to either constitute knowledge or the absence of reasonable diligence. Nonetheless, the Court of Appeal recently stressed, in *DSG v Mastercard*,[70] in overruling the CAT on this point, that, for the purposes of the application of section 32(1)(b), 'the question of whether or not the claimants in this case had reason to investigate and whether they could with reasonable diligence have discovered the relevant concealment requires disclosure and factual evidence to be fairly determined'. The personal characteristics of the claimant may be relevant and the mere availability of documents in the public domain on the internet does not necessarily place a particular claimant on notice re a particular claim or mean they should with reasonable diligence have seen particular documents.[71]

4.2 Binding Force of Competition Authority Decisions

In order for the original mechanism for follow-on damages before the CAT to have greatest success in facilitating litigation,[72] there was provision regarding the binding nature of prior enforcement authority decisions.[73] Section 20 added section 58A to the 1998 Act, which provided that in any action for damages for an infringement of the 1998 Act prohibitions or Articles 101(1) or 102 TFEU, a court will be bound by a decision of the CMA or CAT that any of the prohibitions have been infringed,[74] if the requisite appeal process has taken place or the period for appeal lapsed.[75] Nonetheless, there have been difficulties in determining the scope of the effect of a prior binding infringement decision.[76] A particular problematic issue concerns the precise nature and consequences of a competition authority's findings, and this may involve factually complicated determinations by the CAT, as evidenced by *Enron Coal Services Ltd (in Liquidation) v EWS Ltd*.[77] Furthermore in *Emerson Electric Co v Morgan Crucible Co plc*,[78] the CAT stressed that 'the Tribunal's jurisdiction in proceedings

---

[69] [2020] EWHC 415 (Comm).

[70] [2020] EWCA Civ 671, paras 63–71.

[71] ibid para 70.

[72] See J Dodds and B Rayment, '*WH Newson Holding Ltd and Others v IMI Plc*: New Developments in the Jurisdiction of the UK Competition Appeal Tribunal' (2013) 34(8) ECLR 395 and also the subsequent Court of Appeal ruling [2013] EWCA Civ 1377. See Miguel Sousa Ferro, 'Antitrust Private Enforcement and the Binding Effect of Public Enforcement Decisions' (2019) 3(2) Market and Competition Law Review 5.

[73] See Court of Appeal in *Enron Coal Services Ltd (in Liquidation) v English, Welsh and Scottish Railway Ltd* [2011] EWCA Civ 2.

[74] Section 58A(2) of the Competition Act 1998.

[75] Section 58A(3). See also art 16 of Regulation 1/2003 in relation to Commission decisions. See discussion in *Enron Coal Services Ltd (in Liquidation) v English, Welsh and Scottish Railway Ltd* (n 73).

[76] See *Enron Coal Services Ltd (in Liquidation) v English, Welsh and Scottish Railway Ltd* [2009] CAT 7 and Court of Appeal, [2009] EWCA Civ 647, and also the subsequent Court of Appeal ruling in the same case [2011] EWCA Civ 2 (n 73). See also *Emerson Electric Co v Morgan Crucible Co Plc* [2011] CAT 4.

[77] Case No 1106/5/7/08. This was reinforced in *Enron Coal Services Ltd (in Liquidation)* (n 76), [2011] EWCA Civ 2 (n 73). See T Woodgate and I Filippi, 'The Decision that Binds: Follow-on Actions for Competition Damages after Enron' (2012) 33(4) ECLR 175.

[78] [2011] CAT 4.

under section 47A is limited to resolving issues of causation and quantum of loss resulting from an already established infringement'.[79] This ruling was subsequently upheld by the Court of Appeal.[80]

The dangers in seeking to rely on an infringement finding as binding were also demonstrated in *Gibson v Pride Mobility Products Ltd*,[81] a case concerning an application for a CPO. The fundamental difficulties here lay in the related issues of the scope of the infringement decision and the requisite boundaries of a follow-on action and the impact of the decision on the various sub-classes of claimant. It was noted that the claimant's difficulties here stemmed in part from the enforcement approach of the OFT, which had focused on 'the low lying evidential fruit'[82] in its investigation and findings.

The Consumer Rights Act revised the scope of section 58A of the Competition Act 1998, with effect from 1 October 2015 (in relation to decisions made after that date). It now provides that prior infringement decisions are binding both in relation to proceedings before the courts and the CAT under either section 47A or section 47B.[83] In addition, section 58A made final infringement decisions by the European Commission binding on the CAT and courts[84] but this rule has now been removed following the UK' withdrawal from the EU.[85]

4.3 The Existence of a Specialist Court/Tribunal

The existence and functions allocated to a specialist competition court or tribunal are clearly major factors in the institutional design of a legal system to deal with competition litigation.[86] The Enterprise Act 2002 introduced the specialist competition court in the UK, the Competition Appeal Tribunal, initially to hear only follow-on damages actions. The Consumer Rights Act 2015 enhanced the role of the CAT as the specialist forum for competition law disputes in the UK and introduced an opt-out collective redress mechanism in relation to competition law infringements.[87] It was evident that the High Court had continued to be a primary venue for competition damages claims. A central aspect of the reform was the extension of the competence of the CAT under section 47A of the Competition to stand-alone actions in addition to 'follow-on' actions. Claimants will not have to wait until an infringement decision by the CMA becomes final before raising an action before the

---

[79] ibid para 59, upheld by Court of Appeal [2012] EWCA Civ 1559.

[80] ibid.

[81] [2017] CAT 9; see further below at 4.7.

[82] ibid para 109.

[83] In relation to the CAT, the revised s 58A effectively replaced s 47A(9) of the 1998 Act. Note that s 47A has been revised to refer only to infringements of the Chapter I and II prohibitions by the Competition (Amendment etc) (EU Exit) Regulations 2019 (SI 2019/93).

[84] Section 58A(4); see Case C-344/98 *Masterfoods* [2000] ECR I-11369. See *Royal Mail Group Ltd v DAF Truck and Others* [2020] CAT 7.

[85] See the Competition (Amendment etc) (EU Exit) Regulations 2019 (SI 2019/93).

[86] See B Rodger, 'Introduction' in B Rodger (ed) *Landmark Cases in Competition Law: Around the World in Fourteen Stories* (Kluwer Law International 2011) 17. See also Bailey (n 9). See D S Savrin, 'Specialized Antitrust Courts: A Practitioner's Observations' in B Hawk (ed), *Annual Proceedings of the Fordham Competition Law Institute* (Fordham Competition Law Institute 2013) 116–17 and P Roth, 'Specialized Antitrust Courts' also in B Hawk (ed), *Annual Proceedings of the Fordham Competition Law Institute* (Fordham Competition Law Institute 2013) 105.

[87] See B Rodger, 'The Consumer Rights Act 2015 and Collective Redress for Competition Law Infringements in the UK: A class Act?' (2015) 3(2) JAE 258.

CAT.[88] Furthermore, the CAT now has power (at least in proceedings in England and Wales and Northern Ireland) to grant injunctions.[89]

The practical role of the CAT was significantly enhanced by the (belated) adoption of the Section 16 Enterprise Act Regulations 2015.[90] The 2015 Regulations allowed the High Court to transfer cases to the CAT for its determination of 'so much of any proceedings as relates to an infringement issue'[91] relating to either the Chapter I prohibition or Article 101 TFEU. This may involve transfer of a specific competition law issue in a wider dispute as in *Agents Mutual Ltd v Gascoigne Halman*,[92] or the transfer of the dispute itself, as has taken place frequently, including for instance the numerous transfers in the range of truck cartel claims which originated in the High Court.[93] There is an inherent risk here that a dramatic increase in the CAT's workload may present new challenges for the CAT's role and its specialist nature.

Nonetheless, despite the increasing significance of the CAT, the role of the appellate courts remains important, and the Court of Appeal in particular has played a major role reviewing the CAT ruling regarding certification of applications for collective proceedings in *Merricks v Mastercard*. The Court of Appeal overruled the CAT's refusal to allow an appeal, on the basis that this was a decision in collective proceedings related to the award of damages,[94] and subsequently rejected the CAT's determination that the application was not suitable for certification. This dispute, subsequently on appeal before the Supreme Court, will be considered further below. Interestingly, the importance afforded the specialist CAT and simultaneously the significance of the Court of Appeal can be observed in the ongoing proceedings also involving Mastercard (and Visa) whereby the Court was required to consider appeals in three separate, related cases. The Court of Appeal remitted to the CAT to use its expertise to determine remaining issues of exemption and quantum,[95] and the Court of Appeal's findings were affirmed on appeal to the Supreme Court.[96] Indeed, the Supreme Court's developing involvement in competition litigation generally is notable and it is likely to have an increasingly significant role in helping to shape the private enforcement landscape in the UK in the coming ten years.

4.4 The Availability of Effective Disclosure Mechanisms

In England and Wales the Civil Procedure Rules mandate that a party must disclose all documents which are relevant to the litigation, including those that harm its own case or

---

[88] See P Akman, 'Period of Limitations in Follow-On Competition Cases: When does a Decision become Final?' (2014) 2(2) JAE 389. See r 119 of the revised CAT rules (The Competition Appeal Tribunal Rules 2015, SI 2015/1648). See *Gibson v Pride Mobility Products Ltd* [2017] CAT 9.

[89] Section 47A(3). There is also provision for a fast-track procedure in para 31 of Sch 8 to the 2015 Act.

[90] SI 2015/1643.

[91] See s 16(6) of the Enterprise Act 2002. See also *Unwired Planet International Ltd v Huawei Technologies Co Ltd* [2016] EWCA Civ 489, [2016] 5 CMLR 11.

[92] [2017] CAT 22. There is no right of appeal from a CAT ruling in these circumstances.

[93] See eg Case 1343/5/7/20 (T) *DS Smith Paper Limited and Others v MAN SE and Others*.

[94] *Merricks v Mastercard* [2018] EWCA Civ 2527.

[95] *Sainsbury's Supermarkets v Mastercard Inc; Asda Stores Ltd v Mastercard; Sainsbury's Supermarkets Ltd v Visa Europe Services Inc* [2018] EWCA Civ 1536, paras 363–67.

[96] [2020] UKSC 24, although appeal was successful on the 'broad axe' issue regarding pass-on requirements as discussed further below at 4.5.

support the opposing party's case.[97] There are limits on pre-trial disclosure.[98] There was a ruling on disclosure in 2014 in the *National Grid Electricity Transmission Plc v ABB Ltd*[99] case following the supply of gas insulated switchgear cartel. The applicant, the owner of the UK electricity system, sought further information under CPR Pt 18 from various companies about how the cartel had operated in the UK market. The application was granted in part where the requests were reasonable, proportionate and necessary to understand how the infringement found by the Commission had actually operated in the UK and where the potentially relevant information was in the knowledge of only one side in the litigation, emphasizing the importance of disclosure to equality of arms in the competition litigation context.[100] In ordering disclosure in *Peugeot and Others v NSK Ltd*[101] the effective enforcement of follow-on damages claims was stressed.[102] The disclosure mechanisms (particularly in England and Wales) have been a significant factor in the historical attractiveness of the UK courts to litigation relating to multi-state competition law infringements. Article 5 of the Antitrust Damages Directive was aimed primarily at those Member States with limited provision for pre-trial disclosure and only the explicit requirement of proportionality expressly required to be implemented by changes to court rules.[103]

The most controversial provision in the Directive concerned the protection of leniency applicants' documentation from access by claimants through court disclosure processes.[104] The limitations on access to leniency documentation had been examined by the European Court in *Pfleiderer*[105] and that ruling was considered and applied in *National Grid Electricity Transmission plc v ABB Ltd and Others*.[106] The High Court weighed the relevance of the leniency materials against the difficulty the claimant would have in obtaining the materials from other sources.[107] The High Court confirmed that there could not be a 'blanket objection to disclosure',[108] and the courts would assess, on a document by document basis, the extent to which the materials sought are necessary for proving the damages claim.[109] Nonetheless, the Directive as implemented deviates from the ECJ jurisprudence and restricts access in private litigation to leniency documentation in a way which is unfortunately likely to limit claimant incentives and likelihood of success in follow-on claims.[110]

---

[97] Civil Procedure Rules, Pt 31, in particular Pt 31.6(b). See rr 60–65 of the Competition Appeal Tribunal Rules 2015.

[98] See *Hutchison 3G UK Ltd v O2 (UK) Ltd* [2008] EWHC 50 (Comm). See also r 18 of the CPR.

[99] [2014] EWHC 1055 (Ch). See also for instance *WH Newson Holding Ltd v IMI plc* [2013] EWHC 3788 (Ch); *Emerald Supplies Ltd v British Airways Plc* [2015] EWCA Civ 1024. See also *Infederation Ltd v Google Inc* [2015] EWHC 3705 (Ch).

[100] In Scotland note the process of specification of documents. If not forthcoming, ch 35 of the Court of Session Rules allow for an application for commission and diligence for recovery of documents to compel a party to disclose withheld documents.

[101] [2018] CAT 3.

[102] See para 30; see also para 31.

[103] CPR 31C and CAT practice direction relating to Disclosure and Inspection of Evidence in Claims made pursuant to Parts 4 and 5 of the Competition Appeal Tribunal Rules 2015.

[104] See eg A Singh, '*Pfleiderer*: Assessing its Impact on the Effectiveness of the European Leniency Programme' (2014) 35(3) ECLR 110.

[105] Case C-360/09 *Pfleiderer v AG Bundeskartellamt* [2011] ECR I-5161, paras 30 and 31. See also Case C-536/11 *Donau Chemie et al* [2013] 5 CMLR 19.

[106] [2012] EWHC 869 (Ch).

[107] ibid para 44.

[108] ibid para 50.

[109] See N H Endendorf and N Maierhofer, 'The Road after *Pfleiderer*' (2013) 34 ECLR 78.

[110] See art 6(6). See C Rey, 'The Interaction between Public and Private Enforcement of Competition Law, and Especially the Interaction between the Interests of Private Claimants and those of Leniency Applicants' (2015) 8(3) GCLR 109. See arts 6 and 7 of the Directive generally.

4.5 Damages Awards

The underlying basis for the award of competition law damages, as with other types of tort or delict claim, is compensation for loss suffered.[111] This was confirmed by the European Court jurisprudence in claims based on EU competition law in *Crehan* and *Manfredi*, and reaffirmed by Article 3 of the Antitrust Damages Directive, which highlights the right to full compensation based on the principles of equivalence and effectiveness.[112]

In the legal systems of the UK there is no specific and separate requirement of 'antitrust' standing. Essentially on a case by case basis the courts will determine which parties are entitled to seek compensation on the basis of an infringement.[113] The Antitrust Damages Directive contains various provisions regarding the extent of liability, passing-on, indirect purchasers and quantification of harm which seek to ensure the general effectiveness of the EU right to full compensation. The UK Regulations made specific provision to implement the rebuttable presumption that cartels cause harm in Article 17 (2), although the presumption is limited to the existence rather than the extent of damage.

2 Travel Group PLC (in Liquidation) v Cardiff City Transport Services Ltd[114] was the first successful, final award of damages as quantified by the CAT; it was followed in 2013 by a damages award in *Albion Water v Dŵr Cymru Cyfyngedig*.[115] In the former case, the CAT applied the basic test for causation in English law.[116] Generally the test for 'factual causation' is the 'but for' test.[117] The CAT held that the infringement cost 2 Travel 41,255 passengers in the relevant period, and the loss was quantified as £33,818.79; being the lost profits which would have been generated by those passengers. Various other claims in the case, for considerably larger sums of money,[118] were rejected on the basis of counter-factual reasoning that the claimed losses were not caused by the infringement. Similarly, the award of damages by the CAT in *Albion Water v Dŵr Cymru Cyfyngedig* involved a relatively straight-forward application of the causation test to ensure that Dŵr Cymru: (a) was liable to pay Albion £1,694,343.50 in respect of Albion's claim for loss arising in relation to the supply of water to Shotton Paper; and (b) was liable to pay Albion £160,149.66 in respect of Albion's claim for loss arising from the lost opportunity to supply water to Corus Shotton.[119] In the first follow-on claim for damages to reach trial before the tribunal, causation was central to the rejection of the claim brought by Enron Coal Services Limited (in liquidation) against English Welsh & Scottish Railway Limited.[120] The tribunal concluded that the claimant had

---

[111]   See S Peyer, 'Compensation and the Damages Directive' (2016) 12 European Competition Journal 87.

[112]   Article 4.

[113]   See for instance the claimant as recognized by the CA in *Crehan v Inntrepreneur Pub Company (CPC)*, [2004] EWCA Civ 637; [2004] ECC 28. See also *Safeway Stores Ltd v Twigger* [2010] EWCA 1472. See also *Jetivia SA v Bilta (UK) Ltd (in liquidation)* [2015] UKSC 23, [2015] 2 WLR 1168; and A Robertson, 'Pulling the *Twigger*: Directors and Employees Back in the Firing Line for Damages after *Jetivia* in the Supreme Court?' (2015) 35(8) ECLR 325.

[114]   [2012] CAT 19.

[115]   [2013] CAT 6.

[116]   See Lianos and Geradin (n 1) ch 4. See also *Arkin v Borchard Lines Ltd and Others* [2003] EWHC 3088 (Comm); M Kolmes and P Lennon, 'Causation: The Route to Damages' (2004) 25 ECLR 475.

[117]   See para 2-09 of M Jones (ed), *Clerk & Lindsell on Torts* (20th edn, Sweet & Maxwell 2010); B Pillans, 'Causation' in J Thomson (ed), *Delict* (Greens/SULI 2007).

[118]   A claim of at least £6.8 m in respect of the loss of a capital asset; and a £10 m claim for the lost value of a commercial opportunity.

[119]   The CAT ordered interest on those sums payable at an annual rate of 2 per cent above the base rate from date of infringement until payment. An additional claim for exemplary damages was rejected.

[120]   *Enron Coal Services Limited (in liquidation) v English Welsh & Scottish Railway Limited* [2009] CAT 36.

only a speculative prospect of supplying the third party and had therefore failed to prove that the breach of statutory duty by English Welsh & Scottish Railway Limited caused any claimed loss.

Sainsbury's Supermarkets Ltd v Mastercard Inc and Others[121] involved a damages claim in respect of Mastercard's multilateral interchange fee (MIF). The tribunal held that there was an infringement of Article 101 TFEU and that Sainsbury's were entitled to recover nearly £70 million in damages. The CAT considered in detail the quantification of damages, in only the third, and most complicated case, in which it has awarded and assessed damages. The general principles informing the calculation of the overcharge damages award[122] are compensation/reparation, the balance of probabilities and 'where there is an element of estimation and assumption—as frequently there will be—restoration by way of compensation is often accomplished by "sound imagination" and a "broad axe"'.[123] The CAT also reflected on the passing-on defence and underlying compensation principle,[124] particularly where indirect purchasers were involved. There was also a detailed calculation of the appropriate levels of interest to be added to the damages awards,[125] and a subsequent ruling on the effect of taxation on the damages award and interest to be paid on the damages.[126]

Nonetheless, the view that damages are awarded *only* for the purpose of compensation in the UK courts has been rejected.[127] The Court of Appeal in *Devenish*[128] had indicated that the English courts should adopt a strictly compensatory approach and that there would be little scope for restitutionary, exemplary, or other forms of multiple damages awards. However, the CAT subsequently awarded £60,000 for exemplary damages in *2 Travel Group PLC*.[129] No fines had been imposed on Cardiff Bus due to the small undertaking immunity under section 40(4) of the 1998 Act, and the CAT distinguished *Devenish* as the defendants in that case had benefited from leniency, and the court had recognized the importance of not discouraging whistleblowing.[130] Nonetheless, section 47C(1) of the Competition Act, introduced by the Consumer Rights Act, proscribed the award of exemplary damages by the tribunal in collective proceedings.[131] Paragraph 36 of the implementing Regulations provides that a court/tribunal may not award exemplary damages in competition proceedings, removing the potential for such awards in any context before the UK courts. However, the confirmation by the Supreme Court (and earlier the Court of Appeal) in *Merricks v Mastercard Inc*[39] of the availability under the new collective proceedings mechanism of aggregated damages absent any relationship to actual losses incurred by individual consumers, appears to be inconsistent with the compensation principle.

---

[121]   Case 1241/5/7/15 (T) *Sainsbury's Supermarkets Ltd v Mastercard Inc and Others* (n 42).

[122]   ibid para 423.

[123]   ibid. See also *Asda Stores Ltd v Mastercard Inc* [2017] EWHC 93 para 306 (Popplewell J); and see also for instance Lord Briggs in *Mastercard Inc v Merricks* [2020] UKSC 51 at paras 47–51.

[124]   At paras 479 ff, in particular para 480.

[125]   At paras 527–47 and the conclusions in particular at para 546.

[126]   [2016] CAT 26. See [2020] UKSC 24.

[127]   J Edelman, *Gain-Based Damages, Contract, Tort, Equity and Intellectual Property* (Hart Publishing 2002). See Lord Nicholls in *Att-Gen v Blake* [2001] 1 AC 268 at 285.

[128]   See *2 Travel Group* [2012] CAT 19 (n 114).

[129]   ibid; C Veljanovski, 'CAT Awards Triple Damages, Well Not Really: *Cardiff Bus*, and the Dislocation between Liability and Damages for Exclusionary Abuse' (2012) 33 ECLR 47.

[130]   Lord Briggs delivering the majority judgment in *Mastercard Inc v Merricks* (n 123); see earlier [2019] EWCA Civ 674, para 494.

[131]   See also the Antitrust Damages Directive (n 22) recital 13 and art 3.

Finally, in 2018, we witnessed the first judgment by a UK court[132] awarding damages in relation to a cartel under Article 101 TFEU.[133] The claimant had sustained losses as a result of the operation of a global power cables cartel. In relation to quantification, the court stressed that it would take a pragmatic approach,[134] and that inability to prove the exact sum of loss would not preclude recovery, on the basis that assessment of damages in all areas of civil liability involved some form of estimation and the adoption of assumptions. Accordingly, a broad-brush approach by the court would be appropriate, albeit the final sum awarded would need to be grounded in evidence.[135] The overcharge was assessed as the difference between the price actually agreed and price the claimant would have agreed absent the cartel. The court undertook a broad-brush analysis of the overcharge, and damages of circa £13 million plus interest[136] were awarded, although this was later reduced on appeal to under £12 million.[137]

4.5.1 The Passing-on Defence and Indirect Purchasers

Chapter IV (Articles 12–14 in particular) of the Directive tackles the problematic issue of the passing-on of overcharges, specifically requiring changes in the UK to ensure the burden of proof was on the defendant in line with Article 13 of the Directive.[138] Moreover, an indirect purchaser would only need to establish: (1) an infringement by the defender; (2) that it resulted in an overcharge to the direct purchaser; and, (3) the indirect purchaser has purchased goods or services which are the object of the infringement. There has been considerable academic literature in this context over the years,[139] although no case law practice in the UK until *Sainsbury's Supermarkets Ltd v Mastercard Inc and Others*,[140] in which there was considerable reflection by the CAT on the pass-on defence,[141] particularly where indirect purchasers are involved, albeit the Directive was inapplicable. The CAT confirmed for the first time the recognition of overcharge claims by indirect purchasers and the existence of a passing-on defence for defendants.[142] The CAT stressed 'that the pass-on "defence" ought only to succeed where, on the balance of probabilities, the defendant has shown that there exists another class of claimant, downstream of the claimant(s) in the action, to whom the overcharge has been passed on. [Otherwise] we consider that a claimant's recovery of the overcharge incurred by it should not be reduced or defeated on this ground'.[143] The Supreme Court, emphasized the compensatory principle but stressed that in applying the broad axe in determining the level of mitigation of loss, the evidentiary burden did not require a greater degree of precision on the part of the defendants (than the claimants) in quantifying the precise level of pass-on which had been made by the claimants.[144]

---

[132] *Britned Development Ltd v ABB AB* [2018] EWHC 2616 (Ch).
[133] See *Crehan v Inntrepreneur Pub Co* (CPC) [2004] EWCA Civ 637.
[134] *Asda Stores Ltd v Mastercard Inc* (n 123) applied.
[135] At paras 10–12 and 24–25.
[136] The claim for compound interest was held to be unarguable.
[137] [2019] EWCA Civ 1840. Note also that this was considerably lower than the sum claimed for.
[138] See Rodger, 'United Kingdom' (n 32).
[139] See C Petrucci, 'The Issues of the Passing-on Defence and Indirect Purchasers' Standing in European Competition Law' (2008) 29 ECLR 33. See B Rodger, 'Let's Talk about Consumers: Competition Law Compensation for Indirect Purchasers' Losses: A UK perspective' (2021) Antitrust Law Journal (forthcoming).
[140] Case 1241/5/7/15 (T) *Sainsbury's Supermarkets Ltd v Mastercard Inc and Others* (n 42).
[141] ibid paras 479 ff. See in particular para 480.
[142] ibid para 484: 'The pass-on "defence" is in reality not a defence at all: it simply reflects the need to ensure that a claimant is sufficiently compensated, and not over-compensated, by a defendant.'
[143] ibid para 484.
[144] [2020] UKSC 24, paras 175–226, particularly paras 225–26.

4.6 Collective Redress Mechanism

It is generally recognized that effective justice requires appropriate collective redress mechanisms to ensure that ultimate consumers can seek compensation for overcharges as a result of competition law infringements. Consumers should be able to seek compensation for being overcharged as a result of an abuse of dominance or a cartel-type arrangement. There has been considerable academic study and literature in relation to collective consumer redress generally, led by Rachel Mulheron,[145] and empirical work which has highlighted major gaps in redress for consumers specifically in relation to competition law infringements.[146]

Section 47B of the Competition Act allowed follow-on damages claims to be brought before the CAT by a specified body on behalf of two or more consumers with claims in respect of the same infringement[147] —a form of 'consumer representative action'. There was only one section 47B claim: *Consumers' Association v JJB Sports plc*[148] in relation to *Football Shirts*.[149] Ultimately, this action, with only 144 consumers becoming party to it, was settled and withdrawn on the basis of compensation up to a maximum of £20 per individual consumer.[150] The clear limitations of the specialist representative action, notably the low participation rates in opt-in schemes due to a lack of incentives,[151] were widely acknowledged. Subsequently, in 2012 the Department for Business, Innovation and Skills ('BIS') consulted on proposals to reinforce the system of private enforcement in the UK.[152] The BIS recommendations were included in reforms made to the existing Competition Act regime by the Consumer Rights Act 2015. The Act was given royal assent on 26 March 2015 and the changes came into effect on 1 October 2015.[153] The new, revised section 47B of the Competition Act 1998 provides for both opt-out and opt-in collective proceedings before the CAT. The UK Parliamentary debates were influenced by concerns about the consequences of potentially introducing an American style litigation process and culture. Accordingly, it was stressed during the passage of the Bill that 'safeguards' would be built

---

[145] See for instance R Mulheron, *The Class Action in Common Law Legal Systems: A Comparative Perspective* (Hart Publishing 2004); R Mulheron, 'Recent Milestones in Class Actions Reform in England: A Critique and a Proposal' (2011) 127 Law Quarterly Rev 288; R Mulheron, 'Opting In, Opting Out, and Closing the Class: Some Dilemmas for England's Class Actions Law-Makers' (2011) 50 Canadian Business LJ 376; R Mulheron, 'A Missed Gem of an Opportunity for the Representative Rule' (2011) 23 EBL Rev 49. See also M Ioannidou, *Consumer Involvement in Private EU Competition Law Enforcement* (OUP 2015).

[146] *Reform of Collective Redress in England and Wales: A Perspective of Need* (Report submitted to the Civil Justice Council of England and Wales, February 2008).

[147] Section 47B(1) and (4).

[148] Case No 1078/7/9/07.

[149] As *Replica Football Kit* had become known in the CAT follow-on case. See discussion in B Rodger (ed), *Landmark Cases in Competition Law: Around The World in Fourteen Stories* (Kluwer Law International 2012) ch 13.

[150] If receipts had been retained see http://www.which.co.uk/news/2008/01/jjb-to-pay-fans-over-football-shirt-rip-off-128985.jsp.

[151] See M Hviid and J Peysner, 'Comparing Economic Incentives Across EU Member States' in B Rodger (ed), *Competition Law Comparative Private Enforcement and Collective Redress Across the EU* (Kluwer Law International 2014) ch 6.

[152] See 'Private Actions in Competition Law: A Consultation on Options For Reform' BIS 12/742 (April 2012).

[153] The Competition Appeal Tribunal Rules, SI 2015/1648. However, according to r 119 of the revised CAT rules, the old Competition Act provisions and Tribunal rules on limitation of actions (and the suspensive effect of appeal proceedings) continue to apply to all claims (including in collective proceedings) to which s 47A applies where the claim arises before 1 October 2015. See *Gibson v Pride Mobility Products Ltd* (n 88). Generally see B Rodger, 'The Consumer Rights Act 2015 and Collective Redress for Competition Law Infringements in the UK: A Class Act?' (2015) 3(2) JAE 258.

into the UK collective action model.[154] These safeguards are effectively: a requirement for the CAT to certify that a representative is suitable to bring proceedings; [155] a ban on exemplary damages awards; and, the prohibition of damages-based agreements.[156] The amended section 47B of the Competition Act provides for the CAT to make a CPO[157] in relation to a claim only on the basis that there is: an authorized representative;[158] the claims raise the same, similar, or related issues of fact or law; and, are suitable for collective proceedings.[159] A CPO must include:[160] (a) authorization of the person who brought the proceedings to act as the representative in those proceedings; (b) description of a class of persons whose claims are eligible for inclusion in the proceedings; and, (c) specification of the proceedings as opt-in collective proceedings[161] or opt-out collective proceedings.[162] It should be noted that in such proceedings, any non-UK domiciled class member[163] must opt-in by notifying the class representative.[164] Section 47B(8) provides for authorization of the class representative in collective proceedings whether or not that representative is a 'class member'.[165] Another crucial provision is section 47B(8)(b), which specifies that authorization will only be granted if the Tribunal 'considers that it is just and reasonable for that person to act as a representative in those proceedings'. Collective settlements may be approved under section 49A where a CPO has been made and the CAT is satisfied that the settlement is just and reasonable, and there are parallel provisions in section 49B for collective settlements where a CPO has not been made. The legislative provision is sparse on the central issues regarding opt-out collective proceedings: eligibility as a collective proceeding; whether it should be on an opt-in or opt-out basis; and, the appointment of a suitable class representative. Each of these issues is dealt with in fuller detail in Part V of the Competition Appeal Tribunal Rules 2015. The relevant certification process provision is set out in Rules 77–79. Rule 78 deals with the authorization condition and rule 79 with the eligibility condition.[166]

Despite the existence of the new opt-out collective redress scheme the difficulties in obtaining successful collective redress for consumers has been exemplified by the first two cases under the new regime. In *Gibson v Pride Mobility Products*,[167] the application for a CPO was adjourned for the applicant to return with an amended claim form. The fundamental difficulties here lay in the related issues of the limited scope of the infringement decision and the requisite boundaries of a follow-on action,[168] and the consequent impact of the decision on the various sub-classes of claimant. In order to grant a CPO the tribunal, inter alia, required the applicant to propose revised sub-classes and a methodology which focused on the effects of the agreements

---

[154] See for instance Baroness Hayter of Kentish town, Grand Committee, House of Lords, 3 November 2014, col 579. See C Hodges and R Money-Kyrle, 'Safeguards in Collective Actions' (2012) 19(4) Maastricht Journal of International and Comparative Law 477.
[155] Baroness Neville-Rolfe, Grand Committee, House of Lords, 3 November 2014, cols 570–81.
[156] More accurately, a provision that declares them to be unenforceable.
[157] As required under s 47B(4) of the 1998 Act. See s 47B(5)(a) and (6) in particular.
[158] In s 47B(5)(a) of the 1998 Act.
[159] ibid s 47B(6).
[160] ibid s 47B(7).
[161] ibid s 47B(10).
[162] ibid s 47B(11).
[163] ibid s 59(1B).
[164] ibid s 47B(11)(b).
[165] ibid s 47B(8)(a).
[166] See *O'Higgins* [2020] CAT 8, discussed below.
[167] [2017] CAT 9.
[168] Because of the transitional provisions, the applicant was required to bring this action as a follow-on action.

which were the subject of the infringement decision.[169] The claim was subsequently withdrawn and the applicant held liable for the defendants' costs of the proceedings.[170]

In *Merricks v Mastercard Inc*[171] the claims were held by the tribunal not to be certifiable under Rule 79 of the Tribunal Rules as eligible for inclusion in collective proceedings. Merricks sought to bring proceedings on behalf of a class defined as individuals who between 22 May 1992 and 21 June 2008 has purchased goods and/or services from businesses selling in the UK that had accepted Mastercard cards provided those individuals were (a) resident in the UK at the time and (b) aged 16 years or over. The claim was for an aggregate sum of approximately £14 billion including interest and the class was considered to be around 46.2 million people in a follow-on claim based on Mastercard's setting of the multilateral interchange fee which applied as a fallback between banks in the UK. The case failed on the suitability test on the basis that the applicant had failed to put forward: (1) a sustainable methodology to be applied in practice to calculate a sum which reflected the aggregate of the individual claims; and (2) a reasonable and practicable means for establishing the individual loss to be used as a basis for distribution.[172] On appeal, the Court of Appeal rejected the CAT's reasoning and adopted a more purposive approach to certification proceedings, recalibrating the process in the balance of potential collective redress applicants. In considering the nature of the aggregated damages, the Court of Appeal noted that the Canadian approach[173] at the certification stage did not involve a detailed analysis of expert opinion, and the threshold for certification was not an onerous one. The Court considered that the applicants had provided a methodology for calculation of the aggregate damages and there was data likely to be available to operate it, and at this stage they need only show prospect of success before completion of disclosure and filing of evidence, not that the claims were certain to succeed. The CAT had set too high a hurdle for certification and there was 'no requirement … to approach the assessment of an aggregate award through the medium of a calculation of individual loss'.[174] The second main issue concerned the proposed mechanism for distribution of the aggregate damages award. The Court stressed that section 47B did not require aggregate awards to be distributed on a compensatory basis as envisaged by the CAT.[175] The CAT Rules 1992 and 1993 provided that distribution on the basis of individual loss where readily calculable is the most obvious and suitable method, but the Court emphasized that the power to make an aggregate award would be largely negated if 'calculation of individual loss was a pre-requisite for any authorised method of distribution and therefore for certification'.[176] The opt-out CPO mechanism was 'obviously intended to facilitate means of redress which could attract and be facilitated by litigation funding and had parliament considered it necessary to limit this new type of procedure by what would be required for the assessment of damages in an individual claim then it would have said so'.[177] On the contrary the provisions for distribution of an aggregate award are open-ended

---

[169] [2017] CAT 9, paras 112–18.
[170] https://www.catribunal.org.uk/sites/default/files/1257_Dorothy_Gibson_Order_250517.pdf.
[171] [2017] CAT 16.
[172] https://competitionpolicy.wordpress.com/2017/08/10/has-the-cats-mastercard-decision-killed-off-opt-out-class-actions-by-indirect-purchasers/#more-1175.
[173] ibid para 40.
[174] ibid para 46.
[175] ibid paras 56–62.
[176] ibid para 57.
[177] ibid para 60.

and '[t]he vindication of the rights of individual claimants is achieved by the aggregate award itself'.[178] The ruling emphasizes the need for the practical effectiveness of the collective redress scheme itself, and that the mechanisms created for CPO applications should be workable and not create insurmountable barriers to collective redress by consumers. The Supreme Court delivered its ruling in December 2020, and a favourable majority judgment, delivered by Lord Briggs,[179] upheld the Court of Appeal's ruling and returned the case to the CAT to reconsider the CPO application in light of its findings that it had erred in law. Lord Briggs, in line broadly with the Court of Appeal's approach,[180] emphasized context and purpose: 'Collective proceedings are a special form of civil procedure for the vindication of private rights, designed to provide access to justice for that purpose where the ordinary forms of individual civil claim have proved inadequate for the purpose.'[181] The most serious of the errors of law by the CAT identified by Lord Briggs at paras 72–74 concerned the methodology and evidence to calculate damages at trial.

The minority judgment (by Sales and Leggatt LJJ), concurred with Lord Briggs (and the earlier Court of Appeal ruling) on the issue of distribution of aggregate damages.[182] Again, the CAT had erred in law in deeming the compensatory principle to be essential for determining the outcome of that process. As Lord Briggs noted, 'section 47C of the Act radically alters the established common law compensatory principle by removing the requirement to assess individual loss in an aggregate damages case, and that nothing in the Act or the Rules puts it back again, for the purposes of distribution'.[183]

Despite early case law setbacks in *Gibson* and *Merricks*, there are a number of ongoing CPO application proceedings before the CAT, notably in relation to numerous follow-on claims against Mastercard and Visa and in relation to the trucks cartel[184] The downside is that they generally reflect, as is historically the case in private competition litigation in the UK, the predominance of business claimants, and not ultimate consumers; although the ongoing claim by train commuters in *Justin Gutmann v First MTR South Western Trains Limited and Another*,[185] is notable.[186] It is hoped that the favourable ruling by the Supreme Court in *Merricks* on the broad axe approach required for quantification of pass-on and ultimate losses for certification of CPO applications, in line with the Court of Appeal's approach, and the rejection of the compensation aligned damages distribution model required at first instance by the CAT, may help to incentivize future consumer-based claims.

Of course, the nature of the representative, and whether they will be over—or adequately incentivized to pursue this type of litigation, is also crucial. The CAT has already been requested to determine a 'carriage issue'; i.e. which of two potential representatives should be approved to proceed in relation to collective proceedings in *O'Higgins FX Class representative Ltd v Barclays Bank and Others*, and *Philip Evans v Barclays Bank and Others*[187] both follow-on actions in relation to two Commission infringement decisions, FOREX (three

---

[178] ibid.
[179] *Mastercard Inc v Merricks* (n 123) para 82 (Lord Briggs).
[180] ibid para 64.
[181] ibid para 45.
[182] ibid paras 148– 50 (Sales and Leggatt LJJ).
[183] ibid para 76.
[184] See generally https://www.catribunal.org.uk/cases.
[185] Case 1305/7/7/19, registered 27 February 2019.
[186] See also Case 1339/7/7/20 *Mark McLaren Class Representative Limited v MOL (Europe Africa) Ltd and Others*.
[187] [2020] CAT 8.

way banana split) and FOREX (Essex express). The CAT refused to rule on the matter as necessarily a discrete preliminary issue and noted that: 'the United Kingdom's collective proceedings regime is still in its infancy, with multiple novel questions being decided in this tribunal and in the higher courts'.[188] In anticipation of the Supreme Court ruling in *Merricks*, all CPO applications had been stayed/sisted pending the outcome. In addition to the substantive certification point, a key issue for determination is the appealability of the CAT's CPO rulings. There is a danger that appeals at the CPO stage will mean that the collective proceedings will become protracted and considerably delay any form of justice for consumers.

4.7 Funding Private Enforcement

The availability of contingency fees for lawyers in the USA has been central in incentivizing the raising of class actions on behalf of consumers.[189] Hviid and Peysner have stressed that any opt-out system would also benefit from the availability of contingency fees.[190] In England and Wales, there has been a considerable shift in the use of alternative legal fee arrangements over the last fifteen years.[191] Conditional fee arrangements, involving a success percentage uplift (of up to 100 per cent) of a standard fee, are common, albeit following the Jackson Report,[192] the Legal Aid, Sentencing and Punishment of Offenders Act 2012 (LASPO) prohibited the recovery of success fees and ATE insurance premiums from the unsuccessful party.[193] Following the introduction of the Damages-Based Agreements Regulations 2013,[194] DBAs, where a lawyer's fee is contingent upon the success of the claim and is calculated as a percentage of the compensation received by the claimant, have been permissible generally in civil cases, to incentivize lawyers to pursue more risky and work-intensive cases. In Scots law the award of costs generally flows from success. Most litigation in Scotland is funded by the parties themselves. However, solicitors may enter into speculative fee agreements with their clients whereby the client is only liable to pay the solicitor's fees if the litigation is successful.[195] Scots law also allows third party funding of litigation.[196] Following publication of the Taylor Report into the Expenses and Funding of Civil Litigation in Scotland in September 2013,[197] the Civil Litigation (Expenses and Group Proceedings) (Scotland) Act 2018 makes provision for success fee agreements and Third Party funding of litigation.[198]

---

[188] ibid para 56.

[189] See for instance KC Wildfang and S P Slaughter, 'Funding Litigation' in A Foer and R M Stutz (eds), *Private Enforcement of Antitrust Law in the United States, A Handbook* (Edward Elgar Publishing 2012) ch 10.

[190] See generally C Hodges, J Peysner, and A Nurse, 'Litigation Funding: Status and Issues' Joint Report University of Oxford & University of Lincoln (Sponsored by Swiss Re) (2012); J Peysner, *Access to Justice: A Critical Analysis of Recoverable Conditional Fees and No Win No Fee Funding* (Palgrave MacMillan 2014).

[191] Hodges, Peysner, and Nurse (n 190).

[192] Review of Civil Litigation Costs: Final Report (December 2009) https://www.judiciary.gov.uk/wp-content/uploads/JCO/Documents/Reports/jackson-final-report-140110.pdf.

[193] See *Coventry and Others v Lawrence and Another* [2015] UKSC 50.

[194] SI 2013/609.

[195] Allowed for by s 61A of the Solicitors (Scotland) Act 1980.

[196] *Quantum Claims Compensation Specialists Ltd v Powell* 1998 SC 316.

[197] See Review of Expenses and Funding of Civil Litigation in Scotland, Report by Sh P J A Taylor (September 2013) http://scotland.gov.uk/About/Review/taylor-review/Report.

[198] In ss 1 and 10, respectively.

The government decided to prohibit DBAs in collective actions cases before the CAT. Section 47C(8) of the amended Competition Act provides that 'a damages-based agreement is unenforceable if it relates to opt-out collective proceedings.'[199] Accordingly, a central conundrum is how prospective opt-out collective proceedings can be financed. There was an attempt to amend the legislation in Parliament to exclude such third-party litigation funding agreements.[200] However, the government accepted that third party funding may be necessary to ensure effective consumer redress.[201] This was stressed by the CAT in *Merricks v Mastercard*: 'the Government in promoting the legislation therefore clearly envisaged that many collective actions would be dependent on third party funding, and it is self-evident that this could not be achieved unless the class representative incurred a conditional liability for the funder's costs, which could be discharged through recovery out of the unclaimed damages.'[202] A key concern, alleviated in that ruling, concerned the recovery of success fees and ATE premiums from the losing defendant. The only explicit arrangement for fees in opt-out collective actions can be found in section 47C(6) of the Competition Act 1998 (as amended by the CRA) and CAT rule 93(4). These rules provide a route for costs and success fees to be recovered after the class members have received their damages, and the dicta in *Gibson* and *Merricks*[203] on the specific costs issues were positive from a third party funding perspective. Nonetheless, despite the favourable Supreme Court ruling in *Merricks*, there remains a concern that the cost recovery rules may inadvertently result in the collective proceedings mechanism being used primarily for common claims by businesses rather than consumers.[204]

5 Learning from the USA

The analysis of the UK legislative and case law background may at least partly explain the trajectory followed by competition law private enforcement in the UK, such that a (specific) competition and litigation culture has developed where appropriate institutions, rules, processes and mechanisms are established.[205] It appears that the developing culture and jurisprudence in the UK has similarities with the US system, although at a much earlier developmental stage. There are a range of mechanisms which facilitate private antitrust lawsuits in the USA, inter alia, the availability of treble damages, an opt-out class action mechanism, discovery, and contingency fees.[206] Essentially, the US legal system has for a considerable period promoted access to the courts for consumers.[207]

---

[199] Amending s 58AA of the Courts and Legal Services Act 1990. See r 113 of the CAT Rules 2015. See R Mulheron, 'The Damages-based Agreements Regulations 2013: Some Conundrums in the "Brave New World" of Funding' (2013) 32 Civil Justice Quarterly 241.

[200] Baroness Noakes, Grand Committee, House of Lords, Report, 3 November 2014, col 575.

[201] ibid 582.

[202] [2017] CAT 16, para 127.

[203] *Merricks v Mastercard* (n 94) and *Gibson v Pride Mobility Products Ltd* (n 88) para 145.

[204] For fuller discussion see A Render and S Peyer, 'Are Cases Too Good to Litigate? Cost Recovery in Antitrust Collective Actions in the UK' (2020) 41(1) ECLR 3.

[205] See S Vande Walle, 'What Keeps Plaintiffs Away from the Court? An Analysis of Antitrust Litigation in Japan, Europe and the US' in D Vanoverbeke, J Maesschalck, S Parmentier, and D Nelken (eds), *The Changing Role of Law in Japan: Empirical Studies in Culture, Society and Policy Making* (Edward Elgar Publishing 2014).

[206] See for instance A E. Foer and J W Cuneo (eds), *The International Handbook on Private Enforcement of Competition Law* (Edward Elgar Publishing/American Antitrust Institute 2010).

[207] See A Andreangeli, 'Collective Redress in EU Competition Law: An Open Question with Many Possible Solutions' (2012) 35(3) W Comp 529; A Andreangeli, 'A View from Across the Atlantic: Recent Developments in

The key element in the US is the opt-out nature of the class action mechanism, provided for in Rule 23 of the US Federal Rules of Civil Procedure. Although the opt-out basis is crucial in ensuring widespread compensation, in applying Rule 23 the courts have had to reconcile this underlying aim of efficient adjudication with other potentially conflicting principles, such as party autonomy and due process requirements. Although opt-out class actions have been central to the enhanced role for private antitrust enforcement in the USA over the last forty years at least, the class certification process in that context should not simply be viewed as a rubber-stamping process. Moreover, it is evident that the courts dealing with class certification motions undertake a 'careful scrutiny'[208] as to whether the requirements in Rule 23 are satisfied, and case law and academic commentary indicates a significantly more rigorous approach to certification in recent years,[209] which may reign in any of the perceived excesses of the US opt-out class action mechanism.[210] The misconceptions about the US class action mechanism—the perceived lack of supervision of class counsel in the US class system and the fee incentives to lawyers—has meant that the debate in Europe generally, and in the UK specifically, has been driven by a generalized (and unsubstantiated) fear about the creation of a system driven by ambulance-chasing lawyers maximizing self-interest at the expense of the class,[211] 'blackmailing' defendants into settling for vast sums.

Antitrust damages actions play a significant role in the overall antitrust enforcement landscape and it is an important reference point from which lessons can be drawn. The primary lesson is that in order to facilitate the availability of compensation in damages actions a range of institutional factors and mechanisms have combined to ensure that private enforcement of US antitrust law is effective. Nonetheless, there has been academic scepticism of the extent to which private antitrust enforcement continues to be encouraged and facilitated in the USA. The more scrupulous approach in this context may indeed discourage class action claims and thereby weaken the class action as an enforcement tool and method of ensuring collective consumer redress. Rathod and Vaheesan concluded that private enforcement had been undermined by the business victim mythology which had shaped attitudes of, inter alia, judges to limit the scope of private enforcement rights, and they advocated strongly against the import into Europe of an 'anti-private enforcement' message based on 'empirically unsupported narrative of "excessive litigation" in the United States'.[212]

the Case Law of the US Federal Courts on Class Certification in Antitrust Cases', ch 7 in B Rodger (ed), *Competition Law Comparative Private Enforcement and Collective Redress Across the EU* (Kluwer Law International 2014) and B Rodger (ed), *Private Enforcement of Antitrust—Regulating Corporate Behaviour through Collective Claims in the EU and US* (Edward Elgar Publishing 2014).

[208] *AmChem Products Inc v Windsor*, 83 F.3d, 610 at 616.

[209] Subject to 'scrupulous scrutiny': see *Re Hydrogen Peroxide Antitrust Litigation* 552 F. 3d 305 (3rd Cir. 2008).

[210] See eg S Rajski, '*In Re: Hydrogen Peroxide*: Reinforcing Rigorous Analysis for Class Action Certification' (2011) 34 Seattle UL Rev 577, 603–604; J M Jacobson and J Choi, 'Curtailing the Impact of Class Certification on Antitrust Policy' (2011) 66 NYUANSAL 549,554. Moreover, the indirect purchaser rule at the federal level militates against indirect purchaser claims which are most likely to be raised by end consumers. See Rodger, 'Let's Talk about Consumers (n 139) and A Gavil, 'Consumer Welfare without Consumers, *Illinois Brick* after *Apple v Pepper*' (2019) 7 Journal of Antitrust Enforcement 447.

[211] See inter alia M Helveston, 'Promoting Justice through Public Interest Advocacy in Class Actions' (2012) 60 BF L Rev 749, 777; also J Tidmarsh, 'Rethinking Adequacy of Representation' (2009) 97 Tx L Rev 1137, 1156–58.

[212] See J Rathod and S Vaheesan, 'The Arc and Architecture of Private Enforcement Regimes in the United States and Europe: A View from Across the Atlantic' (2015) 14 UNHLR 303.

6 Impact of UK Withdrawal from EU

There are a number of factors which may have implications for the continued role of the CAT (and High Court) as a key international forum for international competition litigation following the UK's withdrawal from the EU.[213] The first category of issues concerns the scope and effect of EU competition law. First, EU law will be treated as a foreign law. Secondly the territorial scope of EU law infringements no longer extends to the UK.[214] Thirdly, and most significant in practice as discussed earlier, section 58A of the Competition Act has been revised to the effect that EU Commission decisions will no longer be binding on the CAT and courts in the UK. These are likely to limit the incentives of litigating EU-wide (and beyond) cartels in the UK, making it more difficult for consumers to raise collective actions based on prior Commission infringement decisions. Moreover, the private international law rules within the EU have a considerable role to play in determining the rights and obligations arising out of anti-competitive activity, particularly in relation to wide-scale international cartels.[215] The rules determining the civil jurisdiction of the courts in the EU, and consequently where in the EU an action based on a competition law infringement may be raised, were until 31 December 2020 provided in the recast Brussels IA Regulation,[216] and there have been numerous rulings by the CAT and High Court on aspects of the provisions of the Regulation in a competition law context.[217] The Rome II Regulation,[218] also provides rules for determining the applicable law in non-contractual obligations. However, the significance of the Brussels IA Regulation, and the consequent attractiveness of the English courts as a forum for international competition litigation, lay in the rules of automatic recognition and enforcement of judgments under the Regulation, where for instance a defendant is domiciled, and has assets in another EU jurisdiction. The reciprocal nature of the EU-wide recognition and enforcement provisions under the Regulation have been lost, and pending the adoption of a satisfactory replacement mechanism, the attractiveness of the CAT as a forum for international litigation may be reduced.[219]

---

[213] The issue of the revised s 60A interpretative requirements in relation to the Competition Act prohibitions post withdrawal from the EU (by the Competition (Amendment etc) (EU Exit) Regulations 2019 (SI 2019/93)) is significant, but less so in this specific context.

[214] *Iiyama Benelux BV v Schott AG* [2016] 5 CMLR 15 (Ch); *Iiyama (UK) Ltd v Samsung Electronics Co Ltd* [2016] EWHC 1980 (Ch); [2016] 5 CMLR 16 and [2018] EWCA Civ 220; *Media-Saturn Holding GmbH v Toshiba Information Systems* [2019] EWHC 1095 (Ch).

[215] See B Rodger, 'EU Competition Law and Private International Law: A Developing Relationship' in I Lianos and D Geradin (eds), *Handbook on European Competition Law: Enforcement and Procedure* (Edward Elgar Publishing 2013) ch 8. See also J Basedow, S Francq, and I Idot (eds), *International Antitrust litigation, Conflict of Laws and Coordination* (Hart Publishing 2011).

[216] Regulation 1215/2012, [2012] OJ L351/1.

[217] See *Roche Products Limited v Provimi Limited* [2003] EWHC 961 (Comm); *Emerson Electric Co v Mersen UK Portslade Limited* [2012] EWCA Civ 1557 *Deutsche Bahn AG v Morgan Crucible co plc and Others* Case 1173/5/7/10 [2013] CAT 18, [2013] EWCA Civ 1484.

[218] Regulation 864/2007, [2007] OJ L299/40.

[219] While the courts may still exercise jurisdiction, there will be less certainty, and the mechanisms for recognition and enforcement across the EU Member States will not be as simple as under the Brussels IA regime. There remains at this stage continued uncertainty regarding future arrangements, whether the UK will accede to the Lugano Convention or ratify the Hague Convention on the Recognition and Enforcement of Foreign Judgments in Civil or Commercial Matters 2019.

7 Conclusions

Competition law and policy in the UK has undergone a radical transformation—a 'sea-change'—in the last twenty years.[220] The Competition Act 1998 marked the start of the transformation[221] to a more legalistic, prohibition-based set of provisions with clear sanctions and remedies. Institutional mechanisms and bodies have been introduced (the follow-on damages action, the CAT itself, the opt-out collective proceedings mechanism) which have sought to facilitate private enforcement. There has been an increase in practitioners involved in competition law, greater awareness of competition law rights and remedies[222] and more case law, although settlements continue to obscure much of this practice.

The United Kingdom provides an example of a change in the legal and enforcement architecture leading to shifts in competition law enforcement trends. The old 'unique and idiosyncratic model'[223] of British policy-making was chronicled in Wilks' history of the Monopolies and Mergers Commission (MMC), *In the Public Interest*,[224] in which he compared the historical British civil service approach with the 'legal evangelism' of US antitrust enforcement.[225] However, that book was published as the UK Parliament was passing the Competition Act 1998. That event marked the start of the transformation of the UK regime from a purely bureaucratic, public interest model of competition policy-making to a more legalistic system, including, alongside the old market investigation process, a prohibition-based set of provisions with clear sanctions and remedies, involving a key role for the Competition Appeal Tribunal with a range of functions,[226] notably its role in relation to follow-on damages actions. The shift from the historical public interest based paradigm in the UK to a more rights-based, legal prohibition approach has parallels in the Japanese context.[227] The legalization of the competition law context in terms of the introduction of substantive rules, institutions and processes at the UK level, and how this can create a more effective competition law rights based culture, also reflect a general shift identified by Kelemen[228] towards the US system of 'adversarial legalism' in the EU.

Over the last twenty years the courts in the UK have become increasingly attractive as a forum for international private litigation involving infringements of domestic and EU competition law rules. This is partly as a result of the introduction of a range of legal, procedural and institutional mechanisms, including the specialist CAT. The UK's attractiveness as a forum reflects the experience of the established competition law plaintiff and defence Bar in London, the availability of alternative forms of funding and incentives to litigate, and the experience and quality of the judiciary in competition law-related litigation. The repeated and ongoing involvement of the Supreme Court in competition-related disputes reflects the established nature of competition law and litigation in the UK. Nonetheless, there remains the underlying perennial conflict about achieving the appropriate equilibrium between

---

[220] See Rodger and MacCulloch (n 6); and Rodger (ed), *Ten Years of UK Competition Law Reform* (n 2).
[221] See Wilks (n 7).
[222] See S Vande Walle, 'What Keeps Plaintiffs Away from the Court?' (n 205).
[223] Wilks (n 7) ch 6.
[224] ibid.
[225] ibid ch 3.
[226] See Bailey (n 6).
[227] See S Vande Walle, *Private Antitrust Litigation in the European Union and Japan* (Maklu 2013) 41–48 generally.
[228] See R D Keleman, *Eurolegalism: The Transformation of Law and Regulation in the European Union* (Harvard University Press 2011).

facilitating the effectiveness of competition law rights on the one hand and avoiding excessive cost and potential liabilities for business as a result of excessive litigation on the other
hand.[229] It is uncertain to what extent the various Directive provisions will further facilitate
damages actions, although the greatest threat to the continued significance of the UK courts
as an international forum arises from the recent exit of the UK from the EU. There has been
some, at least partial, experiential learning from the antitrust private enforcement in the
USA, and a number of ways in which competition law claims have been encouraged and
facilitated here: improved limitation and discovery provisions; provision for binding infringement decisions; a specialist court; successful damages actions; and, subject to limitations, experimentation with creative forms of funding claims, notably through Third Party
funding.

Overall, in assessing the impact of the legal and case law developments over the last
twenty years in terms of consumers and access to justice, it is notable that the successful
stand-alone High Court cases (under Chapter 2/Article 102) were all business to business
claims. This is the same for the CAT's case law generally, with the limited exception of *Replica
Kit*. The CAT's jurisprudence has primarily focused on procedural issues, notably limitation, although final damages awards have been emerging in recent years. Nonetheless, the
CAT mechanism has also been utilized more recently (aided by the fast-track procedure) by
smaller business claimants.[230] Although applications for CPOs have been raised by business
parties (notably re *Trucks* and *Visa/Mastercard*)[231] there is also evidence of increasing resort to the collective redress mechanism in final consumer based claims in *Gibson/Merricks*
and *Gutmann/Maclaren*. The Supreme Court ruling in *Merricks* should help to facilitate
effective consumer redress by reducing the hurdles at the early stage of applications for a
CPO, and thereby translate the limited general successes in creating a vibrant private enforcement framework in the UK from business claimants to consumers in the third decade
of the modern UK competition law.

---

[229] See Rathod and Vaheesan (n 212).
[230] See eg Case 1303/5/7/19 *Melanie Meigh (trading as The Prinknash Bird and Deer Park) v Prinknash Abbey
Trustees Registered.*
[231] See also for instance Case 1329/7/7/19 *Michael O'Higgins FX Class Representative Limited v Barclays Bank
PLC and Others.*

13

The Quiet Decline of the UK Cartel Offence

A Principled Victory in the Face of Practical Failure

Angus MacCulloch

1 Introduction

The introduction of the Cartel Offence in the UK was met with much excitement by many in the UK competition law community. Much scholarly ink was spilled discussing the nature and shape of the offence introduced by the Enterprise Act 2002.[1] It is safe to say that the original offence was not without controversy, but in this chapter I do not intend to focus on the detail of that debate.[2] Here I intend to examine, not the rise of the cartel criminalization in the UK, but its decline. We have not, yet, seen the official fall of this new empire, but its continued relevance is definitely in doubt.

The nature of the Cartel Offence introduced into the UK will be set out in section 2. An attempt will be made to explain the choices which were made in its controversial structure. In section 3 I shall look at the practical failures which led to the first seeds of the institutional doubt which has plagued the UK Cartel Offence in its mid-life. Following that mid-life crisis there was a process of legislative reform that, while being well intentioned and having some positive aspects, had significant flaws and has proved in practice to have very limited impact. The institutional appetite for the Cartel Offence appears to have been fundamentally damaged.

In the section 4 I shall examine a parallel but much more positive process—that is the scholarly debate around criminalization. While enforcement activity in the UK was beset with problems, the scholarly community was making real progress, and reached a point of consensus that was perhaps surprising given the controversy in relation to the Cartel Offence's first phase. There has now developed a broad consensus as to the key features and overall 'shape' of workable cartel criminalization to guide future reform of criminalization in other jurisdictions. This new understanding is, rather ironically, perhaps too late to help restore confidence in the UK Cartel Offence.

---

[1] See eg J Joshua, 'The UK's New Cartel Offence and its Implications for EC Competition Law: A Tangled Web' (2003) 28 European Law Review 620; A MacCulloch, 'The Cartel Offence and the Criminalisation of United Kingdom Competition Law' [2003] JBL 616–; and J Lever and J Pike, 'Cartel Agreements, Criminal Conspiracy and the Statutory "Cartel Offence" Pt I' [2005] ECLR 90; Pt II, [2005] ECLR 164.

[2] For a retrospective look at the genesis and first phase of the Cartel Offence in the UK see Angus MacCulloch, 'The Cartel Offence: Is Honesty the Best Policy?' in Barry J Rodger (ed), *Ten Years of UK Competition Law Reform* (Dundee University Press 2010).

Angus MacCulloch, *The Quiet Decline of the UK Cartel Offence* In: *The UK Competition Regime.* Edited by: Barry Rodger, Peter Whelan, and Angus MacCulloch, Oxford University Press. © The Contributors 2021. DOI: 10.1093/oso/9780198868026.003.0013

In the final section, section 5, I turn to a prospective view. There have been unexpected, and largely unseen, benefits that stem from the introduction of the Cartel Offence in the UK. These have mostly been in the context of civil antitrust enforcement. While these potential benefits in civil enforcement cannot justify criminalization in themselves, they do indicate that criminal investigatory powers have brought benefits to the competition law regime as a whole. Without active criminal cases it must, however, be questioned whether this use of criminal investigatory powers can be justified. For example, the focus on individual responsibility during the investigation phase has led to a growth in Competition Disqualification Undertakings as effective sanctions.[3] The growing scholarly consensus does, however, suggest a way forward for the UK to prioritize certain types of cartel cases, and to give UK enforcement agencies a pathway to rebuild the institutional confidence in the Cartel Offence that currently seems lacking.

2 The Introduction of the Cartel Offence

The introduction of the original Cartel Offence into UK law was part of a wider policy to increase the deterrent effect of UK competition law as a whole. The criminal offence was not viewed as an extension of the criminal law, but rather as a new form of deterrence to complement the existing competition law armoury. It would create a deterrent for individuals who were involved in the most serious of competition law violations.[4] This 'instrumental' approach to the introduction of the Cartel Offence followed from the strong orthodoxy that had developed in the competition law literature around 'optimal deterrence' in competition law sanctions.[5] It was seen as vitally important that the competition regime developed sufficient sanctions to deter both undertakings, and the individuals within them, from engaging in cartel activity.

Section 188 of the Enterprise Act 2002 set out that an individual would commit an offence if he or she: 'dishonestly agrees with one or more other persons to make or implement, or to cause to be made or implemented, arrangements of the following kind relating to at least two undertakings'. The agreements must be one which 'if operating as the parties to the agreement intend' would (a) fix prices, (b) limit supply, (c) limit production, (d) divide supply, (e) divide customers, or (f) bid-rig. The offence therefore only seeks to capture hard core horizontal cartel activity, and only individuals who 'intend' to 'dishonestly', 'make or implement' those agreements.

The apparently complex drafting of the new offence had two main purposes: first, to narrow the offence to cover only 'hard core' cartels; and, second, to avoid overlap between the offence and the Article 101 TFEU prohibition. This latter concern was to ensure UK law's compliance with the Article 3 of Regulation 1/2003.[6] That provision seeks to avoid conflict between national competition law and the EU prohibitions. By targeting individuals, as

---

[3] For a fuller examination of the use of Competition Disqualification Orders and Undertakings see ch 11 above.

[4] See Hansard, HC, Standing Committee B, Enterprise Bill, Fifth Sitting, Tuesday April 23, 2002, col 169.

[5] See eg J M Connor and R H Lande, 'The Size of Cartel Overcharges: Implications for US and EU Fining Policies' (2006) 51(4) Antitrust Bul 983; and W P J Wils, 'Optimal Antitrust Fines: Theory and Practice' (2006) 29(2) World Comp 183.

[6] Council Regulation 1/2003/EC on the implementation of the rules on competition laid down in Articles 81 and 82 of the Treaty [2003] OJ L1/1.

opposed to the economic entities captured by EU law, the UK Cartel Offence was a complement to the EU prohibition rather than being in conflict with it.[7] The Cartel Offence also focuses on the 'intention' of the parties rather than the object or effect of the agreement.[8] This absence of conflict was confirmed by the Court of Appeal in *IB v The Queen*.[9] As the Cartel Offence does not go to the 'validity' of the cartel agreement itself it cannot be considered as 'national competition law' within the terms of Article 3 of Regulation 1.[10] Another perceived advantage of the offence's focus on intention and form, as opposed to effects, was the perception that it would reduce the potential for complex economic evidence being raised before juries in criminal trials.

The other key feature of the offence which raised concerns at the time, and was to prove to be its most controversial aspect, was the inclusion of the dishonesty requirement.[11] There was concern that the need to prove dishonesty, in relation to the intricacies of cartel behaviour, much of which would be an unfamiliar world for jurors, would prove to be challenging for prosecutors. How would they set about proving that cartel members should have known that their behaviour was dishonest?[12] As we shall see shortly, those concerns were well founded. But the dishonesty requirement also served another important function within the offence. As the actus reus of the offence was broad (namely, 'making or implementing' hard core cartel arrangements), there was a need to narrow the offence through the mental element to avoid the over-criminalization of otherwise benign behaviour. Those who made or implemented an arrangement caught by the offence, but thought it was legitimate - perhaps because it benefitted from the Article 101(3) TFEU exception, or simply where they were unaware of the nature of the arrangement - could seek to argue that they had not done so dishonestly. Notwithstanding the concerns about the need for, or efficacy of, the dishonesty requirement,[13] it was made a keystone of the new offence.

The new UK offence created an exciting new tool for the OFT, but it was a significant departure from any experience they previously had in relation to bringing administrative enforcement proceedings. Their task was now to use their new powers effectively to enhance the deterrent effect of the UK competition regime. Before the Cartel Offence was introduced, an OFT commissioned Report, 'Proposed Criminalisation of Cartels in the UK'[14] predicated that the number of likely prosecutions was at the lower end of six to nine per annum.[15] It was also suggested that the 'cases themselves will probably be complex and the majority will be high profile'.[16] The prediction as to numbers was optimistic, but the prediction of complexity proved too accurate.

---

[7] See Melanie Johnson, Hansard, HC, Standing Committee B, Enterprise Bill, Fifth Sitting, Tuesday April 23, 2002, col 167.

[8] The contemporary debate around the nature of 'object' agreements following Case C-67/13 *Groupement des cartes bancaires (CB) v European Commission* EU:C:2014:2204 indicates that subjective intention can be an element in 'object' cases, but it is a much wider concept.

[9] [2009] EWCA Crim 2575.

[10] ibid 34, 35, and 38. See also Peter Whelan, 'European Cartel Criminalization and Regulation 1/2003: Avoiding Potential Problems' in Adriana Almăşan and Peter Whelan (eds), *The Consistent Application of EU Competition Law: Substantive and Procedural Challenges* (Springer 2017).

[11] See eg MacCulloch (n 2) and A Stephan, 'How Dishonesty Killed the Cartel Offence' (2011) 6 Criminal Law Review 446.

[12] See MacCulloch (n 1).

[13] See MacCulloch (n 2) and Stephan (n 11).

[14] A Hammond and R Penrose, 'Proposed Criminalisation of Cartels in the UK', OFT365 (November 2001).

[15] ibid 3.6.

[16] ibid 3.7.

3 The Cartel Offence: A Mid-life Crisis

3.1 A Quiet Decline

The high point of the Cartel Offence in the UK was arguably the conviction of several defendants in the *Marine Hose* case in 2008.[17] That conviction was the result of effective international cooperation between the OFT and the US DOJ regarding UK nationals who were
initially arrested in the US in relation to the activities of an international cartel, and were
eventually returned to the UK, as a part of a US plea bargain. Their repatriation was subject
to their admissions of involvement in the cartel to the UK authorities, while still in the US,
and their arrest as they returned. All four pled guilty in the UK as required by their plea
deal. This was the high point as the original sentences imposed were at the top end of those
provided for in the sentencing guidelines and the sentencing remarks indicated the seriousness which the trial judge placed on the nature of the cartelists' wrongdoing.[18] From this
point on events began to take a less positive turn.

The three that plead guilty in *Marine Hose* all sought to challenge the sentences of 2½ or
3 years imprisonment handed down in 2008. When the case was heard before the Court of
Appeal it became obvious that the reality of the *Marine Hose* convictions was well outside
the norms of most UK criminal cases.[19] The Court was obviously troubled by the fact that
the appellants sought to appeal the length of their sentences, but were also keen to ensure
that they were not reduced too much. This was clearly an unusual argument to be heard in a
criminal appeal; but, it stemmed from a feature of the US plea deal—a minimum term of US
imprisonment had been agreed under the plea deal, and if a lesser term were served in the
UK additional time would need to be served in the US. The sentences set out in the US plea
agreement ranged from 30 months to twenty months.[20]

The Court of Appeal was concerned that it did not hear argument from the appellants'
counsel, as it would expect in a normal appeal. Because of the US plea bargain the Court did
not look at the personal mitigation of the applicants in detail, but did note that they were of
'good character', they had cooperated with the authorities (including giving evidence in the
US case), they had pled guilty at the first opportunity, and had lost their livelihoods. There
was recognition that these factors would, in normal circumstances, have led to certain discounts in sentence.[21] More interestingly, the Court stated they were 'much pressed with the
argument that this case could not conceivably be one of the worst cases of its kind'.[22] This
comment raises an interesting question—how bad a cartel was this? It may not have been
the largest in terms of monetary value, with an EU fine of €131m,[23] and it was certainly not
on the scale of *Trucks* (€3.8 billion) or *Monitor Tubes* (€1.4 billion).[24] However, the Cartel

---

[17] CMA, 'Marine Hose: Criminal Cartel Investigation' (14 November 2008) https://www.gov.uk/cma-cases/
marine-hose-criminal-cartel-investigation accessed 12 February 2020

[18] Judge Rivlin QC, *R v Whittle, Brammar & Allison*, Sentencing Remarks, Crown Court at Southwark (11
June 2008).

[19] *R v Whittle, Brammar & Allison* [2008] EWCA Crim 2560.

[20] ibid 26.

[21] ibid 29.

[22] ibid 30.

[23] European Commission, 'Antitrust: Commission fines marine hose producers €131 million for market sharing
and price-fixing cartel', IP/09/137 (28 January 2009).

[24] European Commission, 'Cartel Statistics' https://ec.europa.eu/competition/cartels/statistics/statistics.pdf
accessed 15 April 2020.

Offence is, as we shall discuss later, not focused on the economic harm caused by the cartel. It is perhaps tempting for the courts to look to the sheer size of a cartel as some form of proxy for its seriousness, but that is not itself a sufficient gauge. The Cartel Offence rightly looks beyond the traditional economic harms of cartels; such as overcharge to customers.[25] It focuses on the personal culpability of an individual for their role within the cartel. If we consider the role of Whittle, for example, within the Marine Hose cartel it is difficult not to see his pivotal role as being an example of a high level of culpability. He originally worked within one of the cartel firms, but formed his own consultancy company to facilitate the operation of the cartel full-time. Using code names and communicating with email accounts not associated with the infringing companies, he facilitated the big-rigging process and monitored it through monthly reports.[26] All of these factors indicate that all those involved knew of the nature and scale of their wrongdoing and were taking steps to hide their activity from detection and continue to reap its unlawful benefits. Whittle was paid directly by each cartel participant for his role, but also accepted a so-called 'commission', which I would characterize as kickbacks, to allow individual cartelists to succeed on particular bids and 'cheat' the other members.[27] This is a clear example of the worst form of personal responsibility for managing and personally benefiting from clandestine cartel activity. Beyond coercion or threats, this is the highest level of culpability.

There is nothing the CoA judgment to explain in substance why they adopted the view that this case was not at the most serious end of the spectrum of cartel activity; other than they were 'much pressed' with argument to that effect.[28] The CoA indicated 'considerable misgivings' about disposing of the case in light of the argument heard, but reduced the sentences to bring them into line with the US plea agreement.[29] Notwithstanding the reductions, the CoA also indicated that if the proceeding had not been constrained by the US deal they might have, 'been persuaded to reduce the sentences further'.[30] Unfortunately, they did not give any further justification for this approach. The Court stressed that this finding was not to be of value as a guideline sentence, because of its very particular, and unusual, US/UK nature. As for future guidance they highlighted the factors set out in the Hammond Penrose Report which proceeded the introduction of the offence.[31] It is difficult to see why many of these factors—gravity and nature, duration, culpability etc.—were not, as described above, at the 'top end' in relation to many aspects of the Marine Hose cartel.

While Marine Hose was perhaps a shaky start for the Cartel Offence it can probably be seen as its high point to date. That is because the Cartel Offence's next significant outing was such a low point; one that in practice may have caused such existential harm that the appetite for criminal prosecutions has never recovered. Much of the decline of the UK Cartel Offence can be traced back to the failure of the 'BA Four' prosecution.

It was clear from the outset that the BA case was going to important for the success of the nascent offence,[32] but its ignominious collapse during the trial itself was rightly seen

---

[25] See eg Connor and Lande (n 5).
[26] Sentencing Remarks (n 18) 11–12.
[27] ibid 12.
[28] ibid 30.
[29] ibid 31 and 32.
[30] ibid 31.
[31] Hammond and Penrose (n 14).
[32] See eg A Stephan, 'The Trial that will Make or Break the UK Cartel Offence Begins Today: The British Airways Four' CCP Competition Law Blog (1 April 2010).

as a disaster for both confidence in the Cartel Offence and in the OFT as a prosecution authority.[33] The OFT withdrew the prosecution case, offering no evidence against the accused, as it became apparent that it had not disclosed a significant number of emails to the defence, some of which may have been exculpatory in nature.[34] There was no suggestion that this was a deliberate act by the authority, rather the problem appears to have stemmed from material not being provided to the OFT by Virgin, who had blown the whistle on the cartel and applied for civil leniency.[35] The disclosure failure was ultimately fatal to the prosecution. It is clear that such a high profile failure has had a significant impact on the future of the offence itself, and the OFT's willingness to bring prosecutions in high profile cases. The OFT undertook an arm's length review of the case, Project Condor, in which it found that the threshold for prosecution, in terms of both evidence and public interest, was met.[36] However, '[w]ith the benefit of hindsight it was not ideal as the OFT's first contested case'.[37] The lessons surrounding evidence management and internal governance were important ones for the OFT to learn, but for the purposes of this chapter the most significant finding was that some features of BA case could have potentially 'undermine[d] the credibility of the prosecution with a jury'.[38] The particular features of this case that led to difficulties were that: 'the alleged cartel was a bilateral one in which the immunity applicant and its witnesses (who were also immune from prosecution) were equally implicated in the alleged offence. The reliability of the witnesses might be questioned'.[39] The defence case in the trial was that this was a 'world turned upside-down' where those who insisted that they had not acted dishonestly were tried on the basis of evidence given by those, including the Chief Executive of Virgin, who admitted acting dishonesty, but had been granted immunity and were getting away 'scot-free'.[40] The prosecution may well have found it challenging to present this as a just result to a jury.

Subsequent investigations under the Cartel Offence were often much more modest cases, in terms of both size and profile. A number of investigations were formally opened, and then closed on the basis of insufficient evidence.[41] The only other contested trial was in relation to a number of relatively small UK firms in the Galvanised Steel Tank (GST) cartel. The cartel investigation focused on three companies, Franklin Hodge, Galglass, and Kondea, which were involved in price-fixing, bid-rigging and market sharing, from 2005 to 2012, in the UK market for galvanized steel water tanks—a product often used in sprinkler fire systems for

---

[33] See A Stephan, 'Collapse of BA Trial Risks Undermining Cartel Enforcement' *CCP Competition Law Blog* (12 May 2010).

[34] OFT, 'OFT withdraws criminal proceedings against current and former BA executives' OFT Press Release 47/10 (10 May 2010).

[35] For a review of Virgin's role in the failure to disclose as a leniency applicant see, OFT, 'Virgin Atlantic Airways immunity review' OFT1398 (December 2011) https://webarchive.nationalarchives.gov.uk/ 20131101181358/ http://oft.gov.uk/shared_oft/ca-and-cartels/OFT1398.pdf.

[36] OFT, 'Project Condor Board Review' (December 2010) 1 https://assets.publishing.service.gov.uk/media/ 556876fce5274a1895000008/Project_Condor_Board_Review.pdf.

[37] ibid 2.

[38] ibid.

[39] ibid.

[40] See Alistair Osborne, 'BA-Virgin Case Exposes the Wacky World of Whistle-blowing' *The Telegraph* (30 April 2010).

[41] See OFT, 'Agricultural Sector: Criminal Cartel Investigation' https://www.gov.uk/cma-cases/agricultural-sector-criminal-cartel-investigation; OFT, 'Automotive Sector: Criminal Cartel Investigation' https://www.gov.uk/cma-cases/automotive-sector-criminal-cartel-investigation; and OFT, 'Commercial Vehicle Manufacturers: Criminal Cartel Investigation' https://www.gov.uk/cma-cases/commercial-vehicle-manufacturers-criminal-cartel-investigation.

commercial premises. After one cartel participant, CST, sought leniency the CMA began a criminal investigation and were able to use their powers to make an audio-visual recording of a cartel meeting in July 2012. Initial charges were brought against Peter Nigel Snee on 13 January 2014 in relation to price fixing and bid rigging.[42] Mr Snee went on to plead guilty to the charges. Two other men, Stringer and Dean, were charged in relation to the same cartel investigation on 30 June 2014.[43] The trial began in June 2015 and resulted in the latter defendants being acquitted, the CMA Press Release stating that, 'the jury were not persuaded that Mr Stringer and Mr Dean acted dishonestly.'[44] This gives us little to go on, but it is implicit that the CMA blamed the difficulty in proving the dishonesty of cartelists for the failure to secure a conviction.[45] The reaction of Peter Snee to his fellow cartelists' acquittal, after his guilty plea, was also not recorded. Snee was later sentenced to six months imprisonment—suspended for twelve months—and 120 hours of Community Service.

The reporting of the acquittals suggested that the defendants did not contest the facts as to their behaviour, but the defence presented them as being, 'motivated by honest considerations, including maintaining standards and keeping their businesses afloat in an increasingly competitive market',[46] and, were 'designed to avoid bankruptcy and redundancies, rather than to increase profit'.[47] It was also reported that a statement was released by Mr Dean's solicitor that the key issue in the trial 'was whether there was greed'.[48] That theme is reported to have been portrayed in 'theatrical style' in closing arguments.[49] It was reported that the jury were told that not every untruth was criminal (a compliment to your mother-in-law, may not be true, but would not be criminal), and the defendants 'worked hard and lived unflashy lives, driving second hand cars and paying off mortgages. The "evil" underpinning dishonesty - greed - was not present.'[50] The jury took less than 3 hours to decide that they were not dishonest and therefore acquit them of the charge.[51]

The arguments surrounding dishonesty have been well rehearsed in the competition law literature,[52] but for ease of reference the test in England and Wales was that as set out in *Ghosh*.[53] It was confirmed by *R v George, Burns, Burnett and Crawley*[54] that proof of dishonesty was required of an individual, but that there was no requirement for mutual dishonesty between the parties. The *Ghosh* test had two parts. First, the 'objective' test—whether according to the

[42] OFT, 'Man Faces Charge in Criminal Cartel Investigation', OFT Press Release 04/14 (27 January 2014).

[43] CMA, 'Two Men Face Charges in Ongoing Criminal Cartel Investigation', CMA Press Release (11 July 2014).

[44] CMA, 'CMA Statement Following Completion of Criminal Cartel Prosecution' (24 June 2015).

[45] See their post acquittal statement, ibid.

[46] See Chris Bryant, 'Defendants Acquitted in Criminal Cartel Trial' (Bryan Cave Leighton Paisner LLP (3 July 2015) https://www.bclplaw.com/en-US/insights/defendants-acquitted-in-criminal-cartel-trial.html accessed 5 August 2020. For the nature of the arrangements see CMA Decision, 'Galvanised Steel Tanks for Water Storage: Main Cartel Infringement' Case CE/9691/12 (19 December 2016), and CMA Decision, 'Galvanised Steel Tanks for Water Storage: Information exchange Infringement' Case CE/9691 (19 December 2016).

[47] King & Wood Mallesons, 'Water Tank Directors Cleared of Dishonest Criminal Cartel Conduct' (King & Wood Mallesons (3 July 2015) https://www.kwm.com/en/uk/knowledge/insights/water-tank-directors-cleared-of-dishonest-criminal-cartel-conduct-20150703 accessed 5 August 2020.

[48] ibid.

[49] Norton Rose Fulbright, 'Criminal Cartel Offence in UK: Public Attitudes' (Norton Rose Fulbright, June 2016) https://www.nortonrosefulbright.com/en-gb/knowledge/publications/3436c26a/criminal-cartel-offence-in-uk-public-attitudes accessed 5 August 2020.

[50] ibid.

[51] ibid.

[52] See the discussion in section 2 of this chapter.

[53] *R v Ghosh* [1982] EWCA Crim 2. The *Ghosh* test was overturned by the UKSC in *Ivey v Genting Casinos (UK) Ltd t/a Crockfords* [2017] UKSC 67. I shall return to this point later in the chapter.

[54] *R v George, Burns, Burnett and Crawley* [2010] EWCA Crim 1148.

ordinary standards of reasonable and honest people what was done was dishonest? And, secondly, the 'subjective' test—did the defendant himself realize that what he was doing was by those standards dishonest? In the context of the Cartel Offence we are largely concerned with the objective test. Did the jurors think that what these down-to-earth cartel participants— who led unremarkable lives, without greed, and drove second-hand cars—did was dishonest? The jury were not convinced by the prosecution case. There is no explicit reference to greed in the *Ghosh* test, but the references to greed and motivation in this case give an indication of the narrative that the defence presented to the jury; ordinary people, like you, working hard to save their businesses in difficult times. That narrative would not have worked in relation to BA case, but there you can perhaps see a related strategy. In that case it was far more difficult to portray the cartel participants as 'everymen', but the defence could seek to rely on the apparent intrinsic unfairness of one half of bilateral arrangement being threatened with a lengthy term of imprisonment, while their co-conspirators walked away on the basis of an immunity deal. Both of these cases highlight the dilemma in Cartel Offence case selection. It is vital that the prosecutor is able to build up a clear evidential picture of not just an overview of the cartel, but of the individual's culpability within that arrangement. It was simply not sufficient to show that a 'bad' cartel existed, you also needed to prove that there were 'bad' people inside the cartel. Their actions must be such that they demonstrated they were acting in a manner that deserves sanction. It may be that the competition law community are absolutely convinced with regard to the opprobrium deserved of individuals within cartels,[55] but that was not the view of the jury in GST. If you cannot show that those involved were acting beyond the moral pale, it will be very difficult to secure a conviction.

The final noteworthy case in the story of the original iteration of the UK Cartel Offence is the Precast Concrete Drainage Products cartel. There is, however, relatively little public information available on the criminal case. In March 2016, Barry Cooper, a director of Stanton Bonna (UK) Ltd, was charged with the Cartel Offence. Over a year later, in June 2017, the CMA decided that charges would not be brought against any other individuals in relation to that three party cartel. It is not clear how the cartel came to the attention of the OFT. The criminal investigation formally began in March 2013, but the OFT had clearly been tipped off earlier and had consequently begun surveillance of a number of cartel meetings, between August 2012 and March 2013, which were recorded and became a part of both the criminal and civil investigations. None of the participants had sought individual leniency when the investigation was initiated. Once the civil cartel investigation was underway, in November 2013 Stanton Bonna (UK) Ltd applied for civil Type B leniency, a lesser form of leniency available after an investigation has started, and began to cooperate with the investigation. That leniency was partial and, after the criminal case had concluded, Stanton Bonna (UK) Ltd, along with another cartel member CPM Group, entered into settlement discussions with the CMA. The other participant in the cartel, FP McCann, contested the CMAs characterization of their involvement in the cartel throughout the investigation, arguing that they had been competing throughout. It is, then, perhaps rather surprising that Barry Cooper, the senior executive from Stanton Bonna (UK) Ltd who had attended the recorded meetings, was the only individual charged with the Cartel Offence.[56] Mr Cooper

---

[55] At this point there is an antitrust tradition to refer to a particular US Supreme Court judgment, but I shall resist that temptation.

[56] CMA, 'Man Charged in CMA Criminal Cartel Investigation' CMA Press Release (7 March 2016).

pleaded guilty to the charge on 21 March 2016. It was not until June 2017 that the CMA announced that none of the other active participants was to be charged.[57] The only insight we have into the inner workings of the cartel is the evidence presented by the CMA in the civil infringement decision. From that it is somewhat puzzling why Cooper was singled out. One might assume that he was the ringleader of the 'pigeon club', as it was known by some participants,[58] but that does not appear to be the case. The evidence presented by Cooper and his counterparts from CPM Group, who were both cooperating with the CMA investigation, which was corroborated by the recordings, did not present him as the ringleader. In fact, in the meetings themselves it was not Cooper who directed the discussions. The evidence from CPM Group was that the representatives from CPM Group and FP McCann usually took the lead as they were 'the two more powerful characters' who 'kept things in check, maintaining discipline during the meetings'.[59] The main characteristic which distinguished Cooper appears to have been that he was more forthright in his knowledge of the unlawful nature of his activities, he took more explicit steps to hide the nature of the arrangements from senior figures in the company, and did more to ensure his staff did not depart from the arrangement. Cooper had undertaken competition compliance training in 2006, but had avoided signing the compliance documents as he knew he was breaking their terms.[60] He was eventually required to sign the documents in 2011 and, even though he knew that he was breaching its terms, he did so.[61] His internal conflict in signing those compliance documents was apparent in the evidence he gave to the CMA. In the civil decision the CMA noted that his evidence was to some extent 'internally inconsistent and contradictory', but it was consistent as to the key aspects of the cartel, and was supported by other evidence.[62] The final element that distinguishes his participation was that Cooper was the sole individual responsible for cartel activity in his undertaking. He monitored all activity, and ensured that others in the company implemented the cartel arrangement; even going so far as to reprimand them if they departed from its policy.[63] Without better evidence it is difficult to draw firm conclusions, and without access, in particular, to the recordings of the meetings, it is hard to shake off the suspicion that there may be a 'the customer is our enemy' moment somewhere on those tapes,[64] but if there was, why did the CMA not use it bolster its civil case? The evidence we do have points to the fact that Cooper was central to the cartel, largely being personally responsible for the activity in relation to his undertaking, and with good evidence, especially in relation to the avoidance of signing the compliance documents, that he knew what he was doing was unlawful. That may well have given the CMA confidence that they could make out a clear case for dishonesty in relation to his individual conduct. There was not the same evidence in relation to the other individual participants at the cartel meetings.

---

[57] CMA, 'Supply of Precast Concrete Drainage Products: Criminal Investigation' Case CE/9705/12 Update (13 June 2017).

[58] CMA Decision, 'Supply of Products to the Construction Industry (Pre-cast Concrete Drainage Products)' Case 50299 (23 October 2019) 4.57.

[59] ibid 4.79.

[60] ibid 2.84.

[61] ibid.

[62] ibid 2.88 and 2.89.

[63] See eg the comments from the FP McCann employee in the CMA Decision (n 58) 4.60.

[64] This is a reference to the infamous tapes of the Lysine Cartel meetings in the US in the 1990s see John M Connor, '"Our Customers Are Our Enemies": The Lysine Cartel of 1992-1995' (2001) 18 Review of Industrial Organisation 5.

An examination of the Cartel Offence prosecutions to date leaves us with a pretty disappointing picture. A few relatively minor successes, and a significant, and embarrassing, failure. It is no surprise that the CMA seems to have adopted the position that the best way forward was not to only to learn from the mistakes that had been made in these early cases, but also to press for reform. Its focus for reform was the dishonesty element of the Cartel Offence that they had found so troublesome in relation to their prosecution cases at trial. Despite their limited success bringing prosecutions before the courts, the CMA were much more successful in their pressure to reform the offence.

3.2 The Reshaping of the UK Cartel Offence

The early failures of the UK Cartel Offence led quickly to criticism and calls for reform.[65] That process began with a consultation and BIS proposals for reform.[66] The main proposal for the Cartel Offence was to remove the dishonesty element.[67] It was, however, impossible to simply excise that part of the offence without creating another set of problems. The requirement to prove dishonesty made it more difficult for the prosecution to make out their case, but it also stopped the offence from 'overreach'—where it would catch otherwise benign behaviour which had the explicit or tacit approval of civil antitrust prohibitions. There are two main types of behaviour with which we might be able to illustrate this issue. Firstly, horizontal agreements, that fall within the terms of the offence, but because of their positive aspects are authorized by competition law; for instance, the joint selling of sports TV broadcast rights, or credit card interchange fees. These beneficial agreements need to be 'carved out' of the criminal offence. The other group is less obvious, but also important. As the Cartel Offence prohibits both the 'making' and 'implementing' of cartel arrangements, it is important to distinguish between those who knowingly implement the cartel arrangement, and those that simply follow instructions from their managers and, without knowledge of the arrangement, operationalize a cartel. An example of that would be the salespeople in Stanton Bonna who complied with the instructions of their manager without knowing the pricing policy came from the 'pigeon club'.

The BIS proposal was to remove the dishonesty element, and it consulted on four potential options to subsequently narrow the potentially wide scope of the offence: 1) the introduction of prosecutorial guidance; 2) the introduction of a 'white list' of permitted agreements; 3) the introduction of a 'secrecy' element; or, 4) defining the offence to not include agreements made openly. The Government's preferred option was to remove agreements made openly from the offence.[68] The response to the consultation process showed no consensus, with several of the options getting support, but the Government decision was to retain their preferred choice of option 4.[69] The removal of the dishonesty element was largely

---

[65] See eg my contribution to the 10-year retrospective on UK Competition law reforms: Angus MacCulloch, 'The UK Cartel Offence: Is Honesty the Best Policy?' in Barry J Rodger (ed), *Ten Years of UK Competition Law Reform* (Dundee University Press 2010), and M Furse, 'The New Cartel Offence: "Great for a Headline But Not Much Else"' 32(5) European Competition Law 223.

[66] Department for Business, Innovation & Skills, 'A Competition Regime for Growth: A Consultation on Options for Reform' BIS/11/657 (March 2011), and Department for Business Innovation & Skills, 'Growth, Competition and the Competition Regime: Government Response to Consultation' URN 12/512 (March 2012).

[67] 'Growth, Competition and the Competition Regime' (n 66) section 7.

[68] ibid 7.26.

[69] ibid 7.12–7.25.

accepted by most commentators,[70] and the remaining debate surrounded the changes that would be necessary to replace that element and make the Cartel Offence more effective. When the Enterprise and Regulatory Reform Bill was introduced to the Parliament in April 2013, the new carve-outs of 'openness' and 'publication' were included. However, towards the end of the Bill's passage through Parliament other amendments were introduced with almost no scrutiny.

The final version of section 47 of the Enterprise and Regulatory Reform Act 2013 which received Royal Assent made useful amendments that improved the offence, as discussed above, but also introduced a number of problematic new provisions.[71] Alongside the removal of the dishonesty element from section 188(1) of the Enterprise Act 2002, section 47 of the ERRA 2013 introduced new 'carve outs' to the offence by inserting ss.188A and 188B into the 2002 Act. Section 188A(1)(a) sets out an 'openness' carve out: if the parties to an agreement give customers 'relevant information' about the arrangement before they enter into 'agreements for ... supply'.[72] A separate 'publication' carve out, under section 188A(1)(c), is available if relevant information is published before the arrangement is implemented. The 'relevant information' is defined in section 188A(2) to include the parties to the arrangement, its nature, and why it might be an arrangement to which the section 188(1) offence might apply. Concerns were raised in the consultation about commercial confidentiality, but the information that needs to be published is not detailed or likely to be commercially sensitive.[73] These are effective protections for beneficial arrangements. Rather than carving out behaviour which was found not to be harmful, or some other form of complex examination of the arrangement or the parties, it uses a simple proxy: do all of parties in a transaction know of the existence of the arrangement before committing to any obligations? To borrow from Louis Brandeis—'sunlight is said to be the best of disinfectants'.[74] It is reasonable to say that if the parties bring an arrangement to the attention of the public, and in particular to any customer before the supply of the relevant product, they should escape criminal law sanctions. That is not to say they are acting entirely lawfully—just that the criminal law is no longer the most appropriate remedy. It is also reasonable to assume that the publicity accorded to the arrangement through these mechanisms will alert customers and the competition authorities to a potentially problematic arrangement. Customers might want to reconsider their purchase, and the CMA may wish to examine the arrangement more closely. If public, and official, scrutiny is not a concern for the parties to the arrangement, there are more appropriate regulatory tools than the criminal law available; for example, the Chapter I prohibition. As discussed below, the criminal law should be reserved for the most egregious, and morally reprehensible, of violations; the parties are not likely to invite scrutiny of such arrangements. It is the simplicity of this 'carve out' which commends it. If the parties to a horizontal agreement are confident in its legitimacy, they have a means to protect themselves from any risk of criminal prosecution. In return they open up their arrangement to

---

[70] In the academic community at least, the responses to the BIS consultation were very mixed. See CMA, 'Consultation Outcome: A Competition Regime for Growth: Options for Reform' (16 March 2011) https://www.gov.uk/government/consultations/a-competition-regime-for-growth-a-consultation-on-options-for-reform accessed 11 August 2020.

[71] On the reform process and s 47 ERRA 2013 see Peter Whelan, 'Section 47 of the Enterprise and Regulatory Reform Act 2013: A Flawed Reform of the UK Cartel Offence' (2015) 78(3) Modern Law Review 493.

[72] Section 188A(1)(b) provides an analogous defence in relation to big-rigging.

[73] See Whelan (n 71) 507.

[74] Louis Brandeis, *Other People's Money and How the Bankers Use It* (Friederick A Stokes 1914) ch 5.

potential scrutiny. Whelan commends this approach as being a useful 'rough cut' between 'cartel activity caught by the (reformed) UK Cartel Offence and morally wrongful behaviour' as seen in the usual deception of a clandestine cartel.[75]

The defences introduced in section 188B are more problematic: those in section 188B(1) and (2) introduce some concerns, but in practice are unlikely to be significant; however, the new defence in section 188B(3) has been described as an 'absurdity'.[76] The defences in section 188B(1) and (2) are complements to the 'openness' and 'publication' carve outs found in section 188A. They cover 'gap' situations where the relevant information has not been provided, but the parties to the arrangement can show there was no intention to conceal them. Under (1), they must show they 'did not intend that the nature of the arrangements would be concealed from customers at all times before they enter into [supply] agreements'. Under (2), they must show they 'did not intend that the nature of the arrangements would be concealed from the CMA'. The rationale behind these defences is that they cover the 'gap' between the arrangement being made and the section 188A defence being completed. The most obvious example is under (2): to make out the defence you must first make an arrangement, and then subsequently publish its existence in the required form.[77] There must be a 'gap' between those two steps in which the offence of 'making' the arrangement has occurred, but the defence of publication has not been made out. The section 188B(2) defence covers that gap, as long as the parties can prove that they did not 'intend' to 'conceal' the arrangement from the CMA. The timing of the discovery of the arrangement will be important—the longer the 'gap' the more difficult it will be for the parties to show that concealment was not their intention. The same is true under (1) where the gap will be slightly different: here it would be between the agreement being made and a supply agreement being entered into. The parties would have to prove they had no intention, during that time, to conceal the nature of the arrangement. While the gap in (2) could be due to a simple delay in formal publication, the failure to alert customers in (1) must always be an error or oversight of some form. That failure will be difficult for those at the heart of the arrangement to explain, but in a larger commercial undertaking it may well be possible that full information about the nature of the arrangement is only available to a few people in the wider organization. The carve out will potentially be useful for individuals who are at a distance from the cartel arrangement. If we think back to the sales teams in Pre-Cast Concrete cartel, it was apparent that the sales team in some firms were kept in the dark as to the cartel, section 188B(1) may give them a defence. At the time high-level management made the arrangement, those sales people will be able to show that they did not intend to conceal that arrangement from customers with whom they transacted. My interpretation of (1) will need to be tested, but it appears that it may cover that situation. One might hope that the CMA would not seek to prosecute an 'innocent' implementer of a cartel arrangement, but this would, on the face of the Act, give such an individual the comfort of a defence.

The most problematic defence introduced by section 47 of the ERRA 2013, is now to be found in section 188B(3) of the 2002 Act. It is such a bizarre provision it is worth setting out in full:

[75] Whelan (n 71) 511.
[76] Andreas Stephan, 'The UK Cartel Offence: a Purposive Interpretation?' (2014) 12 Criminal Law Review 879, 883.
[77] For the correct form see the CMA, 'Cartel Offence Prosecution Guidance' CMA9 (March 2014).

(3) It is a defence for an individual charged with an offence under section 188(1) to show that, before the making of the agreement, he or she took reasonable steps to ensure that the nature of the arrangements would be disclosed to professional legal advisers for the purposes of obtaining advice about them before their making or (as the case may be) their implementation.

A complete defence to the UK Cartel Offence has been created for any individual who merely takes 'reasonable steps' to disclose the nature of the cartel arrangement to 'professional legal advisers' for the 'purposes of obtaining advice'. Quite frankly this beggars belief. It might be possible, at a very generous reading, to understand why Parliamentary drafters would want to protect an assiduous businessperson who: develops a novel, and highly beneficial, new business arrangement; consults his solicitors for legal advice; receives advice that the arrangement would benefit from the provisions of Article 101(3) TFEU, or sections 9 or 11 of the Competition Act 1998; and, then, seeks protection from the apparent application of the Cartel Offence. But a legitimate defence in that situation exists—publication under section 188A(1)(c). My reaction to the defence was to refer to it as 'Get Out of Jail Free' card;[78] Stephan, as noted above, described it as 'manifest absurdity';[79] and, Whelan, in a more measured way, as 'particularly troubling'.[80] One significant problem would be enough to condemn the defence, but there are several very obvious issues. If an individual obtains advice that the behaviour is clearly a criminal offence and they should not embark on that course of action, but chooses to go ahead regardless - it is still a good defence. If you disclose the nature of the arrangement to a legal adviser seeking advice, but do not wait for, or pay attention to, their response—it is still a good defence. If you post a letter to a foreign lawyer disclosing the agreement, but fail to provide a return address—is that enough? Any of these failings would be enough for the defence, as it is drafted, to be considered seriously flawed. But its most fundamental failing is that it is simply not required. Legal advice is irrelevant to the question of individual culpability for cartel activity. The 'publication' carve out in section 188A is an effective, and simple, means to give those who believe they are behaving legitimately the requisite protection, no matter why they believe their arrangement should not be considered unlawful. There is no need for further protection. Section 188B(3) should be removed from the statute book as soon as possible. Stephan makes an interesting argument that it may be possible to construe the defence in such a way as to mitigate its most significant failings,[81] but such an interpretation would stretch the limits of potential statutory interpretation. It would better if the section 188B(3) defence is repealed.

The 2013 reforms are a classic 'curate's egg'—partly good, partly bad. The removal of the troublesome dishonesty element was inevitable; it will not be missed by prosecutors, its potential will be missed by the defence bar.[82] The removal of dishonesty, which had the function of differentiating legitimate and illegitimate conduct, necessitated the introduction of

---

[78] Angus MacCulloch, 'Get Out of Jail Free: s 188B(3) of the Enterprise Act 2002' *Who's Competing Blog* (15 November 2015) https://whoscompeting.wordpress.com/2013/11/15/get-out-of-jail-free-s-188b3-of-the-enterprise-act-2002/ accessed 12 August 2020.

[79] Stephan (n 76).

[80] Whelan (n 71) 517.

[81] Stephan (n 76).

[82] See eg the many law firms who supported its retention in their responses to the CMA Consultation (n 70).

a new 'carve out' mechanism into the offence.[83] The carve outs in section 188A are a simple and elegant way of achieving that purpose, without adding significant added complexity to the provision. If you are open about your activity, with either your customers, or the CMA via publication, you cannot commit an offence. Openness may of course leave your undertaking open to investigation under the antitrust prohibitions, or private actions for damages, but that will not be an issue when the behaviour is legitimate. Thus partly good. The new defence in section 188B(3) is, on the other hand, the bad. If there was a legitimate concern that led to its late introduction in the Act, its wording has surely gone beyond that purpose. It is only a shame that Parliament gave it such minimal scrutiny. It should now be repealed.

4 A Developing Consensus in the Academic Debate

The introduction of the Cartel Offence in 2004 generated a great deal of commentary.[84] Most of that discussion focused on the additional deterrence that the new Cartel Offence would introduce, and how it would complement the existing antitrust fines imposed on undertakings. There was also considerable interest in the extent to which individual penalties could transform the incentives for leniency within cartels.[85] That debate was largely instrumental in nature and only looked at the Cartel Offence as a tool of competition law. It gave little heed to the fact that new offence was not simply another piece of administrative competition law; it was a part of the criminal law. The debate transformed once it was clear that the offence was not generating the prosecutions and convictions that were envisaged when the offence was introduced.[86] Even before the setback of the collapse of the BA Four case, and the soul searching which then followed, much of the academic debate focused on the dishonesty element of the Cartel Offence and its appropriateness.[87] After the failure in the BA prosecution the tide turned for dishonesty; even though the collapse of the trial was because of a discovery failure, the main line of defence led by the accused clearly related to the honesty, or otherwise, of the cartel participants' behaviour. The debate then widened out to consider how the UK Cartel Offence might be reshaped to make it workable, not only in terms of a what should be required for the prosecution to make out their case, but also in the terms that the offence properly captured the culpability of those individuals involved in a cartel. It is to that principled debate that I now turn.

The problems faced by the CMA in securing convictions in jury trials indicate the importance of capturing the culpability of individuals within a cartel. Much of the blame for those prosecution failures has been placed on the requirement to prove dishonesty, but, even without dishonesty, it will be necessary for the prosecution to make out a clear case to a jury why a cartel participant deserves to face the moral stigma of a criminal conviction, and

---

[83] It is with no little irony that after the ERRA 2013 reforms the UKSC redefined the dishonesty test in *Ivey v Genting Casinos* [2017] UKSC 67. As this reform essentially removed the 'subjective' element of the *Ghosh* test it would not have made a significant difference in cartel offence cases.

[84] See eg Joshua, MacCulloch, and Lever and Pike (n 1).

[85] See Christopher R Leslie, 'Cartels, Agency Costs, and Finding Virtue in Faithless Agents' (2008) 49 Wm & Mary L Rev 1621.

[86] Six to ten prosecutions per year were envisaged in the Hammond/Penrose Report (n 14).

[87] See eg C Beaton-Wells and A Ezrachi (eds), *Criminalising Cartels* (Hart Publishing 2011); and MacCulloch (n 65).

the possibility of the law's most stringent sanction—a term of imprisonment. If a prosecutor cannot convince the jury of this, there will always be the real risk of acquittals. Williams explains this as the 'bootstraps' problem—the Cartel Offence sought to harden the moral opprobrium of cartels, by declaring them as criminal; but the original offence presupposed that 'ordinary' citizens on juries would consider cartels as dishonest and therefore morally wrong.[88]

One of the reasons put forward as the primary rationale for the introduction of the dishonesty element in the original offence was to avoid the necessity of introducing complex economic evidence in jury trials.[89] But the desire to avoid economic analysis did not sit well with the instrumental approach to deterrence which lay behind the introduction of the Cartel Offence. If the economic harm caused by a cartel is not the rationale that lies behind the moral opprobrium, what is the criminal heart of cartel activity? It is also worth stressing at this point that the economic harm of cartels is in most cases the responsibility of undertakings operating on markets; the Cartel Offence does not apply to those undertakings. The offence applies to individuals within undertakings. They are to a greater or lesser extent isolated from the impact of the economic activity of the firm.[90] In the Galvanised Steel Tank trial the acquitted defendants' case was built upon the argument that they did not benefit personally from the cartel.[91] If we are to effectively explain why the individual deserves condemnation we must focus our attention on the individual's actions as an active cartel participant.

When one turns to look at the morality of cartel behaviour in the criminal law context there are a number of interesting arguments. A useful starting point is the work of Green in relation, more widely, to white-collar crimes.[92] He has developed a three-part test for situations in which the criminal law has traditionally determined that behaviour deserves the intervention of the state. Those three tests are: 1) culpability, 2) social harmfulness, and 3) moral wrongfulness. That framework can be used to place the criminality of cartel behaviour inside the framework of the criminal law; as opposed to merely looking for justification from a competition law perspective. We can look at each of these elements in turn.

4.1 The Culpability of Cartel Participants

Before an individual feels the full force of the criminal law, it should be proved that they are personally culpable. This is perhaps the least controversial element in relation to the UK Cartel Offence. Section 188(2) of the 2002 Act contains the requirement that to fall within the office the arrangement must be a 'hard core' cartel arrangement 'if operating as the parties to the agreement intend'. That intention element goes to the culpability of the individual. Intent is common feature of such offences. The individual must have intended to commit the actus reus of the offence.

---

[88] R Williams, 'Cartels in the Criminal Law Landscape' in C Beaton-Wells and A Ezrachi (eds), *Criminalising Cartels* (Hart Publishing 2011) 289–312.

[89] MacCulloch (n 1).

[90] On the problems with harm see, Bruce Wardhaugh, 'A Normative Approach to the Criminalisation of Cartel Activity' (2012) 32(3) Legal Studies 369.

[91] See KWM (n 47) and NRF (n 49).

[92] Stuart P Green, *Lying, Cheating, and Stealing: A Moral Theory of White-Collar Crime* (OUP 2006).

4.2 The Social Harmfulness of Cartel Behaviour

The social harmfulness of white-collar crime can be more difficult to explain, when one compares it to more commonly understood street crimes.[93] In a cartel the criminal behaviour is highly disguised, exists alongside legitimate behaviour, and has very diffuse effects. We have discussed the economic harm of cartels above, and that it is not the sole reason for cartel criminalization. The criminal law will normally look at harm as part of its justification. Criminal law, however, does not see all harms as being equal. Many events could be perceived as causing harm, but only the most serious will be seen as appropriate for the attention of the criminal law. One of the key distinctions is that between private harms— which are left to be resolved through private remedies, such as contract and tort—and public harms - that 'properly concerns the community as a whole, rather than just the individual citizens within such community'.[94] It is therefore important that if competition law wants to call on the innate criminality of a cartel, we should make a clear argument that cartels cause harm that goes beyond the private interests of financial interests of individuals, and goes to a broader form of public harm to the wider community. The 'public' nature of the cartel harm requires us to examine the inherent wrongfulness of cartels.

4.3 The Moral Wrongfulness of Cartels

The attempt to establish the inherent wrongfulness of cartels is at the heart of the contemporary understanding of cartel criminalization. If competition lawyers cannot articulate why cartels are intrinsically wrong, they should not claim the support of the criminal law.[95] The academic literature in the UK has shown a surprising confluence of views in regard to this fundamental question. This is in stark contrast to the divergence of opinion in demonstrated in wider responses to BIS Consultation on the ERRA reforms. If you canvas the academic literature you see that many authors have seized upon a common set of ideas that seek to capture the heart of cartel criminality. While we all have sought out our own perfect term, there is perhaps value in the wisdom of the crowd. If we look at the language proposed we can arguably see that there is shared understanding of the problem that we seek to address.

The most interesting attempts to characterize the wrong of cartels have included Harding & Joshua's arguments around 'delinquency'[96]—where the cartelist through the subterfuge they employ to avoid detection shows that they are acting outside the 'norms' of acceptable business behaviour. In his sole authored work, Harding continues to develop that idea by suggesting 'defiant willingness' to describe cartel behaviour.[97] Williams uses the concept of 'exploitation' to describe the advantage that the cartelist seeks to gain through their

---

[93] ibid 35 and 36.

[94] ibid 34.

[95] For a more wide-ranging examination of wrongs in competition see Nicolas Cornell, 'Competition Wrongs' (2020) 129 Yale Law Journal 2031.

[96] Christopher Harding and Julian Joshua, *Regulating Cartels in Europe* (2nd edn, Oxford University Press 2010) ch 3.

[97] Christopher Harding, 'The Anti-Cartel Enforcement Industry: Criminological Perspectives on Cartel Criminalisation' in Caron Beaton-Wells and Ariel Ezrachi (eds), *Criminalising Cartels* (Hart Publishing 2011).

activity.[98] The most popular analogy to be used, and the one which I now find by far the most convincing is that of 'cheating'. It has been proposed by Beaton-Wells,[99] Wardhaugh,[100] and Whelan.[101] I admit to being late to join this group, but now have the zeal of a convert.[102] I have rehearsed the arguments in favour of cheating being the most appropriate model elsewhere, but I shall attempt to summarize them briefly here.[103]

Green's white-collar crime model is, again, a useful structure based on the common law understating of the criminal cheat. It encompasses a situation where, 'X must (1) violate a fair and fairly enforced rule, (2) with the intent to obtain an advantage over a party with whom she is in a cooperative, rule-bound relationship'.[104] It is the nature of the relationship which is key to the conception of the cartel as a cheat. Much of the common law case law stems from gambling and games of chance, for a recent example we can look to *Ivey v Genting Casinos*, where the UKSC examines cheating in casino Baccarat.[105] In the context of a cartel the 'game' can be seen as the rules of the market itself—there is an expectation that all the market participants accept those 'rules' to facilitate trade and ensure there is a level playing for their mutual benefit. The cheat is where the cartel participants step outside the 'norms' of the market in order to gain an unfair advantage over their peers. It is important to stress that the wrong is not gaining an advantage, that is the expectation in a market, but it is that the cartel participant steps outside the normal expectations of the marketplace to seek that advantage.

As was noted above, not all wrongs or harms are best dealt with through the criminal law - crime should focus on 'public' wrongs. In what way can we then characterize the wrongful cheating of cartel participants as a public wrong? Again we can turn to the fundamental importance we place on the market as a public institution. This was explained by Wardhaugh who sets out that the market has taken a central role in the economic system upon which we all rely.[106] The market creates a 'fair environment for exchange'[107] which society uses to ensure the proper allocation of resources. By stepping beyond the expectations of the market the cartel participants not only harm other market participants, but also the wider public interest in the functioning of the market as a public institution.

4.4 The Value of Consensus

This specific conception of the 'public' wrongfulness of cartels is my own, but one can see that there is now a more widely accepted agreement that there are certain expectations of

---

[98] Rebecca Williams, 'Cartels in the Criminal Law Landscape' in Caron Beaton-Wells and Ariel Ezrachi (eds), *Criminalising Cartels* (Hart Publishing 2011).

[99] Caron Beaton-Wells, 'Capturing the Criminality of Hard Core Cartels: The Australian Proposal' (2007) 31 Melbourne University Law Review 675.

[100] Bruce Wardhaugh, *Cartels, Markets and Crime* (CUP 2014) ch 1.

[101] Peter Whelan, *The Crminalization of European Cartel Enforcement* (OUP 2014) ch 4.

[102] See Cerian Griffiths and Angus MacCulloch, 'Dishonesty and Cheating in Fraud and the Criminality of Cartel Behaviour' CLaSF Workshop, Granada (September 2018).

[103] Angus MacCulloch, 'The "Public" Wrong of Cartels and the Article 101 TFEU "Object Box"' (2020) 65(3) Antitrust Bulletin 361.

[104] Green (n 92) 57.

[105] *Ivey v Genting Casinos (UK) Ltd t/a Crockfords* [2017] UKSC 67.

[106] Wardhaugh (n 100) 25–26.

[107] ibid 45.

the market, and that those who participate in cartel activity act against the market as an institution, rather than simply in a manner that harms their individual customers. The value in having a more widely accepted description of the wrongfulness of cartels is twofold. First, those who seek to justify the use of criminal law sanctions against cartel participants can explain why those, most stringent, sanctions are an appropriate response to that behaviour. Until now that rationale has not been set out very clearly. Second, the lessons learned from having a clear idea of why a criminal sanction is appropriate gives investigators, and ultimately prosecutors, a narrative to explain to a jury why the behaviour of the cartel participants falls below expected standards of behaviour, and how it damages us all. Without a common conception of the criminal cartel problem it was difficult for investigators to understand exactly what evidence needs to be gathered to build a good criminal case, as opposed to that evidence that they were used to gathering for a civil antitrust investigation. That evidence will go to the fact that those individuals knew that they were stepping outside the norms of the market and they did so to gain an advantage; not necessarily to line their own pockets, for this is not a question of greed, but to protect their commercial interests from the rigours of the market. It is the market that protects us all, but those individuals sought to deny us that protection in order to advantage themselves.

5 The Future of Criminal Investigations and the Cartel Offence in the UK

At the time of writing there are few reasons to be optimistic about the operation of the UK Cartel Offence. There have been very few prosecutions, and while there have been convictions, they have only come from guilty pleas. Where cases have gone to trial, those charged have been acquitted.[108] If I were a member of the defence bar, I might advise my clients to take their chances at trial—the CMA do not have a good record as a prosecutor.

While that record cannot be denied there are still reasons for some guarded optimism. That is not to say that we can expect a sudden upsurge in cases, or a reversal of the current position. However, we have some indication that there are building blocks in place, which may allow the UK authorities, and the wider competition law community, to develop an environment in which future criminal prosecutions might be more likely to be successful. There are a number of interrelated strands which we must continue to develop to build that more positive environment.

5.1 The New Cartel Offence

With the clear exception of the defence of seeking legal advice, the changes to the Cartel Offence introduced by ERRA 2013 are largely to be welcomed. The removal of the dishonesty element of the original offence was an inevitability given the problems that it caused in the first cases to go to trial. There are questions which can legitimately be raised about the OFT and CMA's case selection and preparedness for being a prosecutor, and there were

---

[108] See *Galvanised Steel Tanks* (n 46).

always going to be issues as it developed its expertise in a very different legal environment; but, that phase is now over.

There will be a significant lag period where 'legacy' cases, discovered after the introduction of the new offence but including behaviour that proceeded it, are discovered. It will only be when cartels that began after 1 April 2014 begin to come through the system that we can observe how the new offence will cope. These cases will now be coming to the attention of the CMA.

The new offence may be easier to prove, in that the evidence will only need to show that there was an intention to make or implement an arrangement of a certain type, but as we have seen defendants are willing to make strenuous defences based on arguments that what they did was not 'wrong' or motivated by personal greed. The focus on the ordinary nature of the defendants and their motives in *Galvanised Steel Tanks* prosecution is an example of this defence strategy, but it has been apparent in both live cases in the UK.[109] The presence of the dishonesty element in those cases made such a line of defence of obvious value, but there is no reason to suggest that such an approach will not be retained under the new offence. If the defence can present the accused as an everyman who is just doing their best to look at their business and save jobs it will still be a powerful message to the jury.

For a successful prosecution to be brought the CMA must focus on the right sort of cases for prosecution. That choice goes beyond technical questions about whether there is evidence about the nature of the arrangement. A good case for prosecution is also one that not only surpasses the technical evidence threshold, but is also one that shows clearly why it is a good case for criminal prosecution. The criminal law has a different focus to that of the antitrust prohibitions. A cartel may present with very strong evidence of a Chapter I infringement, but that does not necessarily mean that it will also present with evidence of a strong criminal case. The nature of criminal enforcement is that it will be reserved for the most serious cases; that is its very purpose. In practical terms a criminal case must also come before an antitrust infringement process. That challenge means that the CMA must be aware of the potential for a criminal investigation at the very early stages of any Chapter I investigation. It should also be alert to the flags, discussed below, that indicate that a cartel case has the elements which might make it a good case for criminal investigation, and ultimately of prosecution. It is in this regard where there are more reasons for optimism. There is evidence that the CMA increasingly understands the importance of individual culpability and a wider narrative of wrongfulness.

5.2 Individual Culpability

One of the most obvious distinctions between criminal investigations under the Cartel Offence and traditional antitrust investigations is their focus on individual behaviour. Recent CMA practice has shown that it has taken steps to make that its focus in more cases.

We have already examined the Cartel Offence cases. In *Galvanised Steel Tank* and *Pre-Cast Concrete Drainage* the CMA,[110] at an early stage in the process, identified the potential for a criminal case and used their criminal investigatory powers to focus on the individual

---

[109] See the discussion in section 3.1.
[110] See section 3.1.

actions within the cartel. In those cases that was through the making of covert recordings of the cartel activity. Those recordings were no doubt invaluable, not only in proving the nature of the arrangement, but also proving the role played by certain individuals. But that was not the only evidence of individual behaviour which was focused on in criminal investigations such as *Pre-Cast Concrete Drainage*. There was also evidence addressing the leadership of meetings and who shaped discussions.[111] As I have identified, there were other elements of individual culpability which singled Mr Copper out for the bringing of a criminal charge: 1) he signed competition compliance documents while being involved in cartel activity, and 2) he reprimanded staff who unknowingly made sales outside the parameters set by the cartel arrangement. This type of evidence is not required for a Chapter I prohibition case. It does not matter who did what within an undertaking, only what the undertaking did as a whole. While there has always been the potential for a 'smoking gun' email to emerge during any infringement investigation, there now appears to be a more concerted effort to gather the right sort of evidence to support a criminal case. The experience in these cases will also have helped investigators to understand what evidence is most effective before a jury.

The growing importance of individual culpability in relation to competition law is also seen in another interesting area: Competition Disqualification Orders and Undertakings. There is no need to go into the detail of those Orders and Undertakings here, as it is covered in detail above by Peter Whelan in Chapter 11. As that Chapter indicates, Director Disqualification also acts as a form of individual deterrence within the UK competition regime, working as a complement to fines on undertakings, and the ultimate sanction of imprisonment. One of the key features which must be addressed by the CMA in considering making an application for a CDO is that 'the director's conduct contributed to the breach of competition law'.[112] This shows that across the full panoply of competition law enforcement in the UK the individual conduct of a Director may be of importance in any investigation, not just in classic cartel cases. This renewed focus on individual behaviour in wider competition investigations will build expertise and experience which will feed into potential Cartel Offence cases in the future, and will ensure that in early Chapter I investigations potential evidence of individual responsibility will be gathered.

The renewed focus on individuals has not, yet, led to Cartel Offence prosecutions, but there have been increasing numbers of Competition Disqualification Undertakings (CDUs) alongside Chapter I infringement cases. Whelan has noted a surge of cases in the last four years.[113] Many of those cases were in relation to small scale price fixing arrangements, and it is clear that the use of CDOs or CDUs act as an effective complement to potential Cartel Offence cases. They are not only a complement in terms of deterrence, they also ensure that investigators will, well before decisions about the ultimate form of a case are finally taken, attempt to gather good evidence of individual culpability that could be of value in either a CDO or a criminal case.

I have stressed the importance of investigation and evidence gathering in this section. There is however also a note of caution to be struck. One unusual feature of Chapter I cases

---

[111] *Pre-Cast Concrete Drainage* (n 58) 4.79.

[112] Competition and Markets Authority, 'Guidance on Competition Disqualification Orders' CMA 102 (6 February 2019) 2.10.

[113] See ch 11 above.

like *Galvanised Steel Tank, Balmoral Tanks*,[114] and *Pre-Cast Concrete Drainage* is that we see evidence gathered using criminal investigation powers, usually covert recordings of cartel meetings, used in antitrust infringement decisions. That has proved to be very useful in those cases, and the use of the enhanced investigatory powers in those cases was justified. If we do not see new criminal prosecutions being brought before the courts in the future, the continued availability of those criminal powers of investigation may be brought into question.

5.3 The Narrative of Wrongfulness

The enhanced focus on individual culpability during investigations and evidence gathering is only part of the change required to develop effective pathways toward successful prosecutions. The prosecution must be able to present that evidence in a way that convinces a jury that a conviction and term of imprisonment is deserved (and not simply legally warranted).

It is here that the developing understanding of the criminal nature of cartel activity is of assistance. Having a shared understanding of the nature of cartel criminality gives the wider competition law community an opportunity to develop a clearer narrative of what it is about an individual's behaviour in a cartel that means they deserve punishment. The conception of 'cheating' the market is potentially therefore very helpful. If investigators and prosecutors have that conception in mind when building their cases, and ultimately prosecutors present their evidence to a jury using that narrative to explain the criminal wrong that lies at the heart of cartel activity, they are more likely to carry the jury with them. A single narrative used over time in a number of cases, and highlighted in competition advocacy by the CMA, may also help to develop a better understanding of the cartel problem in the business community and more widely in the public consciousness.

It is hopefully not mere coincidence that the recent CMA 'Cheating or Competing' campaign[115] is an example of how this message can be built up, through adverts, videos, and posters, and carried through into investigations and prosecutions. As Howard Cartlidge, the CMA's Senior Director of Cartels, said in the press release, 'The CMA is cracking down on businesses that collude to rip off customers by fixing prices, sharing out markets amongst themselves or rigging bids. Our message to them is that we know cheating when we see it, even if you don't.'[116] The campaign uses covert recordings captured in previous criminal investigations, such as *Pre-Cast Concrete Drainage*, and *Residential Estate Agency Services*.[117] Effective advocacy of this nature is to be encouraged. It should raise awareness of the cartel problem in the business community, but it must also be carried through by the CMA into its enforcement efforts. If the CMA consider cartel activity as a species of cheating they will have the intellectual support of many in the academic community. That narrative of wrongfulness must also be used to help CMA investigators shape the evidence they gather, and then have CMA prosecutors use that evidence to build up cases which can convince a jury that cartel participants are criminal cheats. If they can do that effectively it will help

---

[114] *Balmoral Tanks Ltd & Anor v Competition And Markets Authority* [2019] EWCA Civ 162.

[115] CMA, 'Cheating or Competing?' https://cheatingorcompeting.campaign.gov.uk/ accessed 18 September 2020.

[116] CMA, 'New CMA Campaign Urges Firms to Compete, Not Cheat' (26 February 2020).

[117] CMA Decision, *Residential Estate Agency Services*, Case 50543 (17 December 2019).

to reduce the impact of the common lines of defence that cartel activity is not for personal greed, or is to save jobs. That is less relevant is the narrative of harm focuses on cheating the wider public.

6 Conclusions

The UK Cartel Offence has, in many ways, not been a great success. It was a bold change in enforcement practice for the UK regime, and it appears the UK competition authorities were underprepared for the enforcement challenges it would bring. The wider competition law community had also failed to appreciate how much the adoption of criminal powers, and contested trials, would necessitate a re-examination of many of the fundamental questions which underlie competition law. Those early failures have, through the changes brought in by the ERRA 2013 and the wider debate surrounding the wrongfulness of individual cartel activity, been addressed to a great extent. The problem now is not the lack of a clear pathway to rebuild the UK Cartel Offence, it is whether there is the institutional appetite, particularly within the CMA, to re-invest in criminal enforcement. There is still significant reputational risk in further failure, and one hopes that there are those within the CMA who are willing to try again. The CMA's focus on cartels as 'cheating' and their willingness to use other individual sanctions, such as CDUs, gives some hope that there is still stomach for the fight.

14

Competition Law and the Digital Economy in the UK and Beyond

Liza Lovdahl Gormsen

1 Introduction

The digital economy, or 'data economy',[1] only has few boundaries. One can debate whether we are going through a digital revolution or evolution, but either way our economy is going digital. The evolving digital economy can be associated with an increased use of advanced robotics, AI, the Internet of things, cloud computing, big data analytics, and three-dimensional (3D) printing. In addition, interoperable systems and digital platforms are essential elements of the digital economy. According to the EU's Executive Vice President Margrethe Vestager, 'a digital economy is—necessarily—a platform economy.'[2] Platforms consists of algorithms, which are widely employed throughout our economy and society to make decisions that have far-reaching impacts, including their applications for education, media, finance, healthcare, tourism, transportation and employment to mention some.[3] Algorithms feed off data. More data than ever is being generated at a much faster pace with more precision. Data can be a product where firms compete to sell data.[4] It can also be an input, which firms need in order to compete in a particular market.[5] Data can affect entry conditions by making it more or less difficult for a firm to enter or compete. Having a data advantage can lead to great innovations, but it can also create huge concentrations in various markets. Whether any particular practice of a platform is anti-competitive is fact-driven and highly dependent on the actual market dynamics in the specific markets at issue. Antitrust laws permit evaluation of concerns about unlawful exercises of market power by multi-sided platforms and relevant characteristics such as network effects, multi-homing and data as a source of market power, tool of exclusion or an entry barrier.[6] Antitrust laws are good at responding to changes in the economy by taking tested and well-functioning theories of harm and applying them to a new set of facts. The digital economy undeniably

---

[1] 'A Deluge of Data is Giving Rise to a New Economy' *The Economist* (20 February 2020).
[2] Margrethe Vestager, 'Building a Positive Digital World' European Commission (29 October 2019) https://wayback.archiveit.org/12090/20191129200144/https://ec.europa.eu/commission/commissioners/2014-2019/vestager/announcements/building-positive-digital-world_en accessed 1 May 2020
[3] 'Big Data: A Tool for Inclusion or Exclusion? Understanding the Issues' Federal Trade Commission (January 2016) https://www.ftc.gov/reports/big-data-tool-inclusion-or-exclusion-understanding-issues-ftc-report accessed 1 May 2020.
[4] *CoreLogic/DataQuick* [2014] 131 0199: FTC challenged merger that would have combined one of only three providers of national assessor and recorder bulk data (real estate); consent required merged firm to license data to a new competitor.
[5] *Verisk/EagleView* [2014] 141 0085: FTC challenged merger of the only two significant competitors for rooftop aerial measurement products for insurance (aerial image libraries are a key input to the product); parties abandoned after complaint issued.
[6] The terminology of antitrust and competition law is used interchangeably throughout this chapter.

Liza Lovdahl Gormsen, *Competition Law and the Digital Economy in the UK and Beyond* In: *The UK Competition Regime*. Edited by: Barry Rodger, Peter Whelan, and Angus MacCulloch, Oxford University Press. © The Contributors 2021. DOI: 10.1093/oso/9780198868026.003.0014

poses challenging new facts and raises a huge number of interesting questions. With limited space however, the focus in this chapter will be on: (i) data and its relevance in the antitrust analysis; (ii) enforcement in digital markets and (iii) regulation of some parts of the digital economy in the UK.

To be true to the title of this book *The UK Competition Regime: A Twenty-Year Retrospective*, this chapter will make the discussion geographically focused on the UK. Given the truly global nature of the digital economy, the discussion will be contextualized within the wider debate in the EU and beyond. Despite the fact that the UK has left the EU, it is reasonable to expect that the enforcement of competition rules will follow the same or a very similar approach as Brussels. Thus, references to EU competition policy in the digital economy are included whenever relevant. References to reports delivered in other jurisdictions such as the United States of America and Australia are also included for comparative purposes.

2 Antitrust and the Digital Economy

The digital economy describes markets characterized by rapid innovation and technological change, the features of which variously include the creation, exploitation of, and reliance on intellectual property rights; the need for complementary products, services or platforms to work together; and a high degree of technical complexity and technological sophistication.[7] In the UK, this poses a unique challenge for the Competition and Markets Authority (the 'CMA'), as seen in its *Online Platforms and Digital Advertising* market study published in July 2020 (the 'CMA report').[8] The latter showed how the digital economy is undermining conventional notions about how businesses are structured, how firms interact and how consumers obtain services, information and goods. Competition law in the UK and elsewhere respond to changes in the economy by taking tested and well-functioning theories of harm and apply them to a new set of facts. The UK is not alone in intensifying its scrutiny of the digital economy. Over the past decade, the European Commission (the 'Commission') has taken enforcement action against some of the world's biggest platforms.[9] In April 2019, the Federal Trade Commission (FCT) took action against Surescripts—a two-sided platform business that connects prescribers, pharmacies and payers—alleging that Surescripts illegally maintained its monopoly in e-prescribing markets by using exclusivity and loyalty agreements to prevent multi-homing.[10] Using competition law to assess exclusivity and loyalty agreements is not new and competition authorities are well equipped to look at these kinds of conducts. Another example is network effects, which are relevant when considering data, but network effects are not new. It is not novel for competition authorities to have to consider when the positive aspects of network effects (e.g. innovating a

---

[7] Alison Jones, Brenda Sufrin, and Niamh Dunne, *EU Competition Law: Text, Cases and Materials* (7th edn, Oxford University Press 2019) 57.

[8] Competition and Markets Authority, *Online Platforms and Digital Advertising: Market Study Final Report* (CMA Report) (1 July 2020) https://assets.publishing.service.gov.uk/media/5fa557668fa8f5788db46efc/Final_report_Digital_ALT_TEXT.pdf.

[9] For example, the European Commission has taken enforcement action against Google in a number of cases: Case 40411 *Google Search (Ad Sense)*; Case 40099 *Google Android*; Case 39470 *Google Search (Shopping)*.

[10] *Federal Trade Commission v Surescripts, LLC*, 1:19-cv-01080-JDB https://www.ftc.gov/system/files/documents/cases/surescripts_redacted_complaint_4-24-19.pdf accessed 1 May 2020.

network to bring people together) outweigh the negative impact of network effects (e.g. excluding access to the network). What is new however, is the required understanding of the technology as much as the economics.

It is important to recognize that not all digital platforms are the same; there are important differences in business models between them. Conduct by a digital platform owner that may raise competition concerns is usually intertwined with the incentives and abilities produced by the kind of business model being employed on the platform. Think of data-driven firms like Facebook or Google, which provide a service to users in exchange for their data rather than charging a monetary price.[11] Data is a fundamental input that advertising-funded platforms require for the successful operation of their revenue-making segment (that is, targeted advertising). Measuring consumer welfare in terms of price does not sit well with business models where end consumers do not pay a monetary price.[12] The notion of 'no price, no harm' may have shielded some technology companies from competition enforcement for some time due to a narrow interpretation of consumer welfare focusing on price. This way of measuring consumer welfare has been criticized for considering a static view of the market and pursuing short-term consumer interests only.[13] With the economy going digital, it has been argued that markets have become less consumer friendly, prices have gone up and there has been raising concentrations in certain markets.[14] It is clear that not all concentrations are bad. An increase in concentration following productivity and innovation, and therefore an outcome of disruption, is good. However, when concentration is driven by barriers to entry it is unhealthy.

2.1 Digital Platforms, Data, and Anti-competitive Conduct

Digital platforms can be divided into two high-level categories: traditional platforms and aggregation platforms. Both traditional platforms and aggregation platforms depend on data—big data. The latter is the amalgamation of volume, velocity, variety and veracity of data.[15]

Traditional platforms include computer or cloud operating systems. Third-party developers may offer applications and services on the platform. They have a direct relationship with their customers and are not intermediated by the platform. Interoperability is a typical competition concern for traditional platforms. Aggregation platforms are distinguished by their ability to aggregate users and suppliers on either side of the platform and control

---

[11] Some people may not be convinced that consumers are not paying a monetary price, as the actual price extracted probably includes indirect costs of advertising on Facebook passed on to customers by the advertisers. It also includes attention i.e. time spend and time can be converted into a monetary value.

[12] 'Most of the literature on the antitrust consumer welfare standard assumes that the variable of interest is price: other things being equal, an increase in consumer welfare occurs if the price falls, and a decrease in consumer welfare occurs if the price rises.' See Herbert Hovenkamp 'On the Meaning of Antitrust's Consumer Welfare Principle' University of Pennsylvania, Inst for Law & Econ Research Paper No 20-16 https://ssrn.com/abstract=3525385.

[13] Bruno Lassere and Andreas Mundt, 'Competition Law and Big Data: The Enforcer's View' (2017) 1 Italian Antitrust Law Review 92; Tim Wu, 'After Consumer Welfare, Now What? "The Protection of Competition" Standard in Practice' Competition Policy International (April 2018) 5–6.

[14] Thomas Philippon, The Great Reversal (Harvard University Press 2019); Lina M Khan, 'Amazon's Antitrust Paradox' (2016) 126 Yale Law Journal 564; Matt Stoller, Goliath (Simon & Schuster 2019).

[15] Also called the four Vs; see Ariel Ezrachi and Maurice E Stucke, Digital Competition (Harvard University Press 2016).

the relationship between them. Strong network effects,[16] huge economies of scale,[17] and scope[18] typically protect aggregation platforms. Because aggregation platforms distribute digital goods over the Internet, they enjoy zero marginal costs for serving users. They are typically monetized in two ways either by share of sales or by advertising. Those aggregation platforms that connect consumers and vendors, such as online marketplaces, app stores and ridesharing services take a cut of the sale. Others such as social networks and search engines offer a free (zero price) service to users and provide access to those users to advertisers. Their control of the relationship between users and suppliers may lead to two antitrust harms: exploitation and exclusion. Exploitation occurs when the aggregator exercises market power over one side of the platform, control access by the other side, and extracts all the rents. Exclusion occurs when they stifle companies that compete with them for user demand.

Aggregation platforms can easily employ both antitrust harms simultaneously. For example, when a company like Facebook combines first party data, which is data collected on its own platform Facebook.com, and third party data—data collected from apps other than Facebook.com to serve ads, in particular targeted ads, it has the ability to exclude competitors in the upstream market for online display advertising such as content publishers.[19] In Germany, the Bundesgerichtshof has banned Facebook from collecting first and third partly data without providing the user with a choice as to whether such data collection can happen. Following the judgment, users actively have to agree to such data collection.[20] While the combination of data elicits data-driven efficiencies, leading to better ad targeting and enhanced user experience, it could fuel traditional and data-driven network effects to such an extent that little room remains for effective competition in the online display advertising market. Advertisers are attracted to the possibility of targeting a large audience with remarkable precision (based on the richness of Facebook's datasets), and consequently competitors suffer. This effect could be a mere consequence of economies of scale and scope. However, the collection and combination of data from third party websites and apps with data gathered from Facebook's properties (first party data) renders no benefit to users. Such combination of data does not benefit the delivery of the individual services—quite the contrary. It reduces quality because of the subsequent changes undermining the privacy standards. The counterfactual is given by Facebook's good privacy standards before it became dominant,[21] and its lax privacy policy following its cemented dominance in the market for social network. Facebook's explanation—a better layout—for degrading its privacy policies was not accompanied with significant improvements on the services. A better layout is not a significant improvement and does not require data aggregation. Users are interested in interacting with their online connections and see engaging content consistent with their

---

[16] The positive effect that an additional user has on the value of the platform to others.
[17] The cost advantage that arises as more users join the platform.
[18] Efficiencies created by diversifying production.
[19] Facebook is a multi-sided platform that caters to at least four sides (users of its social network, advertisers, app developers and content publishers), enabling interactions that would not be possible but for its intermediation. For a good overview of multi-sided platforms, see David S Evans, 'Some Empirical Aspects of Multi-Sided Platform Industries' in David S Evans (ed), *Platform Economics: Essays on Multi-sided Businesses* (Competition Policy International 2011).
[20] At the time of writing only the press release was available but not the judgment. See https://www.bundesgerichtshof.de/SharedDocs/Pressemitteilungen/DE/2020/2020080.html?nn=10690868.
[21] Liza Lovdahl Gormsen and Jose Tomas Llanos, 'Facebook's Anticompetitive Lean in Strategies' *Social Science Research Network* (17 June 2019) 22–24 https://papers.ssrn.com/abstract=3400204.

interests. The data gathered from Facebook's properties is more than enough to this end. Not only that, such combination is likely to be seen as a degradation of quality of the social networking platform. The combination of data reduces the degree of competition in the on-line display advertising market, thereby protecting Facebook's dominance in the social network market. As a consequence, barriers to entry are raised and incentives to compete and innovate are reduced (especially considering Facebook's actions to impair the growth of entrants). Since Facebook is the entry point for advertisers, there is no incentive for others to innovate e.g. with more privacy friendly tools, and there are no incentives for Facebook itself to innovate because there is no competitive pressure. These detrimental effects on competition and harm to social network users likely outweigh efficiencies that may be claimed in the form of improved ad targeting to the benefit of Facebook's advertising customers. It must be noted, however, that the combination of data is not the only factor leading to anti-competitive outcomes. Direct and indirect network effects also play a paramount role.

Much can be done under the GDPR to combat the combination of data gathered from Facebook's different services. This combination violates the purpose limitation and data minimization principles[22] and the consent users provide in this regard is questionable, as the majority of users have no idea what they have consented to. Digital platforms usually obtain data from consumers by offering a binary choice in form of accepting or rejecting the terms and conditions. The latter are typically drafted in a way that does not allow consumers to fully understand what exactly they are accepting. Even if consumers choose to review such terms and conditions it is unlikely that they will have the background and expertise required to understand how much data—personal data—they provide to the platform.[23] While GPDR and privacy laws seem best suited to deal with issues of consent and personal data, competition law still has a role to play. From a competition law perspective, there is the issue of coercion when consumers face a binary choice expressed in 'take it or leave it' terms and conditions set by a dominant undertaking. Both Article 102 of the Treaty on the Functioning of the European Union (TFEU) and section 18 of the Competition Act 1998 (CA 1998) recognize 'unfair trading conditions' as an abuse of dominance. The situation becomes critical in the absence of alternatives offering a better choice for users in what and how much data to provide. This also has an impact in the market as the dataset held by the dominant platform continues to improve and harder for actual and potential competitors to replicate it. The goals of privacy law and competition law may not necessarily be identical, but they have 'family ties'.[24] Both GDPR and competition policy converge in the sense that both pursue market integration by applying a common framework across the EU.[25]

Facebook could be forced to respect the aforementioned principles and obtain actually valid consent to carry out said combination as has now happened in Germany.[26] Limiting the scope of data extraction is relevant for antitrust purposes as digital platforms create

---

[22] Regulation (EU) 2016/679 of the European Parliament and of the Council of 27 April 2016 on the protection of natural persons with regard to the processing of personal data and on the free movement such data, and repealing Directive 95/46/EC (General Data Protection Regulation), art 5, 1(b), 1(c).

[23] Stigler Committee on Digital Platforms. Final Report (George J Stigler Center for the Study of the Economy and the State, 2019) (Stigler report) https://research.chicagobooth.edu/-/media/research/stigler/pdfs/policy-brief---digital-platforms---stigler-center.pdf?la=en&hash=AC961B3E1410CF08F90E904616ACF3A3398603BF.

[24] Francisco Costa-Cabral and Orla Lynskey, 'Family Ties: the Intersection between Data Protection and Competition in EU Law' (2017) 54(1) Common Market Law Review 11.

[25] ibid.

[26] See n 22.

barriers to entry into the market because of the importance and greatness of the datasets they possess.[27] Owing to data advantages, potential competitors are unable to pose a challenge to the market position from giant market players. Limiting the scope of data to be extracted from consumers would serve two purposes. First, applying adequate standards for the protection of privacy and second, to prevent digital platforms from expanding their market power into neighbouring markets.

As demonstrated by the Facebook example, digital platforms have the ability to extract data in consumer-facing markets (i.e. search engine or social media) as a raw material that will improve their market position in the advertisement market. Useful information on this matter can be found in the CMA report.[28] The latter highlighted the importance of the dataset held by Google and Facebook in consumer-facing markets such as being able to target consumers based on specific interests or background information. This allows both Google and Facebook to have a significant competitive advantage in the digital advertisement market as businesses seeking to advertise and to reach the widest possible number of consumers are likely to advertise on Google and Facebook. Thus, these two platforms are unlikely to have significant competitive pressure as the dataset itself is a barrier to entry.[29] Other jurisdictions have arrived at similar findings as the CMA. The Australian Competition and Consumer Commission (the 'ACCC') conducted a digital platforms inquiry.[30] Its final report, published in July 2019, concluded that both Google and Facebook generate revenue in digital advertisement as a consequence of their position in consumer-facing markets. Another advantage of the dataset is improving users' experience. This attracts more users to the platform and incentivizes current users to spend more time in the platform, providing more data and ultimately allowing the platform to improve.[31]

The greater the data the platform extracts in consumer-facing markets, the better it becomes at selling advertisement. This strategy works as a vicious circle as one market complements the other and makes the dataset bigger and bigger. Thus, competitive pressure either disappears or becomes insignificant. However, when this conduct has already taken place, antitrust laws can readily be used on the basis that consumer harm (exploitative conduct) is arising from the imposition of unfair terms on the downstream market—the social network market—leads to a weakening of the competitive market structure on the upstream market for online display advertising (exclusionary conduct).[32]

On the other end of the spectrum, if a rigid data protection rule is enacted that forces digital platforms to dramatically reduce the amount of data they extract from consumers this could have a negative impact for both the market and consumers. There are three important considerations to analyse if barriers are created for the extraction of data. First, consumers could end up worse-off because platforms use their data to overall improve their services and consumers' experience. In other words, less data could mean a slower

---

[27] Michael Gal and Oshrit Aviv, 'The Competitive Effects of the GDPR' (2020) 16(3) Journal of Competition Law and Economics 349, 351–53 3–4.

[28] CMA Report (n 8) paras 2.3–2.10.

[29] ibid para 43.

[30] Digital Platforms Inquiry—final report (Australian Competition and Consumer Commission, July 2019) (ACCC Final report). https://www.accc.gov.au/system/files/Digital%20platforms%20inquiry%20-%20final%20report.pdf.

[31] ibid 7.

[32] This is a very different theory of harm to the one employed by the Bundeskartellamt in their Facebook decision where it relied on data protection law to find an infringement. See Case B6-22/16 Verwaltungsverfahren GEM § 32 ABS 1 GWB.

improvement of the services. It will be up to policymakers to strike a fair balance between the protection of personal data and any improvement in service. Secondly, if data is considered a property right and therefore triggers a payment for consumers, it could bring no meaningful change in the market. In the absence of specific and clear guidance (i.e. a proactive role) from the enforcer, platforms can assign a nominal value to the data. Even if the enforcer is proactive, it should not be forgotten that platforms generate vast revenues in the advertisement market. The CMA report is particularly persuasive in this point when analysing the UK market as it concluded that approximately £14 billion was spent on digital advertising in the UK in 2019. From this amount, approximately £7 billion corresponded to search advertising and approximately £5 billion to display advertising.[33] Google has generated around 90% or more of UK search traffic each year over the last ten years and generated over 90% of UK search advertising revenues in 2019.[34] The CMA report also found that Facebook and Instagram—owned by Facebook since 2012—generated almost 50% of the total revenues in display advertising in 2019. The amount of revenues generated by Facebook and Instagram was approximately five times higher than the revenue of its next competitor, YouTube, which is owned by Google.[35] Considering the large amount of resources held by dominant market players, then it is unlikely that paying for the data extracted from consumers will be problematic as a nominal value could be assigned. Almost certainly it will not be an issue for digital platforms to pay extra to maintain the status quo. Thirdly, a measure that severely limits the collection of data could harm both dominant and non-dominant platforms. This could work in favour of the biggest market players as they will still be in a much more favourable position because they will remain in control of the largest datasets. A possible option is to create specific rules (i.e. data sharing rules) applicable only to platforms with significant market power as suggested by Professor Furman in *Unlocking Digital Competition* (the Furman Review).[36] However, this could be questioned on grounds of fairness and may harm incentives to invest and innovate.

Google and Facebook could be regarded as two examples of how the extraction of data and possession of a relevant dataset can be used as a tool to engage in potential anticompetitive conduct, as rivals will find it very difficult to compete because of their inability to replicate the dataset. The CMA report explores the intersection between competition and data protection further as it considers privacy as a parameter for competition.[37] This same parameter is applicable to search engines and social media as it is expected that online platforms will compete, among other competition parameters, on privacy settings.[38] For example, a healthy and competitive market will allow consumers to compare and select a search engine or a social media based—among other elements—on the basis of the amount of personal data they must provide to access the platform. This shows an intersection between competition policy and privacy policy expressed as better privacy settings. As explained before, data privacy regulation and competition policy analyse data issues from different perspectives, but there is an overlap between them as unfavourable privacy

---

[33] CMA Report (n 8) para 16.
[34] ibid para 18.
[35] ibid.
[36] *Unlocking Digital Competition* (March 2019) para 2.117 https://assets.publishing.service.gov.uk/government/uploads/system/uploads/attachment_data/file/785547/unlocking_digital_competition_furman_review_web.pdf (Furman Review).
[37] CMA Report (n 8) paras 3.12, 3.158.
[38] ibid.

policies could reflect a potential competition issue. It has been argued that the expectation is to enable the market to generate competition for privacy.[39] However, as the CMA report explains, it is not entirely clear if consumers behave in this way in reality. This means that they do not always diligently analyse privacy policies from platforms.[40] The data paradox theory suggests that although consumers are concerned about their privacy in the online world, they seem to behave in a contradictory way as they usually accept almost any privacy terms offered from platforms even if it means providing—what it seems to be—a disproportionate amount of data to use the platform.[41] Various possible explanations have been provided for this paradox theory, some of them are lack of choice as these are highly concentrated markets (i.e. no alternative provider) or nudging strategies based on the exploitation of cognitive limitations attributed to consumers (i.e. unwillingness to be engaged with privacy terms or making it harder to access such terms), and this issue is further explored in the CMA report.[42] However, it is significant to look beyond the sheer volume of data that any company holds and understand the rights of the company vis-a-vis the data. It is important to distinguish between data itself and what companies do with the data. The latter is what is of interest to antitrust enforcers. A lot of data is non-rivalrous meaning that no one person has the data—it is accessible to all—and it flows from various sources. However, some data is rivalrous meaning it belongs to a company and can be used to exclude customers and competitors upstream. Thus, it is important that antitrust enforcers understand from a technical perspective (i) what any number of various data sets enables the company to do with the data; (ii) assess whether the data is rivalrous or non-rivalrous; (iii) whether the use of big data matches a traditional theory of harm and (iv) define at what point the data advantage becomes insurmountable to the detriment of consumer welfare.

The issue as to how to regulate data still remains unresolved. The CMA report recommends setting up a Digital Markets Unit (DMU), which would enforce a code of conduct.[43] This code is meant to operate as digital regulation and it is based on, among other high-level principles, 'trust and transparency'.[44] This principle—while not entirely an original proposal from the CMA, but more an adaption from the principles suggested by the Furman Review,[45]—includes an obligation for platforms to provide information to consumers explaining how the platform extracts and processed personal data.[46] The potential problem with this proposal is that it may not tackle the issue on the extraction of data. The provision of information to consumers on how the platform operates and is funded—while it is certainly a problem of transparency—may not be the key issue to solve the problem with data. For all practical purposes, data is the price paid by consumers to access a platform funded by digital advertising. Even if more information is provided to consumers there is still a risk that they may misunderstand it or simply choose not to be engaged with the terms and conditions, as explained by the CMA report regarding the data paradox theory.[47] A more comprehensive and bolder approach from the competition authority could consist of analysing

---

[39] Costa-Cabral and Lynskey (n 24) 7–8.
[40] CMA Report (n 8) paras 4.46–4.58.
[41] ibid.
[42] ibid.
[43] ibid paras 7.22–7.89.
[44] ibid paras 7.85–7.89.
[45] Furman Review (n 36) para 2.38.
[46] CMA Report (n 8) para 7.87.
[47] ibid paras 4.46–4.58.

the possibility of monetizing data, in the sense that—in specific circumstances—it could trigger a payment for consumers. The role of data goes far beyond the provision of information for consumers and the root of the problem must be tackled, namely the massive extraction of data at little or no cost for most dominant platforms.

The Digital Markets Taskforce (DMT) accepted the CMA's recommendations in its advice to government set out in its report *A New Pro-competition Regime for Digital Markets* (DMT report).[48] Part of the DMU's role will be to understand the role of data in specific business models.[49]

2.2 Data Sharing and Data Portability

The Furman Review outlined some of the challenges involving the sharing of data and how the DMU should strike a fair balance between different competing interests such as protecting incentives to innovate (i.e. developing a dataset) and preventing free riding (i.e. making access to the platform too easy).[50] This is a key issue as data sharing involves forcing online platforms to provide access to their infrastructure, which is likely to be the reason of their own success.[51]

In this regard, data sharing is not a remedy without costs. The Furman Review was particularly cautious regarding the sharing of data between platforms as it suggested that giving access to the infrastructure amounts to a very intrusive intervention.[52] However, the purpose of this measure is to develop a competitive market. The expected benefit arising from achieving this goal should be measured against the cost of implementing an intrusive remedy based on access. In this regard, the Furman Review proposed limiting the type of data that will be shared. This involves designing data openness in a cautious way by reducing intervention to the core of the business model. One possible way to achieve this is to limit access to raw data. This is data that has not been classified or treated by the platform as opposed to processed data. The latter has necessarily been subject to development, meaning that the platform has invested resources to foster the dataset.[53] Giving access to this type of data may discourage innovation as it may allow inefficient entry into the market (i.e. free-riding). In this regard, the Furman Review concludes—in very abstract terms—that the DMU should decide how to implement data openness by balancing benefits and costs. The DMT report acknowledges data openness as a means to promote competition.[54] Accordingly, data mobility, interoperability and data access can be used to address the factors, which are the source of market power of a firm with significant market status (SMS).[55] The DMT talks about data openness, data mobility, and data access as remedies.

A similar concern arose in Europe as the EU's Executive Vice President Vestager has highlighted the necessity of making data accessible in the digital economy:

---

[48] *A New Pro-competition Regime for Digital Markets* (December 2020) https://assets.publishing.service.gov.uk/media/5fce7567e90e07562f98286c/Digital_Taskforce_-_Advice.pdf (DMT report).
[49] ibid paras 6 and 3.7.
[50] Furman Review (n 36) para 2.66.
[51] ibid.
[52] ibid para 2.87.
[53] ibid para 2.91.
[54] DMT report (n 48) para 1.3.
[55] ibid para 1.3.

Europe's businesses hold huge amounts of data that isn't working as hard as it should, be-cause it's scattered. But if we bring that data together, it can help businesses build better products, and compete more successfully. And the competition rules have an important role to play here, by giving companies guidance on the types of data sharing that are good for competition—and the red lines they shouldn't cross. Because we need to help busi-nesses pool and share data, but in a way that can benefit our whole society.[56]

Vestager's position is not surprising, as the report on *Competition Policy for the Digital Era* (the 'EC policy report'),[57] prepared for the Commission in 2019, discussed the issue of data sharing. The latter has the potential to lead to both pro- and anti-competitive outcomes, thus a scoping exercise of the different types of data pooling and subsequent analysis of their pro- and anti-competitive aspects is therefore necessary to provide more guidance.[58] It is important to understand the potential role of measures such as data sharing and data portability in addressing competition law concerns. It is important to distinguish between mandating data sharing and data portability through *ex-ante* regulation and ordering data sharing and data portability to restore a competitive environment to its pre-merger or pre-conduct state. It requires the authorities to understand specific legal violations and how data sharing and data portability would remediate the competitive harm (e.g. preserve or restore competitive conditions) in the affected markets.

In relation to data portability, the EC policy report suggested a more stringent regime to be imposed on dominant platforms in order to overcome particularly pronounced lock-in effects.[59] More demanding regimes of data access, including data interoperability, can be imposed (i) by way of sector-specific regulation (as in the context of the Payment Services Directive 2015/2366/EU)—in particular where data access is meant to open up secondary markets for complementary services; or (ii) under Article 102 TFEU—but then confined to dominant firms.[60] It is necessary to distinguish between different forms of data, levels of data access, and data uses. In a number of settings, data access will not be indispensable to compete, and public authorities should then refrain from intervention. There are other settings, however, where duties to ensure data access—and possibly data interoperability—may need to be imposed. This would be the case, in particular, of data requests for the pur-pose of serving complementary markets or aftermarkets, that is, markets that are part of the broader ecosystem served by the data controller. However, in these cases competition authorities or courts will need to specify the conditions of access. This, and the concomitant necessity to monitor, may be feasible where access requests are relatively standard and where the conditions of access are relatively stable. Where this is not the case, in particular where a dominant firm is required to grant access to continuous data (i.e. to ensure data interoper-ability), there may be a need for regulation, which must, at times, be sector specific.[61]

---

[56] Margrethe Vestager, 'Shaping a Digital Future for Europe' European Commission (3 February 2020) https://ec.europa.eu/commission/commissioners/2019-2024/vestager/announcements/shaping-digital-future-europe_en accessed 1 May 2020.

[57] Jacques Cremer, Yves-Alexandre de Montjoye, and Heike Schweitzer, 'Competition Policy for the Digital Era. Final Report' (European Commission 2019) (EC policy report) https://ec.europa.eu/competition/publications/reports/kd0419345enn.pdf.

[58] ibid.

[59] ibid 77.

[60] ibid 9.

[61] ibid 9–10.

In principle, mandating a platform to share their infrastructure with rivals seems to be a fast and effective way to develop competitive markets. However, if data collection can be reproduced, it cannot be seen as an 'essential facility' under *Oscar Bronner*.[62] In those circumstances where data can be replicated, forcing access to a platform's data would therefore likely be disproportionate. Ensuring portability and 'multi-homing' in these circumstances is therefore the preferable option. That said, even if replicating the dataset were possible, it could be highly costly and uncertain.[63] Smaller platforms could—in theory—develop their own infrastructure.[64] This could be fostered by facilitating access to the dataset held by dominant players. However, because of the way in which technology markets operate, it is unlikely that a rival will ever be able to develop a competitive dataset. Without regulatory intervention, it may never happen. This is one of the conclusions from the Stigler Committee on Digital Platforms' final report in 2019 (the 'Stigler report'): 'It is unlikely that these problems will self-correct, meaning new and revised rules and incentives will be needed to prevent market power from entrenching a few dominant tech firms as economic and social gatekeepers.'[65] Secondly, depending on the situation it may be inappropriate to facilitate access to the infrastructure. Market players may have reduced incentives to innovate. Thirdly, designing access remedies could be costly. Enforcement costs are high because constant supervision becomes more relevant. This is not just limited to enforcing access itself (i.e. willingness to deal with competitors), but also to supervising the terms of access (i.e. prices). This was an issue in the telecoms sector where the Commission has had to apply a very broad notion of refusal to deal merging it with constructive refusal to deal as part of the same infringement.[66] An access remedy is intrusive. Refusal to deal could potentially go beyond a simple rejection of access, as the authority could create novel theories of harm generating less predictable enforcement patterns.[67] This was particularly problematic when the Commission enforced competition law in the utilities sector. This was in line with the Commission's objective of achieving the single market in the EU. This development is less relevant for the UK—as an erstwhile EU member—but still useful to understand possible future developments in EU competition policy. Considering some of the similarities between utilities and online platforms such as the existence of a single infrastructure (i.e. platform) and the need to regulate access to such platform, it would not be surprising if a similar pattern of competition enforcement is applied by the Commission in the digital sector.

In the US, the Stigler report proposed instead a schematic two-fold strategy, consisting in the first place, of enacting legislation for the protection of consumers' data. A second step consists of giving supervisory powers to the digital authority (i.e. regulator) to develop and enforce policy on data portability.[68] The digital regulator, as proposed by the Stigler report, should have a pro-competitive remit in charge of, among others, rulemaking on data portability.[69] Some ideas included in the Stigler report to achieve data portability involve, for

---

[62] *Oscar Bronner GmbH & Co KG v Mediaprint Zeitungs- und Zeitschriftenverlag GmbH & Co KG, Mediaprint Zeitungsvertriebsgesellschaft mbH & Co KG and Mediaprint Anzeigengesellschaft mbH & Co KG* ECLI:EU:C:1998:569.
[63] Lassere and Mundt (n 13) 97–98.
[64] *Oscar Bronner* (n 62).
[65] Stigler report (n 23) 120.
[66] *Konkurrensverket v TeliaSonera Sverige AB* ECLI:EU:C:2011:83.
[67] Pietro Merlino and Gianluca Faella, 'Strategic Underinvestment as an Abuse of Dominance under EU Competition Rules' (2013) 36 World Competition: Law and Economics Review 513.
[68] Stigler report (n 23) 109.
[69] ibid 273.

example, putting the regulator as an intermediary that streamlines the flow of data between consumers and platforms.[70]

Mandating data sharing is a contentious issue and perhaps this a good excuse for the Australian ACCC, as its conclusions in this regard are surprisingly inconclusive, because it decided to further analyse this subject. It considered there to be insufficient evidence to determine how likely it is that data portability will diminish barriers to entry into the market in the short term.[71] As explained earlier in this section, the Furman Review also took a cautious approach, as it proposed in abstract terms that the DMU should strike a fait balance between the protection of innovation and the promotion of competition in the digital sector.

A way to factor in foreclosure concerns arising from accumulation of data, as well as from restriction of access to such data, must be found. This analysis should consider not only the breadth of the data accumulation, but also the extent to which it is truly indispensable for other companies to compete, for instance, in view of other available sources. Foreclosure effects should be based on strong economic evidence, as opposed to being based on mere theoretical arguments that concentration of data allows a platform to behave independently of its customers and competitors. Once the theories of harm are clearly defined, acceptable commitments should be adjusted accordingly; for instance, behavioural remedies including data access and portability commitments may prove effective to dispel concerns in digital ecosystems. The EC policy report considers data portability as a proper solution when a gatekeeper impedes access to data.[72] In practice, however, portability is sometimes not viable because the standards applied are not harmonized. On some occasions, the manner in which data is provided to the requesting party makes it impossible to use it. Moreover, privacy and security concerns may limit data sharing.

2.3 Killer Acquisitions

Another antitrust concern with digital platforms is the so-called 'killer acquisitions'. The terminology killer acquisitions is borrowed from the critically acclaimed research by Cunningham, Ederer, and Ma entitled 'Killer-acquisitions'. The authors explain the strategy applied by pharmaceutical companies consisting of the acquisition of nascent rivals engaged in the development of new pharmaceutical products. The purpose of this kind of acquisitions is not the production of efficiencies but shutting down the development of new products.[73] Such acquisitions are strategic in an anti-competitive sense, with the purpose of protecting the market position of a monopolist or a dominant market player.

Killer acquisitions are nothing new in the digital sector. In fact, as explained below, competition enforcers are aware of this situation, as the various policy reports have shown. The antitrust concern with killer acquisitions is whether incumbent firms may acquire smaller upstart companies to pre-empt future competition, for example to block potential competitors, protect a monopoly or otherwise harm competition.

---

[70] ibid 110.
[71] ACCC Final report (n 30) 11.
[72] EC policy report (n 57) 91.
[73] Colleen Cunningham, Florian Ederer, and Song Ma, 'Killer Acquisitions' Social Science Research Network (22 March 2019) <https://ssrn.com/abstract=3241707>.

Competition enforcers are also aware of this strategy. CEO of the CMA, Andrea Coscelli, has expressed concerns about digital mergers:

> Over the last decade, Amazon, Apple, Facebook, Google, and Microsoft combined … have made over 400 acquisitions globally, with more than half of these – close to 250 – just in the most recent 5 years. Some of these acquisitions have had exceptionally high valuations. However only a handful of these mergers have been scrutinised by competition authorities, and none have been blocked. As an economist, these statistics naturally lead me to question whether we as competition authorities have got the balance right. Is it right that across all 400 of these acquisitions, there has not been a single prohibition? On this basis, is it possible to argue that we've correctly balanced the risks of under- and over-enforcement?[74]

The statement reflects a curious situation where merger review seems to have reached 100% compliance (i.e. manifested in the fact that no merger was blocked) and yet it seems to be 100% ineffective as some digital markets are hugely concentrated, as different competition enforcers across different jurisdictions have demonstrated.[75] Transactions like *Facebook/WhatsApp* or *Microsoft/Skype* have been reviewed by antitrust regulators and often are considered critical only in hindsight. As the Furman Review clearly outlines, there is a dichotomy in merger control between false positives (i.e. vetoing mergers that are not harmful to competition) and false negatives (i.e. allowing mergers that are anti-competitive). The Review mentions that the problem in the digital sector is, almost certainly, related to under-enforcement of competition.[76]

It is not surprising that the Stigler report, taking the American perspective on digital killer acquisitions, has found similar evidence as it concluded that as a consequence of windfall profits generated by incumbent online platforms, they are able to scout, purchase and shut down potential nascent rivals. The Stigler report cites the Facebook/WhatsApp acquisition as a possible example of a killer acquisition.[77]

Changing the concept of potential competition is not only a question of catching more competitive concerns so that they can be addressed, but also about applying a sufficient level and standard of proof. Could a transaction actually be prohibited under the substantial lessening of competition test if we were looking towards an even longer forecasting horizon or if products or services offered by the startup are—at best—partial substitutes at the moment of the transaction? If market entry still requires relatively lengthy and complex innovative work, i.e. depends on a series of factors in relation to which it is not certain that they might all occur in the sufficiently near future, the prospective analysis of the effects of the concentration could become purely speculative. That said, the reports commissioned in the UK, the EU, the USA, and Australia have all proposed changes to the merger control regime to different extents. The proposals can be subdivided into three different categories. First, the most far-reaching involve altering the burden of proof by requiring the merging

---

[74] Andrea Coscelli, 'Competition in the Digital Age: Reflecting on Digital Merger Investigations' Competition and Markets Authority (June 2019) https://www.gov.uk/government/speeches/competition-in-the-digital-age-reflecting-on-digital-merger-investigations.

[75] CMA report (n 8) para 2.14. ACCC, ACCC Final report (n 30) 74–76, 80–84. See Commission decision on Case AT.39740—*Google Shopping* 59–60, 72–73, 57–58.

[76] Furman Review (n 36) para 3.43.

[77] Stigler report (n 23) 75.

parties to prove the pro-competitive effects of the merger, otherwise the merger is prima facie anti-competitive. This proposal was put forward by both the Stigler report and the EC policy report. Secondly, the middle-ground approach proposed by the Furman Review maintains a case-by-case analysis, but with reference to a new test renamed the balance of harms approach. Thirdly, the ACCC's Final report proposes simple changes to the merger control regime in relation to the elements to be reviewed by the competition enforcer.

The inversion of the burden of proof in merger control consists of an effective presumption of illegality applicable to all mergers. Despite the EC policy report expressly rejecting that such presumption exists, the parties are meant to provide evidence of the pro-competitive effects of the merger:

> In particular, in the context of highly concentrated markets characterised by strong network effects and subsequently high barriers to entry (a setting where impediments to entry which will not be easily corrected by markets), one may want to err on the side of disallowing types of conduct that are potentially anti-competitive, and to impose the burden of proof for showing pro-competitiveness on the incumbent.[78]

The Stigler report has explained this proposal as follows:

> The agency will need a simple and efficient merger review process so that businesses can move forward without undue delay, and the agency does not expend more resources than necessary. These concerns indicate that the burden of proof must primarily be placed on the merging parties who have the incentive, data, and resources to quickly deliver the right information to the authority.[79]

The Stigler report has proposed this measure to dominant platforms with bottleneck power (i.e. single service provide that forces consumers to single-home).[80]

The main advantage of creating a presumption of illegality is the elimination of the risk of killer acquisition from happening again in digital markets. However, the question is whether the measure is proportionate to the aims it seeks to achieve. Integration may also be a source of efficiencies. These acquisitions often have a sound efficiency rationale and are pro-competitive, for example, if acquirers, due to their know-how and superior financial possibilities, successfully bring products or services into the market, or improve their availability and quality. Also, innovation is often motivated by the prospect of selling a startup, once it has developed a promising product, to a larger company wishing to expand or improve its offer. Barring or limiting such possibilities may deter startups and innovation beyond the alleged anti-competitive effects of a transaction. Moreover, not every potential competitor succeeds in establishing its market presence, whether in the digital field or otherwise. Thus, it is questionable whether changing and expanding the concept of potential competition would do justice to complex cases and theories of harm. The dangers of applying this presumption are that it may lead to false positives with dire consequences in markets where innovation is the main driver. One side of the analysis should consider that

---

[78] EC policy report (n 57) 51.
[79] Stigler report (n 23) 112.
[80] ibid 105–106.

costs of monopolization or leveraging into neighbouring markets. The other side should consider the upside of the efficiencies generated such as the development of new innovative products or services for the benefit of consumers. The question that policy-makers are encouraged to answer is how to achieve a fair balance between these two considerations.

The EC policy report considers that the EU merger regulation does not require legislative update without providing further detail.[81] However, the inversion of the burden of proof in merger control is likely to require legislation such as secondary EU law because it will be a significant change in the way mergers are analysed and also an important variation on the scope of the parties' rights. If that is the case, this could effectively mean creating sector specific rules for the digital sector on merger control. According to Article 2, Council Regulation (EC) No 1/2003 on the implementation of the rules on competition laid down in Articles [101] and [102], the burden of proving an infringement shall rest on the party or authority alleging an infringement.[82] The CJEU has clarified the burden of proof in *Baustahlgewebe v Commission*: 'where there is a dispute as to the existence of an infringement of the competition rules, it is incumbent on the Commission to prove the infringements found by it and to adduce evidence capable of demonstrating to the requisite legal standard the existence of the circumstances constituting an infringement'.[83]

In recent case law, the CJEU has addressed claims involving an alleged inversion of the burden of proof in competition enforcement cases rejecting such inversion.[84] In *Bertelsmann v Impala*, the CJEU held that there is no presumption that a concentration is either compatible or incompatible with the single market.[85] It also emphasized that the decisions from the Commission on merger control must be based on evidence: 'Furthermore, it is true that, as is apparent from the Court's case-law, the decisions of the Commission as to the compatibility of concentrations with the common market must be supported by a sufficiently cogent and consistent body of evidence'.[86]

Establishing a presumption of the anti-competitive character of a merger could lead to a conflict not just with Regulation 1/2003, but also with well-established case law from the CJEU, as the parties could be required to prove that the concentration is not incompatible with the single market. Thus, this proposal requires further consideration if it is to be implemented.

A moderate middle-ground approach was suggested by the Furman Review, as it proposed updating the merger control test based on balance of harms. According to this test the competition enforcer will consider whether the concentration is expected to do more harm than good depending on their impact in the market.[87]

As will be explained and analysed below, while from the main text of the report it is not possible to fully grasp what such assessment would entail, the footnotes provide a substantive explanation:

---

[81]   EC policy report (n 57) 124.

[82]   Article 2, Council Regulation (EC) No 1/2003 of 16 December 2002 on the implementation of the rules on competition laid down in Articles 81 and 82 of the Treaty.

[83]   Case C-185/95 P *Baustahlgewebe v Commission* [1998], para 58.

[84]   Case C199/92 P *Hüls v Commission* [1999] ECR I-4287, paras 149 and 150. See also Case C235/52 P *Montecatini v Commission* [1999] ECR I-4539, paras 175 and 176.

[85]   Case C-413/06 P *Bertelsmann and Sony Corporation of America v Impala* ECLI:EU:C:2007:790, para 48.

[86]   ibid para 50.

[87]   Furman Review (n 36) 99.

The balance of harms test would have similarities with the government's recognised approach for making regulatory decisions, which draws on the principles of cost-benefit analysis. This can combine qualitative and quantitative analysis and judgement, with various techniques for addressing the challenges of uncertainty. This approach is frequently used for significant and complex government decisions, for example for public health proposals, environmental protection, or a major infrastructure project.[88]

In connection with the balance of harm approach mentioned before, the Furman Review also addressed the presumption of illegality suggested in both the Stigler report and the EC policy report. It rejected this proposal on the basis that a merger could also be a source of efficiencies and the inversion of the burden of proof could be disproportionate.[89]

There are two important issues in the Furman Review, which can be contrasted with the EC policy report and the Stigler report. Firstly, the enforcer would be given a broader test to analyse the merger on a case-by-case basis. The most relevant aspect is that the enforcer would still be in charge of reviewing the pros and cons of the merger. This is a major difference compared to inversion of proof, as it would discharge the enforcer from its role of conducting an analysis of the merger and transfer it to the merging parties. Another element is that it opts for a case-by-case analysis of digital mergers as opposed to a general presumption of illegality. Thus, the Furman Review argues in favour of a proactive role by the authority as opposed to a secondary and passive character proposed by the Stigler report and the EC policy report. A first impression is that the centre stage is given to the parties for them to prove that the merger is in fact pro-competitive, and until then the concentration is regarded as incompatible and therefore void. If the competition enforcer is meant to provide evidence of the anti-competitive character of the merger this enables it to have a much more active role over the analysis of the merger. Secondly, the broad scope of analysis provided by the balance of harms approach enables the competition enforcer to exercise a certain level of discretion. As mentioned before, it is expected that merger control will be more similar to a cost-benefit test applied by the government before enacting regulation or developing policy. This sophisticated level of analysis will require further clarification and guidance to enable officials to apply it in a comprehensive and transparent way. Thus, the use of merger guidelines in this regard becomes essential otherwise enforcement could become less predictable and ultimately much costlier for the merging parties.

The ACCC Final report proposed a less severe overhaul of the merger control regime. It suggested a legislative update comprising of an amendment of the merger factors (i.e. elements to be considered by the ACCC when reviewing a merger), namely first, the likelihood of the merger removing a potential competitor and, second, the nature and significance of the assets (including data and technology) being acquired. The ACCC Final report acknowledges that in spite of the fact that the first factor was already taken into account it will still propose legislation to include such requirement.[90] If that is the case then it is questionable if this suggestion would make any difference in the merger control regime. The inclusion of the second factor was justified by the ACCC as a way to expand its scope of analysis and include data as a relevant asset to be analysed in the merger.[91]

---

[88]   ibid.
[89]   ibid 101.
[90]   ACCC Final report (n 30) 107.
[91]   ibid 108.

It is unclear if the suggested changes will tackle killer acquisitions. If these proposals are contrasted with suggestions in the USA and the EU, such as inverting the burden of proof, they could be criticized as going too far or being disproportionate, however the ACCC's suggestions are located on the other extreme as they do not propose a meaningful change in the merger landscape and there is a significant risk that they will be largely ineffective.[92]

The ACCC has also proposed the creation of a protocol of notification that should be negotiated with large platforms. This protocol should include the type of acquisitions that require notification.[93] The idea that platforms shall notify future acquisitions is also reiterated in the Stigler report[94] (applicable to firms with bottleneck power) and the Furman Review[95] (applicable to firms with SMS), although both reports frame this notification as an obligation and not as a negotiated protocol. Thus, the ACCC also takes a softer stance in this regard.

The balance of harm approach, suggested by the Furman Review, was accepted by the DMT, which proposed some suggestions applicable to SMS firms.[96] The CMA will retain jurisdiction to assess merger control in the digital sector.[97] There are five relevant traits to be highlighted from the DMT report. First, SMS firms will have a new reporting obligation regarding all the transactions entered into.[98] This will require informing the CMA shortly after every transaction. While this may not necessarily trigger a formal review process, it will allow the CMA to check thresholds applicable to mandatory notification.[99] Secondly, the DMT suggested the implementation of clear-cut thresholds for merger control in the case of mandatory notification; however, it did not provide a conclusive answer but just some recommendations.[100] The DMT suggested that the materiality of a merger can be assessed by reference to the transaction value and the connection of the transaction to the UK (i.e. UK nexus) by considering revenues, assets, or end users in the UK.[101] Thirdly, the merger control regime should not be limited to the core activities of the SMS platforms but instead it should have a wider approach as acquisitions made in adjacent markets may impact the core activities.[102] Fourthly, the DMT proposed creating a prohibition on closing for the mergers fulfilling the requirements for mandatory notification.[103] The parties will be unable to implement the transaction until and unless they receive clearance from the CMA.[104] Fifthly, the DMT suggested a different standard of proof to assess mergers. This would entail reviewing mergers on a lower standard based on a 'more likely than not' test.[105] This is the same test applied by the CMA in a phase 1 investigation on whether to refer the merger for a phase 2 investigation.[106] The question the CMA tries to answer when making

---

[92] ibid. However, the ACCC highlights that it is considering other proposals such as inverting the burden of proof in merger control as a future and separate recommendation.

[93] ibid 109–110.

[94] Stigler report (n 23) 114.

[95] Furman Review (n 36) 12.

[96] DMT report (n 48) paras 4.134–4.159.

[97] ibid para 4.134.

[98] ibid para 4.135.

[99] ibid.

[100] ibid paras 4.136–4.145.

[101] ibid para 4.140.

[102] ibid para 4.141.

[103] ibid paras 4.146–4.148.

[104] ibid.

[105] ibid para 4.153.

[106] ibid para 4.154.

such reference is if the merger is likelier to generate a substantial lessening of competition.[107] This new test could prove to be controversial as the number of transactions being caught by it could be significantly larger. However, it is not a radical reform if compared to the inversion of the burden of proof in merger control.

The multi-jurisdictional analysis shows that if the UK follows the advice from the DMT report a middle ground regime will be implemented, updating the merger control analysis by applying a balance of harm approach. Thus, it does not go to the extreme of vetoing mergers based on a prima facie anti-competitive presumption, as proposed by the Stigler report and the EC policy report. The DMT report takes a more nuanced approach, as it recognizes the problem of killer acquisitions, but proposes to deal with it by adopting a balance of harm test. This is a more reflective stance regarding the enforcement of mergers in the digital space and may benefit the UK following Brexit, where the EUMR will not apply to the UK.

3 Enforcement in the Digital Space

Antitrust intervention in Europe has proven most successful in connection with the most egregious behaviour: the monopolization of multibillion-euro businesses, such as the client PC and server OS markets,[108] the browser market,[109] online search and paid search markets,[110] and some mobile app and OS markets.[111] UK and other European cases will be discussed in more detail in this section, and contrasted with enforcement in the US.

The CMA has begun to focus on application of the competition rules in digital markets over the last couple of years. Its enforcement has been less intrusive to date than the Commission as will be explained below. In a case involving price collusion, the CMA fined Trod Ltd. £163,371 for fixing prices with another competitor. The CMA found evidence of the agreement (i.e. previous communications between the parties) and then the illegal behaviour was implement by using re-pricing software.[112] In 2017, in a case involving a ban on online sales, the CMA fined Ping Europe Limited £1.45 million for banning UK retailers from selling its golf club online.[113] The prohibition of a ban on online sales was in line with a previous decision issued by the CJEU in Pierre Fabre on the same matter.[114] In 2019, the CMA fined Casio £3.7 million for including a resale price maintenance clause ('RPM clause') on the online selling of pianos. Casio also used software to monitor the setting of the prices.[115]

Regarding future regulatory and enforcement patterns in the digital world, the CMA report has endorsed the proposal from the Furman Review to establish the DMU. The DMU will be placed as a unit within the CMA and will regulate firms against a new code of

---

[107] ibid.
[108] Case AT.37792 *Microsoft*.
[109] Case AT.39530 *Microsoft (Tying)*.
[110] *Google Shopping* (n 75).
[111] Case AT.40099 *Google Android* (n 9).
[112] Case 50223 [2016] *Online sales of posters and frames*.
[113] Case 50230 [2017] *Online sales ban in the golf equipment sector*.
[114] *Pierre Fabre Dermo-Cosmétique SAS v Président de l'Autorité de la concurrence and Ministre de l'Économie, de l'Industrie et de l'Emploi* ECLI:EU:C:2011:649.
[115] Case 50565-2 [2019] *Online resale price maintenance in the digital piano and digital keyboard sector*.

conduct, which sets clear expectations for platforms on what represents acceptable behaviour when interacting with competitors and customers.[116] This means that the CMA will be in charge of regulation and the enforcement of competition rules in the digital sector. [117]

Trying to gauge future enforcement patterns in the UK is hard, especially in the context of the exit of the UK from the EU. The CMA has tried to alleviate some of the concerns on the implementation of competition policy and future enforcement. While the issue on how far national law will diverge from EU law—if at all—is still a highly contested debate that lies beyond the scope of this chapter, the analysis of enforcement would be incomplete without a reference to the Guidance on the functions of the CMA in the context of Brexit published in January 2020 (the 'Brexit Guidance').

The Guidance largely replicate some aspects of the withdrawal agreement. There are two important elements from the Brexit Guidance regarding competition law enforcement. First, proceedings or investigations initiated by the Commission before the end of the transition period on 31 December 2020 will remain subject to the EU's jurisdiction.[118] The same rule applies to references made under the provisions of articles 4(5) and 22 of the Merger control regulation.[119] Similarly, the UK may acquire jurisdiction over cases that were initiated at the EU level before the end of the transition period but are likely to have an impact within the UK.[120]. Secondly, the Commission will retain jurisdiction to supervise and enforce elements from commitment decisions and remedies imposed in the UK. However, both competition enforcers may agree on a transfer of responsibilities.[121] Even after the end of the transition period both authorities will still require fluent and constant communication. This is a natural consequence of the entrenchment of EU law into national law. This means that the prospects of divergence on enforcement patterns could be understood— from a technical perspective and not a political or ideological view—as unlikely in the near future, even if the UK decides to maintain a distant relationship with the EU in other areas.

The EU has undertaken competition enforcement in digital markets in a much more aggressive way compared to the UK. In the Google Shopping case, the Commission fined Google €2.42 billion for displaying its own comparison-shopping website on Google's search engine platform in a much more prominent way.[122] The Commission considered that Google was leveraging its market power from general search engine into price comparison websites, a different market segment.[123] The decision itself cuts across different areas and has a myriad of relevant topics for discussion, however the analysis below is focused on the theory of harm developed by the Commission and how it reflects possible future competition enforcement patterns in digital platforms. Google's objective with this practice seemed to be the exploitation of inertia in consumers by using its own search engine (i.e. platform) to nudge consumers into using another service provided by Google. In this specific case, artificial intelligence—an algorithm—was demoting rivals' websites. This is one of the findings of the Commission: 'Comparison shopping services are prone to

[116] DMT report (n 48).
[117] Press Release, 'CMA advises government on new regulatory regime for tech giants' https://www.gov.uk/government/news/cma-advises-government-on-new-regulatory-regime-for-tech-giants.
[118] ibid 4.17.
[119] ibid 3.9.
[120] ibid 4.19.
[121] ibid 4.23.
[122] Google Shopping (n 75).
[123] ibid.

being demoted by the ... algorithm due to the characteristics of those services.'[124] This same behaviour was in line with the exploitation of inertia in consumers as they tend to select search results based on their location (i.e. first search results) as these are more prominently displayed. The Commission decided:

> 597 [t]he Conduct is likely to reduce the ability of consumers to access the most relevant comparison shopping services. This is for two reasons.
>
> 598. In the first place ... users tend to consider that search results that are ranked highly in generic search results on Google's general search results pages are the most relevant for their queries and click on them irrespective of whether other results would be more relevant for their queries...
>
> 599. In the second place, Google did not inform users that the Product Universal was positioned and displayed in its general search results pages using different underlying mechanisms than those used to rank generic search results ... while the 'Sponsored' label may suggest that different positioning and display mechanisms are used, that information is likely to be understandable only by the most knowledgeable users.[125]

The Google Shopping decision has far reaching consequences. It should not only be seen as just another competition infringement, but also as containing a hidden prescriptive element. This decision could be understood as mandating the design of algorithms in the future. This can be analysed from two different perspectives. First, one of the essential reasons that triggered competition enforcement in this case was the existence of Google's dominant position and the consequences derived from it. Google was accused of leveraging its market power from general search engines into comparison-shopping websites. The notion of leveraging as applied by the Commission is closely related to ordoliberalism. According to ordoliberals, the market structure should be protected from dominant undertakings as this affects the right to compete in the market. The CJEU, for example, has been sympathetic towards this school of thought. In *Michelin I* it held:

> A finding that an undertaking has a dominant position is not in itself a recrimination but simply means that, irrespective of the reasons for which it has such a dominant position, the undertaking concerned has a special responsibility not to allow its conduct to impair genuine undistorted competition on the common market.[126]

The approach taken by the CJEU seems to resemble a broad approach to the notion of abuse of dominance. A broad approach is not necessarily negative, as it could be helpful to quickly adapt competition enforcement in new markets such as digital markets. According to the Van den Bergh case, the Ordoliberal approach has clear implication on the enforcement patterns:

> The competitive system has already been harmed by the simple presence of a dominant firm and should not be further weakened. For example, a refusal to supply can be prohibited

---

[124] ibid para 352.
[125] ibid paras 597–99.
[126] *NV Nederlandsche Banden Industrie Michelin v Commission of the European Communities* ECLI:EU:C:1983:313, para 57.

as an abuse of a dominant position, irrespective of the fact that such conduct is perfectly lawful when practiced by its non-dominant competitors.[127]

Secondly, the consequences of this decision are far reaching as Google's future developments over its own platform will not just need to consider its own profitable interest, but also the development of a competitive digital market. This includes designing an algorithm that does not restrict rival's access to its platform. This position brings into conflict two important interests (i) a restriction on future innovation and (ii) the promotion of a competitive digital market. The Commission opted for the latter, which shows that competition law is currently being enforced in a dynamic way in markets involving digital platforms.

Hefty fines were also imposed in Google Android (€4.34 billion) involving the tying of different Google products in mobile phone systems and the granting of commercial incentives to mobile phone operators to pre-install Google products and the restriction on the development of apps without Google's previous approval.[128] In 2019, Google was fined again (€1.49 billion) for restricting rivals' from offering advertisements in Google's own search engine results. The Commission decision, however, still remains unpublished.[129] A common element in the Google saga and—perhaps the root of the 'problem'—seems to be Google's dominant position in general search engines. As explained before, perhaps this specific market segment has become so relevant in the digital economy that there is little doubt about its public utility character. This could be analysed in the same way as telecoms and energy in the sense that there are economic reasons to regulate the platform (i.e. controlling market power) and social considerations (i.e. relevance for consumers). With or without sector specific regulation in the EU, the Commission seems to have already decided what its role is going to be in the digital economy, the gatekeeper in digital platforms by enforcing competition law in a dynamic way. This same analogy is not applicable in the case of the UK as EU competition policy pursues a political goal: market integration. It could be argued that the pursuit of this goal enabled the Commission to apply competition law in a much more dynamic way in the utilities sector. As explained below, the enforcement of competition in the utilities sector for the promotion of competition is likely to be replicated in digital markets at the EU level.

In the US, the Federal Trade Commission has brought cases to protect future competition and reach acquisitions of nascent/potential competitors. For example, in Mallinckrodt (Questor) in 2017, the Federal Trade Commission alleged under Section 2 of the Sherman Act that Questcor illegally acquired the US rights to develop a competing drug, Synacthen, for no other purpose than to eliminate a nascent competitor that threatened its Acthar monopoly.[130] In CDK/Auto Mate in 2018, the Federal Trade Commission sued to block a merger under section 7 of the Clayton Act of two digital technology platforms where the firms were current competitors, but one was a market giant (close to a duopolist) while the other was far smaller.[131] The complaint alleged harm to current competition, but focused even more sharply on harm to future, or nascent, competition. Moreover, the FTC has ordered "data

---

[127] Roger Van den Bergh, *Comparative Competition Law and Economics* (Edward Elgar Publishing 2017) 109.

[128] *Google Android* (n 9).

[129] Case AT.40411—*Google Search (Ad Sense)* (n 9).

[130] Press release: 'Mallinckrodt Will Pay $100 Million to Settle FTC, State Charges It Illegally Maintained its Monopoly of Specialty Drug Used to Treat Infants' Federal Trade Commission (18 January 2017) https://www.ftc.gov/news-events/press-releases/2017/01/mallinckrodt-will-pay-100-million-settle-ftc-state-charges-it.

[131] *CDK Global, Auto/Mate* [2018]—171 0156.

divestitures" in merger cases when needed to reset the market. It also ordered licensing and certain product interface in the 2010 Intel case.[132] In the latter case, the FTC alleged that Intel engaged in number of anti-competitive practices to block and slow design of competitive chip products and strengthen its monopoly. Perhaps in response to claims of under enforcement of antitrust rules, the FTC launched in February 2020 a retrospective merger review over unreported mergers and acquisitions consummated between 2010 and 2019.[133] The requirement was addressed to five big market players, Amazon, Apple, Facebook, Google, and Microsoft.

4 Regulation

The digital economy is to a high degree affected by innovative services in sectors that rely on core digital technologies, including digital platforms, which are making a growing contribution to economies, as well as enabling potential spillover effects to other sectors. While innovation is positive, there appears to have been a regulatory reluctance in the name of innovation—at least in the UK—to do much about the antitrust issues arising in the digital economy. The regulatory stagnation of certain sectors of the digital economy is not surprising. Think about the political opportunity that has presented itself by keeping social media platforms unregulated. Now politicians can circumvent electoral law and the BBC and reach voters directly. Unlike the BBC, social media platforms have no duty to balance their content, thus politicians can control the narrative entirely. However, the tide may be about to change. Andrea Coscelli, the CEO of the CMA, stressed that the development of the digital market is a wider public policy concern not just limited to competition issues: 'Making digital markets work well is also an area of priority highlighted by the UK government in its recent 'Modernising Consumer Markets' Green Paper which is well-aligned with our Annual Plan'.[134] In the same vein, Executive Vice President Vestager has argued that 'there's really no such thing as "cyberspace"—no separate, digital world that can just play by its own rules. What happens online doesn't just stay online—it affects our freedom, our rights, our safety in the real world. And so businesses ought to have the same responsibilities in the digital world as they do offline'.[135]

4.1 Regulatory Initiatives around the World

Various reports, commissioned by the UK, the EU, the USA, and Australia have proposed different regulatory strategies for digital platforms.[136] For the UK, both the Furman Review

---

[132] Intel Corporation [2010]—061 0247.

[133] Press release: 'FTC to Examine Past Acquisitions by Large Technology Companies' Federal Trade Commission (11 February 2020) https://www.ftc.gov/news-events/press-releases/2020/02/ftc-examine-past-acquisitions-large-technology-companies.

[134] Andrea Coscelli, 'Regulation and Competition Enforcement—a Combined Approach' Competition and Markets Authority (7 September 2017) https://www.gov.uk/government/speeches/fordham-competition-law-institute-annual-conference-2018-keynote-speech.

[135] Margrethe Vestager, 'Technology with Purpose' European Commission (5 March 2020) https://ec.europa.eu/commission/commissioners/2019-2024/vestager/announcements/technology-purpose_en.

[136] Furman Review (n 36); EC policy report (n 57); Stigler report (n 23); ACCC Final report (n 30).

and the DMT report suggested an enforceable code of conduct applicable to firms with SMS.[137] This recommendation was also put forward in the CMA report. The Stigler report has proposed the creation of sector specific regulation as a long-term goal.[138] The ACCC Final report proposed a digital regime as a supplement of competition. The discussion below will begin with the proposals for the UK, as outlined in the Furman Review and the DMT report, with references made to the developments occurring in other jurisdictions regarding the possible implementation of digital regulation.

The DMT report endorsed the development of pro-competitive interventions.[139] It argued that these interventions are required as the code of conduct may not be able to address underlying competition problems such as the source of market power.[140] However, the DMT clarified that the pro-competitive interventions should be applied as a consequence of a detailed assessment.[141] With the only exception of ownership separation, there should not be limits to the interventions from the DMU including interoperability and obligations to provide access.[142] The DMT report clarified that full ownership separation remedies should be implemented only by the CMA.[143] For this purpose it proposed that the DMU should be able to make a market investigation reference.[144]

The proposal of a more nuanced approach in the UK is expressed in an enforceable code of conduct on the basis of the following advantages:

> a system where industry has greater clarity and confidence over what constitutes acceptable practice and the rules that apply. This will secure good consumer outcomes upfront, and help foster an environment where there is a greater certainty for investors, where small businesses can be created and grow, and innovation by all parties is supported and rewarded … The best way to achieve these outcomes is through introduction of a digital platform code of conduct, that clarifies acceptable conduct between digital platforms and their users, and is developed collaboratively by the proposed new digital markets unit with platforms and other affected parties'.[145]

The enforceable code of conduct would combine self-regulation subject with State intervention, also known as meta-regulation. Coglianese and Mendelson explain:

> meta-regulation focuses very much on outside regulators but also incorporates the insight from self-regulation that [firms] themselves can be sources of their own constraint. Meta-regulation refers to ways that outside regulators deliberately—rather than unintentionally—seek to induce [firms] to develop their own internal, self-regulatory responses to public problems.[146]

---

[137] Furman Review (n 36) para 2.17 and DMT report (n 48) paras 13 and 1.3.
[138] This proposal is divided between a general digital regulatory regime (i.e. general application except new entrants or small market players) and a special digital regulatory regime (i.e. applicable only to firms with bottleneck power).
[139] DMT report (n 48) paras 4.60–4.65.
[140] ibid para 4.63.
[141] Ibid para 4.65.
[142] ibid para 4.68.
[143] ibid para 4.70.
[144] ibid para 4.71.
[145] Furman Review (n 36) para 2.24.
[146] Cary Coglianese and Evan Mendelson, 'Meta-regulation and Self-regulation' in Robert Baldwin, Martin Cave, and Martin Lodge (eds), *The Oxford Handbook of Regulation* (Oxford University Press 2010) 146–69.

Meta-regulation is a regulatory strategy that has been extensively studied.[147] While its application gives greater freedom to regulated firms it is to some extent constrained by State
supervision. A key element and an advantage of meta-regulation is that firms are given the
option to design their own rules and the best way to achieve compliance.[148] This is particularly relevant in market sectors where a high level of intrusion could have a detrimental impact on the industry as a whole. Giving voice to market players allows greater flexibility that
will be hard to achieve if heavy detailed regulation is put in place. A code of conduct is also
cost efficient for the State, as the industry itself will likely bear some of the costs of its design. This regulatory strategy has, however, numerous shortcomings.[149] First, it is unlikely
to work effectively if the regulated firms are ill intentioned (i.e. likely to reap benefits from
loopholes in the rules) and well-informed (i.e. high level of knowledge or having highly
skilled advisors) as they could use all the tools available to protect their market position.[150]
Secondly, another risk is the possibility that firms will influence the design of the rules to
protect their own interests. As the reports show, the platform economy is prone to a high
level of concentration.[151] Thus, there is a good reason to be sceptical towards the fact that
dominant digital platforms will voluntarily alter their behaviour to promote competition.
Thirdly, the potential failure of meta-regulation will generate intervention from the State to
implement an all-encompassing regulatory regime similar to utilities. Before implementing
meta-regulation, it will be necessary to analyse the behaviour of market players (i.e. past
practices) so that the likelihood of success of this strategy can be predicted.

The Furman Review briefly detailed the rationale for its code of conduct preference instead of a regulatory regime similar to utilities:

> utilities regulation typically allows a regulated rate of return for the monopoly operator,
> and seeks to ensure open and fair access that allows competition in the market that rely
> upon the network . . . But utilities regulation of this kind involves trade-offs: it accepts the
> monopoly position of the utility operator while looking to minimise the resulting conse-
> quences for competition and consumers.[152]

This statement takes a rather narrow view of the purposes and role of utility regulation. The
latter can be understood as a transitory stage aiming at the development of a competitive
market. Applying a sector specific regulatory regime does not necessarily mean that there
will always be a monopoly in place. The role of regulation is precisely to open segments of
the market that are prone to monopoly. Thus, regulation is not an end in itself, but a means
to achieve competition. Moreover, there is evidence to suggest that digital platforms are
prone to a winner-takes-it-all outcome.[153] Sector specific regulation seeks to address this
issue. It is not a matter of accepting the monopoly position, but looking into the best possible way to deal with it by opening specific market segments to competition. On the other

---

[147] Robert Baldwin, Martin Cave, and Martin Lodge, *Understanding Regulation* (Oxford University Press 2010)
137–64.
[148] Coglianese and Mendelson (n 146).
[149] ibid.
[150] Robert Baldwin and Julia Black, 'Really Responsive Regulation' (LSE Law, Society and Economy Working
Papers 15/2017).
[151] Furman Review (n 36) paras 1.95–1.99. EC policy report (n 53) 23. Stigler report (n 23) 34–35.
[152] Furman Review (n 36) paras 2.14, 2.15.
[153] *Google Shopping* (n 75).

hand, digital regulation akin to utilities regulation allows for a broader level of intrusion in the market, albeit not free from costs. One advantage of regulation enforced by a central regulator—also known as a regulatory strategy based on command and control—is certainty.[154] Guidance and enforcement patterns issued by the regulator provide clarity on the expected behaviour from market players. For example, a digital regulator could clarify the terms of access to a dataset and the extent of data that will be provided to avoid breaches of privacy. Thus, it will be involved in a standard setting process. Another advantage is deterrence, where the regulator is engaged in a constant monitoring process and the imposition of penalties if necessary. For example, constant supervision should also include approval of pricing practices and supervising requests for access to the infrastructure. In another words, the data regulator/data unit will have a broad remit to police the industry. The regulator is also expected to have a high level of specialism. Thus, the specificities of the market will, in principle, be better addressed by a pool of experts as opposed to a competition enforcer that operates across the board. However, the greatest disadvantage of implementing a command and control regime is capture whereby[155] the regulator could end up protecting the interests of an industry.

The CMA endorsed the Furman Review on an enforceable code of conduct subject to three high level principles: fair trading, open choice and trust and transparency.[156] However, from the CMA report it is unclear if the likely direction of the regulatory regime will be closer to meta-regulation or a fully-fledged regulatory regime similar to utilities. Among other reasons for this is the fact that the CMA report seems to be contradictory regarding future enforcement patterns in digital markets. On the one hand, it criticizes competition law as being rigid, slow and allegedly ex-post. This is because—according to the CMA report—competition enforcement requires lengthy investigations and it takes several years before a decision is reached and remedies implemented.[157] The CMA has argued that the code of conduct will allow anti-competitive behaviour to be challenged in a faster way before it has even harmed competition.[158] This statement is partially true. As explained before, meta-regulation provides flexibility and quicker solutions, however there could be a trade-off between flexibility and effectiveness. The weak point of meta-regulation is precisely its self-regulatory character. This requires a high degree of compliance and willingness from digital platforms to make the regulatory regime work effectively. Absent this element, then meta-regulation loses much of its potential pro-competitive outcomes. On the other hand, the CMA also acknowledges that the DMU will be able to impose substantial financial penalties.[159] These penalties will be subject to judicial review.[160] This effectively implies that the DMU will require to investigate, issue a statement of objections, provide evidence and adjudicate in a case involving a potential infringement. In essence, this proposal seems to be not so different—if at all—to the lengthy competition regime criticised by the CMA report. It could also mean that digital platforms will be subject to a regime similar to utilities but also to some extent to meta-regulation.

---

[154] Baldwin, Cave, and Lodge, *Understanding Regulation* (n 150) 106–14.
[155] ibid.
[156] CMA report (n 8) para 7.74.
[157] ibid paras 7.33.
[158] ibid para 7.31.
[159] ibid para 7.100.
[160] ibid para 7.99.

As will be explained below, the other reports commissioned in the US, EU and Australia all seem to point at a clear direction: there are serious problems in the digital sector. The UK has made its own contribution towards finding a solution to fix markets in this sector. As mentioned previously, the UK government and the CMA have both demonstrated their intention to follow as closely as possible the recommendations from the Furman Review. However, as explained before, the proposals outlined in the Furman Review are far from being the magical elixir for the digital market. A more critical and reflective role is essential from the CMA in this regard. Two examples can be given to explain the necessity of a bolder approach from the CMA. First, its decision to largely rehearse the solutions proposed by the Furman Review in its report on digital platforms. For example, the CMA report is not bold enough on its analysis of the potential disadvantages of the enforceable code of conduct compared to a fully-fledged regulatory regime similar to utilities.[161] Secondly, the CMA's unwillingness to undertake a market investigation into online platforms and digital advertisement is unfortunate. There is plenty of evidence provided by third parties and also gathered directly by the CMA in relation to the critical issues in the digital market. In sum, the challenges from the digital market requires a bolder, more confident and critical competition enforcer.

In the US, the Stigler report outlined its regulatory proposal in the following way:

> a new Digital Authority runs the risk of being captured by industry, becoming a new barrier to entry rather than a promoter of competition. This risk can be minimized, albeit not eliminated, by a careful institutional design. This is one reason why we envision – at least initially – to have the Digital Authority as a subdivision of the FTC, an across-industry authority with a better-than-average record of avoiding capture.[162]

To prevent capture, the report made several proposals such as granting autonomy to the digital authority, giving a broad remit, including rulemaking powers in the following areas: general consumer protection, privacy policies, data portability and access to data and algorithms for external auditing and research.[163] A similar concern surfaced in Australia as the competition enforcer proposed that the specialist digital platforms agency as a branch within the ACCC:

> A new regulator or agency would take considerable time to build the skills already possessed by existing regulators and, being so targeted, would run a clear risk of regulatory capture. Rather, more effective and targeted oversight would be provided by supplementing the functions of existing enforcement and regulatory agencies … which are already working very well together.[164]

The ACCC expects that the digital branch will benefit from the experience and relationships the competition enforcer already has with other regulatory agencies. It expects that this institutional design will make capture less likely.

---

[161] ibid paras 7.129–7.133.
[162] Stigler report (n 23) 13.
[163] ibid 310–15.
[164] ACCC Final report (n 30) 29.

While the Furman Review proposed the creation of a digital markets unit, it did not make a specific recommendation as to where the DMU should be located or whether it should be a new institution.[165] It is now clear the DMU will sit within the CMA.[166]

Like the Furman Review, the EC policy report was not keen on utility like regulation either: 'In these fast moving and diversified markets, we believe regulations organizing the whole sector—akin to the type of regulation used for traditional utilities—to be inappropriate. Rather we must adapt the tools of competition policy to the new environment'.[167] There are very powerful reasons to believe that the Commission will follow this recommendation, as this will effectively ensure it remains as the only EU institution with an overarching influence on competition enforcement. The creation of an EU digital authority would require intense debate and involve a convoluted political process. The EC policy report opts instead for maintaining the status quo and—perhaps unintentionally—advocates for a similar enforcement pattern akin to the utilities sector. Such a suggestion would probably suit the Commission's agenda, as it would remain fully in charge of the EU policymaking strategy. The EC policy report highlights the fact that EU competition law is still fit for purpose, but it proposes updating some aspects:

> We are convinced that the basic framework of competition law, as embedded in Articles 101 and 102 of the TFEU, continues to provide a sound and sufficiently flexible basis for protecting competition in the digital era. However, the challenges stemming from the rise of the Internet, the 'new economy' and, today, the digital economy do require an adaptation of the way this basic framework is applied. The specificities of platforms, digital ecosystems and the data economy require adaptation and refinement of established concepts, doctrines and methodologies, and competition law enforcement itself.[168]

For example, the report proposes overhauling the notion of consumer welfare by considering any strategy as anti-competitive if it reduces competitive pressure in the market, unless consumer gains can be proven. Other proposed reforms include updating the notion of market definition,[169] how market power is measured and inverting the burden of proof.[170] Another way to view these proposals is to consider them as a sector specific competition regime. Thus, this will generate a general competition regime (i.e. EU competition law) and a special competition regime for digital platforms. It would—in practice—be hard to distinguish between the special competition regime and digital regulation. The EC policy report does not analyse contemporary enforcement of competition law in telecoms and the energy sector. Otherwise it may have arrived at a different conclusion, as the Commission has already applied competition law as a form of regulation in those areas. In practice, the proposal seems to suggest that EU competition enforcement will effectively be a regulatory regime for digital platforms.[171]

---

[165] Furman Review (n 36) para 2.9.

[166] CMA Press Release (n 118).

[167] EC policy report (n 57) 19.

[168] EC policy report (n 57) 39.

[169] The Commission is currently reviewing its Notice of the definition of the relevant market, Commission notice on the definition of relevant market for the purposes of Community competition law (97/C 372/03).

[170] EC policy report (n 57) 42–53.

[171] For example, in *Deutsche Telekom* (Case C-280/08) the Commission acted as a regulator of regulators when it held that behaviour amounted to margin squeeze in spite of the fact that the German telecom's regulator had

The Commission has also taken the initiative on the regulation of digital platforms by proposing three key reforms: First, the Digital Services Act Package, which is a sort of all-encompassing legislative proposal on online platforms. Some of its intended contents lie outside the scope of competition policy as it aims to protect consumers from online harms more generally.[172] Secondly, an ex-ante regulatory regime on digital platforms.[173] While the specific details of this initiative will remain unknown until the draft proposal is ready and published, this will clarify how EU law will interact with national law on this same subject. Thirdly, the proposal involving a so-called competition tool.[174] This seems promising as it could expand the scope of powers of the Commission to propose recommendations involving structural remedies in areas lying outside the scope of EU competition rules and involving competition issues affecting the functioning of the internal market. While it is at the moment not entirely clear where the boundaries of EU competition law are meant to be placed, this is likely to be a proposal in line with the EC policy report as it will allow the Commission to oversee digital regulation at the national level.

As can be seen, opting for a code of conduct—as proposed by the various UK reviews and reports —or a fully-fledged regulatory regime has advantages and disadvantages on both sides. The code of conduct has flexibility and this is a relevant consideration in a market that relies heavily on innovation such as the digital sector. On the other hand, a regulatory regime is likely to create rigid and prescriptive rules. This is an intrusive but necessary measure to allow the promotion of competition. It should not be forgotten that the regulatory strategy is just a tool to achieve competitive markets. Therefore, there is no single perfect solution to deal with digital platforms. This means that policy-makers will have to select the strategy that they are better placed to supervise by minimizing disadvantages and maximizing effectiveness. Under the right conditions and careful planning any of the two strategies could have a good chance of succeeding. In principle, the DMT proposal is to be welcomed because it provides greater flexibility to an industry that relies heavily on innovation. The extent of this flexibility should be measured against its effectiveness. The DMT report is to be welcomed, as it will be a decisive step in determining what to expect from the UK's strategy on digital platforms. Until these reforms are passed then the path ahead will remain as it is now, a bit uncertain but with a strong desire to improve digital markets.

5 Conclusion

With digital technologies underpinning ever more transactions, the digital economy is becoming increasingly inseparable from the functioning of the economy as a whole.

previously approved prices. For a detailed analysis of this subject see Giorgio Monti, 'Managing the intersection of Utilities Regulation and EC Competition Law' (LSE Law, Society and Economy Working Papers 8/2008) http://www.lse.ac.uk/law/working-paper-series/2007-08/WPS2008-08-Monti.pdf.

[172] See publication from the Commission announcing the Digital Services Act Package and public consultation: https://ec.europa.eu/digital-single-market/en/digital-services-act-package.
[173] The Commission has published an inception impact assessment on this regard: https://ec.europa.eu/info/law/better-regulation/have-your-say/initiatives/12418-Digital-Services-Act-package-ex-ante-regulatory-instrument-of-very-large-online-platforms-acting-as-gatekeepers.
[174] See press release on the competition tool as introduced by the Commission and request to the public for comments: https://ec.europa.eu/info/law/better-regulation/have-your-say/initiatives/12416-New-competition-tool.

As Andrea Coscelli has argued the 'digital economy is transforming the way we live our lives: people are in contact with companies 24/7 on their devices, business models are changing at pace, and innovation is the key to success across all markets.'[175] The digital economy is, as Executive Vice President Vestager calls it, a platform economy. It is clear that data are, maybe by far, the most salient feature in digital platforms. It is still highly debatable if data are 'more like oil or sunlight' as The Economist described it.[176] Either way, how to deal with data remains a challenge for competition policymakers. It is clear that data rich companies have an advantage and unlimited data processing is unsustainable. Digitalization currently accounts for 4% of the carbon footprint—a number which is predicted to increase to 8% in 2025. Since the importance of data will only grow, we need to be willing to take decisive action.[177] The CMA has concluded that it will not conduct a market investigation into the digital advertising market; instead the DMU will be established within the CMA, and it will have the power to enforce a code of conduct against firms with a SMS. This will take time. In the meantime, it is essential that the CMA is bolder in its enforcement action, as the CMA report indicated huge problems in the market for digital advertising. Regulation and enforcement action are not mutually exclusive—simply very different ways of dealing with digital markets. Antitrust intervention takes time. This means that it may fail to achieve its structural goals altogether, but regulation is difficult in fast moving innovative markets. Data sharing and portability are positive aspects, but not necessarily likely to overcome scale advantages that are typically present with respect to big data. One thing that is clear is that that cross-collaboration between various regulators, such as the CMA, Ofcom, the FCA, and the ICO is needed for effective regulation of competition in the digital economy in the UK in the future.

---

[175] The CMA's Digital Market Strategy (Competition and Markets Authority, 2019) https://www.gov.uk/government/publications/competition-and-markets-authoritys-digital-markets-strategy/the-cmas-digital-markets-strategy#our-five-strategic-aims.

[176] 'Are data more like oil or sunlight?' The Economist (20 February 2020).

[177] Vestager (n 56).

Index

For the benefit of digital users, indexed terms that span two pages (e.g., 52–53) may, on occasion, appear on only one of those pages.

Tables and figures boxes are indicated by *t* and *f* following the page number

abuse of a dominant position *see also* Article 102
      (abuse of a dominant position); Chapter II
      prohibition (abuse of a dominant position);
      exclusionary abuses; exploitative abuses and
      excessive pricing
   assessment of dominance xv–xvi, 80–86
   Competition Commission (CC) 210–11
   concurrency regime 49–50, 256–57, 270–71, 272–
      74, 275–76
   damages 325, 326
   digital economy 360–61, 377–79
   director disqualification 299–300
   enforcement 1, 4–5, 9, 316–18
   fair hearing, right to a 237–41, 243–49, 252
   institutions xvii, 209, 228
   killer acquisitions 370
   merger control 4–5
   OFT 9, 209–10
   pharmaceutical companies 9, 82–85
administrative proceedings
   administrative, definition of 234
   civil rights and obligations 236, 237
   criminal charges 236–37
   fair hearing, right to a 231, 234–37, 239–41, 242,
      243–44, 245, 253
   integrated agency model 232, 235, 238, 239–41
   remedies 253
adverse effect on competition (AEC) test
   consumer detriment threshold, replacement
      with 167–68
   consumer policy 154
   enforcement 3, 25
   market investigation regime (MIR) 3, 144–45, 146,
      149–50, 153
   public interest 166
   state action 154–55
   vertical restraints 152
   well-functioning market 151
algorithms 359–60, 377–78, 379
anti-competitive agreements *see also* Article 101
      (anti-competitive agreements); Chapter I
      prohibition (anti-competitive agreements)
   concurrency regime 256–57, 264–65, 270–72, 274
   enforcement 1
   fair hearing, right to a 237, 238
   institutions xvii, 209, 228
   OFT 209–10
   public interest 238

Antitrust Damages Directive 17, 23, 313–15, 319–
      20, 322–24
appeals *see also* Competition Appeal Tribunal (CAT)
   Competition Commission Appeals Tribunal
      (CCAT) 210–12
   institutions 204–5, 228
   ministers, role of 18–19
appreciable effect on competition 94–96, 101–2
Article 101 (anti-competitive agreements) 22–23
   adverse effect on competition (AEC) test 3
   Brexit 23–24, 53–54, 280–81
   Cartel Offence 338–39
   concurrency regime 49–50, 280–81
   hub-and-spoke cartels 40
   Market Investigation Regime (MIR) 3, 152,
      153, 162
   resale price maintenance (RPM) 64–65
   single economic unit, agreements between 61
   vertical agreements 55, 56–58, 74, 76
Article 102 (abuse of a dominant position) 22–23
   adverse effect on competition (AEC) test 3
   Brexit 23–24, 280–81
   concurrency regime 49–50, 280–81
   discrimination 99, 103
   excessive pricing 113–14, 129, 132
   exclusionary abuses 79, 109
   multi-marketing settings, exclusion in 92, 109–10
   retroactive rebates and bundled discounts 88–89
Australian Competition and Consumer Commission
      (ACCC) 370, 371–72, 374–75, 380–81, 384

barriers to entry
   abuse of a dominant position 80, 81, 82, 83, 85–
      86, 109
   data collection/extraction 359–60, 363–64
   digital economy 359–60, 361, 362–63
   discrimination 103–4
   exclusionary abuses 98
   Market Investigation Regime (MIR) 152, 153
   multi-marketing settings, exclusion in 93–94
   vertical agreements 57
behavioural economics 155–61
   behavioural economics, definition of 157
   biases 156, 157, 159–60, 161
   consumer policy 155–56, 158–60, 167–68
   Energy investigation 155–56, 159–60
   intermediate markets 160–61
   Investment Consultancy investigation 160, 161

behavioural economics (*cont.*)
  market failures, identification of 157
  market investigation regime (MIR) 154, 155–61
  rationality 157
  reimagining markets, dangers of 159–60
  remedies 159–60
  Retail Banking investigation 155–56, 159–60
  scope 160–61
behavioural remedies 142, 159–60, 165, 370
biases 156, 157, 159–60, 161, 163–64
  confirmation bias 176–77, 185–86, 188–89, 227
  framing biases 157
  independent and impartial tribunals 234–35, 246
  loss aversion biases 157
  processing power biases (bounded rationality) 157
  time inconsistency biases 157
block exemptions 56–57, 60–61, 73, 74, 76
Brexit 23–24
  cartels 39
  climate change 223–24
  Competition Act 1998 xv, 1, 23–24, 28, 54, 73
  concurrency regime 265, 280–81
  cooperation 192
  digital economy xix, 360, 377, 386–87
  director disqualification 291
  dual capture mergers 191
  enforcement 25, 26, 28
    CMA 221–22, 226, 228
    Competition Act 1998 xv, 1, 23–24, 28, 54
    private enforcement 311–12, 334
  exclusionary abuses 79–80, 110–11
  fair hearing, right to a 151, 251–52
  Financial Conduct Authority (FCA) 53–54
  foreign law, EU law treated as 334
  horizontal agreements xv, 53–54
  killer acquisitions 376
  legal certainty 76
  merger control 14, 24, 25, 169–70, 190–93, 198–99, 377
  prosecutorial system, adoption of 24
  recast Brussels IA Regulation 334
  resources 222
  retroactive rebates and bundled discounts 92, 109
  Rome II Regulation 334
  state aid, scrutiny of 221–22
  transition period 377
  vertical agreements xv, 56, 69, 73, 78
  workload, changes in 221
bundled discounts xv–xvi, 87–92, 109
burden of proof 134–35, 371–72, 373–75

Cartel Offence *see* UK Cartel Offence
cartels xv, 30–39, 54, *see also* UK Cartel Offence; hub-and-spoke cartels
  2014-2020, enforcement action between 36–39
  collusive tendering 31–32, 35, 38
  Competition Act 1998 30–39
  concerted practices 31–32, 33, 34
  damages 324, 326

  enforcement 2, 4, 7–8, 16, 30–39, 315
  facilitation doctrine 272
  fair hearing, right to a 237–41, 243–44
  fines 30–35, 36–39
  horizontal agreements xv, 30–39, 54
  increase in enforcement activity 30
  information sharing agreements 32–34
  investigations xv, 30–31, 54
  large cartels 30
  leniency process 30–32, 34, 50, 51
  National Audit Office (NAO) 7–8, 35–36
  OFT 7–8, 16, 30–35, 54
  price-fixing cartels 311
  private enforcement 16, 315
  Restrictive Trade Practices Act 1976 32–33
  trade associations 36–37
  under-enforcement, criticism of 35–37
CAT *see* Competition Appeal Tribunal (CAT)
CC *see* Competition Commission (CC)
Chapter I prohibition (anti-competitive agreements) 22–23, 53–54
  cartels 30–33, 36–37
  concurrency regime 49–50, 256–58, 263, 270–72, 274
  director disqualification 290–91
  enforcement 3, 312, 316–17, 322
  fair hearing, right to a 237, 238–39, 243–44, 250–51, 252–53
  Market Investigation Regime (MIR) 144, 152, 153, 162
  multi-marketing settings, exclusion in 94, 95–96
  resale price maintenance (RPM) 63, 64–66
  trade associations 43
  vertical agreements 55, 56–58, 74, 76–77, 78
Chapter II prohibition (abuse of a dominant position) 9, 22–23
  cartels 30
  concurrency regime 49–50, 256–58, 263, 270–71
  director disqualification 290–91
  discrimination 103
  enforcement 3, 16–17, 312, 316–17
  exclusionary abuses 79, 109
  exploitative abuse 129
  fair hearing, right to a 237, 238–39, 243–44, 250–51, 252–53
  Market Investigation Regime (MIR) 162, 163
  multi-marketing settings, exclusion in 94, 95–96, 109–10
  vertical agreements 56
Civil Aviation Authority (CAA) 258–59, 266–67, 274
civil rights and obligations 234–35, 236–37, 246
classical economic theory 157
climate change 223–24, 226, 228, 386–87
CMA *see* Competition and Markets Authority (CMA)
collective redress mechanism 312, 322, 327–31
  certification 17
  Collective Proceedings Orders (CPOs) 315–16, 327–30, 336

damages 325, 327–28
  opt-outs/opt-ins xviii, 17
collusion
  cartels 31–32, 35, 38
  fair hearing, right to a 244, 246–47, 249, 252
  hub-and-spoke cartels 40, 41, 42
  vertical agreements 57
Commission
  Brexit 53–54
  cartels 36
  data sharing and data portability 368, 369
  DG Comp 23, 24, 173
  digital economy 21, 360–61, 377–79, 385–86
  exclusionary abuses xv–xvi, 79–80
  exploitative abuses 113, 122, 128, 136
  fines 30–31, 377–78
  Google Android case 379
  Google Shopping case 377–79
  investigations xv, 30–31
  killer acquisitions 373
  leveraging 378–79
  Regulation 1/2003 22–23
  retroactive rebates and bundled discounts 87–89
  Vertical Guidelines 61–62, 74
Competition Act 1998 22–23, *see also* **Chapter I
    prohibition (anti-competitive agreements);
    Chapter II prohibition (abuse of a dominant
    position); enforcement under Competition
    Act 1998**
  Brexit xv, 1, 23–24, 28, 54, 334
  cartels 30–39
  CAT 211–12
  Chapter I prohibition 312
  Chapter II prohibition 16–17, 109, 312
  Competition Commission (CC) 228
  concurrency regime 19, 49–50, 256–60, 262–
    76, 277
  Covid-19 pandemic 52–53
  decision-making 209–13
  director disqualification 284, 291
  discrimination 99, 102–3
  entry into force xv, 30, 232, 284
  exploitative abuses xvi, 113–36
  fair hearing, right to a 231–34, 237, 243–47, 249
  horizontal agreements xv, 29–54
  hub-and-spoke cartels 39–43
  Human Rights Act 1998 243–47
  list of legislation replaced 29
  margin of appreciation 250–51
  Market Investigation Regime (MIR) 138–39, 151
  Monopolies and Mergers Commission (MMC) 201
  OFT 209–10, 228
  private enforcement xv, 16–18, 312–13, 318, 335
  public interest 238–39
  representative actions 312, 327–28
  royal assent 54
  time limits 318
  trade associations 43
  vertical agreements xv, 55, 56–58, 62–71, 73, 76–78

Competition and Markets Authority (CMA) 22–23
  21st century challenges 220–24
  2014-2020, enforcement action between 36–39
  abuse of a dominant position 9, 83, 232
    assessment of dominance 80, 81, 85–86, 109
    exclusionary abuses 79, 109, 110
    exploitative abuses 113–14, 117–26, 134
  accountability 215, 216, 251
  advocacy role 219–20
  annual State of Competition report,
    proposals for 19
  appointments 215
  behavioural economics 154, 155–61, 215, 226
  blog 306–7
  Brexit 24, 53–54, 221–22, 226, 228
    concurrency regime 280–81
    digital economy 377
  cartels 10, 30, 35–39, 54, 214
  Case and Policy Committee (CPA) 227–28, 229
  case decision groups (CDGs) 216–17, 227–28, 229
  CAT 218, 224, 225–27, 229
    Brexit 24
    enforcement 25–26
    fair hearing, right to a 232, 244, 250, 253
  commitments 79
  Competition Act 1998 29
  composition 215–16
  concurrency regime xvii–xviii, 20, 49–50,
    214, 255–81
  confirmation bias 176–77, 185–86, 188–89, 227
  consumer benefits 214–15, 219, 223–24, 225
  conventional competition cases 151–52, 162–63
  Covid-19 pandemic 52–53, 222–23, 226, 228
  decision processes 215–17, 227–28
  design 215–17, 227
  digital economy 20, 22, 27, 360–61
    Brexit 377
    Data Markets Unit 366–67
    Digital Markets Unit (DMU), proposal for xix,
      220–21, 376–77
    enforcement 6, 220–21, 226, 228
    fines 376
    Furman Report 383–84
    Online Platforms and Digital Advertising market
      study xix, 360–61, 364–66, 386–87
    regulation 376–77, 383–84, 386–87
  director disqualification 10, 283, 285–87, 292–94,
    295–308
  enforcement 6, 25–26, 27
    directorates 216
    internal procedures 4
    Market Investigation Regime (MIR) 137, 141–42
    private enforcement 321–22
    proposals 27
  Enterprise and Regulatory Reform Act 2013 8–9,
    214–20, 247
  establishment xvii, 11, 35–37, 139, 201, 214
  evidence, admission of relevant 250–51
  excessive pricing 113–14, 117–26, 134, 218

Competition and Markets Authority (CMA) *(cont.)*
exclusionary abuses 79, 109, 110
exploitative abuses 113–14, 117–26, 134
fair hearing, right to a 231, 232, 243–44, 247, 248–49, 250–51, 253
fines 29, 35, 36–39, 117–26, 226, 227–28, 376
guidelines 150–51
increase in CA 1998 decisions 217–18
independent decision-making xvii, 216–17, 227–28
inquisitorial approach 226–27
intelligence 182, 184–85, 192, 216
interactions with regulators 264–65, 278, 279–80
interim measures, anticipated use of 214, 224, 225
international reputation 219–20
investigative powers 214, 215–16
judicial review 142–43, 148–50
judicial scrutiny, weakening 27
leadership 279–80
mandate 203, 214–15
margin of appreciation 248–49
Market Investigation Regime (MIR) xxxviii, 11–12, 23, 25, 27, 137–68
market studies 139–41, 145–46, 215–16, 226, 227–28
Memoranda of Understanding (MOUs) 264
merger control xvi–xvii, 13–14, 24, 169–99, 217, 218–19, 227
Non-Ministerial Department, as 215
OFT
   cartels 35
   Competition Commission xvii, 201, 214, 215–16, 217, 227, 228
   merger control 184
performance 217–20, 226
political interference 215
precedent 218, 219, 228
priorities 203, 215, 216, 223–24
prosecutorial system, proposal for 226–27, 229
public faith in markets, loss of 220, 224, 226, 228
public interest 11–12, 166–67, 214
raising awareness 219–20
reform xv, 220–28
   21st century challenges 220–24
   coherent institutional reform 226–28
   own proposals 224–26, 229
   Tyrie letter 224–27, 229
remedies 141–42, 146–48, 226
resale price maintenance (RPM) 63–67
resources xvi–xvii, 198–99, 215, 217, 219
retroactive rebates and bundled discounts 89, 90–92
Secretary of State, relationship with 215
Senior Responsible Officer (SRO) 216–17
staff 217, 219, 227–28
   continuity 227
   independence 227–28
   morale 217
   transition from OFT 217
   turnover 217, 219
standard of review 224, 225–26, 229
state action 154–55
technical support 279
trade associations 43
under-enforcement, criticism of 35–37
vertical agreements 55–56, 69, 71, 75, 76–78
workload, increase in 280–81
Competition Appeal Tribunal (CAT) xvii, 211–12, 228
abuse of a dominant position 9, 83–85
   exclusionary abuses 79
   exploitative abuses xvi, 113–29
adversarial approach 212
Brexit 251–52, 334
cartels 31–32, 33, 34, 37, 39–40, 41–42
CMA 24, 25–26, 232, 244, 250, 253
collective actions 17, 327–31
Competition Act 1998 211–12
composition 207, 211–12
concurrency regime 20
Consumer Rights Act 2015 212, 321–22
Court of Appeal, appeals to 212, 322
damages 16, 17–18, 212, 312–13, 315–16, 324–25
enforcement 2, 4, 25–26, 218, 224, 225–27, 229
Enterprise Act 2002 201, 211–12, 321–22
Enterprise Act Regulations 2015 322
Enterprise and Regulatory Reform Act 2013 8
excessive pricing xvi, 113–29
exclusionary abuses 79
exploitative abuses xvi, 113–29
fair hearing, right to a xvii, 231–32, 241–53
follow-on actions 312, 313, 315–16, 321–22
full jurisdiction requirement 247, 252–53
hub-and-spoke cartels 39–40, 41–42
inquisitorial approach 212
judicial appointments 211–12
judicial review 142–43, 148–50, 212, 225–26
Market Investigation Regime (MIR) 11, 137, 148–50, 168
merger control 12–13, 170–72, 178
merits reviews xvii, 4, 212, 225–26, 231, 248, 250, 251–53
new evidence, allowing 244–46, 251–52
non-monetary claims 313, 315
OFT 4, 212–13, 244, 245, 246–47, 248
private enforcement xviii, 16–18, 335–36
recruitment 211–12
representative claimants, designation of 16, 313
significant market power decisions 212
stand-alone actions 313, 318
standard of review xvii, 225–26, 229
substitution of judgment 250
workload 322
Competition Commission (CC) 184, 210–11, 217
administrative approach 207
airport monopolies 213
appointments 211
behavioural economics 156–57
cartels 35

case numbers 213
Competition Act 1998 228
composition 211–12
concurrency regime 20
culture 207
enforcement 2–3, 4–5
Enterprise Act 2002 228
EU law 3
guidance 211
information, power to demand 211
inquisitorial approach 207
judicial review 211
Market Investigation Regime (MIR) 3, 10–11,
    23, 138–39
    energy market case 12
    Market Investigation Guidelines 156–57
    OFT 10–11, 139
    retail banking case 12
    rule of law 163–64
merger control 4–5, 12–13, 170–72, 213
    CMA 184
    delay 189–90
    halting integration 177
    referrals 188–89
ministers, role of 18
Monopolies and Mergers Commission
    (MMC) 201, 207, 210–11
OECD 18
OFT 10–11, 139, 210, 213, 228
peer reputation 213
performance 212–13
public interest 15, 166–67, 210–11, 228
reporting to Secretary of State 210–11
structural interventions 213
territorial limitations 165
witnesses, power to demand 211
Competition Commission Appeals Tribunal
    (CCAT) 210–12
competition test xvi–xvii, 209–13, 228
    consumer interest xvii, 224–25, 229
    economic analysis 209, 211
concerted practices 31–32, 33, 34, 40, 41–42
concurrency regime xv, 1, 255–81
    abuse of a dominant position 49–50, 256–57, 270–
        71, 272–74, 275–76
    advisory letters 269–70, 274
    anti-competitive agreements 256–57, 264–65,
        270–72, 274
    case allocation 265–69, 279–80
    Chapter I prohibition 49–50, 256–58, 263, 270–
        72, 274
    Chapter II prohibition 49–50, 256–58, 263, 270–71
    Civil Aviation Authority (CAA) 258–59, 266–
        67, 274
    CMA xvii–xviii, 20, 49–50, 255–81
        enforcement 214
        interactions with regulators 264–65, 278, 279–80
        Memoranda of Understanding (MOUs) 264
    Competition Act 1998 19, 49–50, 256–60, 262–77

Concurrency Regulations 257–58, 260–61, 264–
    65, 266
Concurrency Working Party 19, 257–58, 260–
    61, 264–65
cooperation between agencies 264–65, 278, 279–80
Department for Business, Energy and Industrial
    Strategy (BEIS) 263, 277–78, 279
effectiveness 255, 259, 276–78
enforcement xv, 1, 19–20, 25, 26
enhanced concurrency 259–78, 279–80
EU law 256–58, 265–66, 280–81
Financial Conduct Authority (FCA) 258–59, 265,
    268, 275
horizontal agreements 49–50
improvements 20
information, gathering and sharing 260–61, 263–
    64, 279–80
initial problems 19
Littlechild Report 255–56, 281
Market Investigation Regime (MIR) 256–57, 263
NHS Improvement (NHSI) 258–59, 268–69, 276
Northern Ireland Authority for Utility Regulation
    (NIAUR) 258–59, 272–73, 275–76
Ofcom 258–59, 270–71
Ofgem 258–59, 267, 271–73, 275–76
OFT 255–58, 265–66
Ofwat 258–59, 273–74
origins and evolution of concurrency 255–59
ORR 258–59, 273
Payment Systems Regulator (PSR) 258–59, 275
primacy provision 259–60
priorities 264–65, 266
regulated markets, enforcement activity in 269–
    76, 277–79
Regulation 1/2003 19
reports 259–61, 263, 264–65, 268, 278, 279,
    280, 281
sectoral regulator orders 261–62
UK Competition Network (UKCN) 260–61,
    263, 264–65
UK Regulators Network (UKRN) 19
under-enforcement 259–60, 276, 277–78
vertical integration 49–50
warning letters 269–70
conditional fee arrangements (CFAs) 331
confirmation bias 176–77, 185–86, 188–89, 227
consumer detriment 167–68, 179, 224
consumer policy 155–56, 167–68
    competition policy, tension with 158–60
    Market Investigation Regime (MIR) 153–54, 168
    political trade-offs 158–59
    utilitarianism 158–59
Consumer Rights Act 2015
    CAT 212, 321–22
    damages 17–18, 325
    fair hearing, right to a 249
    Lever Amendment 17–18
    private enforcement xviii, 17–18, 313, 321
    time limits 318

consumer welfare
  behavioural economics 158
  CMA 214–15, 219, 223–24, 225
  digital economy 20–21, 360–63, 385–86
  Market Investigation Regime (MIR) 144–
    45, 167–68
  private enforcement xviii
  resources 219
contingency fees 331
costs 332
Covid-19 pandemic
  CMA 52–53, 226, 228
  Competition Act 1998 27–28, 52–53
  Coronavirus Task Force 52
  crisis cooperation agreements 223
  digital market 222
  enforcement xv, 1, 25, 26, 28, 223
  excessive and unfair pricing 222–23
  failing firm defence in mergers 223
  free competition, policy of 27–28
  guidance 52
  horizontal agreements 51–53
  individual exemptions 52–53
  national champions 223
  public interest 223
  public policy 51–53
  Regulation 1/2003 52
  scarcity 52–53
  temporary measures 27–28, 52
criminal cartels see Cartel Offence (UK)
criminal proceedings
  criminal in nature infringements, meaning of 232–
    40, 244–45, 250
  fair hearing, right to a xvii, 231–43, 244–45, 248–
    49, 250
  oral hearings 235
  presumption of innocence 241–42, 244–45
  punitiveness 234–35
  silent, right to remain 235, 241–42
  standard of proof 236, 246
culpability
  Cartel Offence 340–41, 343–44, 349, 351, 355–57
  director disqualification 304–6, 307–8
culture 206–8

damages 16–18, 209–10, 324–26
  abuse of a dominant position 325, 326
  Antitrust Damages Directive 17, 23, 313–15, 319–
    20, 322–24, 335–36
  cartels 326
  CAT 16, 17–18, 212, 312–13, 315–16, 324–25
  causation 324–25
  CMA 226
  collective actions 325
  damages-based agreements (DBAs) 331–32
  exemplary damages 325
  follow-on actions 312, 313, 320–22
  overcharging 325, 326
  passing-on defence 326
  restitutionary damages 325

data see data collection/extraction; data sharing and
    data portability
data collection/extraction 361–67
  advertising 362–63, 364
  algorithms 359–60
  barriers to entry 359–60, 363–64
  big data 361
  climate change 386–87
  coercion 363
  combination of data collected 363
  consent to data collection 362–64
  consumer-facing markets, extraction of data in 364
  expansion of platforms 363–64
  first party data and third party data,
    combining 362–63
  improving consumers' experience 364–65
  input, as 359–60, 361
  limiting data 363–64
  market power 359–60
  minimization principles 363
  paradox theory 365–67
  payment for collection 364–65
  privacy 20–21, 362–64, 365–66
  product, as 359–60
  purpose limitation 363
  take it or leave it approach 363
  targeting consumers 362–63, 364
  terms and conditions, acceptance of 363
  variety, velocity, veracity, volume 361
data protection 363, 364–65, 366–67
data sharing and data portability 367–70, 386–87
  access to infrastructure 367, 369–70
  free riders 367
  Furman Report 367, 370
  innovation 367, 370
  interoperability 368
  intrusive remedy, access as an 367, 369
  limits on sharing 367
  lock-in effects 368
  multi-homing 369
  privacy 370
  proportionality 369
  raw data 367
  refusal to deal 369
  regulation 368–70
  security 370
  transparency 367
de minimis threshold 56–57, 60–61, 74, 77–78, 101–
    2, 172
decision-making 203–4, 209–13, 228
  bifurcated agency model 204
  bifurcated judicial model 204
  CMA 215–17, 227–28
  Competition Act 1998 209–13
  fairness 203
  group decision-making 204
  independent decision-making xvii, 216–17, 227–28
  inquisitorial systems 204
  integrated agency model 204
  new powers of decision 209–13

Department for Business, Energy and Industrial
      Strategy (BEIS) 263, 277–78, 279
deterrence
    CMA 219, 228
    director disqualification xviii, 283–90, 294–95,
      296–98, 300–2, 303–5
    fair hearing, right to a 237–39, 244–45
    fines 285, 287, 307–8
    merger control 175
    OFT 209–10, 212–13
    performance 205
    private enforcement 311
    transparency 306–7
DGFT *see* **Director-General of Fair Trading (DGFT)**
digital economy 359–87, *see also* **digital economy,
      regulation of; killer acquisitions**
    abuse of a dominant position 85–86, 360–
      61, 377–79
    advertising 22, 361–67, 379, 384, 386–87
    aggregation platforms 361–63
    algorithms 377–78, 379
    anti-competitive conduct 361–67
    barriers to entry 359–60, 361, 362–63
    Brexit xix, 360, 377, 386–87
    cartels 21
    challenges xv, 1, 6, 20–22
    cloud operating systems 361–62
    CMA xix, 20, 22, 27, 360–61, 376
      Brexit 377
      Data Markets Unit 366–67
      Digital Markets Unit (DMU), proposal for xix,
        220–21, 376–77
      dominance, assessment of 85–86
      enforcement 6, 220–21, 226, 228
      Online Platforms and Digital Advertising market
        study xix, 360–61, 364–66, 386–87
    Commission 21, 360–61, 377–79
    commitments 85–86
    consumer-facing markets 364
    Consumer Green Paper 20–21
    consumer welfare 20–21, 360–63
    data protection 363, 364–65, 366–67
    economies of scale 361–63
    enforcement xix, 376–80, 386–87
    EU law 376, 377–78
    exclusionary conduct 361–62, 364
    exclusivity agreements 360–61
    exploitation 361–62, 364
    fines 20–21, 379
    Furman Report 21, 220–21, 364–65, 366–
      67, 376–77
    inertia of consumers, exploitation of 377–78
    innovation 20–21, 22, 379
    intellectual property rights (IPRs) 360–61
    interoperability 359–60, 361–62
    loyalty agreements 360–61
    Market Investigation Regime (MIR) 28
    market power 21, 359–60
    merger control 6, 21, 22, 169–70, 190–91, 195–98
    MFN provisions 85–86

    multi-homing 359–61
    network effects 360–63
    platforms 359–60, 361–67, 386–87
    reform 224
    response to challenges 21–22
    social networks 361–63, 364, 365–66
    substantial lessening of competition (SLC)
        regime 85–86, 196, 198, 199
    targeting consumers 364
    territorial limitations 166
    transparency 366–67
    tying 379
    United States 360–61, 379–80
    Unlocking Digital Competition. Treasury xix
    vertical agreements 55–56, 59, 61–67, 75, 77
digital economy, regulation of xix, 21–22, 380–86
    Australian Competition and Consumer
        Commission (ACCC) 380–81, 384
    authority, need for stronger digital 384–85
    capture of regulators by industry 384
    CMA 376–77, 383–84, 386–87
    code of conduct, proposal for an enforceable 380–
        84, 386
    command and control 382–83
    Commission 385–86
    Digital Markets Unit (DMU), proposal for xix,
        376–77, 383
    EU law 380–81, 384, 385–86
    Furman Report 380–81, 382–84, 385–86
    Green Paper 'Modernising Consumer Markets' 380
    innovation 380
    judicial review 383
    market power 380–81
    meta-regulation 381–82, 383
    overseas initiatives 380–86
    platforms 380, 382–83, 384, 385–86
    privacy 382–83
    promotion of competition 382
    reports 380–81, 384
    sectoral regulators 382–83, 386–87
    self-regulation 381, 383
    specialism 382–83
    spillover effects 380
    Stigler Report 380–81, 384
    United States 380–81, 384
    utility regulation 382–83
director disqualification 283–310
    abuse of a dominant position 299–300
    aggravating factors 294
    assistance and co-operation, provision of
        material 296–97
    cartels 39
    civil/administrative (non-criminal) enforcement,
        as xviii, 283–310
    CMA 10, 283, 285–87, 292–94, 295–308
    Company Directors Disqualification Act 1986 290–
        93, 295–96, 302, 303–4, 305–6
    Competition Disqualification Orders
        (CDOs) 290–300
    culpability 305–6

director disqualification (*cont.*)
   duration 292
   effectiveness 301–2, 303–4
   five-step procedure 294–96
   guidelines 294–97
   number of CDOs 297–98, 303–4, 307–8
   standard of proof 292–93
   transparency 306–7
   unfitness, decisions on 290–93, 305–6
   Competition Disqualification Undertakings
      (CDUs) 293, 296–300
     duration 293, 298–99
     list of CDUs 309–10
     number of CDUs 297–98, 301–2
     register 293
     transparency 306–7
   complementary role 285–86, 287–90, 291, 297–98
   corporate culture 287–89
   costs 293
   criminal cartels 10, 283–84, 287–89, 297–99, 306–7
   criminal enforcement xviii, 10
   culpability 304–6, 307–8
   deterrence xviii, 283–84, 285–90, 294–95, 296–98,
      300–2, 303–5, 306–8
   development of UK approach 290–300
   Director Disqualification Orders (DDOs) 285–93,
      302, 305–6
   effectiveness 287–90, 301–4, 307–8
   efficiencies 303
   enforcement practice 293–300
   Enterprise Act 2002 291, 293
   fairness 304–5
   fines 283–84, 285–90, 294–95, 307–8
   guidelines 294–97, 306
   hierarchy of conditions 295–96, 302
   indemnification 287
   internal punishment 289–90
   jurisdictions, consideration by other xviii, 300–7
   legal basis xviii, 290–93
   legitimacy 304–8
   leniency/immunity process 287–90, 294–
      95, 296–97
   links with conduct of director 301–2, 303–4, 308
   mitigating factors 294
   negligence 303, 307–8
   normative role xviii, 285–87
   OFT 283, 285–86, 294–96, 297–98, 302–4, 306
   press statements and news releases 306–7
   pressure from companies, resisting 289–90
   previous infringements, involvement in 296–97
   procedural fairness 304
   public interest 295–96
   publicity 306–7
   rationale 284–90
   reputation 287–89, 303
   retirement, closeness to 287
   sanction effect 287–89
   strict liability 303, 307–8
   transparency 294, 304, 306–7

   undertakings 293, 296–300, 301–2, 306–7
   unfitness, decisions on 290–92, 305–6
Director-General of Fair Trading (DGFT) 207–8
   abolition 210
   appointment 208
   competition portfolio 208
   consumer portfolio 208
   culture 207–8
   economists, appointment of 209
   executive decision-maker, as 228
   fines 30
   penalties 210
   Registrar, absorbing role of 208
   resources 208
   Restrictive Practices Court, abolition of 210
   Secretary of State 208
disciplinary infringements 234–35, 237–38, 242–43
disclosure 322–23
discounts xv–xvi, 87–92, 109
discrimination xv–xvi, 98–105, 110
disqualification *see* **director disqualification**
distribution arrangements 55–56, 57, 59, 69–71
dominance *see* **abuse of a dominant position; Article**
      102 (abuse of a dominant position)
dominance, assessment of xv–xvi, 80–86
   barriers to entry 80, 81, 85–86, 109
   digital platforms 85–86
   exclusivity 81
   general approach 80–81
   market definition 80, 109
   market share 80, 81, 85–86, 109
   OFT 80–81, 109
   pharmaceutical markets 82–85
   substantial and durable market power 80, 85–86, 109
due process 232, 235, 242, 245–46, 247

economic analysis 209, 211, 227
economic nationalism 220
economics *see* **behavioural economics; economic**
      analysis
effectiveness
   Antitrust Damages Directive 324
   concurrency regime 255, 259, 276–78
   director disqualification 287–90, 301–4, 307–8
   enforcement 1
   fair hearing, right to a xvii
   private enforcement 311–12, 335–36
   remedies 142
efficiencies
   data collection/extraction 362–63
   decision-making 203
   director disqualification 303
   efficient competitor test 87–92, 103–4, 109
   exclusionary abuse 87–109
   killer acquisitions 372–73
   Market Investigation Regime (MIR) 161
   merger control 176
   multi-marketing settings, exclusion in 95
   vertical agreements 60–61, 75

enforcement *see also* concurrency regime;
     enforcement under Competition Act 1998;
     private enforcement
  Brexit xv, 1, 23–24, 28, 386–87
  cartels 9–10, 30–39
  CMA 137, 141–42
  digital economy xix, 376–80, 386–87
  director disqualification 293–300
  directorates 216
  discrimination 98, 102–3
  exclusionary abuses xv–xvi, 79
  fair hearing, right to a xvii, 231–40
  horizontal agreements 29–54
  Market Investigation Regime (MIR) 141–42, 162
  merger control xvi–xvii, 12–13, 170–72, 176–77,
       178, 179–81, 183–91
  over-enforcement 371
  registration-based to enforcement-based structure,
       from 232–34
  resources 203, 215, 217, 219
  under-enforcement 35–37, 53–54, 204, 371
enforcement under Competition Act 1998 1–28
  1998 to 2002, objectives of regime introduced
       from xv
  abuse of a dominant position 1, 4–5, 9
  adverse effect on competition (AEC) test 3
  anti-competitive agreements 1
  antitrust xv, 6–10, 25–26
  assessment of regime 25–28
  appeal system xv
  Brexit xv, 1, 23–24, 25, 26, 28
  cartels 2, 4, 7–8
  CAT 2, 4, 25–26
  chilling effect 4, 25–26
  CMA 4, 6, 25–26, 27, 216
  Competition Commission (CC) 2–5
  concurrency regime xv, 1, 19–20, 25, 26
  conduct of infringement cases 26
  Covid-19, effect of xv, 1, 25, 26, 28
  criminal enforcement 9–10
  criticism 1, 2–6
  digital economy, challenges of xv, 1, 6, 20–22, 26, 28
  director disqualification 10
  effectiveness and utility of regime 1
  EU law 2, 3, 6–7
     Brexit xv, 1, 23–24, 25, 26, 28
     legal framework 22–24
     Merger Regulation 4–5
  financial penalties 6
  future 25–28
  horizontal relationships 2–3
  institutional issues 2–3, 25
  investigation of markets, system for 1
  judicial control 1
  judicial review 4
  Market Investigation Regime (MIR) 3, 10–
       12, 25, 28
  merger control 1, 2, 4–5, 6, 12–14, 25
  ministers, role of xv, 1, 2, 4–5, 18–19, 26–27

monopolies 2, 3
National Audit Office (NAO) 3, 4, 7–8
new regime 2–6
objectives 1, 2–6
Office of Fair Trading (OFT) 2–3, 6–8
  Competition Appeal Tribunal (CAT) 4
  judicial review 4
  merger control 4–5
performance of new regime 6–20
private enforcement xv, 16–18
prohibition system 6
public interest xv, 15–16
Regulation 1/2003 3, 6–7
restrictive agreements, control of 1, 7–8
scepticism about competition analysis 5
sectoral regulators xv, 1, 2, 3, 19–20
soft enforcement policy 7–8
vertical relationships 2–3
World Class Competition Regime White Paper 2
Enterprise Act 2002
  behavioural economics 156
  cartels xviii–xix, 4, 337, 338, 347–49
  CAT 4, 201, 211–12, 321–22
  Competition Commission (CC) 228
  concurrency regime 256–59, 261–62, 276
  decision-making 209–13
  director disqualification 291, 293
  enforcement 2, 4
  fair hearing, right to a 231, 250–51
  judicial review 142
  Market Investigation Regime (MIR) 10, 12, 137,
       138–39, 143, 210
  market studies 140
  merger control xvi–xvii, 1, 4–5, 12–13, 169–99
  OFT 209–10, 228
  private enforcement xviii, 16, 312
  public interest 15–16, 166–67
  vertical agreements 55, 72–73
Enterprise and Regulatory Reform Act 2013 3–
       4, 5, 7–9
  cartels 35, 346–48, 352, 354–55, 358
  CAT 8
  CMA 8–9, 214–20
  commitments 8
  concurrency regime xvii–xviii, 19, 255, 256–62, 281
     case allocation 265–66
     enhanced concurrency 259–78, 279–80
     regulated sectors 270
  enforcement 3–4, 5, 7–9, 25
  fines 8
  Market Investigation Regime (MIR) 10, 11–12,
       137, 138
     cross-market references 143–44
     procedure 168
     public interest 143–44
  merger control 5, 12–13, 14, 170, 198
     consultation 175–76, 182
     fine-tuning 175–81
     initial undertakings (IUs) 178

Enterprise and Regulatory Reform Act 2013 (*cont.*)
  interim measures 177, 178
  missed opportunities for radical change 181–93
  review of impact 179, 181, 190–91
  ministers, role of 18–19
  Office of Fair Trading 8
  partial settlements 8
  pharmaceutical companies 8–9
  prosecutorial system 8
  public interest 143–44, 166–67
  Regulation 1/2003 8
entry barriers *see* **barriers to entry**
equivalence. principle of 324
essential facility doctrine 99–100, 369
EU competition law *see also* **Brexit; Commission; Regulation 1/2003**
  Antitrust Damages Directive 17, 23, 313–15, 319–20, 322–24, 335–36
  Commission Notice on Co-operation with National Courts 313–14
  commitments 8
  Competition Act 1998 22–23
  Competition and Markets Authority (CMA) 22–23
  Competition Commission 3, 23
  concurrency regime 256–58, 265–66, 280–81
  consistent interpretation, principle of 23
  Consumer Rights Act 2015 321
  digital economy 376, 380–81, 384, 385–86
  direct effect 22–23
  effectiveness 313–14
  enforcement 2, 3, 4–5, 6–7, 22–24
  exclusionary abuse xv–xvi, 79, 110–11
  integration 22–23
  killer acquisitions 371–72, 373–74, 376
  Market Investigation Regime (MIR) 23
  merger control 4–5, 23
  preliminary rulings 313–14
  primacy of EU law 57, 73
  private enforcement 17, 23, 313–15, 319–20, 335–36
  retroactive rebates and bundled discounts 87–89, 90–91, 109
  vertical agreements xv, 56–57, 73–74, 76, 77–78
European Commission *see* **Commission**
European Competition Network (ECN)
  Brexit 221
  concurrency regime 265, 266
  enforcement 3
  investigations 22–23
  Market Investigation Regime (MIR) 1
  ministers, role of 18
European Convention on Human Rights (EHRC)
  fair hearing, right to a 231, 232–53
  Market Investigation Regime (MIR) 161–62
  peaceful enjoyment of possessions 249
excessive pricing *see* **exploitative abuses and excessive pricing**
exclusionary abuses 79–111
  Article 101 106–7, 110

  Article 102 79, 106–9, 110
  barriers to entry 98
  Brexit 79–80, 110–11
  bundled discounts xv–xvi, 87–92, 109
  CAT 79
  CMA 79, 106, 109, 110
  Commission xv–xvi, 79–80
  commitments 79, 98
  Competition Act 1998 xv–xvi, 109
  contract-oriented strategy 107–8
  digital economy 361–62, 364
  discrimination xv–xvi, 98–105, 110
  dominance, assessment of xv–xvi, 80–86, 109
  efficiencies 87–109
  EU law xv–xvi, 79–80, 81, 110–11
  exclusivity 97–98, 107, 110
  foreclosure, standard of 87–109, 110
  generics 105–6, 107
  guidance 79
  intent, evidence of 107–8
  legal test for abuse 87–109
  MFN and equivalent clauses xv–xvi, 97–98
  multi-marketing settings, exclusion in xv–xvi, 92–97, 109–10
  OFT 79, 97, 105–6
  pharmaceutical sector xv–xvi, 79, 105–9
  private enforcement xv–xvi, 79
  public enforcement xv–xvi, 79, 110
  retroactive rebates xv–xvi, 79, 87–92, 109
exclusivity agreements 97–98
  digital economy 360–61
  discrimination 105
  dominance, assessment of 81
  exclusionary abuse 97–98, 110
  foreclosure 97–98, 110
  MFN provisions 97–98
  vertical agreements 62, 77–78
exemptions
  block exemptions 56–57, 60–61, 73, 74, 76
  individual exemptions 52–53
  vertical agreements 57–58
exploitative abuses and excessive pricing xvi, 113–36
  Advocate General opinions xvi
  Albion Water 115–17, 136
  Article 102 113–14, 129, 132
  ATTHERACES 127–28, 133, 134, 136
  burden of proof 134–35
  CAT xvi, 113–29
  Chapter II prohibition 129
  CMA 113–14, 117–26, 134, 218
  comparable products 117–26
  core principles 129–36
  Court of Appeal xvi, 121–26, 129–30
  decisional practice and case law 114–29
  fairness 117–26, 130, 134–36
  fines 117–26
  High Court cases/appeals from High Court cases 32, 126–29
  margin squeeze 115–17

Napp case 114–15, 136
OFT 114–15
overseas authorities and courts xvi
patents 114–15
pharmaceuticals 113–15, 117–26
Phenytoin case 117–26, 129–30, 136
predation 114
predominance of evidence approach 114–15
price regulation 113, 114–15
sectoral regulation 115–17
extraterritoriality 164–65

Facebook
advertising 364–65
consumer-facing markets 364
Federal Trade Commission (FTC) 379–80
first party data and third party data,
combining 362–63
General Data Protection Regulation 363
Germany 21
killer acquisitions 371
privacy 365–66
services in exchange for data, provision of 361
unfair trading practices 21
fair hearing, right to a 231–53
abuse of a dominant position 237–41, 243–49, 252
administrative decisions/proceedings 231, 234–37,
239–41, 242, 243–44, 245, 253
anti-competitive agreements 237, 238
cartels 237–41, 243–44
CAT xvii, 231–32, 241–53
Chapter I prohibition 237, 238–39, 243–44, 250–
51, 252–53
Chapter II prohibition 237, 238–39, 243–44, 250–
51, 252–53
CMA 231, 232, 243–44, 247
abuse of a dominant position 232
accountability 251
anti-competitive agreements 232
CAT 232, 244, 250, 253
evidence, admission of relevant 250–51
margin of appreciation 248–49
civil rights and obligations 234–35, 236–37, 246
collusion 244, 246–47, 249, 252
common law 233–34, 241–44
criminal in nature infringements, meaning of 232–
40, 244–45, 250
criminal proceedings xvii, 231–43, 248–49
deterrence 237–39, 244–45
disciplinary infringements 234–35, 237–38, 242–43
due process 232, 235, 242, 245–46, 247
enforcement xvii, 231–40
European Convention on Human Rights
(EHRC) 231, 232–53
full review, notion of 236
Human Rights Act 1998 231, 232–34, 242–47
independent and impartial tribunals 234–35, 246
integrated agency model 232, 235, 238, 239–
41, 244–45

interpretation 234–40
judicial review 236–37, 247, 248, 250–52, 253
legal representation, access to 243
natural justice 242, 243
new evidence, allowing 244–46, 251–52
oral hearing, right to an 233, 235, 236–37
penalties/sanctions 236–40, 244–45, 246–
47, 252–53
pharmaceutical industry 244–48
presumption of innocence 241–42, 244–45
procedural safeguards 235–37
public interest 235–36, 237, 238
punitiveness 237–39, 244–45
regulatory infringements 234–35, 238
review of infringement proceedings 231
standard of proof 231, 241, 244–45, 246–47
witnesses, cross-examination of 245–46
fairness *see also* fair hearing, right to a
decision-making 203
excessive pricing 117–26, 130, 134–36
exploitative abuses 117–26, 130, 134–36
Financial Conduct Authority (FCA) 53–54, 258–59,
265, 268, 275
fines
Brexit 53–54
cartels 30–35, 36–40
CAT 212
CMA 29, 35, 36–39, 117–26, 226, 227–28
concurrency regime 263
deterrence 20–21, 285, 287, 307–8
digital economy 20–21
director disqualification 283–84, 285–90, 294–
95, 307–8
enforcement 6
Enterprise and Regulatory Reform Act 2013 8
exploitative abuses 117–26
Market Investigation Regime (MIR) 167
OFT 212–13
remedies 167
resale price maintenance (RPM) 63–65
tying 379
follow-on actions 24, 312–13, 315–16, 320–
22, 327–28
foreclosure
data sharing and data portability 370
discrimination 100–4
exclusionary abuses 87–109
multi-marketing settings, exclusion in 95–96
retroactive rebates and bundled discounts 87–92
fuller effects analysis 61–62, 74
fundamental rights 161–62, *see also* European
Convention on Human Rights (EHRC); fair
hearing, right to a; Human Rights Act 1998
funding private enforcement 331–32
Furman Report
concurrency regime 277
data sharing and data portability 367, 370
digital economy 21, 364–65, 366–67, 376–77
data sharing and data portability 367, 370

Furman Report (*cont.*)
   killer acquisitions 196, 197, 371, 373, 375–76
   regulation 380–81, 382–84, 385–86
   killer acquisitions 196, 197, 371, 373, 375–76

global financial crisis 2008 5, 15, 174, 220
Google
   abuse of a dominant position 21, 100–1, 102, 316–17, 378
   advertising 364–65
   Brexit 221
   Commission 21
   data in return for services, exchange of 361
   data protection 365–66
   discrimination 102
   killer acquisitions 371
   targeted customers 364

hard-core restraints 60–61, 74
horizontal agreements
   Brexit xv, 53–54
   cartels xv, 30–39, 42, 54
   Competition Act 1998 xv, 29–54
   concurrency regime 49–50
   Covid-19 pandemic 51–53
   enforcement 29–54
   hub-and-spoke cartels xv, 39–43
   levels of enforcement xv
   National Audit Office (NAO) xv
   notification and exemption 46–49
   Paroxetine case 29–30, 43–46
   pay-for-delay agreements in the pharmaceutical sector 29–30, 43–46
   Scotland 50–51
   trade associations 29–30
   under-enforcement 53–54
hub-and-spoke cartels xv, 39–43
   collusion 40, 41, 42
   concerted practices 40, 41–42
   Dairy Products case 42
   definition 40
   diagrammatic form 40
   fines 39–40
   Football Shirts case 39–40, 41
   horizontal agreements xv, 39–43
   OFT 39–40, 41, 42
   other jurisdictions, agreements in 42
   Toys and Games case 39–40, 41
   United States 42
   vertical agreements 56–57, 63
   warehouse clubs 42
human rights *see* European Convention on Human Rights (EHRC); fair hearing, right to a; fundamental rights; Human Rights Act 1998
Human Rights Act 1998
   appeals 204–5
   Competition Act 1998 243–47
   declarations of incompatibility 232–33
   enactment 232–33
   fair hearing, right to a 231, 232–34, 242–47

illegality, presumption of
   merger control 372–73, 374
   vertical agreements 56, 59–60, 61, 74–75
impartiality *see* biases; independent and impartial tribunals
independent and impartial tribunals 234–35, 246
information
   asymmetries 156
   concurrency regime 260–61, 263–64, 279–80
   failure to provide necessary information 146
   power to demand 211
   sharing agreements 32–34
institutions enforcing competition law, reform of 201–29, *see also* Competition Appeal Tribunal (CAT); Competition and Markets Authority (CMA); Competition Commission (CC); Director-General of Fair Trading (DGFT); Monopolies and Mergers Commission (MMC); Office of Fair Trading (OFT)
   abuse of a dominant position xvii, 209, 228
   advisory duties 203, 228
   advocacy duties 203
   anti-competitive agreements xvii, 209, 228
   appeals 204–5, 228
   climate change 223–24, 226, 229
   Competition Commission Appeals Tribunal (CCAT) 210–12
   competition test 209–13, 228
   cultures 206–8
   decision-making 203–4, 209–13
   design 202–6
   economic analysis 209, 211
   first interest determinations, quality of xvii
   mandates 203
   Market Investigation Regime (MIR) 137, 138, 139–44
   ministers 201, 203
   Monopolies and Restrictive Practices Commission (MRPC) 206–7, 208
   Monopolies Commission (MC) 207–8
   organizational changes xvii
   organizational design 203–4
   penalties 201, 209, 228
   performance 205–6
   precedent, lack of 208
   priorities 203
   private enforcement 312–15
   privatization of public utilities 208
   prosecutorial system, replacement of xvii
   public interest xvii, 206, 209
   reform 137, 139
      21st century challenges 220–24
      case for reform 220–28
   Registrar, post of 207
   resources, sharing 203
   responsibilities, list of 203
   Restrictive Practices Court (RPC) 207, 208
   Secretary of State
      case decisions, withdrawing from 209, 211

monopoly references 208
  veto 208
sector regulators, role of 208
trade-offs 203
integrated agency model
  case selection, investigation and
    adjudication 204
  fair hearing, right to a 232, 235, 238, 239–
    41, 244–45
intellectual property rights (IPRs) 142, 360–61, *see*
    also patents
intelligence 177, 216
inter-brand competition 59–60, 65–66
interim measures
  CMA 214, 224, 225
  concurrency regime 263
  Consumer Interest Authority, proposal for 225
  cooperation, incentivizing 225
  executive control, loss of 225
  interim measures orders 178–79
  judgments 315–16
  Market Investigation Regime (MIR) 167
  merger control 177–79, 198–99
  phase 2 market investigations 225
International Competition Network (ICN) 18
interoperability 359–60, 361–62, 368
intra-brand competition 59–60, 61–62, 73
investigations *see also* **market investigation**
    regime (MIR)
  cartels xv, 30–31, 54, 338
  CMA 214, 215–16
  Commission 30–31
  enforcement 1
  European Competition Network (ECN) 22–23
  Monopolies and Restrictive Practices Commission
    (MRPC) 206
  references for full market investigations 215–16
  Secretary of State's power to request
    investigations 214
  specialized investigative agencies 204

judicial review
  appeals 204
  CAT 142–43, 148–50, 212
  CMA 142–43, 148–50
  Competition Commission (CC) 211
  digital economy 383
  enforcement 4
  Enterprise Act 2002 142
  fair hearing, right to a 236–37, 247, 248, 250–
    52, 253
  full merits review 142–43
  list of challenges 148
  Market Investigation Regime (MIR) 137, 139, 142–
    43, 148–50, 163–64
  market studies 142
  merger control 24, 142–43
  number of challenges 148
  Secretary of State 142
  sectoral regulators 142

killer acquisitions 370–76
  abuse of a dominant position 370
  balance of harms test 373–74, 376
  bottleneck power, dominant platforms
    with 372, 375
  burden of proof 371–72, 373–75
  concentrations 371–72, 373, 374
  definition 370
  efficiencies 372–73
  EU law 371–72, 373–74, 376
  Furman report 371, 373, 375–76
  illegality, presumption of 372–73, 374
  innovation 372–73
  Merger Regulation 373, 376
  monopolies 370, 372–73
  over-enforcement 371
  pharmaceutical sector 370
  pre-emption of future competition 370
  proportionality 372–73, 375
  protocol of notification, proposal for 375
  Regulation 1/2003 373
  rivals, buying up small 370–76
  standard of proof 371–72
  Stigler Report 371–72, 374, 375–76
  substantial lessening of competition (SLC)
    regime 371–72
  under-enforcement 371
  United States 360–61, 371–72, 375
  windfall profits 371

legal certainty
  Article 101 74
  block exemptions 76
  fair hearing, right to a 234
  Market Investigation Regime (MIR) 161–62, 164
  merger control 173–74
legal representation, access to 243
leniency process
  cartels 30–32, 34, 50, 51, 341–43, 344–45, 350
  concurrency regime 263, 270–71, 274
  director disqualification 287–90, 294–95, 296–97
  documentation 323
  OFT 7
  vertical agreements 63–64
loyalty agreements 360–61
loyalty rebates 88–89, 90, 92

mandates of institutions 203, 207, 214–15
market investigation regime (MIR) 10–12, 137–68
  2010-2020, overview of 145–50
  adverse effect on competition (AEC) test 3, 144–45,
    146, 149–50
    concentrations 153
    consumer detriment threshold, replacement
      with 167–68
    consumer policy 154
    enforcement 3, 25
    future developments 167
    vertical restraints 152
    well-functioning market 151

market investigation regime (MIR) (*cont.*)
Aggregates 152, 153
background 138–39
behavioural economics 154, 155–61
CAT 11, 137, 148–50, 168
CMA xvi, 27, 137–68
Competition Commission (CC) 3, 10–11, 12, 138–39
complex monopolies 138–39
concurrency regime 256–57, 263
consumer policy 153–54, 168
consumer welfare 144–45, 167–68
conventional competition cases 151–52, 162–63
demand-side features 139, 150–51, 153, 154
digital economy 3, 28
early identification of cases 11
economic context 168
Energy Market case 12, 154, 155, 168
enforcement 3, 10–12, 25, 28, 141–42
Enterprise Act 2002 10, 12, 137, 138–39, 140, 143, 146
Enterprise and Regulatory Reform Act 2013 10, 11–12, 137, 138
 cross-market references 143–44
 market studies 139–40
 procedure 168
extended competition cases 152–53
Funerals 154
future developments 167–68
identification of adverse effects on competition 141
impartiality 141
information, failure to provide necessary 146
inquiry groups 141
institutional framework 137, 138, 139–44
interim measures 167
Investment Consultancy Services 154, 155
judicial oversight 163–64
judicial review 137, 139, 142–43, 148–50
length of process 25
list of investigations 147*t*
Local Bus Services 153, 155
market power 150–51, 152, 153, 155
market studies (Phase I) 139–41, 145–46
merger control 11, 144, 150
ministerial decision-making xvi–xvii, 10
Movies on Pay-TV 152
National Audit Office (NAO) xvi, 138, 145–46, 168
national security public interest grounds xvi–xvii
number of investigations 146, 168
Office of Fair Trading (OFT) 3, 10–11, 137, 139
Payday Lending 154, 155
policy goal 144–45
policy issues 164–67
political context 168
Private Healthcare 152, 153, 155
Private Motor Insurance 152, 155
procedure 139–44
public interest 11–12, 140–41, 144, 145–46, 150–51, 166–67

references, making (Phase I) 138, 139–41, 145–46, 168
reform xvi, 137
regulatory arbitrage cases 151, 162–63
remedies 140, 141–42, 146–48, 154, 167
reports 140–41
Retail Banking 12, 154, 155, 168
rule of law 161–64
scope of regime 137, 138
sectoral regulation 139–40, 142, 168
state action 154–55
Statutory Audit Services 153, 155
substantive provisions 143–44
terms of reference 141
territorial limitations 164–66
time limits 11, 140, 141
transparency xvi–xvii
trends 150–55
undertakings 141, 145, 167
vertical agreements 55, 77–78, 138–39
working group, establishment by Competition Commission and OFT of 11
World Class Competition Regime White Paper 10–12
market share 82, 83
dominance, assessment of 80, 81, 85–86, 109
multi-marketing settings, exclusion in 92
market studies 215–16, 226, 227–28
CMA 139
Market Investigation Regime (MIR) 139–41, 145–46
OFT 210, 213
merger control 169–99, *see also* **killer acquisitions; Merger Regulation; Monopolies and Mergers Commission (MMC)**
accountability 175
agenda for further reform 190–98
anticipated mergers, imposition on interim measures on 179
banking investigation 219
behavioural remedies 219
Brexit 14, 24, 25, 169–70, 190–93, 198–99
CAT 12–13, 24, 170–72, 178
CMA xvi–xvii, 13–14, 15, 169–99
 Brexit 24
 digital economy 22
 enforcement 217, 218–19, 227
 new approach 14
 resources xvi–xvii, 198–99
 statutory remit xvi–xvii
Competition Commission (CC) 12–13, 170–72, 213
 CMA 184
 delay 189–90
 enforcement 4–5
 halting integration 177
 referrals 188–89
concentrations in digital economy 359–60, 361–62
concurrency regime 280

confirmation bias 176–77, 185–86, 188–89
deterrence 175
digital economy 21, 169–70, 190–91, 195–98, 199
   concentrations 359–60, 361–62
   enforcement 6
economic growth 175–77
efficiencies 176
emerging challenges 190–98
energy investigation 219
enforcement 1, 2, 4–5, 6, 12–14, 183–90
Enterprise Act 2002 xvi–xvii, 1, 4–5, 12–13, 169–99
Enterprise and Regulatory Reform Act 2013 12–13, 14, 170, 198
   consultation 175–76, 182
   enforcement 5
   fine-tuning 175–81
   interim measures 177, 178
   missed opportunities for radical change 181–93
   review of impact 179, 181, 190–91
EU law 23
Fair Trading Act 1973 169, 170, 172–73, 175, 199
foreign takeovers 190–91, 193, 199
funerals market 218–19
Green Paper 190–91
halting integration 177–79, 198–99
higher rate of enforcement 183–85
hold separate measures 177–78
horizontal/vertical distinction 21
initial enforcement orders (IEOs) 177–78, 179
initial period 171–75
initial undertakings (IUs) 177–78
interim measures 177–79, 198–99
investigations 184–85
judicial review 142–43
legal certainty 173–74
length of proceedings 5
lieu of a reference (UILs), in 180–81, 183–86, 198, 218
Market Investigation Regime (MIR) 11, 144, 150, 163–64
material influence, threshold of 13, 15
media plurality 171
Merger Assessment Guidelines 172
ministerial decision-making xvi–xvii, 4–5, 170–71, 173–75
Monopolies and Mergers Act 1965 170
National Audit Office (NAO) 190
national security 171, 190–91, 194–95
National Security and Investment Bill 190–91, 195
nationalism 169–70, 192–95, 199
news, presentation of 171
notification, voluntary system of 14, 171
   anticipated mergers, imposition on interim measures on 179
   BIS consultation 182
   full mandatory system, proposal for 182, 192
   hybrid mandatory system, proposal for 182
   information, delays caused by requests for 190
   mandatory system, lack of 182–83, 192

non-notified mergers, strict approach to 179
   number of referrals 187–88
   opportunities for change 181–82
   pre-emptive actions 182
   pre-notification discussions 189–90
   quasi-mandatory review 198–99
   time limits 179–80
   weaknesses 182
number of decisions 213
OFT 12–13, 170–73
   Competition Commission 176–77, 184
   delay 189–90
   enforcement 4–5
   halting integration 177–78
   referrals 171–72, 186–89
   undertakings in lieu (UILs) 180–81
outcome, completed decisions by 188*f*
Phase I enforcement powers xvi–xvii, 12–13, 170–71, 172, 176–77
   CMA 218–19
   confirmation bias 188–89, 189*t*
   decline in investigations 184–85
   duration of investigations delay 189–90
   Goldilocks model 179–80
   hold-separate orders 178
   initial enforcement orders (IEOs) 178
   initial undertakings (IUs) 178
   reviews 190–91
   substantial lessening of competition (SLC) regime 180–81
   time limits 179–80, 189–90
   undertakings in lieu 180–81, 183–86, 187–88
Phase II enforcement powers xvi–xvii, 12–13, 170–71, 172, 174, 176–77
   CMA 218–19, 227
   confirmation bias 188–89, 189*t*
   interim orders 178
   likelihood of referrals 187*t*
   marginal cases 189
   rate of referrals 187–88
   references, number of 187*f*
   reviews 190–91
   standard of proof 171–72, 186, 188–89
   time limits 179–80, 189–90
political bias 169
predictability xvi–xvii, 169
pre-emptive action 177, 178–79, 182
pre-notification discussions 22, 189–90
private enforcement 24
procedure 175–76
prohibitions 184
public health emergencies 171, 174–75
public interest xvi–xvii, 15, 140–41, 169–71
   Commission 192–93
   enforcement 4–5
   foreign takeovers 193, 199
   Merger Regulation 192–93
   public interest intervention notice (PIIN) 174–75
   residual public interest regime 173–75

merger control (*cont.*)
  radical change, opportunities for 181–83
  rate of enforcement 183–85
  referrals 171–72, 186–88
  reform, agenda for further 190–98
  relevant merger situation, concept of a 172–73, 177–78
  remedies 177, 184, 219
  resources 176–77, 183, 188
  stability of the UK financial system 171, 174
  statistics 183–90
  Stericycle decision 178
  substantial lessening of competition (SLC)
      regime 14, 170–72, 175, 176
    digital mergers 199
    enforcement 4–5
    interim measures 177
    Phase I decisions 180–81
    Phase II referrals 188–89
    screening 184–85
    standard of proof 183
  Tebbit doctrine 170–71, 175
  territorial jurisdiction 13
  time limits 179–81, 183
  transparency xvi–xvii, 4–5, 169, 173–74, 175, 183, 198–99
  turnover threshold 23
  unconditional clearances 188–89
  undertakings 12–13, 177–78, 180–81, 183–86, 187–88, 198, 218
  unwinding powers 179
Merger Regulation
  Brexit 24
  enforcement 4–5, 25
  killer acquisitions 373, 376
  merger control 14, 173
  public interest 15–16, 192–93
  turnover threshold 23
meta-regulation 381–82, 383
MFN *see* most-favoured-nation (MFN) provisions
ministers, role of xv, 1, 2, 4–5, 201, *see also* Secretary of State
  appeals 18–19
  change of emphasis 18–19
  Competition Commission (CC) 18
  Competition and Markets Authority (CMA) 19
  decision-making xvi–xvii, 10
  enforcement xv, 1, 2, 4–5, 18–19, 26–27
  Enterprise and Regulatory Reform Act 2013 18–19
  European Competition Network (ECN) 18
  expertise, reduction in 18
  independence from institutions 203
  International Competition Network (ICN) 18
  merger control xvi–xvii, 4–5, 170–71, 173–75
  OFT 18
  populism 26–27
  public interest 15, 26–27
  Regulatory Appeal Review 18–19
  specialists 18

withdrawal of ministers from day-to-day operations and decision-making 18
  World Class Competition Regime White Paper 18
MIR *see* market investigation regime (MIR)
MMC *see* Monopolies and Mergers Commission (MMC)
monopolies *see also* Monopolies and Mergers Commission (MMC)
  Competition Commission (CC) 213
  competition test 211
  complex monopolies 138–39
  digital economy 382–83
  enforcement 2, 3
  killer acquisitions 370, 372–73
  Monopolies Commission (MC) 207–8
  multibillion-euro businesses, monopolization of 376
  price 99–100
  public ownership 206
  Secretary of State, references to 208
Monopolies and Mergers Commission (MMC)
  Brexit 24
  Competition Act 1998 201
  Competition Commission (CC) 201, 207, 210–11
  concurrency regime 255–56
  culture 207
  enforcement 4–5, 335
  initiation of inquiries 208
  mandate 207
  Market Investigation Regime (MIR) 138–39
  Monopolies and Restrictive Practices Commission (MRPC) 207
  OFT 24
  public interest 29, 207
  referrals 207
  reform 209
  Secretary of State, referrals by 207
  sector regulators, role of 208
Monopolies and Restrictive Practices Commission (MRPC) 206–7
  composition 206
  culture 206–7
  investigative body, as 206
  investigative procedure 206
  mandate 207
  Monopolies Commission (MC), renamed the 207
  negotiations 208
  public interest 206–7
  public ownership, monopoly creation under 206
  referrals 206
  reports 206
Monopolies Commission (MC) 207–8
moral wrongfulness 351, 352–54
most-favoured-nation (MFN) provisions
  concurrency regime 268
  exclusionary abuses xv–xvi, 97–98
  Market Investigation Regime (MIR) 152, 162–63
  narrow provisions 72
  vertical agreements 62, 67–69, 76–78

Vertical Block Exemption Regulation (VBER) 162–63
wide provisions 72, 152
MRPC *see* **Monopolies and Restrictive Practices Commission (MRPC)**
multi-homing 359–61, 369
multi-marketing settings, exclusion in xv–xvi, 92–97, 109–10

National Audit Office (NAO)
cartels 35–36
concurrency regime 263
enforcement 3, 4, 7–8
horizontal agreements xv
Market Investigation Regime (MIR) xvi, 138, 145–46, 168
merger control 190
UK competition authorities: the UK competition regime 35–36
national security xvi–xvii, 15–16, 171, 190–91, 194–95
nationalism 169–70, 192–95, 199
natural justice 242, 243
network effects 360–63
NHS Improvement (NHSI) 258–59, 268–69, 276
Northern Ireland Authority for Utility Regulation (NIAUR) 258–59, 272–73, 275–76
nudging 156–57, 365–66, 377–78

Ofcom 258–59, 270–71, 386–87
Office of Fair Trading (OFT) 207–9, *see also* **Director-General of Fair Trading (DGFT)**
abuse of a dominant position 9, 80–81, 83, 109, 209–10
anti-competitive agreements 209–10
appointments 210
behavioural economics 156–57
Brexit 24, 53–54
cartels 9–10, 16, 30–35, 54
   Cartel Offence 339–42, 354–55
   enforcement 7–8, 30–35
   hub-and-spoke cartels 39–40, 41, 42
case closures 212–13
CAT 4, 212–13
CMA 35, 184
Competition Act 1998 209–10, 228
Competition Commission (CC) 35, 213
   Market Investigation Regime (MIR) 10–11, 139
   merger control xvii, 176–77, 184, 201, 214, 215–16, 217, 227, 228
   referrals 210, 213
competition role 210
concurrency regime 255–58, 265–66
consumer role 210
corporate entity, as 210
Counter-Inflation Act 1973 207–8
Covid-19 pandemic 52–53
criminal cartels 210, 213
culture 207–8
damages 209–10

decision-making 228
deterrence 209–10, 212–13
director disqualification 283, 285–86, 294–96, 297–98, 302–4, 306
enforcement 2–3, 4
   advocacy 7–8
   cartels 7–8, 30–35
   financial penalties 6
   leniency policy 7
   Market Investigation Regime (MIR) 3
   merger control 4–5
   private enforcement 321
   prohibition system 6
   restrictive agreements, control of 7–8
Enterprise Act 2002 209–10, 228
Enterprise and Regulatory Reform Act 2013 8, 201
exclusionary abuses 79, 97
exploitative abuses 114–15
fines 6, 32, 212–13
horizon-scanning 208
hub-and-spoke cartels xv, 39–40, 41, 42
informal commitments 8
investigations 30
leniency policy 7
Market Investigation Regime (MIR) 3, 10–11, 137
market studies 210, 213
merger control 3, 4–5, 12–13, 170–73
   Competition Commission 176–77, 184
   delay 189–90
   halting integration 177–78
   hold-separate orders 178
   initial undertakings (IUs) 178
   intelligence function 177
   referrals 171–72, 186–89
   undertakings in lieu (UILs) 180–81
Monopolies and Mergers Commission (MMC) 24
multi-marketing settings, exclusion in 92–94, 109–10
National Audit Office (NAO) 35
OECD 18
organisational model 207–8
penalties 209–10, 228
performance 212–13, 217–18
precedent 209–10, 212–13
Price Commission 207–8
references, initiating 171–72, 186–89, 208
reform 209
Regulation 1/2003 3
resale price maintenance (RPM) 63
restrictive agreements, control of 7–8
Restrictive Practices Court (RPC) 24, 207
restructuring 213
retroactive rebates and bundled discounts 89–90
reviews of performance 35
sector regulators 213
staff retention and recruitment issues 212–13
super-complaints by consumer groups 210
trade associations 43
transparency 210
vertical agreements 57

Ofgem 258–59, 267, 271–73, 275–76
OFT *see* Office of Fair Trading (OFT)
Ofwat 258–59, 273–74
oligopolies 138–39, 151, 152, 156
oral hearing, right to an 233, 235, 236–37
ordoliberalism 378–79
ORR 258–59, 273

parallel enforcement *see* concurrency regime
Paroxetine case 29–30, 43–46
   abuse of a dominant position 82, 83–85
   actual or potential competition 44–45
   CMA 29–30, 43–46
   Competition Appeal Tribunal (CAT) 43–46
   object, restriction of competition by 45–46
   patents 43–46
   pay-for-delay agreements 29–30, 43–46
   pharmaceutical sector 29–30, 43–46
patents 82–83, 84–85, 114–15
pay-for-delay agreements in the pharmaceutical
      sector 29–30, 43–46
Payment Systems Regulator (PSR) 258–59, 275
peaceful enjoyment of possessions 249
penalties/sanctions
   CAT 212
   DGFT 210
   fair hearing, right to a 237–40, 244–45, 246–
      47, 252–53
   institutions 201, 209, 228
   market studies 146
   OFT 209–10, 228
   proportionality 236–37
performance of institutions 205–6
   CMA 217–20, 226
   Competition Commission (CC) 212–13
   OFT 212–13, 217–18
pharmaceutical markets *see also* pharmaceutical
      markets, dominance in
   Enterprise and Regulatory Reform Act 2013 8–9
   killer acquisitions 370
   pay-for-delay agreements 29–30, 43–46
pharmaceutical markets, dominance in 9, 83–85
   assessment of dominance 82–85
   barriers to entry 82, 83
   CMA 83, 117–26
   comparable products 117–26
   excessive pricing 113–15, 117–26
   exclusionary abuses 79, 97
   exploitative abuse 113–15, 117–26
   fairness 117–26
   fines 117–26
   generics 117–26
   market definition 83–85
   market share 82, 83
   Paroxetine 82, 83–85
   patents 82–83, 84–85
   Pharmaceutical Price Regulation Scheme
      (PPRS) 115, 118, 119
   presumption of dominance 82

populism 26–27, 110–11
Precast Concrete Drainage Products cartel 344–45,
      348, 355–56, 357–58
precedent
   CMA 218, 219, 228
   concurrency regime 266
   institutions 208
   OFT 209–10, 212–13
   performance 205
presumption of innocence 241–42, 244–45
price *see also* exploitative abuses and excessive
      pricing; resale price maintenance (RPM)
      Clauses
   abuse of a dominant position 82, 83, 85–86, 87–88,
      89–90, 92–93, 95
   cartels 31–32, 36–38
   concurrency 48–50
   cover pricing 7, 31–32, 34
   digital economy 6, 20–21
   discrimination 100, 102–4, 110
   energy market 12
   exclusionary abuses 105–6, 107
   excessive pricing 9, 43–44, 46, 48, 51–52
   fixing prices 34–35, 37–38, 311
   future pricing 33, 37, 41
   hub-and-spoke cartels 41–42
   information exchange 34
   monopolies 99–100
   OFT 7, 33, 34
   parity clauses 69, 75, 98
   price relationship agreements 62, 67–69
   remedies 20–21
   trade associations 43
   unfair pricing practices 220
   vertical agreements 55–56, 62, 72, 75–77
privacy
   data collection/extraction 20–21, 362–64, 365–66
   data sharing and data portability 370
   digital economy 382–83
private enforcement xv, 16–18, 311–36, *see also*
      damages
   abuse of a dominant position xv–xvi, 79, 316–18
   Antitrust Damages Directive 17, 23, 313–15, 319–
      20, 324
   binding force of national competition authority
      (NCAs) decisions 320–21
   Brexit 311–12, 334
   cartels 16, 315, 318–19
   case law, overview of UK 315–18, 336
   CAT xviii, 16–18, 335–36
      Consumer Rights Act 2015 321–22
      Court of Appeal 322
      damages 16, 17–18, 312–13, 315–16
      Enterprise Act 2002 321–22
      Enterprise Act Regulations 2015 322
      EU law 321
      follow-on actions 312, 313, 315–16, 321–22
      non-monetary claims 313, 315
      representative claimants, designation of 16, 313

stand-alone actions 313, 318
   time limits 318, 319, 336
   workload 322
causation 324–25
Chapter I prohibition 316–17, 322
Chapter II prohibition 316–17
collective redress mechanism 327–31
   CAT 327–31
   certification 17
   Collective Proceedings Orders (CPOs) 315–16, 327–30, 336
   opt-outs/opt-ins xviii, 17
compensatory functions 311–12
Competition Act 1998 xv, 16–18, 312, 318, 335
consumer representative actions 312, 327–28
Consumer Rights Act 2015 xviii, 17–18, 313, 318
deterrence 311
disclosure 322–23
effectiveness 311–12, 335–36
Enterprise Act 2002 xviii, 16, 312
EU law 313–15, 335–36
   Antitrust Damages Directive 17, 313–15, 319–20
   Brexit 311–12, 334
   Commission Notice on Co-operation with National Courts 313–14
follow-on actions 312–13, 315–16
funding private enforcement 331–32
increase in cases 315
institutional developments 312–15
interim judgments 315–16
legislative developments xviii, 312–15
merger control 24
Merricks case xviii, 17, 311–12, 322, 329–30, 332, 336
Monopolies and Mergers Commission (MMC) 335
opt-outs/opt-ins xviii, 17, 313, 331–32
price-fixing cartels 311
private enforcement xv–xvi, 79
public interest 335
Replica Football Shirts litigation 16
representative actions 16, 313
specialist court/tribunal, existence of a 321–22
specific issues 318–32
time limits 318–20
United States antitrust enforcement regime xviii, 311–12, 332–33, 335–36
privatization 208, 255–56, 258
promote competition, duty to xvii, 256–57, 261–62, 379
proportionality
   data sharing and data portability 369
   disclosure 322–23
   discrimination 102
   killer acquisitions 372–73, 375
   multi-marketing settings, exclusion in 95
   penalties/sanctions 236–37
   remedies 142
prosecutions
   Brexit 24

Cartel Offence xviii–xix, 346–47
CMA 226–27, 229
decision-making 204
Enterprise and Regulatory Reform Act 2013 8
institutions, replacement of prosecutorial systems by xvii
Public Accounts Committee (PAC) 215
public faith in markets, loss of 220, 224, 226, 228
public interest
   adverse effect on competition (AEC) test 166
   Cartel Offence 341–42
   CMA 11–12, 166–67
   Competition Commission (CC) 15, 166–67, 210–11, 228
   competition test, replaced by 209
   concurrency regime 258
   consumer interest 215
   culture 208
   definition 206
   director disqualification 295–96
   economic analysis 209, 211
   economic nationalism 220
   enforcement xv, 15–16, 335
   Enterprise Act 2002 15–16, 166–67
   Enterprise and Regulatory Reform Act 2013 166–67
   fair hearing, right to a 235–36, 237, 238
   global financial crisis 15
   grounds for intervention 15
   institutions xvii, 206, 209
   Market Investigation Regime (MIR) 11–12, 144, 150–51, 166–67
   merger control xvi–xvii, 4–5, 15–16, 192–93
   ministers, role of 15, 26–27
   Monopolies and Mergers Commission (MMC) 29, 207
   Monopolies and Restrictive Practices Commission (MRPC) 206–7
   promotion of competition, replacement by xvii
   public interest intervention notices (PIIN) 140–41, 174–75
   Secretary of State's power to request investigations 214
   significant impediment to effective competition (SIEC) 192–93
   wider public interest 15–16
publicity
   Cartel Offence xviii–xix, 346–48, 349
   concurrency regime 260–61, 278
   director disqualification 306–7

rationality 157, 163, 215
rebates xv–xvi, 79, 87–92, 109
reform
   21st century challenges 220–24
   access remedies 20–21
   Cartel Offence xviii–xix, 337, 346–50, 354–55
   CMA 220–28, 229
   coherent institutional reform 226–28

reform (*cont.*)
enforcement xv
institutions 220–28
Market Investigation Regime
  (MIR) xvi, 137
merger control 190–98
Tyrie letter 224–27, 229
Registrar, post of 207, 208
regulation *see also* **concurrency regime; digital
  economy, regulation of**
data sharing and data portability 368
fair hearing, right to a 234–35, 238
prices 113, 114–15
regulatory arbitrage cases 151, 162–63
remedies 146–48
Regulation 1/2003 22–23, 54
adverse effect on competition (AEC) test 3
burden of proof 373
Cartel Offence 338–39
concurrency regime 19
Covid-19 pandemic 52
enforcement 3, 6–7
Enterprise and Regulatory Reform Act 2013 8
killer acquisitions 373
vertical agreements 57–58
remedies *see also* **damages**
behavioural economics 159–60
behavioural remedies 142, 159–60, 165, 370
CMA 141–42, 146–48, 226
complex remedies 159–60
consumer policy 154
divestitures 142
effectiveness 142
enforcement 2
extraterritoriality 164–66
fines 167
injunctions 212, 321–22
intellectual property remedies 142
intrusive remedy, access as an 367, 369
Market Investigation Regime (MIR) 140, 141–
  42, 146–48
merger control 177, 184
proportionality 142
reasonableness 142
regulatory remedies 146–48
structural remedies 142, 165
timing 142
representative actions *see* **collective redress
  mechanism**
resale price maintenance (RPM) Clauses xv, 56–57,
  59, 60–61, 62–67
advertising prices 65
Competition Act 1998 63–64, 65–66, 77
digital economy 376–77
EU law 63–64, 66–67
fines 63–65
interbrand competition 65–66
online selling restraints 62, 63–67, 75, 77
territorial restraints 75

resources
Brexit 222
budget cuts 219
CMA xvi–xvii, 198–99
consumer benefits 219
DGFT 208
enforcement 203, 215, 217, 219
merger control 176–77, 183, 188
Restrictive Practices Court (RPC)
CAT 207
composition 207
culture 207, 208
OFT 24, 207
Restrictive Trade Practices Act 1976 29
retroactive rebates and bundled discounts xv–xvi,
  79, 87–92
above-cost rebates 87
Brexit 92, 109
conditional rebates 87–88, 89–90
efficient competitor test 87–92, 109
EU law 87–89, 90–91, 109
foreclosure standard 87–92
loyalty rebates 88–89, 90, 92
negative effects on competition concept 87
predation 90, 92
rule of law and market investigation regime (MIR) 161–64
accessibility of law 161
Aggregates investigation 163–64
bias 163–64
conventional competition issues 162–63
fundamental rights 161–62
intelligibility, clarity and predictability 161
judicial oversight, weakness of 163–64
judicial review standard 163–64
legal certainty 161–62, 164
Private Healthcare investigation 163–64
Private Motor Insurance investigation 162–63
rationality 163
regulatory arbitrage 162–63
rule of reason 88–89

safe harbour 57–58, 60–61, 74, 76–78
sanctions *see* **penalties/sanctions**
Scotland, horizontal agreements in 50–51
search engines 361–62
Secretary of State
case decisions, withdrawing from 209, 211
CMA 215
DGFT 208
judicial review 142
monopoly references 207, 208
reporting 210–11
veto 208
sectoral regulators *see also* **concurrency regime**
CMA 214
culture 208
data sharing and data portability 368
digital economy 382–83
enforcement xv, 1, 2, 3, 19–20

exploitative abuse 115–17
    judicial review 142
    Market Investigation Regime (MIR) 139–40, 142, 168
    market studies 139–40
    OFT 213
    privatization of public utilities 208
    recommendations 142
self-regulation 381, 383
significant market power decisions 212
social harmfulness 351, 352
social media 361–63, 364, 365–66, 380
soft law 7–8, 137, 269–70
standard of proof
    digital economy 199
    fair hearing, right to a 231, 241, 244–45, 246–47
    killer acquisitions 371–72
state aid 221–22, 226
Stigler Committee on Digital Platforms
    data sharing and data portability 369–70
    digital economy 380–81, 384
    killer acquisitions 371–72, 374, 375–76
substantial lessening of competition (SLC) regime
    dominance, assessment of 80, 85–86, 109
    interim measures 177
    killer acquisitions 371–72
    merger control 4–5, 14, 170–72, 175, 176, 177, 180–
        81, 183, 184–85, 188–89, 199
    Phase I decisions 180–81
    Phase II referrals 188–89
    screening 184–85
    standard of proof 183

territorial limitations 164–66
    behavioural remedies 165
    digital economy 166
    extraterritoriality 164–65
    relevant market 165
    remedies with extraterritorial effect 164–65
    resale price maintenance (RPM) 75
    Statutory Audit market study 165–66
    structural remedies 165
    vertical agreements 75
trade associations, horizontal agreements between
    cartels 36–37
    Chapter I prohibition 43
    Competition Act 1998 43
    concerted practices 43
    decisions of undertakings 29–30, 43
transparency
    Cartel Offence xviii–xix, 346–48
    CMA 216
    data sharing and data portability 367
    digital economy 366–67
    director disqualification 294, 304, 306–7
    Market Investigation Regime (MIR) xvi–xvii
    merger control 4–5, 169, 173–74, 175, 183, 198–99
    OFT 210
tying 138–39, 379
Tyrie letter 224–27, 229

UK Cartel Offence 337–58
    2013 reforms xviii–xix, 337, 346–50
    academic debate, developing consensus in 337,
        339, 350–54
    actus reus 339, 351
    advice, disclosure to legal advisers for 349
    BA Four prosecution 341–44, 350
    benefits of Cartel Offence 338
    bootstraps problem 350–51
    carve outs 347–48, 349–50
    Chapter I prohibition 356–57
    cheating 340–41, 352–53, 357–58
    CMA 10, 214, 342–43, 344–45, 348, 349–
        50, 354–58
    Competition Disqualification Orders 356
    Competition Disqualification
        Undertakings 338, 356
    concurrency regime 263
    criminalization debate 337, 339, 350–54
    culpability 340–41, 343–44, 349, 351, 355–57
    decline 337–58
    defences 348, 349–50
    delinquency 352–53
    deterrence xviii–xix, 338, 356
    director disqualification 10, 283–84, 287–89, 297–
        99, 306–7
    disclosure 341–42, 349
    dishonesty xviii–xix, 338, 339, 341–48, 349–51
    drafting 338–39, 349
    enforcement 4, 9–10
    Enterprise Act 2002 xviii–xix, 337, 338, 347–49
    Enterprise and Regulatory Reform Act 2013 346–
        48, 352, 354–55, 358
    EU law, conflicts with 338–39
    evidence of individual culpability xviii–xix
    future 354–58
    Galvanised Steel Tank (GST) Cartel 342–43, 355–56
    hard-core cartels xviii–xix, 338–39, 351
    horizontal agreements 346, 347–48
    implementing cartel arrangements 346, 355
    imprisonment 350–51, 357
    individual responsibility 338, 355–57
    introduction of offence 337, 338–39, 350
    investigation phase xviii–xix, 338
    jury trials, economic analysis in 351
    knowledge 346
    legacy cases 355
    leniency process 341–43, 344–45, 350
    making of cartel arrangements 346, 355
    Marine Hose case 340–41
    mental element 339
    moral wrongfulness 351, 352–54
    OFT OFT 9–10, 210, 213, 339–42, 354–55
    openness xviii–xix, 346–48
    overcharging 340–41
    Precast Concrete Drainage Products cartel 344–45,
        348, 355–56, 357–58
    priorities 338
    public interest 341–42

UK Cartel Offence (*cont.*)
  publication xviii–xix, 346–48, 349
  reform xviii–xix, 337, 346–50, 354–55
  reshaping of the offence 346–50
  secrecy 346–47
  social harmfulness 351, 352
  white list of permitted agreements 346–47
  wrongfulness xviii–xix, 351, 352–54, 357–58
UK Competition Network (UKCN) 260–61,
    263, 264–65
UK Regulators Network (UKRN) 19
undertakings
  Competition Disqualification Undertakings
    (CDUs) 293, 296–300
  director disqualification 293, 296–300, 301–
    2, 306–7
  initial undertakings (IUs) 177–78
  lieu of a reference (UILs), in 180–81, 183–86,
    187–88, 198
  market studies 145
  merger control 12–13, 177–78, 180–81, 183–86,
    187–88, 198
United States
  adversarial legalism 335–36
  antitrust enforcement regime xviii, 311–12, 332–33
  business victim methodology 333
  class action mechanism 332–33
  class certification process 332–33
  contingency fees 331
  damages 333
  data divestitures 379–80
  digital economy 360–61, 379–81, 384
  Federal Trade Commission (FTC) 360–61, 379–80
  hub-and-spoke cartels 42
  killer acquisitions 360–61, 371–72, 375
  opt-out class action mechanism 332–33
  retrospective merger review 379–80
  Sherman Act 379–80
  Stigler Committee on Digital Platforms 369–70
  treble damages 332–33
utility regulation 382–83

vertical agreements 55–78
  absolute territorial protection (ATP) 59
  assessment of compatibility xv
  barriers to entry or expansion 57
  block exemptions 56–57, 60–61, 73, 74, 76
  Brexit xv, 56, 69, 73, 78
  Commission Vertical Guidelines 61–62, 74

Competition Act 1998 xv, 55, 56–57, 62–71
  Brexit 73
  EU law 56–57, 73
  exemptions 57–58
  most-favoured-nation (MFN) Clauses 76–77
  object restrictions 77
  primacy of EU law 78
  resale price maintenance (RPM) 63–64, 65–
    66, 77
  substantive assessment 56
de minimis principle 56–57, 60–61, 74, 77–78
digital economy 55–56, 59, 61–62, 63–67, 75, 77
distribution arrangements 55–56, 57, 59, 69–71
efficiencies 60–61, 75
EU law
  block exemptions 76
  Brexit xv, 56, 73, 78
  CMA 73
  following xv, 56–57, 73–74, 77–78
  internal market xv, 56
  modernization 55, 57–62
  primacy of EU law 57, 73
  Verticals Regulation 76
evolution of the law 56–62
exclusivity provisions 62, 77–78
fuller effects analysis 61–62, 74
future 73–77
guidance 76–77, 78
hard-core restraints 60–61, 74
hub-and-spoke agreements 56–57, 63
illegality, presumption of 56, 59–60, 61, 74–75
inter-brand competition 59–60
intra-brand competition 59–60, 61–62, 73
leniency process 63–64
Market Investigation Regime (MIR) 55, 77–78
MFN clauses 62, 67–69, 76–78
national competition authorities (NCAs) 57
object restrictions 58–60, 74, 75
online selling, vertical restraints
    affecting xv, 63–67
price relationship agreements 62, 67–69, 76–77
resale price maintenance (RPM) xv, 56–57, 59, 60–
    61, 62–67, 75, 77
safe harbour 57–58, 60–61, 74, 76–78
single economic unit, agreements between 61
territorial restraints 75
UK jurisprudence 62–73
vertical restraints 57, 152
Verticals Exclusion Order 56–62, 77